PENDULUM OF WAR

PENDULUM OF WAR

The Three Battles of El Alamein

Niall Barr

THE OVERLOOK PRESS
Woodstock & New York

First published in the United States in 2005 by
The Overlook Press, Peter Mayer Publishers, Inc.
Woodstock & New York

WOODSTOCK:
One Overlook Drive
Woodstock, NY 12498
www.overlookpress.com
[for individual orders, bulk and special sales, contact our Woodstock office]

NEW YORK:
141 Wooster Street
New York, NY 10012

Cataloging-in-Publication Data is available from the Library of Congress

Manufactured in the United States of America
FIRST EDITION
ISBN 1-58567-655-1
ISBN 1-58567-738-8 (pb)
2 4 6 8 10 9 7 5 3 1

This book is dedicated to
the memory of

John Pimlott
colleague, mentor and friend

CONTENTS

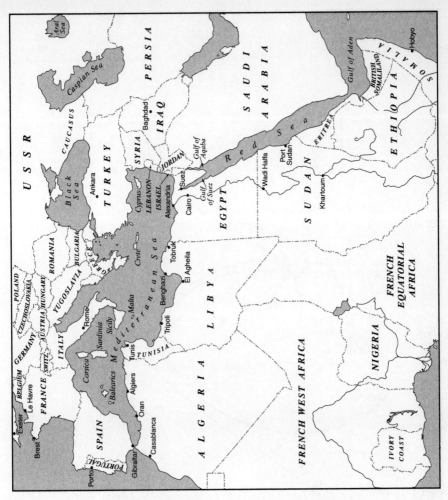

Map 1: The Mediterranean and Middle East theatre.

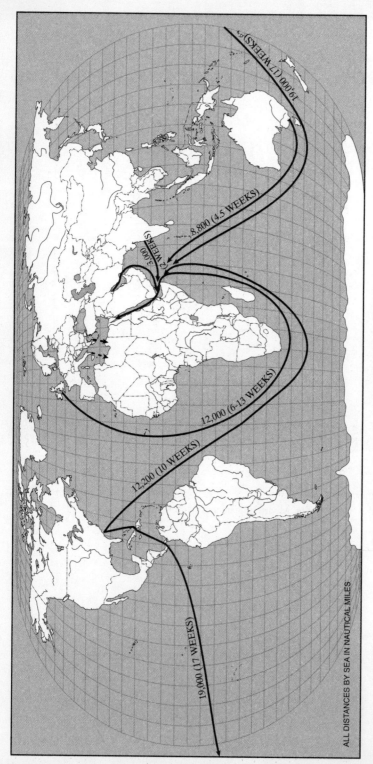

ALL DISTANCES BY SEA IN NAUTICAL MILES

19,000 (17 WEEKS)

8,800 (4.5 WEEKS)

3,000 (2 WEEKS)

12,000 (6-13 WEEKS)

12,200 (10 WEEKS)

19,000 (17 WEEKS)

Map 2: The sea lines of communication to the Middle East base

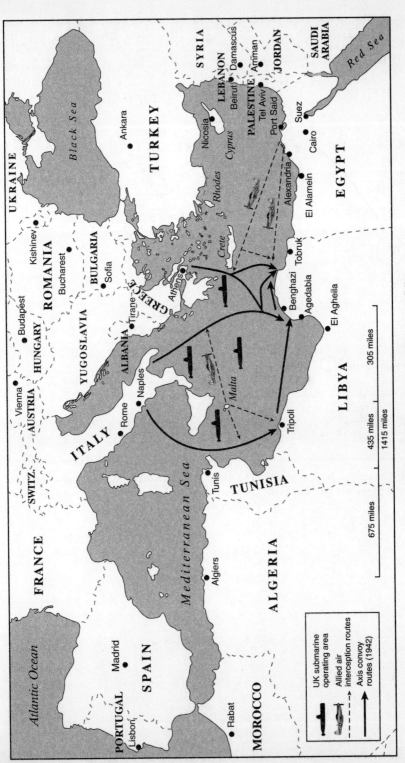

Map 3: The Axis lines of communication to Libya

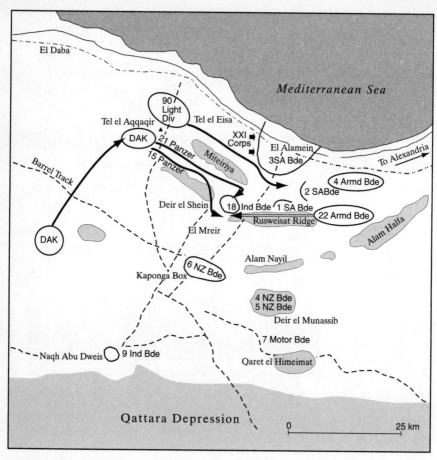

Map 4: The crucial day, 1 July 1942. The Africa Korps is held by the 18th Indian Brigade at Deir el Shein and the 90th Light Division's drive to the coast is frustrated by fire from the Alamein box.

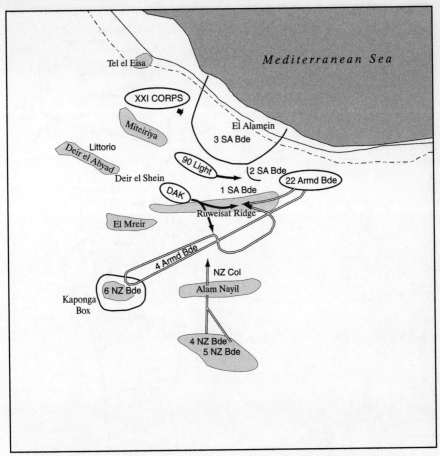

Map 5: On 2 July, Rommel renews the attempt but the Afrika Korps is stopped by
the combined action of 'Robcol' and the British armoured brigades.

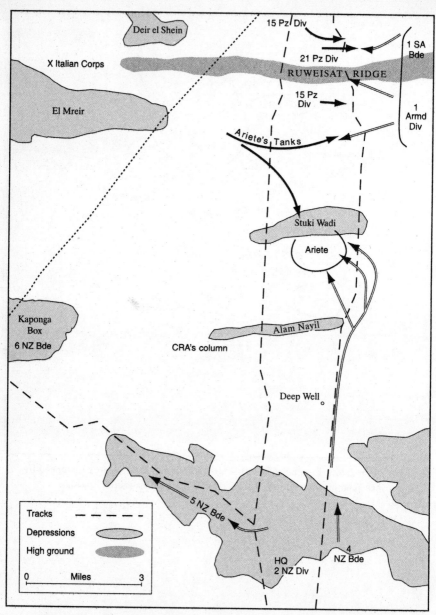

Map 6: The route of Ariete on 3 July. While the Afrika Korps is held on the Ruweisat ridge, the Ariete Division's artillery is overwhelmed by a column from the New Zealand Division

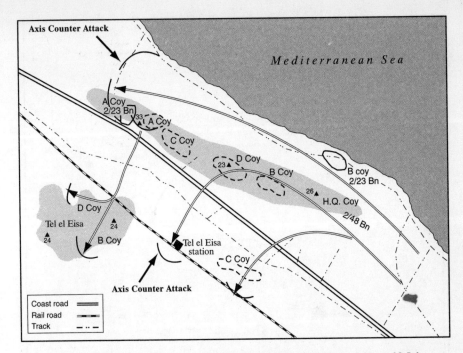

Map 7: 26th Australian Infantry Brigade's attack on Points 26 and 33 on 10 July which destroyed the Sabratha Division.

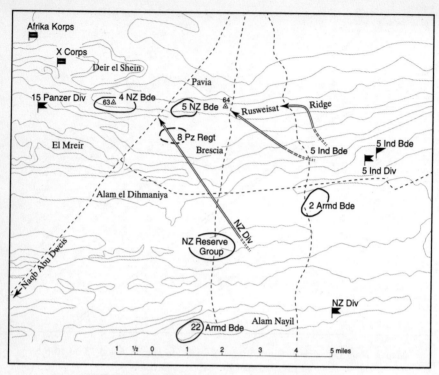

Map 8: Operation Bacon. The 2nd New Zealand Division's attack onto
the Ruweisat ridge on 14–15 July.

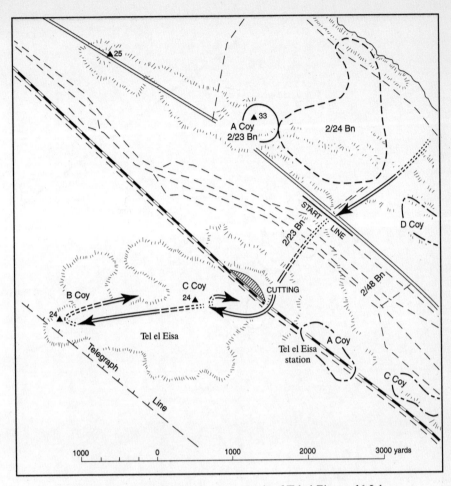

Map 9: The fierce fighting for the mounds of Tel el Eisa on 16 July.

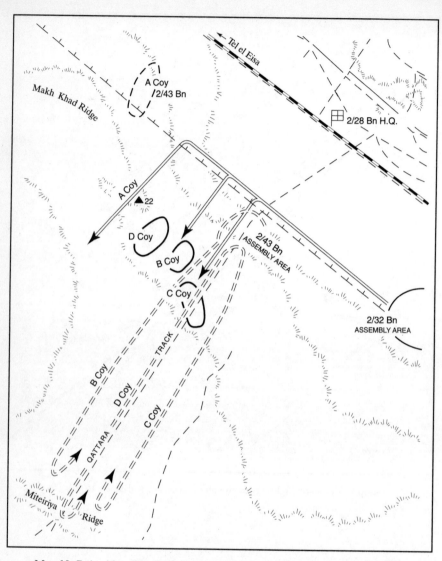

Map 10: Ruin ridge. The first attempt to secure the Miteiriya ridge on 17 July.

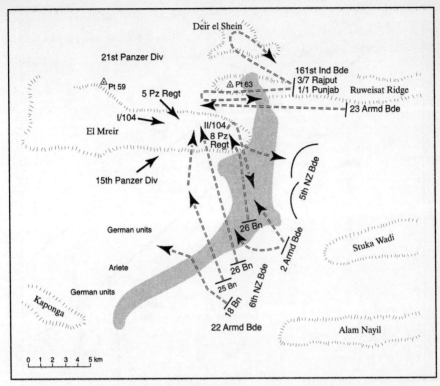

Map 11: Operation Splendour. The sadly ill-coordinated attacks of 6th New Zealand Infantry Brigade, 161st Indian Brigade and 23rd Armoured Brigade on 22 July.

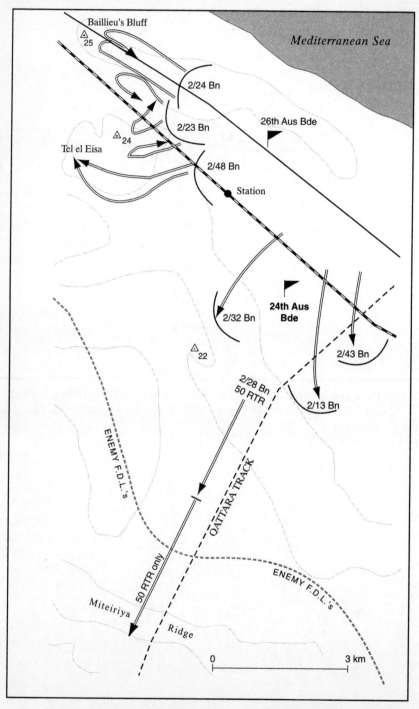

Map 12: The Australian part in Operation Splendour. A series of battalion attacks to take Tel el Eisa and the confused attempt by 50th Royal Tank Regiment and the 2/28th Battalion to seize Ruin ridge.

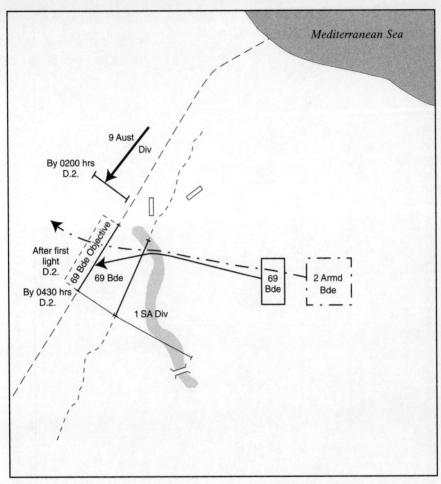

Map 13: The plan for Operation Manhood (taken from 30 Corps Operation Order no. 68). The last gasp of Eighth Army's offensive in 26–27 July.

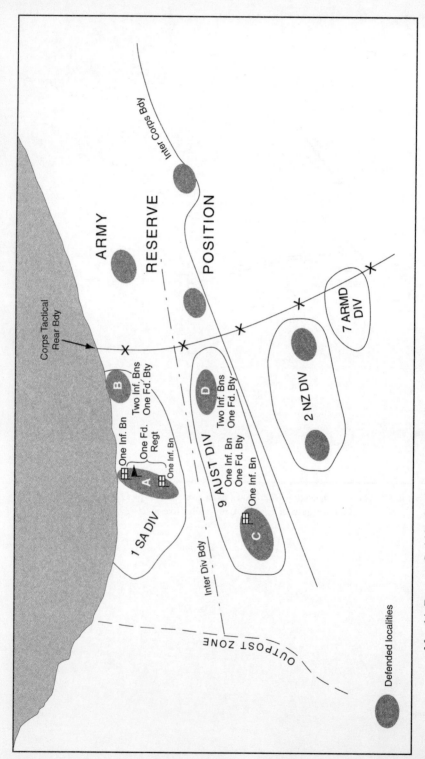

Map 14: Dorman–Smith's plan for a 'modern defensive battle' (taken from 30 Corps Operation Order no. 63).

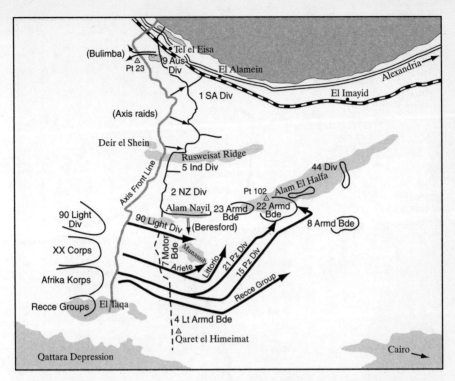

Map 15: Montgomery's first desert victory: Alam Halfa. The drive of the Afrika Korps towards the ridge is shown as are the less well-known thrusts mounted during Bulimba and Beresford.

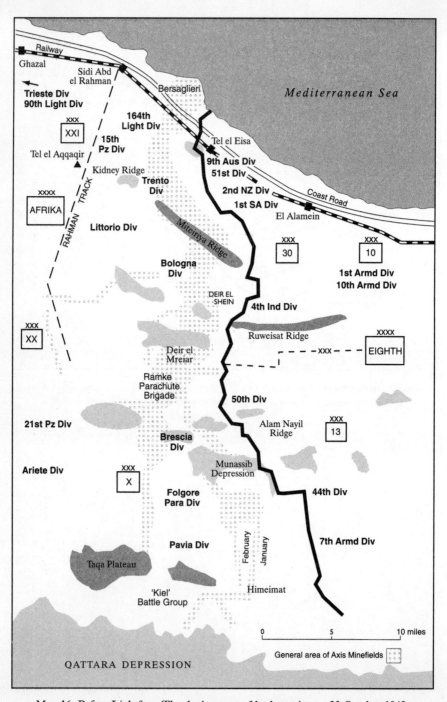

Map 16: Before Lightfoot. The deployment of both armies on 23 October 1942.

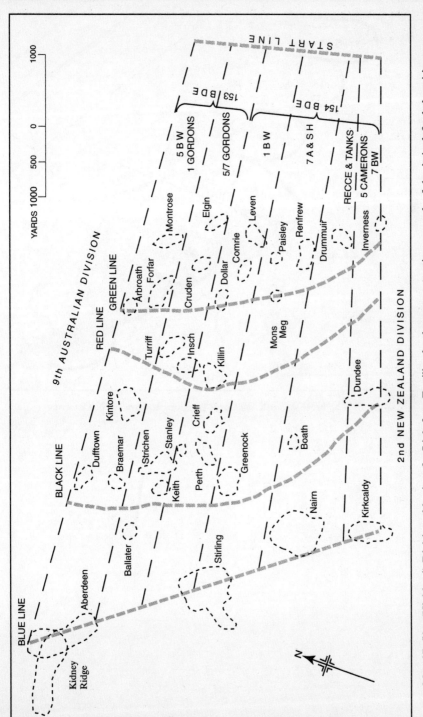

Map 17: 51st (Highland) Division objectives for Lightfoot. Familiar, local names were given to each of the Axis-defended positions.

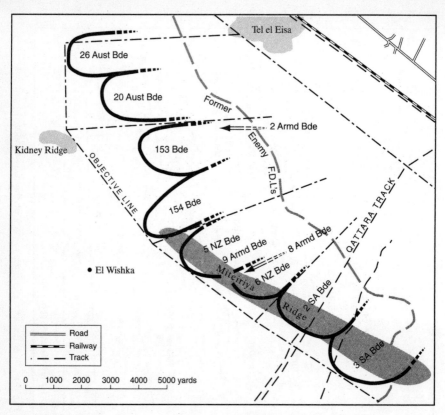

Map 18: The break-in battle. 30 Corps positions at dawn on 24 October.

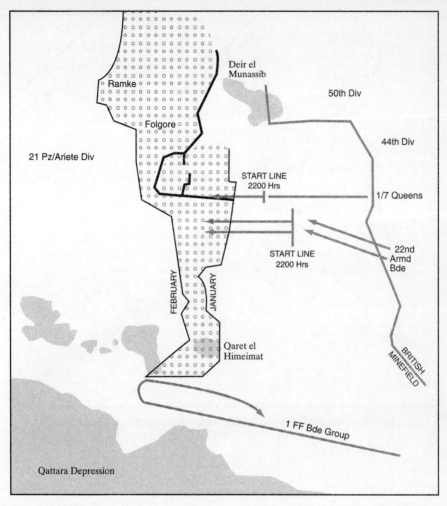

Map 19: 22nd Armoured Brigade's stalled attack in the 13 Corps sector on 23-24 October.

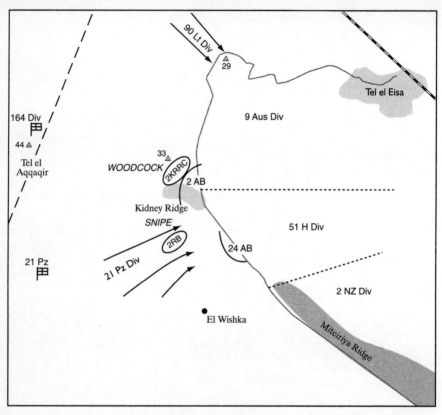

Map 20: The fierce actions fought around Snipe and Point 29 on 27 October 1942.

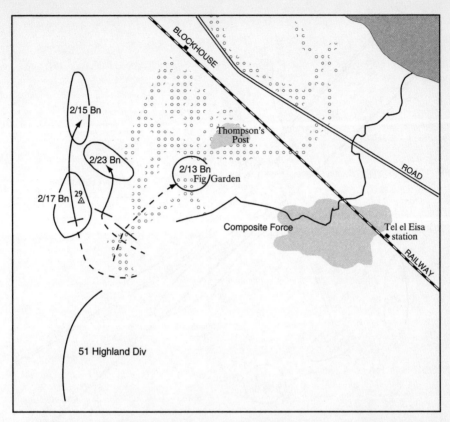

Map 21: Attack towards the coast. The Australian drive north on 28–29 October.

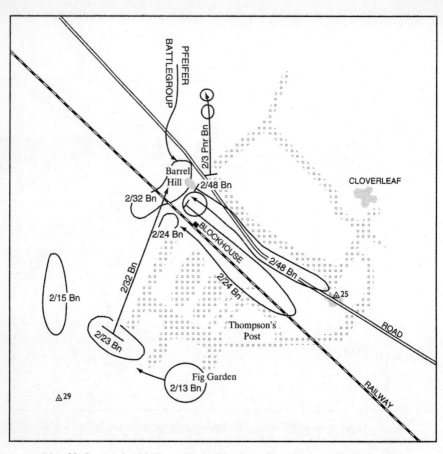

Map 22: Round the Mulberry Bush. The Australian attack on 30–31 October which finally cut the coast road and provoked intense German counterattacks throughout the day.

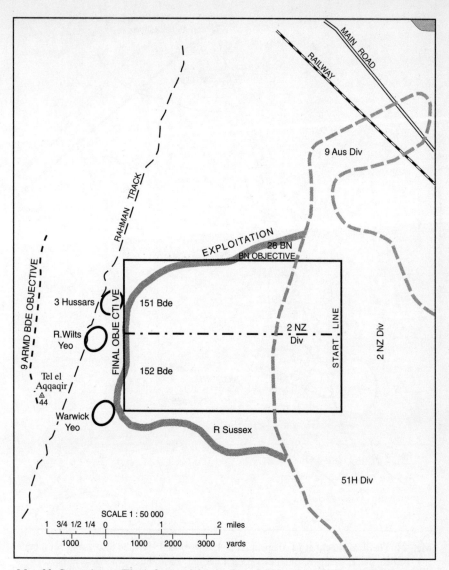

MAIN ROAD

RAILWAY

9 Aus Div

RAHMAN TRACK

9 ARMD BDE OBJECTIVE

EXPLOITATION

28 BN
BN OBJECTIVE

FINAL OBJECTIVE

3 Hussars

151 Bde

START LINE

2 NZ
Div

2 NZ Div

R.Wilts
Yeo

152 Bde

Tel el
Aqqaqir
△
44

Warwick
Yeo

R Sussex

51H Div

SCALE 1 : 50 000

1 3/4 1/2 1/4 0   1   2 miles

1000   0   1000   2000   3000   yards

Map 23: Supercharge. The infantry night attack on 2 November 1942 was followed by 9th Armoured Brigade's dawn charge of the Axis gun screen. The armoured battle raged for the rest of the day.

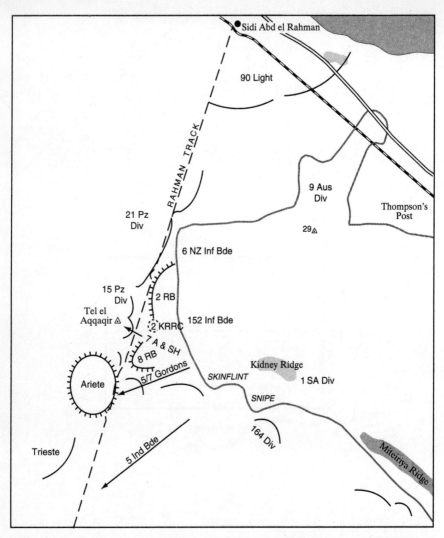

Map 24: The final attacks at El Alamein on 3–4 November 1942. The increasingly desperate British attacks finally resulted in a breach but only once the Axis forces had begun to withdraw.

A Crusader tank with its 'sunshield' (*Imperial War Museum E 18461; reproduced by permission of the Imperial War Museum*).

The opening bombardment of Eighth Army's offensive on 23 October 1942 (*Imperial War Museum E 18472; reproduced by permission of the Imperial War Museum*).

An Italian 47mm anti-tank gun pit (*Imperial War Museum E 18736; reproduced by permission of the Imperial War Museum*).

Rearming a Sherman (*Imperial War Museum E 18993; reproduced by permission of the Imperial War Museum*).

An Australian convoy passes wrecked Valentines of 40th Royal Tank Regiment. (*Tank Museum Collection, Bovington*).

General von Thoma meets Montgomery at his tactical headquarters, 4 November 1942 (*Imperial War Museum E 19132; reproduced by permission of the Imperial War Museum*).

LIST OF ILLUSTRATIONS

Auchinleck stands beside the desert road at El Daba, 28 June 1942 (*Imperial War Museum E 13881; reproduced by permission of the Imperial War Museum*).

The railway halt at El Alamein (*Imperial War Museum E 15165; reproduced by permission of the Imperial War Museum*).

The crew of a six-pounder anti-tank gun portee in early July (*Imperial War Museum E 14113; reproduced by permission of the Imperial War Museum*).

The crew of a 25-pounder field gun in action, 2 July 1942 (*Imperial War Museum E 14075; reproduced by permission of the Imperial War Museum*).

Valentine tanks of 23rd Armoured Brigade being unloaded at Port Tewfik (*Imperial War Museum E 14134; reproduced by permission of the Imperial War Museum*).

Two of the 99 Valentine tanks lost by 23rd Armoured Brigade on 22 July 1942 (*Tank Museum Collection, Bovington*).

Churchill with Auchinleck, Gott and Dorman-Smith, 5 August 1942 (*Imperial War Museum E 15384; reproduced by permission of the Imperial War Museum*).

Montgomery with Brian Horrocks and 'Pip' Roberts (*Imperial War Museum E 15787; reproduced by permission of the Imperial War Museum*).

Sappers with detectors practice at the Eighth Army Mine Clearance School, September 1942 (*Imperial War Museum E 18097; reproduced by permission of the Imperial War Museum*).

A platoon from 5th Seaforth Highlanders march in the desert during training (*Imperial War Museum E 17626; reproduced by permission of the Imperial War Museum*).

ACKNOWLEDGEMENTS

The inspiration for this book came from my first visit to El Alamein in October 1995. In the company of the much more experienced and knowledgeable John Pimlott and Duncan Anderson, I helped to conduct a party of officers and men of the US Third Army on a battlefield tour of Montgomery's famous battle. The desert was a haunting yet beguiling place and I could not fail to be moved by the pristine cemeteries of the three powers that had fought over such an isolated and desolate spot. My interest in the subject of the desert war was kindled and, after two subsequent visits to the battlefield, I became convinced that there remained a story to tell about the bitter campaign fought on the sands around El Alamein.

I cannot thank enough all my former colleagues of the War Studies Department, Royal Military Academy Sandhurst, for the many impromptu discussions and debates on all aspects of the battle which we have had over the years and for their continued interest in the project. I would particularly like to thank Duncan Anderson, Stephen Hart, Klaus Schmider and Lloyd Clark for their help, humour and encouragement. Duncan as well as Christopher Pugsley have been instrumental in widening my perspective upon the campaign.

I have also been fortunate indeed to work with my colleagues in the Defence Studies Department at the Joint Services Command and Staff College. We work in a very busy environment yet I have felt a very strong sense of individual and collective support from all my colleagues. I am deeply grateful to the Department for its generous funding of this project. Professor Anthony Forster helped me greatly in securing grants to complete the work. I would also like to thank all the students I have taught at Staff College, and particularly those who have taken my option and elective on the war in the Mediterranean, for their own insights into this and many other subjects. I am especially grateful to Steven Waites, Dan Clayton and Mark Rickaby for the production of the maps.

I am indebted to my friends and colleagues, Keith Blackmore, Warren Chin, Grant Elliott, Saul Kelly, Greg Kennedy, Jenny Macleod, Gary Sheffield and Chris Tuck, who read and commented on the manuscript.

Their ideas and kind advice have contributed immeasurably to the book. Needless to say, any errors or omissions are mine alone.

I am also very grateful to Professor Hew Strachan and Professor David French for their support. Their sustained interest has been of immense help and encouragement to me.

I would like to express my thanks to the Arts and Humanities Research Board which gave me a substantial Research Leave Award. The extended sabbatical gave me the time and space I needed to finish the book. I am also deeply indebted to the Australian Army History Unit which awarded me a Research Grant. This enabled me to visit Australia and New Zealand which immeasurably strengthened the source material for the work. I would also like to thank Roger Lee, the Head of the Australian Army History Unit, and Peter Stanley, the Principal Historian of the Australian War Memorial, for their many kindnesses during my stay in Canberra.

No work of this nature would be possible without the help of the librarians and archivists who are the custodians of the great wealth of material on the battles of El Alamein. I am particularly indebted to Andrew Orgill and the staff of the Central Library, Royal Military Academy Sandhurst, as well as Andrew Noble and the staff of the Library of the Joint Services Command and Staff College. I would also like to thank the staffs of the Public Record Office, Kew, the John Rylands Library, Manchester, the Royal Artillery Institution, Woolwich, the Royal Signals Museum, Blandford Forum, the Royal Logistics Corps Museum, Deepcut, the Imperial War Museum, London, the Liddell Hart Centre for Military Archives, London, the Australian War Memorial, Canberra, and the National Archives of New Zealand, Wellington. All have offered friendly advice and kind support.

I have been very fortunate in working with Will Sulkin, Jörg Hensgen and Rosalind Porter. Their advice, support and patience have been invaluable. Richard Collins's work on the manuscript was a model of thoroughness and efficiency.

I would like to thank my wife, Cara Brandi, for her sustained help, support and encouragement. She has borne my frequent absences, both mental and physical, with equanimity and has always taken me away from the sands of history just when I needed it. I thank her from the bottom of my heart. Our two sons, Freddie and Finlay, have given us much joy and acted as a powerful encouragement to finish this work.

This book is dedicated to the memory of John Pimlott, former Head of the Department of War Studies at the Royal Military Academy Sandhurst. His humanity, enthusiasm for military history and dedication as a teacher remain an inspiration to me.

INTRODUCTION

At midnight on 4 November 1942 the British people finally heard good news about the course of the war with Germany. The BBC were able to announce that the British Eighth Army had achieved a decisive victory over the Italian and German Panzerarmee west of the little railway halt of El Alamein in Egypt.[1] The tattered remnants of Rommel's once proud Afrika Korps were in full retreat.

Yet just four months before, the Eighth Army had been streaming back towards El Alamein after suffering one of the worst military defeats ever inflicted upon a British army. In the desperate days of June and July 1942, the entire British position in the Middle East had hung in the balance. The war fought in the Libyan Desert (referred to by the British as the Western Desert) from 1940 until 1942 had seen British forces race up and down the desert for nearly two years in a process that came to be known as the 'desert pendulum'. The final battle at El Alamein ensured that the desert pendulum would not swing again.

Winston Churchill emphasised the importance of this victory, and the subsequent Anglo-American landings in French North Africa, in a speech at the Mansion House on 10 November 1942. He said: 'This is not the end. It is not even the beginning of the end. But it is, perhaps, the end of the beginning.'[2] Churchill had put into a few masterful phrases what was seen as the real meaning of the victory. After so many disappointments and defeats the victory at El Alamein seemed to be a true watershed in Britain's fortunes during the war. The turn of the tide, so long expected, seemed to have finally arrived. This book explores the many swings of fortune which occurred at El Alamein in an attempt to understand the true nature of this pivotal campaign.

This view of the fighting at El Alamein in October and November 1942 as a major turning point in the fortunes of the Second World War was vigorously disseminated both during and after the war. In his monumental *The Second World War*, Churchill pressed the point home yet further when he famously stated: 'It might almost be said: "Before Alamein we never had a victory, after Alamein we never had a defeat."'[3] The hugely significant caveat 'It might almost be said' tends to be ignored in most renditions of this statement. In fact,

Churchill had a significant interest in developing and maintaining this version of events – that all was defeat before Alamein and all was success after it – however much that might mangle historical truth. After all, it was Churchill who, as the British war leader, had gone to Egypt in August 1942 and shaken up Britain's Middle East command in the hope that the changes might lead to victory.

Some of the commonly accepted explanations for the renaissance in the fortunes of Eighth Army have become part of the British mythology of the Second World War. The first and most popularly recognised explanation concerns Churchill's appointment of a new Eighth Army commander in the person of Lieutenant-General Bernard Law Montgomery on 12 August 1942. Montgomery's version of events as published in his *Memoirs*,[4] supported to a large extent by Winston Churchill's *The Second World War*,[5] have convinced many that his assumption of command radically changed the fortunes of Britain's desert army. Desmond Young caricatured this argument in his biography of Montgomery's erstwhile opponent, Erwin Rommel:

> The general impression in England, even to-day, seems to be that, having fallen back completely routed from the frontier, it [the Eighth Army] remained cowed and cowering at El Alamein while a panic-stricken staff in Cairo burnt mountains of paper and made ready for a retreat into Palestine or East Africa. Then, so runs the popular legend, General Montgomery arrived out of the skies and, having re-created or, indeed, created it, at once turned defeat into victory. The legend is unfair to the Eighth Army: it is also contrary to the facts.[6]

The impact of Montgomery's personality on Eighth Army has been minutely examined[7] and in the popular imagination the desert war seems to have been almost a personal contest between Montgomery and Field Marshal Erwin Rommel.

Indeed, the battle for the military reputations of the commanders in the Second World War began even before the conflict had ended. Montgomery and Rommel both took full advantage of the publicity machines of their day, and both wrote their own versions of events to justify their actions and add to the lustre of their record and reputations. Even though Rommel was eventually defeated comprehensively at El Alamein, his reputation remains undimmed. Similarly, the reputations, actions and personalities of Generals Auchinleck and Montgomery have been minutely analysed and justified in an attempt to explain the dramatic course of events in Egypt from May to November 1942. However, the reputations of these generals have been fought over so many times that the field of their military biographies now seems as much a wasteland as the Western Desert itself. The importance of the generals' reputations means that unpleasant reverses and defeats are not allowed to obscure the fact that Auchinleck was the real 'victor at Alamein', Rommel a true 'desert fox' and that Montgomery was the 'master of the battlefield'. The historical emphasis placed upon the character, abilities and reputations of the army commanders has had unfortunate effects upon our understanding of the campaign at El Alamein as a whole. While the importance of Montgomery's command style in his cultivation of himself as the all-knowing master to rebuild the morale and confidence of his army cannot be doubted, this interpretation cannot provide a complete explanation as to how Eighth Army rebuilt its ability to fight and win.

The fierce argument over the names of the various battles at El Alamein is second only to the controversy over the reputations of the desert generals. This is unsurprising since the two quarrels are closely linked. Just as wars are fought for political objectives, so the naming of battles is an intensely political process in which victories can be magnified and defeats ignored or explained away. Although the battle of El Alamein which began on 23 October 1942 has entered the public consciousness as the sole 'Battle of El Alamein', the campaign that took place around El Alamein from July until November 1942 was much more than one single battle.

The confused fighting of July has never received a completely appropriate name. For obvious reasons, the Axis powers had no wish to dignify this episode with a title as it signified the end of their dream to reach Alexandria and Cairo. In return, the British government had no real desire to name the actions which marked the end of the humiliations of Gazala and Tobruk but which did not include the decisive victory that Churchill so desperately desired. Ultimately, the British officially recognised 'First Ruweisat' and 'Second Ruweisat' but these titles only properly relate to two of the many combats which were fought in July.

Major-General Eric Dorman-Smith, Auchinleck's erstwhile Chief of Staff, did mark 1 July 1942 as 'The Battle of El Alamein' in his diary and many historians have subsequently accorded the July fighting the title of 'The First Battle of El Alamein'. Many supporters of Montgomery's reputation consider this a 'ludicrously silly assertion'[8] and merely part of a misguided attempt to restore Auchinleck's reputation and belittle Montgomery. General Charles Richardson later wrote, 'I can state from my continuous presence as GSO 1 (Plans) throughout those weeks that no battle entitled to that name "First Alamein" ever took place.'[9] However, if these deeply held views are accepted, it leaves the problem of what to call one of the fiercest series of engagements ever fought during the desert war.

There is little doubt that the fighting in July was often messy, confused and seemingly random to the troops who took part. New Zealand troops who fought in July spoke of the actions of 'Ruweisat ridge' and 'El Mreir' while Australian soldiers remembered 'Tel el Eisa' and 'Ruin ridge'. The actions of the New Zealand and Australian Divisions were separated by more than twenty miles of desert and seemingly unconnected to each other yet all of these battles involved intense fighting. The July battles were generally known at the time as the 'Battle of Egypt' which gave it a defensive ring rather like the Battle of Britain. However, 1 July 1942 marked the start of a month of vicious fighting in the desert around El Alamein and thus 'The First Battle of El Alamein' seems as suitable as any other title.

The Axis powers never gave a name to their last offensive at the end of August and quickly passed off Rommel's last attempt to reach the Delta as a 'reconnaissance in force' and thus unworthy of naming as a separate action. The German and Italian soldiers gave it the ironic name of 'The Six Days' Race' since they had rushed forwards and backwards to little purpose. At the time Montgomery considered this, his first victory, to have been an 'historic' engagement and he named it 'The Battle of Alamein' in his diary at the time.[10] Subsequently, he did not wish the failure of Rommel's last throw to be confused with the much greater offensive battle of October so the battle came to be known, at least to the British, by the name of the ridge where Rommel's hopes had foundered – Alam Halfa.

The British offensive, which opened on 23 October 1942, was initially entitled 'The Battle of Egypt' by Montgomery[11] in an unconscious echo of the title of the July fighting, but it soon became known as 'The Battle of El Alamein'. As far as Montgomery was concerned there was only ever one battle at Alamein – and that was *his* Alamein. Historians may have confused the issue subsequently by categorising these actions as 'First' Alamein, Alam Halfa and 'Second' Alamein but this has done little to heal the chronological rift which lies upon the fault line of Montgomery's assumption of command. Whatever titles are given to the fighting of July, August–September and October–November it is clear that three main battles were fought around El Alamein from 1 July to 4 November 1942. The fact remains that the titles accorded to the various engagements are inextricably bound up within the controversies surrounding Auchinleck and Montgomery's reputations.

The emphasis on the personalities of the generals has meant that many accounts do not treat the fighting at Alamein from July to November 1942 as a continuous campaign but almost as two separate and distinct events. Auchinleck's biographers had little interest in the events in the desert once 'their' man was removed in August 1942 while biographies of Montgomery inevitably view the previous course of the desert fighting through the prism of Montgomery's arrival and subsequent success in the theatre. Thus, studies of Auchinleck tend to stop their analysis of the campaign sharply on 8 August when Churchill sacked him; biographies of Montgomery tend to begin just as abruptly on 12 August when the new lieutenant-general arrived in Egypt.

Even beyond the biographies of the commanders, this interpretation of the Alamein battles as two separate campaigns and the Eighth Army of July

and October as two different armies has skewed our perspective of the
fighting. The South African official history, *Crisis in the Desert*, covers the
battle of Gazala and the fall of Tobruk, but finishes its narrative on 10 July
1942 in the middle of the first battle of Alamein because after this date 'the
Eighth Army would never again feel the humiliation of defeat'. The complex
battles of July are often ignored; many writers have concentrated on
Montgomery's two battles in Egypt, preferring to leave July 1942 as the
'forgotten' battle of Alamein. A recent excellent study of the July fighting
made this point explicitly: 'We were an old army fighting an old war . . .
the major achievement of the Eighth Army had been to stop the Axis forces
and to hold them at Alamein until a new and stronger army could strike
back.'[12]

Yet, although some of the units which fought in the October battle were
new to the desert, the core of Eighth Army fought through both battles.
The continuity which underlay the fighting at El Alamein has often been
obscured. It is vital to examine the Alamein campaign as a continuous whole
– from the desperate days of early July to the final victory in November –
so that all of the battles and events can be seen in their proper context.

With the notable exceptions of Waterloo and Normandy, the battles of
Alamein rank as one of the most well-trodden paths of British military
history. Library bookshelves positively groan under the weight of campaign
studies, regimental histories, biographies and autobiographies which take
Alamein and the desert war as their subject. The most influential and
numerous works upon the subject were written in the 1960s by men who
had actually served at Alamein. Some of these works, in particular C. E.
Lucas Phillips's *Alamein*[13] and Michael Carver's considerable collection of
writings on the desert war including *El Alamein, Tobruk* and *Dilemmas of
the Desert War*,[14] remain essential reading. However, none of these writers
had access to the full range of official documents available. Corelli Barnett's
brilliant and iconoclastic *The Desert Generals*,[15] first published in 1960, was,
and remains, highly influential in its defence of the earlier commanders of
the desert war and its trenchant criticism of Montgomery. The title of
Barnett's book, however, explains the major focus of most of these works.
The character and reputation of the senior officers who fought in the desert
campaigns loom large in all of these accounts.

The various official histories of the campaign are models of their type.
The British official account provides a clear and balanced overview but little
detail. The Eighth Army was considered a 'British' army but this term had
a very different meaning in 1942 to the one it has today. The concept of
imperial defence, in which the British Dominions and colonies provided
troops and resources for the British war effort in a process that the British
government and armed forces largely took for granted, now seems a strange
anachronism. Yet the Eighth Army was a force composed of men and women

drawn from all over the British Empire, including Indians, Africans, Australians and New Zealanders. The dissolution of what was the British Empire into quite separate and independent states has led to a division in perspective on imperial forces such as the Eighth Army. For example, the Australian official history, *Tobruk and El Alamein*,[16] and the extensive series of New Zealand official works on the campaign[17] are excellent studies but naturally concentrate upon the endeavours of their own divisions. More recently, Mark Johnson and Peter Stanley's book, *Alamein: The Australian Story*,[18] provides an unsurpassed perspective on the part played by the 9th Australian Division by making full use of official and unofficial sources. However, studies which concentrate upon the activities of one division cannot provide a full picture of Eighth Army and all its component parts.

Strangely enough, few of the more recent works which provide useful accounts of the October battle of Alamein have made full use of the official documents which, in the British case, came into the public domain from 1995 onwards.[19] Yet returning to the original sources written during the campaign is essential to a full understanding of these events. By making extensive use of original British, Australian and New Zealand sources as well as using translated German material, this work is able to assess the Eighth Army as a unified imperial organisation while also revealing important fresh evidence concerning the campaign. Documents of vital historical importance, such as Auchinleck's final military appreciations of 1 and 2 August 1942, can finally become part of the public debate upon the Alamein campaign. In using these sources, this book places the Eighth Army – rather than its commanders – at centre stage.

This book does not concentrate on the battle for reputations that has grown up around the commanders at Alamein but, instead, focuses upon the education of an army from bitter experience on the battlefield. This book analyses the Eighth Army as an organisation which allows the importance of the inner working of the 'brain' of the army – the staff – and the vital contribution of corps and divisional commanders to be properly acknowledged. By exploring the development of Eighth Army's fighting methods from hard-won experience on the field of battle, this book provides a broader and deeper explanation for the final transformation of British fortunes in the desert war than has hitherto been possible.

The study of the British Army as an institution has been at the forefront of recent scholarship on the Second World War. This has moved the historical debate away from military biography and begun the process of examining the social structure, organisation and fighting techniques of the British Army.[20] David French's influential study, *Raising Churchill's Army*, is the first modern work which properly analyses the performance of the British Army in the Second World War.[21] Jeremy Crang has provided an important look at the social structure of the British Army[22] while Timothy Harrison

Place has explored the nature of military training in Britain during the war.[23] This book adds to this growing body of work by examining one British army in one crucial campaign. In understanding how the Eighth Army learnt from its grievous mistakes in combat, and the way those lessons were translated into improved performance, this work analyses the full range of developments which took the Eighth Army from defeat to victory in 1942.

ONE

War in the Desert

On 21 June 1942 Generaloberst Erwin Rommel, the commander of the German-Italian Panzerarmee Afrika, drove down the steep escarpment into Tobruk. The Libyan town did not look like a great military prize that day. All round him was the chaos of a defeated army, with burning supply dumps and parties of prisoners being marched off, while the streets of the small town were littered with rubble. The few buildings left standing were riddled with bullet holes. The wreckage of Italian and British shipping lay twisted and half-submerged in the harbour. Yet, for Rommel, this was the supreme moment of an already glittering military career.

Halfway across the world, Winston Churchill, the British Prime Minister, received the news of Tobruk's fall while standing in the Oval Office of US President Franklin D. Roosevelt. Of the many black moments Churchill had already endured during this war, this was probably the worst. Britain had suffered two years of seemingly unmitigated disaster and defeat since 1940. Narvik, Dunkirk, Dakar, Greece, Crete, Singapore, Rangoon, Gazala and now Tobruk – the litany of British defeats and evacuations simply seemed to go on and on. Churchill later wrote of the fall of Tobruk that:

> This was one of the heaviest blows I can recall during the war. Not only were its military effects grievous, but it had affected the reputation of the British armies . . . I did not attempt to hide from the President the shock I had received. It was a bitter moment. Defeat is one thing; disgrace is another.[1]

British forces had been defeated many times during the war but the battle of Gazala, fought from 26 May to 20 June, saw a numerically superior and better supplied Eighth Army completely outthought and outfought by Rommel's Panzerarmee Afrika. Gazala and the loss of Tobruk represented Britain's complete military humiliation.

Churchill, along with most British observers, was bewildered at the turn of events. During May, when the two armies had confronted one another along the line of defences which the British had built stretching from Ain el Gazala near the coast to Bir Hacheim in the far desert, the odds had seemed to favour the British. Yet this was only the most recent astonishing reversal of fortune that had taken place in nearly two years of war in the desert.

*

On the evening of 10 June 1940, Benito Mussolini, the Italian Duce, stood on the central balcony of the Palazzo Venezia in Rome before a massed crowd. He announced that, from midnight that evening, Italy would be at war with the 'sterile and declining' nations of Britain and France.[2] Allied planning staffs had assumed in the summer of 1939 that Italy would make common cause with Nazi Germany if war came and the Allies had felt a certain sense of relief when Mussolini had announced Italian non-belligerent status on 1 September 1939, the day that Germany invaded Poland.[3] There is no doubt that the Italian Armed Forces were unprepared for war in 1940, let alone 1939, and all of Mussolini's military advisers continued to urge caution. However, by 10 June 1940, the strategic situation seemed to have swung decisively in favour of Hitler's Germany. The Low Countries had succumbed to the German Wehrmacht's lightning-fast offensive and it was clear that France could not remain in the war for long. Mussolini had long entertained visions of breaking out of the 'politico-military' encirclement of the British Empire in the Mediterranean and Middle East.[4] With France on the verge of collapse, Mussolini believed that the time was ripe to strike a blow at the fatally weakened British Empire and gather the spoils.

Mussolini's main strategic concept was for Italy to conduct a war 'parallel to that of Germany'[5] but to achieve Italian – or his own – strategic objectives. He had already decided on 29 May 1940 that, in the case of war, 'Our forces will concentrate on England – viz. on her positions and her naval forces in port and in the Mediterranean.'[6] While the British government faced the prospect of a German invasion of the home island, the Italian Fleet would clear the Mediterranean of the Royal Navy and the large Italian forces present in the colony of Libya would mount an invasion of Egypt to seize control of Alexandria, Cairo and, most importantly, the Suez Canal. By taking advantage of Britain's weakness, Mussolini hoped that the short-comings of the Italian Armed Forces and their unpreparedness for war would not be exposed.

The Italian stance of non-belligerency had ensured that the British authorities in Egypt had attempted to placate Mussolini for as long as possible but this did not obscure the fact that the defence of the Mediterranean and Middle East lay at the heart of Britain's strategic interests.[7] Only through control of Gibraltar in the west and the port of Alexandria in the east could the Royal Navy's Mediterranean Fleet hope to exert some control over the inland sea. The British island base of Malta, which lay only 60 miles off the coast of Sicily, could be used to interdict Italian supply routes to her North African colony. The defence of Egypt against an Italian invasion from Libya protected Britain's vast interests which ran throughout the Middle East region. With the Italian declaration of war, the Suez Canal ceased to be a great artery for British merchant shipping. Nonetheless, the canal enabled the Royal Navy to switch assets from the Mediterranean to the Indian Ocean and Far East. Its retention was still a vital strategic consideration. Britain now found itself engaged in a high-intensity industrialised and mechanised war and the oilfields around the northern Iraqi cities of Kirkuk and Mosul were of immense strategic importance for the oil-fired Royal Navy and highly mechanised army. Not surprisingly, domination of the Mediterranean and control of the Middle East were central to British interests and were considered 'second only to the United Kingdom itself'.[8]

Marshal Pietro Badoglio, the Chief of the Italian Commando Supremo, had advised Mussolini against war. However, the Italian dictator rode roughshod over the objections of all of his Service Chiefs; Italian strategy for the 'parallel war' was never anything more than opportunism.

*

The British Committee of Imperial Defence provided much surer foundations for British strategy in the Mediterranean and Middle East. In June 1939 it had been decided that the Commanders-in-Chief of the three services should coordinate the British defence policy in the Middle East. Thus, Admiral Sir Andrew Cunningham, Commander-in-Chief Mediterranean, Lieutenant-General Sir Archibald Wavell, Commander-in-Chief Middle East, and Air Marshal Sir William Mitchell, Air Officer Commanding-in-Chief, formed the High Command for all British forces in the Middle East. This triumvirate had to reach their decisions through discussion and through consultation with their chiefs of staff.[9] Right from the start, British strategy in the theatre, while far from perfect, was at least based on rational calculation and an awareness of the needs of the three services. As far as was possible, British air, land and naval strategy was coordinated and complimentary from the start of the war in the desert. This cooperation between the three services at the strategic level was of essential importance given the nature of the Mediterranean and Middle Eastern theatres. The activities of the three services simply could not be considered in isolation and the complex interaction between the land, air and sea made the Mediterranean one of the most complicated theatres of operation during the Second World War. The dilemmas and complications of the Mediterranean theatre inevitably led to tensions and arguments but the tri-service nature of the British High Command meant that the British did at least attempt to plan and coordinate their strategic thinking in three dimensions.

Few soldiers in history have had to shoulder the awesome burdens and responsibilities which faced the British Commander-in-Chief Middle East. Lieutenant-General Archibald Wavell took up this new post in August 1939 and immediately had to wrestle with the task of overall command of all British army units over an enormous theatre of operations which stretched over 2,000 square miles and included Egypt, the Sudan, Palestine, Transjordan, Cyprus, British Somaliland, Aden, Iraq and the shores of the Persian Gulf.[10] When Italy declared war, Wavell was faced with an immediate crisis. The defence of Egypt rested on the 36,000 men of Lieutenant-General Richard O'Connor's Western Desert Force which, although highly trained, was still short of equipment. Across the frontier in Libya, Marshal Rudolfo Graziani, at Mussolini's insistence, was gathering the Italian Tenth Army of 140,000 men for an invasion.[11] In Italian East Africa, 130,000 Italian troops were confronted by 9,000 men in the Sudan and 8,500 men in Kenya. In numerical terms at least, the British seemed to be in serious trouble.

With the fall of France, the Royal Navy's position in the Mediterranean also seemed perilous. The combined Anglo-French naval forces had been powerful enough to deter any Italian aggression, but with the French naval units removed from the equation the balance shifted in favour of the Italians. The British Mediterranean Fleet was far smaller than the Italian Fleet, and composed of older and slower ships. The act of destroying the major French Fleet units at Mers el Kebir on 26 June 1940 poisoned Anglo-French relations and simply seemed to emphasise Britain's desperate position in the Mediterranean. The Naval Staffs even considered the abandonment of the island of Malta and the rebasing of the Mediterranean Fleet in Gibraltar. This would effectively have surrendered control of the central and eastern Mediterranean to the Italians and it is fortunate that, in the event, the British did not take complete counsel of their fears. It was decided to fight for control of the eastern, if not the central, Mediterranean. Yet the action fought off Calabria, known to the Italians as Punto Stilo,[12] on 9 July 1940 demonstrated that the Royal Navy could operate in the central Mediterranean in the face of Italian opposition and Admiral Cunningham was determined to continue an aggressive policy to bring the naval war to the Italians in the central Mediterranean at every opportunity.[13]

*

Marshal Graziani was finally forced to invade Egypt on 9 September 1940 and the large Italian forces, which were still largely composed of marching infantry, sweated their way forwards sixty miles to Sidi Barrani where they established a series of fortified camps more suitable for colonial war than against a modern mechanised opponent. The men of the Western Desert Force, who had been preparing to make a decisive stand at the small port of Mersa Matruh, were vaguely disappointed by this turn of events but soon set about achieving complete moral dominance over the Italians by a series of daring raids and fighting patrols. Frustrated with the lack of action and success, Mussolini once again ignored his military advisers and declared war on Greece in October 1940. Unable to cope with one major military campaign in Egypt, the Italian Army was completely unprepared to fight another and the campaign in Greece quickly became an embarrassing debacle. Mussolini's 'parallel' war was already in ruins. He had allowed his strategic ambitions to cloud what little military judgement he possessed.

Meanwhile, Wavell had begun to plan an ambitious 'five-day raid' to strike at the Italian encampments but it was not until December 1940 that he finally unleashed the Western Desert Force in Operation Compass. The British 7th Armoured and 4th Indian Division executed a daring and unconventional attack which completely unhinged the Italian defence. Within two days, the Italian camps, along with the vast majority of their 60,000 defenders, fell into British hands. Graziani began a strategic withdrawal into Libya based on the defence of the fortresses of Bardia and Tobruk but these fell in quick succession to the Western Desert Force in January 1940. The campaign culminated in the climactic battle of Beda Fomm on 5 February 1941 where, after a dramatic chase across unreconnoitred desert, the lead elements of the Western Desert Force caught and trapped the Italian Tenth Army. More than 140,000 Italian soldiers were captured and it seemed that the road to Tripoli was wide open.

O'Connor wanted to continue the pursuit all the way to Tripoli but Wavell now had to find troops for an expeditionary force to Greece and refused to sanction any advance further than El Agheila. After his capture in April 1941, O'Connor would spend the next two years in Italian prisoner-of-war camps agonising about the orders which had halted his advance towards Tripoli.[14] O'Connor always believed that he could have pushed a small force the last 500 miles to Tripoli and prevented the rest of the desert fighting from ever taking place. In reality, such an advance simply could not have been sustained. In advancing the 900 miles to El Agheila, the Western Desert Force had stretched its supply chain well beyond its breaking point and was experiencing, to its cost, the diminishing power of the offensive.

Carl von Clausewitz had explored the changing balance between offence and defence in his great work of military theory, *On War*. In his concept of the 'culminating point of victory', Clausewitz argued that while the advantages which accrued to the defence were permanent, the advantages which aided an attacker, such as surprise, morale and initiative would gradually bleed away in continued movement and exhaustion. A lengthy advance would eventually place a

> burden on an advancing army with every step it takes; so unless it started with exceptional superiority, it will find its freedom of action dwindling and its offensive power progressively reduced. In the end, it will feel unsure of itself and nervous about its situation.[15]

Clausewitz also recognised:

the distance from the sources that must send continual replacements for this steadily weakening army, will increase proportionately with the advance. In this respect a conquering army is like the light of a lamp; as the oil that feeds it sinks and draws away from the focus, the light diminishes until at last it goes out altogether.[16]

This was the phenomenon which Clausewitz called the 'culminating point of victory'. After this point, the balance of advantage would swing to the defender who could then mount a successful counterattack.

Clausewitz's theory was complicated yet further by the nature of the desert environment. The ability to sustain high-intensity operations in the middle of an arid desert for months, indeed years, on end, was only possible due to the mechanisation of warfare. While armies in the past had, with preparation, been able to cross deserts at the cost of great human suffering they had never been able to live, work and fight there for long periods. Not surprisingly, all of the major operations of the desert war were fought within fifty miles of the sea. Only the 'private armies' such as the British Long Range Desert Group were able to operate in the great sand sea of the Libyan Desert for sustained periods.

The barren and hostile nature of the desert meant that both sides had to transport all their supplies into the theatre to sustain their armies. While some water could be found by drilling wells, or accumulated in the ancient *birs* along the coast, all of the other supplies, equipment, ammunition and fuel had to be brought into the desert. This placed an enormous burden on the armies' administrative services which made any sustained advance difficult. Both armies relied on motor transport; without the internal combustion engine the high tempo and speed of the desert campaigns simply could not have been sustained. Given the necessity of bringing all supplies into the theatre, Clausewitz's ideas of the 'culminating point of victory' operated starkly in the desert campaigns. Known to the participants as the desert 'seesaw' or 'pendulum', the 'culminating point of victory' also mitigated against a successful offensive against the enemies' main base. Desert veterans of Eighth Army wryly dubbed these rapidly swaying fortunes as the 'Benghazi Stakes'.

The distances involved in mounting an advance towards Tripoli – or Alexandria – were also unprecedented. Tripoli, the main Axis port and supply base, was 1,415 miles away from the Egyptian city of Alexandria, the home of the Royal Navy's Mediterranean Fleet. The further an army advanced from its main base, the greater the distance – and the consumption of fuel – that its motor transport had to travel to sustain the spearhead units. This law of diminishing returns made a continuous sustained advance of 1,415 miles virtually impossible.

The problem of the 'desert pendulum' was given an added layer of complexity by the external lines of communication which brought supplies into the theatre. The British forces in Egypt and the Middle East had to be sustained by supplies despatched from the United Kingdom, the United States or India. British merchant shipping was denied the regular use of the route through the Mediterranean by Italian air and naval power. This meant that only vitally important supply convoys comprised of fast ships were ever pushed through the Mediterranean in the face of opposition and the vast majority of British convoys from the United Kingdom had to take the alternative route around the Cape of Good Hope in a journey covering a distance of 12,000 miles, which took between ten and 13 weeks. The supplies were then landed at the small and congested port of Suez on the Red Sea. The British Middle East Command was thus sustained by the longest umbilical cord in the history of military logistics. Other convoys plied the route from India, a mere 3,000 miles away, and others sailed from the United States and Canada, which were 12,200 miles away. Thus, from the perspective of the quartermasters in Cairo, North America was little further than the United Kingdom. The sheer length of these supply lines placed enormous strains upon Allied shipping capacity and made forward planning in the Middle East an inexact science:

> If you cabled for something, it might and usually did, take two to three months to manufacture and collect at an English port, a week to load (if bombing did not interfere), ten weeks at the lowest at sea, another two weeks perhaps to unload at a small and most congested port, a day or so to a Base Depot, and from there four or five hundred miles by rail or road to the fighting troops in the desert.[17]

The length of these sea lines of communication, combined with the inherent delays in scheduling dozens of convoys involving hundreds of ships, meant that any build-up of supplies for an offensive in the desert could take months rather than weeks to organise. However, there were some significant advantages to the British lines of communication. Although the British supply lines were interminably long, they were also relatively secure once the menace of Italian submarines operating in the Red Sea was finally eliminated in April 1941. Since the German U-boat command concentrated its attentions upon the North Atlantic, convoys bound for Suez were relatively unmolested once they passed Gibraltar. Although there were some inevitable accidents and losses, once a convoy had been despatched, British planners could be reasonably sure that it would arrive at Suez.

The same could not be said for Italian lines of communication. The route for Italian merchant shipping across the Mediterranean from ports such as Naples, Brindisi or Taranto was a short crossing to the main Libyan ports of Tripoli or Benghazi. However, Italian convoys were vulnerable to attack by British submarines, aircraft and surface ships based in Malta and Egypt. The British ability to interdict the Italian lines of communication meant that the Italian air and naval units faced a constant battle to protect convoys bound for North Africa. Nonetheless, if conditions were favourable, Italian convoys could reinforce the army in Libya far more quickly than the British could support their forces in Egypt.

The peculiarly complex logistic demands of the armies in the desert also placed strict limitations upon their size. It was certainly possible to deploy and sustain large numbers of foot-bound infantry in the theatre but, as the Italian Army had found to its cost during Operation Compass, large quantities of such troops were of little value against a smaller number of highly mobile armoured and mechanised formations. Yet even relatively small mechanised forces required large quantities of motor transport, maintenance services and fuel to keep them operational in the desert. In turn, these demands required increased shipping capacity to the extent that, even though the forces deployed in the desert were comparatively small (and indeed dwarfed in comparison to the forces deployed on the Eastern Front between 1941 and 1945), they required a logistic effort out of all proportion to their size. The complex interaction between logistic demands, lines of communication and the race to build up supplies for offensives played a critical part in the outcome of the fighting in the desert for the next two years.

*

The wholesale destruction of the Italian Tenth Army in Libya created a real crisis for Italy. Mussolini had entered the war to achieve his own strategic vision for a renewed Italian Empire but the failure of Italian arms in Libya, Greece and East Africa meant that he had become increasingly dependent upon Hitler's Germany.[18] In effect, Italy became little more than a German satellite and Mussolini's 'parallel' war in the Mediterranean was subsumed into a much wider German dominated conflict.[19]

Adolf Hitler, the German Führer and the dominating will of Germany's strategic ambitions, had not shown much interest in the Mediterranean theatre since the war began. Negotiations with General Francisco Franco, for a joint German–Spanish attack upon Gibraltar came to nothing in October 1940,[20] and German intervention in the theatre was finally forced by Italian failure. With the British threatening to conquer the entire Italian possession of Libya, Hitler felt forced to act. Fliegerkorps X of the Luftwaffe was ordered to bases in Sicily with the main objective of attacking British naval forces. Under Operation Sunflower, a small 'special military blocking' force, consisting initially of only the 5th Light Division, was sent over to Tripoli in February 1941.[21] Its purpose was purely defensive, although Generalmajor Hans von Funck, who visited Libya in early February, doubted whether German intervention could prevent disaster.[22]

However, the advent of the Luftwaffe in the Mediterranean theatre was felt almost immediately. Advance units of Fliegerkorps X attacked and seriously damaged the aircraft carrier, HMS *Illustrious* on 10 January 1941, serving notice that operations in the central Mediterranean had just become a much more dangerous proposition for the Royal Navy.

Meanwhile, Hitler had appointed a commander of considerable drive and energy to command what became known as the Deutsches Afrika Korps. Generalleutnant Erwin Rommel[23] had not followed the conventional career path of a German officer. He had started his military career as an infantry lieutenant and first experienced combat on the Western Front in 1914. However, his greatest military exploits in the First World War were fought against the Italians where he led a stormtroop battalion in the battle of Caporetto (24 October–10 November 1917). He managed to find a place in the 100,000-strong Reichswehr Army in the inter-war years and spent much time at infantry training schools. However, Rommel's career would have been permanently stunted under normal circumstances as he never attended the German Staff College which opened the path to higher command. However, his book *Infantry Attacks*[24] caught the eye of Hitler and he became the commander of Hitler's bodyguard battalion in 1938. At the end of the Polish campaign, Hitler gave Rommel command of the 7th Panzer Division. The spectacular performance of his 'Ghost' Division caught the attention of Joseph Goebbels, Hitler's Minister of Propaganda, and Rommel soon became Hitler's version of the 'Darling Child of Victory'.[25] Although Rommel owed his promotion and his post as the German commander in Africa to Hitler's influence, he was a very talented tactical commander who understood innately the opportunities inherent in armoured warfare. Rommel was a daring and bold commander who, although he was far from infallible, never hesitated to punish mistakes made by his opponents.

Rommel arrived in Tripoli on 12 February 1941 and possessed a much more radical view of his task than to act merely as the commander of a passive blocking force. Instead, he wanted to drive the British out of Egypt and establish German control over the Middle East and in the process gain for himself imperishable military glory. The Italian forces in Libya had suffered humiliation and the arrival of German forces to support them did nothing for morale; Rommel was never noted for his tact in his relations with Italian superiors and subordinates. He began his habit of ignoring orders from General Gariboldi, the new Italian Commander-in-Chief Libya, and indeed his German superiors at Oberkommando des Heeres,[26] by launching an attack on the British 2nd Armoured Division at El Agheila on 31 March 1941. The British commanders on the ground responded with confusion and soon the British forces were in full retreat. The Afrika Korps bundled the Western Desert Force out of Cyrenaica in a matter of days and, by 11 April, German and Italian forces had already surrounded the port of Tobruk. Perhaps the worst loss suffered by the British during the debacle was the capture of Lieutenant-General Richard O'Connor and Brigadier Combe on 7 April, two of the most experienced and skilled of Britain's desert commanders, when they were travelling up to the front to restore the situation.

The British loss of Cyrenaica was due primarily to Rommel's audacity in mounting an attack with inadequate forces. Wavell had quite consciously stripped bare the Western Desert Force in order to provide troops for the Greek expeditionary force. The 2nd Armoured Division which held El Agheila was inexperienced and new to the desert but, perhaps most importantly, Wavell had based his calculations on excellent intelligence of German troop movements and intentions which had shown clearly that the Afrika Korps would not be ready to mount an attack before May.

All important radio traffic of the German Armed Forces was encrypted before transmission through the use of an 'Enigma' machine. Due to the sophistication of this electro-mechanical device, the Germans believed that their radio traffic, while it might be intercepted, was undecipherable. However, British code-breakers at Bletchley Park in Hertfordshire, working on the leads given to them by Polish intelligence, had managed to break some Enigma traffic in 1940. Intelligence gained from the 'Enigma' decrypts was known as 'Ultra' and remained highly secret throughout the war – and for many years afterwards. Although the use of Ultra intelligence was still in its infancy in 1941, from 28 February Brigadier Shearer, Wavell's chief intelligence officer, was receiving intelligence based on the radio messages of Fliegerkorps X and the Fliegerführer Afrika. The disaster in Cyrenaica was an early demonstration that, although Ultra intelligence was of great value, its correct application could be fraught with difficulties. Even possessing direct intelligence of German orders and intentions could still be misleading.[27] Rommel had ignored orthodox military planning and achieved an astonishing success precisely because of his boldness.

Rommel's first offensive in Libya had certainly been full of sound and fury but although German and Italian forces made repeated attacks, the 9th Australian Division put up a tenacious defence of the fortress of Tobruk throughout the summer and autumn of 1941. Rommel's forces remained stalled in front of the fortress and in defensive positions on the Egyptian frontier. Rommel could not advance into Egypt with a British bastion in his rear and, without the port capacity that Tobruk represented, any such attempt would have been doomed to failure. The transfer of Fliegerkorps X to Greece in May 1941 meant that, while the Royal Navy suffered terrible punishment from its attentions during the evacuation from Crete, pressure was slowly lifted from Malta and it was possible to restore its offensive capability.

The source of Rommel's frustration was wider than he realised. The complex interaction of air, land and sea combined with competing strategies and operations had so far foiled his desire to reach Alexandria and the Suez Canal. Rommel's surprise offensive in March 1941 had coincided with a period of great weakness in the Middle East for Britain. Wavell had to deal almost simultaneously with Rommel's attack and the evacuation of Greece, followed by the German airborne attack on the island of Crete. Yet the single most dangerous problem was Raschid Ali's rising in Iraq which saw the Iraqi Army mount a siege of the RAF's No. 44 Training Squadron at the Habbaniya airfield. Had this succeeded, the small German squadron which flew to Iraq would probably have been sufficient to bolster the Iraqis against British attempts to restore the situation.[28] Britain came dangerously close to losing its control of the Middle Eastern oil supplies. Immediately after the situation was restored in Iraq, Wavell had to mount an offensive into French-controlled Syria to prevent the German use of its airbases. Meanwhile, the war in Ethiopia and East Africa was still being waged. The period March to June 1941 saw numerous challenges to Britain's position in the Middle East, but none of the threats was individually sufficiently dangerous to overwhelm the British.

Wavell came under intense pressure from Churchill to relieve Tobruk but the two ill-considered and ill-prepared attempts of Operations Brevity, in May, and Battleaxe, in June, simply saw the Western Desert Force break its head against Rommel's frontier defences. Even though Wavell had achieved the remarkable feat of holding the British position in the Middle East together when threatened with complete disaster, Churchill had lost patience with his taciturn commander. Wavell left the Middle East Command in June 1941 and was replaced by General Claude Auchinleck, who had impressed Churchill while in charge of Southern Command in England during 1940 and as Commander-in-Chief India in 1941.

Auchinleck began to organise the forces of the Western Desert Force for a more deliberate offensive to relieve Tobruk. General Alan Cunningham, who had just completed the successful campaign in Italian East Africa which saw the liberation of Ethiopia, was given command of the newly created Eighth Army. The build-up of men and materiel took a number of months and it was not until 18 November that Operation Crusader was finally launched. Rommel was taken by surprise: he had been about to launch his own effort to take the fortress. Operation Crusader saw a series of confusing, swirling and bloody armoured battles around Sidi Rezegh which wore both sides down to the point of near collapse. In an attempt to break the deadlock, Rommel drove with the Afrika Korps towards the Egyptian frontier in what became known as the 'dash to the wire', but this daring move failed to stampede Eighth Army. It was no accident that the basing of Force 'K', composed of two Royal Navy light cruisers and two destroyers, at Malta in October saw Rommel's supply situation deteriorate to the point of collapse at the same moment as Auchinleck launched Operation Crusader in

November 1941 to relieve Tobruk. On 9 November, the actions of Malta-based aircraft and submarines in combination with the surface ships of Force 'K' had forced the Italians to halt all convoys to Tripoli. With his supply line strangled, Rommel had no prospect for resupply and he had little choice but to withdraw to El Agheila to save his force from destruction.

However, as the depleted British forces cautiously followed up the Axis withdrawal, the desert pendulum swung once again. The loss of Force 'K' in an uncharted minefield off Tripoli on 18 December and the deployment of Fliegerkorps II, under the command of Albert Kesselring, to Sicily the same month broke the British stranglehold over the Axis line of communication. Kesselring had explicit orders to 'neutralise' Malta and the British capacity to interfere with Italian convoys withered. This enabled Rommel to rebuild his strength far faster than Eighth Army which now had to wrestle with the problems of supplying its forward troops over a distance of 900 miles.

The surprise Japanese attack on the United States Pacific Fleet at Pearl Harbor on 7 December 1941 widened the war into a truly global conflict. Hitler's declaration of war upon the United States, combined with Roosevelt's policy of 'Germany First', meant that Britain would soon have the direct military support of a powerful ally. However, the Japanese threat to British possessions in the Far East also robbed Auchinleck of the fruits of victory in Cyrenaica. At the very moment when the injection of reserve forces could have stabilised the front at El Agheila in preparation for a further British offensive, Auchinleck was forced to send troops and resources to the Far East. This left the forward units of Eighth Army weakened and ripe for a counterstroke.

In January 1942, Rommel's newly renamed Panzerarmee Afrika drove the Eighth Army back to Ain el Gazala, just west of Tobruk. The loss of the Cyrenaican airfields made the Royal Navy's task in running convoys through to Malta yet more difficult. Churchill began to harass Auchinleck with demands for an immediate offensive to recapture Cyrenaica and thus relieve the pressure on Malta which, under Fliegerkorps II bombardment, had become the most bombed place on earth. Meanwhile, the Axis commanders began to plan their own offensive to take Tobruk.

The plans for Operation Venezia had been thrashed out between Marshal Count Ugo Cavallero, the Chief of the Italian General Staff, Field Marshal Albert Kesselring, the German Commander-in-Chief South, and Rommel, the commander of the Panzerarmee Afrika. Official Axis policy was that, once the Panzerarmee had defeated the Eighth Army and seized Tobruk, its advance would be halted on the Egyptian border. This operational pause would enable the Panzerarmee to be resupplied for a sustained advance into Egypt. Meanwhile, air and naval assets would be redeployed for Operation Herkules, the long-planned conquest of Malta. Once the island fortress was in Axis hands, the supply routes to Africa would be considerably safer and convoy timings much more reliable. The Panzerarmee would then be unleashed in an invasion of Egypt with the Suez Canal as its ultimate objective. The agreed Axis strategy was ambitious but, for once, coordinated.

The Eighth Army stood on the Gazala line with 100,000 men, 849 tanks and 604 aircraft. The Panzerarmee Africa attacked with 90,000 men and only 561 tanks (228 of which were inferior Italian designs) and 542 aircraft. Although Eighth Army's position was defensive it remained poised to seize the initiative. It had in fact been planning its own offensive, codenamed Acrobat, to defeat the Panzerarmee and finally destroy the Axis presence in North Africa. It was a strong force in apparently formidable positions. Enormous 'mine marshes' had been laid to channel any advance by the Axis forces. Its fighting units were fresh and rested, the ranks filled with many desert veterans well used to tangling with Rommel's Panzerarmee Afrika. Some of its armoured units had just been re-equipped with the powerful new American Grant tank which easily outclassed all of the German and Italian models. Meanwhile, the new British six-pounder anti-tank gun – a match for the German 50mm Pak 38 – was just reaching the Royal Artillery's anti-tank batteries.[29] Rommel's men would no longer have quite the qualitative advantage in weaponry which they had enjoyed during the previous year.

Eighth Army also held what it believed was a major advantage in intelligence. It was well aware of Rommel's plans for an early offensive. Using Ultra intelligence sourced from the decryption of German Enigma radio transmissions, the code-breakers at Bletchley Park were able to give the intelligence staff of General Headquarters Middle East and the Eighth Army clear warning of Rommel's intention to launch an offensive against the Gazala line late in May 1942. However, Enigma intelligence could not help the Eighth Army intelligence officers, nor Lieutenant-General Neil Ritchie, the commander of Eighth Army, to divine Rommel's plan of battle.

On the afternoon of 26 May, the main units of the Panzerarmee Afrika began their long drive into the desert. By dusk, British patrols had observed the long columns of tanks, trucks and guns heading towards Bir Hacheim. Yet, even though Eighth Army had thus been well warned not only of the German attack but now of its probable direction, little was done to capitalise on the intelligence.

The next day, the concentrated power of the Afrika Korps descended on the strung-out elements of the 7th Armoured Division and scattered them. At 10.00 hours, German armoured cars overran 7th Armoured Division Headquarters. Such a lapse in security was inexcusable and, although Major-General Messervy escaped, 7th Armoured Division had ceased to function as a unit.[30]

4th Armoured Brigade, after inflicting considerable loss on the advancing

15th Panzer Division, retired north to El Adem having lost much of its strength, and that afternoon 2nd and 22nd Armoured Brigades also engaged in a fierce action with the panzer divisions. But the British armoured brigades were coming into action individually and without their supporting motor infantry and anti-tank guns. This meant that they simply did not have the stamina or strength to sustain the fight. Yet, by the end of 27 May, the Panzerarmee was beginning to run into serious difficulties. The panzer divisions had lost a third of their strength in the heavy fighting, and their forces were now scattered over a wide area – on the British side of the minefields. This meant that the Axis supply columns were completely out of touch and unable to reach the fighting units.[31]

By the end of 28 May, General Ritchie was confident that the tide of battle was flowing in his favour. The units of the Afrika Korps remained separated and were still having to fight off the attentions of the British armoured brigades. By 29 May, Rommel's forces were in a critical situation. Eighth Army seemed to have trapped the Afrika Korps against its minefields and it appeared that the main striking force of the Panzerarmee would wither and die over the next few days. Hemmed in by the minefields to the south and the British armoured brigades to the north and east, Rommel concentrated his forces in an area that became known as the 'Cauldron'. The Axis forces deployed a heavy anti-tank gun screen to hold off the British armoured forces and began to cut a gap in the minefields to the east to restore communication with the rest of the Panzerarmee Afrika.[32]

It was only on 30 May that Rommel realised his route to the west was barred by the 150th Brigade, well dug in and supported by 30 tanks from the 1st Army Tank Brigade. Now desperate to cut a gap in the minefields, Rommel shifted forces from the north and east and threw them against the beleaguered 150th Brigade. Meanwhile, the British armoured brigades had put in numerous piecemeal attacks but met with the concentrated fire of the Axis anti-tank gun screen and made no progress. None of them had succeeded in preventing Rommel from switching troops to launch against the 150th Brigade.[33]

The slow reactions of Eighth Army Headquarters meant that the eventual recognition of the plight of 150th Brigade came too late for any effective action to be taken. Ritchie seemed to be making decisions in slow motion; it was not until the night of 1–2 June that he finally decided to attack the Axis forces holding the Cauldron. The hastily organised sortie achieved nothing but loss. This failure, and the belated realisation that 150th Brigade had been destroyed, led Ritchie to make fresh plans for an attack on the Cauldron – but in '48 to 72 hours'. Ritchie had lost the initiative and his best chance for defeating Rommel.[34]

Rommel wasn't willing to wait patiently for Ritchie to develop his attack. Having secured his supply lines, he sent the 90th Light and the Trieste

Divisions south to deal with Bir Hacheim. He knew that, once this outpost had fallen, little could prevent his onward rush to Tobruk and the encirclement of the British forces holding the weakened Gazala line.

Stuka dive bombers hammered the Free French defenders of Bir Hacheim in swirling sandstorms while the soldiers of the 90th Light and Trieste Divisions probed the defences. General Koenig's Free French put up fierce resistance but while battle raged at Bir Hacheim little pressure was exerted against the Axis defenders of the Cauldron. Although small British columns continued to raid and harass the Axis supply lines, this could not dislodge the really dangerous Axis forces or save Bir Hacheim. Both sides were reorganising and preparing for the next blow.[35] However, Ritchie's passivity doomed Bir Hacheim to slow strangulation and capture. One by one, piece by piece, Rommel's army was destroying the units of the Eighth Army.

When, finally, the Eighth Army acted to crush the German forces in the Cauldron, it was far too late. Operation Aberdeen, which began at 02.50 hours on 5 June, was an unmitigated disaster. The armour of 7th Armoured Division and the infantry of 10th Indian Division were tasked with mounting the attack, but with the armour under the control of 13 Corps, and the infantry under the control of 30 Corps, there was no coordination of their movement. Eighth Army yet again dissipated its strength in piecemeal attacks which dissolved against a tough Axis defence. The attacks made by 7th Armoured and 5th Indian Divisions in fact reached their objectives under cover of a heavy artillery barrage relatively easily. It was only at dawn that they realised their mistake: the German defences lay further to the west and the heavy bombardment had fallen on empty desert. The attack had been a blow into the air.

The German reaction was fierce and caused heavy losses amongst both the armour and infantry. The Indian infantry battalions that had advanced deep into the German positions were all overrun and captured. The artillery batteries which had been brought forward and concentrated for the barrage were caught without armoured support and destroyed by the advancing German panzers. The gunners fought and died by their guns, but by the end of the day more than 100 anti-tank guns and field guns – four complete artillery regiments – had been destroyed at little cost.[36] By the end of this fiasco, Eighth Army had not only lost the initiative but had lost its ability to control Rommel.

After days of aerial bombardment and fierce fighting, Bir Hacheim was finally evacuated by the Free French on 10 June, who managed to escape with most of their force intact. With his southern flank secure, Rommel could now return to his planned northward thrust. Fatal disaster struck Eighth Army on 12 and 13 June, when both sides' armour met in action once more around the 'Knightsbridge' area. Again, the British armoured units suffered from fatal lapses in command. Confusion descended upon the commanders of the British divisions at the very moment that the Germans attacked. General Messervy lost touch with his headquarters and General Norrie, which meant that the strung-out British armoured brigades were left uncertain of their orders. In the swirling fight that developed, the Germans gained the upper hand and capitalised upon it; the panzers encircled the British armour and attacked from three sides. Confused and fierce fighting in the middle of a severe dust storm continued during 13 June which saw the Knightsbridge position captured and the British armoured brigades reduced to mere shadows. By the end of 13 June, Eighth Army could muster only 50 cruiser and 20 infantry tanks, and, what was worse, because the armoured brigades had been forced to withdraw, could not recover the hundreds of wrecked and damaged tanks which littered the battlefield.[37] This disaster sealed the fate of Eighth Army.

Without the power to halt, let alone defeat the Panzerarmee, Eighth Army fell back to the Egyptian frontier. This exposed the fortress of Tobruk, which had been held against Rommel for much of 1941, to a full-scale attack. In January 1942, a conference of the three Commanders-in-Chief Middle East – Admiral Andrew Cunningham, Air Marshal Arthur Tedder, and General Sir Claude Auchinleck[38] – had come to the 'firm and unanimous decision that Tobruk should not again be held'.[39] Churchill had insisted that the port must be held. Now, that the prospect of the Axis capture of Tobruk actually loomed, an unhappy series of misunderstandings between Churchill, Auchinleck and Ritchie resulted in muddle. Eighth Army was withdrawn, against Auchinleck's wishes, to the Egyptian frontier where it could rest, reorganise and, most importantly, rebuild its armoured formations, while the 2nd South African Division and supporting troops were left in Tobruk to accept a 'temporary' siege.

While the staff of Eighth Army were calculating in terms of a one- or two-month siege which would enable them to rebuild their armour quietly on the frontier, Rommel was planning a lightning-fast attack to seize the prize which had been denied him the previous year. On 20 June, wave after wave of German and Italian bombers attacked Tobruk with impunity. At dawn, Rommel's tired men moved into the attack against the fortress. The defences were not what they had been. Many of the mines had been lifted and placed in the ineffectual Gazala line, while some of the troops were inexperienced and stunned by the ferocity of the attack. By midday, the vital crossroads of King's Cross was in Axis hands and it was only a matter of time before the fortress fell. Major-General H. B. Klopper, commander of the 2nd South African Division, vacillated between fighting on, breaking out and surrender. The decision was made for him when German panzers broke through to the port. Almost 35,000 men[40] were taken prisoner and vast quantities of supplies and stores were either captured or destroyed. The port which had held out for over nine months against Rommel the year before – and in which Churchill had invested a good deal of political capital – fell after just two days.[41] And with the capture of Tobruk, Rommel's forces were now free to mount an invasion of Egypt.

Colonel Bonner L. Fellers, the American military attaché at the US Embassy in Cairo, had paid close attention to the fighting at Gazala and lost faith in the abilities of the British Eighth Army. On 20 June, Fellers reported to Washington:

> With numerically superior forces, with tanks, planes, artillery, means of transport, and reserves of every kind, the British army has twice failed to defeat the Axis forces in Libya. Under the present command and with the measures taken in a hit or miss fashion the granting of 'lend-lease' alone cannot ensure a victory. The Eighth Army has failed to maintain the morale of its troops; its tactical conceptions were always wrong, it neglected completely cooperation between the various arms; its reactions to the lightning changes of the battlefield were always slow.[42]

This was a damning but accurate analysis of the Eighth Army at Gazala. The United States had become the 'arsenal of democracy' in 1940 and under the Lend-Lease programme had supplied Britain with vast quantities of equipment and supplies. Yet it appeared that the British were wasting this largesse and incapable of organising for victory.

Churchill was in Washington taking part in a series of high-level meetings to finalise British and American strategic plans for 1942 and 1943 when he heard the news of the fall of Tobruk. The discussions would dictate the shape and course of the rest of the war and set the tone for the alliance. Suffering military disaster in the middle of these negotiations was a grievous blow for Churchill. It called into question British military capacity and thus her value as an ally to the United States. Yet the American response was remarkably generous. General Marshall, the Chief of Staff of the US Army, immediately suggested sending the US 1st Armored Division to Egypt to bolster the British position. This was an offer made in good faith yet to Churchill it may well have suggested a bitter parallel with Hitler's original despatch of Rommel's Afrika Korps to Libya to prop up his failing Italian ally in February 1941.

While Churchill grappled with this strategic humiliation, a certain complacency still persisted within the headquarters of Eighth Army, now based at Sollum on the Libyan–Egyptian border. Ritchie and his staff had long since lost their grip on the military realities of the situation. There was a general feeling both at Eighth Army and at General Headquarters Middle East that Rommel's offensive power must have been dulled after fighting such a fierce battle and that it would be days or even weeks before the Panzerarmee could seriously threaten the frontier. The Combined Staffs working in Cairo decided that the best course of action, given the lack of armoured forces, was to:

> delay the enemy on the frontier with forces which are kept fully mobile while withdrawing main body of 8th Army to the Matruh defences. This coupled with delaying action by our air forces, gives us the best chance of gaining time in which to reorganise and build up a striking force with which to resume the offensive.[43]

Such planning could only be predicated on the belief that Rommel would be unable to mount an immediate threat to Egypt.

Major-General Eric Dorman-Smith, the Deputy Chief of the General Staff Middle East, briefed worried war correspondents in Cairo on 21 June in an hour-long press conference. Although much of his confidence was feigned, Dorman-Smith's soothing words also reflected some of the remnants of optimism left in the British command. *The Times* paraphrased Dorman-Smith's words:

> The disappointment may be tempered by the consideration that in the see-saw of desert warfare . . . the most mobile and hard-hitting force wins . . . Our Commanders . . . are not despondent . . . They are convinced that the next time the pendulum swings it will go in our favour, and the swing will be deeper.[44]

Educating the British public in the 'diminishing power of the offensive' could not disguise the humiliation that Eighth Army had suffered, or the deep crisis that faced the British in the Middle East.

Ritchie's plan of rebuilding his shattered force behind the Egyptian frontier might have worked had the Axis powers held to their original strategy but Rommel had no intention of waiting for the reduction of Malta before invading Egypt. Kesselring met with Rommel on the afternoon of 21 June to discuss future plans and reminded Rommel that the agreed strategy called for Operation Herkules to follow as soon as Tobruk was taken. He also warned Rommel that his supplies during the offensive had only been assured because Malta had been neutralised in preparation for the assault. Kesselring had already ordered his air units back to Sicily for Herkules. The next day, Rommel met with General Count Barbasetti, the Chief of the Italian Liaison Staff, who informed him that General Bastico, the Italian Commander-in-Chief North Africa, had ordered Rommel to halt. Rommel, who had just heard of his promotion to field marshal that day, told Barbasetti that he would not accept this 'advice'.[45]

Faced with opposition from both his German and Italian superiors, Rommel simply short-circuited the Axis command chain. He made a direct appeal to

Mussolini on 22 June, which was then passed on to Hitler. The Führer had never been an enthusiastic supporter of Herkules, perhaps a legacy of the costly operation on Crete, and was happy to postpone the operation indefinitely. Hitler also believed that the British had lost the opportunity to grab Tripoli from the Italians in January 1941, so he had little hesitation in sanctioning Rommel's continued advance. He signalled to Mussolini that 'It is only once in a lifetime that the Goddess of Victory smiles.' Mussolini was only too happy to be convinced and, against the protests of Cavallero, gave his blessing to Rommel. News of Mussolini's approval arrived in the first hour of 24 June; the units of the Panzerarmee had been on the march since 22 June. The entire Axis strategy for the Mediterranean theatre had been placed on a new course.[46]

Yet Rommel's decision to pursue the Eighth Army was based not only on his own intuition and thirst for military glory but also on crucial American reports of British frailty. On 19 June 1942, the British code-breakers working at Bletchley Park decrypted and translated another Enigma transmission from something called the 'Good Source'. The message discussed the British view of German tank tactics.[47] This account provided a clear description of the battle drill employed by the German panzer divisions when assaulting British defended positions. The 'Good Source' had previously supplied Italian and German military intelligence with detailed information concerning the plans and operations of Eighth Army as well as its battlefield performance. The unwitting 'Good Source' was none other than Colonel Fellers, the military attaché in the US Embassy in Cairo.

Not surprisingly, the United States had taken a real interest in the fighting in North Africa. British experience in fighting the Germans and Italians was of enormous value to an army which knew that it would have to fight the German Army yet had few direct means of collecting intelligence of German methods. Fellers had pursued his task with real vigour and had made many contacts within Eighth Army. A stream of US liaison officers were sent up to the front to report on the fighting. Fellers thus often knew a great deal about the ongoing operations and sent detailed reports back to Washington on the course of the fighting, the nature of the tactics and the operational situation. Unfortunately, unbeknownst to Fellers or the authorities in Washington, the Italian Military Intelligence Service (SIM) had broken the American diplomatic cipher. An Italian agent had obtained a position as a cleaner in the American Embassy to the Vatican in Rome and managed to gain access to the safe where the cipher keys were kept. Access to the State Department's diplomatic code allowed the Italians to break any messages sent in it. The information received from the 'Good Source' was quickly sent on to the intelligence staff of the Panzerarmee Afrika.

The British were first alerted to the problem through their own decryption of German Enigma traffic. On 19 June, Churchill wrote on the bottom

of one of the top-secret translations he received informing him of important German signals: 'Is this still going on?' – as by that date the British
knew that high-grade information was being passed to the Germans through
the US Embassy in Cairo. The Prime Minister was informed:

> US authorities having now changed their cipher, no further leakage should
> occur as from 25th July 1942.
>
> If leakage continues, then there must be a traitor with access to American
> telegrams in Cairo transmitting by secret wireless from Egypt but available
> evidence does not support this likelihood.[48]

Not surprisingly, once the British realised the extent of the problem, they
– and the Americans – moved quickly to plug the leak. The State Department
changed its diplomatic code and Fellers returned home in late July 1942.

Unfortunately, at just the moment the British finally realised that the
American diplomatic code had been compromised, Rommel was receiving
the most important material that he ever gained from his 'Good Source'. A
subsequent report by SIM noted that: 'On 20 June there came to our knowledge the full picture of the sharp crisis through which the British forces
were passing.'[49] Fellers had visited Eighth Army during June 1942 and sent
back a stream of reports to Washington detailing the British defeat in the
desert. On 16 June, Fellers reported the full extent of the British tank losses
during Gazala:

> The British began the present operations on 26 May with 742 tanks . . . On
> 15 June at least 372 had been replaced. A total of 1142 tanks was thus thrown
> into battle . . . The British losses up to the present amount to at least 1009
> tanks . . . On 10 June there were only 133 tanks of all types in all the depots
> of the Middle East.[50]

By 20 June this invaluable intelligence was in Rommel's hands. He now knew
that, weakened though his panzer divisions were, the British had virtually
no tanks left to stop them. The same day, Fellers sent one of his most detailed
reports back to Washington, providing Rommel with all the operational intelligence he needed. Fellers detailed what British estimates of Axis strength
were, but also gave a full listing of the remaining British forces and estimates of their losses of tanks and artillery:

> The units left to the Eighth Army are: the South African Brigade, of low
> combat efficiency; a brigade of the Fiftieth Division; the second group of
> Free French; a grouped Indian Division; the fresh and complete New Zealand
> Division, which has no replacements available; the Ninth Australian Division,
> which is still in Palestine and in Syria. In the Middle East it is estimated that

one weak armored brigade can be ready at the frontier by the first week in July . . . A very optimistic estimate of the British tank force at the front is 100 tanks. Of this optimistic figure, only a small proportion are tanks of the American medium type and the rest are instead of the British cruising type, of no value . . . When it began operations, the Eighth Army had 21 regiments of 25 pounder artillery, three medium artillery regiments. The British have lost 8 full regiments . . . Consequently it is safe to estimate that they have lost from 40 to 50% of their artillery.[51]

This report was not strictly accurate. Fellers made no mention of the remnants of 7th Armoured Division, including 7th Motor Brigade, and he referred to a South African Brigade instead of the complete 1st South African Division which was now digging in at El Alamein. Although the 50th Division had lost its 150th Brigade at Gazala, it remained a viable combat formation. However, the report did accurately assess the crisis facing Eighth Army's tank strength and the loss of its artillery. Perhaps most important of all was the knowledge that the complete 9th Australian Division had yet to move into the theatre. If the Panzerarmee was to destroy Eighth Army at its weakest, it had to strike now. Detailed intelligence of this nature very rarely finds its way into the hands of a commander and Rommel was determined to make full use of it. Fellers ended his report with a grim conclusion:

1. The army has been defeated primarily because of the incompetency of its leaders; 2. If Rommel intends to take the Delta, now is the time; 3. The British must make haste to offer at least a respectable resistance to the forces of the Axis; 4. To hold the Middle East the British must be supplied immediately, in order of importance, with a large number of bombers, tanks, artillery.[52]

With a complete picture of British recriminations, low morale, of the crippling British losses and the existing order of battle, Rommel could make an informed calculation concerning the risks of continuing his pursuit of the British. His drive into Egypt was not the blind rush of a gambler, but based on the full knowledge of the British weakness.[53]

Armed with the knowledge that the British might well be on the point of collapse, Rommel was determined to take the opportunity to drive on to Cairo and Alexandria. If he held his army back while Malta was captured the British would have time to regroup and repair the effects of the defeat he had inflicted upon them. If he continued his pursuit, Rommel believed that he could bounce the remnants of the Eighth Army out of every defensive position on the road to Alexandria. Rommel now believed his victorious troops could drive the British out of Egypt altogether.

The calm rebuilding of the Eighth Army behind the frontier very soon turned into a confused rout. Although Ritchie had planned to fight a delaying

battle on the Egyptian frontier, with the loss of almost all of the armoured
force this was impossible. Ritchie was ordered to impose as much delay on
the Panzerarmee as possible while falling back on Mersa Matruh. The
Middle East Defence Committee instructed Ritchie 'to prepare to fight a
decisive action round Matruh and to delay the enemy as far west as possible'.[54]
In fact, the retirement from the frontier which was meant to delay the
Panzerarmee rapidly turned into headlong flight. Rommel's men experienced little or no delay in their equally headlong pursuit. Rommel knew
that speed was essential: if the British were given any respite they might be
able to recover. He drove his men on and on, deeper into Egypt. The
remnants of Eighth Army fell back towards the little coastal town of Mersa
Matruh, where, in 1940, General Wavell had decided he would stand in 'the
worst possible case'. That case had now become reality. Ritchie was determined to fight the final battle at Matruh; to save Egypt and his army or
suffer irretrievable defeat.

TWO

The Swing of the Pendulum

On 25 June 1942 General Claude Auchinleck, the British Commander-in-Chief Middle East, and Major-General Eric Dorman-Smith, better known as 'Chink', boarded a Boston bomber at Cairo West aerodrome. They were flying out to Maaten Baggush, the Headquarters of the Eighth Army. Auchinleck was a troubled man. He had flown up to Eighth Army just three days earlier to discuss the crisis with its commander, Lieutenant-General Neil Ritchie, but his present flight had a very different purpose. Auchinleck had already signalled the Chief of the Imperial General Staff,[1] General Alan Brooke, with his intentions: 'Am taking over command 8 Army from RITCHIE this afternoon . . . Shall use DORMAN SMITH as my Chief of Staff leaving CORBETT to represent me at GHQ.[2] Auchinleck's decision to take direct command of the army represented a real upheaval of the British command chain, a sign in itself of the deep crisis facing Middle East Command. Auchinleck had asked Dorman-Smith to act as his 'DCGS in the field' by dealing with all of the wider strategic issues concerning Middle East Command while he would command the army through the established staff at Army Headquarters. This left Lieutenant-General Tom Corbett, the Chief of the General Staff Middle East, as Auchinleck's deputy in Cairo.

Auchinleck believed that the seriousness of the crisis warranted his taking direct command over the remnants of the Eighth Army, and that only he could restore the situation. He may well have been right. Auchinleck had, after all, once before taken over command of Eighth Army – in December 1941, when General Alan Cunningham had suffered a nervous breakdown. At that time, once the crisis of Operation Crusader was past, he had controversially handed the command of the army to Neil Ritchie, his chief staff officer at Middle East Headquarters. Ritchie was an excellent staff officer but he had very little operational experience and Auchinleck had always attempted to look over his shoulder, giving avuncular advice from Cairo which did nothing to develop Ritchie's authority over the army. By taking field command again, Auchinleck had succumbed to the terrible temptation felt by most strategic commanders – of getting involved with the demands of battlefield command. From the moment he boarded the Boston bomber,

Auchinleck had effectively surrendered his strategic command of the Middle East; no one man could effectively fill both posts. While Auchinleck concentrated his main attention and care on the battered remnants of the Eighth Army, General Headquarters Middle East was effectively rudderless.

Auchinleck seems never to have understood just how vulnerable this made his position. He had in fact offered his resignation to Brooke on 23 June:

> The unfavourable course of the recent battle in CYRENAICA culminating in the disastrous fall of TOBRUK impels me to ask you seriously to consider the advisability of retaining me in my command . . . Personally I feel fit to carry on and reasonably confident of being able to turn the tables on the enemy in time. All the same there is no doubt that in a situation like the present, fresh blood and new ideas at the top may make all the difference between success and stalemate.[3]

Auchinleck had even suggested his replacement: General Harold Alexander. But the replacement of the Commander-in-Chief Middle East at the height of the crisis would have been yet another political and military disaster for Churchill and it is not surprising that the offer was rejected. Brooke replied in a generous tone, mentioning that the Prime Minister had already expressed 'his entire confidence in you' before Auchinleck's telegram reached London and that he 'shared his views. My thoughts are with you in the difficult situation which confronts you.'[4] It would appear that Auchinleck simply meant to clear the air with this telegram, but by taking full personal responsibility for Gazala and Tobruk, Auchinleck had made himself a hostage to fortune.

Churchill was delighted when he heard that Auchinleck had taken direct command. Indeed, the Prime Minister had consistently urged Auchinleck to do so even before Gazala began. Churchill sent his Commander-in-Chief and new Army Commander a heartening message:

> I am very glad you have taken Command. Do not vex yourself with anything except the battle. Fight it out wherever it flows. Nothing matters but destroying the enemy's armed and armoured force. A strong stream of reinforcements is approaching. We are sure you are going to win in the end.[5]

The fact was that Auchinleck could not help but vex himself with his responsibility for the entire Middle Eastern theatre. However, these wider concerns were of secondary importance; from now on Auchinleck had to try to stem the tide which threatened to engulf Eighth Army.

As the engines of the Boston roared for takeoff, Auchinleck and Dorman-Smith settled themselves down on the empty floor of the bomber and began to discuss possible solutions to the plight facing Eighth Army. There were too many questions and not enough answers:

If it was no longer possible to regroup Eighth Army for battle at Matruh, could that Army be pulled out and re-deployed elsewhere . . . Could it be reorganised, re-educated, re-vitalised in the time gained by retreat? What was Rommel's Afrika Korps really worth after a month's hard fighting?[6]

Auchinleck and Dorman-Smith hoped, almost against hope, that with a new commander and just a little time, Eighth Army would be able to halt Rommel's victorious Panzerarmee Afrika before it reached Alexandria and Cairo. The dilemma was very real. Could the battered and exhausted remnants of the Eighth Army hold on against the much depleted but still advancing elements of the Panzerarmee Afrika? Given the disasters which had already been suffered by the Eighth Army, the situation looked bleak. Yet in their discussions on the floor of the bomber, Auchinleck and Dorman-Smith thrashed out a series of ideas which they believed would give Eighth Army a fighting chance.

The most important decision was to abandon Mersa Matruh and withdraw the Eighth Army to the area around El Alamein, which lay 150 miles further east. Virtually all British planning up to this point had understood a last-ditch stand at Mersa Matruh as the 'worst possible case'. In 1940, General Archibald Wavell had recognised that, if the Western Desert Force was pushed back to Mersa Matruh, the crucial naval base at Alexandria and the population of Cairo would be exposed to air attack. Given this vulnerability, which would force the evacuation of the Mediterranean Fleet from its main port, he had believed that any further retreat would lead to disaster. When Auchinleck took command in the Middle East in June 1941, he had ordered the construction of some fortifications at El Alamein, but it was still generally considered that the loss of Matruh meant the loss of Egypt.

Auchinleck and Dorman-Smith now realised that, in all likelihood, the Eighth Army would be destroyed if it fought at Matruh. Both men knew that 'El Alamein offered by far the strongest position in the Western Desert as both its flanks rested on impassable obstacles'.[7] It was far better to pull the army back to here, where the Qattara Depression pushed up towards the coast. With its impassable salt marshes on one flank and the sea on the other, there remained only a narrow neck of desert 40 miles wide. While the defences at El Alamein and in the desert to the south were still sketchy, the position did limit the opportunities for Rommel's characteristic outflanking sweep through the desert. Given the reduced state of Eighth Army forces, El Alamein offered them an even chance of holding Rommel before he reached Alexandria.

When the Boston landed at Maaten Baggush, Auchinleck and Dorman-Smith drove straight to Ritchie's headquarters. The same headquarters had been occupied by Lieutenant-General Richard O'Connor eighteen months before when he had planned his masterful attack on the Italians at Sidi

Barrani. The headquarters was now witness to a more doleful occasion. Auchinleck went inside and, without undue ceremony, he curtly informed Ritchie that he was taking over command of the Eighth Army. Ritchie was sacked. There is no doubt that Ritchie felt badly treated. A mutual friend wrote to Auchinleck after Auchinleck too had been sacked:

> I have seen Neil . . . He talked to me at some length about his battles but it was too close to the event, so far as he was concerned, for me to get very much out of him. It was rather like . . . asking a boxer in his dressing room who had just been rather badly mauled, what he thought of boxing generally. One is apt to get blood on one's clothes.[8]

Ritchie had been placed in an impossible situation when he was given command of the Eighth Army. Ritchie had impressed all who he worked for, including Brooke and Auchinleck, as an effective and intelligent staff officer. However, he simply did not have the necessary experience to succeed as the commander of Eighth Army.[9]

By sacking Ritchie without ceremony – there was no time, given the crisis – Auchinleck did not make a clear break between Ritchie's command and his new command. Generals have habitually sought scapegoats for disasters and sacked subordinates fairly and unfairly as a means of deflecting criticism. To search for scapegoats was not in Auchinleck's character, but, by not doing so, he unwittingly took the mantle of a scapegoat upon himself. Auchinleck had never taken such 'political' thinking seriously and he did not do so now. Instead, he concentrated on what he believed was necessary to halt and defeat Rommel.

The situation which greeted Auchinleck and Dorman-Smith at Maaten Baggush was very grave indeed. Ritchie's deployment for the coming battle was dangerous and there was no time now to change it. Dorman-Smith had 'writhed' in the War Room at General Headquarters Middle East 'as Ritchie's dispositions for the Matruh battle revealed themselves. Everywhere dispersion, nowhere concentration.'[10] 10 Corps Headquarters were taking over from the exhausted staff of 30 Corps and were tasked with holding the area of Matruh itself. The 10th Indian and 50th Divisions held the old minefields and defences of Matruh which Ritchie had decided to use as a 'fortress' like Tobruk, even though these positions were incomplete, badly laid out and unlikely to halt the Afrika Korps. 13 Corps, under Lieutenant-General William H. E. 'Strafer' Gott, was deployed nearly 20 miles to the south, to control the rocky escarpment which dominated the desert at that point. The fresh 2nd New Zealand Division, which had only just arrived from Syria, had been deployed in the Mersa Matruh defences until its commander, Lieutenant-General Bernard Freyberg, had complained. It was now deployed around Minqar Qaim – a position which was described as being in the middle of nowhere.[11] Even further south, watching the flank of the army, were the remnants of 1st Armoured Division. The 20-mile gap between the two main formations of Eighth Army was patrolled by two very small columns – Gleecol and Leathercol – which were formed from battalions of the 29th Indian Brigade. Auchinleck realised that there was really nothing to stop the Afrika Korps from motoring straight through the gap and enveloping the Eighth Army from the rear.[12] If 10 Corps was encircled in Mersa Matruh it might well meet the same fate as the 2nd South African Division at Tobruk.

Dorman-Smith saw that there could have been a different approach to the coming battle. He later observed:

> Correctly both of Eighth Army's Corps should have been deployed for battle, shoulder to shoulder, on the open desert south of the northern escarpment, with only a token force in the Matruh defended perimeter. No heed should have been taken to the now inapposite previously prepared defensive positions or the incomplete minefields. Had this been done and the armour moved from the southern flank into centrally located Army reserve, Rommel's impetuous advance would have met a powerful force in place of a vacuum dividing two strong but uncoordinated wings.[13]

Such a plan would certainly have presented Rommel with a much more serious problem at Matruh, but there was no time now to change the dispositions. Eighth Army could either stand and fight on the ground it occupied, however dangerous the deployment, or turn and run for Alamein.

Auchinleck had been convinced of the need to retire to Alamein during the flight to Baggush, but he was not a man to give up without a fight. He decided that, although Eighth Army had to retain its 'freedom of action' and not be 'pinned down at Matruh',[14] he would nonetheless fight at Matruh in an attempt to halt Rommel. If any danger of encirclement threatened, he would withdraw. It is likely that the political significance of Matruh influenced his decision. Auchinleck later noted that 'The loss of Matruh would be a further shock to Egyptian morale, and Axis propaganda would certainly hail it as another triumph.'[15] Even though Matruh was no more than a small fishing village and port, its loss would have serious political repercussions in Cairo and London. Auchinleck decided to fight and see what developed.

Unfortunately, this compromise was probably the worst option because it meant that any withdrawal would have to be made while in contact with the enemy. There might well have been just enough time to withdraw from Matruh, evading contact with Rommel's spearheads, if Eighth Army had moved quickly. Auchinleck's decision made a messy fight almost inevitable.

Late in the evening of 26 June, the German 90th Light Division advanced towards the minefield barrier south of Mersa Matruh. A 13 Corps Intelligence Summary stated:

They . . . advanced in very close order actually through the minefield, not the gap; the mines apparently failed to explode. A thrust of this nature late in the day has often been employed by the Germans in the past and is intended to cause the maximum possible confusion when darkness falls. The object was to a certain extent obtained in that the enemy's numbers were at first over-estimated – there appear to have been only in fact 30 tks – and the direction of his advance was not clearly followed.[16]

The advance achieved exactly what it had intended; Leathercol was dispersed after a short action, and the Germans penetrated through the weak minefield without loss. Further south, 21st Panzer Division inflicted similar damage to Gleecol and passed through the minefield. The Afrika Korps had operated exactly as Dorman-Smith had feared. The way was open for a further, more dramatic, advance the next day. As the remnants of the 29th Indian Brigade withdrew to the east, there was now a 20-mile gap between the two corps of Eighth Army and communications between them were already beginning to break down. Conflicting reports had come into various headquarters but most agreed that the Germans had at least 100 tanks in their spearheads.[17] The correct figure of 30 tanks was not established until the damage had already been done; Eighth Army believed it was facing an aggressive enemy with an overwhelming advantage in armour.

The next day, 90th Light continued its advance to the east, skirting Mersa Matruh. It came under heavy artillery fire but was still able to attack and virtually destroy an isolated battalion of 151st Infantry Brigade. The 9th Durham Light Infantry fought hard but was overwhelmed. The same dynamics of isolated British units being overwhelmed one by one still seemed to be playing out at Mersa Matruh. Once brought under heavy artillery fire, the 90th Light Division eventually veered off to the south and rested until the afternoon.

Meanwhile, as 21st Panzer Division advanced east on the north side of the escarpment, 15th Panzer advanced south of it. While 15th Panzer was halted and attacked by the 4th Armoured and 7th Motor Brigades, 21st Panzer motored on to reach the bottom of the escarpment beneath the positions of 2nd New Zealand Division at Minqar Qaim. At noon, Rommel ordered 21st Panzer to attack the forces at Minqar Qaim and insisted that the 90th Light Division should cut the coast road by evening. The Italian Littorio Division moved up in support of 21st Panzer Division, while the rest of the Italian XX Corps followed up behind the 15th Panzer Division.

Unfortunately, Auchinleck had sent messages to both Gott and Holmes that morning with instructions that, if it became necessary to withdraw, they should pull out together and aim for Minqar Omar 30 miles to the rear. There they were to halt and delay Rommel's forces again. The codeword for this withdrawal was 'Pike'.[18] However, concerted action by the two British corps commanders was already almost impossible, especially given communication difficulties. Separated by almost 20 miles of desert filled with hostile units, neither corps could really assist the other and any properly coordinated withdrawal was beyond their power.

Gott took matters into his own hands. He had already issued contingency withdrawal plans to his units even before he received Auchinleck's instructions, and, during the afternoon, Gott seems to have believed that the 21st Panzer Division's attack against Minqar Qaim threatened to encircle and split his command in two. With 1st Armoured Division in action against 15th Panzer, and now the 2nd New Zealand being attacked from the flank and rear by 21st Panzer, Gott decided to withdraw on his own authority.[19]

That evening Gott issued orders for withdrawal, but the situation descended into chaos. General Bernard Freyberg, the commander of 2nd New Zealand Division, had been wounded and Brigadier Leslie Inglis, commander of 4th New Zealand Infantry Brigade, had hurriedly taken over command of the division. Orders for the New Zealand Division to withdraw were transmitted but became garbled and confusion reigned. 1st Armoured Division was able to withdraw relatively unmolested, but the New Zealanders found themselves surrounded at Minqar Qaim, without armour support and with only thirty-five rounds per gun for their artillery. Inglis decided that he had to mount a break-out and planned to use his trusted 4th New Zealand Infantry Brigade to clear a gap for the rest of the division to pass through. Unfortunately, the transport for the division had been chased off by 21st Panzer Division and was unreachable by radio. With every available vehicle crammed with men, the New Zealanders began their move. 4th New Zealand Infantry Brigade crashed through the German lines and inflicted heavy casualties on the 104th Panzergrenadier Regiment. After numerous adventures, the New Zealand Division was able to regroup by the next night.[20]

While Gott had sent notification of his withdrawal to Eighth Army Headquarters, who had immediately issued the codeword 'Pike' to 10 Corps, General Holmes and his headquarters were out of radio contact with Eighth Army until early on 28 June. Holmes remained unaware that 13 Corps was withdrawing and instead planned a counterattack to seize the line of the northern escarpment at Bir Sarahna. While this would not fully close the gap between the two corps, it would have increased the Afrika Korps' difficulties considerably. The attack went ahead, but achieved little and the 50th Division failed to reach the escarpment.

By the morning of 28 June, 10 Corps was cut off at Mersa Matruh while the units of 13 Corps motored for Fuka. Throughout the day, while the Afrika Korps drove hard to get as far east as possible, 10 Corps remained immobile and a victim of the garbled communications with Eighth Army. It was nearly noon before Holmes received an important order from Auchinleck:

No question of fighting it out. No time to stage deliberate attack along road
for which there is probably no objective. You will slip out to-night with whole
force on broad front, turn east on high ground and rally El Daba. 13 Corps
will cover you.[21]

Of course, 13 Corps was now miles away and utterly incapable of covering
anyone. That evening, 21st Panzer Division overwhelmed the remnants of
the 29th Indian Brigade at Fuka, leaving 10 Corps very nearly beyond help.

That night, the columns of the 10th Indian and 50th Divisions attempted
their break-out. There were innumerable confused actions in the darkness as
the Indian and British troops came across German tank leaguers and
attempted to break clear. 10th Indian Division in particular lost many men
and vehicles during the break-out. Even though the majority of the troops
of 10 Corps managed to escape, both divisions had been shattered. The
remnants streamed through the Alamein position to reform near Alexandria.[22]

Auchinleck had taken direct command over Eighth Army because he
believed that he would be able to master the situation better than Ritchie
who, by late June, was clearly out of his depth. Yet the battle of Mersa
Matruh had turned into another fiasco for the British. Caught by Rommel's
spearheads between defence and withdrawal, Eighth Army had never really
had a chance to fight properly. The result had been the loss of two badly
needed infantry divisions. Rommel seemed as unstoppable as ever.

With the loss of Mersa Matruh, Auchinleck had to develop a new plan.
Wavell's 'worst possible case' had now happened, and there were no existing
plans which envisaged the continued retreat of Eighth Army. Auchinleck
asked Dorman-Smith to prepare a new appreciation to cover the new 'worst
possible case' – the loss of Egypt. Auchinleck was still thinking as a strategic
commander and wanted the broadest picture from his erstwhile Chief
of Staff. Even at the risk of losing Egypt, Auchinleck was determined that
the Eighth Army should not be destroyed. He correctly identified that the
continued existence of Eighth Army remained Britain's 'centre of gravity'
in the Middle East. Clausewitz had defined the centre of gravity as 'the hub
of all power and movement, on which everything depends'.[23] No matter what
territory was given up, as long as Britain had a field army in existence,
Auchinleck believed the position would be retrievable. Indeed, Auchinleck
already knew that considerable reinforcements were on their way to Suez.
General George C. Marshall, the Chief of Staff of the US Army, had promised to send 300 Sherman tanks and 100 self-propelled artillery pieces. The
American 'Halpro' force of heavy Liberator bombers that had been destined
for China was rerouted to Palestine. Meanwhile, the British 8th Armoured,
44th (Home Counties) and 51st (Highland) Divisions were en route to Suez.
If the fight against the Panzerarmee could be maintained until at least some
of these reinforcements reached Suez, then defeat might still be turned into

victory against a dangerously overstretched Axis army. However, if the Eighth Army was encircled and destroyed by Rommel, the entire British position in the Middle East would probably collapse, and the Axis could gain possession of the entire area and all its riches.

Dorman-Smith's appreciation, tightly written in the approved Staff College format, acknowledged the Panzerarmee's superiority in armoured manoeuvre warfare. The objective for Eighth Army must be to ensure that its armoured strength could be rebuilt through a defence of the Red Sea ports. At the same time, the necessity to interdict Rommel's supply lines by action from Malta was also acknowledged. The importance of the Desert Air Force was recognised, given the weakness of the armoured formations: 'Our only offensive weapon is our air striking force . . . it alone enables us to retain any semblance of the initiative.'[24] The intention was to keep the 'E.[ighth] Army in being as a mobile field force and resist by every possible means any further attempt by the enemy to advance eastwards'.[25] Thus, Auchinleck planned to fight and delay Rommel's advance as much as possible. There was to be a battle at Alamein. However, the appreciation did not detail this fight beyond mention of imposing the 'utmost delay possible without entailing encirclement or destruction'.[26] Since the appreciation was examining the contingencies necessary in the worst possible case, and being written under great pressure, Dorman-Smith did not even sketch out a likely battle plan. He did, however, outline the potential retreat from the Alamein line: 'Should withdrawal from El Alamein position be forced on us, Eighth Army (less 1 South African Division)' would withdraw towards Cairo. Meanwhile, the 1st South African Division would withdraw on Alexandria where it would be joined by the 9th Australian Division just arriving from Palestine. The fight around Alexandria, the Delta and Cairo would be 'step by step'.[27]

Dorman-Smith's appreciation was an example of sound contingency planning. However, it did contain some deep flaws. In the last two months, Eighth Army had already attempted to make at least three controlled withdrawals while imposing delay upon Rommel; all three had ended in fiasco. There was little reason to expect that the planned withdrawal towards Alexandria and Cairo would not encounter disaster en route. Just as importantly, any withdrawal to the gates of Alexandria and Cairo would be strategically disastrous. Much of Eighth Army's ability to regenerate as a force depended not on reinforcements but on the Egyptian base. Even if Rommel could be held at the gates of these cities, his continued advance into Egypt would entail the disruption or destruction of many of the base depots and workshops. The loss of even a part of that capacity could fatally weaken the Middle East Command's ability to repair, reorganise and re-equip the troops already in Egypt. At the same time, it was highly unlikely that the Egyptian government and army would passively stand by and not assist in their 'liberation' from the British. On the whole then, a gloomy outlook. Of course,

Dorman-Smith's plan was no more than theoretical; as a trained staff officer, he knew that though plans had to be made covering all eventualities most were never executed. But neither he nor Auchinleck had any idea of the despondency his appreciation would cause amongst Eighth Army, where at least in some quarters it was assumed that a general retreat had been decided upon. The confusion was increased by the more detailed contingency orders for the formations of Eighth Army prepared by Corbett in Cairo.[28]

Such misunderstandings and communication failures were obviously dangerous and only exacerbated by Auchinleck's command style. Auchinleck had taken charge of Eighth Army but had not stamped his authority and personality upon its officers and men; nor had he fully informed them of his intentions. In some crucial respects, Auchinleck was not commanding Eighth Army. The Eighth Army had not got used to Auchinleck as its commander, yet with Dorman-Smith as an unofficial Chief of Staff, Auchinleck had already clouded the chain of command and the division of responsibilities. Tom Corbett was, meanwhile, acting not only as Auchinleck's chief staff officer at General Headquarters Middle East, but also as his representative, and holding himself ready to take command of Eighth Army in the event of retreat. Confusion was almost inevitable in such circumstances. Impeccable staff college appreciations were worthy and important planning aids for a commander attempting to consider all possibilities but they could become dangerous documents in the wrong hands. Eighth Army fought the crucial battle on 1 July amongst swirling storms not only of sand and dust but also of doubt and confusion.

During the crisis of the battle for Mersa Matruh, Churchill sent Auchinleck another telegram which contained some helpful points, but also revealed how little the Prime Minister understood of the nature of the fighting taking place in one of the most important theatres of British operations. Churchill had often chivvied both Wavell and Auchinleck about the high ration strength of the forces in the Middle East as compared to the fighting strength of the Eighth Army. He returned to the charge:

> I hope the crisis will lead to all uniformed personnel in the Delta and all available man-power being raised to the highest fighting condition. You have over 700,000 men on your ration strength in the Middle East. Every fit male should be made to fight and die for victory. There is no reason why units defending the Mersa Matruh position should not be reinforced by several thousands of officers and administrative personnel ordered to swell the battalions or working parties. You are in the same kind of situation as we should be if England were invaded, and the same intense drastic spirit should reign.[29]

Churchill's stirring words betrayed his archaic military thinking. At the very moment that Auchinleck was attempting to turn the Eighth Army into a slimmed-down mobile force which could tangle with the Afrika Korps, Churchill was advocating methods which might have worked in Kent or during the March retreat of 1918, but which were hopeless in 1942. Ever since O'Connor's victories against the Italian Tenth Army in 1941, it was clear that the numbers of troops engaged in the Western Desert had been less significant than their firepower, mobility and logistic support. Disrupting the complex administrative and logistic base of the army in Egypt by 'combing out' personnel to 'swell the battalions' would simply result in the complete breakdown of supplies for Eighth Army at the time they were needed the most, and the production of thousands of bewildered men to swell the already crammed Italian prison cages around Benghazi.

Auchinleck's reply was remarkably polite yet still tried to educate the Prime Minister on the reality of modern military operations:

> As to using all my manpower, I hope I am doing this, but infantry cannot win battles in the desert as long as the enemy has superiority in armour, and nothing can be said or done to change this fact. Guns and armour and just enough infantry to afford them and their supply organisation local protection is what is needed. Masses of infantry are no use without guns and armour.[30]

Guns and armour, of course, were what he lacked. Even after the disasters of Gazala and Tobruk, Ritchie had remained confident that the iron laws of time, space, distance and logistics would eventually bring Rommel to a halt. Auchinleck also calculated that Rommel's headlong rush into Egypt would have to slow down eventually: 'By drawing the enemy forward we were lengthening his supply lines and shortening our own – no small advantage since the Eighth Army sorely needed an opportunity to re-equip and reorganise,'[31] he would later write in his despatch. Such thinking accorded with the concept of the 'diminishing power of the offensive'. Yet Rommel had ploughed past the frontier, rushed the defences of Mersa Matruh and was now close to El Alamein. According to British expectations and Clausewitz's theories, Rommel's offensive capacities should have dimmed and the prospects of the Eighth Army brightened. But Rommel's aggressive push seemed as fierce as ever while the strength of the Eighth Army faded away. The desert pendulum, which should have protected the Eighth Army and forced Rommel to halt, had swung much further against them than the British had expected.

The explanation for this seeming contravention of the laws of logistics has to be found in the British campaign plan before Gazala. British planning had assumed that the Eighth Army would resume the offensive in May or June 1942. This offensive, codenamed Acrobat, was intended to defeat Rommel in battle and then push on to Tripoli. It was well understood that the only way of sustaining such an advance over long distances was by developing forward supply dumps which could feed the movement of the Eighth Army all the way to Tripoli. The halt at Gazala enabled the British to build up truly enormous quantities of supplies of ordnance, ammunition and, above all, petrol, in vast dumps at Tobruk and Belhamed. Tobruk contained 10,000 tons of supplies, while No. 4 Forward Base at Belhamed groaned with 20,000 tons of stores, petrol and supplies.[32] Eighth Army's plans for offensive were delayed until 1 June to allow the opening of a new railhead at Belhamed, just south of Tobruk. Once completed, this line would be able to transport more than 2,000 tons of supplies each day and thus ensure that the Eighth Army could mount a sustained advance all the way to Tripoli.

However, these vast supply dumps proved a severe embarrassment to an army in full retreat. In a cruel irony, the railway line to Belhamed opened on 12 June, the very day when it was realised that the depot could no longer be held. On 19 June Ritchie ordered the destruction of the thousands of gallons of fuel that had been laboriously accumulated at Belhamed. As the petrol drained away, so British hopes for their sustained offensive leaked into the sand. Worse was to follow. While ordnance officers had worked hard in Tobruk in the hours before its fall to carry out demolitions, large amounts of food, petrol and ammunition fell into Axis hands in the port. Most of the petrol at Belhamed was destroyed but the Panzerarmee captured enormous quantities of other materiel.

Just as Gazala and Tobruk had been a disaster for the 'teeth' arms, so the retreat to Mersa Matruh and Alamein became a catalogue of disasters for the Royal Army Ordnance Corps and Royal Army Service Corps. Up until 12 June, British quartermasters had been working flat out to transport all manner of supplies up to the front as quickly and efficiently as possible. Just as suddenly, these same personnel now had to move thousands of tons of supplies back the way they had just come. Unsurprisingly, not all could be brought back into Egypt.

Even though the task was undertaken with an energy fuelled by desperation, the enormous congestion on the roads and single-track railway line meant that:

> a good deal of Ordnance material was lost or had to be destroyed, for lack of transport and rolling stock to get it away, 100 tons of clothing being lost at CAPUZZO and another 300 tons between there and MISHEIFA. . . . By 20 June the 8th Army was based on Misheifa and Matruh, which were very congested. Three days later, the main railhead had gone 75 miles further back to Daba though tanks were still being delivered to Fuka a little further forward. Thus by 1 July the situation in Egypt was as serious as it had been at any time since the Fall of France.[33]

Attempting to remove thousands of tons of stores would have been difficult enough during a lull in the fighting but attempting the same task in the midst of military disaster was well-nigh impossible. The speed with which Eighth Army retreated 320 miles in just eleven days made the organised movement of stores back to dumps in Egypt simply too difficult. The chaos produced by this hurried retreat and movement of stores is difficult to imagine. One ordnance officer stated:

> Only those who have witnessed it can appreciate the appearance of muddle and chaos presented by a modern army on a forced move of this kind: the roads congested with traffic, head to tail for 40 miles on end: the hurried backloading of endless mounds of stores which have been brought up by the infinite labour of tired men over many months, and now may never be used: the lorries and trucks milling round the petrol and water points, like animals round a salt-lick: the counter-orders and waste and uncertainty: newly arrived units dumped in the desert in scattered untidy groups of men and vehicles: the crowds thronging the rations dumps . . . for rations or blankets, tents or cookers or water tins: the long procession of lame vehicles or crumpled aircraft or ambulances moving out of harm's way: the interminable waiting on trains or at crossroads: the rumours which have come hot-foot 50 or 100 or 200 miles and grow more garbled every hour: the pervading air of cumbersome disorder. These things have to be seen to be believed: for the hinderparts of a modern army, so helpless and so obese, have neither beauty nor an air of efficiency to sustain them.[34]

It is perhaps not surprising that most British accounts of the retreat to Alamein do not dwell on the chaos which developed; the truth was simply too embarrassing. In fact, even in the midst of such confusion, the Royal Army Ordnance Corps and Royal Army Service Corps did work wonders. Thousands of tons of stores were moved back into Egypt; workshops and dumps that had been hundreds of miles behind the lines were reactivated as forward supply dumps. There was administrative chaos behind the Eighth Army during the first two weeks of July, but eventually by the end of the month normal function had been restored. The fact that Eighth Army and its logistic base survived such chaos at all seems little short of a miracle.

Yet if Eighth Army had been subjected to sustained air attack during this period of retreat, defeat and confusion, the chaos would have turned into horror. The 'miracle' which saved Eighth Army from such a disaster had two complementary sources. In pushing his Panzerarmee as far and as fast as it could go, Rommel had completely outrun Kesselring's ability to provide air cover. By the summer of 1942, the Luftwaffe was being stretched in too many directions at once. The insatiable demands of the Eastern Front, combined with the need for air cover over Germany, took priority over the Mediterranean theatre. Although the total strength of the Axis air forces present in the Mediterranean theatre far outnumbered the Allied Desert Air

Force, the number of Axis aircraft that could be supplied and maintained in North Africa was strictly limited. This meant that Kesselring only had enough resources to provide air support for the offensive to take Tobruk and then switch his squadrons to the attack on Malta. The Axis air forces had put forth an enormous effort during the battle of Gazala and for the attack on Tobruk but could not sustain this level of activity indefinitely. Furthermore, the air forces had been planning to prepare for the projected invasion of Malta, not the immediate invasion of Egypt. This meant that there was neither the transport nor the supplies to allow the German and Italian fighter and bomber squadrons to move forwards rapidly into Egypt. Even as Rommel's men crossed the Egyptian frontier on 23 June, the air support which they depended upon evaporated.

By pushing deep into Egypt, Rommel forced Kesselring to send squadrons to his aid at the same time as he had to provide squadrons to neutralise Malta. There simply was not enough fuel or transport to bring the squadrons forward quickly and, even though Rommel attempted desperate measures by removing transport from Italian units to give to the Luftwaffe, it took days for the squadrons to reach the forward landing grounds at Fuka and El Daba. Meanwhile, there was now insufficient Axis airpower devoted to the suppression of Malta, which meant that the island could revitalise its battered defences and offensive power. Although the squadrons of the Regia Aeronautica and Luftwaffe struggled forwards into Egypt, the skies above the Eighth Army were completely clear of enemy aircraft from 23 June until 26 June. Even then, the Axis air effort could only be on a very small scale and the Afrika Korps actually remarked on the continued absence of fighter cover. Rommel's impetuous advance meant that his army lacked the air support which could have completed his victory.[35]

If the Luftwaffe was conspicuous by its absence during the retreat to Alamein, the same could not be said of the Desert Air Force. Instead, the squadrons of the Desert Air Force dominated the skies above Eighth Army. Air Vice Marshal 'Mary' Coningham had recognised that the defeat at Gazala and the loss of Tobruk meant that both the Eighth Army and his squadrons would have to make a prolonged withdrawal back into Egypt. Coningham decided to send every possible aircraft into the immediate fight to protect the Eighth Army during its retreat and disrupt the Panzerarmee as much as possible during its advance. Crucially, the squadrons of the Desert Air Force prepared for withdrawal by sending back all unnecessary equipment and personnel at the same time as rear landing grounds were readied for use.

From 23 to 26 June, the fighters and light bombers of the Desert Air Force made a maximum effort to slow the Axis advance even as they 'leapfrogged' back to airfields around Matruh and El Daba. On 26 June, Air Headquarters requested hourly raids by the force of Boston bombers.

Thirteen raids were carried out that day with a total of 111 sorties. This remarkable performance was described as:

> the shuttle service par excellence, besides which all previous records became insignificant. Bostons in large formations were appearing all over the enemy with the uncomfortable regularity of a tolerable suburban train service.[36]

After 26 June, the number of sorties flown declined markedly due to the need to pull back to landing grounds behind the Alamein position, but the night of 25 June marked the introduction of 'round the clock' bombing. Coningham was a keen advocate of 'round-the-clock' bombing so that the Axis troops were given no respite from air attack and had to remain dispersed even during darkness. That night, Fleet Air Arm Fairey Albacores flew slowly over likely concentrations of Axis vehicles and dropped flares to mark the targets. Guided by the light of the flares, 82 Wellington bombers then dropped their bomb loads. Up until this point, the Wellington night bombers of 205 Group had always been used to attack 'strategic' targets but now became an important addition to the day attacks upon the Panzerarmee. While the Desert Air Force put maximum effort into the tactical battle above Eighth Army, the 'Halpro' force of American Liberators, supplemented by some RAF Liberators, Halifaxes and Wellingtons, carried out a series of raids against Tobruk and Benghazi which caused considerable damage to both ports.

Although the operations of the Desert Air Force were marked by considerable success, the retreat into Egypt completely dislocated the machinery for cooperation between the Eighth Army and the RAF. The system of air support was designed so that the RAF responded to calls for support from the army. During the retreat, Air Headquarters received very little information and few requests from the army. In the last two weeks of June, Eighth Army only made twelve requests for air support. This situation meant that Coningham largely fought his own battle; rather than rely on sketchy and old information from the army, the Desert Air Force relied upon its own system of tactical reconnaissance to provide target information.[37] Even though the army and the RAF fought two largely separate battles during the retreat, the intervention of airpower in the land battle was crucial to the survival of the Eighth Army. The Desert Air Force established a dominance in the skies above the desert which set the pattern for the rest of the entire campaign.

The chaos of the retreat was eventually surmounted, but the losses of vital stores and supplies were grievous. Virtually all of the fighting stores, clothing, food, petrol and ammunition which Eighth Army had needed had been based forward around Tobruk and Belhamed. The speed of the German advance and the rumours of catastrophe floating in the ether led to panic withdrawals from some dumps and panic demolitions in others. In dumps from Tobruk and Belhamed, Sollum and Capuzzo to Mersa Matruh and El Daba, the Eighth Army lost thousands upon thousands of tons of food, ammunition, engineer stores, petrol and supplies.

Not surprisingly, statistics of the actual amounts lost are difficult to determine. Nine thousand nine hundred and fifteen miles of electric cable were lost in Tobruk. Fifteen hundred tons of stores were 'abandoned' at Sollum, while at least 3,000 tons of stores were blown up at Misheifa. Two thousand one hundred and sixteen tons of ammunition loaded on 189 railway trucks were blown up at the last moment at El Daba. Indeed, it was in ammunition that the Eighth Army suffered the most grievous losses. The quantities of ammunition which were either captured or destroyed were staggering:

> . . . The forward Ordnance officers in charge of dumps had a most unenviable time. 'To blow or not to blow' that was their question and it was made no easier in certain cases by orders which envisaged the possible arrival of a hypothetical train to back-load what was left. One thing is certain: our losses of ammunition in Tobruk, in Cyrenaica and at forward railheads during the period between May 27 and 1 July were very high, whether they were 'denied to the enemy' or fell into his hands intact.[38]

Estimates suggest that as many as 782,403 shells and 12,827,000 rounds of small arms ammunition were destroyed, lost or captured during the retreat:

Ammunition Losses 27 May to 1 July

Type	Rounds Lost		Tons of ammunition lost
6-pounder QF	41,631	Tobruk	5,827
75 mm (all types)	81,578	Capuzzo	613
25-pounder (all types)	512,752	DV	1,445
37mm	146,442	El Hamra	1,751
Total shells	782,403	Total	9,636

Small Arms Ammunition (SAA)	
SAA .303 Mk VIII	3,808,000
7.92mm	5,283,000
.450	3,736,000
Total SA	12,827,000[39]

When the Eighth Army reached the Alamein line, it had been bled almost dry of the supplies and ammunition it would need to fight a further battle.

As Eighth Army had haemorrhaged its lifeblood, so the Panzerarmee had received a substantial transfusion of supplies. The normally iron laws of logistics which should have forced Rommel's army to grind to an undignified halt had been bent. It was estimated that in July 1942 the Germans had as many as 6,000 usable lorries which had formerly belonged to the Eighth Army. Similarly, German and Italian artillery units, which had lost numerous guns during Gazala, supplemented their firepower with captured British 25-pounder field guns and ammunition. The spearhead units of the Panzerarmee, eating 'Imperial Tinned Peaches' and driving Canadian Ford trucks with Iraqi petrol in their tanks, pushed on towards Alamein.

There were, of course, factors which could not be overcome by the capture of supplies. The cutting edge of Rommel's army, the Afrika Korps was severely depleted. While the units had begun the battle of Gazala at almost full strength, they were now severely reduced in numbers. On 29 June, 90th Light Division could only muster 1,679 men. The next day, the Afrika Korps reported that it only had 55 battleworthy tanks left. The Italian XX Corps was in an even worse state; only 15 tanks were still available.[40] Moreover, the men who made up these units were physically and mentally exhausted after moving and fighting for weeks. Nonetheless, the wholesale capture of British arms, equipment and supplies pushed the culminating point of Rommel's advance further than either side had believed possible. The oil in the Panzerarmee's lamp was draining, but there was still just enough to keep the light burning.

If the Eighth Army had lost thousands of tons of supplies, the situation in its tank workshops was, if anything, even more dire. Clausewitz could not possibly have considered the realities of mechanised warfare in his theories, yet the main factor which debilitated the Eighth Army was its tank losses. During the Gazala battle, British tank losses had been astronomical. Disastrously, British armoured regiments had often been forced to withdraw from the battleground, leaving hundreds of damaged but repairable tanks behind. Estimates suggested that 1,188 tanks had been knocked out in 17 days of fighting. Nonetheless, Royal Army Ordnance Corps tank recovery squadrons and tank workshops had worked at full stretch to repair and recondition tanks for the armoured regiments. In many respects, the crisis of Gazala was the Royal Army Ordnance Corps' finest hour because their drivers, fitters and mechanics turned round an enormous number of tanks:

Up to 19 June, the Corps had recovered 581 tanks of which 278 had been repaired and 222 evacuated to railhead. There were on the 19th 81 tanks in workshops. This is a very remarkable figure, daily recoveries varying between 6 and 57 (this was on 29 May) an average of over 23 a day. These figures included 326 American tanks of the Grant and Stuart types.[41]

However, Rommel's sweep round the British minefields had turned the British rear areas into a battlefield. Unsurprisingly, the tank workshops had to be moved out of harm's way. Unfortunately, two of them withdrew into the safety of Tobruk, mainly because 'there was nowhere else for them to go'.[42] This meant that when Tobruk fell the two main tank workshops were captured, along with many other Royal Army Ordnance Corps units.

The hurried withdrawal of 'crocked' tanks by rail back into Egypt, combined with the enormous movement of stores from Egypt to Palestine and the Sudan, and the relocation of base workshops further back in Egypt, created enormous disruption in the system of tank repair and maintenance which had worked very efficiently during Gazala.

The desperate need to recover as many tanks as possible led to a number of individual dramas being played out in the midst of retreat. Lieutenant William M. Nichol was ordered to take his tank transporter company into the desert five miles west of El Alamein to recover damaged tanks coming out of the battle on the morning of 30 June. Once he arrived with his recovery section at his destination, Nichol learned that the covering armoured car patrol had been withdrawn. He stayed with his transporters and began to recover Grant tanks with their crews while under heavy shellfire. Even though his route to safety became blocked by Axis forces, Nichol managed to recover 12 Grant tanks and their crews before using a dust storm as cover to escape pursuing Axis armoured cars. Nichol and his men of the 1st Tank Transporter Company saved a substantial number of Eighth Army's Grant tanks that day.[43]

On 1 July, Eighth Army stood on the Alamein line with 137 tanks in its units and 42 in transit from the base workshops to the front. But on the same day, there were more than 902 tanks sitting in the base workshops, of which only 34 were serviceable. Because of the disruption and loss of spare parts, many of these tanks were simply irreparable. Eighth Army had somehow managed to recover many of the tanks which had been knocked out during the fierce armoured battles but now had no way of returning them to the fight. The first week of July was reckoned to be:

> the nadir of our efforts at maintaining armour in the Middle East. Actually it chanced to coincide with the moment of our greatest need in the history of Egypt; that we survived such a moment is one of the things that history may some day record with as frank an astonishment as it will doubtless record the events of June and July 1940 in the history of Britain.[44]

The condition of Eighth Army was indeed desperate as the men of Rommel's Afrika Korps motored on through the dust and the haze of their own exhaustion. The entire position of the British Empire in the Middle East hung in the balance.

On the evening of 30 June, just as Rommel organised his men for a head-long dash at the Alamein defences, Major Friedrich von Mellenthin, his intelligence officer, received a signal giving him special hope for success. That day, Alex C. Kirk, the American Ambassador to Egypt, sent a gloomy telegram to the State Department in Washington:

> Fellers considers that within the next few days it will be possible for Rommel to arrive at Cairo and Alexandria unless the British can obtain immediately reinforcements of anti-tank and air artillery. Fellers considers that the situation could be redeemed if hundreds of bombers with anti-tank guns were being flown in.
>
> In my own opinion, I cannot escape the feeling that the scales might be turned even now by some supreme effort.[45]

Although Kirk had suggested that there might be a glimmer of hope for the British, this was the kind of intelligence that a military commander could normally only dream of receiving. Rommel now knew that he had been right to tear up the agreed Axis strategy and drive into Egypt. He knew it was only a matter of time before the American reinforcements for which Fellers was pleading actually arrived in Egypt. Rommel's fighting formations and transport columns were being subjected to increasingly heavy bombardment from the air but none of these problems would matter if he could drive through the last defensive positions held by Eighth Army around Alamein. Rommel was confident that, after one last supreme effort of will, Egypt would be his.

THREE

The Armies at El Alamein

On 28 June Auchinleck stood by the roadside and watched his defeated army stream past. He was shocked to see that 'lorry after lorry carried bulging loads of non-essential, near luxury gear of no conceivable fighting value'.[1] Auchinleck became determined that there should be no luxury at his new headquarters; he, along with all of the staff of Eighth Army Headquarters, would share the same rations and hardships of the men in the front line. Throughout the time of his command of Eighth Army, Auchinleck slept in the open beside his operations caravan.

Auchinleck, the 'sepoy General', was, with the exception of William Slim, who commanded the Fourteenth Army in Burma, unique amongst the higher commanders of the British Army during the Second World War in coming from the Indian rather than the British Army. His formative experiences as a soldier had been on the North West Frontier of India. It was said of Auchinleck that he was at his happiest as a subaltern sharing the hardships of his Indian soldiers. He had had little contact with the British troops attached to Indian brigades. By the time of his appointment as Commander-in-Chief Middle East, Auchinleck had already served as Commander-in-Chief of the Indian Army, the highest post normally available to an Indian Army officer. Auchinleck was noted for his personal courage, his intelligence and his unshakeable character but as a higher commander in charge of British forces he possessed one flaw that could not be overcome: he did not possess an intimate knowledge of the British Army. He had been brought from India to command the Norway expedition in 1940, and had commanded Southern Command in 1940–41, but he had not built up the same web of connections within the British Army that every senior British Army officer had developed over the course of their careers. This meant that Auchinleck did not know the cliques, factions and social mores of the British Army as intimately as he did those of the Indian Army. Commanders like Archibald Wavell had the advantage of knowledge of both military worlds which meant that they could choose subordinates from both pools. Auchinleck's relative ignorance of the British Home Army goes some way to explaining his often criticised choice of subordinates.[2]

Auchinleck decided that his new headquarters must be close to the troops. While his decision to enforce austerity upon the staff of Eighth Army Headquarters seems to have caused little complaint amongst officers already used to the hard and spare life of the desert, Auchinleck's choice of location for his new headquarters was very definitely controversial.

Lieutenant-Colonel Charles Richardson, Auchinleck's newly appointed General Staff Officer 1 (Plans) found his way to the new headquarters at the junction of some camel tracks located just to the north east of the Ruweisat ridge. Richardson was not impressed with the location:

> Why General Auchinleck or Jock Whiteley chose it, and why we stayed there for so long has never been explained. Certainly it was a track junction, not that that was particularly significant since one could normally drive anywhere by compass bearing. It was liberally supplied with camel dung and the attendant clouds of flies. It was unsuitably close to our forward troops . . . It was miles away from the headquarters of the Desert Air Force with whom we had to co-operate closely. I came to the conclusion that General Auchinleck decided not to withdraw from it, lest units deduce that further withdrawals were 'in the air'.[3]

The camel dung and flies certainly added to the air of austerity that hung about the place but there were actually very good reasons why Auchinleck placed his headquarters well forward. The RAF were scandalised that the new headquarters was not co-located with their own at Burg el Arab. Since November 1941, the Main Headquarters of Eighth Army had indeed been co-located with Air Marshal Coningham's Desert Air Force Headquarters. This had the benefit of enabling rapid transmission of targeting information from the army to the air force but it had severe drawbacks for an army commander attempting to deal with a fast-moving battle. Ritchie's headquarters during Gazala had been too distant to exert real control over the fighting. Similarly, Coningham's new headquarters at Burg el Arab was more than 40 miles from El Alamein.

Dorman-Smith later provided sound military reasons for the location of Eighth Army's Main Headquarters in such an unsavoury spot:

> The artillery plan was all tied up under Army. The admin was largely under Army. But the fighting front was 40 miles and two L. Generals H.Q.s seemed essential. At that time we had no real reserve but what there was was direct under Army. . . . The organization was very closely knit. Auchinleck could confer at his own H.Q.s (with full conveniences for planning – intelligence interception of our + enemy R.T. traffic etc) in 30 minutes with the Corps commanders. 8 Army HQ was only 12 miles from the front + in the middle of the Army.[4]

Auchinleck decided that, in this moment of crisis, he needed to be close to his corps commanders so that he could actually direct the battle. This meant face-to-face contact with his two corps commanders, Gott and Norrie. As Michael Carver explained: 'While commanders were on the move from one place to another and when they were in conference together, nothing happened.'[5] Additionally, Auchinleck did not want communication difficulties with short-ranged wireless sets to interfere with his command of the army. Auchinleck's choice of location for his headquarters minimised these delays and increased his control over Eighth Army.

However, Dorman-Smith's account suggests a well-organised and smooth-running headquarters when the reverse was the case. On 30 June, Auchinleck 'lost confidence' in Brigadier 'Jock' Whiteley's abilities to function as Brigadier General Staff of Eighth Army. The truth was that Whiteley was physically and mentally exhausted. He had been running the staff of Army Headquarters during the agonies of Gazala and Tobruk. When Richardson met him on 25 June he noted that Whiteley 'was lying flat out in his caravan with an exhausted look in his eyes and a very red face'.[6] Yet rather than replace Whiteley, Auchinleck decided simply to hand over his functions to Dorman-Smith. The original intention had been for Dorman-Smith to act as a 'DCGS in the field'. This meant that Dorman-Smith would have dealt with any wider Middle East matters as well as higher-level planning while leaving Whiteley in harness as the chief staff officer of Eighth Army. Even this arrangement was awkward but, rather than dismissing the exhausted Whiteley and officially naming Dorman-Smith as Brigadier General Staff Eighth Army, Auchinleck kept Whiteley in place. Whiteley was frozen out of all of the important decision-making yet left in office, which made his position very awkward indeed. 'Chink' meanwhile relished the challenge of taking on all the important staff work. Eighth Army during July 1942 was commanded by Auchinleck but he depended upon Eric Dorman-Smith for much of his inspiration.

Eric Dorman-Smith remains one of the most controversial figures of British military history. He was considered by some, including Archibald Wavell, to be one of the most brilliant and inventive staff officers of his generation but by others, including Brooke, to be a dangerous 'menace'. There were no half measures with 'Chink'. His was a mercurial and lightning fast intelligence which thrived on difficult problems but, although he might come up with ten solutions, only one might be brilliant and the other nine positively dangerous. Dorman-Smith was only too aware of his intelligence and made no attempt to suffer fools gladly. He had been psychologically scarred by his service in the First World War to the extent that he had nothing but contempt for what he considered as the brave but stupid officers who populated the inter-war British Army. Highly ambitious, he had commanded a battalion in Egypt, and, just like Montgomery, was known as a stickler for efficiency and hard training. Yet 'Chink' was far more a staff officer than a commander. He seized on staff problems and worked out their 'solutions' faster than anyone else, but he seems to have become less and less aware of the difficulties which subordinate commanders faced in translating those orders into reality.[7] There is no doubt that Dorman-Smith relished his informal post at Eighth Army but there was a real problem with this situation. Dorman-Smith's informal post offered him power without responsibility. He produced the ideas and voluminous plans for Eighth Army's coming attacks but never took on the mantle of a chief of staff who took the responsibility for ensuring that every commander involved in the plans understood his role.

Unfortunately, while Auchinleck and Dorman-Smith understood one another and the informal arrangement between them, the rest of the staff at Eighth Army Headquarters did not. It is also quite clear that Auchinleck also froze out other members of the Eighth Army Headquarters staff. Each evening, Auchinleck had an 'Evening Prayer' session in his caravan which was a discussion between Auchinleck, Dorman-Smith, Whiteley in his uncomfortable role as the sidelined Brigadier General Staff, Richardson tasked with plans, Lieutenant-Colonel Hugh Mainwaring in charge of Operations, Lieutenant-Colonel David Belchem in Staff Duties and Lieutenant-Colonel 'Spud' Murphy in charge of intelligence, including the precious information gained from the 'Usual Most Secret Sources' – 'Ultra'. Richardson later related that, 'The prayer meetings were very depressing; nothing constructive by way of seizing the initiative ever emerged . . . I could offer nothing and felt totally impotent.'[8]

It is quite clear that Auchinleck did not give Richardson the full set of tasks that he might have been expected to fulfil in his staff and to a large extent froze him out of important decisions. Neither Whiteley nor Richardson was privy to Auchinleck's plans or thinking. Meanwhile, Dorman-Smith, whom Richardson regarded as a 'dangerous supernumerary adviser', was actually operating as Auchinleck's chief inspiration and, albeit informally, as the principal staff officer of Eighth Army. This arrangement, exacerbated by Chink's personality, led to confusion and enmity at Eighth Army Headquarters. Auchinleck's own staff did not understand the complex and ambiguous relations which operated and neither did the rest of the army.

The army which Auchinleck attempted to command from his unconventional headquarters was a polyglot force formed from the wreckage of Gazala, Tobruk and Mersa Matruh along with the welcome addition of a few fresh formations recently arrived from other sectors of the Middle East. When it stood at El Alamein, Eighth Army was not a unified army with a strong sense of collective identity but a collection of units with sometimes competing identities. It was, above all else, a multinational force. Soldiers from across the British Empire and allied governments served in its ranks.

Up to July 1942, Eighth Army incorporated greater or lesser numbers of British, Indian, Australian, New Zealand, South African, Free French, Polish and Greek soldiers. However, the status of these troops and their relationship to Eighth Army Headquarters could differ. While Indian Army troops were still largely led by British officers and each Indian brigade continued to have one British or 'Imperial' battalion within its ranks, the forces of the Dominions of Australia, New Zealand and South Africa were formed exclusively from those countries. Eighth Army had no jurisdiction over discipline, training or administrative matters for the Australian, South African and New Zealand troops within its ranks. More importantly, Lieutenant-General Sir Leslie Morshead and Lieutenant-General Bernard Freyberg, the Australian and New Zealand divisional commanders respectively, each had the right to refer any orders he disagreed with to his own government, thus circumventing the normal chain of command. Major-General Dan Pienaar, the commander of the 1st South African Division, did not possess the same right of referral to his government but remained independent in terms of discipline, training and administration. This gave the commanders of the 9th Australian, 2nd New Zealand and 1st South African Divisions a very different constitutional and military relationship from the other forces within Eighth Army. These complex constitutional and administrative arrangements made sustained collective training very difficult. Dominion forces could be encouraged but not ordered to train with their British comrades.

The difficulties in commanding a multinational and multi-ethnic force were complex enough but the Eighth Army had also struggled with the problems of combining its armoured, infantry and artillery units into an effective all-arms team. The real difficulties in producing effective all-arms cooperation which both sides experienced in the desert were exacerbated by the British Army's approach to doctrine, its pre-war impoverishment, structural and organisational weaknesses, and key deficiencies in its equipment.

By 1939, the British Army had accumulated a great deal of experience in desert fighting. The inter-war army could draw on the experience of Allenby's campaigns in Sinai and Palestine during the Great War as well as the pathfinding work of Major Ralph Bagnold and the other members of the Zerzura club who had explored Egypt's Western Desert in the inter-war years.[9] In 1937, the War Office published a military report on the Egyptian desert, largely written by Bagnold, which provided a detailed account of the problems and solutions to military movement in the desert.[10] The Western Desert Force, consisting of what became 7th Armoured Division and 4th Indian Division, had exercised intensively in the desert and represented perhaps the finest-trained, if not the best-equipped, force that Britain possessed in 1939. Indeed, the Western Desert Force of 1940 might be compared with the BEF of 1914 in terms of its quality, training and expertise.

The signal victory which the Western Desert Force achieved over the

Italian Tenth Army during Operation Compass seemed to demonstrate that the British Army had learnt the right lessons from the debates concerning armoured warfare and mobility which had dominated military thinking throughout the inter-war years. The conduct of the campaign appeared to correspond closely to the spirit of mobility, flexibility and the emphasis on surprise enshrined in the British Field Service Regulations 1935.

In many respects, the methods adopted during Compass mirrored the doctrine enshrined in those regulations.[11] The formations of the Western Desert Force were commanded in a strikingly modern way. O'Connor, and the divisional commanders operating under his command, proved audacious and willing to improvise in order to outthink their opponents. The cruiser tanks of 7th Armoured Division, infantry tanks, anti-tank guns, infantry and artillery were welded together into an effective all-arms team which completely outfought their Italian opponents. However, the long report which detailed the initial lessons from Compass ended on a sober note. It noted that valuable experience had been gained by commanders, staff, regimental officers and all ranks who undertook the operation: 'Not only in their own particular sphere but also – which is so important and so valuable – in working in close co-operation with arms of the Service other than their own.'[12]

The report recognised that the Italian Tenth Army had lacked soldierly qualities and that its troops had given way too easily to 'demoralisation'. It speculated that a German army would have been a much more formidable opponent and that:

> While we have learnt many lessons and gained much valuable experience, we must guard against any tendency to apply them rigidly or unimaginatively in future circumstances which may prove very different from those encountered in the Western Desert of Egypt and Libya in December 1940.[13]

These were prophetic words indeed. While Operation Compass seemed to vindicate the pre-war training, doctrine and concepts of operation of the Western Desert Force, the situation changed literally overnight when the Afrika Korps arrived in Tripoli in February 1941. Although the regular soldiers of the Western Desert Force did not suffer the enormous casualties of their forebears in 1914, the easy familiarity and the high levels of trust and understanding which had allowed an almost instinctive approach to orders were soon lost in the breakneck expansion of the army, competing demands for troops in far-flung theatres of operation and the turbulence of defeat.

There were also deeper structural reasons for the poor performance of the British desert forces in the face of German intervention. Even once British rearmament got underway in 1936 in the face of the evident threat from Nazi Germany, the Royal Navy and Royal Air Force received the lion's share of the budget; the army remained third in the list of priorities. When the army was faced with the need for rapid expansion in 1939, there were simply not enough weapons and equipment to go round.[14] If the pre-war impoverishment of the British Army had pernicious effects upon the ability of the forces in the desert to adapt to the challenge of fighting the Afrika Korps, the compound effect of multiple defeats only made the situation worse.

From the perspective of July 1942, when the most recent crisis had been surmounted, a Royal Army Ordnance Corps officer wrote:

> In the First Mechanised War expeditionary forces were cheerfully bundled neck and crop out of countries minus every tank, lorry and gun they had possessed and in many cases without even their rifles and equipment.[15]

The evacuations from France, Norway, Greece and Crete, combined with the retreat from Cyrenaica in April 1941, meant that the British Army lost vast quantities of vital stores and equipment. British industry was already struggling to produce sufficient quantities of equipment for the vastly expanded army and these disasters meant that reserves were almost wiped out each time British forces had to be evacuated. These losses made it very difficult to supply the desert army with all the arms and equipment it needed and there were critical shortages of vital equipment during the first two years of the desert campaign.[16]

At the same time, the British Army was being stretched to the limit to cope with the competing demands and priorities of a war of national survival. In order to meet those demands the British Army expanded tenfold from 1939 to 1942 in a process which saw the raising of a vast range of new units. Fresh units sent to the desert were often ill-trained and unprepared for the challenges ahead. Most of the officers and men, quite unlike the desert veterans of 7th Armoured Division, had to learn about the problems of desert movement and navigation for the first time. While most units sent from Britain had received barely enough training in their own arm, the time and resources allocated to all-arms training was completely inadequate.[17] Far from the expanded Western Desert Force and then Eighth Army learning in a progressive way from previous experience, most units had to relearn the same lessons.

The Eighth Army also experienced an incredibly rapid turnover of units and personnel within formations. Units were transferred from brigades, divisions and corps with bewildering speed and could then be sent to different sectors and even theatres. The Commander-in-Chief Middle East had had to find troops for operations in Ethiopia, Greece, Syria, Iraq and, after December 1941, for Australia, Singapore and Burma as well. These demands meant that veteran units were often replaced with units fresh from the United Kingdom without the same level of expertise or desert knowledge. As Britain's armed forces expanded, the pre-war regulars were augmented by Territorial units and then by the mass of wartime-created units filled with willing and unwilling conscripts.[18] This gave an unevenness of experience within Eighth Army for which it could be difficult to compensate. The Western Desert Force had been renamed Eighth Army in November 1941 in recognition of its expansion to a two corps force, but that very expansion had diluted the level of experienced units within the force.

Indeed, the issue of training within Eighth Army had been a serious problem since February 1941 when the original Western Desert Force had been broken up. On 7 July 1942, Whiteley published some 'Notes on Main Lessons of Recent Operations'. He clearly felt the need to give advice to junior officers and assist them in assimilating the lessons of the battle of Gazala, and hopefully rectify some of the most glaring errors. The extraordinarily basic level of his comments may be judged from a piece of doggerel which prefaced his notes:

> Always <u>maintain your objective</u>,
> <u>Offensive</u> your action should be;
> <u>Surprise</u> 'gainst the foe is effective;
> And <u>concentrate</u> on him, he'll flee.
> <u>Economise</u> always your forces;
> <u>Security</u> seek from alarms.
> Make <u>mobile</u> your columns – like horses;
> And <u>co-operate with all arms</u>.[19]

Such banalities suggest that Eighth Army had totally lost its way. The image of young, inexperienced Eighth Army officers parroting the principles of war while trying to outfight the hardened veterans of the Afrika Korps is a desperate one. In fact, the image was far from the reality. The units of Eighth Army had fought with determination and resolve and there had been many highly experienced officers and men within its ranks on 25 May – who did not need schoolboy doggerel to help them understand battle tactics. Nonetheless, even by the crude test of the 'principles' of war, Eighth Army's performance at Gazala had been disastrous. Whiteley's notes did include much helpful advice on the need for rapid decision-making, the seizure of initiative and the tactical handling of troops.[20]

The problem was that such ideas were well understood within Eighth Army yet they had still suffered defeat. The difficulties which had afflicted Eighth Army lay not in the quality of its troops or its junior leaders but in its organisation, command and tactical methods. Even in the heat of battle during May and June, commanders and officers understood that matters had gone badly wrong and that much needed to be changed within Eighth Army. The problem lay in how that knowledge could be disseminated and translated into improved technique.

Timothy Harrison Place has detailed the great amount of effort which the British Army expended in official publications to educate this vastly expanded Army. These included training manuals, Army Training Instructions and Notes from Theatres of War.[21] One of the real problems for training within the Eighth Army was that while the pre-war Field Service Regulations 1935 (the closest approximation to a commonly understood doctrine) were sound, and most of the training manuals issued by the War Office were helpful, most desert veterans believed that the unique conditions of the desert required a new approach and that many of the official publications produced in London were obsolete. Eighth Army itself already possessed a number of official and semi-official channels through which to disseminate 'lessons learned' and changes in tactical thinking. After each major operation, General Headquarters Middle East had prepared 'Notes on Lessons from Operations' for dissemination to the desert and home forces. On every occasion, these notes had stressed the importance of initiative, rapid command decisions, cooperation between arms and a host of more detailed lessons. Pamphlets such as Whiteley's were distributed to every officer in the army. For much of the desert campaign, however, it can virtually be assumed that they were simply too busy to read them.

A difficulty which had afflicted Eighth Army since its inception was the inability to continue effective training in the midst of high-intensity operations. Units were so busy moving, fighting and recovering from operations that there was little time available for training. Once a unit had been acclimatised in a training camp in Egypt, it might receive little or no further training after it arrived at Eighth Army. The problem was exacerbated by the distances involved in the campaign. Units fighting around Tobruk or the Egyptian frontier were more than 350 miles away from the training camps in Cairo and Alexandria. This meant that very little training actually took place in the desert and most troops learned very much 'on the job'. This led to an informal approach to training and a lack of common understanding throughout the army.

Under the combined pressures of defeat and overstretch, it was quickly realised that the doctrine, equipment, training and tactical ability of the Afrika Korps were superior to those of Eighth Army. Eighth Army was increasingly forced into a series of tactical expedients and experiments. Those expedients had led to disaster at Gazala. The British armoured brigades had fought independently of their supporting infantry and often separately from one another. British infantry brigades had been locked into static defensive 'boxes' that the Panzerarmee had reduced one by one. If Eighth Army persisted in these techniques at El Alamein it would be destroyed.

Auchinleck and Dorman-Smith had debated a whole series of changes to Eighth Army's tactical technique and organisation during their flight to Baggush. Both men were imbued with the pre-war British military thinking that stressed the importance of mobility and manoeuvre in war. Certainly, the recent fighting had demonstrated the sheer futility of attempting a fixed defence in open desert. Auchinleck and Dorman-Smith's thinking was not necessarily as radical as has been suggested but they certainly were taking substantial risks in introducing so many doctrinal changes to an army struggling to survive. Their first decision concerned the use of artillery. They agreed that the artillery, which had been badly dispersed during Gazala, must be centralised under 'divisional, Corps and even Army control'.[22]

During the First World War, the Royal Artillery had provided the cutting edge of the British armies in France. In the inter-war period, the Royal Artillery remained central to the British concept of the all-arms battle and the artillery regiments of British infantry divisions still provided critical support for the formation in defence and attack.[23] However, the Royal Artillery encountered real difficulties in providing that support during the desert campaigns and the British use of artillery reached a painful nadir during the battle of Gazala.

The report on the use of Eighth Army's artillery during Gazala lamented:

> The superiority of 8 to 5 in artillery with which the Eighth Army accepted battle on 27 May has failed to produce the results expected, though almost without exception guns have been fought with the utmost gallantry and determination. The principle reasons have been:-
>
> (a) Defeat in detail, owing to employment in small bodies not under command of the highest Artillery Commander who can exercise collective control.
> (b) Failure to make a fire plan based on adequate reconnaissance, or in some cases to make a fire plan at all.
> (c) Confusion in the minds of many officers as to the two roles of the 25-pr as a Field Gun and as an Anti-Tank weapon.
> (d) Failure to use the Anti-Tank Artillery in accordance with the principles laid down in MIDDLE EAST TRAINING PAMPHLET NO 15 INSTRUCTION NO 2 (TACTICAL HANDLING OF ANTI-TANK UNITS).[24]

This training instruction demonstrated that British artillery officers knew precisely what had gone wrong but had been unable to prevent serious mistakes.

The basic artillery unit was the regiment which consisted of two twelve-gun batteries each of three troops.[25] The distinction in nomenclature between field regiments (which were generally integral to an infantry division) and

Royal Horse Artillery regiments (which were generally attached to armoured divisions) made no difference to their organisation or function. All field and Royal Horse Artillery regiments in the Middle East were equipped with the excellent 25-pounder field gun. This was a new gun which first came into service in 1940. The gun had been designed to have an anti-tank capability and, when in action, sat on a circular firing platform which enabled 360-degree traverse.[26]

However, the Royal Artillery's provision of medium and heavy guns was inadequate. Throughout most of the desert war, Eighth Army had to rely on just two medium regiments (7th and 64th Medium Regiments). These regiments were initially equipped with obsolete First World War pieces, the old 60-pounder gun and six-inch howitzer, until well into 1941 when they were re-equipped with the new and highly effective 4.5-inch and 5.5-inch medium guns.[27] At no time did Eighth Army ever possess heavy or super-heavy artillery pieces. This meant that in many artillery engagements, Eighth Army was effectively outranged and undergunned compared to its Axis opponents.

During the desert war the power of Royal Artillery had gone into decline which had serious effects on the ability of Eighth Army to fight effectively. The concentrated use of artillery demanded three essentials – good regimental and divisional level training to weld artillery batteries into effective large-fire units, effective communications and targets which were relatively static.[28] Pre-war training had instead emphasised rapid observed fire by troops or batteries as a means of engaging the fleeting targets expected in mobile warfare. While one battery could be ranged onto a target in a matter of minutes by its forward observation officer, it took much longer to survey the target and coordinate the guns for a regimental or divisional shoot. This level of coordination was only possible with effective radio communications and proper training.

Unfortunately, static targets were in short supply in the desert campaigns. Since the desert itself held no tactical significance, and since most formations were mechanised, targets tended to be fleeting. With forces dispersed and mobile, it was difficult to plot a target accurately and range a large number of guns onto it in the time required. At the same time, commanders needed immediate artillery support because of the fluid nature of the fighting – it was often argued that four guns in action now was better than 32 guns in half an hour. One possible solution to the German's habitual use of powerful anti-tank gun screens was to suppress them with heavy concentrations of artillery fire. However, by the time the screen had been identified and guns brought to bear, the fighting might have moved on to another patch of desert. These tactical problems of time and space bedevilled the use of Eighth Army's artillery in the desert.

The desert war also saw the reintroduction of direct fire as an important artillery tool. Tank and anti-tank gun weapons used direct fire to achieve their effect but the British operated at a severe disadvantage in this area. The Royal Artillery's anti-tank regiments provided the backbone of anti-tank defence for infantry and armoured divisions. Each regiment was equipped with 48 guns but, unfortunately, this was the two-pounder anti-tank gun which, by 1942, was obsolete. When the gun[29] was formally approved in January 1936, there is little doubt that it was the best anti-tank gun in the world.[30] It was mounted on a three-legged carriage which allowed rapid all-round traverse although this made the gun heavy and laborious to bring into action. A semi-automatic breech mechanism meant that it had a very high rate of fire and its shot had excellent penetration effects against all existing tanks. By 1940, the gun's performance was less impressive and by 1941, once German tanks had been up-armoured (fitted with additional plates of armour), it was dangerously obsolete. This meant that anti-tank gunners could only knock out German tanks at very close ranges. One British report noted that in an attack during Operation Crusader:

> the GERMAN tanks cruised about very slowly outside the effective range of the 2-pr., continuously shelling the position with 75mm guns. They gradually goaded our A.Tk guns to fire, and when satisfied that all had been located, they knocked them out quickly with fire from gun tanks and supporting artillery. Then just before dusk they moved forward with infantry close behind, and overran the centre of the position.[31]

The lack of an effective anti-tank gun meant that the 25-pounder field gun, the mainstay of the field artillery regiments, was increasingly used in the anti-tank role. This robbed the artillery of its ability to develop concentrated fire.

As early as 1938 the need for a more capable replacement had been foreseen and a six-pounder anti-tank gun was designed and tested. The new 'Roberts' gun[32] was due to enter production in 1940 but more than 500 two-pounder anti-tank guns had been lost in France and the dearth of anti-tank guns, combined with the fact that the existing factories tooled for the two-pounder could produce two guns to one from the factories scheduled to produce the six-pounder, meant that the transfer of production, with all the attendant delays in tooling up the factories, was postponed. This decision appeared to make sense during the crisis of 1940 when any anti-tank gun was better than none, but it meant that the forces in the desert had to struggle on with the two-pounder anti-tank gun long after it had become obsolete.[33] The six-pounder gun was not brought into production until November 1941 and did not reach full production of 1,500 guns per month until May 1942. By that time, Eighth Army had just received its first allocation of the new gun but had had no time to train the gunners in its use. The New Zealand anti-tank gunners at Minqar Qaim were issued with new six-pounders still in their packing grease.[34] Nonetheless, the introduction of the six-pounder was very important because it provided infantry with an effective anti-tank defence and enabled the 25-pounder field guns to be used in their proper role.

German air superiority in the desert had also hampered the use of large groups of artillery. The Luftwaffe had demonstrated the potential of tactical airpower used in the support of the ground offensive in 1939–40, but the impact of airpower was all the greater in the desert theatre.[35] There was no natural cover or camouflage whatsoever to employ against observation and attack from the air. Once deployed to Libya, the Luftwaffe quickly gained air superiority which placed British ground formations in a real dilemma. While standard British tactical doctrine stressed the concentration of formations, and the importance of fighting divisions as divisions, this became very difficult if not impossible in a hostile air environment where there was no natural cover. Columns of tanks or trucks which moved close together in the desert simply became an inviting and vulnerable target to the Luftwaffe's 'flying artillery' of Ju87 Stuka dive bombers and Ju88 medium bombers. The only way to keep casualties and disruption to a minimum was to disperse troops and transport over very wide distances. The Germans, given a benign air environment, could afford, on occasion, to be lax about their desert dispersal. For the British, the constant threat of a surprise Stuka raid on a concentrated formation led to strict discipline in the enforcement of dispersion at all times.[36] The need for dispersion made the employment of standard artillery tactics very difficult indeed. A field artillery battery position or field artillery regiment which kept in close proximity became a sitting duck in the desert. Guns, particularly once in action, were easily spotted from the air and just as easily suppressed or destroyed.[37] The German Army had relied on Luftwaffe support for counter-battery work as early as France 1940, and it made the concentrated use of artillery on the British pattern very difficult in the desert.

Even worse, the dispersion necessary in the desert placed impossible demands upon the British signals organisation which simply could not provide secure, reliable communications over the new and unprecedented distances required. Both armies fighting in the desert relied primarily on radio communications for command and control. Wireless had first been used extensively during the First World War, but the advent of voice radio during the inter-war years seemed to offer a new era of immediate tactical communications for commanders. Armoured formation commanders in particular sensed the possibilities; even when closed down in a tank, and out of sight of each other, an entire regiment of 50 tanks could be controlled by one man's voice.

Indeed, the fast-moving combats fought in the desert were only possible with reliable wireless communication which enabled instant control of multiple vehicles. The British Army had led the way in 'voice control' of armoured formations with its 1927 Experimental Force, which had developed and tested many important concepts of armoured warfare, and the principle of wireless 'nets' where every transmitter and receiver in a regiment or battalion was tuned into the same frequency was well established by the outbreak of war.[38]

However, just as the British divisional organisation had been developed for use in Western Europe, so its signals organisation and equipment had been configured to provide communications in that environment. In 1939, the British Army was expected to rely on field telephones linked by cable or telegraph for communication. Wireless communications were designed only for tactical use at short distance and within units.[39] Much of this establishment had been forced upon the Royal Signals by the fact that, as with most equipment, the Royal Navy and Royal Air Force had first call on the limited resources available for wireless in the British services. Indeed, the supply of wireless communication within the British Army reached crisis proportions during early 1941. This was partly because of the enormous losses of precious communications equipment in the innumerable evacuations carried out by British forces in the early years of the war, and also because of the lack of production capacity in Britain which again saw the lion's share go to the other two services. This meant that there were never enough wireless sets to go round, and links between units and formations which would have been possible with more sets were simply not available.[40]

An associated problem was that the available sets lacked power, range and flexibility. The problem was that, in the Western Desert, units could not use lines, cables and telegraph – except in very particular circumstances such as those affecting the besieged forces inside Tobruk. In the mobile battles fought in the desert, telephones and cables were a hopeless anachronism: by the time they had been laid the unit and the fighting would have moved on. This threw the entire communications burden for command and control of units in a fast-moving mobile battle onto inadequate wireless communications.[41]

One example of the impact of the low priority placed on signals within the British Army was demonstrated in the design of British tanks, the key fighting platform in the desert. Against the advice of the Royal Signals, British tanks were designed to operate with only one battery. This had to operate the engine and power the wireless set. Not surprisingly, this placed undue strain on the tank engine and increased the unreliability of the wireless. Throughout 1941, British wireless communications in the desert were unreliable, intermittent and short-ranged.[42]

The limitations of short-range wireless communications decreased the size of formation which could be reliably and easily commanded in battle, particularly given the dispersal imposed by the hostile air environment.

These problems led almost naturally to the development of the Jock column and later the brigade group as the largest unit which could be easily handled. In particular, a commander could not rely on concentrated artillery firepower because, even had the Royal Artillery insisted on fighting on a divisional basis, communications between the artillery and infantry it was meant to support would be too unreliable. The lack of effective long-range radios made the coordination of large numbers of guns over large distances almost impossible. Increasingly, British commanders came to demand that their artillery was in close support and under their command – anathema to British orthodoxy but often the only useful manner of using artillery given the weaknesses inherent in British equipment, the dispersion enforced by a hostile air environment and poor wireless communications.

Auchinleck had become convinced that, in desert warfare, the brigade group rather than the division should be used as the main unit for manoeuvre and combat. Each infantry or armoured brigade group was thus provided with its own all-arms package of supporting weapons. However, such decentralisation of supporting arms meant that divisional commanders lost the ability to concentrate their artillery against important targets. The natural tendency in desert fighting to devolve control of the guns to brigade level or even lower to ensure immediate support certainly gave flexibility and mobility to small unit commanders (and the immediate fire support they needed) but it also robbed the artillery of its main role – which was to provide concentrated firepower.[43]

Now, in the crisis of late June 1942, Auchinleck had made the critical decision to reconcentrate the artillery. This was only possible because of the benign air environment provided by the Desert Air Force and the fact that the units of Eighth Army now had at least a mix of six-pounder and two-pounder guns for anti-tank protection. Nonetheless, the central position of the Royal Artillery in British fighting technique had been restored. It remained to be seen with what effect.

The dominant weapon in the desert remained the armoured formations. The tank represented the ideal balance of mobility, protection and firepower for the tactical conditions in the desert. Yet if the tank could exploit the possibilities for limitless manoeuvre that the desert offered, the anti-tank gun and the mine provided the correct antidote to the tank. Unfortunately, the British developed organisational structures which depended far too heavily upon the tank alone and gave insufficient importance to the combination of all-arms.[44]

By May 1942, each British armoured division was officially composed of one armoured brigade and one infantry brigade. The armoured brigade consisted of three armoured regiments and one motor infantry battalion, while the infantry brigade was a standard formation of three infantry battalions. This should have corrected the previous overly tank-heavy organisation but at Gazala the armoured brigades had fought quite independently of their infantry brigades. Tom Corbett noted bitterly:

> Ritchie's armour fought without its vital motor infantry component. In one case the Motor Bde was never nearer than about 50 miles to its armoured component, in the other the Motor Bde was used for static defence.[45]

By the time El Alamein was reached, the 1st Armoured Division was actually composed of three weak and disorganised armoured brigades with composite armoured regiments. The attached infantry brigades had been lost during the fighting. Thus, throughout the July fighting, the British armoured forces fought in brigade groups devoid of supporting infantry with the exception of their single motor infantry battalions. Rather than spread the remaining effective tanks thinly amongst three weak brigades, Auchinleck decided:

> to concentrate the precious Grant tanks, and when these were used they should always have the maximum available artillery support. The lighter tanks, and the armoured cars should be re-grouped to form a Light Armoured Division, the 7th was indicated, to be used on the flank of the main battle.[46]

The remaining Grant tanks were distributed to the 2nd and 22nd Armoured Brigades. However, there were simply not enough Grant tanks to equip all the armoured regiments and this meant that they had to adopt a compromise organisation in which each regiment had one or two 'heavy' squadrons equipped with Grants and at least one 'light' squadron armed with Crusaders. After the first days of fighting at El Alamein, the 4th Armoured Brigade was taken out of the line to reorganise it as a light armoured brigade, thus making use of the large numbers of armoured cars and light tanks available.

British armoured forces had also been outmatched technically by the Afrika Korp's tanks. By July 1942, Auchinleck had recognised that all the current British designs used in the desert were obsolete. In a memorandum concerning the employment of armour he wrote:

> We . . . have two types of A. F. V. The Grant type which is the fighting equivalent of the German tank and the Crusader and Stuart types which are roughly the equivalent of the Italian tanks in armament and fighting power. The Valentine tank, since it cannot fight the German tank on equal terms, must be regarded as a less mobile member of the second group.[47]

The British had used a multitude of tanks during the desert campaign. However, the fact that Eighth Army had, by mid-1942, used seven different designs of tank not only complicated the maintenance of the armoured forces but proved that no one design had stood the test of battle. The A13 and A9 cruiser tanks had been replaced by the Cruiser Tank Mk VI (A15), known as the Crusader. The Crusader Mk II was the main British 'cruiser' tank in use in 1942 but its performance left much to be desired. This meant that British tank regiments throughout 1941 and into 1942 were solely reliant on a cruiser tank designed for exploitation rather than close fighting, and a tank whose protection could not be properly upgraded. The Crusader looked impressively sleek and was a fast tank with a maximum speed of 27 mph but had been designed so hurriedly during 1939–40 that none of the multitude of lessons learned from combat experience could be incorporated into its design. The tank had also been rushed into production which meant that many teething problems remained when it entered service. Reliability remained a problem throughout its service life. Its 49mm front armour compared favourably with German tanks in 1941, but was becoming inadequate by 1942. In the cramped turret the Crusader mounted the inadequate two-pounder gun with a coaxial Besa machine gun, which meant that it was seriously outranged by German tanks and had no answer to German anti-tank guns.[48] It was soon realised that 'Cruiser tanks are not suitable for attacking enemy holding positions with A. Tk guns. In such attacks casualties will be disproportionate to the results achieved.'[49]

British infantry tanks were designed to have heavy armour to protect them against intense fire but because their role was infantry support they were not required to travel much above walking pace. The Matilda, Infantry Tank Mk II (A12), had reigned supreme during Operation Compass as its 78mm front armour was immune to the Italian anti-tank and field guns. It, too, was armed with the two-pounder gun and a coaxial machine gun. It was noted during 1940 that:

> One of the outstanding features of the operations has been the marked effect upon the morale of the enemy who for the first time found himself confronted with a tank virtually immune to all forms of fire.[50]

While the Germans had also panicked when first confronted with the Matilda during the Arras counterattack in France, they soon learned that its armour was vulnerable to the fire of their Flak 38 88mm anti-aircraft gun. In Operation Battleaxe, the advancing Matildas were destroyed at long range by only a few 88mm guns. The Matilda was slow, with a maximum speed of just 15 mph, and difficult to maintain.[51] The Infantry Tank Mk III, known as the Valentine, was essentially a more reliable and easily maintained version of the Matilda that had been designed by Vickers in 1938. It was a small and easily concealed tank with a maximum of 65mm armour, but it was also slow, with a maximum speed of 15 mph, and again carried the two-pounder gun. The small turret was cramped and could only just squeeze in two crew members.[52]

The Stuart tank was the American M3 Light Tank. It first saw service with Eighth Army in November 1941. Although called a 'light' tank, the Stuart resembled the British Crusader in terms of its weaponry and armour. The Stuart was armed with a 37mm M5 gun of comparable performance to the two-pounder and had a maximum of 51mm of armour plate. It was fast, with a maximum speed of 36 mph, and so reliable that its British crews nicknamed it the 'Honey'. But though the Stuart was a useful tank for reconnaissance it did not give the British any particular battlefield advantage.[53]

Minute comparisons of differences between the German and British tanks of the early desert campaigns generally miss the most important and fundamental point. While the British initially thought in terms of a tank versus tank encounter, encouraged by pre-war theorists such as Fuller and Liddell Hart, not to mention Percy Hobart – who had first trained 7th Armoured Division before the war – the combats in the desert were a combination of tank versus tank and tank versus anti-tank gun and artillery. The German panzer divisions operated as all-arms groupings which the British found very difficult to counter. The British inability to deal with the German tactics of tank units supported by a mobile anti-tank gun screen, which in turn was supported by infantry and artillery, has generally been ascribed to a cavalry ethos which would countenance no other tactic than the all-out charge. Such views have actually obscured the harder and more unpalatable truth.

The real problem was that all the British tanks in service with Eighth Army in July 1942, with the exception of a small number of close-support versions which were armed with a three-inch howitzer, primarily designed to fire smoke, were armed with the same two-pounder anti-tank gun. This meant that, by 1941, British tank crews could only effectively engage German tanks at 500 yards range while German tank crews in Mk IIIs could engage at ranges up to 1,000 yards.[54] Indeed, the two-pounder had never really been suitable as a tank-mounted weapon because it was not a dual-purpose gun. The small bore of the gun did not allow the use of an effective high-explosive shell. British tank designers, having absorbed the importance of mobility and firing on the move, mounted the gun so that it was perfectly adapted for firing on the move, but when the tank stopped to fire, the mount remained less steady than a fixed mount designed to be fired at rest.[55] This meant that the vast majority of British tanks, whatever their role, could fire only a solid anti-tank round capable of penetrating German tanks at close range but of no use whatsoever against German infantry or anti-tank-gun positions.

This resulted in a real dilemma for British tank crews. Lieutenant-Colonel H. E. 'Pete' Pyman, the veteran commander of 3rd RTR, later explained during Operation Crusader:

At the battle of SIDI REZEGH, I saw a squadron of Crusaders which I had commanded until a week previously destroyed by German anti-tank guns in ten minutes. They were gallantly charging an anti-tank screen. It was the only way in those days. It was very costly and very ineffective.[56]

British tanks which found themselves confronted by German tanks had to attempt to close the range so that they could use their two-pounder guns effectively. The German tanks would invariably withdraw and pull back onto their waiting screen of anti-tank guns.[57] The British tank crews then had either to retreat – as quickly as possible – or else find some local cover where they could go 'hull down' (whereby only their turret was visible) or advance. Simply remaining on the spot was not an option. Unfortunately, no matter what they did, they often failed to spot the anti-tank guns which then proceeded to knock them out.

Unfortunately for the British tank crews of the early period of the desert war, the Afrika Korps very quickly perfected the techniques which had first come to prominence in the Battle for France. The panzers of the 15th and 21st Panzer Divisions very rarely operated alone but instead worked in concert with their infantry, anti-tank guns and artillery. British reports noted that:

> the enemy's use of his A.Tk guns, pushed right up with or in front of his tanks, was a notable feature of most engagements. They are most inconspicuous and very boldy handled, and he appears to use them for the protection of his tanks in advance, withdrawal and during replenishment.[58]

The Afrika Korps was equipped with two of the best anti-tank guns of the war. The main one was the 5cm Pak 38 which had a very low profile and could knock out most British tanks at 1,000 yards range.[59] However, great use was also made of the famous 88mm anti-aircraft gun, which could destroy British tanks at 2,000 yards range.[60]

British reports observed that:

> Our tactics have been dictated by the superior range of the German gun, which has made it most expensive for our tanks to be within effective range . . . Regiments have always endeavoured to get hull down positions and to await attack where possible.
>
> It has been most expensive to make a head on attack from the front and should never be done except in extreme circumstances, as it was found that the enemy destroyed our tanks before his tanks were within our effective range (800x to 1000x). He was penetrating our tanks at 1500 yds.[61]

Although British tank crews often believed that their tanks were being knocked out by German tanks, frequently the culprits were well-camouflaged anti-tank guns. Even so, the 'charge' against a German anti-tank gun screen was often the only response that seemed possible. If the range could be brought down to 500 yards then the British tanks might – just might – have a chance of suppressing the anti-tank gunners with a spray of machine-gun bullets and a hail of solid shot. Of course, most of the time, this simply led to heavy casualties amongst the British tank crews for little gain. The fact was that British tanks simply had no answer to the German anti-tank guns and their crews.

The Grant tank which entered service with the Eighth Army in April 1942 was thus more than just another tank with which to harass the Royal Army Ordnance Corps tank workshops. It was a version of the American M3 Medium Tank, armed with a 75mm gun mounted in a sponson on the side of its hull and a 37mm gun mounted in a British-designed turret. If a little slow, the Grant was roomy, reliable and well-armoured with a maximum of 50mm of armour plate.[62] The combination of stout armour and a much heavier gun meant that, for the first time, British tank crews had a weapon that enabled them to outmatch their German opposition. Just as importantly, the 75mm gun could fire an effective high-explosive round, which meant that British crews, rather than charging anti-tank guns, could stand off at long range and shell suspected positions in exactly the same manner as the Germans. The main problem with the Grant was that it was a very high-standing tank and, since its main armament was mounted in the hull, it could not take up proper hull down positions. Nonetheless, even though the Grant was clearly a flawed and transitional design, British crews were delighted with it when they first received it in May 1942.

The Grant tank was also a major industrial achievement in its own right. Overshadowed by the quantities of Sherman tanks produced, and the speed in which American industry was able to churn out Liberty ships or aircraft by 1944, the production of the M3 tank represented a race against time. The National Munitions Program of 30 June 1940 had demanded that 1,741 medium tanks would be produced within 18 months. In fact, the M3 design was finalised in March 1941 and the pilot models of the M3 were built in early April 1941.[63] In less than a year, the United States had gone from possessing no serious competitor to German tanks to churning out a flawed, compromised, yet powerful tank design.

However, the very speed of the M3 programme led to real difficulties for the Eighth Army in attempting to use, modify and repair American tanks thousands of miles from the factories producing them. Even before the Grant went into action, British ordnance experts had discovered numerous flaws in it. Perhaps the most important was that the American M72 armour-piercing shell fired by the Grant's 75mm gun was of little use against German armour. The archaic steel shot simply shattered against German face-hardened plate armour. British ordnance experts hit upon an ingenious solution to give the Grant's main gun a much better performance.[64] The British had captured large stocks of German 75mm armour-piercing rounds, and these were used to 'cap' the American explosive charge. It was found that these composite rounds fitted perfectly, and, thanks to the hardened German steel projectile, gave very good penetration results against German armour plate. Thus, ironically, the Grant tanks that went into battle at Gazala in May 1942 were firing British-designed composite German/American ammunition from an American modification of a French gun. Unfortunately, during the retreat from Gazala, the large stocks of composite ammunition, which had absorbed much time and effort in their production, were captured. This meant that the Grant tanks in action at Alamein were forced to use the much inferior American ammunition, which limited their combat effectiveness.

Far worse for the troubled officers of the Royal Armoured Corps in July 1942 was the almost total lack of spare parts for their force of Grant tanks. The American factories were concentrating on manufacturing as many complete tanks as possible and this limited the spare parts available. By 1 July, there were more than 100 Grant tanks lying in Eighth Army base workshops ready for repair, but there was a critical lack of spare guns and engines. Until another convoy carrying spares and more tanks arrived from America in September, the Grant tanks in the Eighth Army inventory were a wasting asset. Yet it was not for nothing that the officers and men who crewed the Grant tanks called them 'ELH', or 'Egypt's Last Hope'. In a campaign in which RAC crews had been trained to accept that their weapon was the decisive element on the battlefield, the Grant stood out as the most powerful tank available to the British. The few Grants left to Eighth Army were precious. Armour commanders were unlikely to hazard their last few ELHs in what they considered a risky operation. British tank crews had also become cautious. Too many crewmen had charged invisible anti-tank gun screens too many times. At Gazala, where British tank strength had been wiped out in a matter of hours, British tank crews had learned the most important lesson the hard way – their tanks could not take on German opposition on their own. The unsupported charge of anti-tank guns – which had seemed the only alternative with tanks armed with two-pounders – would not happen again. In fact, it was the very advantages which the Grant tank conferred on its crews which made such caution possible. A Grant tank could duel and spar with its German opposite number at long range; a Crusader could not. But the timing of the introduction of the Grant had been unfortunate, in that the first examples reached Eighth Army just before Gazala. There had been little time to assimilate the new tank into the armoured regiments or develop universal tactics for its use.

The other major problem facing Auchinleck was how to use the remaining infantry formations in Eighth Army. Infantry divisions formed the backbone of the British Army during the Second World War. They were composed of infantry battalions, reconnaissance regiments, engineers, signallers, and field artillery regiments. The standard infantry battalion was composed of a head-quarters company and four rifle companies. The headquarters company held all the supporting weapons integral to the battalion in its signals, anti-aircraft, mortar, carrier, pioneer and administrative platoons. The rifle companies had an official strength of three officers and 97 other ranks organised in four platoons of three sections. Each section was led by a corporal and had two men to look after the Bren light machine gun and five riflemen.[65] Not surprisingly, battalions on active service rarely reached the full official strength. The battalion transport was divided into three echelons: the F (fighting) Echelon contained the most essential vehicles for communications, extra ammunition and the support weapons, while the A and B Echelons carried the reserve ammunition, stores and catering equipment and were kept well back until needed.[66] The full amount of transport required to lift a battalion and all its equipment was considerable and amounted to at least 72 vehicles.[67]

The full combat power of a British division could only be developed by using the division as a formation, enabling the infantry battalions to fight with the support of the concentrated firepower of the field artillery regi-ments. However the British 50th Division had been shattered at Mersa Matruh and the only formed infantry divisions left to Eighth Army were the 1st South African and 2nd New Zealand Divisions. The Commonwealth Divisions mirrored British practice in most respects although they had rejected the concept of brigade groups and held to the policy of fighting as divisions. However, the British had encountered real difficulty in employing their forces of infantry properly in the desert.

The 7th Armoured Division report after Operation Compass had explained that:

> Like crabbed age and youth, unarmoured and armoured vehicles do not go
> well together, and the more open the country the more embarrassing is such
> a combination apt to become to those whose task it is to handle it. The Western
> Desert probably contains less of what we call 'Infantry country' than anywhere
> else in the world.[68]

During daylight hours, infantry that was not well deployed and dug in was highly vulnerable to fire from tanks, artillery and indeed other infantry. It was only at night when tanks were blind that infantry making a 'set-piece' attack came into their own. Similarly, infantry forces while on the move in their vast caravans of trucks made excellent targets for tanks and armoured cars. However, Eighth Army never possessed sufficient trucks to make all its infantry completely mobile. Battalions of infantry without sufficient transport to lift all the men and their equipment were, in General Tuker's memorable phrase, mere 'tank fodder'[69] in the desert.

The British solution to this problem was to deploy infantry brigades in dug-in positions known as 'boxes' which could offer all-round defence. This meant that an infantry brigade could ensure that its positions were difficult and costly to take but there was insufficient depth to a single brigade position. Since supporting arms were parceled out to each brigade, there were never sufficient numbers to defend the position properly if a serious attack developed. Once a brigade position was under heavy bombardment, it was virtually impossible to resupply with ammunition or reinforce, which meant that the brigade had to fight a lonely battle with diminishing strength against an enemy who could easily resupply and maintain the tempo of his attack. Once the Afrika Korps began an attack on a brigade 'box' it was only a matter of time before the brigade's resistance crumbled. Meanwhile, other brigades dug into similar boxes were too far away to offer any support to their beleaguered comrade. Brigade boxes represented the nadir of British tactics in the desert. They were immobile, frittered away valuable men and weapons in penny packets, and were incapable of mutual support.

Auchinleck decided to make the remaining infantry of Eighth Army fully mobile by ordering all troops that could not be lifted by existing transport back to the Delta. The infantry-defended 'boxes' were to go. Infantry formations of whatever size would not be left immobile where they could be 'first isolated and then by-passed or reduced at leisure. Mechanised infantry formations should retain their potential mobility.' This was a highly controversial order but it was designed to ensure that there would be no hostages to fortune at Alamein. Auchinleck emphasised that:

> Divisions and Corps should be prepared to move to each other's assistance and not as had so often been the case in recent fighting remain supinely watching their specified front while decision was being reached at the expense of their relatively close neighbours.[70]

These decisions, which stemmed from Auchinleck and Dorman-Smith's discussions in the Boston bomber, showed that both men were already thinking ahead to the day when Eighth Army would bring the Afrika Korps to a halt. During the Gazala fighting, the weak Italian infantry divisions had been cleverly posted by Rommel so that they held British troops in position, but were actually protected by the British minefields, making any attack on them difficult. Auchinleck had wanted to mount an attack on the Italian infantry opposite the 1st South African Division near the coast, but this had proved impossible. Both men resolved that if the Afrika Korps could be halted, they would seek to concentrate Eighth Army's offensive effort against the Italian infantry formations. This would wear down the Panzerarmee

Afrika's strength and force Rommel to protect the Italians rather than mounting attacks of his own.[71] These ideas of more flexible, mobile warfare would inform the way that Auchinleck fought at Alamein, but their execution also introduced great difficulties.

While Auchinleck and Dorman-Smith had already learned important lessons from the Gazala fighting and were determined not to repeat the mistakes which had led to disaster, they had no time to explain these ideas to the corps and divisional commanders who would have to implement the changes. Auchinleck's first orders to the Eighth Army were peremptory instructions to reverse what had become orthodoxy within Eighth Army. Infantry formations, which had just been convinced of the virtues of the 'box' and had trained hard to implement the tactical policy of static all-round defence, were now told to dispense with supernumeraries and make their formations mobile. Armoured formations, which had not yet settled down in their previous organisation, now had to adapt to a different one. The introduction of such root and branch reforms, however necessary, in the middle of a chaotic retreat and hard fighting led to bewilderment and strong arguments amongst the commanders of Eighth Army. Meanwhile, the confident veterans of the Afrika Korps had never needed to alter their doctrine and approach to battle during the fighting in Africa.

The first German units which arrived in Tripoli in February 1941 had no prior experience of desert conditions. This resulted in some initial problems with equipment designed for operations in Europe rather than desert sand. The standard wood-burning stove was useless, for example (since there was no wood), and German trucks were found to be much inferior to British ones. Their twin rear tyres were frequently damaged by stones becoming jammed between them. Rommel recognised from the start that British lorries, which were fitted with proper desert tyres, were far more suitable and encouraged his men to make use of them as much as possible. These were relatively minor equipment problems that were overcome rapidly through improvisation.

More importantly, a German report on the initial lessons gained in Libya confirmed that 'the principles laid down for tank warfare have been entirely justified and should be applied unchanged. The desert is ideal tank country with unlimited space for manoeuvre.'[72]

The Germans may not have possessed deep knowledge of desert conditions but they did possess a clear and well-defined doctrine for armoured warfare that had been developed and refined during the Polish and French campaigns. When the 5th Light Division arrived in Libya it was able to employ those methods without change.

It was also significant that the Wehrmacht only committed three divisions to Libya during 1941. The 15th Panzer Division, 21st Panzer Division and 90th Light Division were fully mechanised formations and part of the elite Panzerwaffe. While the majority of the German Army throughout the Second World War remained marching infantry with horse-drawn supply columns,[73] such formations were not sent to Africa in 1941.[74]

The all-arms combination of the panzer divisions had been tested and proved during the early years of the war. Each division consisted of a reconnaissance unit, a panzer regiment composed of two tank battalions, a rifle regiment of three battalions and an artillery regiment. There was also a generous allocation of anti-tank and anti-aircraft guns along with engineers and support services within each division. All these different units were bound together not only by a strong collective sense of belonging to an elite but by their excellent radio communications.[75]

The Afrika Korps possessed a great advantage over the British in the quantity and quality of its signals equipment. From the inception of the Panzerwaffe in the late thirties, there was a recognition, based mainly on the British experiments in the 1920s, that for effective command and control of a fast-moving armoured formation, powerful wireless communications would be required. The most obvious difference between British and German practice lay in the high-powered (and thus long-range) tubular aerials which festooned German armoured cars and command vehicles. The generous provision of high-powered wireless equipment in the panzer divisions of the Afrika Korps provided the 'glue' for the flexible use of combined arms which became the trademark of Rommel's formations in the desert.[76]

The panzer divisions in Africa were equipped with three main types of tanks. The Panzer II[77] was a lightly armed and armoured tank[78] which was only useful for reconnaissance purposes. The backbone of the panzer regiments was provided by the Panzer III. This was a large roomy medium tank with a crew of five which had been successively up-armoured and up-gunned since its conception in 1936. The Panzer III Ausf G was the most common marque found in Libya during 1941 and was armed with a short 50mm gun[79] and two machine guns. Just before Gazala, the Panzerarmee Afrika received its first few Panzer III Ausf Js which were armed with the more powerful 50mm L/60 gun.[80] This was known to the British as the Mk III 'Special'. The Panzer IV had been designed as a support tank and was armed with a short, low-velocity 75mm gun designed primarily to fire high-explosive shells and two machine guns.[81] The Panzer IV was a highly effective tank and gave the panzer battalions the much needed ability to suppress and destroy anti-tank guns and infantry positions. Thus, if a German panzer formation came upon a British defence of anti-tank guns, 25-pounder artillery pieces and even tanks, if the Germans could drive off the British tanks, then the Panzer IVs could shell the British anti-tank and artillery positions in a leisurely fashion from 2,000 yards – well out of range of the British ability to hit them. Perhaps the most important feature of the Panzer IIIs and IVs which equipped the Afrika Korps was their good all-round capability and reliability. Although they were up-armoured and up-gunned, the Germans found no need to change the existing designs. This made maintenance simpler.

The 90th Light Division was officially separate from the two panzer divisions of the Afrika Korps but generally served alongside them. 90th Light was essentially a motorised infantry division which operated in a collection of battlegroups, each heavily armed with artillery and anti-tank guns. The division consisted of four infantry battalions, two anti-tank battalions and one artillery battalion. Each of the infantry battalions were 'entire arsenals', being liberally equipped with submachine guns, light machine guns, mortars and infantry guns. Every section had a captured 7.62mm Russian field gun which doubled as an excellent anti-tank gun. Thus, although not an armoured formation, 90th Light could develop enormous firepower against either a British infantry or armoured formation.[82] The men of these divisions were already part of the elite Panzerwaffe of the Wehrmacht, and this sense of superiority was only enhanced by their status as 'Afrikans'. Just as importantly, although each of the divisions required constant replacements through the course of the fighting, the divisions themselves remained in Africa. This meant that, at any one time, each division possessed a cadre of personnel with experience and knowledge of desert warfare. There was no doubt in anyone's mind that, even reduced to brigade strength, the veterans of the Afrika Korps formed the most powerful and formidable striking force in the desert.

The Panzerarmee Afrika might be described, with only some exaggeration, as two or even three different armies. At the core of the Panzerarmee Afrika lay the German Afrika Korps, which always formed the main striking power of the army. However, on the Italian side the Ariete Armoured Division and the Trieste and Littorio Motorised Divisions of XX Italian Motorised Corps habitually served alongside the Afrika Korps and provided an important addition of strength. These divisions gained well-deserved reputations for determination and skilled fighting during the desert campaigns but were poorly equipped with obsolete weapons in comparison to their opponents and their German allies.

The Italian armoured fighting vehicles used by these divisions were hopelessly out of date by 1942. The Italian M.13/40 tank, which formed the mainstay of the Ariete Division, was slow, underpowered, poorly protected and armed with an inadequate 47mm gun.[83] Just as British tank commanders were often forced to try to close the range with their German opponents, so the main Italian armoured tactic had to be a 'headlong dash' to bring the range down to 400 yards, where their guns had a chance of penetrating British tanks. The 75mm Semovente assault guns provided greater firepower but were also poorly armoured.[84] All the Italian armoured and mechanised formations suffered from a crippling shortage of signals equipment which made the proper use of mobile tactics very difficult and also severely hampered cooperation with the German formations.[85]

The officers and men of the XX Motorised Corps were properly trained and well-motivated soldiers. The same could not be said of the bulk of the Italian contribution to the Panzerarmee which came in the form of poorly equipped and badly trained infantry divisions of X and XXI Corps. The Italian Army persisted in emphasising mass and numbers of soldiers even in the face of repeated evidence that, in the technological warfare of the desert, such Great War assumptions no longer held true.[86] This meant that poorly motivated, sketchily trained and badly equipped Italian infantry divisions continued to serve in the Panzerarmee. Yet the organisation of the standard 'binary division' containing only two regiments each of three battalions meant that an Italian infantry division lacked the staying power and numbers of their British counterparts which contained three brigades each of three battalions.[87] These Italian divisions were of questionable value; their morale was understandably weak and they lacked the motor transport necessary for desert warfare. Rommel therefore relied heavily upon the German element of his force. The difficulties, which the British encountered in combining armour and infantry formations effectively, were shared by the Panzerarmee but their importance and any potential solutions were obscured by German contempt for their Italian allies.

Both armies racing for El Alamein had potential strengths and weaknesses. However, Rommel's Panzerarmee Afrika had been able, in battle after battle, to maximise its advantages and ruthlessly exploit the weaknesses it had found in its opponent. After suffering a series of grievous defeats, the Eighth Army was about to turn and fight on the last possible defence line before Alexandria while also attempting to alter its tactical technique. No one could predict whether, this time, Rommel would be able to find and exploit the faults in the Eighth Army in the same way that he had done so successfully many times before.

FOUR

The Crucial Day

History will establish that one of the greatest hours of the 8 Army was when it stood at bay under AUCHINLECK, NORRIE and GOTT at ALAMEIN[1]

Scraps of burnt paper floated down all over Cairo on 1 July 1942. In the courtyards of General Headquarters Middle East, British Troops Egypt and the British Embassy, office staff were burning thousands of confidential documents to prevent them from falling into the hands of the Axis. The bonfires burnt badly, and many half-burnt secret papers flew down onto the surrounding streets. Days later, Cairenes could still buy peanuts in paper cones made from charred secret documents, much to the annoyance of British officials.[2] The pall of smoke which hung over Cairo and the charred remains of important documents on 'Ash Wednesday' were only some of the visible signs that the British in Egypt had panicked.

The 'Flap', as it became known, had started when Egypt learned of the fall of Mersa Matruh. Rumours, fanned by Axis propaganda, spread like wildfire through Egypt. Rommel was now at the gates and it seemed to the population as if he would enter Alexandria and Cairo at any moment. The Mediterranean Fleet, now under threat of bombing and the aerial mining of Alexandria harbour, abandoned its main base and sailed for ports in the Canal Zone and Palestine. Flotsam and jetsam from the fighting at the front jammed the roads nose to tail into Alexandria. Meanwhile, women and children were being evacuated onto packed trains to Upper Egypt, the Sudan and Palestine. The British hold over Egypt was visibly trembling. Much of the Egyptian population, amongst them military officers like Gamal Abdel Nasser and Anwar Sadat, waited expectantly for their Axis 'liberators'.

Scenting not only an historic opportunity but an historic moment, Mussolini flew to Derna. His entourage took up 12 plane loads and included his clerical staff and cook. Mussolini's barber was unfortunate enough to be killed when his plane crash landed.[3] All of the details of Mussolini's triumphal entry into Cairo were organised and it seemed as if Mussolini would not need to wait too long for his moment.

Much of the panic and disruption taking place behind Eighth Army was the first symptom of Auchinleck's absence from General Headquarters Middle East. Corbett had ordered all officers to wear pistols and instituted a curfew in Cairo without explanation or any reassurances, which only fanned the flames of the worst rumours. On 1 July, it was Corbett who ordered that all confidential papers had to be destroyed and Auchinleck's presence at his desk would probably have kept the rumours and fear floating round Cairo in check. Yet that very day Corbett had signalled to Auchinleck: 'Have everything well in hand here. Prepared for defeat of enemy and our advance westward. Good luck.'[4] Corbett had in fact been unable to control the 'Flap' to any extent and his ebullient message to Auchinleck did nothing to assuage the nervous worry at Eighth Army Headquarters. Auchinleck could no longer worry about what was happening behind his army; he had much more pressing matters to concentrate upon on this crucial day.

Auchinleck now had to ensure that the Eighth Army was able to fight and win on the Alamein 'line' and halt Rommel's career towards the Delta. However, the existing positions which had been dug at Alamein did not inspire confidence in anyone. Lieutenant-Colonel Charles Richardson was sent to find out how Lieutenant-General Willoughby Norrie planned to hold the Alamein position. Norrie had been sent back with 30 Corps Headquarters to prepare the Alamein defences in the short time available. Richardson arrived at Norrie's headquarters and spoke to him: '"Alamein position?" said Norrie. "There isn't any position. We need sixteen divisions to hold this line."'[5] Norrie had every reason to be pessimistic. The reports of journalists, on the contrary, were unreasonably optimistic. This caused a predictable reaction amongst the troops:

> When the Riflemen heard the suave voice of the BBC announcer reporting that the Eighth Army had reached the Alamein 'Line', they looked round at the empty desert, indistinguishable from the miles of sand to east and west, and commented only as Riflemen can.[6]

There was no 'line' at Alamein on 1 July, only a widely scattered series of boxes.

The name El Alamein arises from the railway halt which British engineers built there in the 1920s. As the route of the track was surveyed, the engineers placed two flags in the sand to mark the halt. The local Bedouin tribesmen christened the spot 'el Alamein', meaning 'two flags'.[7] In 1942, the place was empty apart from a small group of railway buildings standing in the desert. To the north of the railway, just by the coast road, there rose a shoulder of rock; this formed a small line of hills sloping away to the salt marsh on the coast. To the south, the ground was composed of seemingly empty and undifferentiated desert covered with clumps of camel thorn. However, the surface of the desert could change rapidly over the course of a few hundred yards from a rocky limestone bed with a thin covering of sand to areas of deep soft sand. The desert was also marked by two low ridges, imperceptible to the eye from a distance. The Miteiriya ridge was roughly 10 miles south from the railway line and stretched in a broad arc across the desert. The Ruweisat ridge was a low rock hump running west to east 20 miles south of the railway halt. Further south, the landscape changed into a much rougher, rockier landscape, culminating in a series of high hills which overlooked the cliffs on the edge of the Qattara Depression.

It was not until Auchinleck assumed command of the Middle East in July 1941 that this stretch of desert was identified as a useful defence line for Egypt. Little thinking that a year later his defensive plan would form the bastion of Egypt's defence, Lieutenant-General Sir John H. Marshall Cornwall laid out three boxes across the 'bottleneck' of Alamein. The most important box was built in a rough semi-circle of fifteen and a half miles around the railway halt. The defences were designed to be held by a division and comprised 37 company positions and included a Corps headquarters dug into the rock of the ridge near the coast. These defences, which resembled a mini-Tobruk, should have been impressive but remained unfinished and without stocks of water or ammunition. There had been many more pressing tasks since July 1941.

Halfway across the desert, a further box was laid out at Bab el Qattara, where the defences were augmented by the natural escarpments which surrounded the position. In the south, the box at Naqb Abu Dweiss commanded the approach to a pass which led down into the depression itself. The boxes were at least 15 miles apart and could never be held independently. The assumption of July 1941 was that a strong armoured force would manoeuvre between these defended localities, but by July 1942 Eighth Army no longer had the necessary armour.

Norrie had been worried by the great distance between the three boxes and the paucity of troops to hold them, and he decided to construct a further box at Deir el Shein, halfway between Alamein and Bab el Qattara, in an attempt to cover the gap. Norrie explained later that, as he was laying out the defences of the Alamein line:

> it appeared essential to fill in the gap between the EL ALAMEIN position and the central 'Box' at QARET EL ABD. There was no armour or mobile tps to do this, so a proposal was put forward to construct a locality about DEIR EL SHEIN. . . . Although far from ideal, it was the best available.[8]

No matter how many boxes or defences might have been dug at Alamein, the strength of Eighth Army fell far short of Norrie's pessimistic estimate of 16 divisions. Indeed, the manner in which formations arrived at Alamein in disconnected elements revealed the disorganisation within Eighth Army. The 1st South African Division had retired from the Gazala line and had been sent straight back to the Alamein line. They then spent nearly two weeks 'improving' the defences of the Alamein box by drilling out new positions, roofing in existing ones, laying thousands of yards of barbed wire and burying thousands of mines. The irony of their situation did not escape them. More than 20,000 of their countrymen had been captured in Tobruk, a larger and more powerful fortress. They were now attempting to put into order a much smaller and less impressive set of defences. Major-General Dan Pienaar, the commander of the 1st South African Division, was deeply unhappy about Auchinleck's order to 'thin out' the infantry formations and send the 'super-numeraries' back to the Delta. Auchinleck ordered Pienaar to send out two mobile columns, each composed of a brigade of infantry and two batteries of guns, to watch the desert to the west and south of the box. This meant that Pienaar could only afford to hold the Alamein defences with one weak brigade. Auchinleck was determined not to leave any troops to be encircled and captured but this meant that only the western side of the Alamein box could actually be held by troops of the 3rd South African Brigade.

Although the box was weak in infantry, it was strong in artillery. The artillery of the 1st South African Division, composed of 1st and 3rd South African Field Regiments, was reinforced by the 7th and 64th Medium Regiments. The 4.5-inch and 5.5-inch medium guns could hit targets over 15 miles away from the box and the divisional artillery could lay down concentrated fire on any attacker. Auchinleck had begun the process of concentrating the fire of Eighth Army's artillery.

Meanwhile, the remnants of 50th Division were organised into three eight-gun columns and deployed behind Alam el Onsol to help cover the gap between El Alamein and Deir el Shein where 18th Indian Brigade was deployed in the box. Ten miles further south, the 6th New Zealand Brigade were deployed in the Bab el Qattara box, while the 4th and 5th New Zealand Brigades reorganised themselves, after their breakout from Minqar Qaim, around Deir el Munassib. In the far south, the 9th Indian Brigade held the box at Naqb Abu Dweiss but was short of water and petrol and felt considerably isolated. As late as midday on 30 June, although all of these infantry positions were garrisoned, none of the British armoured units had reached Alamein. The remnants of the 1st and 7th Armoured Divisions, with the 2nd, 4th and 22nd Armoured Brigades, were still 50 miles away at Fuka and motoring towards Alamein with only a hazy idea of where they were meant to be deployed. The situation was dangerous and tense for Eighth Army. Until the armoured formations, however weak, could reach their allotted positions to support the infantry defences, the Alamein line was simply too thin to hold against the onrush of Rommel's armoured spearheads.

Rommel knew that speed was critical if he was to bounce the British out of their last defensive line. It was almost as if the exhausted soldiers of the Panzerarmee Afrika were being borne bodily forwards by their commander's strength of will. On the morning of 30 June, Rommel had ordered the concentration of his troops to the south of Sidi Abd el Rahman from where they would mount their attack. Rommel hoped to hit the Alamein defences that day but delays made it impossible. Rommel's knowledge of the defences was sketchy. He expected to find the 50th Division holding the defences of the Alamein box while his intelligence placed the 10th Indian Brigade at Deir el Abyad. It is clear why Rommel's intelligence officers made these errors. Fellers had mistakenly reported that there was one 'South African Brigade, of low combat efficiency'[9] when in fact the 1st South African Division was still intact and 'one brigade organic to the 50 Division' present in Eighth Army. In fact, the Alamein box was held by the much fresher South Africans, and the 18th Indian Brigade was in position at Deir el Shein, three miles further east of Deir el Abyad. Panzerarmee intelligence assumed that 1st Armoured Division would take up position in front of 2nd New Zealand Division on the southern flank. Given what seemed to be a similar British deployment to that at Mersa Matruh, Rommel decided to replicate his plan of attack. While he would mount a feint attack towards the southern flank of Eighth Army, he planned to penetrate the centre of the Eighth Army, bypassing the Deir el Abyad and Alamein boxes, and encircle the Eighth Army just as he had done at Matruh.

90th Light Division was tasked with skirting around the Alamein box, and then driving to the sea to cut it off, which, as von Mellenthin noted, were 'exactly the same orders as at Mersa Matruh'.[10] Meanwhile, the two panzer divisions, followed by the Italian XX Corps, would manoeuvre round Deir el Abyad and attack the 1st Armoured Division and 2nd New Zealand Division from the rear. Rommel knew that there was little chance of breaking Eighth Army in a hard frontal assault but he believed that, with luck and daring, his troops might encircle it and panic it into 'headlong flight'[11] as at Mersa Matruh.

In the small hours of 1 July, Auchinleck hurriedly scribbled down his ideas for the coming battle. While his headquarters moved back from El Imayid, he visited Norrie in the Alamein box. Auchinleck was determined to turn the tables on Rommel. He sketched out his battle plan on a scrap of paper yet kept to the strict military format of the Appreciation that he had learned at Quetta Staff College. 'My Draft for Counter-Offensive' noted that

1. The enemy has concentrated opposite 1 SA Div with obvious intention to attack early with bulk of his forces.

Intention

2. I intend to defeat the enemy and destroy him.

Method

3. (a) 30 Corps will stop enemy advance eastwards.

(b) 13 Corps with 1 Armd and NZ Div will attack NORTHWARD against enemy RIGHT flank and rear between 86 and 88 Grid lines inflicting the maximum destruction on the enemy . . .

(c) ~~5 Ind Div under 13 Corps will protect 8 Army SOUTHERN FLANK~~

4. (c) 13 Corps will withdraw south of positions from BAB QATTARA defended locality for use as mobile reserve.

Small det will be left in locality to deceive enemy and prevent the occupation for as long as possible.

13 Corps will remove as many reserves now in post as far as possible.[12]

While Dorman-Smith's appreciation of 28 June had explored the worst-case scenario of a continued retreat from the Alamein position, Auchinleck's hurried scribbles on the early morning of 1 July prove that he was determined to fight it out at Alamein. Rommel's feint, attempting to make the British believe he aimed to strike the southern flank of Eighth Army, had failed; Auchinleck had been informed by Ultra decrypts and was prepared to meet it. While the men of the 1st South African Division in the Alamein box, 18th Indian Brigade at Deir el Shein and the roving columns in the desert in between, held the attack of the Panzerarmee, Auchinleck hoped to use the tanks of 22nd Armoured Brigade and the infantry of 2nd New Zealand Division as a striking force to crush the flank and rear of the Panzerarmee as soon as it had launched its own assault. However, although Auchinleck knew and understood Rommel's intentions, his knowledge of his own army was lacking. Eighth Army Headquarters knew that 2nd New Zealand Division were dug in at Bab el Qattara, only 10 miles south of the southern flank of 30 Corps but Eighth Army had completely lost contact with 'Strafer' Gott. Dorman-Smith subsequently related his thoughts on 1 July concerning the commander of 13 Corps: 'Gott! Where in hell was he? Why couldn't signals find his HQs? Where was 13 Corps HQs?'[13] Auchinleck's plans for an immediate counterattack would founder that day in part because one of his Corps Headquarters was out of reach.

Communications difficulties and the continuing chaos present amongst units which were still struggling to take up their positions at Alamein help to explain the real sense of confusion and doubt in the minds of commanders, officers and men during this critical day. While Dorman-Smith and Norrie now understood Auchinleck's intentions, there had been no time to convey the points contained in Auchinleck's 'My Draft for Counter-Offensive' further down the ranks. Auchinleck had issued a pugnacious Special Order of the Day on 30 June to all ranks of the Eighth Army, stating: 'The enemy is stretched to the limit and thinks we are a broken army . . . He hopes to take Egypt by bluff. Show him where he gets off.'[14] Like Haig in the dark days of April 1918, he may have hoped that such a message would galvanise the officers and men of Eighth Army. However, there is little evidence that it was widely read by the soldiers it was meant to reach.

The two panzer divisions of the Afrika Korps rolled forward well behind schedule on the morning of 1 July 1942. The British defences of the Alamein line were about to be tested. But General Walter Nehring and his men were in for a shock. They believed that they were outflanking a British box at Deir el Abyad and would be able to drive deep behind the Eighth Army's positions before encircling the defences of El Alamein itself. As the tanks, half-tracks and trucks of 15th and 21st Panzer divisions rumbled across the open desert and were about to start climbing up the long, low Ruweisat ridge, they came under fire from an unexpected direction. Rommel's hurried plans to bounce the British out of the Alamein positions had allowed no real time for reconnaissance. There had been no time to probe the British line, and the positions of the 18th Indian Brigade at Deir el Shein, to the north west of the Ruweisat ridge, had been completely missed.

As Nehring's men came under fire from the dug-in defenders, he decided to mount a full-scale assault on the Indian position. It was clear that if the box at Deir el Shein was bypassed, the position north of the Ruweisat ridge held by the 1st South African Division would have to be eliminated. Once the defences of Deir el Shein were reduced, the panzer divisions would have a clear road and an unobstructed supply route behind the British defences. An offensive-minded commander like Nehring was not going to allow a weak British position to prevent his thrust from reaching the British rear.

The tired tank crews, panzergrenadiers and gunners of the two German divisions quickly shook out into formation, according to the battle drills which they had practised so many times, and began their attack. The troops of Eighth Army were all too familiar with the tactics practised by the Afrika Korps. The standard procedure was to open fire with:

a company with Panzer IV at 1800 metres: under protective fire from these tanks and the artillery, assault guns, anti-tank guns and infantry with full equipment . . . are brought up. The infantry opens MG fire on artillery and anti-tank guns at long range.

As soon as fire concentration is superior to enemy defence, tanks attack in three waves, part of the infantry following, 180 metres behind the last wave.

Artillery, tanks and infantry, thrown in to support the assault attack, fire as long as possible with some use of HE shells.

Flanks are protected by reconnaissance forces.[15]

This battle drill had become second nature to the men of the 15th and 21st Panzer Divisions and, even though they had been radically reduced in strength, they were still powerful enough to deal with a single brigade. Once the panzers began their attack, it was only a matter of time before the positions of 18th Indian Brigade were overrun.

The men of 18th Indian Brigade, however, were unlikely to recognise the German battle drill; they were a new formation in Eighth Army. The condition of this brigade was an example of one of the great problems which had afflicted Eighth Army throughout its existence. While the German troops of 15th and 21st Panzer Division were dog-tired, they were, in many cases, the same men who had attacked Eighth Army on 26 May and who had fought through the grinding Crusader battles of November and December 1941. Indeed, some had even arrived with Rommel in February and March of 1941. They were truly desert veterans, buoyed up by a sense of invincibility, mutual trust and shared experience.

The men of 18th Indian Brigade had no similar sense of shared belonging. In the course of two confusing months, they had passed through the command of three armies – Tenth, Ninth and Eighth. As the crisis in the desert had deepened, General Headquarters Middle East had become desperate for formed bodies of troops whatever their state of equipment, training or readiness. At the beginning of June the brigade had made the long journey from Erbil in Iraq through Mosul and Damascus to Acre in Palestine, spending only one week in Palestine before it was ordered, on 25 June, to the Western Desert. The long rail journey had not been without mishap either: the three trains which carried the three battalions of the brigade had been bombed at Galal station (25 miles west of El Daba) when they stopped there on 26 June. The trains had then been moved back to Alamein and the tired officers and men of the brigade found themselves dumped unceremoniously at the Alamein halt on the morning of 27 June. Meanwhile, the brigade headquarters and the brigade's artillery regiment, which had both gone ahead by road, were out of touch and presumed lost at Mersa Matruh. Lieutenant-Colonel K. F. May, the senior battalion commander had taken charge and sought orders from Norrie.[16] He had ordered the brigade to Deir el Shein at once, where it went with no time to adjust.

Using a shuttle service of borrowed trucks, the brigade had finally deployed at Deir el Shein by midnight on 28 June. The brigade was told to expect an attack within 48 hours and the men had set to work digging themselves in immediately. Lieutenant-Colonel May later commented, 'Time was against us from the start.'[17] Over the next few days, supporting arms found their way in dribs and drabs to Deir el Shein and by the evening of 30 June, the brigade had been provided with 25 25-pounder, 18 six-pounder and 16 two-pounder guns. Brigadier Mead Dennis, the artillery commander of 30 Corps, later emphasised, 'although there were 25 x 25-prs, they were disorganised bits of three separate Regts, and communications were almost non-existent, owing to all wireless batteries being down and cable having been expended'.[18] With such handicaps there could be no question of coordinating the fire of the guns. This meant that 18th Indian Brigade could not rely on the concentrated artillery fire which was so essential to breaking up any determined assault on their positions. For the past three days the men had spent 18-hour days digging in, wiring the position and laying mines around the perimeter. The brigade engineer officer had found himself short of many thousands of mines and the South Africans and New Zealanders had helped out with compressors to dig through the unforgiving rock floor of the desert. They also provided more mines to bulk out the defences. Yet by 1 July, despite the back-breaking labour, there were still gaps in the mine-field on the eastern side, and the wire was no more than a triple coil obstacle. None of the battalions had any reserve ammunition beyond that which they had brought all the way from Iraq, and the artillery pieces and anti-tank guns were very short of ammunition.[19]

As the brigade waited for the coming storm, an order was received to evacuate the position the next day – informed by Auchinleck's new policy of not allowing any immobile troops in Eighth Army, which could be cut off and destroyed by Rommel's army. Auchinleck had made it clear to Norrie that he wanted 18th Infantry Brigade to be given enough troop-carrying transport to make them completely mobile. Given its straitened circumstances, Eighth Army simply did not have the 80 or so lorries required. Instructions on the thinning out of defensive positions were issued to the brigade, and, ironically, one battalion of the brigade was to have been sent back to El Amiriya on the night of 1–2 July.[20] These orders were never carried out.

The one great advantage that the men of 18th Indian Brigade enjoyed was the nature of the position itself. Norrie commented:

Digging on the ridge itself was very difficult owing to its rocky nature but there were some patches of sand about DEIR EL SHEIN which made digging easier. The position was a sort of saucer, with good OPs on the edges.[21]

The Arabic word *deir* translates roughly as 'depression' and Deir el Shein was only one of many large depressions scattered across the desert at Alamein. These depressions often had quite steep lips where they joined the floor of the desert which could offer good firing positions across the relatively flat desert, but the troops deployed in the depression itself were thus protected from observation unless the enemy literally stood on the edge of the depression itself. Thus, the fighting troops of the brigade could fire out of the depression, while the artillery pieces, headquarters and ancillary staff remained out of view of an attacker, although by no means immune to indirect artillery fire.

The morning of 1 July was very dusty and the constant movement of

British units driving past the box on their way to various rendezvous points kicked up yet more dust and made observation very difficult. Norrie commented that 'July 1st was an unpleasant day, both as regards dust storms and visibility.'[22]

The brigade first sighted the Afrika Korps as a large cloud of dust moving forwards from the south west. At about 10.00 hours that morning, the Axis artillery, which had fired numerous ranging shots, began to shell Deir el Shein and concentrated their fire mainly on the Essex Battalion which was holding the north east corner of the box. The Afrika Korps then played a *ruse de guerre* they had employed a number of times before to demoralise their opponents. Two blindfolded officers who claimed to be from the 50th Division arrived at brigade headquarters in a Bren carrier at about 11.15 hours. They said that they had been sent by the German commander to order the brigade to surrender within half an hour to avoid 'needless bloodshed'. Not surprisingly, brigade headquarters sent back the message 'We will fight it out'.[23] The two officers were then sent back to 10th Division Headquarters for interrogation. They revealed that 15th Panzer had about 60 tanks, with plenty of captured artillery and anti-tank guns.

The polite exchanges of possible surrender terms took some time, but by early afternoon the Afrika Korps, under the cover of a heavy bombardment, began to probe the position for weaknesses. Although perhaps six vehicles were disabled on the minefield, the Germans soon found a gap and were able to take advantage of the cover provided by a slight depression a quarter of a mile west of the Essex B Echelon positions. After some reorganisation, German assault engineers advanced under the cover of a bombardment thickened by heavy mortar fire, and attempted to place Bangalore torpedoes under the wire to blow a gap. However, the 'men, cooks, mess staff, clerks, MT personnel and QM and his staff' of the Essex B Echelon were 'firing steadily' and took a toll on the advancing German engineers.[24]

However, with ammunition running low, the firing began to slacken. This enabled the Germans finally to blow a gap in the wire and drive some Panzer IIIs and IVs into the position. The dug-in field guns opened fire at point-blank range and knocked out some of the panzers but the Germans continued to press their advantage. The panzers moved straight for the brigade head-quarters where they were engaged by the seven Matilda tanks that had arrived on the evening of 30 June. The Matildas were no match for the German panzers: soon all seven were in flames.[25]

Norrie had ordered 1st Armoured Division to render 'every assistance' to 18th Indian Brigade but the harsh reality was that the British armour was in no position to do anything.[26] 4th Armoured Brigade had reached its deployment area but most of its vehicles had become stuck in soft sand and it took almost all day to drag them out.[27] The 18th Indian Brigade had first called for help early in the afternoon but had sent its message in high-security cipher rather than by the more rapid but less secure radio telephone. The vital message was given no priority and it was not until 17.00 hours that 30 Corps Headquarters realised 18th Indian Brigade was in serious trouble.[28] Major-General Herbert Lumsden, commander of the 1st Armoured Division, related that:

> Owing to the difficulty of . . . locating our own troops and the enemy accurately, it was not until 1900 hrs that 22nd Armd Bde contacted the enemy tanks in the neighbourhood and South of the DEIR EL SHEIN box, inflicting casualties and driving 15 off in a South-Westerly direction. After this very successful action, 22 Armd Bde could see our own troops withdrawing from the box.[29]

The onlooking soldiers at Deir el Shein had a very different perception of the approach of the British armour. Lieutenant-Colonel May later related:

> It was unfortunate that all ranks were told that the 1 Armd Div were coming to their assistance, and that they subsequently saw an armoured force approach the position and then turn away. From then on they seemed to have considered the position hopeless, and to have realised that no further help would be forthcoming. The effect of this disappointment cannot have done other than lower the morale of the whole garrison particularly the Indian troops.[30]

Even though there was now a hole in their position and they were beyond help, the brigade continued to put up fierce resistance. The Germans acted cautiously, no doubt fearing the existence of hidden minefields (which would in fact have been there had more mines been available). It was not until 16.00 hours that the German tanks moved to attack C Company of the Essex, which they finally overran after an hour of fierce fighting. The anti-tank guns, hurriedly emplaced though they were, took a heavy toll on the attacking panzers. The shelling had become more and more intense, and the fighting around the brigade headquarters reached a crescendo of artillery shells, mortar bombs, tank-gun and machine-gun fire. At about 17.30 hours, May noticed hundreds of the 4/11th Sikhs running towards their own wire. He believed that they were waving white turbans in surrender, but this was in fact the Sikhs' attempt to break out of what had become an untenable position.[31] A survivor who managed to escape related that:

> it was decided to evacuate Eastwards just before last light. The enemy tanks were found to be at the East side of the box, but a considerable proportion of our forces succeeded in penetrating this screen.

A small band of Imperial forces decided to remain and were last seen in the fading light firing at the oncoming infantry at 100 yds range.[32]

This small band were the remnants of the 1/4th Essex. Trapped by the encircling panzers and the advancing German infantry, they held out to the last.

Even in this very desperate situation, the Germans mounted their final assault on the Essex 'very deliberately'. After dogged resistance, the Essex were finally overrun at 19.30 hours after a day of very hard fighting. May commented:

> As it was, the final end to the battle was too one sided. Most supporting weapons had shot off their ammunition and the majority of my A/Tank guns were knocked out. Added to which, we had no sticky bombs to hand out to the enemy.[33]

The fight against the Afrika Korps had indeed been one-sided. An ill-prepared and poorly supported brigade filled with inexperienced soldiers had drawn the entire weight of Rommel's two panzer divisions onto their position. Nonetheless, through their resistance, 18th Indian Brigade had accounted for as many as 18 German tanks during the day. Not only had the offensive power of the Afrika Korps been blunted, but the main drive through the British positions which Rommel had wanted complete by the end of the day had been halted. Without this breathing space, it is unlikely that the British troops defending the Alamein line would have been able to shake themselves into the semblance of order which was vital if Eighth Army was to hold off Rommel's tired but victorious troops. The sacrifice of the brigade had bought critical time. Although few, if any, observers recognised it at the time, the resistance of 18th Indian Brigade had stemmed the tide.

Just as the main thrust of the Afrika Korps had been halted, so too had the drive of the 90th Light Division around the Alamein box to the coast. As they moved forwards in darkness on the morning of 1 July, the battlegroups of the division drove up against the defences of the box and were brought under fire by 'machine guns, anti-tank guns, mortars and heavy artillery fire'.[34] Having bumped the defences in darkness, the battlegroups were pinned to their ground by the heavy fire until midday, when a sandstorm enabled them to disengage and attempt to bypass the defences. 90th Light was able to drive forwards for another few miles and actually reached the track that led south to the Qattara Depression. However, just as they reached the track, which marked the halfway point in their drive to the coast, the 90th Light was once again hit by fire as they brushed the defences of the 3rd South African Brigade. In daylight, it was a simple matter for the South African forward observation officers to call down ranging shots from their batteries. Soon, 90th Light Division was being pounded by the concentrated fire of seven batteries of artillery. The division requested more artillery support in an attempt to suppress the hostile batteries, and Rommel drove up to the positions with his *Kampfstaffel*.[35] However, many vehicles of the *Kampfstaffel* were hit, and instead of being able to urge his men on to greater efforts, Rommel had to stem a rout of his own most trusted soldiers. Under the barrage of heavy fire, the German infantry did the unthinkable – they ran for safety. The division's war diary reported:

> A panic breaks out in the Division (1530 hours) which is stopped just in time by the energetic action of the Divisional Commander and Chief of Staff. Supply columns and even parts of fighting units rush back under the ever-increasing enemy artillery fire. The Commanders of the Battle Groups, however, succeed in keeping the majority of their units facing the enemy and bring back the troops which have taken to flight . . . The situation has been clarified and a rout prevented, but the advance has broken down under the concentrated enemy fire.[36]

Although no one in Eighth Army knew what had happened, a major German unit had been close to complete rout in the face of the firepower of the Alamein box. The soldiers of 90th Light Division were pinned to the ground and could not move forwards. Rommel's plan to bounce Eighth Army out of the Alamein line had failed and the swing of the desert pendulum had finally been held.

Eighth Army had been in real peril on 1 July. Had Rommel's men driven through the Eighth Army's positions and reached their rear, it is more than likely that Auchinleck would have interpreted such a penetration as defeat. Throughout the day, Auchinleck was out of contact with Gott and his 13 Corps just as he had been at Mersa Matruh. Throughout the critical hours of 1 July, Gott had believed that Auchinleck intended to mount another withdrawal and remained unaware of Auchinleck's determination to hold Rommel. Had Rommel managed to encircle the Eighth Army on 1 July, at least half of the Eighth Army might well have pulled out in a repeat of Mersa Matruh. Given the breakdown in communications, along with the multiplication of orders and misunderstandings amongst Eighth Army units, any retreat would have turned into disaster.

While the Iraqi oilfields were the true centre of gravity for Britain's position in the Middle East, the loss of Egypt would have been catastrophic. Without the Egyptian base and its workshops, depots and dumps, the British could not have built up the offensive power to restore the situation. Britain's strategic position would have become precarious indeed.

It was late in the afternoon of 1 July when 'Strafer' Gott turned up at Eighth Army Headquarters. Out of radio contact for the entire day, Gott had decided to drive to see Auchinleck himself. Gott was quickly 'put in the picture' by Auchinleck. He was informed that he must not consider himself pinned by the defensive localities, but instead, should operate towards the north west and the Ruweisat ridge in closer contact with 30 Corps. After this briefing, Gott was simply too tired to drive in the darkness back to his own headquarters. He slept beside his car that night before motoring back to his headquarters the next morning. The immediate crisis was over.

The stand of the 18th Indian Brigade at Deir el Shein and 1st South African Division efforts at the Alamein box had halted Rommel's men in their tracks and bought precious time for the rest of Eighth Army to gather itself. Yet these combats had simply been a reminder of much of what had gone wrong with the Eighth Army over the past year. Deir el Shein and the Alamein box represented exactly the kind of position which Auchinleck had been determined to do away with when he took over command of the Eighth Army on 25 June. The supreme irony of 1 July was that Auchinleck and the Eighth Army were saved by the dogged resistance of an isolated fresh brigade employing the bankrupt tactics of the brigade box.

The Afrika Korps, still grouped around Deir el Shein, did not have such a quiet night. Its formations were repeatedly illuminated by flares dropped by Fairey Albacores and bombed by RAF Wellington bombers which brought confusion to its supply columns.[37] Rommel was determined to continue his attack the next day. He had not been able to break the defences of Eighth Army in the first rush, but he still believed that he would be able to reach Alexandria. Eighth Army, however, had not dissolved into flight and there had been no repeat of Mersa Matruh. Far from being over, as Rommel had hoped, the battle for Egypt had only just begun.

FIVE

Ruweisat Ridge

Ruweisat ridge is a bare outcrop of rock lightly covered with sand that stands amongst miles of lonely desert. For most of history this hard stony plateau has stood unremarked upon and unnoticed. Yet, from being an all but nameless low rise in the desert, its features became intimately known by both the Eighth Army and the Panzerarmee Afrika. The long low ridge at Ruweisat became critical terrain and its possession would determine the outcome of the battle. Major-General Tuker explained that the 'ridge had to be held at all costs for its loss would give the enemy observation and a springboard on to the area through which ran the whole communications of the Eighth Army'.[1] Auchinleck later called the Ruweisat ridge 'vital . . . the key to our position'.[2] With the Ruweisat ridge in its hands, the Panzerarmee would outflank the Alamein box and cut off its communications. Similarly, if Eighth Army could secure possession of the ridge, its hump, like a whale's back breaking the waves, would make a perfect jumping-off point for a thrust at the Axis rear. This was why much of the subsequent action during July was fought for this seemingly insignificant rise in the desert. Rommel's continued attempts to break Eighth Army meant that over the next few days, weeks and indeed months, thousands of men on both sides would be killed and wounded in the struggle for possession of this lonely and unremarkable rise in the desert.

The Panzerarmee Afrika faced a real dilemma on 2 July 1942. Rommel had thrust his men on the Alamein line with no reconnaissance or preparation in the hope that the British defence would collapse as it had done at Matruh. Now they faced an unexpectedly stubborn and determined resistance and the possibility arose that, far from thrusting behind a defeated army, the Panzerarmee had placed its head into a noose. Nonetheless, Rommel did not hesitate to order a resumption of the same attacks that had been planned for the day before. In truth, he now had little option but to keep his army on the move in the hope that Eighth Army would break first.

The situation in which Panzerarmee Afrika found itself was becoming progressively worse. The troops of 21st Panzer Division busied themselves by clearing up Deir el Shein in the morning but continuous air attacks during the night had disrupted and scattered supply columns which meant that there was little replenishment possible for the fighting columns in the morning. Worse, there were only 37 tanks left to arm the two panzer divisions.[3] As soon as the sun had come up, the air assault on the Panzerarmee was continued by light and fighter bombers of the Desert Air Force. Coningham's concept of 'round-the-clock' bombing was taking on its full meaning.[4] Rising dust storms prevented flying for much of the afternoon of 2 July but the systematic bombing of the Panzerarmee began to take its toll.

90th Light Division had passed a relatively quiet night and resumed its drive for the coast at 04.00 hours that morning, with Group Menny in the vanguard. Driving along in the darkness the trucks of the division went nearly two kilometres further forward before they drew fire from the Alamein box. Once again, the division was caught in a crescent of fire from at least seven batteries and the advance ground to a halt from 'concentrated enemy fire from all arms'.[5] Four batteries were brought up from the Army Artillery reserve in an attempt to suppress this fire, but the South African defenders of the Alamein box did not even recognise this attack as the 90th Light Division in full cry. Instead the 'attack' was dismissed in its subsequent report as 'Lt shelling continued by both sides on the morning of 2 Jul 42.'[6] It is clear why the two sides had such a different perspective on the same event. While the Germans were pinned to the ground under concentrated artillery fire long before they had reached effective small-arms range, the South Africans, well protected by their series of bunkers, pillboxes and gun pits, were subjected to the scattered and badly directed fire of weak and composite German and Italian batteries. 90th Light Division had lost the power to force a decision.

Rommel acknowledged this painful fact when he changed the role of the Afrika Korps for the day. At 09.00 hours, the two panzer divisions were given urgent orders to finish the mopping up of Deir el Shein and to advance seven kilometres directly east along the Ruweisat ridge and then turn north to the coast instead of south east.[7] The Afrika Korps would sweep round to the coast in cooperation with the 90th Light Division which would now form the inner part of a much larger wheel. With all his German forces now committed in the drive to the coast, Rommel ordered the Italian XX Corps, composed of the Ariete, Trieste and Littorio Divisions, to take up the former role of the Afrika Korps. These Italian armoured and motorised formations would watch the southern flank and, by turning south east once they reached a place on German maps which translates as 'Deep Well', would encircle the southern units of Eighth Army. Rommel hoped that this change of plan would be enough to complete the encirclement of the Alamein positions.[8]

Even in its depleted condition the Afrika Korps was still dangerous and its thrust along the Ruweisat ridge threatened the security of Eighth Army. The German advance got under way at 15.00 hours that afternoon but the delay had given the British armoured brigades precious time to refuel and reorganise. The 90th Light again made no headway in the storm of fire that greeted it, with the Marcks group claiming that it had managed to advance only a further 500 metres eastwards. The division's war diary gloomily commented on its renewed advance that:

> the enemy gave no sign of withdrawing. On the contrary, he gave the impression that he was trying with all his force to stop the Panzerarmee from storming the Alamein position. It seemed that the German forces, exhausted by the heavy fighting and the hardships of the past days and weeks . . . would not be able by their own strength, to force this last British fortification.[9]

Meanwhile, the panzers of the Afrika Korps made a more threatening advance along the Ruweisat ridge. North of this ridge, the men of 1st South African Brigade found themselves under increasingly heavy fire exacerbated by the hard and stony ground which threw off splinters of rock. Its positions were also overlooked by the Ruweisat ridge and high ground to the west. Although this brigade group had been instructed to use mobile tactics, the intensive fire prevented much movement from the scratch and improvised defences. There was only an 'illusion of mobility' in what came to be known by the defenders as the 'Hotbox'.[10] The Hotbox drew fire from both the 90th Light Division and the Afrika Korps that day and even from some Eighth Army guns which mistook the range. Not surprisingly, the brigade felt exposed and the brigadier called for armoured support early that morning; none was forthcoming. Instead, its southern flank was 'protected' by 'Robcol', a scratch force of guns and infantry improvised from the remnants of 10th Indian Division which took up a position on the centre of the Ruweisat ridge. In fact, there was no communication between these two beleaguered forces and both fought independent battles until the evening.

The ability of the German Army in the Second World War to scrape together improvised groups of soldiers to fight in battlegroups has become almost legendary. Most historians have argued that the British Army was unable to compete on similar terms. Inglis had protested against the order to form mobile battlegroups, claiming that they would offer the resistance of 'tissue paper' to the advancing panzers.[11] Indeed, 2nd New Zealand Division sent out two motorised columns that day which reached the Alam Nayil ridge and shelled some far distant Axis transport, but were unable to accomplish anything more dramatic.[12]

The performance of these columns may well have confirmed many suspicions about the value of Jock columns and scratch battlegroups but the performance of Robcol on 2 July gives the lie to the myth that Eighth Army could not fight effectively in such formations. Robcol was a British battlegroup which Brigadier R. P. Waller began to form on 1 July from scattered detachments that had flowed in to the Alamein line. Although the core of the unit was formed from the 11th Field Artillery Regiment which had arrived from Iraq just two days before, Robcol's order of battle[13] shows just what an improvised force it was, with detachments from the 10th Indian Division, and even some of the Gurkhas who had fought with 18th Indian Brigade the day before. The grim joke within Eighth Army was that a 'battle-group' or 'column' was simply a brigade group which had been overrun by tanks. Yet far from offering the resistance of 'tissue paper' to the advancing columns of the Afrika Korps, Robcol played a crucial part in halting the advance of the Panzerarmee on the afternoon of 2 July.

The guns of Robcol had engaged enemy vehicles which could be seen around Deir el Shein during the morning, and the Germans responded with infantry attacks supported with a few tanks. These were easily driven off. The Afrika Korps attack finally got underway during the afternoon but soon ran into fire from both the Hotbox and Robcol. Nonetheless, the panzers and their supporting infantry drove onto the high ground on the right flank of Robcol which gave good observation over the British positions. Fire from these German tanks began to cause heavy casualties amongst the gunners of Robcol, but Lieutenant-Colonel McCarthy, the commanding officer, told his men that 'the guns must fight it out where they stood'.[14] As the German tanks closed in, hosing the gun positions with machine-gun fire, the gunners continued to take a heavy toll of the German tanks.

Robcol fought with the determination of men who realised that this was a last stand. Sergeant Keenan, who had become separated from his unit during the retreat from Matruh, continued to load and fire his gun under heavy fire even when he was the only man left unwounded. Bombardier Johnson lost his left arm but continued to lay and fire his gun while refusing to leave for medical attention. He died the next day.[15]

Robcol would eventually have been overwhelmed, but by late afternoon the tanks of 22nd Armoured Brigade moved in to engage the Germans. 4th County of London Yeomanry, in position on 'North Ridge' (Ruweisat ridge) noted that 'The Bde tanks were engaged for about 3 hours at long range with about 30 enemy tanks – the 6pdr guns appeared to have a very steadying effect on the enemy.'[16] The fact was that the increased performance of the six-pounder anti-tank gun allowed British gunners to engage the German tanks at a distance, keeping them far enough away from the gun positions so that the Germans could neither spot the guns accurately nor use their machine guns to drive the gunners away.

2nd Armoured Brigade had more difficulty in reaching its battle positions and lost a number of tanks to the 88mm guns that covered its avenue of approach. Nonetheless, 15th Panzer Division soon reported that it was being engaged by a greatly superior enemy and had been forced onto the defensive. Just as the Robcol and 1st South African Brigade had worried about their open flanks, so the two British armoured brigades worked around the German flanks. The two panzer divisions made a final effort to push forwards in the evening but by the time 21st Panzer finally broke off its attack, the Afrika Korps had moved only six kilometres forward.[17] The German thrust had been held for another day.

The true significance of the fighting on 2 July 1942 at Alamein is often overlooked by Auchinleck's harshest critics. Auchinleck commented to Brooke later in July:

> The troops have recovered themselves wonderfully, I think, and have acquired a new tactical technique, based really on the proper use of artillery and the retention of mobility, remarkably quickly. They have still a great deal to learn of course, but the gunners have been very good indeed, and the Bosche does not like our shell fire at all, now that it is centrally controlled and directed.[18]

While the fighting on 2 July was not quite as mobile as Auchinleck might have claimed, it certainly represented a radical departure from the previous policy of static infantry boxes. This was why Rommel remarked of the first days of July:

> General Auchinleck, who had meanwhile taken over command himself at El Alamein, was handling his forces with very considerable skill and tactically better than Ritchie had done. He seemed to view the situation with decided coolness, for he was not allowing himself to be rushed into accepting a second-best solution by any moves we made.[19]

A more orthodox employment of forces would have stressed the concentration of each division into a particular defensive sector. While the Afrika Korps was well practised in reducing isolated infantry boxes, a more formal stance of concentrated divisional positions simply would not have covered enough ground to provide a coherent defence.

Auchinleck understood that troops, and particularly artillery, did not need to be concentrated into one locality to have a concentrated effect. Many historians have missed the fact that artillery guns do not need to be physically concentrated to provide devastating support. The shell is the artillery's weapon; the gun merely delivers it. The artillery batteries ranged around the Alamein box were not kept together but were deployed in a broad arc across the desert. The fire of all these guns was coordinated by Brigadier Mead Dennis, the 30 Corps artillery commander, which allowed extremely heavy concentrations of fire to be delivered onto important targets. At the same time, artillery forward observation officers were able to find good targets individually. In fact, the defence of Ruweisat ridge and the Alamein box by 1st and 2nd South African Brigades and Robcol vindicated Auchinleck's new policy of mobile brigade groups. The deployment of these units, however improvised and attenuated, enabled the British to use a combination of arms to full effect. All the available artillery produced a formidable bombardment which halted German movement and disrupted their attacks before they could become truly dangerous. At the same time, once the German tanks and infantry advanced into range, the infantry and anti-tank guns were then able to add their fire to the crescendo of artillery fire. By the late afternoon, when the British armoured brigades intervened in the battle, Eighth Army was using a truly all-arms defence to blunt Rommel's attack. Almost all of the more polished tactics that later became the hallmark of Eighth Army in battles such as Medenine were demonstrated in embryo on the Ruweisat ridge on 2 July 1942.

Eighth Army stood at bay on 2 July using unorthodox but sensible tactics and new weaponry to great effect. Most importantly of all, Rommel's offensive had been stymied for another day. The truth was that Rommel's attack at Alamein could only have succeeded against a comprehensively demoralised force. Robcol's fight demonstrated that, while there was confusion and doubt amongst the higher echelons of the army because of the profusion of plans for retreat, the officers and men of Eighth Army had indeed fought to defend what they saw as 'the last ditch'.

Meanwhile, the Desert Air Force was putting out a tremendous independent effort to stem the Axis tide. Communications between Auchinleck and Coningham remained sketchy and uncertain but although the land and air effort was uncoordinated, there was no doubt that the effect was complementary. The war diary of the 90th Light Division noted:

> The enemy was using all his available aircraft against the attacking Afrika Army. Every 20 or 30 minutes 15, 18 or even 21 Bombers, with fighter protection on the same scale would attack. Even though they were not noticeably successful because the fighting and supply formations were so widely dispersed these heavy and continuous bombing and low-level attacks affected the morale of the troops all the more. Everybody longed for the Luftwaffe, but realised that the German forces could not be brought forward so quickly. Single fighters appeared, and were given an enthusiastic welcome, but these were naturally not in a position to attack such strong formations of bombers.[20]

The medium, light and fighter bombers of the Desert Air Force could not deliver the same tactical effect as the 'flying artillery' of the Luftwaffe in dive-bombing positions but their effect was still profound. From dusk on 1 July until last light on 2 July a total of 180 tons of bombs was dropped by medium, light and fighter bombers.[21] The number of casualties and level of destruction inflicted by a bombing raid could be surprisingly small but the degree of disruption was important. Two British soldiers who had been taken prisoner witnessed a night bombing raid on the Trieste Division on the night of 1–2 July:

The RAF attacked for five hours continuously causing great damage and indescribable confusion. Parachute flares showed up the target brightly and
observer was much impressed by the methodical accuracy of the bombing,
which was accompanied by ground strafing by fighters and the rear gunners
of the bombers . . . Many lorries carrying ammunition were hit and almost
as much damage was done by exploding ammunition as by the bombs.[22]

There is no doubt that this bombing raid disrupted the division and delayed
its march to the front. Although Rommel made increasingly annoyed
enquiries about its location and arrival throughout 2 July, Trieste made no
appearance that day; its men were simply too tired and scattered. The Desert
Air Force provided vital air support during the most dangerous period for
the Eighth Army.

Although the officers and men of Eighth Army had good cause for satisfaction on the evening of 2 July, some dangerous fractures began to appear
within its command structure. 1st South African Brigade Group had understandably felt isolated and under great pressure throughout the day's fighting
and had lost both its brigadier and brigade major. It was estimated that, over
the course of two days, fifteen to twenty thousand shells had pounded the
800 square yards of the position.[23] During the evening they asked for permission to withdraw from the Hotbox. Pienaar telephoned Norrie and informed
him that the position of the brigade was 'now untenable'.[24] Norrie told Pienaar
that he would relieve the brigade, place it in reserve and replace it with
another formation.[25] Pienaar was offended by this suggestion and then phoned
Eighth Army Headquarters and spoke to Dorman-Smith. Dorman-Smith's
account shows clear evidence of a clouded memory[26] but certainly provides
an authentic flavour of the tension in these heated exchanges. Dorman-Smith
responded to Pienaar's request with a peremptory command: 'You'll do no
such thing; you'll stay where you are.'[27] Pienaar then demanded to speak to
Auchinleck who ordered him to hold his ground but mentioned that within
two days the 9th Australian Division would reach El Alamein. Eventually
Norrie worked out the solution that Pienaar could use 'his discretion to withdraw 1 S A Bde'[28] and that its place would be taken by a column of 3rd Royal
Horse Artillery. Norrie attempted to calm the situation by telling Dorman-
Smith that 'Pienaar, after a day of strain, was expressing his excitable nature
by "blowing his top" and all would still be well tomorrow'.[29]

This episode revealed some of the serious problems that lay just beneath
the surface of Eighth Army's command structure. Pienaar's peremptory
demands on the evening of 2 July shook 'Auchinleck's confidence in the
battle morale of the South Africans'.[30] Regardless of the actual morale of
the troops, Auchinleck, Dorman-Smith and Norrie now felt that the 1st
South African Division could not be exposed to 'undue operational strain'.[31]
While Pienaar did not have the same 'charter' of appeal to his government

which Australian and New Zealand commanders possessed, the 1st South
African Division still had to be handled very carefully. After the loss of
the 2nd South African Division in Tobruk, any serious damage inflicted
on the 1st Division would be a political disaster, even if Field Marshal
Smuts, the ebullient South African Premier, was a keen supporter of
Auchinleck. The effect of these exchanges was that Auchinleck believed
that 1st South African Division could not be given any serious or difficult
operational task in the future, and also decided that the 9th Australian
Division would have to be directed to the northern sector of the front to
stiffen the South Africans regardless of the operational situation elsewhere.
There were clear limitations on how and where Eighth Army formations
could be used and under what circumstances. As Dorman-Smith remarked,
the Eighth Army was labelled 'handle with care'.[32]

While Auchinleck was wrangling over the dispositions of the 1st South
African Division, Rommel was desperately trying to find a way out of the
precarious situation which faced his entire army. The Panzerarmee's daily
report to the German High Command emphasised the strong fortifications
of the Alamein position, and the counterattack by the 1st Armoured Division
to explain the lack of progress but proudly announced the haul of 2,000 prisoners taken at Deir el Shein.[33] Of course, the defences of the Alamein box were
never as formidable as represented to the German High Command but nor
did the 90th Light Division ever realise just how close it had come to reaching
the undefended eastern side of the box. The attack had stalled but Rommel
decided to make one last attempt to break through to the Delta the next day.
If this failed, his dream of reaching the Delta would fade to nothing.

Just after midnight on 3 July, Panzerarmee Headquarters issued orders
for this final attempt. The 90th Light Division, which had by now reached
the final stages of exhaustion, was ordered simply to 'hold the positions it
had reached'. Meanwhile, the Afrika Korps would continue to push along
the Ruweisat ridge and aim for the coast. The Italian XXI Corps would keep
up the pressure on the western face of the Alamein box, while the X Corps
would watch the flank of the Afrika Korps at El Mreir. XX Corps was
ordered to keep pushing forwards to Alam el Dihmanlya.[34] Rommel was
placing more trust in the abilities of the Italian Motorised Corps than he
was used to; if the Afrika Korps failed, then perhaps Ariete might encircle
Eighth Army instead.

The panzers made little progress in the morning. However, heavy shelling
of the 3rd Royal Horse Artillery column occupying the Hotbox forced it to
withdraw 'to a posn in rear and South of 2 S A Inf Bde', a fact that was
noted with some satisfaction by Pienaar and his men.[35] This was the only
comfort that the men received, as the South African positions were consistently, efficiently and mistakenly bombed by Boston bombers of the 3rd South
African Air Force Wing throughout the day. Apart from this bitter episode,

the Desert Air Force continued to hammer the Panzerarmee on 3 July and its aircraft flew a total of 780 sorties – an average of one a minute. By comparison, the Luftwaffe flew perhaps 250 sorties over the same period.[36]

Although the panzer divisions were soon halted, the Ariete Division, advancing to the south of Ruweisat ridge, was able to make considerable progress. However, as the division moved forward, its armour and artillery became separated. The armour stayed close to the flank of 21st Panzer Division but the artillery column strayed out into the open desert far to the south. This column was spotted by the roving 'CRAs Column' sent out by the New Zealanders, and Brigadier Weir soon ranged his guns onto the soft target of the Italian guns and their tractors. The fire pinned down the Italian gunners and Weir called up infantry to mount an attack. While the New Zealand artillery kept pounding away, 19 Battalion of 4th New Zealand Infantry Brigade motored up from Deir el Munassib, more than three miles away, and put in a bayonet attack covered by their mortars and machine guns. The entire artillery of the Ariete Division was overrun and an impressive haul of 300 prisoners, 28 guns and 100 trucks was taken.[37] In one blow, much of the remaining power of the Ariete Division had been snuffed out and, far from simply 'swanning' up and down the desert, the columns sent out by the New Zealand Division had achieved a real victory.

Just after this success, Auchinleck received a scribbled note from Gott, his errant Corps commander, which explained many of the difficulties of communication between his corps and Eighth Army Headquarters:

> Unless I stay near my Divs I have the same difficulties of com[munication] as from you to me + they have not the means to overcome them. I explained this on the air to your HQ to-day, + was told 'OK for present', so am not moving. I do consider it essential to remain in close contact with the Div HQs especially NZ.[38]

Gott reported that, as ordered, the New Zealand Division were thinning out of the 'Kaponga' box at Bab el Qattara and had 'reported surrounded on 3 sides an hour ago, but now have 60 prisoners ARIETE + are happy'. Most importantly, Gott mentioned that 'I have NOT concentrated on withdrawal at all. We have been attacking + have been attacked ever since PM yesterday. That is why things have moved slowly.' He reiterated that 'there is no satisfactory solution to the communication problem – it is the spaces involved, bad going, overloaded signals. I will do all I can. I know your intentions + am guided by that if in doubt.'[39]

This small note gives a glimpse into Gott's methods and thinking. Because of the problems of communication, Gott was in many respects fighting an independent battle but he was still being guided by Auchinleck's intent after their meeting on the evening of 1 July. Gott's note also shows that, after being dismayed by the provisional retreat orders written by Corbett, he was now committed to the fight at Alamein.

With the attack evidently stalled, Rommel signalled the Afrika Korps Headquarters that afternoon: 'I demand energetic action by the whole of the D.A.K!.'[40] This was a classic example of Rommel's leadership and the German military belief that willpower could override all obstacles. But it was not to be this time. When the order reached the 21st Panzer Division, the staff gloomily recorded:

> in spite of renewed directives and orders the attack gained no more ground. The forces of the division are exhausted. Lorried Infantry 104 had suffered severely and . . . Numerically the enemy tanks were far superior and did everything in their power to bring the attack to a halt.[41]

Fighting flared up again in the mid-afternoon and the Afrika Korps did gain some ground. At 16.00 hours, after a heavy bombardment which forced Robcol to withdraw after suffering heavy casualties, the two divisions pushed forward only to be met by the British armoured brigades deployed on Ruweisat ridge.

22nd Armoured Brigade had been reinforced by the 9th Lancers that day. The regiment was a scratch formation which had been equipped with all the available repaired tanks from a tank delivery regiment; its A Squadron was a composite of crews drawn from its A and C Squadrons while its B Squadron had 12 Grant and four Crusader tanks. The C Squadron was actually drawn from the 4th Hussars and was equipped with 12 Lees and Grants. Lieutenant-Colonel J. R. MacDonell hoped to be allowed a day to sort out his scratch regiment but when he visited 1st Armoured Division's Rear Headquarters he was told: 'Get down to that ridge as fast as you can – there's an enemy tank attack coming and there's very little to stop it.'[42]

As dusk fell, the panzer divisions clashed with the remaining British armour. The newly arrived 9th Lancers found themselves in the thick of the fighting:

> In the dusk the red tracer behind the armour piercing shells sailed down on the enemy tanks and soon they began to burn. 'One – two – three – there's five – no, six! – no, eight on fire!' an excited voice came on the air. They tried to dodge the fire but within ten minutes twelve tanks were blazing.[43]

After a stiff fight, which 4th Armoured Brigade called 'the hardest day's fighting since the campaign began',[44] the German armour was held at the cost of 17 Grants, 19 Stuarts and three Valentines. These were heavy losses, but also represented a major achievement: Rommel's last thrust had been held.

Late that evening, Panzerarmee Headquarters finally admitted there would be no breakthrough:

Enemy counter-attack must be expected tomorrow, mainly from the east and south-east, but also from the south-west. Corps and divisions will organise themselves for defensive action and will hold their positions . . . Regrouping during the 4th may be expected to take place.[45]

Rommel had clearly received intelligence warning him of Auchinleck's intentions but hoped that his army would be able to hold on. The Panzerarmee Afrika's daily report broke the bad news to the German High Command:

During 3 July the Panzerarmee expanded its penetration of the enemy defence system in a north-westerly direction. In the well fortified positions, reinforced by all sorts of defensive installations, the enemy again offered very stubborn resistance indeed, supported by strong artillery . . . the strength of the enemy, our own decreasing fighting strength and the most precarious supply situation, compel us to discontinue our major attack for the time being . . . the fighting strength of the divisions at present amounts to 1200–1500 men each. The fighting strength of the Italian divisions is also very low.[46]

Rommel had been forced to accept that the flame of his offensive, which had burnt so brightly at Gazala, Tobruk and Mersa Matruh, had finally gone out. Now the Panzerarmee Afrika was 1,400 miles from its main logistic base with no further strength to push through the Eighth Army. The Axis forces could no longer go forward, but neither could they withdraw because of lack of fuel. They could now hardly fight for lack of ammunition. Just as Clausewitz might have predicted, the Panzerarmee Afrika was left feeling 'unsure of itself and nervous about its situation'.[47]

There was indeed good reason for doubt in the minds of the Axis soldiers on the morning of 4 July. Having failed to encircle the Eighth Army, they were now themselves almost surrounded by hostile batteries, infantry and armour. Shortages of ammunition were now critical; 15th Panzer Division had only two rounds per gun and the whole Afrika Korps could only muster 36 tanks. 21st Panzer Division had found 1,500 rounds of 25-pounder ammunition at Deir el Shein and this kept the captured batteries of guns in action when the German-equipped batteries had fallen silent.[48]

Yet even in this disastrous situation, Rommel did not abandon his plans for attack. He added in his report to Berlin that he now planned to 'hold the front and to re-equip in such a way that 2nd New Zealand Division can be surrounded and destroyed'.[49] Having been baulked on the coast, Rommel had already identified the New Zealand Division, which held the southern flank of Eighth Army, as one of the most formidable obstacles to his advance. He planned to withdraw his armoured and motorised formations from the front line and replace them with the Italian infantry divisions which were moving up to the front. Once the panzer divisions had recovered and repaired more of their tanks and been resupplied with ammunition, Rommel would take the offensive again. He believed that, with the New Zealand Division holding what he took to be a static position at Bab el Qattara, it would make an easy target if, and only if, his army could hold out for the next few days and complete its reorganisation.

On 4 July, the Panzerarmee Afrika was in an extremely vulnerable situation. Its dog-tired troops were occupying positions with no fixed defences or minefields, ammunition supplies were critical and many of the Italian infantry formations which were needed to strengthen its defensive lines were still marching up to El Alamein. However, although both of Auchinleck's corps commanders knew his intent 'to attack the enemy without delay and give him no rest',[50] the two armies simply sparred and skirmished throughout the day, and Eighth Army did not land the killer blow on its weakened opponent.

The explanation for this passivity has to be found in the sclerotic communications within Eighth Army which worked against Auchinleck's intent on 4 July, and the fact that the units of Eighth Army were just as tired as the Germans and Italians. Having been prepared to defend against an advancing enemy, it took time for the officers and men of Eighth Army to realise that the roles had been reversed overnight. The two armies had fought each other to a standstill but, unfortunately, this lull played into Rommel's hands: he was able to withdraw the 21st Panzer Division from Ruweisat ridge to begin its regrouping.

By the end of 4 July, Rommel had managed, however slightly, to toughen up the defences of his army. His hopes of reaching the Delta had been dashed and the convoy of Italian troops bound for Alexandria to strengthen the Axis grip on Egypt had to be cancelled. Rommel was now faced with an unenviable set of operational and strategic choices. The Panzerarmee Afrika had advanced far beyond the logistic capacity of the existing organisation to cope and this meant that any build-up of reinforcements and supplies would be tortuously slow. Inventive solutions were attempted; many of the reinforcements Rommel desperately needed were flown in from Crete but heavy equipment and large quantities of supplies could only come by sea.

There were strong military arguments to suggest that Rommel's best course of action was to mount a phased withdrawal back to the Libyan frontier. This would shorten his lines of supply and wrong-foot the already exhausted Eighth Army. However, Rommel's men were equally exhausted, and while captured petrol and supplies had allowed the Panzerarmee to reach El Alamein, there was now not enough petrol to make an orderly and phased retreat. Once his offensive had been held, Rommel found himself trapped at El Alamein; he could not go forward or back. Rommel had staked his personal reputation and standing with Hitler in making the advance into Egypt. His insistence that he should continue had derailed the existing Axis strategy and he could hardly admit failure now. Instead, he had little choice but to hang on grimly at El Alamein, in the hope that his logistic difficulties could be surmounted and that he could find another way out of the labyrinth of his own making.

Auchinleck faced a series of equally intractable dilemmas. The formations of the Eighth Army, with the exception of 2nd New Zealand Division and the 9th Australian Division which would soon arrive at the front, were the exhausted remnants of the force that had fought at Gazala. One option was to sit on the defensive, conserve manpower and build strength for a prepared offensive later in the year. However, it was obvious that the Panzerarmee was now uniquely weak and in a perilous situation so far from its main supply bases. Even with an exhausted and disorganised Eighth Army, this seemed the perfect opportunity to destroy the Axis army. Auchinleck also had too much experience to underestimate the powers of recovery which could be exhibited by the Panzerarmee. To adopt a purely passive defence would give Rommel the time and space he required to rebuild his force and mount a fresh and more dangerous attack.

These perfectly valid operational considerations were overlaid by a worrying strategic dimension making it imperative to destroy Rommel's forces as quickly and as decisively as possible. Although Auchinleck had taken direct command of Eighth Army he still had to consider the wider strategic threats facing the entire Middle Eastern theatre. The defence of Persia and Iraq were as high on his agenda as the defence of Egypt.

*

While Eighth Army was experiencing disaster at the hands of the Panzerarmee Afrika in late June 1942, the German summer offensive in Russia had begun around Voronezh. British planners might have drawn some comfort from the fact that the assault had begun in late June rather than early May, but it became clear that the German objective for their offensive lay in the south; the target was Stalingrad on the Volga and the oilfields in the Caucasus. This information brought renewed nightmares for the British planners in Cairo and the Chiefs of Staff in London. If the German offensive was successful and the Caucasus along with its oil was seized by the Germans, the Wehrmacht might continue its offensive into Iraq and seize Britain's strategic reserves of oil around Mosul and Kirkuk.

Thus, much depended upon the ability of the Red Army to hold the Wehrmacht, but in the summer of 1941 Hitler's invasion of Russia had inflicted enormous damage on the Red Army. The Soviet forces had displayed a breathtaking level of incompetence in defending their Motherland and more than three million Soviet soldiers had been captured in the first six months. Although the Red Army's offensive around Moscow in December 1941 had saved the Soviet capital, there seemed little sign that the Red Army would be any more capable of defeating the German summer offensive in

1942. The Red Army's spring offensive around Kharkov had only recently swelled the Wehrmacht's prison cages with another 250,000 men.[51]

One major difficulty for British calculations concerning the war on the Eastern Front was the dearth of hard military information. Although Britain sent thousands of tanks and aircraft in aid to Russia, the Soviet authorities kept their conduct of the war strictly secret. The British government learned more about the Red Army's deployment and capabilities from intercepted German radio traffic than they did from their Soviet allies. This made it very difficult to make realistic calculations about the Red Army's capacity to hold the Wehrmacht and posed a real dilemma for Auchinleck in July 1942.

British fears of a powerful German attack through the Caucasus were a revival of a deep-seated and long-held British strategic concern. Throughout the nineteenth century the British in India had worried about the threat posed by Russia to the North West Frontier of India. During the Great War, when the Ukraine fell to the Germans in 1917, British planners had worried that a German advance into Persia and Mesopotamia would threaten their position in the Middle East. Thus, worries about strategic threats from the north to their Empire in the Middle East and India were an ingrained part of the British mindset. Not surprisingly, Auchinleck, who had formerly been Commander-in-Chief of the Indian Army and who had served in Meso-potamia during the First World War, was bound to be concerned about any German threat from the Caucasus.

Auchinleck's fears were heightened by the knowledge that he had very few troops to defend the northern front in the face of a German attack. Throughout July, Auchinleck was 'looking over his shoulder' to Persia and the threat from the Caucasus. Of course, in the midst of a desperate battle on the Alamein line, Auchinleck could not devote sufficient time and mental energy to the problem of Persia. It was another example of the risks inherent in trying to fulfil a strategic and operational role at the same time.

The Joint Planning Staff in Cairo considered the problem during June 1942 and prepared a pessimistic report for Auchinleck. In the worst case of rapid German progress, troops from Eighth Army would be needed to re-inforce the Persian front from 15 July onwards. This assessment would mean that Auchinleck would actually have to evacuate Egypt within a matter of weeks to provide sufficient troops for the northern front. Auchinleck requested guidance from Churchill and the War Cabinet on what course of action he should take if confronted with the worst case; which was more important, Egypt or the oil? Churchill replied at length:

We are all only too well aware that the Japanese threat to India and our defeats in the Western Desert have stripped the northern front bare. You also no doubt realise that it is physically impossible to send six, or even four additional divisions from home or from the United States to the northern theatre before the end of October. The only way in which a sufficient army can be gathered in the northern theatre is by your defeating or destroying General Rommel and driving him at least to a safe distance . . . It must be recognised, however, that if you do not succeed in defeating and destroying Rommel, then there is no possibility whatever of making a sufficient transference to the north, and we shall continue to be entirely dependent on the Russian front holding. There is no need to assume that the Russian front will break or that if it does, any substantial forces could operate in Persia as early as October. Indeed, the General Staff's picture was that the advent of winter might prevent any serious threat before the spring of 1943 and even then it would be in terms of a maximum of seven divisions. The Germans would be running serious risks in advancing south-east while the main mass of the Russian armies is undefeated on their front and on the flank of their advancing spearhead. If you beat Rommel decisively, as I am confident you will, and if the Germans do not beat the Russians sufficiently to break into Persia or Syria in 1942, 'Acrobat' will again come under consideration.[52]

The British plan for Acrobat in which the Axis forces in Libya would be destroyed and Tripoli seized had dissolved into the disasters of Gazala and Tobruk. The overall strategic picture for the British was thus filled with intractable problems. Churchill was forced to run serious risks and make enormous strategic gambles because Britain simply did not have sufficient military resources to insure against every threat. However, Auchinleck believed he understood Churchill's intention and assessment of the risks. He replied:

I quite understand the situation and will, as I think you know, do my utmost to defeat the enemy in the West or drive them back sufficiently far to lessen the threat to Egypt. My aim is to destroy him as far east as possible. . . . unless we can destroy the German forces here and so be enabled to transfer troops to Persia we stand to lose Iraq and the oil should the Russian front break. Whether this is a justifiable risk is not within my competence to say, but I understand that you have accepted it and that, therefore, I am to continue to apply all my available resources to destroying the German forces opposing me as soon as possible. I am proceeding accordingly and have 'Acrobat' constantly in mind, though it may seem far off.[53]

The strategic dilemmas contained in these telegrams were of fundamental importance in shaping Auchinleck's conduct of the fighting at Alamein during July 1942. Auchinleck believed that the strategic imperative demanded that he push the Eighth Army to the utmost in an attempt to destroy the Panzerarmee Afrika. Failure to do so might well mean that, in the face of a German attack from the Caucasus, Britain would lose Iraq and its oil. This disaster would cost Britain the war and its Empire.

Unfortunately, Auchinleck was taking counsel of his, and the Joint Planning Staff's, fears. The worst possible case of a German invasion of Persia in the autumn of 1942 – or even the spring of 1943 – as envisaged by the British planners was highly unrealistic. There was no doubt that in June and July 1942, the German summer offensive looked dangerous and the Red Army's response looked as inept as it had in 1941, but extrapolating from that information a rapid Russian collapse and an immediate German advance into Persia relied more on the persistent British nightmare of a threat from the north than from the reality of what the Wehrmacht could actually achieve.

Although the German High Command purported to have a grand strategic plan of an offensive from Russia penetrating into Persia at the same time as Rommel entered the Delta, this too was little more than wishful thinking and there was never any serious military planning attempted to bring this vision into reality. Even had the Russians collapsed, the German military effort would have been largely absorbed in dealing with the aftermath of such a victory. Just as importantly, if the logistic situation of the Panzerarmee Afrika was poor, the prospects of sustaining a German advance into Persia were dire. The Germans had sufficient difficulty in sustaining their forces at the front in Russia, let alone supplying a major offensive through the Caucasus and northern Persia where rail links were non-existent and the few roads were abysmal.

Auchinleck had to weigh and balance these strategic considerations finely. The Germans had already accomplished strategic feats thought to be impossible: the fall of France in just six weeks, the invasion of Egypt and the capture of most of European Russia. Auchinleck would have been foolhardy to have completely ignored the threat to Persia and relied solely on the Russians, particularly when they starved the British of any hard military information concerning their situation.

These strategic imperatives were to bear down hard upon Eighth Army during July and this illustrated the full peril of combining the strategic responsibilities of the Middle East with the operational demands of the Eighth Army Commander into one man's burden. Had Auchinleck still been at his desk in Cairo, it would have been much easier for a commander of Eighth Army to develop sound reasons why no offensive action could be taken, or to dilute Auchinleck's insistent calls for an all-out attempt to destroy Rommel into more tentative attacks. Without any insulation from these strategic imperatives, Eighth Army was pushed to make attacks with highly ambitious objectives that were simply beyond its strength.

In effect, this meant that the responsibility for diluting the implications of Auchinleck's orders for immediate action fell to the corps and divisional commanders, who did not necessarily understand the wider strategic picture but who did understand the level of effort it was possible for the Eighth Army to make. This meant that while some subordinate commanders accepted risky orders and attempted to carry them out to the letter, others interpreted their orders more cautiously.

The root of these problems lay in the fact that Auchinleck had not really been able to grip Eighth Army since he had taken command. His command style suited the demands of theatre command but was not necessarily appropriate for an army commander. He did not get to know the officers and men of Eighth Army intimately. Nor did he attempt to articulate fully the reasons why Eighth Army had to keep stretching to the limit in order to destroy Rommel's army. This meant that the lower formation commanders did not understand why they were committing their troops to an all-out offensive while at the same time troops were being used to prepare an elaborate series of defences behind the front. Auchinleck's inability to use his staff officers effectively or to formalise his command relationship with Dorman-Smith meant that a real gulf opened up between Eighth Army command and the divisional, and lower formation, commanders. These fractures of understanding were to reveal themselves with distressing consequences over the course of Auchinleck's attempt to break Rommel's army.

On the evening of 4 July, Auchinleck issued his clearest instructions to the Army to date. All thought of retreat had disappeared and instead, with the strategic imperative to destroy Rommel or 'drive him to a safe distance', Eighth Army was now to attack. An Eighth Army order noted:

> Today enemy suffered considerably in equipment and prisoners but although showing many signs of lowered morale and fighting power, succeeded in establishing a defensive flank covering the area between the old 18 Inf Bde position and the EL ALAMEIN road in which the greater part of his forces are deployed.[54]

The order went on to state:

> Best evidence shows that the enemy hopes to gain time to recover from his reverses of the last three days. It is not impossible that he may attempt to withdraw though there are no firm signs of this yet. Our task remains to destroy the enemy as far East as possible and NOT to let him get away as a force in being. This can best be achieved by containing the enemy's eastern front and Southern flank and attacking his rear. It is important that the enemy should be given NO rest.[55]

The intention was to continue to hold the northern positions of 30 Corps, taking any opportunity to attack, while 13 Corps operated against the Panzerarmee's right wing and threatened his rear areas. The declared intention to 'attack and destroy the enemy in his present positions'[56] was certainly clear enough, but little actually came of this order on 5 July. The problems of poor communication, lack of flexibility and tempo in responding to a change in orders were to become even more apparent within Eighth Army in the coming weeks.

The 4th and 5th Brigades of the 2nd New Zealand Division moved up to mount an attack but 4th New Zealand Brigade was heavily attacked by dive bombers and badly disrupted. This dangerous attack by Stukas served notice that the Luftwaffe was recovering, however slowly, from the rapid advance of the Panzerarmee. Instead of mounting an attack into the flank of the weakened Panzerarmee, both brigades spent the day under shellfire and harassed by further bombing. The main problem with Auchinleck's conception of the attack was that 13 Corps now had little armour to force a decisive engagement. Almost all the British armour was now with 1st Armoured Division on the Ruweisat ridge. But although 15th Panzer Division was uniquely weak that day, no attack by 30 Corps or its armoured elements developed.

Dorman-Smith witnessed a heated argument between Norrie and Lumsden, commander of the 1st Armoured Division, on 5 July which partly explains why 30 Corps was so inactive during the period of Rommel's greatest vulnerability. Lumsden burst into Norrie's caravan early that morning to demand that his division, which had been fighting for weeks without rest, be relieved. Norrie attempted to placate Lumsden who was 'over-excited and emphatically undisciplined' and Dorman-Smith even wondered why Norrie did not place the armoured commander under arrest. Dorman-Smith duly reported to Auchinleck that little could be expected from 1st Armoured Division for a while. This lack of aggressive action by Eighth Army was worrying because it allowed the Axis units what they desperately needed: time. The Panzerarmee's diary noted that 'no substantial actions took place, so that improvement of the position could go on undisturbed'.[57] As more mines were laid, and the men rested, supplies of ammunition, reinforcements and food began to reach the front. The Italian infantry formations began to flow into the line, and, just as importantly, further Luftwaffe units began to reach the airfields around El Daba and Fuka. The immediate crisis for Rommel had passed.

The 5 July was an encouraging day for Eighth Army in one respect because the 24th Australian Infantry Brigade deployed on the eastern edge of the Ruweisat ridge during the day. The 9th Australian Division had travelled down from Syria in conditions of strict secrecy with all Australian Imperial Force badges, patches and bush hats concealed. The men believed their destination was Homs in Syria but as the convoy passed Damascus:

> their curiosity was aroused which quickly grew to excitement as everyone in the convoy realised something was afoot.
> Through PALESTINE the convoy raced, with speculation and hopes soaring. The WESTERN DESERT? . . . or Home?[58]

The rest of the Australian Corps had sailed back to Australia in December 1941 when the war broke out in the Far East, leaving 9th Australian Division the sole Australian formation in the Middle East. Pressure had mounted from the Australian government to bring it home as well but when the disaster in Libya developed it was agreed that the division should fight in Egypt until the crisis had passed.

After its rest in Syria, 9th Australian Division was an entirely fresh division. It possessed a formidable battle reputation as the 'Rats of Tobruk' who had withstood siege for six months the previous year. In fact, the division still suffered from key shortages in equipment and was not well trained in mobile desert warfare, but nonetheless it represented a real boost to Eighth Army's strength.

However, the presence of the 24th Australian Infantry Brigade on Ruweisat ridge had been achieved only through intense negotiation between Auchinleck and Lieutenant-General Sir Leslie Morshead, the 9th Australian Division commander. Eighth Army had ordered that the division should be formed into brigade groups and that one group should be sent up to the front immediately. Morshead was a fine divisional commander who had skilfully defended Tobruk and he was only too conscious of his rights as an independent Dominion commander. Morshead flew up to Eighth Army Tactical Headquarters and had a stormy interview with Auchinleck. He related that the interview was brusque:

Auchinleck: I want that brigade right away.
Morshead: You can't have that brigade.
Auchinleck: Why?
Morshead: Because they are going to fight as a formation with the rest of the division.
Auchinleck: Not if I give you orders?
Morshead: Give me the orders and you'll see.
Auchinleck: So you're being like Blamey. You're wearing his mantle.[59]

General Sir Thomas Blamey was the commander of the Australian Corps in the Middle East at the time of the siege of Tobruk who had insisted, with the support of his government, despite Auchinleck's protestations, on the relief of the 9th Australian Division.[60] Morshead fundamentally disagreed with Auchinleck's policy of brigade groups and refused to break his division into these formations or send 'surplus' infantry that could not be transported into reserve. Morshead had threatened to invoke his right as the commander of an independent Dominion force to refer any orders he deemed as dangerous to his national government. Obviously such a process would delay the commitment not just of the leading brigade but of the whole division. A compromise was worked out whereby Morshead agreed to the temporary detachment of the brigade to 30 Corps on the condition that the entire division would be brought up as soon as possible and kept under Morshead's command.

Auchinleck reacted badly to this exchange. Both Morshead and Auchinleck were only too well aware that, given the delicate political compromise necessary to ensure the presence of 9th Australian Division in the Middle East, any major disagreement might well lead to the recall of the entire division. In effect, Morshead had firmly emphasised that only he could determine the operational role of 9th Australian Division. Auchinleck had just weathered the worst crisis faced by Eighth Army and desperately needed a fresh brigade to shore up the defences on the critical Ruweisat ridge, only to be told that the brigade was not his to command.

In common with many other British senior officers, Auchinleck never really learned to deal with the distinctive political problems inherent in commanding Dominion divisions. Dorman-Smith later wrote that he came to wish for 'docile, obedient, bull-headed British divisions instead of these brave but temperamental Dominion troops, each totally different from the other contingent'.[61]

The 6 July was another day of relative inactivity, although the South Africans sent out a small raid which upset 90th Light. The supposed drive by 13 Corps into the flank and rear of the Panzerarmee amounted to nothing more than a relatively peaceful drive north by elements of the 2nd New Zealand and 5th Indian Divisions which were met and halted by German armoured cars. Indeed, the day was so quiet in the New Zealand sector that Brigadier Kippenberger kept a minute-by-minute account of his doings that day to stave off the boredom of looking at interminable desert. The fact that he was able to smoke nine pipes of tobacco shows the almost complete inactivity that day in a formation that was meant to be destroying the Panzerarmee. Late in the afternoon, Kippenberger received a message that '1st Armoured Div. attacking from east this evening and expect to reach 880 grid with exploitation in the morning. 5th and 6th Field Regiments to cooperate. New Zealand Division to exploit success tomorrow', but he quite rightly considered this 'Fanciful'.[62]

The 6 July marked a watershed for the Desert Air Force. After a period of frantic activity in which maximum effort had been demanded to help stabilise the situation, air activity began to tail off to a more sustainable level. There had been much argument over army – air cooperation and the bombing of Eighth Army troops had led to considerable controversy over targeting, but the round-the-clock effort mounted by the Desert Air Force had been of crucial importance during the desperate first days at El Alamein.[63]

That evening, Auchinleck reiterated his offensive intentions but the timing had now changed: 'EIGHTH ARMY will attack and destroy the enemy on or after 7 July.'[64] Given the fact that the units of Eighth Army had simply not been able to respond to his orders to attack and destroy the Axis forces,

Auchinleck's plans for a counteroffensive had indeed begun to appear 'Fanciful' and mere wishful thinking.

That night, Norrie was relieved of his command and replaced by Lieutenant-General W. H. C. Ramsden, the commander of 50th Division. Auchinleck had felt that Norrie had handled 30 Corps poorly during the Gazala fighting, but another significant factor may have been that Norrie had had real difficulties with almost all of his subordinate commanders. Indeed, Norrie seems to have lost control of both Pienaar and Lumsden, his two main subordinates, and Auchinleck had had to step in to sort out both of these matters. Nonetheless, it must be said that Norrie has never really received any recognition for his role in deploying Eighth Army at Alamein, or in managing the battle during the first few critical days. Even after all the trouble Pienaar had given, he wrote that he was surprised by the departure of Norrie, whom he 'liked, respected and admired'. Dorman-Smith was also sorry to see him go.[65]

Ramsden had performed well as the commander of the 50th Division. Unfortunately, he had quarrelled badly with Pienaar when both their divisions had been in the Gazala line.[66] Meanwhile, Morshead was aggrieved at being passed over for the command of 30 Corps. Eighth Army was beset with division and friction amongst its higher commanders and, while Auchinleck was able to smooth over some of the difficulties, there remained dangerous cracks just under the surface. Eighth Army was not a unified force operating efficiently under its Commander-in-Chief-turned-Army Commander.

On the night of 7 July, the Australians made their presence felt by mounting a raid on the Ruweisat ridge. D Company of the 2/43rd Australian Infantry Battalion raided German positions and, with engineer support, blew up five anti-tank guns and a number of vehicles:[67]

> Then the company reorganised and was led back. Brilliant and noisy witness to the success lay behind them, on and beyond the ridge. Six hundred yards of flame and smoke and exploding ammunition sending its coloured flashes of light far into the desert.[68]

The raid was certainly very successful and news that the Australians were back in the line caused numerous congratulatory messages to flow in. But a raid could do no more than seize a few prisoners and disrupt local tactical dispositions. It was little enough to show for Auchinleck's aim to destroy his enemy 'on or after 7 July'.[69]

From 6 July onwards, Eighth Army intelligence had detected the strengthening and extension of the Panzerarmee's southern flank.[70] Now, instead of mounting a threat to the Panzerarmee, the New Zealand Division was in danger itself. Auchinleck's attack from the south had turned to naught, but the Panzerarmee had recovered sufficiently after 4 July for their commander to contemplate his own offensive in the south. Rommel hoped to concentrate enough force to isolate and destroy the New Zealand Division at Bab el Qattara. However, on 7 July, the New Zealanders evacuated their 'Kaponga' box, leaving only a few observers to keep watch on enemy movements.

As a result, what should have been a dangerous thrust at the New Zealand Division turned into a comedy of errors for the Afrika Korps. The Panzerarmee did not detect the silent and swift evacuation from Bab el Qattara. As the 21st Panzer and Littorio Divisions concentrated for an attack on the box, and 90th Light pushed forward in the extreme south, it was not until midday on 8 July that a patrol from 21st Panzer Division realised that the box had been evacuated. Even then, the Germans did not push forward and take possession of the defences and on the morning of 9 July Rommel heard a report that Bab el Qattara remained in British hands. He clearly believed that the box was still defended and marshalled heavy artillery and Stukas to support the 'assault'. 21st Panzer and the Littorio Division then mounted a 'text-book' assault on the box which reached the outer defences at 12.50 hours on 9 July. It was only then that the forward troops reported that the box was in fact empty.

Rommel inspected the defences with Generalmajor Georg von Bismarck, the commander of the 21st Panzer Division, and noted that the box:

> lay in extremely favourable terrain and was fortified with well-built concrete strongpoints, gun emplacements and extensive minefields. The New Zealanders had left behind quantities of ammunition and equipment, and we were at a loss to understand why they had given the position up.[71]

Rommel's surprise was shared by many of the New Zealanders who had defended the box, who had liked the security of the concrete shelters and the convenience of the freshwater pipe which ran into the box, but the reasons for its abandonment were clear. Had Rommel's attack fallen on the box while it was still defended by the New Zealanders, the defenders would have eventually met the same fate as the 18th Indian Brigade at Deir el Shein. Instead, it was Rommel who this time had committed his armour, artillery and air reserves to a blow in the air. With a certain amount of deftness, Auchinleck and Dorman-Smith had detected the German move towards the south, and Bab el Qattara had worked well as 'psychological bait'[72] to encourage Rommel to develop his plans for an attack in the south.

Rommel hoped that his attack on the New Zealand Division could be used as 'a base for a break-through'.[73] In fact, Auchinleck had outfoxed his opponent and was about to seize the initiative.

SIX

Tel el Eisa

At 03.30 hours on the morning of 10 July 1942, the men of B and C Companies of the 2/48th Australian Infantry Battalion were silent and keyed up with anticipation as they crossed the start line for their coming attack. Their battalion commander, the redoubtable Lieutenant-Colonel H. H. 'Tack' Hammer had decided to make a silent attack to achieve maximum surprise against the Italian defenders of Point 26. This was the first high point on a ridge which rose 1,300 yards south of the Mediterranean and which overlooked the South African defences in the Alamein box two miles away. Hammer's men were to seize and consolidate their hold on the ridge and then advance south west to capture Tel el Eisa[*] station.[1]

As the men advanced as quietly as possible in the darkness towards the ridge, a lone German plane could be heard circling above them: 'Suddenly the night was lit up like day. The plane had dropped a parachute flare directly over the leading companies. The men froze, expecting the impact of a terrific outburst of fire.'[2] To their surprise nothing happened, and the leading companies soon quickened their pace as they climbed the ridge on either side of the crest. Hammer's plan worked perfectly as the Italian defenders of Point 26 were caught still sleepy and in their pyjamas.[3] The advance to the next triangulation point on the ridge, Point 23, 2,000 yards further on, was not so easy against the now alerted defence but soon the rifle and machine-gun fire of the Italian defenders was drowned out by the drone of hundreds of shells. The guns of all three Australian field regiments and both South African field regiments as well as the 7th Medium Regiment, amounting to more than 100 25-pounder field guns, 4.5-inch and 5.5-inch medium guns in all, began firing their artillery programme in support of the attack:

'Fire!' yells the gun position officer.

The din of the barking guns is indescribable. Everywhere there are gun-flashes; and the sound fills my brain. My eardrums are dulled and my head feels heavy. Automatically I pass over a projectile to Tom, who holds it while Lofty rams; then the cartridge, and I hear the click of the breech. There is

---

[*] 'Tel el Eisa' means 'The Hill of Jesus'.

a roar and a flash as Lofty, watch in hand, at each round orders: 'Fire!' Then a round. Then a cartridge. The air is filled with the reek of cordite.[4]

This was the biggest artillery bombardment of the desert war so far and the shells landed directly on the sketchy defences of the Italian Sabratha Division. The bombardment disrupted the Italian communications and caused panic amongst the inexperienced soldiers. Soon groups of men were throwing their weapons away and running for the rear.

Twenty miles to the south, Rommel was awakened by 'the dull thunder of artillery fire from the north'.[5] Some German veterans recognised the *Trommelfeuer*[6] they had come to dread on the Western Front twenty years before. Auchinleck's policy of concentrating his artillery had already brought defensive success and was now to pay dividends in the attack.

As Hammer's men continued their movement to the second objective, the 2/24th Australian Infantry Battalion began their advance. This battalion was tasked with moving along the sand dunes near the coast and then turning south to assault Point 33, the dominating height at the western end of the ridge. Once this was in their hands, two companies were to push south, cross the railway line and seize Tel el Eisa ridge, another important hill feature which gave observation onto the Alamein defences. Unfortunately, the 2/24th Battalion did not get off to a good start; after the first company had passed, and even before the start line had been reached, the trucks and supporting Valentine tanks from 44th Royal Tank Regiment became bogged down in the salt marsh which lay near the sea. Lieutenant-Colonel Allan Spowers kept his men going and through 'the superhuman efforts of all personnel' the battalion crossed the start line on time.[7] As they advanced on the narrow flat plain between the ridge and the marsh, the battalion initially encountered little resistance from the sleepy Italian soldiers. Soon there was fiercer resistance amongst the dunes, but the carrier platoon, which moved ahead of the battalion, was able to capture two troops of Italian anti-tank guns in a fast frontal assault. After some heavy fighting, the battalion established itself around Point 33, but with most of his supporting tanks and machine guns still bogged down or missing, Spowers decided that he could not launch the second phase of the assault to capture Tel el Eisa ridge.[8]

Meanwhile, two companies from the 2/48th Battalion went forward to seize Tel el Eisa station in the face of heavy fire from both German and Italian field guns. Sergeant J. K. 'Tex' Weston led his platoon in a bayonet charge on one of these battery positions and captured four guns and 106 prisoners. On reaching their new positions, however, the men found that the hard ground and rock made digging in properly almost impossible, and the shallow scrapes they were able to make gave little protection from the shells which pounded them for the rest of the day.[9]

The Australian 26th Infantry Brigade had just mounted a very successful morning attack and seized two key pieces of terrain from the Sabratha Division. Before the attack, Eighth Army intelligence noted that the fact that Rommel had:

> left comparatively immobile ITALIAN infantry in the coastal sector shows that he has momentarily postponed the idea of attacking the ALAMEIN box. There are, however, indications that GERMANS possibly of 200 and 361 Light Infantry Regiments are in the NORTH stiffening the ITALIAN infantry as they did WEST of GAZALA at the end of May.[10]

Auchinleck had decided upon a policy of attacking Italian formations wherever possible, overwhelming them and thus placing a greater strain on the surviving German units to stiffen the defence. He acted upon this principle to crush the Sabratha Division. There was now a gaping hole in the Axis defences. The Panzerarmee Headquarters was deployed a few miles further back, near Sidi Abd el Rahman, and in Rommel's absence, Major von Mellenthin, his chief intelligence officer, was in command:

> early that morning I was startled to see hundreds of Italians rushing past the headquarters in the final stages of panic and rout . . . When a headquarters is threatened the first instinct is to move and safeguard its irreplaceable equipment and documents. It was clear to me, however, that Sabratha was finished – their artillery was already 'in the bag' – and something must be done immediately to close the road to the west. I called on the staff and personnel of headquarters to form a rough battle line, which I strengthened with our anti-aircraft guns and some infantry reinforcements which happened to arrive; we succeeded in holding the Australians, who had captured the mounds of Tel el Eisa, and were seeking to thrust up the coast road.[11]

Although the Crusader tanks of the 9th Australian Divisional Cavalry did attempt to push up the coast road, the Australian attack had never been intended as a breakthrough. There could be no real thought of serious exploitation by the two battalions; they needed to consolidate, dig in and wait for the inevitable Axis reaction. Fortunately for von Mellenthin, the first troops from the 164th Light Infantry Division had just arrived at Sidi Abd el Rahman the previous evening. This division was in the process of being flown over from Crete to Tobruk but the chronic lack of transport meant that its men had had to hitch lifts on whatever supply trucks were moving up to the front. Nonetheless, the half battalion of 382nd Infantry Regiment with some of its anti-tank and infantry guns was enough to begin plugging the gap left by the Sabratha Division.[12]

Meanwhile, Rommel realised that he had been badly wrong-footed and must attempt to restore the situation; all thought of his own projected attack to breach the Alamein line that day had to be discarded. He ordered a battle-group from 15th Panzer Division to move north and counterattack the Australian penetration in an attempt to cut it off from the Alamein defences. 21st Panzer Division, Littorio and 90th Light had to withdraw from their forward positions. Rommel drove north with his *Kampstaffel* and directed the 15th Panzer Division battlegroup into the attack.[13]

The Australians had to endure five separate Stuka attacks during the morning. In each wave, 30 to 40 Stukas swooped down, dropping their bombs amidst the screaming of their sirens. Although these attacks inflicted few casualties, they cut communications and caused disruption.[14] A hasty attack mounted by a small party of German tanks and infantry on the positions of the 2/24th in the sand dunes was seen off easily with artillery fire and anti-tank gun fire.[15] However, by the afternoon, the 15th Panzer Division battlegroup had motored up and was ready to mount its more determined counterattack, though it could muster only 10 tanks.[16] The Axis artillery redoubled its fire on the exposed Australian positions and then the German panzers moved forward, crossed through the heavy shellfire, and drove straight onto the slit trenches of the 2/48th Battalion's forward platoons. The British artillery fire could not stop the panzers but it broke up the repeated attempts of the German infantry to get forward. Spinning round on their tracks, the tanks attempted to crush the slit trenches and their occupants, but the 9th Australian Division's experience at Tobruk had taught the men of 2/48th Battalion that tanks shorn of infantry support were vulnerable to the attentions of determined infantry. The Australian soldiers fearlessly took the fight straight to them. The German panzers made at least three separate attacks on the company positions of the 2/48th battalion and on each occasion, while some men were crushed by the tank tracks, others picked up sticky bombs[17] and slapped them onto the nearest tanks. The Australian gunners of 2/3rd Australian Anti-Tank Gun Regiment had dug in their two-pounder guns and their accurate fire, at very close range, was able to drive off each attack. The anti-tank gunners claimed to have knocked out six German tanks that day and certainly prevented the battalion from being overrun by the battlegroup.

In the early evening, a dangerous attack mounted by 20 tanks and infantry penetrated between the two companies holding out at Tel el Eisa station. Under the pressure of this assault, D Company was forced to withdraw, and Hammer ordered his A Company to counterattack in the darkness. The three platoons advanced in extended order, creeping forward until fired on by a startled German machine gunner. Then, 'yelling like a lot of mad dervishes'[18] and firing all their weapons into the night, they charged the German tanks. This rash charge actually worked and the German tanks quickly withdrew, believing that they were under attack from a much larger force. The Australians then worked hard to enlarge their positions, lay mines and string out barbed wire to deepen and thicken their defensive positions around the narrow and exposed salient that they had just captured.

By the evening of 10 July, after a very long day of fighting, the two battalions of the 26th Australian Infantry Brigade could pride themselves on accomplishing a fine feat of arms. They had seized a key piece of terrain overlooking the Axis rear areas, and given some protection to the Alamein box from Axis artillery fire and observation. Many accounts of the fighting at Alamein consider this day to have been the turning point, not only of the campaign but of the war itself. The South African Official History commented that 'Auchinleck had changed over finally to the offensive, and the Eighth Army was never again to know the anguish and humiliations of retreat'.[19] Dorman-Smith later proudly related how Rommel had played into Eighth Army's hands by concentrating in the south and that the Australian attack was 'a shattering, and almost decisive blow'.[20] In fact, the importance of this attack has been overstated.

The attack was certainly 'shattering' but it had never been designed to be 'decisive'. It was ironic that Morshead, having insisted that he would fight his division as a division, mounted his first attack at Alamein with a brigade group: two infantry battalions supported by tanks, anti-tank guns and artillery. Two battalions, even when supported by tanks and concentrated artillery, were never going to inflict mortal damage on the Panzerarmee Afrika. Instead, the attack closely resembled the 'bite and hold' operations of the Great War in which a British division would mount an attack with strictly limited objectives under the cover of coordinated artillery fire. Once the position was consolidated, the British would seek to cause the maximum damage to the inevitable German counterattack.[21] This was exactly the sequence of events at Tel el Eisa.

Auchinleck had been waiting for the right moment to deliver a blow directly against a weaker Italian formation, and the Sabratha Division's positions at Tel el Eisa had provided the perfect opportunity. Part of the reason why the importance of this attack has generally been overestimated is because of its connection with Captain Basil Liddell Hart's 'Strategy of the Indirect Approach'.[22]

Liddell Hart was one of the foremost British military thinkers and an advocate of mobile armoured warfare during the inter-war years.[23] He was a close friend of Dorman-Smith for many years and the two men engaged in a long and fruitful dialogue concerning the future of warfare and the British Army before, during and after the Second World War.[24] In his 1946 foreword to Liddell Hart's *The Strategy of the Indirect Approach*, Dorman-Smith claimed:

> History will I think show that Auchinleck's handling of the Eighth Army in June and July 1942 not only saved the United Nations from very far-reaching defeat, but also provided students of war with a classical exposition of the application of the indirect approach.[25]

Dorman-Smith later related how, while packing his case for the desert on 25 June 1942, he 'topped off his despatch box with Liddell Hart's book, *The Strategy of the Indirect Approach*. He knew the book well, but it might be helpful now.'[26] Dorman-Smith offered the book to Auchinleck during their flight to Maaten Baggush, announcing 'as we were now about to apply its principles, Auchinleck might like to refresh his memory'. Auchinleck replied that he did not think he would have much spare time for reading.[27]

How much Auchinleck's conception of the fighting at El Alamein related to Liddell Hart's principles remains open to doubt, but there is considerable evidence that Dorman-Smith was influenced by Liddell Hart's ideas – just as Liddell Hart was influenced by him. What is less clear is exactly how directly Dorman-Smith, through his advice to Auchinleck, consciously attempted to apply the principles of the 'indirect approach'.

Liddell Hart's concept of the 'indirect approach' evolved and developed throughout his career as a military thinker, but some essential themes remained constant through the many reissues of the book. Liddell Hart argued that taking a direct approach to a military objective generally produced negative results since moving 'along the line of natural expectation consolidates the opponent's equilibrium, and by stiffening it, augments his resisting power'.[28] Instead, a commander should seek to unbalance his opponent both physically and psychologically by taking the 'indirect approach' – attacking the enemy where he least expected it. Liddell Hart amplified this point by emphasising the importance of 'concentration of strength against weakness'.[29] Eight 'maxims' of war encapsulated most of Liddell Hart's thinking on the 'indirect approach' and were, he believed, the 'Concentrated Essence of Strategy':

1. Adjust your end to your means . . .
2. Keep your object always in mind . . .
3. Choose the line (or course) of least expectation . . .
4. Exploit the line of least resistance . . .
5. Take a line of operation which offers alternative objectives . . .
6. Ensure that both plan and dispositions are flexible – adaptable to circumstances . . .
7. Do not throw your weight into a stroke whilst your opponent is on guard . . .
8. Do not renew an attack along the same line (or in the same form) after it has once failed . . .[30]

The Australian attack on 10 July certainly seemed to fit this pattern. However, although the attack concentrated strength against weakness, and operated against the line of least expectation, there was a serious flaw inherent both in the outcome of the attack and in Dorman-Smith's application of the 'indirect approach'.

Major-General Leslie Inglis, the temporary commander of 2nd New Zealand Division, complained in a letter to Freyberg that:

> The Australian punch seems to me to have taken a wrong direction comparatively harmless to the enemy – perhaps even advantageous to him – and not at all the sort of thing we understood it was going to be. It was eccentric from us and gave us no chance to cooperate from nearly 20 miles away.[31]

The attack of the 26th Australian Brigade at Tel el Eisa effectively committed 9th Australian Division to the defence of a narrow and exposed salient at the extreme northern end of the front for the foreseeable future. This certainly relieved the 'operational pressure' on the 1st South African Division holding the Alamein box, but it effectively removed one of Auchinleck's most powerful infantry formations from any other potentially more decisive operations further south. Even the intended policy of identifying and striking Italian formations had potential pitfalls. By concentrating on the location of Italian formations, Auchinleck and Dorman-Smith seem to have lost sight of the fact that, while it was perfectly possible to destroy weak Italian formations, it was the reaction of the German units of the Panzerarmee Afrika which would determine the outcome of any Eighth Army attack. And while Auchinleck's aim remained the destruction of Rommel's army, the concentration on Italian formations was actually an attritional policy. Targeting the Italian formations would slowly weaken the Panzerarmee so that, eventually, the Afrika Korps and 90th Light could not hold the line but this would take time, and, meanwhile, the German units could do serious damage to any Eighth Army unit which became unbalanced after an attack on an Italian unit. The execution of the 'indirect approach' was not quite as simple as Liddell Hart's maxims seemed to suggest.

However, the Australian attack at Tel el Eisa, quite apart from its territorial gains, quite unwittingly destroyed one of Rommel's most vital units. As the 2/24th Battalion advanced past the sand hills near the sea, a small force was detailed to attack what looked like a deployed headquarters with a varied collection of trucks, vans and radio antennae.[32] The German staff put up as much resistance as they could with their rifles and machine guns, but the Australian infantry were soon supported by mortar fire which pinned the Germans down. After a stiff fight of over an hour some Valentine tanks appeared on the scene and the German staff surrendered. Two German officers and 71 soldiers were marched off to captivity, including the badly wounded commanding officer. The trucks were inspected and a vast haul of documents was sent back to 30 Corps Headquarters for evaluation. No one in the battalion realised the importance of this capture, apart from the rather bland appreciation sent to the battalion by 30 Corps expressing thanks for the 'captured material and documents sent back, much valuable information has been gained'.[33]

In fact, the battalion had overrun and captured Nachrichten Fernsehsendung Aufsklarungs Kompanie 621,[34] commanded by Captain Alfred Seebohm. Far from being an ordinary headquarters, Seebohm's unit was a critical component in Rommel's system of command and control. Since April 1941 Kompanie 621 had provided Rommel with vital tactical intelligence by 'listening in' to British radio traffic, translating and interpreting the messages and sending important signals direct to Rommel. On 10 July, Seebohm had pushed his unit forward in order to improve the reception of British radio traffic. The higher ground around the coast, just 600 metres behind the front line, had seemed like the perfect listening post.

The collapse of the Sabratha Division had caught the unit by surprise. It was trained in defence and had twice before fought off attacks. But now, when Rommel asked for the most recent intercepts on the morning of 10 July he was told by Seebohm's liaison officer that contact had been lost with the company.

'Where is the company positioned?' he asked.
I showed him on the map.
'Then it is *futsch* – lost!' he said, absolutely furious.[35]

Rommel had good reason to be angry. Seebohm and Kompanie 621 had provided him with an unparalleled wealth of tactical intelligence.

The enormous potential advantages of voice radio command and control had also led to significant problems with security. A message sent out 'in clear' by a radio transmitter could be picked up by any radio receiver – whether friendly or hostile, and might well provide up-to-date and tactically useful intelligence and this demanded much tighter security. The use of code or cipher, however, took a great deal of time. A message had to be encrypted, sent and then decrypted at the receiving end. For most purposes, therefore, the armies relied on relatively simple codes in voice communications which could be quickly rendered into plain speech at the receiving end. Unfortunately, the use of code was not nearly as secure as cipher. At the regimental level and below, both code and cipher simply slowed down messages too much, so most radio traffic was 'in clear' with codewords used to disguise important names, units and map references.

Unfortunately, British wireless security during the desert campaign was extremely poor. The combination of lax security in higher level headquarters and the inevitable use of transmissions 'in clear' by lower formations had enabled Seebohm to develop a detailed picture of British units and their methods. British investigators of Seebohm's documents noted:

A very large number of captured codes and documents were found in their files. The practice of forwarding a code name or list to all units in a Division and showing the complete distribution list, has evidently proved of great value to them in determining our exact Battle Order, and assists in identifying units using wireless.[36]

As early as March 1942, documents from an intact truck from one of Seebohm's platoons were captured in Bardia, which should have tipped off the British about what was going on. It apparently did not. There was no major change in British wireless technique. British officers could be heard on air saying such things as: 'I cannot do my show this afternoon as the ground is unsuitable, so I shall do it tonight, it will not affect your show in the morning.'[37] The use of distinctive accents, slang and nicknames over a period of time allowed Seebohm to identify the commanders of particular formations. Lieutenant Hertz, Seebohm's second in command, admitted, 'We don't have to bother much about ciphers, all we really need are linguists, the sort who were waiters at the Dorchester before this war started.'[38] Seebohm and his men had proved not only adept at using captured code books but also in breaking the often very simple code names and words used by British officers in a hurry. They broke the British map code, even though it was changed frequently, and this made locating and then identifying British units a relatively simple matter.

Evidence of Seebohm's startling success could be seen in the last report that he prepared for Rommel. It read almost exactly like the message logbook of Eighth Army Headquarters:

0733 7 Mot Bde is in action with enemy position 866278.
0735 Armoured Bde reports to 1 Armd Div that enemy Recce party in Area 8827 are retiring westwards.
0750 7 Mot Bde reports columns of tanks moving West at 8672275.
0950 7 Armd Div reports to 13 Corps that enemy columns of tanks and AA guns are being encountered during a move in a Southerly and South-Easterly direction.[39]

Obviously, such detailed information on British deployments and intentions had been of vital importance to Rommel.

The value of such information was enhanced yet further by the fact that the highly trained operators of Kompanie 621 were often able to intercept, translate and forward an important message to Rommel faster than the British signals operators who were actually meant to receive the message. Rommel consistently received intelligence and reports concerning the state and location of British units before Eighth Army Headquarters. Indeed, a German officer was able to complain in June 1941 that, 'It is intolerable that I should receive more speedy information about our own troops from intercepted enemy traffic than from your reports.'[40]

Rommel has often been credited with an inspired tactical sense – a 'fingertip feel' for the shifting patterns of battle – but much of this vaunted ability rested on the efforts of Alfred Seebohm and Kompanie 621. It was subsequently discovered by the British that Rommel's greatest success in battle, the destruction of British armour at Knightsbridge on 12–13 June 1942, had only been possible because Seebohm's unit had intercepted 7th Armoured Division communications and worked out its dispositions.[41] The capture of Kompanie 621 and the shock of realisation of the extent of German intercept success 'literally "dumbfounded" Eighth Army'.[42] Almost immediately, it greatly tightened wireless security, stopping the worst leaks. 15th Panzer Division did have a signals intercept unit[43] which, although it received a generous allotment of equipment and personnel, was unable to match the accumulated experience and knowledge of Seebohm and his men. Kompanie 621 was reactivated in September 1942 but never achieved the same success. The 'Good Source' provided by Bonner Fellers had dried up on 29 June, and with the destruction of Kompanie 621 on 10 July, Rommel's 'fingertip feel' deserted him and never returned.

Meanwhile, the vicious territorial fight for the mounds of Tel el Eisa continued. On 11 July, just after dawn, the 2/24th Australian Infantry Battalion attacked the eastern Point 24 on Tel el Eisa ridge. With the support of all three Australian field regiments and a squadron of 44th Royal Tank Regiment, the battalion took the feature and held it against a number of counterattacks.[44] Throughout the day, both battalions of the brigade were subjected to an increasingly heavy bombardment by German and Italian artillery batteries, many of whom had been sent north to help seal off the penetration. A British battlegroup, called 'Daycol', tasked with exploiting south from the salient, encountered heavy fire and was forced to turn back, although with a satisfying haul of 1,024 Italian prisoners.[45] As might be expected, Rommel was planning an attack to retake the lost ground and he ordered the 21st Panzer Division up from the south for action in the north. However, rather than attacking the exposed salient itself, Rommel planned to penetrate the defences of the Alamein box, thereby dealing with the main strongpoint that had frustrated his efforts since 1 July, and simultaneously cutting off the Australian 24th Brigade at Tel el Eisa.[46]

There was a comparative lull on 12 July, although the Australians were forced to endure a bombardment of 'increasing intensity' as the day wore on. Throughout the day, the Australian artillery was called on to break up signs of Axis infantry massing for an attack.[47] In the evening, the German 104th Motorised Infantry Regiment mounted a serious attack on the positions of the 2/24th Battalion which 'exerted extreme pressure on the coastal flank'. After a fight lasting two hours 20 minutes, the Germans were beaten off, leaving more than 600 dead and wounded strewn in front of the Australian positions.[48] Eighth Army intelligence had identified the move of

21st Panzer Division through Ultra and the 'Y' Service, and Auchinleck began considering an operation to seize the Ruweisat ridge while Rommel was occupied with his armour in the north. In 13 Corps, Gott moved the New Zealand Division up to a likely start point for the operation, and from 10 July, 13 Corps were busy with minor adjustments to the front line and planning the operation to seize the Ruweisat ridge. This operation was code-named Bacon. In fact, the New Zealand Division became frustrated by the constant postponements of the operation for no apparent reason.

On 13 July, 21st Panzer Division's attack against the Alamein box went in. Rommel had high hopes of success, writing to his wife, 'Today is to be another decisive day in this hard struggle. Things are already on the move all over the desert.'[49] In fact, Rommel's counterstroke failed comprehensively against the South African defence. 1st South African Division Headquarters was warned of the impending attack of the 5th Panzer Regiment by 'Most Secret Usual Sources' (i.e. Ultra) early that morning, which enabled the defences to be placed on full alert.[50] Heavy shelling and dive-bombing attacks began against 3rd South African Brigade in the early afternoon, but the troops were well protected in their fortifications and losses were small. Meanwhile, full support for the defence was provided by the artillery batteries of 9th Australian and 1st South African Divisions along with 7th Medium Regiment. These guns were able to put down very heavy concentrations of fire which made any progress very difficult and costly for the German infantry. Indeed, the German infantrymen who were meant to go in with the panzers were simply unable to get forward. The South Africans noted that 'the volume of arty fire brought to bear on the enemy broke up the main part of his attacks when they were barely in range of inf weapons'.[51] This meant that the panzers, shorn of their infantry support, just as they had been on 10 July, were unable to mount a fully developed attack. At 17.40 hours, 16 tanks advanced to 300 yards and shot up a number of machine-gun posts, but the South Africans intercepted a message from 34th PAK[52] Regiment to 21st Panzer Division complaining of a minefield which had been located in front of the South African pillboxes and suggested that the attack be called off. The German engineers tasked with lifting the mines were unable to get any further than the South African's outer wire. The panzers mounted another attack late in the evening which met the same reception. The 400 supporting infantry were unable to close with the defences and while 11 tanks took up hull-down positions and shelled the South Africans, three tanks cruised around just outside the wire firing at pillboxes. As long as the artillery of Eighth Army could put down heavy concentrations of fire whenever needed, 21st Panzer could not make any progress.[53]

Having been baulked once again in front of the Alamein defences, Rommel turned his attention directly to the Tel el Eisa salient and ordered the 21st

Panzer Division to attack Point 24. The Australians noticed considerable movements of troops, vehicles and guns south of Tel el Eisa during the day so they had an inkling of what was brewing. Coming out of the evening sun, the Germans attacked with 20 tanks on 14 July against the exposed troops of 2/24th Battalion. The attack 'was pushed in with great speed and determination' and the Germans were able to drive in behind Point 24, thus cutting off the Australian company. After a close fight, the Australians were forced to withdraw back to Point 33 but not without inflicting heavy casualties on the Germans.[54]

At first light on 15 July, the men of 2/24th Battalion realised that the Germans had followed them up towards Point 33 the previous night. Three tanks reached Point 33 but the supporting infantry was dispersed by small-arms fire. The Valentines of 44th Royal Tank Regiment then mounted a counterattack which threw back the enemy tanks, which in turn moved off to hull-down positions to the west. The final German attempt, at 11.30 hours, to retake Point 33 was mounted by two infantry companies unsupported by tanks and was easily broken up by artillery and machine-gun fire.

Throughout these attacks and counterattacks since 10 July, the infantry of Eighth Army had fought with the support of their artillery. Every artillery battery had fired thousands of rounds, often on successive days. For example, 2/12th Australian Field Regiment fired 2,236 rounds on 10 July and 2,164 rounds on 14 July with 'normal rate' expenditure on the less demanding days.[55] The constant demands for fire support had called for 'superhuman efforts' from the gunners, and they never failed to lay down the fire needed.[56]

Although the Axis soldiers facing Eighth Army believed that, compared with their straitened circumstances, the British had inexhaustible supplies of ammunition, in fact the vast expenditure of 25-pounder ammunition was causing a crisis for the quartermasters of Eighth Army. Without the liberal use of its now concentrated artillery fire Eighth Army would not be able to continue its defence or mount an offensive.

While Auchinleck admitted to Brooke late in July that 'we are using a terrible amount of 25 pdr ammo but that cannot be helped'[57] that was not the view of the quartermasters who had to satisfy the voracious needs of Eighth Army. By 12 July 30 Corps were estimating a daily expenditure of 41,000 rounds of 25-pounder ammunition which represented 100 rounds per gun per day. Had this rate of expenditure continued, the entire stock of 25-pounder ammunition held in the Middle East would have been consumed in 10 or 11 days.[58] By 14 July a memo had to be issued on ammunition expenditure that warned:

> In view of the losses of stocks of ammunition of all natures between GAZALA
> and ALAMEIN and the heavy expenditure during operations, it is of the

utmost importance that sniping and indiscriminate shooting at unimportant or ill-defined targets should be rigorously controlled.[59]

In future, it was proposed to limit despatches to Eighth Army to just 15,000 rounds of 25-pounder ammunition each day which was completely inadequate for the demand. The problem was that on 15 July there were only 197,379 rounds in Egypt with another 418,000 en route from Palestine. Another 512,000 rounds were on their way by sea but would not reach Suez until later in the month. Shortages of small-arm ammunition, including the Besa machine gun fitted in British tanks and the Thompson submachine gun, were even more acute. This aspect of the July fighting has been overlooked; the Eighth Army simply did not have the reserves of ammunition, let alone the troops, to mount a sustained attempt to break the Panzerarmee.

SEVEN

Raw Bacon

God will not count your medals, but your scars[1]

Lieutenant-General William H. E. Gott was the doyen of the original desert army. In 1939 he was a lieutenant-colonel in command of the 1st Battalion The King's Royal Rifle Corps, and was promoted brigadier to command the support group of 7th Armoured Division in the heady days of 1940. He was appointed to command the same division in October 1941 and he led it through the bloody 'Crusader' battles later that year. Just five months later he was given command of 13 Corps. Along with Brigadier 'Jock' Campbell VC, the gunner officer tragically killed in a car accident in February 1942, 'Strafer' Gott had become an almost legendary figure to the officers and men of the Eighth Army. Field Marshal Lord Carver, who served as a junior officer on Gott's staff, later commented, 'I worshipped him as the ideal of all that I believed that a senior army officer should be.'[2] This view of Gott was certainly not shared subsequently by every historian. Gott had a difficult relationship with Pienaar, commander of the 1st South African Division, and J. A. I. Agar-Hamilton, the South African official historian, later wrote of him that:

> It has not been unknown for a commander to pass from disaster to disaster, but it is quite without precedent for any commander to pass from promotion to promotion as a reward for a succession of disasters.[3]

This was unfair to Gott who had fought with skill in successive actions. Gott was known as the one British commander who fully understood the challenges of mobile warfare in the desert and who knew how to use the desert as a weapon. However, his fame really came from his calm optimism and his imperturbability even in the worst of situations.

Gott's 13 Corps had not made the impact that Auchinleck had planned for it. 30 Corps had borne the brunt of the battle and had drawn Rommel's armoured reserve northwards to the coast. However, 13 Corps was composed only of the remnants of 7th Armoured Division and the fresher 2nd New Zealand Division. Gott had been waiting for a favourable opportunity. With

Rommel's armour in the north, that opportunity had arrived. Gott, although known for his expertise in mobile desert warfare, would now have to command his corps in an attempt to break into a strongly held enemy position.

Acting Major-General Leslie Inglis, the temporary commander of the 2nd New Zealand Division, had become frustrated with his division's largely passive role since 3 July. Inglis wrote to Freyberg that:

> Gott of XIII Corps is very good, but the strategic direction of the show as a whole beats me and I think Gott agrees. Since we came into the Alamein line I've had orders to go to Dabba [sic] and another time to Sidi Abd el Rahman to exploit attacks by XXX Corps. Those are the occasions on which I probed north West but on neither occasion was there the slightest possibility of exploiting to the named places because the last mentioned Corps gave nothing to exploit.[4]

13 Corps activity had been made contingent on success in the 30 Corps area and, since every attempt to mount exploitation from Tel el Eisa or the Alamein box had failed, Gott had cancelled every projected advance by 13 Corps. This situation was puzzling and confusing to the troops taking part. They had been warned to be ready for action many times but nothing had come of the ambitious orders. On two occasions, the brigades of the New Zealand Division had squared up to a start line and gone in under a bombardment to secure their jumping off points, only to have the operation cancelled.[5] The fact was that any exploitation from 30 Corps could only ever be very small and this meant that 13 Corps had held a considerable portion of Eighth Army in relative inactivity at the very time when simultaneous action by both corps might have been decisive. Inglis went on to say:

> The troops (NZ) are in good fettle. Everytime we've had a go at anything it has come off. What we want now is the General Battle decently tied up to give us a chance of doing something decisive. . . . Information from aloft is scanty and late. I get most of ours personally from Gott, and they seem to leave him a bit vague.[6]

It is clear that Inglis was chafing for an opportunity to demonstrate his ability to command a division in action by taking an important part in an attack which might well break the Panzerarmee Afrika.

Auchinleck had wanted to recapture the Ruweisat ridge in its entirety since at least 4 July when the Panzerarmee's hold on its positions there had seemed so weak. The capture of the ridge would provide good observation over a swathe of the Axis positions and point like a knife at the enemy's heart. Auchinleck and Gott had both seen the potential for an attack which would seize the western end of the ridge and open up the situation for a decisive blow. It was obvious that the 2nd New Zealand Division with its

two fresh brigades would be tasked with mounting the attack. Auchinleck
and Dorman-Smith worked out the framework for Operation Bacon in which
2nd New Zealand Division would advance nearly six miles in a night attack
to seize and hold the ridge. At dawn, the two brigades of 1st Armoured
Division would move up to frustrate any Axis counterattack and take every
opportunity to exploit the success. At the same time, 5th Indian Division
would cooperate from its positions on the eastern end of the ridge by
mounting a brigade attack to seize Point 64, an area of high ground which
lay halfway along the ridge. In its essentials, Bacon appeared bold enough
to cause real damage to Rommel's weakened army.

Since 14 July 1916, when the Fourth Army had mounted a successful
night attack on the Somme, the British Army had developed expertise in
infantry attacks at night. There were many good reasons for this. Although
night attacks could dissolve into complete confusion and demanded
rigorous procedures for keeping direction and distance, attacks during the
hours of darkness also had clear advantages. German defences in the Great
War had relied on the power of machine guns to pin down and kill attacking
infantry which advanced across open ground in daylight, and the events
of 1 July 1916 had proved just how dangerous such a defence could be.[7]
Similarly, in the Second World War, the Afrika Korps' use of combined
arms made German defensive positions very difficult to approach in
daylight but after dusk the situation altered in favour of Eighth Army. Tank
crews were effectively blind at night and the web of anti-tank guns, infantry
and artillery used by the Afrika Korps was much less effective without
direct vision of the target. Thus, most of the advantages that the Germans
held in armour, anti-tank guns and the suppressive fire of their MG 34
machine guns were neutralised during darkness and the advantages that
Eighth Army possessed in its determined infantry could be maximised.
Inglis noted later:

> We knew that the Germans and Italians fought poorly against this kind of
> attack and that their use of tracer ammunition would help to pinpoint their
> defensive localities and assist us to avoid casualties by showing where their
> main lines of fire were.[8]

4th New Zealand Brigade, while under Inglis' command, had developed
expertise in mounting night attacks, both through training and its experiences
at Belhamed in November 1941 during Operation Crusader. 5th New
Zealand Brigade did not have similar combat experience but was still well
trained in night movement across desert. Although Inglis considered a six-
mile advance at night to be 'the maximum distance possible for very good,
well-trained troops',[9] he had little doubt that his two brigades would reach
their objectives on the ridge. This was due to his confidence in the men

under his command but also to the belief that the Axis defences were 'not what the textbooks call "highly organised", but much nearer what they refer to as "hastily organized"'.[10] It was believed that the main line of Axis defences actually ran on or close to the ridge itself, and that the defences that could be seen to the south were only outposts which would not impose much delay on the attacking division.

Nonetheless, from the time that Bacon was first mooted on 10 July it was known that the Axis defences south of the ridge were being thickened up. New Zealand patrols mounted on the night of 11–12 July penetrated three miles into the defences and garnered important information. It was noted that:

> the enemy was working at high pressure to create in the inland sector a centre of resistance to withstand any attack which we might launch. This conclusion was based on the recce reports of digging and laying minefields and the preparation of a screen of guns behind which he was placing defence of infantry.[11]

However, the intelligence picture concerning the location of Axis units and the state of their defences on the Ruweisat ridge remained fairly sketchy. The lack of detailed tactical intelligence highlighted the limitations of Ultra intelligence. Ultra could tell Auchinleck and Dorman-Smith the location of German and Italian units, and sometimes their strength, but it could not provide the detailed tactical intelligence which was vital for mounting a successful operation. Dorman-Smith was aware that Bacon would hit the Italian Brescia and Pavia Divisions but knew little of the defences these forces occupied. The intelligence officers of 2nd New Zealand Division were limited to gaining information from patrols and observing the enemy through field glasses. The lack of visibility in the desert hampered their knowledge of what was happening on Ruweisat ridge. The only time the air was clear enough for detailed observation was for a limited period after sunrise, and then only if there was no morning mist. Once the sun rose there was always heat haze or mirage which made accurate long-distance observation difficult. Unfortunately, the aerial photographs of the Axis defences on the Ruweisat ridge, which should have been a vital part of the intelligence picture, arrived late and so overexposed as to be useless.[12]

On 11 July, it appeared that Operation Bacon was on and the New Zealand Division prepared to move up to the start line for the attack. However, Inglis told Gott that:

> although it would at one time have been easy to occupy the ridge, the enemy had so developed his hold on it that its seizure was no longer practicable except by a major operation with armoured support.[13]

As it turned out, the New Zealand Division received the message that Bacon was off that evening, much to the relief of Inglis who had not wanted to express further concerns to Gott about the practicability of the operation.[14]

Inglis and Lumsden had a series of arguments concerning the role of the 1st Armoured Division in the operation. Inglis believed that his infantry battalions could seize the ridge but would need armoured support to hold their positions after dawn. While British infantry attacks could indeed overrun Axis positions during darkness, it was always difficult to consolidate the defence after a night attack. Artillery observers needed to move up with the infantry to register their guns on fresh targets, while anti-tank guns could not be properly sited until the gunners could see the lie of the ground in daylight. This meant that infantry battalions were vulnerable for some time after dawn and bitter experience had proved that German units counterattacked immediately.

Inglis asked Gott to give him some armour under his own command so that the tanks could operate in close cooperation with his infantry but Lumsden refused on the grounds that his tank crews had not been trained in infantry cooperation. Lumsden's response was partly due to the baleful effect of British doctrine which held that 'cruiser' tanks should operate independently of infantry formations, while infantry should be supported by specialised infantry tanks. Unfortunately, 13 Corps had no infantry tanks, and the few Valentines in 30 Corps were fully occupied supporting the Australians. Lumsden's response also accorded with Auchinleck's recently disseminated policy on Eighth Army armoured forces which made it clear that the main tactical functions of 1st Armoured Division would be:

(a) The neutralisation of the German armour acting in the closest conjunction with the maximum concentration of artillery that can be provided from all resources at the disposal of Eighth Army, irrespective of which Corps is concerned.
(b) Taking part in a decisive attack in conjunction with Valentine tanks and with infantry and supported by the maximum concentration of artillery possible.[15]

The second role conformed closely to the projected plan for Bacon but the limited numbers of precious Grant tanks and the importance of neutralising German armour wherever it might be found made it impossible for Lumsden to agree to tie down his tanks to an infantry support role. Indeed, Lumsden is unlikely to have given Inglis' request much serious thought.

The problem for 2nd New Zealand Division remained this: mounting such a long night advance meant that the battalions would have gone beyond the supporting range of their field artillery batteries. Moreover, the bulk of supporting arms, including artillery and anti-tank guns, would then have to drive six miles across desert still containing pockets of enemy troops before the positions on the ridge could be consolidated. At the Corps Conference held on 13 July, Inglis decided to rely on the assurances which Lumsden 'rather grudgingly' gave him that the 2nd and 22nd Armoured Brigades would advance at first light from their night leaguers. While 2nd Armoured Brigade was 'to close up to the troops on the ridge', 22nd Armoured Brigade was 'to come up on the immediate rear of 4 Bde and seal off the Division's left flank'.[16] These were the orders as Inglis understood them.

Inglis believed that the armoured brigades would be able:

(1) clear up any pockets left by the infantry night attack, (2) to deal with any enemy tanks that might have intervened or been by-passed between the start line and the ridge and (3) to support the infantry on the ridge against counter attack until our own artillery was ready to do so.[17]

In fact, 2nd New Zealand Division had wildly overestimated the capabilities of the two British armoured brigades. The British armoured brigades were to move on a different axis of advance from the New Zealand Division and had no way of knowing how successful the New Zealanders had been until they received the appropriate codewords over the radio. Even starting immediately at first light, the armoured brigades would have six miles of ground to cover before they could reach the new positions of the New Zealand Division. 22nd Armoured Brigade would have a particularly difficult advance since they would be moving along the open left flank of the New Zealand Division, exposed to enfilade fire from any remaining German or Italian positions. It was also unclear how the tanks could mop up pockets of resistance, deal with enemy tanks *and* support the infantry at the same time. The armour was then supposed to 'exploit' the success of the New Zealand Division.

Inglis was expecting too much of the British armour and in fact his plan for the operation flew in the face of the lessons which had been learned during Operation Crusader the previous winter. A set of trenchant and forthright lessons on the use of tanks by Brigadier G. W. Richards was published in January 1942. These notes stated that:

Inf must more clearly appreciate that it is they who have got to hold an objective, and in particular, that they have got to be prepared to hold it against immediate counter-attack, especially tank counter-attack, within a reasonably short time after its capture, and that therefore it is useless to set themselves an objective which they are not confident they can so hold with their own resources.[18]

If this lesson from Operation Crusader was strictly applied, it meant that Eighth Army infantry formations should only mount attacks with limited objectives very much in the manner of the Australian 'bite and hold' operation on 10 July. It was only by moving a strictly limited distance that the supporting artillery would remain in range and that anti-tank guns would be able to close up to the infantry soon after the objective had been taken. The Australians had proven that such tactics could work well but 10 July had hardly been a decisive blow. At the divisional conference Brigadier 'Steve' Weir, the commander of the New Zealand Division's artillery, stressed the fact that the division would be advancing beyond the range of his guns and the infantry brigadiers, Acting Brigadier Burrows and Brigadier Kippenberger, requested that the advance be made in a number of phases. This had become standard practice during the Great War in order to ensure that troops, who might have become disorganised, could reorder themselves before pushing on to the next objective line. Inglis understood that firm consolidation of the objective would be difficult after such a long advance at night but he believed that the serious risks were worth taking in order to make a decisive attack against the Panzerarmee.

Early on the morning of 14 July, the 2nd New Zealand Division received its final set of orders for Operation Bacon. The division was to attack at 23.00 hours that night on a two-brigade front. 4th New Zealand Brigade was to advance on the left, with 5th New Zealand Brigade on the right. Given the oblique angle of the start line to the final objective, 4th New Zealand Brigade would have more ground to cover – almost exactly six miles – to reach its objective on the ridge. The rate of advance was fixed as no more than two miles per hour on a compass bearing of 320 degrees from the start line. It was expected that the battalions would first meet enemy resistance at 01.00 hours and that they would finish their march and be on their objectives by 04.30 hours, thus giving them sufficient time to organise their positions before first light.[19]

The brigades would each advance with two battalions 'up' and one in reserve. 4th New Zealand Brigade was to attack on a front of 400 yards with 18 Battalion forward, 19 Battalion in echelon on the left flank and 20 Battalion in reserve.[20] In 5th New Zealand Brigade, Kippenberger decided to attack on a frontage of 1,000 yards with 21 Battalion on the left, 23 on the right and 22 Battalion in reserve. Unfortunately, the order of deployment was misunderstood by 21 Battalion, which deployed to cover the 1,000 yards all by itself. The leading battalions were tasked with cutting a path through the enemy positions and reaching the ridge. The reserve battalions were to 'mop up' any remaining enemy defenders but any particularly stubborn pockets would be left for the tanks the next morning. This was a true divisional attack with both brigades of the division attacking, supported by all the resources of the division; each brigade had artillery, anti-tank and anti-aircraft guns, machine guns, engineers and signallers under command. Unfortunately, 'No one . . . envisaged the possibility that the supporting

arms might be prevented from moving forward.'[21] The attack was to be silent
to maximise surprise, and the artillery were given normal harassing tasks
along with a limited counter-battery fire programme so that the enemy would
not suspect anything unusual along the front.

The 14 July was a very hot day and the soldiers had to lie in their narrow
slit trenches baking in the heat while under attack from hordes of flies and
the occasional German bomber. After the hot day, the night was cold and
very dark with no moon. As the men made their final preparations, there
was an air of excitement within the division that, finally, they were going to
mount an important attack:

> All ranks were keyed up in expectancy at Div HQ. It was realized that this
> was a major attack which, if successful, as we were sure it would be, and
> advantageously exploited, might well be a turning point in the campaign.[22]

Kippenberger watched his 22 battalion move off from the start line after
the two leading battalions had gone:

> I walked along the line, always a poignant experience before an assault. The
> men were quiet, those I spoke to cheerful and resolute . . . The battalion stood
> up, there was a jingle and rustle of equipment, and then it moved silently
> forward, hearteningly orderly and resolute looking.[23]

Bacon, already cancelled three times, was finally 'on'. Each battalion making
the night assault depended on a small team, called the navigation party, to
keep direction and count the distance marched. Lieutenant Sullivan, in 20
Battalion, led the way with two men checking his bearing and pacing. Sullivan
kept count of the paces by using his rosary to mark every hundred paces.[24]

Just after midnight, when Sullivan and the other navigating officers had
paced two and a half miles, the leading battalions found minefields in their
path. Soon after, the men were illuminated by flares and enemy machine
guns opened up along the front. Just as expected, most of these guns were
firing along fixed lines, and the leading sections of infantry were able to avoid
the bullets while charging onto the Italian posts with grenades and bayonets.
The enemy defences were found to be dispersed and relatively easy to subdue.
Many of the Italian defenders, surprised by the unexpected attack, fled from
their positions. One member of 18 Battalion described the scene as:

> a mad and weird pattern of coloured tracer. There was the hoarse shouting
> of our men using the bayonet and the frightened 'Mamma mia' of the Italians.
> We were moving forward in slow easy stages spending waiting time on our
> stomachs while mortar landed about us.[25]

However, the task of clearing a path through these 'outpost' positions meant that the New Zealand battalions became increasingly dispersed and contact within the battalions broke down. The men of 21 Battalion came upon a leaguer of German tanks which quickly broke up under attack. A number of tanks were set on fire with sticky bombs, and the tanks moved off into the darkness. As time went on, the New Zealand attack dissolved into separate platoons and even section groups of men all bent on reaching the ridge. While 4th New Zealand Brigade managed to keep wireless communications open between brigade headquarters and the battalions, communications within 5th Brigade broke down completely. The batteries supplied for the No. 18 wireless sets ran down very quickly and the cables which were laid back to brigade and division were just as quickly severed. By 05.30 hours, no one within 5th New Zealand Brigade was able to contact any other unit except with runners.[26]

Even with all these difficulties and although some of the battalions had been badly scattered, the attacking troops reached the ridge by about 05.30 hours on 15 July. They were badly disorganised and tired. Brigadier Burrows later recorded:

> It was expected that the outlying enemy posts would not be held in strength, and that the main opposition would be on the ridge itself. The enemy, however, was organised in depth practically from the point on which contact was made to the ridge, a distance of approx 3½ miles.[27]

The soldiers of both brigades had achieved a fine feat of arms. The brigades had fought their way through two divisions of Italian infantry and made a fighting advance of six miles. It was only at dawn that the New Zealanders appreciated how faulty their intelligence picture had been before the attack. Far from meeting the main resistance on the ridge, the scattered 'outposts' had actually been the main defence lines of the Brescia and Pavia Divisions. The two brigades, deploying on the crest of the Ruweisat ridge, had actually broken through to the rear areas of the Panzerarmee Afrika. Burrows described the view that greeted him at dawn:

> To the North was a scene of the utmost confusion. There was an extremely large concentration of enemy transport and in all directions Italians who had thrown away their arms were wandering aimlessly about. We had no means of rounding them up though a considerable number gave themselves up.[28]

While the realisation that their attack had carried them deep into the Panzerarmee gave some cause for satisfaction, the New Zealanders soon found that the ridge was impossible to consolidate on properly.

There was 'a stratum of rock about four inches down and [the] men could not dig'.[29] This made it impossible to make proper trenches or gun pits. The division had achieved real success in reaching the ridge, only to find that the terrain made their position extremely vulnerable. Yet Eighth Army had known beforehand that the Ruweisat ridge was unsuitable for infantry to dig in on. In late June, Norrie had specifically selected Deir el Shein and not the ridge itself for his intermediary box because 'digging on the ridge itself was very difficult owing to its rocky nature'.[30] Norrie had been replaced on 6 July, and the staff officers who knew about the unsuitability of the ridge for consolidation were employed in 30 Corps. 13 Corps, on the other hand, had been operating in the desert south of the ridge, and had no direct knowledge of the nature of the ridge until they actually got there. This seemingly small though vital piece of information was only one example of the two corps of Eighth Army not sharing intelligence and it was to have disastrous consequences for the 2nd New Zealand Division.

The rocky nature of the ground placed the anti-tank gunners in a particularly difficult position and the decision was taken to leave the guns on their portees. The practice of using anti-tank guns 'en portée' had been picked up from the French. (As the term suggests, originally a French expression used to denote the carrying of anti-tank guns on the back of trucks. The habit was relatively short-lived.) Transporting anti-tank guns posed a real problem in the desert. The normal method was simply to hook the gun onto the back of a truck or carrier. However, the design of the two-pounder, the main British anti-tank weapon, featured a three-leg base plate. This enabled all-round traverse but the wheels had to be removed before the gun could be fired. Bringing the gun into action was thus a laborious task, not envisaged by its designer, who had assumed operational conditions on the Western Front similar to those in the Great War. In the desert, this difficulty was magnified by the fact that towed anti-tank guns often suffered serious damage from the rocks and stones of the desert. The natural solution seemed to be to carry the gun, ready for action, on the back of a truck which had ramps and a winch to raise and lower it. Fittings on the truck enabled the gun's trail and spade to be clamped so that the gun was ready for action.[31] This became known as an anti-tank portee.

Using an anti-tank gun portee meant that the gun was protected from the ravages of the desert floor and could be brought into action immediately, a very important consideration in mobile desert fighting. Unfortunately, it also brought severe tactical disadvantages. Rather than being a small indistinct target dug into the desert, the truck-mounted gun made for a much larger and more vulnerable target. Crews were trained to reduce this vulnerability as much as possible by changing position after every few shots and by using whatever cover was available. Yet by their very nature, such tactics could not afford the static infantry in slit trenches the same kind of anti-tank protection as a dug-in gun.

In preparation for the Crusader offensive of November 1941, Lieutenant-Colonel T. H. E. Oakes of the 7th New Zealand Anti-Tank Regiment had intensively trained his crews in the use of porteed anti-tank guns. The regiment had achieved impressive results during the subsequent fighting. L troop, 33rd Battery, managed to knock out at least 24 German tanks on 23 November 1941.[32] Not surprisingly, the use of porteed anti-tank guns became an ingrained practice in the New Zealand Division. However, since that impressive action German tanks had been progressively up-armoured, making the two-pounder gun truly obsolescent. It was generally agreed that the only way to use the gun effectively against the up-armoured German tanks was to use it from defilade positions – holding fire until the tanks had passed the gun position and then firing against the thinner side armour of the tank. With a properly dug-in position, this tactic was just about possible, as the Australians had proved at Tel el Eisa, but with porteed anti-tank guns it was not. By July 1942, the accepted military opinion was that the use of porteed anti-tank guns was a pernicious and dangerous habit. Eighth Army instructions on the point were quite clear: 'The rule is that anti-tank guns will never be fired from their portees except when there is literally no time to bring them into action on the ground.'[33]

On Ruweisat ridge, the New Zealand gunners knew that they needed to dig in and camouflage their guns but found that 'due to the rocky nature of the ground it was hopeless to dig in the gun as we would normally have done. Even the German dead were only thinly covered on top of the ground.'[34] This made the anti-tank guns into highly visible targets which drew fire from all directions: 'any movement of gun or vehicle drew instant fire from Jerry and naturally the infantry did not appreciate portees sculling around in their vicinity. God knows they had had enough for one night.'[35]

While the initial group of anti-tank-gun portees had made the advance with 4th New Zealand Brigade without too much incident, the same was not true in 5th New Zealand Brigade. The first group of anti-tank guns, which had been ordered to follow the leading battalions closely, had become lost and instead followed the transport of the brigade headquarters. This meant that the three battalions of 5th New Zealand Brigade, dispersed and out of contact with each other, had no anti-tank protection as dawn broke. 22 Battalion, the reserve battalion of the brigade, soon suffered disaster. The German tanks which had been encountered during the night had moved off but were still south of the Ruweisat ridge at dawn. As light filtered across the ground, the eight German tanks of 8 Panzer Regiment found the men of 22 Battalion attempting to dig into the rocky ground. With no anti-tank guns and no cover, there was little that the infantrymen could do; they were quickly rounded up by the tanks and hurried off to the west.

The disaster which afflicted 22 Battalion demonstrated clearly the difficulties facing infantry after a night attack. Without their supporting arms, and without the time to dig in, infantry were highly vulnerable to a dawn attack by tanks. This was precisely why Inglis had requested armoured support under his command which might have been able to prevent such a disaster, but it is equally clear that the arrangement to have 1st Armoured Division move 'at first light' could not have helped 22 Battalion. In 4th New Zealand Brigade, the infantry also came under attack from a handful of tanks but the anti-tank gunners were able to drive them off to a relatively safe distance. These tanks sat hull-down throughout the day, shelling and machine gunning the New Zealand positions from long range.

As in every night attack, it took a long time for news to reach the divisional headquarters about what was happening to the leading battalions. At zero hour, the divisional headquarters moved forward to the position just left by the 5th New Zealand Brigade headquarters but communications became difficult very quickly. Even though there were detachments of signallers with each brigade laying telephone cable back to the divisional headquarters these were quickly broken. The radio telephones which they were then forced to use 'became erratic'. The officers at divisional headquarters were soon dependent for news of progress solely on the noise of the attack:

> we could hear sounds of heavy firing and it was obvious that the assaulting troops were being fairly heavily engaged. In particular there was the disturbing sound of constant heavy enemy mortar fire. Later on came the still more disturbing noise of enemy tank gun fire. Both Bdes were able to give the codeword DOG at 0230 hrs, though it was apparent that the outposts were organized in considerable depth and that the advance was proceeding under fairly heavy fire.[36]

While 4th New Zealand Brigade remained in some contact with divisional headquarters, and was able to report 'TIGER' (the codeword that it had reached its objective) at 04.15 hours, it became apparent that all communication with 5th New Zealand Brigade had broken down. Shortly before first light, the brigade major of 5th New Zealand Brigade was able to get in touch and report that:

> Bde HQ was not in touch with leading Bns, but that reserve bn was advancing under fire and Bde Comd was going forward. It was probable that fwd tps were on objective but TIGER was not yet definite.[37]

Clearly, the divisional plan for Bacon had miscarried almost as soon as the attack started. The entire operation hinged on the 2nd New Zealand Division being able to report as early as possible to the 1st Armoured Division that its leading troops had seized their objectives. The armoured brigades would only move at first light if they knew that 2nd New Zealand Division had been successful. But the complete breakdown in communications with the New Zealand infantry brigades and their contact with divisional headquarters had already made this impossible.

But, if communications and control within the Eighth Army formations were difficult, there was panic and confusion amongst the Axis defenders. The New Zealand attack had penetrated almost to the headquarters of 15th Panzer Division, which had considered itself safely behind the lines. Officers at the headquarters had heard the sound of firing from the sector held by the Brescia Division soon after the New Zealand attack began, but the liaison officer at the Brescia Division Headquarters had little to report because there had been no contact with the forward strongpoints:

> The noise of fighting continued, and suddenly the report came in that fleeing artillerymen of Brescia Div had arrived at Div Battle HQ. The three easternmost strongpoints had been overrun without a single report from the Italians.[38]

The weakness of the Italian infantry divisions had once again been revealed and, by first light, the personnel of 15th Panzer Division Headquarters realised that the New Zealanders had penetrated 'as far as Pt 63, very close to Div HQ, and had knocked out some MT and guns belonging to the A Tk unit, which was in protective positions just forward of Battle HQ'.[39] There was little the units of 15th Panzer Division could do but it soon became clear that the 'enemy was not able to bring up any more troops to exploit his initial success'.

The situation remained critical particularly as:

> Throughout the day the remaining Italians were leaving their positions and fleeing to the rear in disorder, taking their rifles with them. There were no officers to be seen. The Italians tried to make some organised stand, but failed because weapons were short and morale gone.[40]

Panzerarmee Afrika was facing a real crisis. 15th Panzer Division found it 'most astonishing that the enemy could not exploit his penetration to a break through by pushing his tanks forward'.[41]

At dawn, the 5th Indian Brigade's assault on Point 64 began but immediately ran into trouble. The 4th Rajputana Rifles was met with heavy fire and fell back in confusion to its start line. Meanwhile, the 3rd Baluch Regiment reached the ridge, but many men had been held up fighting machine-gun outposts and on the barbed wire.[42]

Meanwhile, Nehring attempted to deal with the 'first class crisis' which had arisen. 15th Panzer Division was in action attempting to hold the penetration, while the whole of 21st Panzer Division was still committed in the north. 90th Light Division was ordered to move 33 Reconnaissance Battalion and Group Baade to the north and 21st Panzer Division was to send a battle-group south. It was not until 14.00 hours that 33 Reconnaissance Battalion was sent into action in an outflanking move from the south and west against 4th New Zealand Brigade. By 16.15 hours, one battalion of 100 men under Colonel Bruer from 21st Panzer Division had arrived and was sent into the attack, while Group Baade of 90th Light remained in Bab el Qattara because they had completely misunderstood their orders. Further units of 21st Panzer Division, including its tank battalion, arrived in the late afternoon so that 'the danger of a breakthrough here seems to be eliminated'.[43]

At first light, 2nd New Zealand Division Headquarters advanced, according to plan, to take up a forward position. However, after a mile and a half, the headquarters found that the entire area ahead was filled by the soft vehicle transport for both brigades. The situation was clearly getting worse. The plan had called for the supporting field artillery regiments, anti-tank batteries, anti-aircraft guns, reserve ammunition and signals companies to follow up through the ground taken after first light when the situation should have been stabilised. Instead, all of the supporting arms, transport and ammunition vehicles for the attacking brigades were bunched up in the desert not far from the original start line. As the divisional headquarters moved up, they received a report from 5th New Zealand Brigade that the 'position was not satisfactory and that enemy tanks were operating. We could see shelling not very far ahead.'[44] At this, the chief staff officer ordered the divisional headquarters back to where it had just come from. The situation was becoming disastrous. For a critical time when things had clearly gone wrong, the divisional headquarters was moving backwards and forwards with no clear idea of the situation at the front.

While the attacking brigades had been able to cut large gaps through the defences held by the Italian infantry, they had not been able to subdue all the resistance. Not surprisingly, most of the smaller outposts and defended localities had fallen easily but some of the larger posts had been bypassed during the night. The outposts which remained contained substantial numbers of anti-tank guns, machine guns and infantry. When daylight came, these posts were able to cover the area south of the ridge by fire and shoot up any trucks foolhardy enough to drive forward.

The determined resistance of these isolated posts cut off the New Zealand infantry brigades from their supporting arms. The all-important artillery observers, with one exception, were unable to reach the ridge, and the field regiments were drawn into the fight to clear these outposts rather than supporting the infantry on the ridge. Similarly, the vital additional anti-tank guns of the 7th New Zealand Anti-Tank Regiment were unable to reach the ridge. The isolated Axis posts were also difficult to capture because there was no reserve infantry to clear a path to the ridge. The inability of the New Zealand Division to clear the ground that lay between the objective and start line left its infantry brigades dangerously exposed and isolated on the Ruweisat ridge.

Eventually, around 06.30 hours, Kippenberger arrived at what had been divisional headquarters to find Inglis having a quiet breakfast. The tale he told was not encouraging. He had just escaped from the German tank attack which had overwhelmed 22 battalion, and he had come back to re-establish some sort of communication with divisional headquarters. In a car with a misfiring cylinder, Kippenberger crawled off to find an armoured brigade. He eventually found the tanks and pleaded to the brigadier for help: 'He said he would send a reconnaissance tank. I said there was no time. Would he move his whole brigade?' Lumsden arrived and the three of them clambered onto the brigadier's tank:

> The General asked where we were and the Brigadier pointed out the place on the map. 'But I told you to be there at first light,' General Lumsden then said, placing his finger on Point 63. I jumped down and did not hear the rest of the conversation but in a few minutes the General got down and in a soothing manner which I resented said that the Brigade would move as soon as possible.[45]

Kippenberger's testimony is generally accepted as evidence that the British armoured brigades failed to carry out their orders on 15 July. However, the armoured brigades had not been ordered to mount a night advance but that was the only way they could possibly have reached the objective at first light. Lumsden had become notorious within the Royal Armoured Corps for his use of verbal orders. Major-General Gatehouse later confided to Liddell Hart his impression of Lumsden:

> He prided himself on his quickness, his mobility with a very small H.Q. and his rapid and verbal only orders. Very early I discovered that if such orders 'came off' he was very quick to take the praise, but that if they did not, he would flatly deny having given them.
>
> This is a very serious statement to make, but on the advice of many senior officers in the Cavalry, after one or two experiences of the denials, I made it a point to get any orders he gave me in writing.[46]

In this case, Lumsden did not want Kippenberger to think that he had not ordered his brigades to move up before dawn and Kippenberger's testimony on this point does not make the situation any clearer.

Inglis claims that he never saw the written orders for 13 Corps or 1st Armoured Division, but read today it is clear that they presented a different conception of the type of support the 2nd New Zealand Division could expect.[47] The 13 Corps orders stated that the tasks of 1st Armoured Division were 'To protect the Southern and Western flank of the NZ Div attack from first light 15 Jul' and 'To be ready to exploit NW with armd forces if a favourable opportunity occurs after first light on 15 Jul'.[48] Of course, exactly how the armoured brigades would protect the New Zealand flanks was open to interpretation, and the exploitation that Inglis was relying on to protect his troops was strictly conditional.

The written orders for the British armoured brigades were perfectly clear, although it is impossible to be sure about any conversations between Lumsden and his brigadiers which might have augmented the written orders. 1st Armoured Division's orders stated that:

2 Armd Bde will be prepared to move on centre line of the inter-Corps boundary, with the tasks of
(a) exploiting success of the N.Z. Div to the NW.
(b) countering any enemy counter-attack by the enemy armour against NZ Div which may develop from the NE, North or NW.
22 Armd Bde will be prepared to move on a Centre Line DIMR EL HIMA 891273 – track at 884273 – area of 877277. Ech on the SE flank of 2 Armd Bde Gp.[49]

These orders stated explicitly that the brigades 'will be prepared to move' on receipt of the necessary codewords from divisional headquarters. 'FAITH' would denote that the objective had been captured by the New Zealand Division, while 1st Armoured was 'to be in readiness to exploit in the direction named' on receipt of 'CHARITY'. The envisaged counterattack was expected to be mounted by the 21st Panzer Division which would move from the coastal sector in response to the attack. Implicit in these orders was the assumption that the 2nd New Zealand Division would have to defend its objectives for a number of hours until the armour reached them.

The 2nd Armoured Brigade's orders also noted that it would begin its advance on receipt of the codeword 'RADICAL'. On the morning of 15 July, 2nd Armoured Brigade had received reports that the New Zealand advance had been successful on the left but had encountered tanks on the right but when, at 06.15 hours, Lumsden called Briggs to ask if his brigade was now engaging the enemy, Briggs could only reply that 'the code word had not been received'.[50] Ten minutes later, the brigade was ordered to advance. The armoured regiments sent out reconnaissance tanks ahead of their lead squadrons. British armour which advanced incautiously had all too often found itself under destructive fire from anti-tank guns so this was a reasonable precaution given the unclear situation ahead of them.

Actually reaching the New Zealand infantry on the ridge proved more difficult. By 08.45 hours, the three regiments of 2nd Armoured Brigade had reached the original enemy front line but now had to try and find a way round the pockets of resistance. Little progress seems to have been made yet at 09.16 hours 6th Royal Tank Regiment was ordered to prevent 'inf being attacked by enemy armour'.[51] The problem was that the pockets of enemy left in position after the advance of the New Zealand brigades were resisting strongly. There were still Italian strongpoints around Point 63 which had yet to fall into the hands of the 5th Indian Brigade. Caught in the cross-fire from anti-tank guns, the patrols sent forward by the armoured brigades failed to make much progress.

At 9.30 hours, the 5th Indian Brigade began to make further progress with some tank support from 2nd Armoured Brigade. They managed to overrun another battalion of the Brescia Division, but it was not until 11.30 hours that the Rajputana Rifles were able to attack the Italian strongpoint on Point 64. Bengal sappers from the 4th Field Company blew gaps in the wire and the riflemen stormed through and captured another Italian infantry battalion. More than 1,000 prisoners were taken by the two battalions that day. By midday, the Indian Brigade had reached its objective and cleared the right flank of the New Zealand Division.[52]

During the morning, Major Sawyers of 48 Battery in 6th New Zealand Field Regiment gathered a group of gunners together to attack one of the largest enemy outposts, known as 'Strongpoint No. 2', which was blocking the route to the ridge. It required a fierce bombardment from the entire field regiment to subdue resistance and when the strongpoint finally yielded in the early afternoon, Sawyers and his men captured two 88mm guns, a number of smaller anti-tank guns, and 20 German and 160 Italian soldiers. Inglis had relied on the British armour to 'mop up' these posts, but in reality they were too powerful for the tanks to deal with by themselves. 2nd Armoured Brigade had been right to be cautious. If they had motored forward without paying due attention to reconnaissance, the brigade could easily have been shattered on such a rock.

Some of the smaller Axis posts surrendered after the capture of this strongpoint and 2nd Armoured Brigade found that the collapse of this resistance, combined with the advance of 5th Indian Brigade, had opened a path to the ridge. However, the only viable route was to drive north into the Indian sector and then advance west along the ridge towards the 5th New Zealand Brigade. By 14.00 hours the brigade was informed that the 'forward NZ Bde are cut off from their 25 pdrs and A Tk guns. 1 Armd Div instructed to give all possible assistance.'[53] Unfortunately, at much the same time, a report was received that at least 40 enemy tanks were massing just to the north of Deir el Shein.[54] 21st Panzer Division had moved from the north to an assembly point north of Deir el Shein and these were the tanks that the British armour noticed. This new threat imposed caution on the British armour, as to commit themselves to the defence of Ruweisat ridge in the face of 21st Panzer Division denied them the flexibility and manoeuvrability that they depended upon both to evade anti-tank-gun fire and to ensure that they fought on even terms. It would appear that the two New Zealand brigades, which were now under heavy shellfire with their positions peppered with shrapnel and shrouded in smoke and dust, were unable to see this new and ominous concentration of tanks.

The New Zealand infantry had spent a very difficult day on top of their hard-won objective. With no clear picture of what had happened to their supporting arms or to the British tanks, they found themselves under increasingly heavy shelling from the south and west – including the unreduced pockets that now lay behind them. 4th New Zealand Brigade also had an entirely open left flank which was now filled by the 33 Reconnaissance Battalion of 90th Light Division. Burrows later related, 'The enemy soon realised that we were without our guns and brought his own up. For the rest of the day we had one of the toughest times I have experienced . . . It went on almost without a break . . .'[55] With no cover on the rocky ridge, casualties began to mount alarmingly, particularly amongst the gun crews sitting exposed on their portees. Many of the guns were disabled by the constant shelling and mortaring. By 15.00 hours it was clear to 4th New Zealand Brigade that the Germans were assembling for an attack on their position. Yet at the same time, 2nd Armoured Brigade heard that the New Zealand Division had been able to bring up some of its artillery and anti-tank guns.[56] In fact, this referred to the efforts of 5th New Zealand Brigade, which had managed to bring up some guns and supplies along the same route used by the armour. These could not help the 4th New Zealand Brigade. It was now in real danger of being overrun.

When the German attack went in against the 4th New Zealand Brigade the British armour was not in position to help. At about 16.00 hours, the Axis artillery fire reached the top of its crescendo and then the panzers advanced. Burrows related that:

> Their tanks came in with a slight wind behind them. They set fire to what vehicles they could find in their path, and soon there was an excellent smoke screen across everything. All we could do was sit and wait in our HQ trenches.[57]

Meanwhile, the anti-tank gunners still on their portees found the visibility so poor that it was difficult to identify targets. The whole area was being sprayed by machine-gun bullets fired by the advancing tanks and soon all the portees were put out of action. This left the infantry helpless in the face of the German tanks. Many of the soldiers kept firing with their rifles and Bren guns at the advancing tanks which were now circling their positions. Captain Maxwell, by now in command of the much depleted 20 Battalion, recorded, 'I realised that we were in a hopeless position as there were tanks all around us. The shelling was still going on and . . . I decided that rather than lose the remaining men I had no alternative but to surrender.'[58] Small parties of German infantry then advanced and brought the bitterly disappointed New Zealand prisoners into captivity. Burrows and his headquarters staff were also captured by a group of German armoured cars. However, the Germans were brought under tank fire and, in the confusion, Burrows managed to drop unnoticed into a sangar. He lay still until dark and then managed to make his way back to Eighth Army lines.

Lieutenant-Colonel Reid, of the New Zealand Royal Engineers, managed to escape from the German counterattack with a mixed group of engineers who had been supporting 4th New Zealand Brigade. As they headed away from the battle area they came upon an unexpected sight:

> We saw some of our tanks on the ridge to the south. Imagine our surprise and disgust on topping the ridge to see a large number of them all lying snugly below the crest. Here were the tanks we had been expecting, practically within range of our recent positions, and yet not one of them had come to our assistance. The crews were all very sympathetic with us and just yearning for a fight, but were sorry nothing could be done without orders. It made us mad to think that the tanks had been so close and that we had had no support from them. Had they moved forward over the ridge an hour before, the position undoubtedly would have been saved, as I understand there were no more than sixteen tanks to be dealt with. We were cut off for some hours, and lack of communication and knowledge of the forward situation evidently had been responsible for the hold up.[59]

Understandably, there was great resentment within the New Zealand Division that the British armour had not come to support them. However, the 22nd Armoured Brigade had had a long and hard drive filled with delays caused by minefields and enemy crossfire even to reach the position where Reid found them.[60]

By 17.00 hours, 2nd Armoured Brigade had advanced closer to the ridge but 6th Royal Tank Regiment soon hit some scattered mines and lost two tanks. Once again, the armoured regiments had to halt and feel their way gingerly around the obstacle. Again, such caution must have appeared maddening to the remaining troops of 5th New Zealand Brigade still on the ridge, but to drive on without caution was to risk the loss of large numbers of tanks on hidden mines. It is revealing that the 2nd Armoured Brigade recorded, 'At this period there were 42 enemy tanks on 2 Armd Bde front, in which number the 13 which were attacking the NZ Bde are included.' Once 4th New Zealand Brigade had been overrun, the panzers turned their attention to the British armour. It was reported that, 'The 42 tanks on 2

Armd Bde front hotly engaged, but NZ Bde forced to withdraw with fairly heavy casualties.[61]

When news that 4th New Zealand Brigade had been overrun reached Kippenberger, he had to make the difficult decision whether or not to withdraw his brigade from the positions that had been won and held at such cost throughout the day. Kippenberger learned that his 23 Battalion now had just 190 men and several anti-tank guns left. After dark, Kippenberger informed Inglis that he would not be able to hold his position and he was granted permission to pull back to a ridge 1,200 yards south of Ruweisat ridge.[62]

The battle which had begun with such high hopes and expectations within 2nd New Zealand Division had ended in bitter disappointment. More than 2,000 prisoners, mostly from the Pavia and Brescia Divisions, had been taken, and both these Italian divisions had been shattered. The New Zealanders had suffered 1,405 casualties, the majority of them in 4th New Zealand Brigade. The division had lost an entire brigade which would have to be rebuilt from the small cadre that was left at Maadi, the New Zealand Expeditionary Force's base camp in Egypt.[63]

The New Zealand Official History claimed that its 'examination of the tank role at Ruweisat' was 'undertaken at some length in perhaps a vain effort to explain the inexplicable'.[64] In fact, the absence of the British armour to support the infantry on the ridge was only one failure amongst many during the operation. The British armour advanced cautiously for a reason: there were too many unsubdued enemy positions on both flanks along the route of the New Zealand brigades' advance for the armour to drive forward rapidly that morning. When they did move, they met scattered mines that delayed their progress and forced them to abandon their original axis of advance. By the late afternoon, when the armour had nearly reached the New Zealand positions, 1st Armoured Division discovered a powerful force of German armour massing to the north. This, too, demanded a cautious approach, and ultimately meant that the armoured commanders chose to fulfil their 'independent' role of 'neutralising' the German armour rather than providing support to the infantry. Otherwise, they feared, quite rightly, that they would be caught at a tactical disadvantage in the coming fight and might lose heavily. The New Zealand soldiers, who had taken an enormous risk in reaching the ridge, perhaps had reason to think that the British armour would take a similar risk. That it did not certainly destroyed their trust in British armour but the act was not 'inexplicable'.

The British armoured brigades came to represent a scapegoat for the New Zealand Division. The New Zealand Official History stated:

The Division, however, did not consider itself responsible in any particular for the turn events had taken. It believed it had carried out its part of the battle. Failure to consolidate the bridgehead, to beat off the counter-attacks and to exploit, were attributed to the inaction of the armoured brigades.[65]

In fact, even though the British armour had failed to carry out their task, the New Zealand Division's planning for the operation had been deeply flawed. Brigadier Weir later wrote:

> It was beyond the strength of two Inf. Bdes with one Bn. in reserve, to advance 10,000 yards through defended country, capture a tactical objective at the end of it, clear the intervening country and hold it against a wide open left flank and a right flank which only closed on the objective.[66]

In attempting this ambitious assault, the New Zealand Division became hopelessly unbalanced. The assaulting battalions achieved a great feat of arms by actually reaching the Ruweisat ridge but this meant that they reached their objective without sufficient supporting arms and cut off from the rest of the division. The whole point of Freyberg's heated arguments with Auchinleck during 1941 and 1942 about fighting his division as a division, and his eventual refusal to carry out the order to form brigade groups, was to ensure that all the resources and fighting power of his division could be combined. The plan for Ruweisat ignored this vital principle. Weir later pointed out:

> our tactical doctrine in regard to the attack or the assault was clearly wrong. We did not appreciate:
> (a) How much assault troops could really take in one blow.
> (b) The basic consideration governing a land assault – i.e. capturing clearing and holding all the ground prescribed by the assault.
> (c) The necessity for keeping the Division at all times squarely balanced and cohesive so as not to be dissuaded from our task by anything the Germans did.[67]

The division made such a deep advance on a relatively narrow front that its left flank was open and unprotected – and six miles long. Had the New Zealand Division mounted an attack with limited objectives then these problems would not have arisen. Infantry which had just made a night assault were vulnerable until they had consolidated. The fate of 22 Battalion, which was overwhelmed just after first light, demonstrated this clearly. With the full support of its three field regiments and its entire complement of anti-tank guns, however, the New Zealand Division would have been able to defend itself against any counterattack that the Panzerarmee could have mounted later in the day, even without the support of the British armoured brigades.

This lack of sensible tactical doctrine concerning an infantry assault

stemmed largely from the role which the New Zealand Division had played
in the desert campaigns so far. While the 9th Australian Division had a very
realistic appreciation of what infantry could and could not achieve (along
with a robust attitude to dealing with tank attacks), this was due to the fact
that the Australians had performed a defensive role at Tobruk quite unlike
that of any other Eighth Army infantry. The New Zealand Division had
been trained for open desert warfare in which mobility and rapidity of movement had been stressed. The difference in method revealed itself most starkly
in the way the two divisions used their anti-tank guns. The Australians developed great expertise in the rapid siting, digging in and camouflaging of guns
to achieve enfilade fire against German tanks. In contrast, the New Zealand
anti-tank gunners had been trained in the skilful use of portees in mobile
action. This training, combined with the nature of the ground, placed them
at a severe disadvantage on the Ruweisat ridge.

Inglis commented later that it would 'have been criminally stupid to have
launched them in that particular attack without the assurances of armoured
support'.[68] However, it is clear that Inglis did not understand the limitations
of the British armoured brigades or the particular problems that they would
face in reaching the ridge. Brigadier Richard's notes on tank support warned
that:

Many Inf commanders do not realize that tanks are manned by highly trained
human beings; nor does he understand how essential is ECONOMY in their
use, to save them for really decisive tasks. It has been a common thing for
commanders whose Inf are suffering some casualties from enemy fire to send
for tanks, quite unsupported, to 'clear up the situation'; it is also a common
question to be asked 'how many tanks have you got?' – not 'what is the fighting
state of your units and squadrons?'[69]

Inglis overestimated the nature of the support that he could expect to receive
from the British armoured brigades, and underestimated their difficulties in
providing that support. Weir believed that the division was 'still suffering
from the teachings of "Bir Stella" and "Sidi Cliff" where we "motored
along", deployed, clouted the objective with artillery and raced to the objective'.[70] These exercises in Syria, and the battle experience of the division
during Operation Crusader, had taught the division expertise in the mobile
warfare necessary in 1941, but also meant that the division's tactical doctrine
for assaulting a more static line with defended localities and minefields was
inappropriate.

The New Zealand Division's previous service in the desert had condi-
tioned it to the needs of mobile warfare where a hard blow might well make
an enemy withdraw, since no terrain in the desert had any intrinsic tactical
or operational value. The New Zealand expectation was that a hard blow

followed by exploitation would lead to an Axis withdrawal rather than counterattack. However, at El Alamein, Rommel's army was determined to hold
its ground and Bacon actually became a set-piece assault on a fixed defence.
Rommel would not, could not, leave the Alamein line for strategic reasons
and this determined the nature of the tenacious Axis defence. It also meant
that the New Zealand expectations, and those of Eighth Army, were proved
to be overoptimistic. The Australians, from their experience in Tobruk, were
inured to close and hard fighting against numerous German attacks. The
New Zealanders, from their fighting at Belhamed, had drawn equally valid
conclusions, but ones which were mistaken given the operational situation
at Alamein in July 1942.

Once the crisis had been surmounted and the position stabilised,
Nehring's appreciation of the situation was unhesitatingly critical of
Rommel's plans:

> The measures taken by Armee Command, which during these last days wanted
> to carry out too far-flung a task with too weak forces and to enforce success
> brought with them the danger of the collapse of the fluctuating front . . .
> However the British attack has thwarted the intentions of the C.-in-C. . . . The
> pressure intended for the enemy has been converted into a pressure on us.[71]

Rommel had become desperate to find a way to break the solid positions of
Eighth Army. His search to maintain his offensive had led him to take risks
which were not warranted by the situation, and had opened up the
Panzerarmee for a counterstroke.

Auchinleck and Dorman-Smith's conception for Bacon had almost
worked. They had taken the 'indirect approach' and mounted an operation
to attack the evident weak point of the Panzerarmee Afrika on the Ruweisat
ridge. The attack had seemed to offer the chance for decisive results. Inglis
later wrote to Freyberg that, 'The Ruweisat Ridge show provided a wonderful
opportunity for exploitation by the armour at first light. The enemy was
properly rocked.'[72] However, the operation had not resulted in a breakthrough, and its results had been disappointing.

Dorman-Smith's later assessment of Bacon was revealing. He wrote:

> In desert battles the echeloned headquarters in successive higher control
> learn of the failure, partial success, or full success long before they learn the
> underlying reasons why events took that particular course. Lessons will be
> studied in due course, and the sooner the better, but there is normally little
> time for post-mortems. Auchinleck was disappointed, but not unduly
> depressed at the limited success of 13th Corps for he knew what the impres-
> sion must be on Rommel who had, in four days, all four of his Italian infantry
> divisions over-run.[73]

It was difficult for Auchinleck, in his distant headquarters at the camel tracks, to divine immediately what had gone wrong. Much analysis of actions can only ever be undertaken after the event. However, the rough balance of advantage after Bacon was clear at the time. The Panzerarmee had lost two Italian infantry divisions but this did not materially alter its offensive power. Meanwhile, Eighth Army had lost an experienced brigade of excellent infantry which it could ill afford to lose and the opportunity to inflict a decisive defeat on the Panzerarmee had been squandered. Dorman-Smith's comments also revealed the fatal confusion inherent in his application of the 'indirect approach'. If the objective of Eighth Army was simply to wear down the Panzerarmee to the point at which it could no longer hold the Alamein line then cautious and strictly limited 'bite and hold' operations would have been more effective and much less risky. Yet the objectives for Bacon had been deliberately ambitious in order to destroy the Axis forces in one blow.

Dorman-Smith's search for the weak point of the Panzerarmee Afrika was dependent upon the picture of intelligence garnered from the front and from the precious Ultra messages. However, this picture was shifting constantly and took time to bring into focus. This was the ultimate reason why Bacon was cancelled three times. Dorman-Smith was relying too heavily upon Ultra intelligence to provide him with the weak point which could unbalance his opponent. Rather than making firm operational plans and using the intelligence picture as a guide to shape future operations, Dorman-Smith's plans became intelligence-led in his search for the weak point. And in searching for and attacking the weak point, Dorman-Smith was only ever able to assemble whatever troops lay to hand. The fact was that almost the entire front of the Panzerarmee was weak and while the Afrika Korps excelled in making hasty, risky attacks, Eighth Army did not. The structure and organisation of Eighth Army needed time to plan and prepare deliberate operations. More deliberate planning which refused to be derailed by the shifting intelligence picture could have resulted in more troops being amassed for a set-piece attack. The five days before Bacon had not been used in this way. Instead, the 2nd New Zealand Division had attacked without the benefit of the detailed planning which could have been undertaken, had a calmer atmosphere prevailed at Eighth Army Headquarters.

Bacon is generally cited by historians to demonstrate the woeful state of tank–infantry cooperation within Eighth Army. Certainly, there was no understanding within 2nd New Zealand Division of the difficulties which tank crews faced in combat and seemingly no recognition within 1st Armoured Division of its responsibility to ensure that Eighth Army's infantry did not face an armoured counterattack alone.

However, the operation revealed deeper and more intractable flaws within Eighth Army's method of operations. Worst of all, there was no clear doctrine for mounting an attack on a position held in depth. Auchinleck provided the conception for the operation but took no part in the shaping of the operation by lower formation commanders. Similarly, Gott had exercised little proper control over the divisions under his command and had little influence over 5th Indian Division, which operated under 30 Corps command, even though it was within the same sector as the New Zealand Division. Corps commanders and divisional commanders felt at liberty to place their own interpretation on army orders which made a unified approach to any operation impossible. No one within Eighth Army seemed able to take charge of the many details that had to be thrashed out for a complex operation to succeed.

Perhaps the greatest problem faced by Eighth Army was its inability to share information, so that important intelligence and differing points of view could be aired before an operation began, thus ensuring that every commander understood his role fully. Bacon had been 'on' and 'off' three times before its execution. The planning process for the operation remained in its infancy and was never fully developed. The days of uncertainty before the operation hampered the full dissemination of information and intelligence. Precious time, which should have been spent in army, corps and divisional conferences thrashing out every detail of the operation, was wasted in the uncertainty of whether the operation would be mounted at all. Ultimately, the blame for such problems had to lie with Auchinleck. His conception of operations was bold, but his ability to command Eighth Army was suspect. Flaws inherent in Dorman-Smith's conception of the 'indirect approach', deep weaknesses within Eighth Army's doctrine and fighting methods and Auchinleck's seeming inability to give sufficient drive and direction to the corps and divisional commanders meant that, in spite of its promise, Bacon was half-cooked and doomed to failure.

EIGHT

Ruin Ridge

At 02.50 hours on 16 July, 9th Australian Division's tactical headquarters received an urgent message:

> Enemy is clearly concentrating his whole strength against [the] two flank Div[s] 5 Ind Div and 1 Armd Div with a view to crushing [them] this must NOT repeat NOT happen. Every possible step will be taken starting tonight by our own forces to the north and south to distract attention from the centre. No reason of fatigue or lack of resources will excuse anything less than the most vigorous and sustained action.[1]

While the Panzerarmee certainly felt the pressure placed upon it by Eighth Army, the failure of Operation Bacon clearly rattled Auchinleck more than he admitted subsequently. Instead of punching a hole in the Panzerarmee's defences, he had lost a brigade of excellent troops and the 5th Indian Brigade posted on Ruweisat ridge was now vulnerable to counterattack. The Eighth Army's attack had also drawn all the available German armour to Deir el Shein. The 21st Panzer Division, having made its move from the northern sector at top speed, was ordered to mount an attack at 04.30 hours on 16 July to wrest the captured positions from the beleagured Indians who still held the positions around Point 64.[2] 5th Indian Brigade received due warning of what was to befall them. The German orders were intercepted by Eighth Army's 'Y' Service and a stream of orders was issued, including the urgent message to 9th Australian Division, to prepare for the attack.

The prior warning allowed significant preparations to be made to meet the attack. The 20th Australian Infantry Brigade was ordered to take up a hasty defensive position behind the Indians on Ruweisat ridge[3] but these hurried orders caused another row between Auchinleck and Morshead. Auchinleck had promised that he would not detach any further units from 9th Australian Division and Morshead immediately telephoned Eighth Army Headquarters. He was extremely angry that Auchinleck had broken their agreement and forced the Commander-in-Chief to return the brigade. Soon afterwards, Eighth Army sent the urgent message to 9th Australian Division demanding 'every possible step be taken'. Morshead relented and the orders to 20th Australian Brigade were confirmed, but the incident had further damaged relations between Morshead and Auchinleck.[4]

In a moment of rare comedy, the brigade intelligence officer selected a 'nice piece of empty desert' as a forming-up place. On reaching this point on its drive, the brigade found 'some well scattered and well camouflaged tents sunk deep in the desert. Suddenly the place came to like a poked ant heap. Agitated staff officers and orderlies scurried hither and thither.'[5] The assembled column of trucks had just motored into Eighth Army Tactical Headquarters. This was not marked on any maps and its location was kept secret as a security measure. This certainly improved security but it also isolated Auchinleck from the men actually doing the fighting.

When the Australians reached their positions around the Mubarik tomb, they passed some of the British infantry[6] which had been holding the position since the beginning of July. One Australian soldier commented:

> Everywhere on this, the Ruweisat Ridge, lived English men in the last stages of human misery – never have I seen, nor was I to see, men in such depths of illness and despair.
>
> Put a man in a dugout the shape of a grave; shell and bomb him, kill his friends, let the desert be his scenery, and a stony ridge his lookout; give him a bottle of water each day; make him stay at his sand-swept post, though weak with dysentery or enteric fever, for weeks on end, until sand and stone and shells become his world; for months until he becomes a hopeless weary animal.
>
> Do this, and you have the worn-out English men of the Eighth Army who pointed us the way to Jerry at the Ruweisat Ridge.[7]

Life on Ruweisat ridge was hard. On the Western Front during the Great War, British soldiers could expect to spend no more than a week at a time in the front-line trenches before being relieved. The shortage of infantry which afflicted Eighth Army in July meant that, with a few exceptions, infantry soldiers had to stay in the front line for weeks at a time. Soldiers in both armies were pushed to the limits of human endurance.

Meanwhile, 5th Indian Brigade was collecting as much support as was possible for the coming attack. The guns of Robcol were ordered to cover the front of the Indian Brigade, while 2nd Armoured Brigade, still in position on the ridge, was reinforced by one regiment from 22nd Armoured Brigade and brought up its motor battalion, the Royal Northumberland Fusiliers, and its anti-tank guns, to support the Indians.[8]

The counterattack, launched by both 15th and 21st Panzer, made virtually no ground in the morning, and 5th Panzer Regiment had to report plaintively that it could go no further.[9] Throughout the day, 5th Indian Brigade was subjected to Stuka attacks and heavy artillery fire but it was not until the evening that the panzers attacked again. To the south, Brigadier Kippenberger, whose 5th New Zealand Brigade had had a quiet day after the fighting of the previous day, was witness to the attack. He noted that a group of German tanks moved south from the El Mreir Depression:

> They were met by a group of our own tanks and a typical tank battle broke out, both sides firing briskly at one another from behind cover at about fifteen hundred yards range. We were sitting in the command truck and did not trouble ourselves to go and watch, but one of the Brigade runners did climb the rise to a viewpoint. He came back excitedly and reported that there was a regular battle on, and said with genuine astonishment in his voice: 'Our tanks are fighting like hell!' The implied disparagement was cruelly unjust but in our then state of mind no one thought it was. I went out and watched the affair. Before long the Germans withdrew and an absurdly inaccurate account duly appeared in the Intelligence summary.[10]

In fact, the encounter was far from typical. The Australian infantry of 20th Australian Brigade experienced a very different perspective of the fight: 'The noise of battle grew to a constant roar; and the red flashes of field pieces rippled ceaselessly up and down the ridge. But the attack was held at the front-line; the enemy was thrown back; and, in time, the firing abated.'[11] Early that evening, the dust from the advancing tanks could be seen less than a mile in front of the 5th Indian Brigade. The Germans were attacking, as was their habit, with the setting sun behind them to blind the gunners, but this time they drove straight into a well-planned anti-tank ambush. Major T. Walker, commander of 433rd Anti-tank Battery, had been warned that afternoon of the threat from 'some 50 German tanks and an infantry battalion'.[12] He carefully deployed his force of 16 six-pounder guns to meet the threat. Once the guns had been deployed, there was no time to camouflage the portees so they were simply left strewn over the ridge and were subsequently ignored by the Germans who apparently thought they were derelicts. The tanks of 2nd Armoured Brigade then withdrew behind the screen of anti-tank guns. The trap was set.

As the panzers drove forward, with the sun behind them and the Ruweisat ridge in deep shadow, it was very hard for the anti-tank gunners to see them: 'the tanks melted into the background'.[13] However, the forward observation officers of the four supporting field regiments soon asked for defensive fire to be put down onto the German infantry and the gunners fired some smoke rounds to help the observers identify the bursts fired by their own regiments. Soon the silhouettes of the leading panzers stood out clearly in front of the white smoke screen. By this time, the 4/6th Rajputana Rifles were firing their rifles and machine guns into the German infantry and trucks. Then, 'The enemy, as he rolled forward at walking pace, was caught by simultaneous anti-tank fire from four guns on his south flank, six guns on his north flank and six guns firing almost frontally.'[14] The ambush worked perfectly because the German tank crews concentrated their fire on the distant Grant tanks which were acting as decoys. After dark, the Germans drew off without ever realising 'the trap they were in'.[15]

A full-scale counterattack mounted by both panzer divisions of the Afrika Korps had been stopped in its tracks by the determination of 5th Indian Brigade and its supporting formations. In contrast to the day before, when the British armour had failed to support the New Zealand Division, the combined action of 2nd Armoured Brigade and 5th Indian Brigade resulted in a significant defensive victory that tends to be overlooked in accounts of the fighting at Alamein.[16]

The next day, after a 'searching fire' had driven off a few panzers which had survived the action by 'playing dead', 5th Indian Brigade was able to count its kills. Twenty-four tanks, six armoured cars, one self-propelled gun, 18 anti-tank guns and six 88mm guns had been left by the Afrika Korps strewn in front of 5th Indian Brigade positions.[17] Kippenberger had allowed his bitterness to cloud his description of events. Dorman-Smith claimed, rightly, that the German attack 'failed disastrously' and pointed out that the losses sustained by the Afrika Korps that day were almost half of those lost at Alam Halfa in August 1942.[18] Once again, Eighth Army had proved that, on the defensive, it had found the answer to the Afrika Korps in its combined use of armour, infantry, anti-tank guns and artillery. Yet Operation Bacon had shown how woeful were its attempts to convert those successful techniques into offensive tactics.

Auchinleck and Dorman-Smith were not willing to give up their plans for another offensive just yet. On the night of 15 July, 9th Australian Division held a conference to develop its plans to retake the double Point 24 feature on Tel el Eisa ridge. The attack was to be made by two companies from 2/23rd Battalion with one squadron of Valentines from 44th Royal Tank Regiment.[19]

The attack made good progress and by 07.43 hours, both eastern and western Point 24 had been captured by the rifle companies. Both sides realised the importance of Tel el Eisa but the concentrated artillery fire that both armies could bring down on the position made the exposed feature very difficult to hold. Once the Australians had captured the positions, the Axis artillery then fired an intense bombardment that caused many casualties to the unprotected infantry. Eventually, after suffering heavy loss, the company holding western Point 24 had to be withdrawn to the eastern Point 24, and soon after the remaining troops were forced to retreat to the slopes of Point 33. The two companies had taken 400 prisoners, but could not secure the ground.[20]

Throughout this period, 9th Australian Division had been the recipient of valuable support from 44th Royal Tank Regiment. The division considered that although:

> the bns had never trained with tanks and that the tank crews were mostly improvised, the results were good. This was due in no small measure to the personal contact made between the junior leaders of the two arms and to the fact that the tank units concerned had previously trained in the intimate support of infantry and not in the armd bde role.[21]

44th Royal Tank Regiment had been drawn from 1st Army Tank Brigade which was equipped, trained and organised as an infantry tank formation. Brigadier G. W. Richards had great experience in tank/infantry cooperation and this made a tremendous difference to the effectiveness of his tanks. The Australians were actually learning what tanks could and could not do and a level of trust was beginning to develop between the two units. For the 2nd New Zealand Division, the tank crews of 1st Armoured Division remained strangers and were bitterly distrusted after Ruweisat. The experience of 44th Royal Tank Regiment demonstrated what could be achieved when armour and infantry units developed mutual respect for each other.

There now seemed little chance of widening the salient around Tel el Eisa against a stubborn Axis defence, so Ramsden and Morshead turned their attention to the Miteiriya ridge. South west of Tel el Eisa, a series of almost imperceptible ridges rose out of the desert. The ridge at Tel el Makh Khad gave useful observation from two features known as the 'cairn' and Point 22. Further to the south lay the larger and longer Miteiriya ridge, known all too appropriately to 9th Australian Division as 'Ruin ridge'. Although difficult to discern from a distance, the Miteiriya ridge formed a low elevation running east–west through the desert, almost parallel to the Ruweisat ridge which lay ten miles to the south. In common with Ruweisat, the Miteiriya ridge gave very valuable observation of the surrounding desert. Since Operation Bacon had drawn off 21st Panzer Division to the south, it was now hoped that there might be an opportunity to seize Miteiriya ridge from its Italian defenders. If 30 Corps could gain possession of this feature, its artillery would be able to interdict the desert for miles to the south and the ridge might even act as a jumping off position for the British armour to debouch into the Panzerarmee's rear.

The problem in seizing Miteiriya ridge lay in the distances involved. The 2/32nd Australian Infantry Battalion was tasked with making a silent attack on 17 July upon Point 22 which lay on Tel el Makh Khad ridge. With this first objective secure, the 2/43rd Australian Infantry Battalion would continue the advance to reach Miteiriya ridge. A force of infantry and artillery drawn from 1st South African Division was placed under command 'for further exploitation if the situation were favourable'.[22] The brigade would be supported by the combined artillery of 9th Australian and 1st South African Divisions along with 3rd Field and 7th Medium Regiments, and supported by a squadron of Valentines from 44th Royal Tank Regiment. But in fact the attack was an attempt to make bricks without straw.

Eighth Army was desperately short of reserves. At least one of the brigades of 9th Australian Division had to hold the captured positions around Tel el Eisa. Another had to be kept in reserve to relieve the troops in that dangerous salient. That left just one brigade of three battalions to make any further offensive effort to the south. 1st South African Division still had to hold the defences of the Alamein box, and, after the arguments of early July, Auchinleck was careful not to ask too much of Pienaar and his troops. Further south, the improvised forces of 'Wallgroup', formed from the remnants of 7th Motor Brigade, could hold the line between the Alamein box and Ruweisat ridge, but were not suitable to make sustained attacks.

5th Indian Brigade was completely committed around Ruweisat ridge and although 2nd New Zealand Division, even with the loss of 4th New Zealand Brigade, was still a viable formation, it was in the process of bringing 6 Brigade from its base camp at Maadi. Holding the far south, 7th Armoured Division was able to keep 90th Light Division in check with its roving columns but could do no more. These straitened circumstances meant that 9th Australian Division attacked the Miteiriya ridge with one battalion when at least an entire brigade would have been necessary to achieve results.

The 2/32nd Australian Infantry Battalion, with three companies 'up', crossed its start line on time at 02.30 hours on 17 July, but soon came under heavy fire. When C Company heard the enemy alarm, Private J. M. Welsh remembered,

> Capt Jacoby . . . shouts attack, and the boys magnificently charge forward. Enemy MGs and anti-tank guns, mostly tracer, stream through us, but we keep on. It's a rapid firing tank gun which seems worst to me and I kneel and fire half-magazine in its direction. It stops firing, so we charge forward again. Italians are yelling and squealing; 10 minutes is sufficient to rout out enemy and take over position.[23]

Soon the companies had seized the enemy positions on the ridge, but, in the dark, the men of A Company overshot their objective, Point 22, by 1,500 yards. By the time they realised their mistake they were under such heavy fire that they could not withdraw. By 08.00 hours Italian tanks and infantry began to encircle their positions and eventually forced the entire company to surrender. Meanwhile, the other two companies faced the dilemma which so many infantry units encountered at Alamein. Having captured the ridge, they attempted to dig in on its crest but while doing so they could be observed and fired upon by every Axis post to the south. The battalion was subjected to heavy and systematic shelling by Axis artillery for the rest of the day. Eventually, they had to pull back to the reverse slope and dig in on softer ground. The heavy bombardment had cut all the battalion's communications and it was three hours before it could report its success.[24] This delayed the advance of 2/43rd Battalion which was still under orders to take Ruin ridge.

The Axis defences were alert by the time the battalion attacked and the advancing infantrymen met heavy shellfire. 'The advance continued, like a well carried out exercise. A whine, a cloud of dust, a column of black smoke, a few less men – but those who remained were still advancing.'[25] The left-hand company fought its way through a number of Axis-defended localities and took 19 field and 4 anti-tank guns with 50 prisoners. By the time they reached the ridge, casualties had been heavy and there were only six Valentine tanks left. The rest had run onto a minefield. Even worse, a Stuka attack had destroyed much of the battalion transport and the reserve ammunition. All communications had been cut which meant that no artillery support could be called down. Once again the Australians had managed to penetrate the Italian defences, this time occupied by the Trieste and Trento Divisions, but the same situation the New Zealanders had faced at Ruweisat greeted their efforts to consolidate. No matter how hard they tried, they could only make shallow slit trenches before they hit solid rock. The 'ruin' itself was merely a heap of stones, and 1,000 yards away a group of Axis tanks and vehicles was assembling for a counterattack. The Axis reaction was concentrated, with fire on the front and both flanks of the isolated battalion. The battalion endured the heavy shelling until a few Mk IV tanks took up hull-down positions nearby and also brought the battalion under fire. It was decided to withdraw back to Tel el Makh Khad ridge.[26]

The withdrawal was carried out smoothly and the battalion took up a position on the left flank of the 2/32nd Battalion. However, from the early afternoon, the Axis shelling consisting mainly of 150mm air burst shells 'accurately placed over the positions of the two battalions' increased in intensity.[27] At 16.00 hours the German and Italian troops managed to organise a serious counterattack, which was driven in at the junction of the two battalions. C Company of 2/32nd Battalion was overrun by armoured cars and tanks and many men taken prisoner. Given this pressure, the two battalions fell back independently and were reorganised along the telegraph line which crossed the Qattara track. The South African exploiting force, which had been waiting all day for action, withdrew back into the fortress.

The two battalions had suffered 317 casualties although they had captured 750 Italian prisoners along with a number of anti-tank guns.[28] In fact, the results of this attack were predictable. They had made real exertions to reach their objectives but the attack had inevitably provoked a powerful reaction.

Yet that night, 2/28th Battalion, the reserve battalion of the brigade, was

tasked with reoccupying the position on the Tel el Makh Khad ridge which
the 2/32nd and 2/43rd had lost that day. Amazingly, this manoeuvre
succeeded almost without opposition. The Australian hold on Tel el Makh
Khad ridge was consolidated and strengthened over the next few days.[29]

In an attempt to distract the Axis defenders from the 2/28th Battalion's
attack, the 2/48th Battalion was ordered to mount a raid on the twin Point
24 features at Tel el Eisa. At last light on 17 July, a raid was made by three
sections of carriers which raced forward in the fading light with considerable support from machine guns and artillery. While its distracting effect
on the southern attack was questionable, the raid caused considerable damage
and confusion amongst the Italian and German defenders. The carriers
managed to escape without serious loss. This risky operation was to have an
important sequel in October.[30]

After these multiple attacks, there were no major operations in the next
few days and an uneasy lull settled over the Alamein line. The Germans and
Italians were glad of the rest but nervous about a future blow by Eighth
Army. The pause was indeed only a lull in the storm and Auchinleck and
Dorman-Smith hoped that their next operation, grandiloquently named
Splendour, would finish Rommel and the Panzerarmee Afrika once and for
all.

NINE

Operation Splendour

Frau Rommel must have become worried about her husband in mid-July 1942. His letters to her up until then had generally been optimistic and full of fresh ideas for military exploits, but on 17 July, Rommel wrote:

> Things are going downright badly for me at the moment, at any rate, in the military sense. The enemy is using his superiority, especially in infantry, to destroy the Italian formations one by one, and the German formations are much too weak to stand alone. It's enough to make one weep.[1]

Eighth Army had chewed its way through four Italian infantry divisions by 17 July which seriously weakened the position of the Panzerarmee. This constant attrition forced Rommel to adopt new defensive methods whereby German infantry was interspersed amongst Italian formations in a process Rommel called 'corseting'. The very same procedure had been used by Wellington at Waterloo albeit under very different circumstances where British regulars had been mixed with unsteady German and Dutch troops.[2] Rommel hoped to stiffen his defences and ensure that there would be no easily identified weak points in the Panzerarmee's line.

Since he had abandoned any hope of mounting a serious offensive in the near future, Rommel decided to keep the combined armour of 15th and 21st Panzer Divisions concentrated near Deir el Shein. From this position, they were perfectly poised to meet any breakthrough in the north or centre with immediate and fierce counterattacks.

Dorman-Smith recognised that these changes to Rommel's defensive posture created new problems:

> Future Eighth Army attacks would have to be well mounted and sustained for success, and an important element in success would be i) the drawing off of the enemy armour from the point of attack; ii) direct support of the attack by British Valentines and Grants to assist the break-in and help in holding the ground gained until exploitation could begin.[3]

Yet even if Auchinleck and Dorman-Smith understood the necessity for these preconditions, they did not seem able to transmit their full intention either to the corps or divisional commanders who would execute the coming offensive.

Part of the problem was the continued uncertainty about the next operation. Eighth Army issued Operation Order No. 100 on 17 July proposing an attack that would 'destroy the enemy's army in his present location'.[4] The operation was to be called Splendour and its provisional date was 20 July. In a preparatory phase, 13 Corps was to hold its positions while gaining ground on Ruweisat ridge 'as opportunity offers'. The main attack would be launched by 30 Corps, reinforced by 23rd Armoured and 4th Light Armoured Brigades, and aim to secure a line running from Tel el Eisa through El Wishka and reaching Sanyet el Miteiriya. 13 Corps would provide maximum fire support and exploit north 'as opportunity offers'.[5] On 19 July, however, this operation order was cancelled and replaced by another, Operation Order No. 101. The intention was still to destroy the Panzerarmee but now called for an attack 'in the centre with subsidiary attacks on each flank directed against the enemy's rear'. In this version of Splendour, 13 Corps would mount the main attack with the objective of seizing Deir el Shein, throwing back the enemy's southern flank and also being prepared, in the case of a withdrawal by the Axis, of pursuing towards El Daba and Fuka. Meanwhile, 30 Corps were also to be ready to pursue and to secure Tel el Eisa along with Ruin ridge on receipt of orders.[6] Two days of planning and preparation now had to be turned to a different style of operation. Although Dorman-Smith could keep track of all the changes he was making in planning and dispositions of the army, the corps and divisional staffs could not. Coherent planning and organisation were very difficult for the commanders and their staffs who were faced with seemingly ever changing orders and intentions.

Both 13 Corps and 30 Corps were to attack simultaneously to maximise the impact in breaking the Panzerarmee's power of resistance. 13 Corps was to have the main task with the newly arrived 6th New Zealand Brigade and 5th Indian Division once again making an assault on the centre of the Axis position around the Ruweisat ridge. 6th New Zealand Brigade would make a night assault and take hold of the El Mreir depression which lay just south of Deir el Shein. Meanwhile, 5th Indian Division, using the newly arrived 161st Indian Motor Brigade, would advance along the Ruweisat ridge and capture Point 63. These infantry actions were designed to clear the way for 1st Armoured Division to 'exploit' into the rear of the Axis army. Meanwhile in the north, 26th Australian Infantry Brigade was to attack Tel el Eisa again, while 24th Australian Infantry Brigade was to make another attempt to seize Ruin ridge.[7]

The days leading up to the attack were quiet but there were nightly raids all along the front to harass the German and Italian forward positions. On 20 July, Gott wrote to Freyberg, who was still convalescing in hospital:

We have great hopes of getting a more definite success soon. I don't think the enemy are in very good shape and ours is improving daily. Your chaps are always cheerful and in good heart, and I feel very confident with them in the Corps.[8]

Gott, along with most of Eighth Army's senior commanders, could sense the weakness of the Panzerarmee and believed that a real success was possible. However, Gott's Corps conference, held on 20 July, did not run smoothly. Once again there were disagreements and misunderstandings over the level of cooperation necessary between the infantry and armour. During the meeting, Inglis believed that he was talking to Major-General Alec Gatehouse, the new commander of 1st Armoured Division, but he was in fact speaking to Brigadier A. F. Fisher who had been placed in temporary command of the division. Lumsden had been wounded on 18 July and officially replaced by Gatehouse but he was in Cairo supervising the refit of his 10th Armoured Division. It took time for Gatehouse to get up to Eighth Army and he did not reach 1st Armoured Division Headquarters until the evening of 20 July after the Corps Conference had taken taken place. Gott may have believed that Fisher, as the brigade commander responsible for supporting the New Zealanders, would be best placed to be present at the conference and organise the arrangements personally, but the unfortunate and unavoidable changes of command within 1st Armoured Division led to serious misunderstandings during the subsequent operation.

In the light of the Ruweisat operation, Inglis insisted on closer cooperation between his division and the British armour. He pointed out that the 6th New Zealand Brigade:

> would not be in a posn to defend itself against enemy armour until some hours after first light and insisted that our own armour should be on the Mreir Depression at first light ready to deal with any counter-attacks or tanks which we had over-run.[9]

Although Inglis perhaps exaggerated the length of time after first light that the infantry would be vulnerable, he was quite right to insist on armoured support. Fisher refused to place any armour under the command of 2nd New Zealand Division but he did offer to provide extra liaison officers to be attached to 6th New Zealand Brigade Headquarters. Inglis also pressed for the armoured division's reconnaissance tanks to be up with the leading infantry and Gott agreed to this modification. Fisher gave Inglis an 'assurance that his tanks would not at any stage be more than half a mile from my infantry'.[10] Inglis believed that the:

> Role of Armd Div was made perfectly clear by Corps Comd –
> (a) to attack on our reaching our objective and minefield cleared.

(b) to closely support and frustrate any counter-attack against 6 NZ
    Bde[11]

Already there were deep, albeit hidden, flaws inherent in the operation.
Inglis had accepted the role of the armour and the assurances of Fisher
thinking he was dealing with the commander of 1st Armoured Division
when he was not. This fact alone led to confusion. Gott had made the
armour's role 'perfectly clear' in conference to Fisher but not to Gatehouse.[12]
When the new commander of 1st Armoured Division arrived, he was pitched
into a major operation without sufficient time to grasp the details of the
armour's role before the attack began.

Once again, Inglis accepted considerable risk on behalf of his division.
The task of 6th New Zealand Brigade was to capture the eastern end of
the El Mreir depression after a long night march and 'to breach the minefield and roll up the skin of Anti-tank guns working from South to North
along the enemy forward area'.[13] Its basic task was to clear the way for the
armour but it was understood that 'unless the armour moved quickly and
hit hard, one stripped brigade could NOT hold such wide areas against
full scale counter attack'.[14] Yet assistance from armour could be expected
only after the brigade had reached its objective and the deep minefield in
front of the Axis positions cleared. These preconditions might have
appeared simple in the conference, but both were more difficult to achieve
than either Inglis or Fisher estimated. Both were to result in real delays
and confusion.

With the minefield gapped and the Axis anti-tank-gun screen breached,
the next phase of Splendour would be launched on the assumption that 6th
New Zealand Brigade held the El Mreir depression and 161st Indian Motor
Brigade held Point 63. With these two positions on its flanks cleared, the
newly arrived 23rd Armoured Brigade would drive forward six miles and
push through into the rear areas of the Panzerarmee. The brigade was to
reach and hold a position around Point 59, which lay between Deir el Shein
and the northern escarpment of El Mreir. The idea was to place a British
armoured brigade, with both its flanks protected, in the very centre of the
Afrika Korps' position.[15] If this position could be held against the inevitable
German counterattack, then Rommel would have little choice but to withdraw his army to save it from destruction. The third phase of Splendour
would see 1st Armoured Division debouching from this breach and heading
north east to take the Miteiriya ridge from the rear, or, if Rommel began a
withdrawal, mounting a full-scale pursuit to Fuka.

Gatehouse later related to Liddell Hart important details concerning the
role of 23rd Armoured Brigade on 22 July. Gatehouse maintained that, 'The
only "briefing" I had was from Straffer on the evening of 20th July, and he
dealt almost exclusively with the operation which involved the attack of 23rd

Armd. Bde., on Mreir.'[16] However, in briefing Gatehouse, Gott also revealed that he was not happy with the proposed role for 23rd Armoured Brigade:

> Straffer told me that he did not care about the plan much, and when I heard it, I did not think much of it either, and said so. Straffer gave me his promise that (a) if Pt. 63 was not captured by the Ind. Bde, and (b) if the minefield was not lifted, that the attack of 23 Armd. Bde was off.[17]

It is not surprising that Gott was unhappy about this part of the plan. Sending an inexperienced armoured brigade on a six-mile advance into the teeth of the German defences was to accept considerable risk. Gatehouse extracted an important promise from Gott, that 23rd Armoured Brigade would not be launched on its deep attack unless its northern flank, at the least, was secure and the minefield properly gapped. Gatehouse tried to give the inexperienced formation the best chance of success but the operation would be fraught with danger.

Meanwhile, a full-scale row broke out between Ramsden and Morshead. When Morshead learned the roles allotted for his brigades as part of Splendour, he 'suddenly demurred'.[18] 9th Australian Division was expected to make two attacks in three different directions. In the first phase, 26th Australian Infantry Brigade was ordered to attack the Tel el Eisa feature, which had proved so difficult to consolidate upon in the past, with 2/23rd and 2/48th Battalions. At the same time 2/24th Battalion was to push forward along the coast to take the next area of high ground, known as 'Ring Contour 25',[19] lying to the west of Point 33. Given the necessity of holding onto the vital ground around Point 33, these attacks could only be made in weak company strength – two companies each from the 2/24th and 2/48th Battalions and the 2/23rd Battalion less one company. Meanwhile, 24th Australian Brigade was to make a two-phase attack to reach the Miteiriya ridge. In the first phase, the 2/32nd Battalion would seize Point 22 on Tel el Makh Khad ridge, which remained in Axis hands, and thus secure the assembly areas for the second phase. 2/28th Battalion, supported by 50th Royal Tank Regiment which was detached from 23rd Armoured Brigade for the purpose, would capture Point 21 on the Miteiriya ridge and consolidate its positions.[20] These attacks in fact resembled a bomb burst, going out in all directions with none of sufficient strength to deal properly with the opposition. Such divergent attacks would be difficult to support with artillery, hence the need for a second phase for which it was necessary to redeploy the field artillery for the attack on Ruin ridge. The delay would inevitably alert the Axis defence and ensure that 50th Royal Tank Regiment and 2/28th Battalion met a warm reception.

Morshead disliked the plan and had a stormy two-hour conference with Ramsden on the morning of 21 July in which he 'objected strongly to scope of my attack . . . and several changes in timings'.[21] Morshead 'stood on his constitutional rights and duties insisting on referring to his government before agreeing to attack'.[22] It was after lunch that Auchinleck and Dorman-Smith visited Ramsden and learned of Morshead's objections and his refusal to budge. Ramsden explained that he had tried 'to stop this bloody-mindedness without result' and that Morshead's main objection was 'no confidence in our armour'.[23] This was too much for Auchinleck, who exploded with anger. With difficulty, Ramsden managed to persuade him not to have Morshead report immediately, which might have resulted in an ugly scene and a complete breakdown in the relations between the two men. Instead, he invited Morshead to tea at 30 Corps Headquarters, thus giving Auchinleck time to cool down.

Auchinleck seems to have believed that Morshead objected to his orders because his division, after a fine fighting performance, 'had had about enough of it'.[24] Morshead's diary gives a very different impression. He argued with Ramsden and Auchinleck on the basis that:

> I did not like our plan because of wide dispersions and difficulty to support and pointed out that our immediate objectives were much more difficult than realised by Army and Corps. Commander-in-Chief according to Ramsden was very annoyed and perturbed but he did not show it. He stressed that he realised he must have a willing commander. I stressed that my concern was a task which was reasonably certain of success and could be held and supported, and that my job was to minimise casualties.[25]

Morshead's objections to his division's role could well have been echoed by 2nd New Zealand Division, 5th Indian Division and 23rd Armoured Brigade. They were well founded and he was right to argue the point. Nonetheless, the episode reveals the depth of misunderstanding which had developed between Auchinleck and one of his most capable divisional commanders. Contrary to Auchinleck's assumptions, Morshead was in fact quite willing to engage in further attacks but he wanted those attacks to be well planned, properly supported and far less ambitious. Unfortunately, after persuasion and some flattery, Morshead backed down and agreed to the attacks.

The tense interview was witnessed by Dorman-Smith and his reaction to the discussion revealed his inability to understand the pressures that both Auchinleck and Morshead were facing. Dorman-Smith mused that:

> People who know how to make the infantile do the right thing have a sort of nursery maid genius. Perhaps to be a successful nursery maid is to display considerable genius, but then the maid knows she is dealing with minds which lack the facts on which to base right action and the mental strength to apply what facts they do possess. To be leadable seems to me to betray mental weak-

ness. To lead the leadable seems merely to exploit a weakness which one possesses in some degree oneself.[26]

Dorman-Smith, who actually drafted most of Eighth Army orders, seems to have held many of the subordinate commanders of Eighth Army in contempt with little or no understanding of the responsibility the divisional commanders felt for the men under their command.

The misunderstandings and arguments reflected in Eighth Army's planning process were as nothing next to the problems facing 23rd Armoured Brigade. At the very least, the men of 2nd New Zealand Division and the armoured brigades of 1st Armoured Division were hardened desert campaigners who understood the dangers, risks and opportunities facing them in battle. 23rd Armoured Brigade, on the other hand, was entirely new to the desert and to war. This brigade was a Territorial formation composed of three armoured regiments from the Royal Tank Regiment[27] which had been training in England since 1939.

23rd Armoured Brigade, which formed part of the 8th Armoured Division, had the misfortune to arrive at Suez on 6 July after two months at sea, during the crisis of the fighting on the Alamein line. Its sister brigade, 24th Armoured, had been scheduled to reach Suez earlier, but its ship had developed engine trouble and was still at Durban in South Africa. As soon as his men and tanks had been disembarked, Brigadier Lawrence Misa was informed that his unit 'was to be ready to move to the Western Desert on 15 July'.[28]

There was a general perception within Middle East Command that the level of training received by units in the United Kingdom was insufficient and inappropriate for desert conditions. Unfortunately, units which embarked on ships at a British port generally had no idea whether they would be landing in Egypt, Iraq, India or Burma and Brigadier Misa had not known until 30 June that his brigade would disembark in the Middle East. This made a realistic training programme which was specific to a particular theatre impossible in the United Kingdom. It also meant that Middle East Command believed that every unit, after disembarkation, required a period of at least a month for full acclimatisation and desert training.

Yet even before the brigade had disembarked, Churchill was pressuring General Headquarters Middle East to fling 23rd Armoured Brigade into battle.[29] Churchill had always taken a proprietary interest in the armoured brigades sent to Egypt, and he had demanded immediate action in battle for every fresh armoured brigade since the 'Tigercub' convoy of tanks sent in 1940. In this instance, Auchinleck desperately needed a fresh armoured formation which could lift some of the burden from the exhausted fragments which had fought through Gazala and were still in the line during July. A new armoured brigade appeared to be exactly what was required to exploit the success which Splendour might achieve. 23rd Armoured Brigade would be committed to battle before it was ready.

A major controversy immediately developed over the state of 23rd Armoured Brigade's tanks. None of them was ready for immediate action. German and Italian tanks bound for the desert were transported by rail to an Italian port, loaded on board ship and then taken on the short crossing to Tripoli. German tanks could and, indeed, did drive straight from the docks into action in the desert. Churchill never understood why 'his' tanks could not do the same. This was yet another example of his almost complete ignorance of the realities of military operations. In the case of tanks sent from Britain to Egypt, each and every one had travelled across 15,000 miles of ocean in all kinds of weather. Sea air penetrated the ships' hatches to corrode wireless batteries and other vulnerable items; the gear lever housing on Valentines was particularly susceptible to such corrosion.[30] And even if nothing worse befell the tank, it would not have been maintained for at least two months; its batteries would have run down and, in the case of Valentines powered by diesel engines, the fuel left in its engine would have gummed up.[31]

The officers and men of 23rd Armoured Brigade had taken good care of their tanks in the United Kingdom, with the majority of them overhauled twice in the previous six months. Like the impatient Prime Minister, they expected that their trusted and pampered chargers would be ready for immediate use. But when the tanks were admitted to No. 4 Base Ordnance Workshop, fitters found that the Valentines' engines required overhaul and a whole host of modifications for service in the desert. All this meant that very few tanks were being released by the workshop. Meanwhile, many of the crews had stowed all their personal equipment, along with a full complement of issued equipment, on the tanks. When the tanks emerged from the workshop much equipment was missing. When Brigadier Misa complained about the situation, Major-General Richard McCreery, the Major-General Armoured Forces at General Headquarters Middle East, who had commanded 8th Armoured Division during 1941, visited the workshop to sort out the controversy.[32] Eventually, he insisted that the brigade take the first 164 tanks that came out of the workshop. Among these many were unexamined and missing much of their essential equipment. Most importantly, the majority of wireless sets in the brigade were not 'tropicalised', their batteries and valves unsuitable for the hot conditions in the desert. And even those that were not faulty had not been properly 'netted in' before the brigade was thrown into action.[33]

All the tanks and vehicles for the brigade were issued by 14 July and three days later the brigade had moved up to Hammam, whence it went forward to take up a position south of Ruweisat ridge on 21 July. The crews had had no time to orientate themselves to the seemingly empty desert.[34] Fresh from England, they did not know how to find a hull-down position in the small folds of ground in the desert, how to cope with dust clouds or how to navigate properly in desert conditions. One officer of the brigade later stated that their level of knowledge concerning desert fighting was so poor that:

> Although we saw regular pamphlets about the German Army these gave little idea of the actuality. We were told nothing about their anti-tank guns. Until 22 July 1942 I had no idea that they had a gun that could pierce the armour of a Valentine![35]

Quite clearly the training the brigade had received in England was unrealistic and insufficient to prepare it for the task ahead. What was worse was that the brigade had been trained as part of 8th Armoured Division to fulfil the role of cruiser tanks. Because of the shortage of tanks in Britain, the Valentine, although designed as an infantry tank, had been pressed into service as a 'cruiser' even though it was quite unsuitable for the role. It was well understood in Egypt that only the Grant tank could now properly fulfil the role of main battle tank, but 23rd Armoured Brigade was left with the mistaken idea that its Valentines were still appropriate. There had been time for only one hurried exercise which practised the forming up of one armoured regiment with the brigade headquarters, and demonstrated an attack by the tanks on a 'lightly defended position under cover of 25-pr smoke-screen'.[36] Tank crews serving in either 2nd or 22nd Armoured Brigade could have told their new comrades that no position held by the Afrika Korps was ever 'lightly defended'. Some effort was made to teach the brigade the realities of desert combat. Lieutenant-Colonel G. P. B. 'Pip' Roberts, the commander of the veteran 3rd Royal Tank Regiment, knew many members of 23rd Armoured Brigade and went down to Cairo to give them a lecture on 'Tank fighting in the desert'. He related that:

> There was just one little snag about my lecture. The units were equipped with Valentine tanks, which were vastly different to a Grant tank, being armed with a 2-pounder instead of a 75mm and a 37mm. I'd never fought just with a 2-pounder. I quickly had to do a bit of thinking and, since they would not have their own HE support, stressed the importance of close links and understanding with the gunners.[37]

While Roberts was an experienced tank officer, it might have been better had a member of 44th Royal Tank Regiment, who were equipped with Valentines and serving with 9th Australian Division, given a talk to the assembled newcomers. Misa protested that his unit was not ready to go into action but he was overruled.[38] One regiment, 50th Royal Tank Regiment, was detached from the brigade and sent to 30 Corps to act as infantry support for the coming Australian attack on Ruin ridge. The regiment's war diary recorded its disappointment that it was going to be used as an infantry tank regiment when it had trained in cruiser tactics.

23rd Armoured Brigade was not the only formation which had to prepare hurriedly for action. The 13 Corps Conference was held on 20 July and the 2nd New Zealand Division held its own conference on 21 July, the morning before the battle was due to start. This gave very little time to fix all the details for the coming attack, and no time to iron out any potential problems. Brigadier Fisher, now in his proper role as commander of 2nd Armoured Brigade, attended the conference to sort out the details of the support he would give to the advancing New Zealand infantry, but again an impasse was reached. Clifton noted that Fisher 'said his 22 [sic] Armd Bde could not fight in moonlight and reluctant to move in it. Asked for Regt under my Comd to come round outside minefield . . . but they would not play.'[39]

Fisher's reluctance was understandable. Tank crews, wearing their wireless headsets and with the tank's engine running, were deaf to noises around them. At night in the dark, with the limited vision imposed by their vehicles, tank crews were also blind. This made any movement at night hazardous unless the route had been well marked with lights and scouted ahead of time for any potential problems. Since none of these essentials could be accomplished in the few hours left before the attack, Fisher refused to move his tanks at night. However, this made close tank support for the New Zealand Division impossible, even though Clifton and Inglis knew this was essential to protect them from any German reaction at dawn.

One of the critical elements in the entire plan rested on the ability of the New Zealand engineers to make a number of gaps in the 300-yard deep minefield which was known to exist in front of the Axis positions. 8 Field Company was to clear a route along each of the advancing battalion axes and trucks of armed anti-tank mines were to follow brigade headquarters to consolidate the position. Three 40-foot gaps were to be cleared for 24 Battalion and brigade headquarters, while others were to be made for 26 Battalion. Yet Brigadier Clifton of 6th New Zealand Brigade only received his orders a few hours before the attack was to begin. This meant that the subordinate formations, including the sappers, had very little time for detailed planning or ensuring that every unit understood the plan and their part in it. There was no standard mine-lifting and lane-marking drill which was understood by all the sappers, let alone the other formations, and this was bound to lead to misunderstandings. The New Zealand Engineer History commented, 'Judged by later standards, El Mreir was hastily mounted and loosely organised.'[40]

Although this key element of the plan was insufficiently organised because of the pressures of time, the artillery plan for Splendour formed an encouraging contrast with Bacon. This time, the New Zealand infantry would not outrun the support of their guns and elaborate preparations were made to ensure that the opening bombardment would suppress the Axis defence. All three New Zealand Field Regiments, along with the guns of 64th Medium Regiment and a Royal Horse Artillery battery, would cover the advance of 6th Brigade. The initial bombardment entailed the firing of 2,400 rounds of 25-pounder ammunition; across the whole front of 13 Corps, nine field regiments and one medium regiment in total were taking part.

Splendour was also the first Eighth Army operation which deliberately included the RAF's medium bombers in the tactical plan. During 21 July, the tasks for air support were to attack specific targets which had been identified. In the evening on 21 July, three-quarters of the air effort was to be devoted to the area around Deir el Shein and Point 63 in an attempt to suppress and destroy the Axis artillery and forward positions in this vital area. During the night, the area to the west of El Mreir and Qaret el Abd was to be plastered with bombs to hinder Axis reinforcements and to cause as much disruption as possible to any Axis counterattacks. During 22 July, the focus of air attack would shift to the Miteiriya ridge in order to prepare the way for the Australian attack on the position.[41]

During the day and into the night of 21–22 July, the RAF made continuous and very heavy raids on the agreed targets. 15th Panzer Division noted on 21 July:

> All day long enemy bombers and fighters were over our area, particularly 21 and 15 Pz Divs, on a scale hardly ever before seen. It looked as if the enemy was trying to knock out our HQ and guns in preparation for an attack.[42]

However, when the attacks continued into the night, 15th Panzer Division drew the wrong conclusion. It was believed that heavy night bombing would endanger a large-scale offensive when in fact the bombing areas had been carefully planned so that they would not disrupt the attack. The most serious consequence of the raids was that all communication between Afrika Korps Headquarters and its subordinate formations was disrupted and it took a number of hours before it was restored.[43]

161st Indian Motor Brigade had been transferred from 7th Armoured Division to 5th Indian Division for the attack along Ruweisat ridge. The brigade was, like the 18th Indian Brigade before it, fresh from Iraq and consisted of 1/1st Punjab, 1/2nd Punjab, and 3/7th Rajput Regiments with a battery of six-pounder guns. Its task was to capture Deir el Shein and Point 63 on Ruweisat ridge. At 20.30 hours on 21 July, the brigade mounted its attack but 1/1st Punjab were held up by intense fire in front of Point 63. The 3/7th Rajput Regiments managed to break into Deir el Shein with a bayonet charge. The Indian soldiers reached the gun emplacements of 15th Panzer Division but were counterattacked and eventually ejected.[44] The regiment lost two companies in the attack although they had caused great concern in the Afrika Korps. Unfortunately, even with the efforts of 161st Indian

Brigade to clear the northern shoulder of the attack, Point 63 remained in German hands. At 01.50 hours on 22 July, 5th Indian Division reported to Gott that the attack had not secured Point 63. He then ordered the division to capture Point 63 'in conjunction with the tank attack of 23 Armd. Bde'.[45] This, however, diverged from the agreed plan which was that 23rd Armoured Brigade would not attack unless its northern flank was secured first.

At 17.30 hours, the guns of 13 Corps began the preparatory bombardment and added their noise to that of the aerial bombardment. When the guns of 2nd New Zealand Division began their fire programme in support of the infantry at 20.45 hours, the effect was impressive. The New Zealand Division's War Diary stated:

> It was truly formidable. As the Div Comd and staff watched from G office in the fading twilight of nightfall, we could see the dim skyline darkened with the pall of dust and smoke from the mass of heavy arty concentrations. It was a memorable sight and the noise of gunfire terrific. We had now to wait for news of the progress of the attack.[46]

As the officers at divisional headquarters waited for news, the battalions of 6th New Zealand Brigade began their advance towards El Mreir. Initially the advance went well and each of the battalions made good time towards the objective. 26 Battalion, on the brigade's right flank, had the shortest distance to cover but, owing to the widely separated axes of advance for each battalion, would be out of contact with the rest of the brigade until the objective was reached.[47] The battalion reached the main minefield after 50 minutes and, when a booby trap was tripped, a hail of fire descended on the leading infantry from the German infantry who were dug in on the rim of the depression.[48] The troops ducked and the fire passed harmlessly over their heads. The leading platoons then charged down into the depression and overran most of the German infantry posts. Unfortunately, in crossing the depression the battalion fought its way into the middle of the 8th Panzer Regiment leaguer. The infantry attacked and destroyed some of the tanks with sticky bombs but the others moved off in the dark. Once all supplies of sticky bombs had been exhausted, the battalion had little choice but to hold its positions against an increasing volume of mortar, machine- and tank-gun fire.[49] Unfortunately, when the battalion transport drove up through the minefield, which had been gapped on time by the sappers, the column veered off course and two carriers and an ammunition truck were blown up on mines. Soon, attracted by the pyrotechnics of the blazing ammunition truck, Axis gunners brought down heavy shellfire which destroyed many other trucks. The transport column halted in the confusion and could not get through to the battalion; only four two-pounder anti-tank gun portees reached the battalion some time before dawn.[50] All attempts to contact either brigade headquarters or 24 Battalion, which should have been on the left flank, had failed and the enemy fire was increasing all the time. Lieutenant-Colonel Jan Peart realised that his battalion, without a proper anti-tank defence, would be overrun as soon as there was enough light for the tank crews to see. He decided to withdraw from the exposed position. Just before dawn, the battalion pulled out in two columns and reached the relative safety of 5th New Zealand Brigade lines.[51]

Meanwhile, 24 Battalion had advanced from the start line in good order, but became badly disorganised during its advance. Numerous enemy posts, held by III Battalion of the 115th Panzergrenadier Regiment, were encountered on the 6,000-yard advance and the result of this confused fighting through an area littered with sangars, wire and mines meant that Lieutenant-Colonel Greville reached his objective with just 15 men. Sixty more men from various platoons and companies found their way to the objective over the next hour.[52] Meanwhile, the engineer parties worked hard to clear gaps in the minefield under heavy fire. The task was more difficult than planned because the minefield, part of which had been laid by 18th Indian Brigade in June, was 600 yards wide. The sappers searched every yard of the three gaps with mine detectors and cleared hundreds of mines. Eventually, three 40-foot gaps were cleared and the battalion transport moved up to join the infantry. 24 Battalion thus had its full complement of four six-pounder and seven two-pounder anti-tank guns, along with mortars and machine guns to consolidate the position.[53]

25 Battalion followed, in echelon, to the south west of 24 Battalion and met only light resistance on the way to the objective. Its C Company swung left to deal with heavy fire on the flank and lost touch with the rest of the battalion. It overshot the objective and continued into the rear of the Axis positions. The company eventually halted because RAF flares were lighting up the desert – and because they could see tanks moving in to attack them. Eventually, after these adventures, the company withdrew back onto 5th New Zealand Brigade without ever contacting the rest of the battalion. Meanwhile, the main body of 25 Battalion reached its objective at 01.00 hours and was joined by its transport column.[54]

Brigade headquarters lost wireless contact with the advancing battalions early in the attack and found that the minefield had not been completely gapped on its axis. Eventually, the headquarters found the 24 Battalion gap and followed this through the minefield. At the other end of the gap, groups of 18 Battalion were found withdrawing and under pursuit by five tanks. Clifton detailed three six-pounder portees to guard the gap and these were able to drive away the marauding German tanks. Brigade headquarters finally reached 24 Battalion at 03.30 hours and Clifton ordered 25 Battalion forward into the depression to help in the formidable task of clearing it and establishing a firm defence. Although repeated attempts were made by the liaison officers to call up armoured support, none was forthcoming.[55] By the time brigade headquarters arrived and distributed the reserve support weapons amongst the companies, the moon had set and it was impossible to site them properly in the darkness. Most of the anti-tank guns were left on their portees.

While the New Zealand Division had been plagued by communication failures during Operation Bacon, much effort had been expended to ensure that this did not happen during Splendour. Just before midnight, the divisional headquarters received a report from 26 Battalion stating that it was on its objective but had encountered tanks on the way and that there were still tanks in the depression. The GSO 1 immediately phoned 13 Corps and said it was 'absolutely essential our tanks are on the edge of EL MREIR by first light to deal with enemy tanks milling around in the depression'.[56] At 01.25 hours, Inglis reported to 13 Corps but was less emphatic about the need for armoured support. He mentioned that 'Our 26 Bn is on its objective but they are worried as to the situation in the morning'. At 02.15 hours, the GSO 1 spoke to 2nd Armoured Brigade and restated that it was 'essential that our tanks are at the depression by first light'. Even though 2nd Armoured Brigade had been detailed to frustrate any attack on the New Zealand Brigade at first light, the staff officer of the armoured brigade asked the New Zealanders to 'ring 1 Armd Div to explain necessity for the Bde to move. GSO.1 stressed the urgency of the matter by saying he did not want a repetition of what occurred at RUWEISAT Ridge.'[57]

This duplication of requests should not have been necessary and gave a hint of what was to come. Five minutes later, it was reiterated to 1st Armoured Division that armoured support had to be in the depression at first light to deal with the remaining enemy armour. Inglis then spoke again to 13 Corps outlining the situation. The staff officers at New Zealand divisional headquarters had certainly given a clear and accurate picture of the situation to 13 Corps, 1st Armoured Division and 2nd Armoured Brigade. Not surprisingly, the division 'wanted no repetition of what happened at RUWEISAT and were doing all we could to <u>ensure</u> the armoured co-operation that had been laid on'.[58]

At 02.35 hours 6th New Zealand Brigade was able to report to division that both its leading battalions were on their objective. It appeared to Clifton that 'the objective seemed secure provided any enemy tank attack at first light could be dealt with by our armour. 18 Bn also met tanks but were quite happy. 25 Bn was up in behind the leading Bns of 6 Bde.'[59] The safety of the New Zealand infantry battalions now in the El Mreir Depression rested on the ability of the British armour to reach them before daylight and protect them from the force of German tanks, infantry and artillery which remained in the depression.

However, 1st Armoured Division's orders to 2nd Armoured Brigade placed a very different interpretation on the situation. 2nd Armoured Brigade was contacted at 02.00 hours to ensure that 'they are to be in a posn from which they can deal with a counter-attack by tanks'. No mention was made of actually moving forward to link up with the New Zealand troops. The New Zealand Division had expected that the British armour would roll forward on receipt of its reports but nothing of the sort happened. 2nd Armoured Brigade remained 'prepared' to act, and 'prepared' to meet a counterattack, but none of this would help 6th New Zealand Brigade deal with German tanks.

Meanwhile, the gunners of the New Zealand Field Regiments waited anxiously for the calls from their forward observation officers so that they could begin to protect the infantry in the depression. No calls came in. By noon there was still no word and the gunners had to busy themselves with predicted fire at the second objective.[60] The gunners knew that something had gone wrong but could do little about it.

6th New Zealand Brigade had entered the lion's den. Both the panzer regiments of Afrika Korps were concentrated around the El Mreir depression and it did not take long for the commanders of both formations to organise a counterattack. At 04.30 hours, with the desert still in darkness and only the first flickering of light in the eastern sky, the panzers moved in for the kill. 25 Battalion had just arrived to support 24 Battalion and, with its transport still concentrated around brigade headquarters, the first German tanks opened fire on the mass of New Zealand troops and transport. At least 20 Panzer IIIs had moved into hull-down positions along the northern edge of the depression and began firing blind into the darkness. 21st Panzer Division tersely recorded its successful counterattack:

> 0612 hrs Message from Pz Regt that the situation is confused. Friend and foe are badly intermingled. In the southern part of the depression the Pz. Regt bumps into a large enemy grp consisting of A/Tk guns, tanks and arty and engages them.
>
> 0619 hrs The enemy infantry tries to escape, other units surrender.[61]

Almost immediately, the German fire hit an anti-tank gun portee which burst into flames and, in the light of the fire, the German tanks began picking off the tanks of the liaison officers. Once these were destroyed, the tanks turned their attentions onto the anti-tank guns. The gunners, most of them still mounted on their portees, were almost helpless:

> Even before dawn the enemy brought down crushing fire and some of the 6-pounders fired at gun flashes, some of them from tank guns. The enemy was in all directions and the gun crews could do no more than fire furiously until either they or their guns were disabled – a matter of minutes at the most.[62]

The portees made vulnerable targets and most were knocked out or their crews hit by the hail of machine-gun fire from the German tanks. The area was badly congested and casualties were heavy. The artillery observer officers found that their wireless trucks were hit early in the attack and, anyway, in the darkness there was no way for them to clearly identify targets for the guns to fire upon. Once the anti-tank guns had all been knocked out, the German tanks simply rolled down into the depression, hosing the area with machine-gun fire. The New Zealand infantry stood no chance against this threat and, although some tried to escape, most had no choice but to surrender.

Brigadier Clifton attempted to escape in his jeep but this was quickly knocked out by machine-gun fire. He ripped off his badges of rank and spent the rest of the day helping with the wounded. Just like Burroughs at Ruweisat, Clifton was able to escape during the night and relate the sorry debacle to Inglis at divisional headquarters. Another two New Zealand battalions, along with their supporting weapons, had been overrun and many men captured. 6th New Zealand Brigade had made a deep penetration into the Axis lines and paid heavily for the achievement: 55 officers and 825 men became casualties, the majority of them captured.[63]

Clifton believed that British armour did not intervene until 08.00 hours. In fact, 2nd Armoured Brigade attempted to support 6th New Zealand Brigade earlier in the day. By 06.35 hours, 9th Lancers reported that 15 German tanks had been spotted moving south east to attack 'NZ troops'.[64] On receipt on this report, 6th Royal Tank Regiment finally moved its Grant squadron to attack. However, the tanks came under heavy anti-tank-gun fire from the El Mreir Depression 'which we had presumed to have been eliminated last night'.[65] After losing three tanks to this fire, the squadron withdrew to its original position. At no point were 6th Royal Tank Regiment, or any of the rest of 2nd Armoured Brigade, close enough to assist the New Zealanders. Indeed, even by the time that 9th Lancers reported movement, the resistance of 6th New Zealand Brigade was almost at an end.

At 06.50 hours, 2nd New Zealand Division Headquarters received 'the first news . . . of what we had feared – enemy tanks were attacking and our own armour did not seem to be there'.[66] Inglis immediately rang up 1st Armoured Division for an explanation, but Gatehouse claimed that 'he had NOT been asked for assistance'. Just as puzzling was the response of 6th Royal Tank Regiment to Clifton's later investigation of what had happened to the liaison officer's report: 'there seemed no trace of it being given to the CO in action, or referred to Comd 2 Armd Bde. As one result, the first elements of 6RTR to move out in support did so at 0815 hrs – 3 hrs too late.'[67]

With the knowledge that yet another brigade under his command had been overrun by German tanks, and in the face of temporising by Gatehouse, Inglis was 'angry almost beyond words, and swore that he would never again place faith in the British armour'.[68] Operation Splendour was quickly turning into a debacle, but even with the losses suffered by 161st Indian Brigade and 6th New Zealand Brigade, the sum of disaster was far from complete.

At 06.25 hours, Gatehouse spoke to Gott by radio telephone and reminded him 'of his promise about Pt. 63 (which was not yet captured) and the mine-field (which was not yet properly cleared)'.[69] Gatehouse suggested that the attack of 23rd Armoured Brigade should be cancelled but Gott replied that:

> he remembered his promise but that he was being pressed and felt that the attack must go on. I protested strongly and reminded him that he had never broken a promise to me concerning the employment of armour in all our battles together. He said he was very sorry, but he had to do so now and the attack must go in.
>
> This was the first time in all my contact with Straffer that he gave me the impression of being a very tired man in two minds, whether to carry out an attack or not.[70]

1st Armoured Division War Diary mentions 'Y' reports of German anxiety which might have encouraged Gott to press the attack.[71] However, given that Gott had not been overly impressed with the plan of attack in the first place, this seems unlikely. It is more likely that Gott felt he had to act to support the New Zealanders and to carry out the Army Commander's intention of a decisive attack even if the moment for one had disappeared.

The staff officers in 1st Armoured Division were now alert to the danger that 23rd Armoured Brigade was about to mount an attack over an uncleared minefield. At 06.55 hours, Lieutenant-Colonel Peake suggested that a post-ponement of the attack might be necessary but it was not until 07.50 hours that an order was sent out by 1st Armoured Division, after consultation with 13 Corps, which shifted the centre line of 23rd Armoured Brigade south in an attempt to bypass the minefield. The brigade was ordered to send 'recce ahead looking for mines, and if the mines were insurmountable to treat them as an intermediary objective'.[72] These tactics were standard procedure for the more experienced 2nd and 22nd Armoured Brigades when faced with minefields and the reason why the New Zealanders complained bitterly of their undue caution. However, the faulty radios of 23rd Armoured Brigade never received the order which was issued just ten minutes before the attack began. The failure of 1st Armoured Division's staff work meant that 23rd Armoured Brigade attacked along its original centre line with neither flank secured and drove straight into the minefield.

As 23rd Armoured Brigade prepared for its attack each tank jettisoned its long-range fuel tank. This left three neat lines of discarded fuel tanks marking where the tanks of each regiment had been. At 08.00 hours, the 23rd Armoured Brigade with a total of 106 tanks,[73] formed up with 46th Royal Tank Regiment on the left and 40th Royal Tank Regiment on the right, began

its attack. Each regiment had adopted the narrow column formation in anticipation of driving through the minefield gaps. The tanks motored forward at
10 mph for over 2,000 yards before they came under anti-tank-gun fire. Soon
afterwards, the leading troops of both regiments drove straight onto the Axis
minefield before they found the 30-yard gaps which had been cut by the New
Zealand sappers. As they reached the minefield, the Axis anti-tank-gun fire
and artillery fire increased in intensity. Brigadier Misa decided to send B
Squadron of 46th Royal Tank Regiment south in an attempt to find a way
round the minefield but the squadron soon lost contact with brigade headquarters. The driver of the squadron commander's tank returned the next
day and was able to relate the fate of the unit: every tank had been knocked
out by anti-tank guns. Eventually, both regiments squeezed through the minefield gaps under constant artillery and anti-tank-gun fire and drove forward
to their objectives at Point 59 and the escarpment of El Mreir.

The first that 21st Panzer Division knew of the attack was an urgent
order for the Panzer Regiment to return immediately to its battle assembly
point: 'the enemy has broken through in the sector of I and II/Pz Gren
Regt 104 and, with 12 to 15 tanks, races past in a westerly direction at a
distance of 800 metres'.[74] The attack of 23rd Armoured Brigade caused panic
amongst the German units facing their onslaught. The Valentine tanks of
40th Royal Tank Regiment overran the positions of II Battalion 104th
Panzergrenadier Regiment without realising it and motored on to within
yards of the Afrika Korps Battle Headquarters. Amid scenes of utter panic
and confusion, the staff expected to be overrun any minute and began to
pull out.[75] However, although the headquarters were in confusion, small
groups of German soldiers continued to fight. Günther Halm, a gunlayer
in 104th Panzergrenadier Regiment, along with his gun crew, continued to
fire his 76.2mm Russian gun and knocked out nine of the attacking Valentines.
Halm won the Knight's Cross for his actions on this day.[76]

Soon, the tanks of 21st Panzer Division moved in to counterattack the
Valentines but there was still confusion as the artillery and supporting units
of the division were pulling out:

At this moment Maj. V. Heuduck sends the following W/T message to Corps:
'We shall do the job alright!' This message calmed down the Corps and the
Army, both of whom had looked upon the situation as hopeless. This message
also re-establishes the fighting spirit of the Div.[77]

The drive forward by the tanks of 21st Panzer Division began to restore the
situation and soon the isolated British tanks were under real pressure. By
10.30 hours, the brigade had 15 tanks left and only 12 of these had working
guns. The motor rifle companies of 7th Rifle Brigade, along with the anti-
tank-gun troops of the brigade, were now deployed 1,500 yards from the

objective, but Misa decided to withdraw while there was still time. The withdrawal took place under 'intense fire from Mk III and IV tanks, arty and A. Tk guns and over the minefield'.[78] By 12.30 hours, the shattered remnants of 23rd Armoured Brigade withdrew through 2nd Armoured Brigade. The survivors of the brigade:

> spent the night of 22nd/23rd July in a kind of shock. Round us were the lines of 'jettison' fuel tanks, but only six actual Valentines with them. We had all the fitters, storemen, clerks and drivers . . . but hardly any tank crews.[79]

That night 21st Panzer Division leaguered with just 22 tanks but had the satisfaction of knowing that, along with its anti-tank guns, they had smashed an entire British armoured brigade.[80] 23rd Armoured Brigade had ceased to exist; a composite squadron of seven tanks was all that was left of the 106 tanks that had advanced that morning.[81]

At the same time as 23rd Armoured Brigade began its doomed charge, the 1/2nd Punjab Regiment, the reserve battalion of 161st Indian Motor Brigade, was launched in another attempt to take Point 63. The battalion managed to take the position, which was in its hands by 09.30 hours, but then was forced back by heavy shelling. It was not surprising that the Punjabi regiment could not hold the ground; like the rest of Ruweisat ridge, Point 63 was 'an exposed and very stony feature, and impossible to consolidate in a short period'.[82] Additionally, the Indians were exposed to fire from Deir el Shein and El Mreir which, had Splendour gone according to plan, would have been in Eighth Army hands. During the rest of the day, the 1/2nd Punjab seized the crest of Point 63 another two times, but on each occasion the men were forced back by intense shell and machine-gun fire. The capture of Point 63 had by now assumed an importance which, with the abject failure of Splendour, was inappropriate.

By the afternoon of 22 July, 161st Indian Motor Brigade had suffered heavy casualties and 'was so disorganised that no further advance by them was possible'.[83] However, instead of abandoning the task, 13 Corps insisted that 5th Indian Division make another attempt, using '9 Bde for this task if necessary'. The hurried change of brigades meant that the written orders for 9th Indian Brigade did not reach the units until the following morning. Meanwhile, 9th Indian Brigade had attacked with one battalion, the 3/14th Punjab, which was shelled off the position after a successful attack in the early hours of 23 July. It was only after this final attack that Gott agreed that 'unless the ground to the North and South of Point 63 could be held, the retention of the hill was not worth the casualties which would be entailed'.[84] With the artillery of 15th Panzer dug in around Deir el Shein, any infantry which reached Point 63 was likely to suffer heavy casualties for little gain. Gott later argued that he 'did not consider that Point 63 was lost by 5 Ind Div, because it was not properly gained', even though both 161st and 9th Indian Brigades had 'made gallant attempts to secure this important feature'.[85] Two Indian Brigades had suffered heavy casualties in what had been a forlorn hope.

Once the news of the initial success of 6th New Zealand Brigade attack was reported, the 9th Australian Division activated its series of attacks against Tel el Eisa and Tel el Makh Khad ridge. Just before dawn on 22 July the 2/32nd Australian Battalion advanced against Point 22 on the Tel el Makh Khad ridge and encountered very fierce resistance. Italian armoured cars supported the infantry dug in on the ridge and tanks fired from hull-down positions along the ridge. Eventually, after 'a long and bitter fight', the battalion took their objectives.[86] However, enemy activity soon developed in response. The battalion was subjected to heavy artillery fire and Axis tanks and armoured cars lurked menacingly around its positions. The Australian forward observation officers were busy calling artillery concentrations down on suspected targets throughout the day.

Around Tel el Eisa, the 26th Australian Brigade attacks initially met with unexpected success. The 2/24th Battalion advanced easily to 'Ring Contour 25', soon renamed 'Baillieu's Bluff' after one company commander, and began to consolidate under heavy fire. Eventually, the high casualties inflicted by the intense artillery fire forced a withdrawal back to the original positions around Point 33.[87]

Meanwhile, the 2/48th Battalion had encountered stiff resistance around Tel el Eisa. The right-hand company mounting the attack became disorganised and fell back towards Tel el Eisa station, leaving only one company holding the position. At 09.00 hours a strong counterattack overran a company of 2/23rd Battalion which was holding the eastern Point 24, but the company near the railway cutting managed to hold on. A counterattack was mounted by a squadron of 44th Royal Tank Regiment but the Valentines ran onto mines and, after losing four tanks, pulled back to reorganise. Eventually, the isolated company of 2/48th Battalion was withdrawn and the new positions around the eastern Point 24 consolidated.[88]

During the day it had become increasingly clear that the German resistance around Tel el Makh Khad was too fierce to allow the next phases of the attack to continue. Morshead visited the 24th Australian Infantry Brigade Headquarters a number of times during the day and finally decided at 15.45 hours to cancel the rest of the operation. However, he decided that an attempt at 'exploitation' to reach the Miteiriya ridge should be made that evening. This hasty change of plan left little time for the conference at brigade headquarters and the subsequent 'O' groups at the units. Since this operation was considered 'exploitation' it was decided that the Valentine tanks of 50th Royal Tank Regiment would lead the attack. It was planned that one squadron of tanks, covering a frontage of 600 yards, would be followed by a second wave of tanks with one platoon of the 2/28th and some sappers riding on the tanks. This wave would also be accompanied by the battalion's anti-tank guns and machine-gun platoon. Following behind on foot would be the bulk of the 2/28th Battalion with a final wave of tanks in the rear. This plan followed the standard British doctrine for mounting an attack by infantry tanks with infantry but its execution was anything but standard.

The operation had been so hastily organised that the 'marrying up' of the tanks and infantry, which training instructions stressed had to be done carefully, went badly wrong. When the tanks and infantry arrived at the start line, there was considerable confusion as many of the infantry mounted the wrong tanks and the sappers were not able to climb onto the tanks at all before the column moved off.[89]

At 19.00 hours, the lead Valentine tanks roared forward into action. The tanks soon came under fire and the Australian infantry quickly dropped off to 'consolidate'. Unfortunately, in the ensuing confusion, many of the tanks strayed into an unmarked minefield. Lieutenant Geoffrey Giddings knew its location and when he saw the tanks driving into the minefield, he ran towards them waving his arms to stop them. It was to no avail and, within minutes, twenty Valentines were blown up on mines.[90] Eventually, the depleted squadrons of 50th Royal Tank Regiment and the Australian carriers drove on alone and reached the objective on Ruin ridge. However, the tanks and carriers could do little except drive around in circles dodging the hail of Axis anti-tank gun fire while waiting for the infantry. All communications with 2/28th Battalion had broken down and there was no sign of the battalion. Lieutenant-Colonel Cairns decided that he would have to withdraw.[91] Eventually, the remnants of the tank battalion rallied back behind the minefield after a shattering first exposure to combat. The experience of 50th Royal Tank Regiment demonstrated, if any further example was needed, the folly of committing inexperienced troops to battle without proper preparation.

Meanwhile, the 2/28th Battalion had an equally unfortunate experience. The infantry, trudging forward on foot, were at least 30 minutes late crossing the start line. They soon came under heavy artillery and mortar fire but continued to press forward. As darkness fell, the Valentines drove back through their ranks and the commanding officer of the battalion, who was forward with the leading troops, reached a rise in the ground with what appeared to be some ruins on its summit. He decided that the tanks had gone too far and that this rise must be Ruin ridge. He reported that:

> We struck ridge with what appeared to be a ruin on left, and were all up at 2040 hrs. There seemed to be a large flat on top of ridge, and we were half way across when it began to become dark and we withdrew to reverse slope.[92]

The battalion dug in thinking that it had reached the objective. Unfortunately, when Brigadier Richards visited the battalion that night he discovered that it was still 3,000 yards short of Ruin ridge. With one rise in the desert looking very much like another and faulty navigation, the battalion had lost the opportunity to seize Ruin ridge while the Axis defence was still weak.[93] In truth, the attack had been organised far too hastily. The catalogue of disasters that amounted to Operation Splendour was now complete.

Dorman-Smith's ambitious plan for Splendour had given the British armoured brigades a leading role in achieving a decisive breakthrough. However, both Auchinleck and Dorman-Smith had ignored the condition of Eighth Army and the dilemma facing the commanders of the British armour. Eighth Army had narrowly avoided complete destruction in June and just one month later Auchinleck and Dorman-Smith expected the same troops to destroy their Axis opponents. 1st Armoured Division, with its worn-out tanks and exhausted crews, was not in any condition to act as a decisive armoured spearhead. British armour commanders had also learned caution and, where they felt necessary, to reinterpret the orders they received from higher command.

Just as importantly, 1st Armoured Division had suffered from hasty replacements in command. In taking over command on the evening of 20 July, Gatehouse had never really been given the time to understand the plan, or engage in the details of the planning process. Given the vital role ascribed to 1st Armoured Division in Splendour, this meant that Inglis' faith in the British armour was almost bound to be misplaced. Whilst watching the attack of 23rd Armoured Brigade, Gatehouse was hit by a large shell splinter and had to hand over command of his division to Fisher. 1st Armoured Division went through two commanders in just four days.

23rd Armoured Brigade had followed its orders to the letter. Brigadier Misa had simply attempted to carry his orders out regardless of the risk involved and his brigade actually fulfilled those orders at terrible cost. He was rewarded by being sacked. The only positive note in this unfortunate affair was the appointment of Brigadier G. W. Richards, a highly experienced tank officer who understood the correct use of infantry tanks, as his replacement. 23rd Armoured Brigade had been thrown into battle completely unprepared for the dangers which it would encounter. The complete inexperience of the brigade had meant that the tank crews of the obsolete Valentines had often not even seen the mines or anti-tank guns that knocked out their tanks. It was that very inexperience which meant that the brigade had attacked with a dash and vigour which the watching New Zealanders noted bitterly was lacking in the other, more experienced, British armoured brigades. Yet the fate of 23rd Armoured Brigade was an object lesson in what could happen to a tank formation which advanced incautiously under the guns of the Afrika Korps. Hundreds of British tanks had been lost at Gazala in similar circumstances and the surviving British armour commanders at Alamein saw caution and circumspection in fulfilling ambitious orders as essential if they were not to suffer a similar fate.

Lumsden and Fisher clearly felt that their position was like that of Admiral John Jellicoe's at the battle of Jutland in 1916: they could lose the war in an afternoon.[94] They knew that if they carried out risky orders to the letter, virtually all their precious Grant tanks could be lost on a minefield or on the guns of an anti-tank gun screen in less than an hour – just as the Valentines of 23rd Armoured Brigade had been. They were not prepared to allow that to happen. The problem was that by interpreting radical and daring orders with caution in order to conserve their own tank strength, British armour commanders destroyed any hope of a real breakthrough. The infantry of Eighth Army was allowed to be sacrificed on the teeth of the Panzerarmee Afrika.

The New Zealand Division certainly learned lessons from the disaster of El Mreir. Inglis drew the conclusion that, after a long night advance, infantry could not protect itself against an armoured counterattack for a period of three to five hours. During the march, infantry companies became dispersed; once the objective was reached, time was needed to reorganise and dig in. The anti-tank guns which the infantry brought with them needed to be sited, coordinated and dug in, and this could be done effectively only in daylight. In the interim, Inglis argued, 'our tanks must be right up prepared to support immediately'.[95] Still, Inglis was overly pessimistic about the amount of time infantry needed to 'firm up' on an objective. The Australians at Tel el Eisa had demonstrated that, with experience, it was possible to site and dig in anti-tank guns in darkness.

Clifton drew differing conclusions from his divisional commander. He recognised the particular misfortune that had overcome his brigade: that it was attacked in darkness by tanks which were already in position before the attack began. Clifton believed that just one hour of daylight would have been sufficient to site the anti-tank guns and ensure that the field artillery could have protected the front. However, he also saw the necessity, in that first hour, of close armoured support to protect the infantry. Clifton believed that 'one regiment of any tanks, in the depression with us at 0400 hrs would have won the battle'.[96] He may have been right. The irony of Splendour was that 23rd Armoured Brigade, equipped with infantry tanks, was cruelly misused in the 'cruiser' role and its contribution might have been decisive had its tanks been placed under the command of 2nd New Zealand Division.

After the war, Clifton also aired the doubts shared by many officers of the New Zealand Division but which were impossible to mention at the time:

> I endorse what both you [Kippenberger] and Weir have said, that neither of these regrettable attacks would have occurred if Gen Freyberg had been commanding 2 Div at this fateful time. We lost 3000 of the best Inf in the world to no purpose whatever.[97]

Bernard Freyberg was noted as a tough and experienced officer but also as a realistic, not to say cautious, commander. It is likely that, had Freyberg been in command of 2nd New Zealand Division during July, Morshead would not have been the only Dominion commander to have blazing rows with his corps commander. Yet it is perhaps unfair to level blame at Inglis. He can be forgiven for not wishing to be known as the officer who stood on his rights as a Dominion commander and exercised his 'charter' to refuse orders during his short tenure of the New Zealand Division. However, there is little doubt that, during the unsatisfactory planning process for Bacon and Splendour, Freyberg would have invoked his 'charter' and probably made certain that his division did not undertake such risky operations.

The daily report of the Panzerarmee Afrika highlighted the defensive victory which it had achieved on 22 July even while the high cost was also emphasised to Berlin:

> In these successful defensive engagements Afrika Korps lost heavily, especially in infantry. There were no reserves available to carry on the battle, as all troops were in the front line. . . . The situation is still extremely critical.[98]

During the fighting, Eighth Army troops had overrun and destroyed more than three German infantry battalions. These were troops that the Panzerarmee could ill afford to lose. The Germans expected a renewal of the British attack almost immediately but Splendour had been the greatest effort that Eighth Army could produce. It had shot its bolt. The Axis losses, although heavy, did not outweigh the 130 tanks and 1,000 prisoners Eighth Army lost during Splendour.

Nehring later argued that the crisis of 22 July formed the climax of the July battles for the Afrika Korps. His final comments on the crisis acknowledged the strain that the entire Panzerarmee was facing:

> Officers and men had passed difficult hours rich with crises, which they mastered conscious of the fact that everything was at stake. If D.A.K. collapsed the Panzerarmee was lost. Once again the overtired and exhausted troops fighting in contrary climatical conditions had made superhuman efforts to restore the situation.[99]

That the Afrika Korps had once again survived a supreme crisis demonstrated the tough resilience of the German troops. Eighth Army, by attempting to do too much too quickly, with hasty planning and continued misunderstandings between units which were not properly coordinated at either divisional, corps or army level, had achieved only disaster. The soldiers of Eighth Army had once again displayed courage and determination but had been let down by faulty tactics, poor planning and a fundamental failure of command.

TEN

Emasculation

After the clumsy failure of Splendour, Auchinleck might have been expected to relinquish any thoughts of further attacks. However, the strategic imperative to destroy the Panzerarmee Afrika remained and he attempted one last blow. There was no question that the Panzerarmee was in a parlous state. But Eighth Army was also exhausted. On 25 July, Auchinleck sent a special order of the day to all ranks of the Eighth Army in an attempt to rouse his army to one last effort:

> You have done well. You have turned a retreat into a firm stand and stopped the enemy on the threshold of Egypt. . . . You have borne much but I ask you for more. We must not slacken. If we can stick it we will break him. STICK TO IT.[1]

Ultimately, Auchinleck's final offensive failed, not because the Eighth Army lacked determination but because its units were, after three months of continual fighting, too weary, depleted and disorganised to make a coherent effort.

Dorman-Smith later claimed that he had originally envisaged Splendour as a two-stage attack in which 13 Corps would attack in the centre and draw the reserves of the Panzerarmee onto it, while two days later 30 Corps would then attack the Miteiriya ridge and force a breakthrough. Dorman-Smith claimed even to have suggested that the subsequent attack be called off since Rommel would have had time to shift his reserves after the attacks of 22 July. Most British historians have blamed the failure of the last attack in July on Morshead's row with Ramsden on 21 July.

In fact, the final attack mounted by Eighth Army was a separate, last-gasp attempt to win a breakthrough. Only 30 Corps was involved in Operation Manhood because 13 Corps was now incapable of mounting any further attacks. Manhood returned to the idea of an armoured break-out from the Miteiriya ridge which had been first mentioned in Eighth Army Operation Order No. 100. In this sense it was a return to the original plan for Splendour.

The planning for Manhood was considerably more detailed and 'tied up' than had been the case for either Bacon or Splendour and yet the paucity of resources still resulted in a thoroughly unsatisfactory plan. The first phase of the operation was for the engineers of 1st South African Division to clear two 300-yard gaps in the enemy minefield within the 69th Brigade sector by 00.01 hours on 27 July. The engineers were then to mark and police the gaps – a crucial point which had been completely ignored by 13 Corps in its operations. The gaps were to be reported to a control post and 30 Corps Headquarters to ensure that all units involved were aware of the location of the gaps. The southern flank of the gap was to be protected with anti-tank guns and mines.

Meanwhile, 9th Australian Division would then send a brigade, supported by Valentine tanks, to capture and hold the eastern end of the Miteiriya ridge. This was designed to protect the northern flank of the main attack which was to be made south of the ridge by 69th Infantry Brigade. This brigade, which had been detached from 50th Division for the operation, was to capture and consolidate a three-mile stretch of the Qattara track by 04.30 hours on 27 July. The third phase of the attack would be undertaken when 1st Armoured Division, now commanded by Fisher, with 2nd Armoured and 4th Light Armoured Brigades, would pass through the gap held by 69th Infantry Brigade to 'destroy enemy forces and exploit'.[2] Dorman-Smith provided orders for a multiplicity of circumstances, including a pursuit of the defeated Panzerarmee, which might occur once this happy event had taken place.[3]

The plan contained flaws which compromised the operation from the start. The two infantry brigades were to advance on separate and divergent axes of advance and would not be able to support one another even once they reached their final objectives. The divergent advances made communications between the brigades very difficult and coherent artillery support impossible. Rather than making one large gap in the Axis defences, the two small breaches would provide perfect targets for the inevitable Axis counterattack.

While the corps orders described a role for 9th Australian Division, the task of capturing the Miteiriya ridge was allotted to just one battalion. Once the attack of the 2/28th Battalion had been successful, and only then, the 2/43rd Battalion was to advance and link up with it on the ridge. Again, 9th Australian Division was being asked to cover too much ground. Morshead was reluctant to involve his division in the attack. Available intelligence suggested that the area north east of Miteiriya ridge was lightly held but that there was a high proportion of machine guns and anti-tank guns in the defence. The area was held by German, rather than Italian, troops who had been observed developing the defences.[4] Moreover, this would be the third attempt by 9th Australian Division to take Ruin ridge and the Axis defenders were bound to be alert.

Similarly, although the corps orders delineated a role for 69th Infantry Brigade, this was a rather impressive title for two battalions which had been scraped together out of the wreckage of 50th Division. The 5th East Yorks had been part of the original 69th Brigade, but the Durham Light Infantry battalion was a composite force formed from one company each of the 6th, 8th and 9th Battalions which had originally served in 151st Brigade. All of the men in these scratch companies had served throughout the Gazala battle and the retreat into Egypt. This formation had neither the strength nor the cohesion which might have been assumed from its title.

Just after midnight on 27 July, the 2/28th Battalion advanced in bright moonlight towards Ruin ridge. Even before the supporting artillery concentrations had begun, intense enemy fire caused heavy casualties. Eight hundred yards from the objective, some of the battalion's vehicles were disabled on an unknown minefield. The infantry continued over the field and the sappers worked hard to clear a gap for the transport. However, a German anti-tank gun position which enfiladed the minefield brought down heavy fire, and as the battalion transport moved slowly through the minefield gap, an ammunition truck was hit and burst into flames. Guided by the pyrotechnics display, the German and Italian gunners concentrated their fire onto the gap and knocked out many other vehicles. The minefield gap soon became too dangerous to use and even though observation officers from the supporting batteries, mortar detachments, small parties of men and even lone individuals all tried to deal with the enemy posts on the flanks, the task was beyond them. Perhaps six anti-tank guns (three six-pounders and three two-pounders) did manage to reach the battalion but the rest of the battalion transport, including its vital wireless and ammunition trucks, had to return to the assembly area. Numerous attempts were made to lay telephone cable to the battalion but every one proved fruitless. By 02.42 hours the battalion had transmitted the success signal from its one available wireless set. The infantry companies of 2/28th Battalion had reached their objective but were now cut off from all support.[5]

The Australian soldiers were strangely calm as they dug in on the ridge. They had achieved their objective and Private Sharp commented that 'the chaps were not perturbed'[6] as they expected that supporting infantry and armour would arrive some time after dawn. Numerous attempts were made to reach the 2/28th Battalion, but all failed. Lieutenant Cook, the brigade liaison officer, was ordered to contact the battalion. He drove far to the left of the battalion position onto the ridge, but his jeep was hit by mortar fire and destroyed. He spent the next 22 hours pinned to the ground by heavy fire from nearby machine-gun posts before he was able to get back to brigade headquarters.[7] Given this obviously dangerous situation, Morshead did not commit the 2/43rd Battalion to an advance. Instead, he ordered the Valentines of 50th Royal Tank Regiment to advance onto the Miteiriya ridge to relieve

the 2/28th Battalion. The tank regiment managed to reach the ridge to the
west of the 2/28th Battalion but encountered a ring of German anti-tank
guns and lost 22 tanks in the storm of fire that greeted them. The Valentines
were forced to fall back under heavy fire without ever contacting the beleaguered battalion.

Meanwhile, the two battalions of 69th Brigade had driven down from
Alamein station to their start line in a mood of optimism. The brigade's
advance was timed for 30 minutes after the Australian attack in the hope
that a consecutive attack would have greater impact on the German
defenders. The Durhams could hear the Australian infantry cheering as they
stormed the ridge, but had to wait until they were ordered forward. When
the leading companies did advance, they moved forward into a hail of fire
from an enemy fully alerted by the Australian attack. When they reached
the minefield, the leading sections found that the South African sappers
were pinned down by machine-gun fire which swept the ground.
Nonetheless, the infantry pushed forward over the minefield and closed in
on the German defenders. An officer of the Durham Light Infantry later
recorded frankly that:

> Men went down on all sides like ninepins and nobody had much time to
> wonder whether the minefield was 'live' or not. It may well have been a
> 'dummy' for it was the fierce defensive fire and not exploding mines which
> tore gaps in the ranks of the advancing companies.[8]

Eventually, the British infantry reached their objective and started to dig in.
Casualties in both battalions had been very heavy and the companies badly
disorganised. Both battalions lacked ammunition and their vital supporting
arms. In a tragic repetition of the Australian experience, the brigade's wireless contact broke down and all attempts to re-establish contact through the
minefield gap failed. The column of supporting arms, including the vital
anti-tank guns, never reached the battalions.

Meanwhile, 2nd Armoured Brigade, now commanded by Brigadier John
Currie, moved off at midnight on 26 July to its concentration area. Currie
had not objected to a night march and proved that it was possible for an
armoured brigade to move at night as long as the route was clearly marked
by shaded lights. Unfortunately, although the tanks reached their concentration area in good time and without mishap, questions soon emerged
regarding the location of 69th Brigade and the state of the minefield gaps.
At 06.55 hours, there remained 'considerable uncertainty regarding the location of gap in enemy mines and whether 69 Inf Bde and 2 S A Bde [sic]
are on their objectives'.[9] The zero hour for the armour was moved back to
08.15 hours. Fifteen minutes before zero hour, a report was received from
1st Armoured Division that no gaps had been cleared in the minefield over

a sufficient distance, and it was decided 'on basis of this indefinite information and because of lack of definite knowledge of gaps in minefield'[10] to
postpone the advance of 2nd Armoured Brigade until the information could
be obtained. Yet again, the British tanks did not advance at first light, and
yet again Eighth Army infantry was exposed to a German counterattack.

The German counterattack came in just after dawn against the isolated
2/28th Battalion. Tanks were sighted approaching the battalion position
from the front while another group moved in from their rear. One Australian
officer believed the advancing tanks to be British and was killed when the
German panzers opened fire on his jeep. The few anti-tank guns with the
2/28th were quickly silenced by machine-gun fire and the Australian
infantry soon found themselves helpless and alone. Many of the soldiers
kept firing at the advancing tanks with their rifles and machine guns but
it was a futile gesture. At 09.05 hours the headquarters of the battalion
managed to get their No. 18 set working again and sent the ominous message:
'We are in trouble.'[11] Artillery support could now be brought down to help
the beleaguered battalion, but it was not enough. At 09.43 hours the battalion
asked:

IN – Are there any of our tanks helping us. There are tanks all around us.
OUT – Whose are they?
IN – They are Jerries. You had better hurry. Rock arty in.

Fifteen minutes later, the battalion sent its last message: 'We have got to
give in.' Without their full complement of anti-tank guns and ammunition,
and with no armoured support, the position of the battalion was hopeless.
Private Sharp related that 'The men held their position until the tanks were
practically on top of them, many being crushed by the tanks rolling over
their weapon pits.'[12] Soon, the Australian infantry were forced to surrender
and were rounded up by the German tanks. The battalion was gathered up
and marched off to the rear.

Meanwhile, their comrades in the 2/13th Battalion 'were helpless spectators of this debacle. Held idle in their positions, powerless to bring aid to
their trapped comrades, they were tormented by a sense of frustration.'[13] The
Australian report of the disaster emphasised that the 2/28th Battalion had
'carried out its attack with the utmost determination and skill'[14] but the fact
remained that another battalion had been thrown away in an uncoordinated
attack. The loss was felt deeply in 9th Australian Division. Morshead's fears
about Manhood had been borne out and his comments on the operation were
blistering:

We expected much of 2 Armd Bde with its Grants, and their failure to enter
the battle was a great disappointment, and a very serious one. It is vital that

on the next occasion our armour restores the lost faith in them. Fortunately the Valentines supporting us have never hesitated or wavered and have fought well.

Until we can be certain about our armour we must have more limited and less exposed objectives than those in recent operations. The only justification for recent objectives was that our armour would effectively operate.[15]

The 2/28th Battalion had been overwhelmed but the two battalions of 69th Brigade managed to avoid the attentions of the German tanks for a little while longer. Although two German half-tracks came to investigate their positions at dawn, both vehicles were destroyed and their occupants killed. As the Durhams watched the fate of the Australians, a German officer drove up in a captured jeep and noted their positions. Twenty minutes later, the panzers which had overrun the 2/28th Battalion moved in behind the Durhams and East Yorks, cutting them off from any hope of support. Then two Mk IIIs drove forward to close range and fired long bursts at the helpless infantry crouching in their shell scrapes. Very soon, the men had no choice but to get up, put their hands in the air and surrender.[16] All three battalions involved in the attack had been overrun and captured in a disastrous replay of Ruweisat and El Mreir.

As if operating in slow motion, 2nd Armoured Brigade received reports of the fate of the infantry but did not call off its own attempt to get through the minefield. At 10.45 hours 6th Royal Tank Regiment moved forward to the northern minefield gap but saw that the South African engineers were still lifting mines and halted. In fact the engineers were simply widening the gap but this misunderstanding cost yet more time. Half an hour later, 6th Royal Tank Regiment had moved through the gap, but with 69th Brigade overrun, the Germans were able to bring up anti-tank guns to cover the area and start shelling from both the north and south west. 6th Royal Tank Regiment reported, just after midday, that they were still not clear of the minefield, and were operating on a very restricted front with at least 11 panzers to the west of their position. At the same time, they were being fired on by anti-tank guns. The attack was called off mid-afternoon, but the Germans made withdrawal difficult by working anti-tank guns and infantry around the southern flank of the regiment. It was not until 19.50 hours that 6th Royal Tank Regiment completed its retreat from the enemy minefield.[17]

Major-General Douglas Wimberley, the commander of the 51st (Highland) Division, had arrived in Egypt ahead of his division and spent 27 July at Eighth Army Headquarters. He remembered that:

Auchinleck spent some hours pacing up and down in front of the mess, and for a time he had me to walk with him. He gave the impression of an anxious man, and as the day wore on it became more and more clear that the fighting had not been very successful. Altogether my impression of HQ 8th Army was not one at that time to give great confidence.[18]

Operation Manhood, like the vast majority of Eighth Army's attacks in July, had begun well but ended in dismal failure.

Barrie Pitt wrote of the operation that 'the sad story of the last July attack is quickly told'[19] but while almost every account of the July fighting passes lightly over this last operation, the details of what went wrong in this final attack reveal a great deal about the state of Eighth Army's tactical methods. Brigadier Kisch, the Chief Engineer of Eighth Army, wrote an important report in an attempt to understand the failure of the operation.[20] Kisch posed two important questions: 'Was the field in fact too dangerous for tanks to be put across at 0800 hrs?' and 'Were there grounds for 1 Armd Div to suspect it of being too dangerous?' He answered in the negative to both questions. On the morning of 27 July, he had called in at 1st Armoured Division Headquarters and 'was appalled to learn (at about 1130hrs) that the armour had not yet passed through'. 1st Armoured Division was not prepared to push the tanks through until '"they were 100% satisfied" that the tanks would not run on to mines'. Fisher's stubborn declaration probably originated in the fact that each time 1st Armoured Division had ordered a brigade forward during recent operations the leading tanks had hit mines. Once again, the need to conserve the numbers of Grant tanks in the armoured brigades took precedence over everything else. The Royal Engineers Field Squadron commander from 1st Armoured Division checked the gaps and reported at noon that the gap was clear and that the tanks could now go forward.[21] By this time, 2/28th Australian Battalion had been overrun and 69th Brigade was being savaged by the German counterattack. The South African engineer reports emphasised that, in the northern sector, they had cleared a 15-yard gap for 69th Brigade by 02.00 hours; the transport passed through this narrow gap without any vehicle running onto mines. An hour later, the field company responsible for the northern gap reported to its brigade headquarters that no mines had been found in the northern area. This was the result of some confusion since mines were subsequently found in the northern area in a density of one to every five yards of front. This confusion prompted the liaison officer from 1st Armoured Division to investigate and he reported back to his headquarters that 'he did not consider it safe to bring up the armour'. Yet by first light, the northern area had been rechecked under heavy fire and the original 15-yard gap widened to 120 yards. Meanwhile, the field company responsible for the southern gap found that the minefield in front of them was a dummy field. The area was thoroughly searched but no mines were found and by 04.00 hours a 300-yard gap had been checked and marked. Major Palmer of 3rd South African Field Company, actually approached two officers of 69th Brigade and suggested that their traffic, which was squeezed into the narrow 15-yard gap, could be diverted to the large 300-yard gap to the south.

The southern gap, through which recce vehicles and Honey tanks had been passing freely, was never recognised by 1st Armoured Division, probably because the lone liaison officer had attached himself to the northern clearing party. He had also had the bad experience of being blown up on a mine in the northern area early in the operation. Both South African field companies reported individually to their brigades but not to the one unit, 2nd Armoured Brigade, which really needed clear and accurate information concerning the minefield gaps. This meant that there was no clear and co-ordinated picture of the progress of the gapping operation. The full tragedy of Operation Manhood has therefore rarely been recognised; by 04.30 hours there was a 300-yard gap in the minefield. The tanks of 2nd Armoured Brigade could have reached the forward positions of 69th Brigade without difficulty, and long before the German counterattack developed. Yet because so many separate formations were involved, there was no single headquarters collating the information and making informed decisions. Manhood could have been a striking success instead of the abject failure that it became.

The failure of Manhood placed in stark relief the problems facing Eighth Army during July 1942. For nearly two years, the Western Desert Force and then Eighth Army had operated in the Libyan Desert in fast-moving operations where, with the exception of Tobruk and Rommel's forts at Halfaya Pass, mobility and decentralisation had been used to counter German tactical advantages. During this fighting, the desert terrain sometimes had tactical significance but little operational or strategic value; if a strongly held position was encountered the tactical method of both armies was simply to bypass the resistance and seek a more vulnerable avenue of approach. At El Alamein, for the first time in the desert war, the Eighth Army found itself confronting increasingly well-developed defences, which, because of the static and constricted nature of the front, could not be bypassed.

The Panzerarmee Afrika had been relentless in developing defensive minefields to protect its positions at Alamein. During Operation Bacon, the New Zealanders and British armour had encountered scattered minefields of no great depth. Seven days later, the Axis defences at El Mreir were protected by a minefield 600 yards deep in places. On the night of 26 July, South African engineers had encountered a minefield that – even if much of it was a dummy – was at least 800 yards in depth. On 23 July, important new orders were issued which specified 'the laying out of a "minebox" which is to be made impassable by mines of every kind, to delay the enemy and simultaneously to economize our forces'.[22] The perimeter of this first minebox was to enclose El Mreir and a large area of desert to the south. The concept was simple; if Eighth Army managed to penetrate into the minebox, the advancing troops would be 'hacked to bits' by mines, flanking infantry weapons and artillery fire.[23] This order marked the start of what became known as Rommel's mine gardens.

Each successive attack by Eighth Army had encountered deeper mine-fields and better prepared defences. Still, its formations were completely unused to mounting the complicated but necessary breaching operations involving artillery, infantry and engineers. Breakthrough operations against sophisticated defences had become the stock-in-trade of the British Expeditionary Force during the First World War. British and Commonwealth units amassed crucial experience on the Western Front which enabled them to overcome the most formidable German defences including those of the Hindenburg line in September 1918. Much of this experience – and the organisation necessary for such operations – had been dismissed as irrele-vant for the desert war. Units were used to operating more or less inde-pendently across the open desert, not in the close confines of minefield gaps where one formation had to cooperate closely with the other. They had not trained or prepared for such tasks nor had they yet come to know and under-stand the supporting elements that they now had to rely upon. Manhood had shown that while the units of Eighth Army could undertake their tasks independently, the close cooperation and transmission of information that was vital for success had eluded them every time.

After Manhood, Auchinleck was forced reluctantly to conclude that Eighth Army could not mount any further attacks. It simply did not have the tools or techniques to tackle the increasingly complex task confronting it.

Yet, just as the full tragedy of Manhood is rarely recognised, so the full importance of this operation and the other failures of July in shaping the future conduct of Eighth Army operations has been overlooked. In discussing the debacle of 27 July in which the 2/28th Battalion was lost, the history of one its sister battalions mentioned that:

> this defeat, depressing in the extreme when it occurred, taught the British Army vital lessons upon which the victory of Alamein was to be built. The causes of failure were carefully noted and before the Alamein attack the whole Army trained to avoid the mistakes and surmount the obstacles that had lost us a brave unit on this occasion.[24]

Brigadier Kisch's report on the mine-gapping operation in Manhood was vital for the future development of Eighth Army's engineer operations. Kisch did not spare 1st Armoured Division from criticism and emphasised that 'the 100% freedom from mines sought by the Armd Div is of course impos-sible to assure'.[25] Kisch drew the conclusion that in any future operation where an armoured formation had to cross a suspected minefield, it should be responsible for clearing its own gaps with its own sappers.[26] This formed the basis of all future mine-gapping operations; each formation would be responsible for its own gaps to ensure that there could be no repetition of the confusion and misunderstandings of Manhood.

Manhood represented the last sputtering of offensive effort which Eighth Army could make. Since 10 July, Eighth Army had made attack after attack in an effort to destroy Rommel's army where it stood. The hard fact was that only the very first assault had been an unqualified success and that then committed one of the army's best formations to a narrow and vulnerable salient. No important ground had been wrested from the Panzerarmee Afrika, and much of Eighth Army's strength had been wasted in hasty attacks that broke down in confusion.

Eighth Army had suffered more than 13,000 casualties, including many prisoners, in stemming the tide and mounting its series of unsuccessful attacks during July. The 2nd New Zealand Division had suffered 4,000 casualties while the 5th Indian Division had lost 3,000 men during the month. Axis casualties are very difficult to estimate but at least 7,000 German and Italian troops had been captured during the month of heavy fighting.[27] Neither army had achieved its goal.

G. Isserson, an important Soviet military thinker in the inter-war years, criticised the Allied conduct of operations on the Western Front in 1916–18 and the attempts to penetrate the linear German front. It was, he said a:

> pointless system for hammering in nails. But no wall is brought down by hammering nails into it. In order to knock down a wall, it is necessary to hew its foundations, that is, to brace up under it through fissures which have been formed.[28]

In July 1942 Eighth Army had also been pointlessly hammering nails into the front of the Panzerarmee Afrika. None of the thrusts mounted in Bacon, Splendour or Manhood had been properly organised or powerful enough to spring a fissure in the wall. Each time, the remnants of the Afrika Korps had been able to chop the tip of the nail off. When each seemingly decisive attack failed, Auchinleck and Dorman-Smith fell back on the justification that great damage had been inflicted on their opponent. This could not obscure the fact that Eighth Army simply did not have the resources, organisation or the concept of operations necessary to destroy its opponent.

ELEVEN

Interregnum

And their story lives on far away without visible symbol
Woven into the stuff of other men's lives[1]

On 27 July 1942, as Operation Manhood stumbled towards its dispiriting conclusion, Dorman-Smith sat working in the heat of the operations caravan at Eighth Army Headquarters. Auchinleck had tasked him with preparing another staff appreciation which would cover Eighth Army policy for the immediate future. Auchinleck and Dorman-Smith had been forced to the conclusion that Eighth Army could not make any further offensive effort. The hopes of early July that Rommel and his army might be smashed in a rapid and decisive battle had faded away with each unsuccessful attack. Eighth Army would now have to sit on the defensive and await the arrival of the vast amounts of material now in transit to Suez.

Dorman-Smith considered the options available to Eighth Army and its opponent in the broadest possible terms. Contemplation of a renewed offensive by the Panzerarmee Afrika gave Dorman-Smith no great cause for alarm and his plans for fighting a 'modern defensive battle in the area El Alamein-Hammam'[2] were well advanced. The possibility that Rommel might choose to mount a deliberate attack against the northern sector of the Alamein front could be discounted for the simple reason that Dorman-Smith knew that the Panzerarmee was desperately short of seasoned German infantry. This meant that Rommel would be forced to repeat his operational plan from Gazala by mounting a wide outflanking sweep from the south as his only realistic option. Eighth Army – and Dorman-Smith – had learned from bitter experience that a purely static defence to such a thrust would be dangerous.

There has been much controversy over the nature of the 'modern defensive battle' which Eighth Army planned to fight and much of this is due to the necessarily broad terms of Dorman-Smith's policy paper. Dorman-Smith became very proud of his last appreciation for Auchinleck and this document has often been used to prove or disprove arguments surrounding Auchinleck's future plans for Eighth Army. However, in late July, Auchinleck had decided to reorganise the command and staff work of Eighth Army in advance of the likely visit from General Sir Alan Brooke, the CIGS.

Auchinleck had finally taken the step of relieving Whiteley and replaced him with Brigadier Freddie de Guingand, who had only recently taken up the post of Director of Military Intelligence in Cairo. De Guingand was inexperienced and attempted to refuse the appointment on that basis, but Auchinleck was insistent. Auchinleck had a great confidence in de Guingand's abilities and with him in place Dorman-Smith could return to his post in Cairo and continue work on the proposed changes to the shape and organisation of British forces in the Middle East. This was a job which Dorman-Smith relished and one in which his talents were far better suited than as an erstwhile and unofficial Chief of Staff.

Meanwhile, Auchinleck called his two corps commanders together for a conference on 28 July. Auchinleck, Gott and Ramsden discussed Eighth Army's defence plans in detail and the prospects for an offensive in September. On 30 July, the three men held another meeting which set out the main tasks for the two corps commanders. Dorman-Smith was not privy to all these discussions. He believed that everything had been 'done verbally at the two Corps Commanders' conferences' and that 'there was nothing in writing'.[3] Yet Dorman-Smith became the main source of information concerning Auchinleck's future plans in August 1942, and most historians have emphasised the importance of his appreciation of 27 July rather than the results of Auchinleck's subsequent two corps conferences.[4] Auchinleck's own appreciations have been mentioned only in vague terms by most historians.[5] He did not keep copies of these documents[6] and they were not published alongside Dorman-Smith's appreciation of 27 July in his despatch.

Charles Richardson has painted a bleak picture of Auchinleck at the end of July:

> When I observed him, day after day, sitting in the sand spending long hours staring through binoculars at the distant void horizon I asked myself:
>   'Has he anything left to offer?'[7]

There is little doubt that Auchinleck was tired after the strain of commanding Eighth Army in the field during a month of constant crises and failed attacks. Nor could he get his subordinates to agree with his ideas for the radical transformation of Eighth Army. On 29 July, Major-General Richard McCreery, the Major-General Armoured Forces, and Major-General John Harding, the Director of Military Training, flew up from General Headquarters to discuss Auchinleck's proposals to change the organisation of the British armoured formations in Eighth Army.[8] McCreery and Harding had a 'very bumpy trip' in a Lysander before landing on a rough desert strip and the meeting was equally bumpy.[9]

Auchinleck believed that the fighting during July had exposed a major flaw in the British Army's divisional organisation. Armoured and infantry divisions seemed unable to cooperate properly with each other and the gulf between the armour and infantry now seemed almost unbridgeable. Auchinleck, advised by Dorman-Smith, believed that the answer to this problem was to abolish the distinction between armoured and infantry divisions altogether. Instead, every division was to be re-created as a 'mobile division' composed of one armoured and two infantry brigade groups. However, the particular balance of arms in any one division could be altered depending upon the particular mission to be undertaken. Auchinleck hoped that the distinction between armour and infantry would disappear with this new organisation and that cooperation between all arms would become second nature to every divisional commander and the troops under their command. Auchinleck also wanted to add a fourth tank squadron to each armoured regiment to strengthen them and make the regiment a more sustainable formation even after heavy losses.

McCreery was supposed to be Auchinleck's chief adviser on all matters relating to the use of armour. However, soon after his arrival in March 1942, McCreery had felt sidelined by Auchinleck and he disagreed strongly with these new proposals. McCreery later claimed that, 'I knew the views of all the armoured brigade commanders, and I stuck to my guns, and refused to endorse the many changes in the organisation of the armour.'[10] Auchinleck became very angry and informed McCreery that if he 'would not obey orders he could consider himself relieved of his appointment'.[11] The meeting had not gone well.

There was considerable merit to Auchinleck's idea of 'mobile' divisions with a flexible structure which allowed armour, infantry and artillery to be slotted in as the situation demanded. However, Auchinleck does not seem to have understood the full consequences of attempting to change the basic organisational structures of the British Army in the middle of the war. The War Office had decided upon the concept of distinct infantry and armoured divisions before the war began and, regardless of the changes made in the Middle East, formations would continue to be sent to Egypt as infantry or armoured divisions. Armoured regiments would also continue to arrive as three squadron regiments and this explains much of McCreery's intransigence. He knew that soldiers who had trained together and been inculcated into the ethos and traditions of one regiment would react badly to being moved suddenly to another on arrival in Egypt. Just as importantly, while in theory every divisional commander should have been capable of commanding a mixed force of armour and infantry the reality was rather different.

Douglas Wimberley later explained that soon after he arrived in Egypt he was informed that it was likely that one of his brigades would be sent to an armoured division and that his division would receive an armoured brigade. Wimberley realised that he 'would have to take a firm stand to prevent . . . "the mucking about" of my Division, which had trained as a single fighting formation for two years or more'.[12] Wimberley saw the concept of the 'mobile division' as a clear threat to the powerful *esprit de corps* that he had built up within his division. He eventually decided that he would rather resign than accept the changes. Auchinleck did not realise the depth of feeling that his proposals engendered amongst the officers of Eighth Army.

Although many of his radical proposals met with firm resistance from his subordinates and demonstrated his lack of understanding of the mentality of the British Army, Auchinleck's discussions with his corps commanders on 28 and 30 July showed just how much he could still offer in terms of inventive military thinking. As a result of these discussions, Auchinleck produced two military appreciations which established the framework for the rest of the El Alamein campaign.

Auchinleck's first appreciation, written on 1 August, dealt with the immediate short-term posture for Eighth Army.[13] Auchinleck had been forced to accept that Eighth Army could not mount a fresh offensive until mid-September 'at the earliest', but in the meantime he was determined that Eighth Army would harass its opponent and disrupt its plans 'by every means in its power'.[14] Both corps were to prepare large-scale raids which would be activated if Rommel made the mistake of deploying Italian infantry in vulnerable locations. However, Auchinleck's plans looked beyond Eighth Army operations. A whole series of raids would be mounted through the use of combined forces[15] at the disposal of General Headquarters Middle East. The Royal Navy, in conjunction with the Directorate of Combined Operations, would prepare raids on the coastal flank and the Long Range Desert Group, along with all the other 'private armies', would mount raids from the Qattara Depression. The Desert Air Force would play a key part in all of these projected operations to damage the Axis rear areas and lines of communication. All these operations were designed to stretch the Panzerarmee and its logistic chain as far as possible to delay its build-up of supplies necessary for offensive action. Even taken in isolation, this appreciation proves that Auchinleck and the senior commanders of Eighth Army were certainly not 'looking over their shoulder' to consider further retreat but instead were planning to cause as much damage and disruption to the Panzerarmee Afrika as possible.

Gott also committed his thoughts to paper and his appreciation, written on 1 August, gives a rare insight into his military thinking. Auchinleck and his corps commanders understood that Rommel would mount an offensive as soon as possible and Gott had been tasked with preparing the defences of 13 Corps to meet this eventuality. This document also demonstrates the clear thinking of Gott's principal staff officers, Brigadier 'Bobby' Erskine and Major Freddy de Butts. In fact, Gott's appreciation was a vital document which considered not only the possibilities for offensive action along 13 Corps front but also the coming Axis offensive.

Gott had examined the terrain in his corps sector carefully over the past month and fully understood the critical importance of the Alam el Halfa ridge:

ALAM EL HALFA and GEBEL BEIN GABIR point like fingers to SW and provide all the observation and the good going to the coast road. These features and particularly ALAM EL HALFA are vital for any advance down the Coast to Alexandria – they are also vital to us for holding our present positions.

Given the importance of this terrain, Gott realised that Rommel's most likely course of action was:

An attack with ALAM EL HALFA as his first objective, going round anywhere South of the ALAM NYAL ridge – subsequently cutting the road in the HAMMAN area and thrusting straight for Alexandria. A raid down the Barrel track towards the Delta might be combined with this. This is much the most likely course and the most difficult to meet. An attack anywhere North of ALAM NYAL would meet strong minefields, bad going and prepared positions. There are many possible variations in the details of such a plan but it is the only one which he could carry out with his present shortage of infantry if he is making ALEXANDRIA his objective.[16]

The Panzerarmee Afrika was, by early August, very short of German infantry. It would be unable to sustain the heavy fighting necessary for any break-in battle on the heavily defended northern sector of Eighth Army's front. Given this fact, 'Strafer' Gott, with his long experience of desert warfare and his knowledge of Rommel's methods and tactics, predicted almost exactly the precise scale and scope of Rommel's attack in August 1942. Gott and his staff, rather than Dorman-Smith or Auchinleck – or any other British commander – should be given the full credit for this. The 13 Corps appreciation also revealed the military value of Ultra because the intelligence calculations were based on a very detailed knowledge of German and Italian reinforcements and their likely schedule of arrival in Africa.[17] Of course, Gott and his staff had to assume that all the material and supplies would arrive. Thus, Freddy de Butt calculated that Eighth Army might have to face an offensive by a Panzerarmee Afrika reinforced to 30,000 men and 250 tanks as early as 15 August. Not surprisingly, Auchinleck gave Gott the responsibility of preparing to meet Rommel's coming offensive and enacting Dorman-Smith's concept for a 'modern defensive battle'.

Unfortunately, Ramsden's paper exploring the opportunities for offensive action on 30 Corps' front does not seem to have survived,[18] but the main thrust of his thinking has survived in the instructions and orders he gave to his divisions. On 30 July Ramsden ordered his divisional commanders to:

concentrate on training for the assault in close co-operation with infantry and engineers.

Particular attention will be paid to the following points:

(a) Passage of minefields

(b) Use of smoke

(c) Night operations

Details of training areas will be decided later.[19]

Ramsden was an infantry officer who had served on the Western Front throughout the Great War. Unlike Auchinleck, Dorman-Smith or Gott he had first-hand experience of the tightly controlled and orchestrated break-in battles that the BEF had fought so successfully in 1918. He had already identified some of the failings present in Eighth Army and the remedies that would be necessary to mount a successful attack against the Panzerarmee Afrika's increasingly formidable defences.

On 2 August Ramsden followed up these points with a discussion on the lessons he had derived from the fighting in July. He pointed out that the three recent unsuccessful attacks had failed even though the infantry had achieved initial success. Each time the successful infantry had been driven off or overrun by enemy tanks because the cooperating armour had been held up because of uncleared minefields or unmarked gaps. He went on to outline a number of crucial points for future operations. He insisted that, in future, anti-tank guns must be brought forward with the leading infantry. If this was impossible the infantry had to be halted and 'not left to the mercy of enemy tanks'.[20] Similarly, supporting tanks had to be 'well forward' with the leading infantry so that they would know where the infantry was and whether gaps had actually been made in the minefields. Thorough ground and air reconnaissance of enemy defences was essential to ensure that mopping up cleared up all pockets of resistance. The artillery support provided in all three actions had been satisfactory and commanded centrally. However, ensuring reliable communications and suitable vehicles for forward observation officers was 'under examination'.[21] It was suggested that the engineer effort should be 'centralized in the same way as gunner effort' and that the Chief Engineer of every corps should direct the main engineer activities. Ramsden concluded, 'We must discriminate between a tight battle, in which we are likely to be involved during the next few weeks, and the loose battle, commanded and conducted by General WAVELL.'[22]

Ramsden had been given the responsibility by Auchinleck of planning for Eighth Army's future offensive in the north and his correspondence with his divisional commanders gives an important glimpse into his initial evaluations of the July fighting. The commanders of the Eighth Army already understood many of the basic shortcomings that had been encountered and were taking steps to remedy them. Perhaps most important of all was

Ramsden's recognition that any future offensive mounted by Eighth Army would have to be a 'tight' battle more in the mould of 1918 than the fluid mobile operations previously the feature of the desert war.

Auchinleck's appreciation of 2 August incorporated Ramsden's thinking on the best location to mount Eighth Army's offensive. Just as Gott's appreciation reveals the high quality of his military thinking, Auchinleck's last appreciation, which developed the ideas which had been discussed in conference, clearly shows that he was thinking in a fertile and imaginative way. The fact that this appreciation was headed 'Western Front' underscores the fact that Auchinleck still faced the dilemma of a 'Northern Front' in Persia, but his main object remained to destroy Rommel's army. The paper discussed the relative opportunities for attack across the front of the Panzerarmee. All the avenues presented different difficulties. In 30 Corps' sector, the Panzerarmee Afrika remained deployed in open desert with little in the way of defensible terrain but with strong minefields and field defences. The vital central sector around Ruweisat ridge had been made very strong, while the sector opposite 13 Corps was less strongly held but contained much better defensive terrain. Auchinleck knew that Rommel might expect an attack on the southern flank but, although it might be easier to achieve, a breakthrough there might also open the Eighth Army to a counterstroke. Similarly, an attack on the strong positions around Ruweisat ridge was unlikely to succeed without overwhelming superiority of numbers. Although an attack in the north would meet 'strong opposition organised in depth', Eighth Army could concentrate its artillery and attack the most vital and vulnerable area of the Panzerarmee.[23] Ramsden and Auchinleck had long realised the potential for an offensive with the Miteiriya ridge as its first objective. If Eighth Army could seize this ridge and break out to the south west, the Axis defenders near the coast road could be enveloped and the bulk of the Panzerarmee trapped in the desert to the south.

The deliberations of Auchinleck and his corps commanders produced a plan that was unconventional, at least as far as expectations of desert warfare went, and would maximise Eighth Army's advantages in an offensive timed for mid-September. The plan was:

(i) To make all preparations for a deliberate attack on the extreme NORTH of the enemy's position.

(ii) To disguise this intention by inducing the enemy to believe that when able to resume the offensive we intend to attack in the SOUTH. Overt preparations should be made to this end.

(iii) To attack and harass the enemy communications to the greatest possible extent.

(iv) To perfect the organisation of our main defensive zone in the rear of the EL ALAMEIN position and be ready to meet an enemy attempt to turn or by-pass our SOUTHERN FLANK.

(v) To train and rehearse intensively for the main operation against the enemy NORTHERN flank.

(vi) To prepare our motorised and armoured forces to take immediate advantage of the break through when made.[24]

Gott was to prepare plans to meet the expected advance by the Panzerarmee in the southern sector. Meanwhile, Ramsden was to develop the defences of 30 Corps by preparing battlegroup positions behind the front and study the possibilities for a future attack towards the Miteiriya ridge in the north. Auchinleck had discussed the situation fully with his corps commanders and incorporated many of their ideas although he had not taken Gott's advice that an attack in the south might yield the best results. Thus, Dorman-Smith's appreciation of 27 July, which considered the defensive preparations to cope with an attack by the Panzerarmee, was only part of Auchinleck's much wider thinking.

Charles Richardson's portrayal of Auchinleck as a soldier devoid of ideas and bereft of hope is misleading. Auchinleck's two appreciations, written on 1 and 2 August, prove that, for all his faults as a commander, he was able to produce original and clear-sighted military thought even at the end of a month of continuous fighting. What is most striking about Auchinleck's appreciation of 2 August is that it formed the blueprint for Eighth Army's subsequent success. The appreciation naturally did not deal with the mass of detailed staff work which would be necessary but it set out the broad principles that would animate Eighth Army over the coming months. Every single element of Auchinleck's plan was later followed by Eighth Army under Montgomery's leadership. The complete text of the appreciation provides the final and conclusive proof that Montgomery's much-vaunted 'master plan' for 'his' battle of Alamein actually originated with Auchinleck and his corps commanders.

Auchinleck left Eighth Army headquarters on 2 August to return to his post as C-in-C Middle East in Cairo. Ramsden was left in temporary command of the army to continue the planning process for Eighth Army's offensive, while in the south Gott worked to prepare against Rommel's coming blow. Even in Auchinleck's absence, the staff of Eighth Army continued to work on the problems that would face any break-in attack on the Panzerarmee's northern sector. On 5 August, de Guingand asked 13 and 30 Corps for their views on the subject of 'Training in breaking through minefields'.[25] De Guingand's request and his preliminary thoughts on the matter showed that the senior commanders and key staff officers of Eighth Army were working rapidly to identify and solve the most pressing tactical problems. De Guingand began to develop the detailed thinking that would be necessary to fight the future 'tight' battle. Given the obvious preparations of the Panzerarmee in developing deep minefields as part of their defences, and the recent failures caused by lack of training and proven technique, de Guingand emphasised 'it is essential that we should develop a sound technique for breaking through the enemy's position and should train intensively for this operation'.[26]

De Guingand mentioned that a suitable training ground was to be selected where the entire operation could be rehearsed 'as realistically as possible'. Each corps would then withdraw units to rehearse 'under their own commanders until a high standard of training and co-operation is reached'.[27] It was noted that the Germans used a standard procedure for such tasks which could be modified according to conditions. In the operations around the Cauldron at Gazala, the German and Italian engineers had proved that it was possible to make rapid gaps in minefields. The value of battle drills and standard procedures was finally beginning to be recognised by Eighth Army. Recent operations, de Guingand continued, had shown that points concerning command, inter-communication and responsibility for the gaps cleared, amongst many others, needed to be clarified. He suggested that Eighth Army should develop a standard procedure which could be fully tested during the training period.

De Guingand provided a suggested outline of the methods that might be adopted in mine-clearing during the future offensive:

Stage 1   Intense arty and air bombardment on known enemy posns covering that part of the minefield which is to be lifted. This may be followed immediately by an infantry assault to gain those posns.

Stage 2   Bombardment lifts on to enemy posns to the flank and rear of the gap and on to known enemy gun posns. Covered by this bombardment and by the possible employment of smoke, medium machine guns are pushed forward and are dug in and the preliminary recce of the minefield is carried out and some tanks moved forward in support.

Stage 3   Troops detailed for mine lifting will lift the mines covered by direct fire of MMGs and tanks and indirect fire of arty with direct air support. It may be necessary to reconnoitre the minefield in vehicles before a plan for lifting the mines can be made.

Stage 4   Vanguard of the armoured formations tests the minefield followed by the main guard which must include A/Tk guns.

Stage 5   Advance guard moved forward to its objective. The main body consisting of more tanks, arty fd and A.Tk and inf first consolidate and then enlarge the gap.

Stage 6   The gap having been made the armoured force passes through.

De Guingand's memo formed the original framework for Eighth Army's tactical preparations for the coming offensive. The need for intensive training, cooperation and a standard drill for mine-gapping had all been acknowledged. The hard effort needed for the realisation of these concepts still lay ahead.

The first week in August was a busy time for Gott and his staff as they prepared the detailed work for the 'modern defensive battle' they knew they would have to fight that month. Since the beginning of July, Dorman-Smith, in conjunction with Brigadier Frederick Kisch, the Chief Engineer of Eighth Army, had been planning and preparing a series of defensive zones to give depth to the Eighth Army positions. Kisch, on first seeing Dorman-Smith's plans, is reputed to have said 'it was the first time he had seen brain-power being applied to defence'. In designing this system, Dorman-Smith and Kisch drew from the hard lessons of May and June. At Gazala, Eighth Army had organised a series of brigade boxes which were without mutual support. Not only had the Gazala line been held in a rigid linear method but there had been very little depth to it – which had enabled Rommel to outflank the defences easily. The vast 'minemarshes' of the Gazala line were impressive but large stretches were not under observation let alone covered by fire. This had allowed the German and Italian engineers to gap the minefields easily while in the northern sector the weak Italian infantry divisions actually used the British minefields to protect themselves from attack. Dorman-Smith and Kisch drew upon this depressing experience, along with the defensive methods proven at El Alamein, to design a system with breadth and depth quite unlike any that Rommel had faced before.

Only the northern sector of the front, running from the New Zealand Division's positions at Alam Nayil to the coast, was to be fortified and organised in depth. The southern sector was to be left deliberately 'weak' to encourage Rommel to use his standard tactic of a 'right hook' through the desert. A series of minefields was constructed in the south to impose delay upon any Axis advance, and the 4th Light Armoured and 7th Motor Brigades of 7th Armoured Division were tasked with watching the minefields and imposing the maximum delay upon advancing Axis spearheads.

In designing the defences in the northern sector, Dorman-Smith and Kisch had to balance the need for a robust defence with the desire to release troops into reserve. The plan was for Eighth Army to form two defensive zones. The forward area would be a lightly held 'outpost' zone designed to confuse any attack as to its real strength. Once intelligence confirmed the timing and direction of Rommel's thrust, the units in the northern sector would 'thin out' the forward zone and take up positions in the main line of resistance. This withdrawal was only possible because Dorman-Smith knew that Rommel did not have sufficient infantry to make a serious attack on the northern sector. By stepping back and thinning out the front line in the northern sector, the troops released from defence would then be able to re-inforce 13 Corps in the south. The main positions formed an irregular pattern and each position was designed to hold a grouping of one or two battalions of infantry with artillery. The positions were not necessarily in mutual supporting distance for small-arms fire, but were placed so as to be within artillery supporting distance. Between these positions groups of artillery and armour were formed into mobile battlegroups to draw any Axis spearhead into the web of positions before counterattacking. The Alam el Halfa ridge was recognised as a vital feature which gave observation over 'a wide area of bare and difficult desert to the south' and a succession of strongpoints were prepared on its slopes. Dorman-Smith explained that:

> Minefields ran from each [ridge] like the arms of a starfish so that they gave no support to an invader of this spider's-web system; within which the bulk of the defenders were to keep mobile ready to intervene against an attacker from whatever direction he might come.[28]

This plan was, without doubt, the most controversial of all Dorman-Smith's ideas. It has been called 'disheartening' and an example of defeatism.[29] It has even been suggested that had the defensive scheme been carried out Eighth Army would have dissolved into chaos and rout.[30] What is most remarkable is that few, if any, commentators have recognised the inspiration for Dorman-Smith's scheme. The concept of establishing two defensive zones with a lightly held outpost zone and a web of positions in a main defence zone with mobile battlegroups to counterattack any penetration had been standard German defensive practice since 1917.[31] Dorman-Smith's plan was neither brilliant nor radical; it simply attempted to use German practice and to adapt the tactical method which had worked so effectively for 1st South African Division during the first few days at Alamein.

Dorman-Smith knew that to occupy static positions which had no depth against the Panzerarmee Afrika in full cry was to invite disaster, a second Gazala. Dorman-Smith and Kisch's defensive system was designed to ensure that Eighth Army learned from that lesson and did not repeat it.

Nor was the defensive zone behind Eighth Army the only part of the design. General Headquarters Middle East was tasked with preparing a series of defences around Alexandria, Wadi Natrun and Cairo. All these defences were meant to be part of a 'unified whole; if Rommel eventually decided to by-pass the Eighth Army positions he would merely run into similar defences' further back. The only path that was left deliberately open was the barrel track running towards Cairo (thus dovetailing with Gott's appreciation that Rommel might mount a raid in this direction) but even then he would run into the defences of Wadi Natrun with an alert – and mobile – Eighth Army in his rear.

So there was nothing defeatist or despondent about Dorman-Smith's defensive plan, merely a realistic appreciation of the scale and scope of a likely Axis offensive. The fatal flaw was that neither Dorman-Smith nor Auchinleck explained the plan properly to Eighth Army.

During July, some units of Eighth Army, along with reserve troops, were tasked with digging and preparing the defences. Troops could not understand why they were digging positions in open desert seemingly miles away from the fighting when the Eighth Army plans called for destruction of the enemy where he stood. Worse was to follow when the Operation Instructions for the occupation of the defences were disseminated at the end of July. 30 Corps Operation Instruction No. 71 explained that:

> The enemy may attack us in the Alamein Area before we are ready to resume the offensive. Depending on the scale of the attack and the warning received EIGHTH ARMY will:-
> (a) Fight the enemy on its present posns or
> (b) Thin out the forward zone.[32]

These instructions produced uncertainty within the minds of the divisional staffs of 30 Corps because they did not know whether the defensive scheme would be enacted or not. The conflicting alternatives smacked of the orders in late June to fight or withdraw from the Alamein line even though that was not their intention. The problem was that Dorman-Smith's 'spider's-web' of positions and the linear positions along Eighth Army's existing front could not both be held. This was of particular importance for the 9th Australian Division. Having captured and held the coastal ridge around Point 26, and having fought for the mounds of Tel el Eisa, the division was committed to the defence of an awkward salient. Under the new plan, the Tel el Eisa salient would be 'thinned out' and held only by outposts. It was certainly possible that such outposts might be overwhelmed in any Axis offensive. As far as Dorman-Smith was concerned, the Tel el Eisa salient might have value as a jumping off point for a future offensive, but posed greater problems in defence; by withdrawing from it Eighth Army would gain the 9th Australian Division for use elsewhere. While this was a perfectly valid military view, it ignored the psychology of the Australian soldiers who had fought so hard to capture Tel el Eisa. Morshead's brief note on the corps instructions spoke volumes: 'In the unfortunate event of being ordered to withdraw from our present positions'.[33] As divisional commander he would have to explain to his subordinate commanders the reasons for leaving the ground they had fought for, when he himself did not understand the military reasons for the move. The Australian attack of 10 July represented the one clear-cut success of Eighth Army for that month, and the gains made had been paid for many times in blood. Soldiers are, by instinct, fiercely territorial, and Morshead was clearly dismayed at the thought that he would have to give up the ground that his men had fought so hard to capture.

The plans met a very different reception in 13 Corps. Gott had been instrumental in developing the new tactics and he executed them with energy. He discussed the plan for holding the Alam el Halfa ridge in detail with Inglis, who had no objections to the overall scheme. Once again, the different experience of the New Zealanders and Australians influenced their reactions. While the Australians had fought a tough territorial battle for Tobruk and for Tel el Eisa, the New Zealand Division had operated in the open desert and had few qualms about conducting a tactical withdrawal to wrong-foot the enemy. The New Zealand Division was to thin out its present defences and take position on the critical Alam el Halfa ridge. It is not surprising that Gott selected that division to hold such a vital piece of terrain. He knew the New Zealand Division would be able to do the job efficiently. However, Inglis did not like the details:

> The plan for occupation of ALAM HALFA posn, . . . as now prepared, provides for two Bde boxes out of mutual supporting distance. I want to occupy it as a Div posn with bulk of arty centrally situated and able to cover whole Western and Southern fronts. Corps Comd requests outline plan accordingly.[34]

Gott took account of these reservations and, after he and Inglis had scouted the positions on 2 August, the western end of the defences on Alam el Halfa ridge were redug and the minefields relaid. Gott spent 31 July going round the New Zealand Division sector, 'inspecting 25 posns in detail, and forward OPs in 21 Bn area'.[35] Nothing was left to chance. Meanwhile, Inglis met with the newly promoted Brigadier G. P. B. 'Pip' Roberts, commander of 22nd Armoured Brigade, who was tasked with supporting the New Zealand Division in the event of a German attack. There was time for British armour and the infantry they were to support to discuss and plan coming operations in detail.

The 5 August was an unusual day for the divisional commanders of Eighth Army. At short notice, most of them were ordered to report at 'Tac Army at 1030 hrs'.[36] However, it soon transpired that this was no ordinary army conference. The Prime Minister, Winston Churchill and the CIGS, General Sir Alan Brooke, had activated Operation Bracelet and come to Egypt in person to 'shake up' General Headquarters Middle East and Eighth Army. None of the participants, with the exception of Churchill and Brooke, had a full understanding of the importance of events of that day, when Winston first met the desert forces that had occupied so much of his time and energy for two years.

Auchinleck had been informed of Brooke's impending visit to Egypt in a telegram on 27 July. Churchill wrote:

1. I have not troubled you with messages while you have been so fiercely engaged, but you and your Army have never been out of our thoughts for an hour . . .
5. CIGS is coming out to you early next week. He will be able to tell you about our plans, which are considerable.[37]

This message was sent by a tense Prime Minister still waiting for news of Operation Manhood, no doubt hoping that Rommel's army would be broken by the time Auchinleck replied. The future plans mentioned by Churchill were indeed of the first importance. The British and Americans had finally come to an agreement to commit troops to French North Africa in 1942. This would be 'a combined attack in October on the lines of "Gymnast"'[38] in which British and American troops would seize Morocco and Tunisia in an effort to deny the Axis the North African shore. Churchill noted that:

the President has given the order 'full steam ahead'. Secrecy and speed are vital. You will see how this, if successful, would fit in with 'Acrobat,' if ever the Russian situation and your own achievements render such an enterprise possible.[39]

The British plan for Acrobat, to destroy the Axis forces in Libya and seize Tripoli, had dissolved into the disasters at Gazala and Tobruk. Auchinleck had failed to destroy the Panzerarmee Afrika at Alamein but for Churchill, and the British, to maintain their status in American eyes, Acrobat would have to become a reality – and before Gymnast could be executed in October. Auchinleck should have been warned by Churchill's relative restraint in not troubling him with messages during the fighting in July. Silence from Churchill was never a good sign.

Brooke saw any reorganisation of the command in the Middle East as an essentially military matter which belonged to his remit as CIGS. The next phase of operations in Egypt, however, was of critical political importance to Churchill and he had no intention of allowing Brooke to go to Egypt alone. Indeed, Churchill had been threatening to fly out to Egypt since at least 30 June but Brooke had been able to persuade him that 'the situation must have settled a little before he goes out'.[40] Churchill had expressed frequent impatience with Auchinleck during July and Brooke noted on 8 July that, during a Cabinet meeting, the Prime Minister 'ran down ME army in shocking way and criticized Auchinleck for not showing a more offensive spirit'.[41] Perhaps the final straw for Churchill was the news that Operation Manhood had failed. Brooke wrote in his diary for 28 July:

PM in very depressed mood as result of Auk's second attack being repulsed. Pouring out questions as to why Auk could not have done this or that and never giving him the least credit for doing the right thing. He is quite heart-breaking to work for.[42]

Churchill knew little of the difficulties facing Eighth Army in July 1942 but he knew that although Auchinleck had saved Egypt he had failed to deliver the victory which he so desperately needed.

Brooke's belief in Auchinleck had also faded away. He wrote to Auchinleck on 17 July expressing his feeling that 'it is such a joy to see you gradually regaining the mastery over the enemy'[43] and also reassuring Auchinleck that, although Churchill could be temperamental, he should not 'attach too much importance if occasionally his telegrams are not quite as friendly as they might be'.[44] Auchinleck replied at length on 25 July in a letter which can only have undermined his own position:

> We have succeeded, though only just I am afraid, in regaining some measure of local initiative . . . I was disappointed when our big effort of the 21st/22nd July came to nothing as I had great hopes of it . . . Well, there it is, we undoubtedly gave the enemy a rude shock, . . . but we failed to get our object, which was to break through.[45]

Auchinleck's tone of disappointment cannot have inspired confidence in Brooke. Auchinleck went on to outline the problems of reserves and training in Eighth Army as well as the difficulties inherent in commanding a Commonwealth army but this may have appeared like an apologia to Brooke. This letter may well explain Brooke's later outburst in his diary when he wrote, 'It is very trying having to fight battles to defend the Auk, when I am myself doubtful why on earth he does not act differently.'[46]

Auchinleck also raised the issue of a new commander for Eighth Army and stated that:

> I believe Gott might command Eighth Army well and so far as I can see he shows no signs of weariness and is learning how to handle big formations every day . . . He impresses me most favourably in every way.[47]

Whatever commander was selected for Eighth Army, Auchinleck warned Brooke that:

> He must be a man of vigour and personality and have a most flexible and receptive mind. He must also be young, at any rate in mind and body, and be prepared to take advice and learn unless he has had previous Western Desert experience.[48]

The new commander of Eighth Army would bear a heavy responsibility. Brooke made his final preparations for his journey on 30 July and was shocked to learn that Churchill was planning to follow immediately. Churchill had decided to visit Egypt on his way to the Soviet Union where he was to have a series of meetings with Stalin.

On 3 August, both Prime Minister and CIGS had arrived in Cairo and were beginning a series of meetings with all the main commanders. By the next day, Brooke believed that the main command changes had been settled:

a) new commander for 8th Army Montgomery
b) new CGS to be selected vice Corbett
c) Jumbo Wilson [b. 1881] too old and to be replaced by Gott
d) Quinan unsuitable for 10th Army, to be replaced by Anderson.[49]

These were sweeping changes but left Auchinleck in position as C-in-C Middle East. Brooke was keen to see his protégé, Lieutenant-General Bernard Law Montgomery, assume command of Eighth Army. Although only too aware of Montgomery's abrasive character and quirky habits, Brooke also knew his qualities as a hard trainer of troops and a supremely professional soldier. Auchinleck had agreed to Montgomery as the future commander of Eighth Army and Gott's qualities had been recognised by his promotion to army command, albeit to Ninth Army in Palestine.

On 5 August, Churchill and Brooke flew to Burg el Arab where they were met by Auchinleck, Tedder and Coningham. Dorman-Smith sensed Churchill's hostility immediately. He felt the 'chill; this was not going to be a nice visit'.[50] The cortege drove off but Churchill and Auchinleck were seated in separate cars. The 'sinisterly funeral' convoy drove to El Alamein where Morshead and Pienaar greeted the Prime Minister. The Australian troops gathered round to see the great war leader, but 'Auchinleck was still off stage. The Prime Minister in a tropical suit stumped along alone. The chill could be felt through the desert glow.'[51] As Churchill left, some of the Australian soldiers indulged their mordant sense of humour. One remembered that 'One of the 4th ack-ack blokes yelled out "When are you going to send us home, you fat old bastard?" and all the chaps laughed like hell. The Tommy provosts looked blue murder at everyone then.'[52] It was lucky that Churchill did not hear this shout but some humour was desperately needed when he sat down for breakfast at Auchinleck's Headquarters at the camel tracks. He did not approve of the flies, the spartan mess or the unappetising fried breakfast which was presented to him. He 'looked hot and unhappy'. The atmosphere became worse when Auchinleck and Dorman-Smith gave Churchill a briefing alone in the operations caravan with the current war maps hanging on the walls. Churchill does not seem to have paid much attention to the briefing and Dorman-Smith related that he:

quickly began to demand that Eighth Army should attack afresh. He thrust stubby fingers against the talc; 'Here', he said, 'or here'. We were alone with him, for the C.I.G.S. had gone forward up the line. It was a little like being caged with a gorilla. Eventually Auchinleck said quietly and finally, 'No, Sir, we cannot attack again yet'. The Prime Minister swung round to Dorman-Smith: 'Do you say that too; why don't you use the 44th Division?' 'Because Sir, that division isn't ready and anyhow a one-division attack would not get us anywhere'. Churchill, rose, grunted, stumped down from the caravan and stood alone in the sand, back turned to us. The chill was now icy.[53]

Auchinleck and Dorman-Smith's fates were sealed by this disastrous briefing. They had not been able to tell the Prime Minister of their plans to meet a future offensive by Rommel or the details of their planned offensive in September. Churchill's insistence on offensive action had been baulked by Auchinleck too many times. Auchinleck's persistent delays over Acrobat in the spring of 1942 were coming back to haunt him. Churchill needed a victory and he needed it now. Auchinleck, for every sound military reason, could not give the Prime Minister the assurance of an immediate offensive. Yet if he could not, then Churchill would find someone who would.

After this appalling briefing, Churchill was introduced to Gott, Inglis and Major-General Callum Renton, the new commander of 7th Armoured Division. Churchill then insisted that Gott should accompany him on his drive back to Burg el Arab. This upset the arranged 13 Corps conference between its assembled commanders but the great war leader was not to be deflected and the conference had to be postponed. On the drive to the landing ground, Gott learned more of the Prime Minister's intentions than anyone else that day. Churchill had wanted to meet Gott alone so that he could:

> form an impression of him and also ask him if he felt tired after all his long hard brilliant fighting . . . He inspired me at once with a feeling of confidence and although he said he would be all the better for a few months leave, I accepted his statement that he was fully capable of going on, in view of the imminence of renewed battle, as it then seemed.[54]

Brooke and Auchinleck both favoured Montgomery, presently C-in-C of Southern Command in England, as the next commander of Eighth Army but Churchill insisted on making this important decision himself. Churchill consistently chose military commanders for their personality and particularly their reputations for bravery. Gott had earned the DSO and Bar during the desert campaigns and possessed a legendary reputation amongst the officers and men of the Eighth Army. Churchill wrote to his wife: 'I had a long drive alone with Gott, and I convinced myself of his high ability and charming personality. One knows at once when one can make friends.'[55] Given the importance that Churchill attached to the command of Eighth Army and the necessity to defeat Rommel, the Prime Minister was unlikely meekly to accept military advice on the candidate for the post. That night, Churchill made up his mind: 'I therefore advised the Cabinet that he should be appointed to command Eighth Army, feeling sure this was what the situation required, and the Army would welcome.'[56]

It is not surprising that Churchill made up his mind quickly after meeting Gott. All accounts agree that Gott had a magnetic personality and spread an atmosphere of calm even in the most difficult of circumstances. Yet even in appointing Gott to command Eighth Army, Churchill had misunderstood the situation. There is little doubt that he expected Gott to launch what he wanted – an immediate offensive. But Churchill would almost certainly have been disappointed. Most historians have considered Churchill's appointment of Gott to the command of the Eighth Army a poor decision. His tiredness after two years of constant warfare is often stressed to emphasise his unsuitability. The euphemism of 'tired' was used to describe a multitude of failings during the Second World War, ranging from loss of confidence in a commander's judgement to simple fatigue. Gott had spent two years of hard campaigning in the desert with only two short breaks for leave. Yet he had shown only energy and enthusiasm in the way he prepared 13 Corps for the coming defensive battle.

On 6 August, Churchill and Brooke thrashed out their full set of changes to the Middle East Command. Churchill had decided to sack Auchinleck as Commander-in-Chief Middle East and replace him with Lieutenant-General Harold Alexander. Alexander was a suave, immaculately turned-out Guardsman with a strong reputation for courage, sound tactical skills and an acute sense of diplomacy. He had come to prominence during the Second World War in his role as a 'fireman' during the Dunkirk and Rangoon evacuations. Even in the midst of defeat and despair, Alexander had projected calm, phlegmatic authority.[57] Unfortunately, Churchill entirely misunderstood the roles of C-in-C Middle East and the commander of Eighth Army. He was determined to select Alexander as 'the best possible fighting soldier' and expected him personally to take direct charge of the operations against Rommel. To ensure that Alexander would not be distracted by the strategic concerns of the immense Middle East theatre, Churchill proposed to create a new Iraq–Persia Command that would prepare for the potential threat from the north. This would leave Alexander free to conduct the battle personally against Rommel. Churchill was also determined to clear out some of Auchinleck's subordinate commanders. Corbett, Dorman-Smith and Ramsden were all to be sacked. Meanwhile, Gott would take over command of the Eighth Army.

Gott received the news that day and prepared to take a few days' leave in Cairo before taking up his new command post. But since the 13 Corps conference had not taken place at Auchinleck's headquarters on 5 August as planned, Gott had to delay his departure by holding the meeting on the morning of 7 August. The delay imposed by the rescheduled conference meant that he decided to fly rather than drive to Cairo in the afternoon.

Gott finally held his Corps conference, with Auchinleck in attendance, on the morning of 7 August. All the staff work in preparing the defensive plans in case of an Axis attack was discussed. The planned withdrawal of 7th Motor Brigade in the face of an Axis advance and the plans for the occupation of Alam el Halfa ridge, the coordination of artillery under Brigadier Standford, the artillery commander of 13 Corps, and the battle positions of the 22nd Armoured Brigade were all discussed and laid out in detail. Inglis noted that the conference 'clarified a lot of points'[58] and Major Paul Hobbs, one of Gott's staff officers, remembered:

> the last morning he spent with us presiding at an exercise – 18 red hats round him with me at his back taking notes – all this in a big wig-wam – all his ideas of how the battle should be fought so plainly.[59]

There is no doubt that Gott had put all his subordinates fully 'in the picture' by the end of the conference. All that remained was to prepare the units of 13 Corps to enact the plans for the defence of the Alam el Halfa ridge. The critial decisions for the defence of Egypt had been taken and whoever was selected to command 13 Corps would have the benefit of an army commander who understood the operational and tactical situation intimately. Eighth Army was now ready for any offensive that Rommel might choose to launch.

Gott said his farewells, had a quick lunch with Inglis and then headed for the landing ground at Burg el Arab. He joked that he would return on 11 August after 'a big lunch of prawns at Shepheards and back with the hell of a liver in the evening'.[60] The Bombay transport aircraft was late and did not take off until 16.15 hours. The aircraft was packed with other officers, wounded and press correspondents but flew low along one of the prearranged routes which were considered so safe that planes did not need to be escorted. Churchill had flown along the same route, albeit with an escort, two days before. Ten minutes after take-off, two German Me109 fighters that had been forced down to ground level after a dogfight with British fighters spotted the lumbering Bombay. Rapid bursts of fire from the German fighters quickly damaged the aircraft and wounded the pilots. One of the pilots managed to crash-land the plane and three survivors quickly scrambled out, then went back to rescue those trapped in the wreckage. But the Bombay suddenly burst into flames. Gott, along with 15 other passengers, was killed.[61]

The events leading up to Gott's death had unfolded like a Greek tragedy. Had Churchill not insisted on taking Gott to Burg el Arab to size him up as a potential commander for Eighth Army, the Corps conference planned for the afternoon of 5 August would not have been postponed until the morning of 7 August. Without this delay, Gott would not have been on the unlucky transport plane. Eighth Army had lost its new commander before he was even able to take up the post.

Pienaar's comment on hearing of Gott's death was 'Now I know that heaven is on the side of the British!'[62] But while the South African commander had bitterly disliked Gott, the general mood throughout Eighth Army was one of shock and loss. Gott had been admired and trusted by most of the army's senior officers and, as one of the few ranking generals who had fought throughout the desert campaigns, his loss was mostly regarded as irreparable. Brooke seized the opportunity to convince Churchill that Montgomery needed to be sent out to Egypt as Gott's replacement.

Auchinleck had returned to Cairo on 3 August to take up the reins of General Headquarters Middle East again. His presence with Eighth Army on 5 August was brief and his time taken up with Churchill's visit. On learning of Gott's death, Auchinleck stayed in the desert with Eighth Army and the next day, Colonel Ian Jacob, one of Churchill's entourage, came to visit him. Jacob later recalled that 'it was like going to murder an unsuspecting friend'.[63] Jacob delivered a letter from Churchill which informed Auchinleck that he was relieved of the Middle East Command, offering him instead 'the command of Iraq and Persia'. Churchill sweetened the pill by arguing:

> It is true that this sphere is to-day smaller than the Middle East, but it may in a few months become the scene of decisive operations and reinforcements to the Tenth Army are already on the way.[64]

Auchinleck discussed the proposals with Jacob but concluded that 'he could not accept what was offered'.[65] Auchinleck, had, after all, been Commander-in-Chief of both India and the Middle East, and now he was being offered a truncated command which would be dependent on both the Middle East and India for resources. Auchinleck was only too well aware of the German threat to Iraq and Persia but he also recognised that the command could not receive proper reinforcements and supply without stripping bare Eighth Army. Auchinleck decided that it would be better 'to . . . retire into oblivion'.[66] However, he agreed to think the matter over until Churchill's return from Moscow.

Meanwhile, Alexander arrived in Cairo on 9 August at breakfast time and thus had a few days to prepare before taking command on 15 August. Brooke knew that he had to see Alexander before Churchill did so that he could 'warn him as regards the P.M.'s conception of the Command of the Middle East as opposed to that of the Eighth Army which he mixes together'.[67]

In fact, Alexander never had any intention of directly commanding Eighth Army in the manner of his predecessor. Alexander's role as

Commander-in-Chief Middle East during 1942 has generally been over-shadowed by Montgomery's performance as commander Eighth Army but he nevertheless bore overall responsibility for the campaign. He chose Major-General Richard McCreery, who had only just been sacked by Auchinleck, as his new Chief of the General Staff. He was an inspired choice. Alexander thus ensured that he had an officer with an understanding of armoured warfare at his side. While Auchinleck was still agonising over whether to accept the new Persia–Iraq command, Alexander was the recipient of a short and clear directive signed by Churchill and Brooke:

1. Your prime and main duty will be to take or destroy at the earliest opportunity the German–Italian Army commanded by Field Marshal Rommel together with all its supplies and establishments in Egypt and Libya.

2. You will discharge or cause to be discharged such other duties as pertain to your Command without prejudice to the task described in paragraph 1, which must be considered paramount in His Majesty's interests.[68]

It was Alexander's good fortune to take command of a severely truncated Middle East Command. His responsibilities did not span across 2,000 miles but, instead, were focused on the campaign in Egypt. There was no war in East Africa, no threat to Palestine or Syria. The looming menace of a German attack into Persia was not his concern. But Alexander's remit could only be as seemingly simple and straightforward because Wavell and Auchinleck had wrestled with, and overcome, so many dilemmas and difficulties in the previous two years of war. Shorn of these other responsibilities, Alexander and McCreery were in a position to work hard and efficiently to ensure that the now vast base organisation in Egypt could respond quickly to the growing needs of Eighth Army.[69]

Auchinleck's subsequent reputation was done great harm by his mis-handling of staff work. While he, Gott, Ramsden and Dorman-Smith had been clear on their offensive plans for the future, Corbett, working as Deputy Commander-in-Chief in Cairo, was not. He had continued to labour over the existing Middle East plans and, unfortunately, one of these was the extreme 'worst-case' plan for the retreat of Eighth Army from Alamein. It was based on the contingency plans of late June and bore no relation to Auchinleck or Gott's plans for the future as they stood at the beginning of August. Nonetheless, Corbett continued to work on the worst-case plans during July and sent increasingly detailed instructions to Whiteley who was still, officially at least, the Brigadier General Staff of Eighth Army Headquarters. The forlorn Whiteley was neither party to, nor aware of, his commander's very different planning. In the days just before Whiteley left

Eighth Army, he instructed Charles Richardson to develop the plans for withdrawal. Lieutenant-Colonel Miles Graham, one of the quartermaster's staff, was tasked with scouting the routes for this possible movement.[70] It would appear that neither Auchinleck nor Dorman-Smith was actually aware that this work was going on. As far as the two of them were concerned, any plans for withdrawal were obsolete and outdated. The confusion was, perhaps, the final and most damning example of Auchinleck's lack of grip on staff work and his inability to inject clarity of purpose into his staff. Ironically, Corbett's obsolete plans for retreat badly damaged Auchinleck's subsequent reputation even though they were diametrically opposed to his intentions and plans in early August 1942.

Unfortunately, Corbett's out-of-date plans remained on de Guingand's desk in August. It is little wonder that, in this situation, the new Brigadier General Staff of Eighth Army became dismayed and rather worried. He had before him plans for both future offensive and for withdrawal, with little indication of how to prioritise them. He was new to his job and lacked any clear direction from above. Auchinleck had returned to Cairo and Gott was dead. Ramsden was left in temporary charge of Eighth Army with Morshead at 30 Corps and Freyberg at 13 Corps. Freyberg had only just returned from hospital on 10 August and was still suffering from the effects of his wound at Mersa Matruh. He was not fully conversant with the 13 Corps plans. None of these men, however capable, had understood the next phase of operations as clearly as Gott, who had planned and organised 13 Corps' defence plan in detail. De Guingand was left with a temporary army commander whom he did not know and a contradictory array of forward plans. Eighth Army was certainly not 'looking over its shoulder' but it was bewildered and had lacked a commander for almost a week. What Dorman-Smith called the 'fortnight of confusion' caused by Churchill's sweeping command changes, combined with Gott's death, had produced a dangerous interregnum at Eighth Army Headquarters.

It was into this uncertain situation that, on 12 August, Lieutenant-General Bernard Montgomery, hastily summoned from England to replace Gott, arrived in Egypt. Soon thereafter, Auchinleck gave him a briefing on the current situation. Mongomery claimed in his memoirs that Auchinleck's plan:

> was based on the fact that at all costs the Eighth Army was to be preserved 'in being' and must not be destroyed in battle. If Rommel attacked in strength, as was expected soon, the Eighth Army would fall back on the Delta; if Cairo and the Delta could not be held, the army would retreat southwards up the Nile, and another possibility was a withdrawal to Palestine.[71]

It is impossible to be certain what passed between the two men but Montgomery reports a garbled version of Corbett's obsolete instructions 'in the unlikely event of a retreat'. This was certainly not an accurate portrayal of Auchinleck's plans as they existed in early August 1942. It is more likely that Auchinleck did indeed brief Montgomery as to the existing plans for meeting an Axis attack and the planned offensive in the north. However, Montgomery, both at the time and when writing his *Memoirs*, needed to distance himself from Auchinleck's influence. Montgomery had been selected, as he saw it, as the new broom that would sweep clean; he could not acknowledge the debt he owed to a discredited predecessor.

Montgomery then went to see Alexander. He immediately presented his plan for a *corps de chasse* which he believed would match the role of the Afrika Korps. Major-General John Harding, the Deputy Chief of the General Staff, was called in to a meeting with both Alexander and Montgomery. At that stage Harding did not know of the command changes but Montgomery put him through 'a catechism for about an hour, with Alex not taking any real part in the discussion, and I was quizzed on all the formation commanders down to brigades. At the end he said, "From all this muckage, can you organize for me two desert trained armoured divisions and a mobile infantry division?"'[72]

By that evening, Harding presented Montgomery with a plan for 10 Corps which would consist of two armoured divisions, each with one armoured and one infantry brigade, as well as the 2nd New Zealand Division organised with one armoured brigade and two infantry brigades. Although Montgomery considered his idea for a *corps d'élite* which would be 'strong in armour' and act as the 'spearhead' for the future offensive to be a fresh approach to the problem of desert warfare, it was to a large extent a reinvention of the wheel.[73] 30 Corps had been formed in September 1941 as an armoured corps for precisely this purpose; it was only the heavy losses of armour during 1942 which had recast 30 Corps as a largely infantry formation. The 'new' organisation for the 2nd New Zealand Division was precisely the same as Auchinleck's planned reorganisation of the army into 'mobile' divisions of infantry and armour brigades. Just as importantly, Montgomery who, from his reading, believed the Panzerarmee was separated into 'holding troops' which held static defensive positions and 'mobile troops' which were used for counterattacks, had misunderstood the nature of Rommel's army.[74] The Afrika Korps was not a *corps d'élite* which was held in reserve but the major combat component of the Panzerarmee, which could be used for any task demanded of it. Montgomery arrived in Egypt to stamp his mark upon Eighth Army but he never realised, or admitted, the contribution of his predecessors.

Douglas Wimberley ran into both Alexander and Montgomery at the officers' shop in Cairo buying khaki drill uniforms. Although neither would explain their presence, Wimberley, who had already witnessed the suppressed excitement at General Headquarters, guessed what was happening. He was delighted:

'Alex' had been head student of my year at the Staff College . . . Monty had
been not only my late commander in S.E. England, but had been Brigade Major
to our Brigade in Ireland 20 odd years before, and had taught me at Staff College.[75]

This was just one example of the web of connections which both Alexander
and Montgomery had built up during their careers which would serve them
well in the future.

Montgomery drove up to Eighth Army on 13 August. His meeting with de
Guingand went well; Freddie told Montgomery that 'the Eighth Army wanted
a clear lead and a firm grip from the top; there was too much uncertainty and
he thought the "feel of the thing" was wrong'.[76] Montgomery met with
Ramsden, the acting Army Commander, who explained the current situation
and the future plans for meeting an Axis offensive and the projected attack in
the north in September. Montgomery then dismissed him with: 'All right, I'll
carry on here. You can go back to your corps.'[77] The interregnum was over.

After a day of 'savage thinking', Montgomery addressed his new staff and
gave the clear direction which was most certainly needed. Montgomery told
his staff that he was going to create a new atmosphere: 'The bad old days
were over, and nothing but good was in store for us.'[78] He ordered the
removal of the headquarters from the Ruweisat ridge and insisted that Eighth
Army Headquarters must be linked with the Air Headquarters. He cancelled
all orders for retreat or withdrawal. He informed his staff that he would
immediately start with the planning for an offensive and mentioned the need
for a *corps d'élite* of two armoured divisions and the New Zealand Division.
The term battlegroup would cease to exist and divisions would henceforth
fight as divisions. Perhaps his most important decision was to appoint de
Guingand as his Chief of Staff. This role had not hitherto been used within
the British Army. The accepted role for the Brigadier General Staff, the
senior staff officer at an Army Headquarters, was to act as a first among
equals; the commanding general was still expected to manage his staff.
Montgomery dispensed with this system. As Chief of Staff, de Guingand
would now act as the main conduit for all Montgomery's decisions and the
responsibility and management of all staff work would lie with him. As de
Guingand later recalled:

That address by Montgomery will remain one of my most vivid recollections.
It was one of his greatest efforts. We all felt that a cool and refreshing breeze
had come to relieve the oppressive and stagnant atmosphere. The effect of the
address was electric – it was terrific! And we all went to bed that night with
a new hope in our hearts, and a great confidence in the future of our Army.[79]

There is no doubt that Montgomery's address re-energised the staff of
Eighth Army. Montgomery had begun to execute the 'Projection of

Personality' he had taught at Staff College in the twenties.[80] He projected confidence, determination and a clear direction which was bound to be appealing to a rather jaded and confused group of staff officers.

However, it is difficult in hindsight to disentangle the triumphant 'Monty' of post-1942 fame from the white-kneed lieutenant-general who came to command Eighth Army.[81] Montgomery's last experience of command in action had been with the 3rd Infantry Division during the retreat to Dunkirk. Since then, he had developed a powerful reputation as an energetic trainer of troops and an unconventional commander who drove his men hard. However, he had no experience of actually commanding mechanised forces in action or of the very different dimensions of time and space as they now operated in the deserts of Egypt.[82]

His peremptory orders to burn all plans for withdrawal included both the tactical plan for the 'thinning out' of Eighth Army to take up its defensive positions and Corbett's plans for the retreat of the whole army. As part of this policy of 'no retreat', Montgomery also ordered the removal of all unnecessary transport from the front lines. Any possibility of tactical mobility or rapid redeployment of the front line forces was removed. At one stroke, Montgomery had committed Eighth Army to a static defence in the face of any future Panzerarmee Afrika attack.

Montgomery's response on seeing the spartan mess for Eighth Army Headquarters was also legendary. Kisch had constructed a wire cage around the mess tables in an attempt to keep flies out but instead this had acted as a flytrap. Montgomery burst out: 'What's this, a meat safe? . . . You don't expect me to live in a meat safe, do you? Take it down at once, and let the poor flies out!'[83] Montgomery reacted badly to conditions that were far from unusual in Eighth Army. Auchinleck's Headquarters on Ruweisat ridge had never been intended to be permanent. It only became so when the expected advance in pursuit of a beaten Panzerarmee Afrika never happened. The quality of accommodation and fare was quite usual for the Eighth Army but certainly unusual for a commander straight from England. Nonetheless, Montgomery was correct in moving the Headquarters to Burg el Arab where a proper, more comfortable mess could be arranged and where the staff officers could bathe in the sea after a long day. The crisis at Alamein was over and the Main Headquarters no longer needed to be up in the front line. The move of the mess also acknowledged the important fact that there would be no more fluid fighting; static positional warfare would predominate for the next few months.

Montgomery's reception by the officers and men of Eighth Army was more cautious than perhaps the legend allows. Montgomery met Freyberg on his first day in the desert. Freyberg emphasised the importance of his charter from the New Zealand government. He went on to say:

I have had great anxiety in the past with higher commanders who have a
mania for breaking up military organisation. . . . I have seen two full Generals,
eleven Lieutenant-Generals and innumerable Major-Generals sacked because
they have put their trust in:
1 The 'Jock Columns'
2 The 'Brigade Group' Battle
3 The 'Crusader Tank'.[84]

Along with most of Eighth Army, Freyberg maintained a healthy scepticism
about any new commander fresh from England. Indeed, Freyberg was 'determined not to take part in the Battle of Alamein unless I was given an undertaking that we would fight as a Division'.[85] Not surprisingly, Montgomery's
insistence on fighting 'Divisions as divisions' was music to the ears of
Freyberg and Morshead, neither of whom had agreed with the brigade group
policy. Freyberg noted pointedly that:

after the abolition of the Brigade Group battle there was no disagreement
between the N.Z.E.F. and the C.in C. on questions of battle policy, and harmo-
nious relations were maintained up to the finish of the war.

At the same time, Montgomery's policy of 'no withdrawal' was welcomed
by Morshead who had opposed any withdrawal from the Tel el Eisa salient.
On 14 August, Freyberg held a New Zealand divisional conference at
which he:

told them situation and policy of the 'New Broom'. New Army Comd – New
Corps Comd – big changes at GHQ – probably new Divisional commanders
as well. Told them Army Comd's decision was to fight here – the forward
area is to be strengthened up. Dealt with question of ammunition – dumping
of ammunition, food and water and supply routes.[86]

However, the adoption of static defence meant that the New Zealand Division
could not thin out the forward zone to release troops to hold the Alam el
Halfa ridge. On 14 August, Montgomery demanded that the 44th (Home
Counties) Division be sent up to the front immediately. De Guingand telephoned General Headquarters Middle East with the request but was
informed that the division could not reach the forward area any earlier than
planned. Montgomery then spoke to John Harding who agreed to 'see what
he could do' but added, 'in any case they're not properly trained'.[87] This
reply must have annoyed Montgomery who had had the division under his
command in England. Harding went to see Corbett who responded that the
division was not yet properly equipped but that he should 'see the C-in-C'.
Harding had to ask 'Who is the C-in-C?' and he went to see both Auchinleck

and Alexander before replying to Montgomery that he would do all he could to get the division to the front. Harding did warn, however, that the division should only be given a defensive task.[88]

Freyberg was informed that two brigades from this division would be deployed on the ridge while a third would close the gap between the ridge and the New Zealand Division's positions. Lieutenant-Colonel Gentry, Freyberg's operations officer, commented that the New Zealand Division was not 'in a posn to hold at all costs until that Bde Gp was in', since there would be a vulnerable gap between the New Zealand Division and the positions on the Alam el Halfa ridge which could be exploited by any German armoured thrust. Montgomery's new policy thus did entail some measure of risk. Auchinleck had not brought 44th (Home Counties) Division forward to give its soldiers time to acclimatise. The division had landed at Suez only in mid-July and Montgomery's insistence on bringing it up to the front seemed to repeat the mistake of 23rd Armoured Brigade's too early commitment to battle. Placing an inexperienced division on the vital ground at Alam el Halfa was something of a gamble. However, by 18 August, all the troops of the division had moved forward and occupied the positions on the ridge.[89]

As far as Montgomery was concerned, his arrival in Egypt on 12 August 1942 was the most important event of the month – and possibly the whole war. Yet just two days later an event of immense strategic importance occurred in the Mediterranean theatre far away from the bustle of Eighth Army. The failure of the Harpoon and Vigorous convoys to Malta in mid-June meant that the island could only hold out until the end of September. Even in the face of declining stocks of aviation fuel, aircraft based on Malta continued to strike against Axis supply convoys.[90] Planning began in late June for the next convoy which was essential for Malta's continued survival. On 10 August, the Pedestal convoy of 14 merchant ships, supported by the most powerful naval force ever assembled by the Royal Navy in the Mediterranean, passed the Straits of Gibraltar. After an intense air battle, four merchant ships managed to reach Valetta's Grand Harbour on 14 August. The next day, the vital tanker *Ohio*, carrying 12,000 tons of fuel, with two destroyers lashed to her sides to prevent her sinking, limped into the harbour.[91] The arrival of these ships ensured that Malta could survive for another few months and continue its vital work of intercepting Axis supply convoys.

Montgomery was not the only fresh face to arrive at Eighth Army in August. 13 Corps needed a new commander to replace Gott and Freyberg was initially placed in temporary command on 11 August but he considered his sojourn at 13 Corps 'rather a waste of time'.[92] Montgomery decided to bring his 'own man' out to Egypt. Since his days as a member of the Directing Staff at Staff College, Montgomery had kept a 'black book' filled with the names of officers who had impressed him. Indeed, he saw such patronage and the 'bringing on' of officers as an important role for a senior officer.

Brian Horrocks had commanded the machine-gun battalion in 3rd Division in France and Montgomery had seen to it that he had been given successively a brigade and then a division. The prime importance of patronage within the British Army had been alien to Auchinleck; now Montgomery used his position to build his own team of commanders.

Horrocks, a former school friend of 'Chink' Dorman-Smith, was perhaps more honest in his account of arrival in Egypt than Montgomery.[93] He was naturally very nervous in taking command of a corps which had previously been commanded by Gott. Commanding an active corps was a tremendous opportunity but also a great risk; in the Home Army, the Middle East had become known as the graveyard of lieutenant-generals' careers. When he arrived at Eighth Army's Headquarters on 18 August, Montgomery proceeded to brief him on the military situation. Horrocks remembered this first briefing as:

> One of the most remarkable military appreciations I ever heard. Remember, he had arrived in Egypt only five days before; yet in this short space of time he had acquired a complete grip of the situation.[94]

Montgomery had indeed made an intensive study of the front line on the southern sector in his first few days in command. However, although he never admitted it, Montgomery's 'complete grip of the situation' relied heavily upon the work of Auchinleck, Gott and Ramsden. Montgomery claimed that he 'at once saw the importance of two dominating areas of ground: the Ruweisat Ridge and the Alam Halfa Ridge',[95] yet these had been recognised as vital terrain since 1 July 1942. On the other hand, Montgomery's ability to project confidence and clear vision to his subordinates was a real talent. Horrocks left the briefing with no doubts and happy that he was to serve under his old mentor. Nonetheless, he was inexperienced and was fortunate to have 'Bob' Erskine and Freddy de Butt, who had both been part of Gott's staff, to advise him.

Even the commander of 22nd Armoured Brigade, which now contained almost all of Eighth Army's precious Grant tanks was new. Brigadier G. P. B. 'Pip' Roberts had commanded 3rd Royal Tank Regiment during Gazala and had been in Egypt since 1940, when he was a mere captain. He took command of his new armoured brigade on 4 August and wrote to his father, 'I was suddenly summoned a few days ago to take command of this Bde – very thrilled but naturally a little nervous of my considerable responsibilities particularly at this time.'[96]

The command changes which Churchill and Brooke had initiated thus went very deep in Eighth Army. Eighth Army had a new army commander and, on the vital southern sector, soon to be attacked by the Panzerarmee Afrika, there was a new corps commander, a fresh and untried infantry division and a new brigadier in charge of the most powerful armoured formation. It was not surprising then that Montgomery reacted badly to Callum Renton, the unfortunate commander of 7th Armoured Division, who, on first meeting his new Army Commander, asked 'who would loose the armour against Rommel?'[97] Renton had understood and expected to follow Gott's plan for the predicted Axis attack. 4th Light Armoured Brigade was supposed to retire in front of the German advance while observing and harassing the Axis at every opportunity. The Afrika Korps would then meet the New Zealand Division on Alam el Halfa ridge and its attack would be broken up by artillery and anti-tank gun fire. At this point, with 4th Light Armoured Brigade now on the southern and eastern flanks, 22nd Armoured Brigade would counterattack the German penetration.

Such a manoeuvre had been discussed and practised by all the commanders of 13 Corps and was well within the capabilities of the troops. However, neither Montgomery, Horrocks nor Roberts had experience of commanding their new formations in battle. If the commanders of Eighth Army's armour had been cautious during the July fighting, Horrocks was doubly so. He admitted that he 'hated the idea' of counterattacking against the much-vaunted Afrika Korps.[98] He decided to fight a completely defensive battle and ordered 'Pip' Roberts to dig in his tanks in defensive positions around Point 102 on the Alam el Halfa ridge. Roberts admitted he was glad that all the alternative positions which had been identified under Gott's plan had been scrapped[99] but the static defence ordered by Horrocks was to surrender all possibility of mobility in the coming battle.

While Montgomery undertook a gruelling series of visits to the front line to speak to soldiers throughout Eighth Army, Horrocks also began to make his mark on 13 Corps. He issued a personal memorandum on 23 August explaining his conduct of the battle, German intentions and the preparation necessary for the coming fight. After two operations where they felt the British armour had let them down, most New Zealand soldiers had nothing but contempt for the tanks and did not hesitate to say so. Their new corps commander tried to heal the rift: 'There is a slight tendency for arms to criticise each other – this is natural reaction after a reverse but it must stop now. We are one Corps with complete confidence in each other.'[100] Horrocks also took up a theme beloved by the new Army Commander:

I have noticed that on several occasions when an order is issued from a higher formation staff officers in sub-ordinate formations ring up staff officers at the formation above them and protest against certain aspects of the order – in other words 'bellyache'. This is no good in battle. Orders are not issued without considerable thought and for very good reasons. Staff officers cannot know the wider picture on which a plan is based. The Comd of a sub-ordinate formation always has the right to protest, but this must be done <u>to the Comd above in person or on the telephone</u>, not to the staff.[101]

Eighth Army staff officers had certainly become used to querying orders and this spoke volumes about the nature of staff work during the July fighting. Formations had been ordered into battle at very short notice with orders that had not always been issued after 'considerable thought and for very good reasons'. At the same time, Horrocks was having, by his own admission, 'about the most difficult time I had in the war'[102] because Freyberg queried every order he issued. Horrocks believed that Freyberg was aggrieved at having been passed over for the corps command. The issue of 'bellyaching' was politically more sensitive than either Montgomery or Horrocks realised. The worst offenders had generally been the Dominion commanders who were exercising their constitutional rights as the commanders of national forces.

Churchill returned to Cairo from Moscow on 17 August and could not resist the temptation to revisit the Eighth Army under its new commander. The next day he and Brooke drove out to Burg el Arab to visit Montgomery. Churchill certainly preferred his new headquarters, 'drawn up amid the sand-dunes by the sparkling waves'.[103] Brooke and Churchill went for a swim after their long drive and 'the troops were delighted to see their Prime Minister wading into the water in the untanned nude'.[104] After dinner, Churchill was only too happy to listen to Montgomery's 'masterly exposition of the situation'.[105] The contrast with Auchinleck's last briefing to the Prime Minister could not have been greater.

Churchill toured the front the next day and visited the battle positions of 22nd Armoured Brigade. Although he was impressed by Roberts and delighted to inspect soldiers from his old regiment, the 4th Hussars, the Prime Minister was far from impressed by Horrocks. The 13 Corps commander was perhaps rather too honest in explaining to Churchill the static battle that Montgomery had planned. Horrocks explained that while 22nd Armoured Brigade repulsed the German thrust, the forces of 7th Armoured Division would strike at the Axis soft transport – what Horrocks called a case of 'dog eat rabbit'.[106] Churchill gruffly retorted: 'That's no good . . . Trouble with you generals is that you are defensive minded. Why don't you attack? That's the way to win battles, not by sitting down in defence.'[107] Churchill had once again revealed his ignorance of military affairs but it was fortunate for Montgomery that Horrocks drew the sting of the Prime Minister's dislike. Any ire that Churchill may have had for the passive plan of battle was smoothed away by Montgomery's special orders to the army. Ian Jacob noted:

> The Prime Minister was particularly pleased with two special orders which had been issued to the 8th Army by Monty; and he gave instructions that they should be circulated to the Cabinet on his return. They certainly are the most inspiriting documents and it is quite clear who means to be master in the desert.[108]

The soldiers of Eighth Army would appear to have been less impressed but there is no question that Montgomery had made his presence felt.

Meanwhile, Auchinleck finally decided that he could not accept the new post of the Iraq–Persia Command. He informed Brooke how he felt: 'The scheme is unworkable in practice, and I feel that there is a grave risk of its breaking down under the stress of active operations.'[109] Auchinleck was indeed right to reject the Iraq–Persia Command on military reasoning. There was no possibility that enough troops could be found for the command at the same time that Eighth Army built up for its own offensive. In reality, the command would be entirely dependent upon Cairo for its resources and there was little chance that sufficient troops or materiel would be released to meet the 'worst case' of a German breakthrough in late 1942. The truth was that Churchill and Brooke were still gambling on the Germans being held up in the Caucasus even though Stalin and his generals refused to give them any details of the fighting in Russia. Nonetheless, Auchinleck never understood the political significance of Churchill's offer. In offering Auchinleck an active, if materially unimportant, command, Churchill was seeking to minimise the political consequences of being seen to sack another Commander-in-Chief Middle East. Had Auchinleck accepted the offer, he might well have returned to a more important position later in the war.

Instead, Auchinleck returned to India and eventually replaced Wavell as Commander-in-Chief India. Corbett was sacked by Brooke with the simple words 'It has been decided to replace you.' Corbett noted bitterly that 'one does not dismiss one's gardener without some explanation'.[110] He returned to the command of a division in India. Dorman-Smith returned to the United Kingdom and dropped back to his substantive rank of lieutenant-colonel. While Auchinleck ended his military career in the highest post normally open to an Indian Army officer, Dorman-Smith experienced military 'oblivion'.[111] There is no doubt that the bitterness engendered by the 'Cairo purge' and the interregnum rankled with those affected for the rest of their lives.

Yet although Churchill's command changes appeared sweeping at the time they affected the military situation rather less than has sometimes been stated. Dorman-Smith, writing to Horrocks, later argued:

> The astonishing thing being that out of all this politico-military confusion . . . the 'common doctrine' survived; historically there is no break between a) the July 1942 'Battle for Egypt', b) The July 27th Appreciation; c) Alam Halfa; d) Your Alamein. If we didn't know of the 'Fortnight of Confusion' everything would have seemed to dovetail. Which is what we all went to the Staff Colleges to ensure.[112]

Although Dorman-Smith may have gone too far in his claim of a 'common doctrine', the controversies over the command changes have tended to obscure the fact that Eighth Army itself was relatively unscathed by the turbulence. In fact, the critical document was Auchinleck's own appreciation of 2 August which laid out the need to defeat an offensive by the Panzerarmee and then the measures necessary for Eighth Army's own offensive. Ramsden and de Guingand had both contributed important thinking to this subject long before Montgomery ever arrived in the desert. Auchinleck's 'blueprint' did indeed survive the 'Fortnight of Confusion'.

It is less clear, however, whether Auchinleck would have been able to execute that blueprint with the same resolve and clarity of purpose as the new team of Alexander and Montgomery. The South African official historian J. A. I. Agar-Hamilton's assessment was that:

> Auchinleck as a commander was hopeless but not because he was a fool. He possessed in fact both a first-class military brain and good fighting spirit. What he lacked was leadership. He never seemed able to get anyone to obey him . . . His intellect and his understanding of his trade were alike excellent – his powers of command were nil.[113]

This evaluation of Auchinleck seems fair in the light of the July fighting. There is no question that Auchinleck could identify what needed to be done but encountered real difficulty in translating those ideas into practice. Alexander and Montgomery may have owed more to Auchinleck than they cared to admit but during August 1942 they used their finely developed talents as commanders and leaders of men to inject a new sense of purpose into Eighth Army.

Meanwhile, the slow transit of convoys around the Cape of Good Hope took no account whatsoever of the recent command changes. Vast quantities of supplies began to flow into Egypt from the crowded derricks at Suez. During August alone, 446 guns, 254 tanks, 3,289 vehicles and 72,192 tons of stores arrived from Britain.[114] Amongst the eagerly awaited convoys which arrived at Suez in late August was a ship from America carrying a consignment of new Grant tanks and – just as importantly – spare parts.

This meant that 8th Armoured Brigade could now be equipped with a mixture of new Grants and some of the tanks that had been languishing in base workshops since 1 July for lack of spare parts. Eighth Army was still short of battle-winning tanks but the real crisis in its tank arm had passed.

Earlier in the month, on 2 August, 2nd Armoured Brigade handed over all of its remaining tanks to 22nd Armoured Brigade and, along with the headquarters of 1st Armoured Division, moved back to Khatatba camp. The relief, which Lumsden had demanded for his division on 5 July, had finally taken place. 1st Armoured war diary noted that 'the Div had been in the desert for nine months on end, and the first week was spent in getting personnel on leave and getting generally cleaned up'.[115] Officers and men could now be sent on courses, while proper training began for drafts newly arrived from England. Lumsden returned to his division from sick leave on 15 August but just four days later left to assume command of 10 Corps. The command of the division, after suffering such rapid changes during July, was finally given to Raymond Briggs. Frank Fisher kept his command of 2nd Armoured Brigade.

Every armoured unit within Eighth Army, from experienced desert veterans to the newcomers of 9th Armoured Brigade, now underwent the process of absorbing new personnel, receiving new equipment and carrying out intensive unit training. Lieutenant-Colonel H. E. 'Pete' Pyman, who succeeded 'Pip' Roberts as commander of the 3rd Royal Tank Regiment (which now formed part of 8th Armoured Brigade),[116] explained that:

> The tidying up of the armour in August 1942 was a long and painful process. In my own regiment we took in 17 new officers and 300 other ranks. We were re-equipped with two squadrons of Grant and one of Crusader tanks. . . . in those hot summer days in the desert we set ourselves with great heart to apply [the lessons we had learnt]. . . . Armoured Brigades of three armoured regiments, one regiment of RHA and one bn of motor infantry practised night and day the application of what was now becoming a golden rule AN ARMOURED DIVISION IS A FORMATION OF ALL ARMS.[117]

Even though the armoured divisions still conceived their role as independent from the infantry divisions and only understood the concept of all-arms cooperation within their formation, the significance of this training cannot be overestimated. British armour commanders had long realised the 'golden rule' of all-arms cooperation, and its importance had been stated and restated in 'lessons learned'.[118] However, there was an enormous difference between advising units of its importance and having the time and resources available to ensure that the armour, artillery and infantry of the armoured divisions actually worked and trained together so that all-arms cooperation became second nature. This crash course in sound all-arms tactics could not rectify all the flaws in the British armoured divisions but it was a major step forward.

Even though his wound still required three dressings a day,[119] Gatehouse was given command of 10th Armoured Division which now included 8th, 22nd and 23rd Armoured Brigades. Gatehouse deployed his headquarters on the Alam el Halfa ridge close to Horrocks's Corps Headquarters on 27 August and 8th Armoured Brigade took up a battle position to the south of the ridge on the same day.[120] Eighth Army was now more than ready to meet Rommel's expected attack.

TWELVE

The Six Days' Race

On 29 August 1942, the tanks, half-tracks and trucks of 21st Panzer Division rumbled southwards along desert tracks towards their assembly points. That night, the divisional staff received a short message from the Afrika Korps: 'X Day 30 Aug.'[1] Rommel had finally decided to launch his army in one last attempt to take the Delta. He wrote to his wife: 'There are such big things at stake. If our blow succeeds, it might go some way towards deciding the whole course of the war. If it fails, at least I hope to give the enemy a pretty thorough beating.'[2] After so much tension and worry, Rommel was relieved to have finally made the decision and move onto the attack again.

During August 1942, the Panzerarmee Afrika had faced a range of problems but the worst was undoubtedly what can only be described as a quartermaster's nightmare. Having advanced to El Alamein and survived the repeated attacks mounted by Eighth Army during July, the Panzerarmee had found itself stranded in the desert. Rommel had never expected to spend so long at the gates of Egypt. Now the Axis quartermasters had to try to find a solution to the problems of an army which had long passed its culminating point.

Throughout the July fighting, the Panzerarmee had moved from crisis to crisis and had survived only on a hand-to-mouth basis. Much of the petrol, ammunition, food, mines, tools and even uniforms used by the army had come from captured British stocks. On 1 August, the Panzerarmee reported to Berlin that the supplies reaching the front were sufficient only for the daily requirements of the troops. It was impossible to build up reserves for a major offensive operation. It was not that the supplies did not exist. Indeed, equipment and supplies earmarked for North Africa were piling up in Europe. It was estimated that 2,000 trucks and 100 guns for German formations awaited transport from Italy with a further 1,000 trucks and 120 tanks held in Germany.[3] The problem lay in getting those supplies across the Mediterranean to North African ports and then to El Alamein.

Most of the supplies destined for the Panzerarmee were loaded at Naples because of its better rail connection but Taranto and Brindisi were also used. Ships were also on occasion loaded up at Piraeus, the port of Athens, in Greece. However, after the heavy losses of two years of war, the Italian merchant marine was beginning to feel the strain of the constant runs to North Africa.[4] The Italian Navy, moreover, was finding it increasingly difficult to provide destroyer escorts for convoys and at the same time was hampered by the lack of fuel oil. During August 1942, the Italian Navy was allocated 47,000 tons of fuel oil from Germany and Romania but the projected consumption was 68,000 tons. The shortfall had to be covered by almost literally scraping the bottom of the barrel; amongst other desperate measures, 7,000 tons of oil were emptied out of the Italian cruisers to provide fuel for the convoys.[5] Ultimately, the Panzerarmee depended on the availability of Italian naval escorts for the timing and frequency of its supply convoys.

Powerful escorts for the convoys had once again become necessary because, after the arrival of the Pedestal convoy to Malta, British action in the Sicilian narrows had become more aggressive. Axis supplies bound for North Africa had to run the gauntlet of increased British air and submarine attacks mounted from Malta and Egypt.

Even with these attacks, the Italian Navy still found it possible to escort the majority of supplies safely across the Mediterranean. However, once a convoy had reached Tripoli, Benghazi or Tobruk there remained the problem of getting them to the front. They had to be unloaded from the ships, dumped on the quays and then loaded onto trucks for the long drive to the front. While Tripoli could handle large quantities of materiel, it was nearly 1,400 miles from there to the front. Benghazi, which could also handle reasonable amounts of shipping, was 700 miles from El Alamein. The ports of Tobruk, Bardia, Derna and Mersa Matruh had all been captured during the advance into Egypt but none of them was able to handle large amounts efficiently.[6] Tobruk, the largest of these ports, had been constructed as an Italian naval base and did not have the large wharfs necessary for efficient unloading of merchant ships. This meant that Tobruk could not process more than 20,000 tons of supplies out of the 100,000 tons needed every month.[7] During August, the Panzerarmee demanded that Italian workmen should be deployed to develop the installations at Tobruk and develop landing quays in the small bays and inlets along the coast. However, Tobruk was also under constant attack by British medium bombers and American heavy bombers which made the use of the port very difficult and slowed this development work to a crawl.[8]

Naturally, the movement of supplies from these far distant ports consumed vast quantities of petrol and caused great wear and tear on the motor transport involved. In fact, there was a chronic shortage of motor transport within the Panzerarmee. At any one time, 25 per cent of the Panzerarmee's motor transport was under repair and since 85 per cent of it consisted of captured British vehicles, the lack of spare parts created an enormous problem.[9]

Air transport was the one method which promised to short-circuit the strictures of Clausewitz's diminishing power of the offensive. Troops and supplies could be transported quickly and relatively safely across the Mediterranean in Ju52 transport aircraft. However, the Luftwaffe could never provide sufficient air transport to fulfil anything more than a small percentage of the daily needs of the Panzerarmee. Bulk supplies still had to travel by sea. The soldiers of the German 164th Division, the Italian Folgore Parachute Division and the German Ramcke Parachute Brigade which were flown across to North Africa from Italy and Crete during July and August were welcome additions to the strength of the Panzerarmee but they brought no motor transport of their own. 164th Division had been equipped with obsolete 37mm anti-tank guns and much capacity had to be used in flying over hundreds of 50mm anti-tank guns to equip the division. The arrival of these troops strengthened the defences of the front but at the same time created more difficulties for the quartermasters. Now, though there were more mouths to feed and more requirements for ammunition and equipment, there were no more vehicles to satisfy the requirements. Air transport could never satisfy the complex and voracious appetite of a mechanised army in the field.[10]

Attempts were made to solve the transport problem by making more use of coastal shipping to bring limited quantities of supplies to the smaller ports nearer the front. At the beginning of August, however, there was just one steamer available to ply the coastal route. Since only three Italian destroyers were based in Africa in August 1942, there were constant delays in sailings and some coastal shipping had to wait for eight days before an escort could be found. Although the Panzerarmee requested more Italian barges and at least three Italian coastal vessels for German use, such shipping was highly vulnerable to RAF attacks. On 2 August alone, the RAF sank two barges and two auxiliary vessels in Bardia harbour.[11]

The quartermasters of the Panzerarmee had high hopes that the desert railway from Belhamed to Mersa Matruh, constructed with so much effort by the British, would help to solve some of their transport difficulties. However, it took time to repair the track and signal gear, and the Italian locomotives transferred to North Africa proved to be useless. There were further delays in bringing German diesel locomotives across and decent rolling stock to shift supplies. And even when the railway did come into operation, its use was severely restricted by the attentions of the RAF. Trains could run only at night and constant bombing raids against its installations meant that its capacity was severely reduced.[12]

The ability of the Desert Air Force to mount powerful raids against the Axis lines of supply also severely reduced the quantities of supplies which the Panzerarmee was receiving. During July, 20,000 tons of Axis shipping was sunk mainly as a result of air attack from Malta and Egypt. The losses climbed to 65,000 tons in August.[13] Greater Luftwaffe protection was demanded but this merely took limited air resources from one task to another. The neutralisation of Malta, protection of convoys in the Mediterranean, patrols over the extended desert line of communications and close support of the Panzerarmee Afrika could not all be delivered simultaneously by the overstretched Luftwaffe and Regia Aeronautica units in the Mediterranean theatre.

These structural problems were complicated by organisational tensions between the Italian and German components of the Panzerarmee. The Italian Commando Supremo controlled the movement of shipping across the Mediterranean, and only the German military attaché in Rome, General von Rintelen, had any influence over its decisions. Kesselring, the Luftwaffe's Commander-in-Chief South, was involved solely in questions of air and naval protection for convoys and ports. The Panzerarmee could submit priority lists for supplies but had no say in where the cargo was delivered or the ratio of German and Italian supplies carried.[14]

At the beginning of August, Rommel made a series of demands to von Rintelen detailing the troops, supplies and equipment that would have to reach the front by 20 August before he could mount an offensive. He demanded that the rest of the 164th Infantry Division and the Ramcke Parachute Brigade, along with replacements, should be flown in. Rommel's demands also included a long list of anti-tank guns, tanks, artillery pieces, gun tractors and motor transport along with the complete replenishment of ammunition stocks. Finally, the Panzerarmee would need supplies of all kinds, fuel and spare parts.[15]

Yet even while lacking these resources, Rommel began to contemplate plans for a fresh offensive. On 10 August, he held a conference with Count Barbasetti, the Supreme Commander in North Africa, to discuss the new Italian administrative structure in Africa and to inform him of his intentions. Rommel knew that he would have to attack before the arrival of the British convoys bound for Suez. Any offensive would be likely to fail once the British were reinforced. Rommel also needed to attack before the British defensive minefields became too dense to permit a rapid breakthrough. At the same time, he knew that he could not attack until the scheduled reinforcements had reached the front and the army had received sufficient supplies of fuel. The best time to attack would be 26 August at the time of the full moon to assist in the rapid night march of the Panzerarmee.[16]

Rommel discounted any idea of attacking the heavily defended positions in the northern sector and instead planned to mount his main attack in the south, using his armour and mobile forces to encircle and destroy Eighth Army in a repeat of Gazala. The forces would not be concentrated until the eve of the attack and dummy positions would be used to conceal the movement of the armoured divisions. To maintain the element of surprise there would be no artillery or air preparation and limited infantry attacks would

be mounted along the entire front to confuse Eighth Army. Once the armour
and motorised forces assembled south of Deir el Qattara, they would push
through the British minefields as rapidly as possible. The armour would
drive east and then turn north for the coast road. The plan was to encircle
the British positions and cut them off from their supplies.

In fact, although Rommel later complained bitterly that insufficient effort
had been made to sustain his army in this critical period, during August
1942 the Italian supply organisation met many of the demands – particularly concerning tanks and ammunition. Reinforcements were flown in by
the Luftwaffe and although insufficient motor transport was shipped,
supplies in accordance with Rommel's priority lists for ammunition, tanks
and guns were generally met. By 28 August, the strength of the army had
been rebuilt and compared favourably with the forces that had begun
Operation Venezia on 26 May. The army now held 84,000 German and
44,000 Italian personnel with 234 German and 281 Italian tanks. Three
issues of ammunition were held with the exception of some tank and anti-
tank guns. Given the difficulties inherent in its transportation, this rapid
build-up of men and materiel represented a considerable achievement by
the Axis supply organisation.[17]

However, there remained one critical problem. The army remained
desperately short of fuel. Rommel had met with Marshal Ugo Cavallero,
Barbasetti, Kesselring and von Rintelen on 18 August to discuss his plans
for the offensive and also to sort out the supply problems. On that day, the
German forces in Africa had 3,000 cubic metres of fuel, but since the
consumption was 300 cubic metres per day the stocks would be nearly gone
by 26 August, the date of the projected attack. Rommel insisted that he must
receive an additional 10 consumption units of fuel[18] (6,000 tons) and two
issues of ammunition before he could attack. Rommel emphasised that he
could postpone the operation for only a few days because the full moon was
essential to the success of the plan. Cavallero promised to deliver 6,000 tons
of fuel to the Panzerarmee by X-day and mentioned that 750 tons of Italian
fuel would be brought up for German use. Kesselring gave additional guar-
antees that, in an emergency, he would undertake to fly 500 tons of fuel
across from Greece every day to ensure that the army had sufficient
supplies.[19]

On 22 August, Rommel informed Commando Supremo that he would
not be able to attack unless 2,000 tons of fuel and 500 tons of ammunition
were landed at Tobruk and Benghazi by 25 August. The army would need
a further 2,000 tons of fuel unloaded at Tobruk on 27 August and finally
another 3,600 tons of fuel and 2,000 tons of ammunition delivered to Tobruk
and Benghazi by 30 August.[20] These were heavy demands to make of a supply
chain that was already operating at full stretch.

The next day Cavallero replied that the tanker *Alberto Fassio*, carrying

1,140 tons of fuel and 500 tons of ammunition, had arrived that morning in Tobruk harbour. More was on its way: 225 tons of fuel was due on 25 August, 2,470 tons of fuel and 242 tons of ammunition on 28 August, 2,956 tons of fuel and 580 tons of ammunition on 1 September, and 1,000 tons of fuel and 1,650 tons of ammunition on 4 September. Meanwhile, stocks of fuel were being kept in reserve in Italy to replace any losses by British action. However, Cavallero also warned that these deliveries represented the maximum effort that could be made, and the timing was dependent on the escorts necessary for the convoys. The Italians continued to lose shipping as a result of British action, which made meeting Rommel's demands very difficult.[21]

It was no accident that Italian tankers seemed to be sunk with depressing regularity. The British air and naval effort from Malta and Egypt was necessarily limited but it was focused on sinking high-value targets like tankers. The use of Ultra came into its own in the war against Italian tankers. German and Italian radio traffic gave complete details of ports of departure and expected times of arrival. This enabled attacks to be planned very carefully and targeted precisely. The security of Ultra intelligence was guarded by the requirement that every convoy had to be visually sighted by an aircraft before an attack could be mounted. While by no means all of the attacks were successful, Ultra enabled the British to focus their limited resources on such targets as tankers and thus have a disproportionate and sometimes crippling effect upon the Panzerarmee's logistic chain.[22]

The effects of attacks from Malta were magnified at the end of August as a result of the Panzerarmee's desperate need for fuel. The sinking of the tanker *Pozzarico* with its cargo of 1,010 tons of fuel on 21 August meant that Italian stocks were reduced to the bare minimum. The Germans were forced to loan 500 tons of fuel to their allies. Delays in getting convoys across the Mediterranean meant that Rommel was forced to postpone his attack again. The movement of the forces into the assembly areas, which was due to start on the night of 26–27 August, had to be put off. By the evening of 28 August, there were only 2,400 cubic metres of fuel for German use, which represented four consumption units.[23]

The next day, the Panzerarmee announced that, because the fuel and ammunition had not arrived, the offensive had been altered into a local operation to destroy the enemy forces in the Alamein position. Of course, nothing had really changed and Rommel was still gambling his entire force on a successful outcome. Kesselring had placed 1,000 tons of Luftwaffe fuel reserves at the disposal of the Panzerarmee and promised to fly more fuel across from Crete and Greece.

During the build-up to the offensive, Rommel's doctors became increasingly worried about his health. The field marshal was now suffering from low blood pressure which precipitated fainting fits brought on by chronic stomach problems. On 21 August, Rommel informed Berlin of his condition and requested that a replacement be sent out as soon as possible. Rommel asked for Panzer General Heinz Guderian as his replacement.[24] Guderian had masterminded the creation of the panzer corps in the 1930s and had led the XIX Panzer Corps to victory in 1940. However, during the Barbarossa campaign of 1941 Guderian had quarrelled violently with Hitler and he remained out of favour. Berlin replied to Rommel's request by saying that no suitable replacement with tropical experience could be found and that he had to steel himself to continue until the offensive had been carried through.

Ultimately, Rommel made the decision to attack in the full knowledge that there was insufficient fuel in Africa to make the attempt. Nehring commented:

> the fuel situation is bad . . . The German Pz divisions have 1.5 fuel units that means if the ground conditions are normal and if there is no fighting they can travel 150 kms; after that they are immobile.[25]

Not only was Rommel gambling on repeating another Gazala but he was relying on the mere promise of fuel to complete his advance to the Delta.

Rommel issued orders on 22 August for the attack. The Afrika Korps, 90th Light, Ariete and Littorio were to assemble between Qaret el Diyura and the El Taqa plateau by the evening of X-day. At 22.00 hours that night, the attacking armoured divisions were to pass through the Axis minefields to the north of Himeimat and drive east through the night in the hope of taking Eighth Army by surprise. Strong detachments of engineers were to clear passages through the enemy minefields as rapidly as possible. By 03.30 hours the divisions were to have assembled on the far side of Eighth Army's minefields to replenish and refuel at Samaket Gaballa. As the main striking force of the Afrika Korps advanced, its right flank would be screened by a group of reconnaissance units and its left by the Italian armour. 90th Light was to penetrate the minefields further north near the Munassib Depression and act as the hinge between the static northern front and the advancing Afrika Korps. By 04.30 hours, the whole force would wheel to drive north east, bypassing the Alam el Halfa ridge, and heading for the British rear at the eastern end of the Ruweisat ridge. Once the Afrika Korps had made this daring move, the 'British centre and the north wing together with the reserves in their rear were to be cut off and destroyed'.[26] It was a bold plan but it required speed, surprise and enough fuel to make it work.

Meanwhile, it was hoped that Eighth Army would be distracted from this main thrust by diversionary attacks and raids mounted along the front. 164th Division and the Italian divisions of X and XXI Corps were to keep the front of Eighth Army busy with strong raiding parties composed of Italian combat engineers with flamethrowers to take prisoners and cause disruption. Folgore Division was to attack from El Taqa to capture Height 216 and hold it against attack. Meanwhile, a battlegroup formed from elements of the Ramcke Brigade, XX Corps and the Brescia Division were to capture the heights to the south west of Alam Nayil. The Panzerarmee also requested the support of Fliegerführer Afrika and the Italian 5th Aerosquadra in putting up continuous fighter patrols to protect the formations in their assembly areas and during the attack. Stukas and fighter bombers would then be used to support the advance of the motorised formations.[27] These orders failed to recognise the growing dominance of the Desert Air Force over the skies above El Alamein. The Panzerarmee had for too long operated with the assumption of air superiority. Air power was an integral part of the doctrine and tactics of the Afrika Korps in attack and defence. This time, it would be lacking.

As the sun sank below the desert horizon on 30 August, the panzer divisions of the Afrika Korps began their move forward. Approaching the British minefields, it seemed that they had succeeded in achieving surprise but those hopes were to be dashed when, just before midnight, they contacted the units of 7th Motor Brigade.

Lieutenant-Colonel Michael Carver, the chief staff officer of 7th Armoured Division, had become frustrated at the constant postponements of the looming Axis offensive. Ultra decrypts had confirmed the outline of the Axis plan and the fact that it was timed to coincide with the full moon. Reconnaissance flights on 30 August had reported heavy concentrations of transport in the southern sector and estimated that there were as many as 3,000 vehicles and 105 tanks there. Even though these were underestimates, the Axis attempts to conceal their movement and concentration had failed badly. Soon after midnight, Carver received reports from the outlying battalions of 7th Motor Brigade that Axis artillery was shelling the minefield gaps used by the advanced armoured cars.[28] Carver immediately requested an RAF bombing raid on the area west of the British minefields.

Just as Eighth Army had waited impatiently for Rommel to begin his offensive, so the Desert Air Force was tensed for maximum effort. Coningham's squadrons were ready to execute his three-pronged air campaign. Round-the-clock bombing against the main enemy concentrations would give the Axis forces no rest while the attacks against the Panzerarmee's lines of communication served to isolate the battlefield. Meanwhile, the day-by-day challenge for air superiority would be met by offensive fighter sweeps and attacks on the Axis forward landing grounds.[29] Coningham had rested his squadrons as much as possible during August while concentrating the maximum force for the coming test. Nonetheless, the Kittyhawk squadrons were badly understrength, as were the three squadrons of Spitfires. The Hurricane fighter squadrons were up to strength but, being slower aircraft, were less useful for escorting bomber formations. However, the bombing squadrons of Bostons and Baltimores were up to strength and some new B25 bombers were reaching the front. Every landing ground had built up large reserves of fuel, ammunition and supplies for the coming struggle. Group Captain Beamish wrote:

> Morale was very high throughout the force. The whole of the Air Force was in a high state of efficiency and prepared to operate at maximum intensity for a considerable period . . . the battle could not open under better conditions.[30]

The effectiveness of the Desert Air Force's preparations was soon to be tested and it would not be found wanting.

At roughly 12.30 hours, the first Fleet Air Arm Fairey Albacores arrived over the southern sector of the front and began dropping flares to illuminate targets for the following Wellington bombers of No. 205 Group.[31] Coningham had encouraged the 'pathfinder' Albacore flights also to carry bombs to give them 'a personal offensive interest'.[32] Major H. Woods, commanding a company of the 1st King's Royal Rifle Corps holding the high ground at Himeimat, witnessed the attack:

> It was one of the most awe-inspiring sights I shall ever see, I think – there were seldom less than 20 flares in the air at any one time and the whole valley with its mass of the Afrika Korps stationary was lit up like a huge orange fairyland.[33]

Numerous night bomber sorties were made that night and 38 tons of high explosive and incendiaries dropped on the Panzerarmee.[34] Under normal circumstances, night bombing raids against dispersed formations in the desert often accomplished little more than disturbing the sleep of those on the ground. This time, the bomb-aimers found perfect targets beneath them: the bombs rained down on concentrated groups of tanks, half-tracks and trucks as they bunched together in the minefield gaps and clustered around the western edge of the British minefield.

Although the three battalions of the 7th Motor Brigade were strung out in company positions along a front of 13 miles and confronted by the entire Afrika Korps, they still put up stiff resistance. The magnesium flares dropped by the Albacores gave the British anti-tank gunners clear targets to pick out among the advancing transport, while riflemen, machine guns, mortars and artillery all added their fire to delay and disrupt the German engineers struggling to clear the minefields. Carrier patrols went forward to create mayhem amongst the parties of German engineers. Eventually, the increasing pressure forced the heavily outnumbered companies of riflemen to pull back.[35] By 04.39 hours 21st Panzer Division could report 'enemy fire decreasing noticeably. Enemy infantry withdrawn.'[36] However, the light tanks and armoured cars of 4th Light Armoured Brigade covered the withdrawal of the motor battalions and both units conducted a steady fighting retreat in the face of the German advance.

Rommel's timetable had been seriously delayed. It was not until 05.00 hours that the German engineers were able to make a safe gap in the minefield and start pushing the lead elements of the Panzer regiments forward. By that time, as 21st Panzer Division ruefully recorded, enemy night bombers had attacked them 18 times.[37] Worse was to follow. Two Wellingtons of No. 104 Squadron, while searching for targets, observed and bombed a tented camp in the battle area. They scored a direct hit on the battle headquarters of the Afrika Korps.[38] Nehring himself was wounded by bomb splinters and had to be evacuated while two staff officers died of their wounds.[39] Staff Colonel Fritz Bayerlein took over command of the Korps but, just twenty minutes later, Generalmajor Georg von Bismarck, the able commander of 21st Panzer Division, was killed and his chief staff officer badly wounded by mortar fire when they went forward to encourage the troops of the leading infantry battalion.[40] The command and control of the Afrika Korps was thus badly disrupted at the very moment it was needed most.

Further north, the series of raids mounted by Italian engineers and German paratroops had scored some successes although Eighth Army Headquarters quickly realised that they were merely intended to distract attention from the main thrust in the south. The most successful raid was conducted by a battalion of German paratroops from the newly arrived Ramcke Brigade. Under the cover of a heavy artillery bombardment, the paratroops overran the forward positions of D Company of the 2nd Battalion, West Yorkshire Regiment, on the Ruweisat ridge. However, after a heavy bombardment, the paratroops were forced back. It was the last action of the West Yorkshires at Alamein. After a month of being 'scorched by the heat, plagued by flies and exhausted by endless digging and patrolling', the battalion was finally relieved on 7 September.[41]

By 08.00 hours, both divisions of the Afrika Korps had pushed four kilometres east of the minefields and were preparing to begin their drive further east. Rommel arrived at Afrika Korps Headquarters to consider the options that remained open to him. At this point, given the delay imposed by air attack, minefields and the resistance of 7th Armoured Division, it was clear to Rommel that 'All possibility of taking the enemy by surprise – an essential condition for the success of the operation – had now disappeared.'[42] The unexpected delay had increased fuel consumption and there was still no news of the tanker expected to reach Tobruk that morning. The dangerous fuel situation had become a crisis, but Rommel was now committed to the offensive. Breaking off the attack would mean halting, turning around and withdrawing through narrow minefield gaps in the face of active opposition.

Perhaps not surprisingly, Rommel decided to continue the offensive but with a modified plan. There was insufficient fuel to make a wide sweep to the east, as he had originally intended, so he instructed the panzer divisions to turn north east immediately. Their objective was now Point 102 on the Alam el Halfa ridge.[43]

Although this modified plan seemed to be a realistic option and far preferable to the abandonment of the Panzerarmee's last chance to destroy Eighth Army, it was, albeit unwittingly, the worst decision that Rommel could have made. Far from achieving surprise, he had chosen to attack in exactly the way that Gott had originally envisaged he would. 22nd Armoured Brigade and 44th (Home Counties) Division were dug in on Alam el Halfa ridge just waiting to receive Rommel's armour. There would be no repetition of Gazala. This time, Eighth Army was ready.

Throughout the morning and early afternoon, the mass of advancing Axis tanks and vehicles was harassed by the tanks of 4th Light Armoured Brigade. Eventually, the advancing panzer divisions threatened to outflank 7th Motor Brigade's positions, and Brigadier Bosvile asked for permission to move back to his reserve position just to the north of the Ragil Depression. This would place the brigade five miles south of 22nd Armoured Brigade and in touch with 4th Light Armoured Brigade further south at Samaket Gaballa. Renton agreed to this eminently sensible proposal but Horrocks was furious. He had expected 7th Armoured Division to fight a much longer delaying battle within the minefields. Carver had 'an acrimonious conversation with him, in which he complained that we were not imposing enough delay and were too concerned with preserving our forces'.[44] Horrocks insisted that Bosvile's 7th Motor Brigade return to the second British minefield. Renton now spoke to Horrocks and refused to carry out the order since it would only cause confusion but he did agree to send the Crusader squadron of the 10th Hussars back to the west. This heated exchange betrayed Horrocks' inexperience. The two desert veterans knew that the Motor Brigade was 'still too vulnerable to all types of fire when passing through minefield gaps in unarmoured trucks'.[45] They had been right to ensure that their troops negotiated the gaps in darkness before the Afrika Korps had pressed them too hard. The Crusaders of the 10th Hussars did go forward to impose delay on the Italian armoured divisions but soon found themselves forced to speed away to the north east to avoid being cut off by the Afrika Korps. In fact, Renton's 7th Armoured Division conducted a model fighting withdrawal. A great deal of delay and disruption had been caused to the Afrika Korps. The division had fulfilled the role Dorman-Smith and Gott had planned for it. Dorman-Smith later wrote to Liddell Hart saying: 'Renton tells me that Monty operated the Defence plan we arranged in early August and it went like a charm . . . Good to think of.'[46]

Although 7th Armoured Division had imposed serious delay on the Axis advance, the light bomber force of Baltimores and Bostons was unable to mount the sustained series of attacks that had been planned. An early sortie by 18 Baltimores encountered intense and accurate anti-aircraft fire but still managed to drop 11 tons of high explosive south of Deir el Munassib. However, just as Rommel was being forced to consider modifying his plan, swirling dust on the landing grounds began to dislocate the programme of daylight bombing. A growing dust storm prevented effective operations:

> Never had the Panzers, which were concentrating to the east of the minefield near the Ragil Depression, presented such inviting targets, but the bomber force was compelled impotently to stand by.[47]

The German and Italian landing grounds were less affected by dust that day and both dive bombers and fighters produced increased activity. Nonetheless, the 240 fighter and 70 dive-bomber sorties mounted by German and Italian aircrew had little impact on the ground battle.

Montgomery soon became convinced from the reports reaching him at Burg el Arab that the 'main enemy armoured movement was on Southern flank'.[48] 23rd Armoured Brigade was given to 13 Corps and moved south to cover the gap between the New Zealand box and the positions of 22nd Armoured Brigade around Point 102, the high point on the Alam el Halfa ridge. 9th Australian, 2nd New Zealand and 5th Indian Divisions had to make do with one squadron each of 40th Royal Tank Regiment as their sole armoured support. In the early afternoon, Montgomery left Army Main Headquarters and went to visit his corps commanders. This was the first use in battle of Montgomery's new innovation in command. While de Guingand presided over Eighth Army's Main Headquarters at Burg el Arab, Montgomery came forward with his tactical headquarters. This squared the circle between the Army Commander's need to gain an immediate impression of the fighting through regular discussions with his corps commanders and the desire to maintain close links with the Desert Air Force and General Headquarters Middle East in Cairo. Nonetheless, with Burg el Arab 40 miles behind the front, Montgomery spent considerable amounts of time driving up to the front and back.

As the Afrika Korps turned towards Alam el Halfa ridge, the heavy sandstorm had reduced visibility to less than 100 metres. The light bomber force remained grounded and the artillery observers could only wait anxiously for targets they could not see. Nonetheless, 22nd Armoured Division had been waiting in its positions at Point 102 since the early hours of that morning after receiving the codeword 'Twelvebore'. During the morning, as reports of the enemy movements became clearer, Roberts had ordered the Crusader squadrons of 4th County of London Yeomanry and 5th Royal Tank Regiment to patrol to the south to prevent the deployment of an anti-tank-gun screen if the enemy was intending to bypass the Alam el Halfa ridge and to draw the panzer divisions onto the brigade's positions.[49] Generals Horrocks and Gatehouse were watching the advance of the panzer divisions from the positions of the 44th (Home Counties) Division further east. Gatehouse contacted Roberts: 'I don't want you to think that we are in a blue funk here or anything like that, but if these fellows continue on as they are doing you will have to come out and hit them in the flank.'[50] Roberts ordered both the 4th County of London Yeomanry and 5th Royal Tank Regiment to move out to engage the enemy in the flank but the order was quickly rescinded when it became clear that the panzers were turning north and advancing straight towards the brigade's positions on the ridge.

21st Panzer Division, with its 5th Panzer Regiment in the van, wheeled and headed straight for Point 102 and soon more than 120 panzers were advancing in three waves towards the ridge. 5th Panzer Regiment was ordered to 'Push on quickly, forward forward, do not send anything to the left, swing out to the right is the policy'.[51] The main concentration of the 21st Panzer Division advanced towards the anti-tank guns of the 1st Rifle Brigade and the positions of the 4th County of London Yeomanry. Roberts had given his tank crews strict instructions to hold fire until the panzers were within 1,000 yards but soon the leading German tanks came within range. However, some of the panzers gave the British tank crews a shock. Amongst the mass of German tanks were brand new Panzer Mk IV Ausf F2s, armed with a long-barrelled, high-velocity 75mm gun. These outranged the British Grants.[52] Within minutes all the Grants of A Squadron, 4th County of London Yeomanry, had been knocked out, leaving a gap in the defences. Yet the advancing German tanks had fallen into a trap.

The anti-tank gunners of B Company 1st Battalion the Rifle Brigade, crouched by their six-pounder guns and held their fire until the German tanks were just 300 yards away. The German tank crews had focused on the threat from the distant British tanks and had ignored the possibility of a British anti-tank gun screen. It was the same trap that had been set for the panzers on 16 July by 433rd Anti-Tank Battery on the Ruweisat ridge and it was just as effective. Although one platoon of guns was overrun and captured, Sergeant Griffith's team managed to knock out five tanks. The 1st Rifle Brigade claimed a total of 19 tanks during the action.[53] Heavy concentrations of artillery fire were brought down in the middle of the advancing panzers and this, combined with the anti-tank gun fire, brought them to a halt. The Royal Scots Greys were brought forward from reserve but by the time they had moved up to plug the gap the panzers had been held.

21st Panzer Division reported to the Afrika Korps that:

The enemy seemed to be firing heavy DF [Defensive Fire] forward of the whole Pz Regt from a strong system of field positions. Enemy tanks were firing from reverse slope positions in little hollows mainly on the left flank. The Pz Regt's left-hand unit had faced left and was in action against an enemy force in well-built and camouflaged positions.[54]

The German tank crews had not expected to meet this kind of resistance and halted in front of the Rifle Brigade and 4th County of London Yeomanry positions. Some tanks continued to follow orders and kept moving to the right, searching for a weaker point in the defence. They managed to bypass the 5th Royal Tank Regiment's positions but under Roberts' orders the remnants of 4th County of London Yeomanry blocked this tentative thrust by nightfall.

Throughout the action, 21st Panzer Division had called vainly for confirmation of 15th Panzer Division's front line. This uncertainty had engendered greater caution than usual. As darkness fell, 21st Panzer Division drew off towards the Ragil Depression to the south. The action had been short but sharp: 21st Panzer Division claimed 12 British tanks knocked out and six anti-tank guns destroyed.[55] 22nd Armoured Brigade estimated a tally of 30 enemy tanks although this was later found to be too high.[56] Nonetheless, the effectiveness of Eighth Army's defensive techniques had been proven once again.

Colonel Lungerhausen, who had by now taken command of 21st Panzer Division, judged that any 'frontal attack on the enemy positions forward of the division will be very costly'. But his chief staff officer also suggested, rather optimistically, that if the panzer divisions could take the Alam el Halfa ridge, 'the enemy would be forced to abandon the whole Alamein line'.[57] During the evening, Bayerlein, now commanding the Afrika Korps, suggested to Rommel that both panzer divisions should withdraw from contact, drive east and then swing round to take Point 102 from the flank.[58] This is almost certainly what the Afrika Korps would have attempted the next day but the fuel tanks of the panzers were nearly empty.

The evening report from 21st Panzer Division to Afrika Korps was not encouraging. There were only 0.25 units of fuel for the panzers and 0.4 units for the wheeled elements. The unexpected delays in the British minefields, the action against 7th Armoured Division throughout the day and the soft sand encountered during the advance all meant that the panzer divisions had used far more fuel than expected.[59] The shortage made any outflanking move impossible and, indeed, placed the whole of the Afrika Korps in a very precarious situation. As von Mellenthin commented: 'an armoured division without gasoline is little better than a heap of scrap iron'.[60] The panzer divisions could not manoeuvre without fuel and without manoeuvre they could not dislodge Eighth Army from the Alam el Halfa ridge.

As the panzer divisions took up all-round defensive positions in the Ragil Depression and sent out recovery parties to secure their knocked-out tanks, the first RAF night bombers could be heard overhead. With the weather clearing towards evening, the Wellingtons and Albacores were able to mount constant raids on into the night against both the Axis transport moving slowly through the minefield gaps and the panzer divisions grouped in the Ragil Depression. Wellington crews from No. 148 Squadron:

> resolved that this . . . operation would be one Axis forces would never forget. When aircraft arrived over target fires were still burning from first sortie. Aircraft 'K' observed one big concentration of hundreds of vehicles. Four sticks scored direct hits and five well-laden trucks were seen blazing. A few black objects (presumably personnel) [were] seen running about among trucks and rear gunner took advantage of this excellent opportunity to fire 1,000 rounds. Fires and a black pall of smoke observed all over the target area when crews prepared to leave. Twenty six different fires started and explosions seen all over area. Flying debris filled the air and crews reported havoc caused.[61]

The constant attacks were already beginning to affect the morale of the German and Italian troops exposed to this battering. Most of all, the Axis soldiers were dismayed by the complete absence of friendly night-fighters and the protection they would have afforded.

Before dawn on 1 September, the 2/15th Australian Infantry Battalion mounted a battalion raid codenamed Operation Bulimba.[62] This had been designed as 'an immediate counter-stroke to an enemy attack further south'.[63] It is also possible that Bulimba was a hangover from Auchinleck's appreciation of 1 August in which preparations were to be made in both 30 and 13 Corps for large-scale raids. Orders issued to the 2/15th Battalion on 24 August envisaged an attack by the battalion supported by one squadron of Valentine tanks from 40th Royal Tank Regiment. The objective was to seize Point 23, a small rise in the desert two and a half miles south west of Tel el Eisa. The battalion was to make a breach in the enemy line and then form a 'bridgehead' through which a small exploiting force composed of two squadrons of Crusader tanks, supported by one troop of field guns, two troops of anti-tank guns and a platoon of lorried infantry, would pass and raid enemy communications leading south from Sidi Abd el Rahman.[64]

The battalion had spent long hours each evening standing to in readiness only to have the raid postponed every night as Rommel struggled to launch his offensive. Morshead was worried about the raid from its inception. He considered that it was another case of 'sending a boy on a man's errand'.[65] He was right. The 'raid' looked alarmingly similar to any one of the many piecemeal attacks which the 9th Australian Division had mounted in July. One battalion was too weak a force to hold a sizeable 'bridgehead' open in the face of an enemy counterattack and the 'exploiting' force was far too small to have any real effect.

Nevertheless, the attack began at 05.35 hours with the two leading companies closed up in night attack formation. Rehearsals carried out a few nights before meant that the soldiers knew their task intimately. The initial advance was silent; then, 15 minutes after it began, timed artillery concentrations fired by the divisional artillery crashed out in support. The leading infantry crossed the enemy minefield and found the German defenders 'both dazed by our arty and surprised by the inf attack'.[66] Most of the enemy posts surrendered easily but some put up a considerable fight. By 06.30 hours, the battalion had achieved considerable success and established the battalion headquarters beyond the enemy minefield. However, events soon took a turn for the worse. Lieutenant-Colonel R. W. G. Ogle was severely wounded when his carrier ran over a mine and command of the battalion had to be given to Major C. H. Grace. Communications between the battalion headquarters and the leading companies broke down. Meanwhile, though the engineers accompanying the leading troops had managed to clear gaps in the minefields under 'constant enemy fire',[67] the passage of the supporting tanks through them went badly wrong. The squadron leader, Captain J. L. Lumby, was killed soon after his tank had driven through the minefield, and his second in command shared the same fate. The rest of the squadron were understandably reluctant to follow through a narrow gap under heavy anti-tank gun fire and two of the tanks hit mines when they turned abruptly attempting to avoid anti-tank gun fire while in the gap.[68]

Reserves of the German 164th Light Division began to mass for a counterattack and the positions held by the Australian companies came under increasingly heavy fire. Supporting mortar carriers and reserve ammunition lorries attempted to pass through the gap but, in a depressingly familiar situation, came upon an unexpected minefield and had to return to their assembly point. By 08.35 hours, the forward elements of the leading companies were on their objectives on Point 23, but no more progress was possible. The attack had made a penetration but it 'was not really deep enough to be regarded as a breach in his line. And it was not very securely held.'[69]

Major Grace took the difficult decision to withdraw his battalion because he did not think the positions could be held against a determined counterattack. Nor did he think the breach could be held open to allow the exploiting force to pass through. The withdrawal took place smoothly although some wounded men had to be left behind. 2/15th Battalion had suffered 36 per cent casualties and Bulimba had failed.[70] This operation represented the only effort of 9th Australian Division during Rommel's offensive. If Bulimba had been planned as a counterstroke it was hopelessly inadequate. Montgomery's 'no withdrawal' order had raised the morale of the Eighth Army but it had also forced one of the army's best divisions into a passive role. Bulimba also demonstrated the contrast between Eighth Army's offensive and defensive capabilities. The day before, the troops of 13 Corps had fought an expert defensive battle that proved the methods first tested in July had been finely honed. In contrast, clearly much needed to be done to achieve success in the attack.

The members of 2/15th Battalion might have consoled themselves with the thought that the operation had served to test techniques for the coming offensive. Sadly, Major Grace's report stated that 'few new lessons, if any, emerged from the operation'.[71] 'While it is practicable for inf with hy arty to get on to their own objectives', he went on, 'some foolproof method of getting their own sp weapons and reserve amn up to them is necessary.'[72] No such foolproof method was forthcoming. However, the divisional report discussed a whole range of important points including the width and marking of minefield gaps which eventually found their way into Eighth Army practice.

The Afrika Korps met with no success on 1 September either. Kesselring made good his promise to fly in emergency fuel. However, as Nehring recorded, Kesselring's efforts produced a 'grotesque result'.[73] Of 400 cubic metres flown to Benghazi, Derna and Tobruk, more than 75 per cent was 'swallowed up by the transport'. Probably no more than 25 per cent actually reached the front. The lack of petrol throughout the army meant that the lorries transporting the fuel had to fill their tanks first in order to transport it to the front. Nonetheless, the small quantities that reached the panzers were enough to prevent complete disaster.

At 05.00 hours on 1 September, Montgomery noted that the 'enemy *schwerpunkt*'[74] was directed on the 44th Division and 'thence Northwards on to RUWEISAT Ridge'.[75] This information must have been gleaned from Ultra intelligence and was now, in fact, out of date. Rommel had been forced to alter his original plans. Yet it was only at noon that day that Montgomery decided to 'regroup so as to form reserves and make troops available for closing the gap between N.Z. area and Himeimat, and seizing the initiative'.[76] Montgomery ordered 151st Brigade of 50th Division to move into localities G and H, 2nd South African Brigade was to move to Locality D, while 5th Indian Brigade was to reinforce the New Zealand area. 7th Medium and 149th Anti-Tank Regiment were to be transferred to 13 Corps. However, these moves were not to be complete until the evening of 2 September. At the same time, 13 Corps was ordered to begin to 're-establish minefield, working south from N.Z. area' on the night of 2 September. Horrocks and Freyberg began planning this operation to gain observation over the Axis routes through the minefields. 30 Corps was to thin out and form reserves while 10 Corps was to 'be prepared to take command of all reserves available and push through to DABA. 9 Aust Div possibly coming [under] 10 Corps.'[77] These orders were issued verbally to Ramsden and Horrocks on the afternoon of 1 September, but Lumsden did not receive them until 11.00 hours on 2 September. Given that it had been obvious since 10.00 hours on

31 August that the main Axis attack was being made in the south, Montgomery's reaction was painfully slow. The fact that he had previously ordered all surplus transport away from the front line units also made the regrouping a slow process.

What is perhaps most surprising about Montgomery's decisions on 1 September is that the Eighth Army Commander was having to think on his feet. He had not planned to seize the initiative before Rommel attacked and there was no clear plan for a counterstroke in place. Given the level of intelligence which Eighth Army possessed before the Axis attack, there had been plenty of time to prepare a properly worked-out plan for a counterstroke and time to issue warning orders to units. Montgomery had focused entirely on meeting the Axis attack and, when it was clear that the initiative was there to be seized, all planning for a counterstroke had to be improvised. Most accounts of Alam Halfa emphasise Montgomery's insistence that the armour was not to be loosed and that there was to be no counterattack. Montgomery changed his mind once the battle had begun but had prepared no contingency plans for such an eventuality.

The plans of Auchinleck, Dorman-Smith and Gott for meeting an Axis counterattack have been much criticised yet they specifically envisaged the thinning out of Eighth Army's forward positions, the provision of sufficient transport and the rehearsal of the thinning out process to enable the regrouping to take place rapidly. The meaning of 30 Corps' warning order of 30 July becomes clear in the context of Montgomery's decisions of 1 September. That order had stated:

Depending on the scale of the attack and the warning received EIGHTH ARMY will:-
(a) Fight the enemy on its present posns or
(b) Thin out the forward zone.[78]

Auchinleck, Dorman-Smith and Gott had understood that the thinning out of the forward zone and the regrouping to form mobile reserves had to take place as soon as possible. This order had caused dismay amongst the divisional commanders of Eighth Army at the time and yet the same orders were given by Montgomery on 1 September when they were already too late to be effective.

Gott's last appreciation had envisaged the possibility of luring 'the Enemy out in front of his minefields to fight on ground disadvantageous to him. But such a plan would surrender the initiative to the enemy which might be difficult to regain.'[79] Rommel had, quite of his own volition, taken the bait and was now bogged down in exposed positions in front of the Alam el Halfa ridge. Montgomery now attempted to regain the initiative but in an improvised and ineffective manner.

21st Panzer Division had been ordered to 'strengthen [its] defence with all possible means' while, given the lack of fuel, only 15th Panzer Division was ordered to renew the attack on Alam el Halfa.[80] Although that division mounted a number of probing attacks during the day, these were held by the intervention of 8th Armoured Brigade which moved up in support of 22nd Armoured Brigade. However, a screen of German anti-tank guns prevented any link-up between the two brigades. In the afternoon, 8th Armoured Brigade attempted a coordinated attack on the German gun screen under cover of smoke but was 'not fully successful'.[81] The brigade lost 13 Grants to the German anti-tank guns but claimed the destruction of eight Mk IIIs and one Mk IV.[82] 44th (Home Counties) Division had not been engaged at all the previous day but some of its anti-tank guns were in action on 1 September against the tanks of 15th Panzer Division.[83] Nonetheless, the defences of the division were not seriously tested. For a second day, the Afrika Korps made no headway against Eighth Army's defence.

Although the panzer divisions fired artillery concentrations against the targets on the ridge that they could see, these efforts were dwarfed by the volume of fire which Eighth Army directed against them. Brigadier 'Steve' Weir, commanding the New Zealand artillery, had gathered together an impressive array of field and medium regiments. After being briefed by Montgomery on the expected course of the Axis offensive, Weir realised that the positions of 2nd New Zealand Division would form the southern pivot of the Alamein line and that its artillery 'would play a vital part in harassing the wheel of the Afrika Corps'.[84] Weir conducted three rehearsals with his divisional artillery and quickly realised that there were insufficient guns for all the probable fire tasks. He appealed to Brigadier Standford, who commanded the artillery of 13 Corps, for more and Standford managed to find him three extra field regiments which were transferred from 30 Corps.[85] Then, on the first day of Rommel's offensive, Weir asked for more artillery and got the 7th Medium Regiment and one more field regiment from 30 Corps.[86] He now had seven field regiments and two medium regiments at his disposal which, in conjunction with the divisional artillery of 44th (Home Counties) Division, began to hammer the German and Italian troops to the south.

Meanwhile, the light bomber force was able to mount 125 sorties against the 'great pool of enemy vehicles and armour lying in the open desert' between the Munassib and Ragil depressions. These raids were mounted in the face of dense and accurate anti-aircraft fire which brought down three aircraft. However, the streams of flak could not prevent 76 tons of bombs being dropped on the inviting targets. Just as worrying for the Panzerarmee were the unmistakable signs of strain on the Stuka pilots which the Afrika Korps had come to rely upon for 'flying artillery' support. The constant bombing of their landing grounds had disrupted their operations while the

Me109 fighter force rarely checked the constant threat from Desert Air Force fighters. Increasingly dense and effective anti-aircraft fire forced many Stuka pilots into bombing level or into jettisoning their bombs when enemy fighters approached. Deprived of their specialist role, the Stukas became slow lumbering bombers of little value.[87]

During the day, 21st Panzer Division had noted that 'enemy movement was increasing'.[88] This almost certainly referred to 8th Armoured Brigade as it moved up to gain touch with 22nd Armoured Brigade. By the evening of 1 September, the Afrika Korps was confronted by all the armour of Eighth Army in secure defensive positions. Yet the German tanks had fuel for a few kilometres only, which ruled out the possibility of manoeuvring around them.

The RAF night bombers weighed into the fight again that evening and the Afrika Korps lamented that:

> the attacks, which increase in strength every night show a definite and effective tactical method. It is estimated that 200 aircraft took part in the attacks during the night 1/2 September and dropped about 1600 bombs.[89]

In fact, these were overestimates. Only 64 Wellingtons and 26 Albacores from No. 205 Group had attacked targets that night but once again they started many fires amongst the clumps of transport below.[90]

That night, the Panzerarmee's daily report explained that its troops had gone over to the defensive 'because the POL promised for 1 September has not arrived. The steamer *Sanandrea* has not arrived and the *Abruzzi* is still at sea.'[91] Rommel was to learn only the next day that Malta-based Beaufort anti-shipping aircraft had sunk the *Sanandrea* on the day he had begun his attack. The *Abruzzi*, carrying 611 tons of fuel which had been expected at Tobruk on 1 September, was badly damaged by an air attack that night and had to be beached 100 miles west of Tobruk three days later. None of the fuel carried by these tankers ever reached North Africa.[92] The combined air and naval attacks on the Axis supply lines were strangling the Panzerarmee.

Throughout the morning of 2 September, the Afrika Korps, 90th Light and Littorio Divisions remained deployed in their exposed defensive positions and waited for the expected counterattack. None came. Meanwhile, the Panzerarmee received still more bad news. The fate of the *Abruzzi* and the *Sanandrea* finally became clear and, worse, word came that the *Picco Fascio*, with 1,100 tons of fuel on board, had been sunk early that morning. There was now no hope of receiving sufficient fuel to continue the attack. Rommel had to take the painful decision to begin a withdrawal. His hopes of victory had disappeared like a mirage.

At 10.00 hours that morning, the Afrika Korps received new orders:

1. The superiority of the enemy air force and the lack of supplies – especially fuel – compels us to break off the offensive.
2. The Panzerarmee will withdraw westwards in stages. It is intended to organise defence on a level with the minefields north of Qaret el Himeimat.
3. Each division will form a battle group of one battalion, one panzer company, two light batteries and one Panzerjager company.[93]

These orders came as a shock for most of the officers and men. They had expected to go back onto the attack after a temporary pause and did not understand the wider reasons which forced the withdrawal. Rommel decided to make the best of the painful retreat by incorporating the British minefields which had caused so much delay into his own defensive system. Mount Himeimat, which offered superb observation over a wide area, would also be retained. The battlegroups were to act as an operational reserve and help to cover the retreat of the main elements.[94] All these preparations proceeded unhindered by Eighth Army with the exception of continuing air raids and artillery fire.

On the night of 2 September, the Panzerarmee had to inform Berlin and the Commando Supremo of its failure. The daily report noted that there were only three consumption units between the harbours and the front which would give the troops only one consumption unit per day until 5 September. Over the past few days, although 4.2 consumption units had arrived, 5.5 units had been lost. The report explained that the inadequate supply situation combined with the following reasons forced the Panzerarmee to withdraw:

> The plan of operations was based on the assumption that during the moonlight night of 30/31 August advanced elements of the motorised group . . . would reach assembly areas 40–50km to the east of their starting points, travelling through terrain which was reported to be only weakly defended and partially mined . . . progress was greatly delayed owing to the hitherto unidentified minefields and obstacles, some of which were organised to a depth of several kilometres.[95]

The Panzerarmee's failure to reconnoitre properly had cost it dearly. Dorman-Smith and Kisch's plan had worked perfectly. In addition:

> the heavy air attacks which the enemy has carried out day and night since the operation began have caused serious losses to personnel and material. They have also affected the morale of both the German and Italian troops . . . systematic harassing attacks by the enemy air force on the supply columns, railway and coastal shipping have further upset the supply situation.[96]

The Panzerarmee had been repulsed by an unexpected combination of rigid defence by the Eighth Army and continual attacks by the Desert Air Force. The reason why withdrawal was forced upon it, however, was the deeper strategic attack that cut off its supply of fuel.

Montgomery noted early on 2 September that: 'Panzer Army was not going to take the offensive. Possibly short of petrol, supplies, and so on', yet it was not until the evening that he decided:

> Panzer Army ringed in. Important not to rush in to the attack. 13 Corps given two main tasks:
> (1) to shoot up, and harry and destroy enemy MET. To tear the guts out of the enemy by destroying his vehicles and soft stuff. Savage rabbit tactics against all enemy MT by everyone.
> (2) To gradually and methodically close the gap, working Southwards from the NZ area; at same time mobile forces to operate northwards from HIMEIMAT.[97]

By the time Montgomery had developed this plan, the Axis withdrawal had been underway for a number of hours. There was a fundamental flaw in this approach to regaining the initiative. The Panzerarmee's soft transport could be hit from the air and bombarded by artillery but the 'savage dog' of the Afrika Korps lay between the transport columns and the armour of Eighth Army. This meant that only the light forces of 7th Armoured Division were able to harass the Axis supply columns. With any further advance forbidden, the rest of Eighth Army could not intervene. Roberts remembered that by the morning of 2 September, 'the nearest enemy vehicle was at least 3000 yards away and we could take no action other than harassing fire by the artillery and occasionally by the tanks'.[98] This notion, that the Panzerarmee was to be brought to its knees by raids on its supply transport, was strikingly familiar: it was exactly what Ritchie had ordered when Rommel had first become trapped in the Cauldron at Gazala.[99]

After the fighting had died down on the Alam el Halfa ridge, Alec Gatehouse had an unpleasant interview with Lumsden. Although Gatehouse had been in command of all three armoured brigades while Lumsden was forming 10 Corps Headquarters, Lumsden visited Gatehouse's headquarters in 'a very highly strung state and was extremely rude'. Lumsden demanded to know why:

> When Rommel had withdrawn into the Deir el Ragil I had not pursued, and annihilated him. I informed him that previous to the battle I had had a long briefing by the Army Cmdr. (Monty), and that this had been one of the main points insisted upon – viz. not to be drawn on a wild goose chase on to the

muzzles of waiting 88 m.m. guns – as Rommel had so often managed to make his enemy do in the past.

H.L. would not believe me and when I repeated I had had definite orders on this point, and that I heartily agreed with them, he quivered with rage and left my H.Q. in a hurry.[100]

Clearly, not all the desert veterans were champing at the bit to charge after Rommel. It was easy, both at the time and afterwards, to suggest that a more aggressive approach would have yielded greater dividends. Montgomery's approach ensured that, at the very least, neither he, nor his armoured commanders, made any fatal mistakes.

The Eighth Army was unlikely to regain the initiative or prevent the withdrawal of the Panzerarmee but Montgomery's approach meant that he was running very little risk of a second Gazala. There was also a great difference between Gazala and Alam el Halfa in the power of the Desert Air Force. Even as the Eighth Army remained passively on the defensive, the light bombers of No. 3 Wing flew 176 sorties on 2 September, breaking their previous record of 155 sorties on 3 July. Group Captain Beamish argued: 'In effect, the guns and armour of the Army made a ring and the air gave the punch inside the ring.'[101] Montgomery's approach was cautious but it maximised the damage inflicted on the Panzerarmee for very little cost.

The night bombing of the Panzerarmee reached a climax that night as the Wellingtons and Albacores redoubled their efforts by dropping 112 tons of bombs – an average of one bomb every 40 seconds.[102] The Afrika Korps again overestimated the numbers of aircraft involved[103] but this may be explained by the amount of damage inflicted. Some units which had experienced the worst of the raids found that most of their vehicles had been wrecked by the following morning. On 3 September, the withdrawal of the striking elements of the Panzerarmee took place without any serious intervention by Eighth Army. 15th Panzer Division was able to mount its withdrawal without interference; only weak British forces were probing forward in front of the Afrika Korps.[104] However, the withdrawal required desperate measures. The fuel tanks of all the transport vehicles left in the assembly areas to the west of the Axis minefields had to be drained and the fuel given to the units conducting the withdrawal. Such measures, combined with the small quantities of Kesselring's fuel which reached the front, enabled the withdrawal to take place. By mid-afternoon that day, Montgomery had received aerial reconnaissance reports noting that 'three large enemy columns were moving West through the minefield area; that a large concentration of M.T. was assembling East of the minefields, and was feeding itself out into these columns'.[105] The chance of inflicting a real defeat on the Panzerarmee had already passed.

Although Kesselring planned an ambitious series of air strikes on the

Desert Air Force landing grounds and the formations of the Eighth Army in an attempt to redress the balance, the Desert Air Force was able to report that day that the 'enemy air effort was reduced'. Instead, the light bombers of the Desert Air Force were able to break all records by flying 200 sorties against the withdrawing columns of the Panzerarmee.[106]

No. 205 Group was asked to make 'the maximum Wellington effort' on the night of 3–4 September because, with the obvious signs of withdrawal, it was believed that it might be the last opportunity to catch the heavy concentrations of enemy transport. The medium bomber squadrons were beginning to suffer from the fatigue and strain of unremitting operations. Nonetheless, 71 sorties were mounted which still caused considerable damage. The bomber force tasked with attacking Rommel's line of communications scored another important success. The *David Bianchi*, a tanker of 1,500 tons, was sunk by torpedoes launched by a special striking force of three A[nti] S[urface] V[essel] Wellingtons, two ASV Liberators from No. 221 Squadron and two bomber Wellingtons from No. 38 Squadron. The *Padenna*, another tanker in the convoy, was sunk by a submarine, HMS *Thrasher*, which was guided to the ship by a Wellington.[107]

That night, Montgomery's plan to 're-establish the minefield, working south from the N.Z. area' went ahead. What became Operation Beresford had had a fairly long gestation period and seems to have begun in Horrocks' mind as a substantial raid. On 31 August, Horrocks discussed with Freyberg the possibility of pushing south from the New Zealand box for about 4,000 yards and Freyberg told both Clifton and Kippenberger that 'Corps want substantial raid' which would involve infantry tanks. By the next day, Freyberg was worrying that 'we are perhaps being too supine' and that night 13 Corps gave orders for the attack.[108] However, by 2 September, the scale of the projected raid had changed into a full attack although Freyberg was 'not keen on poking further South as is suggested'. The attack was to be mounted by 26 Battalion from the 6th New Zealand Brigade to cover the western flank, with the three battalions, 2nd Battalion, Royal East Kent Regiment (the Buffs), 4th and 5th Battalions, The Queen's Own Royal West Kent Regiment, of the 132nd Infantry Brigade in the centre and 21 Battalion and the Maori Battalion[109] of 5th New Zealand Brigade on the eastern flank. The planned relief of the New Zealand Division by 44th (Home Counties) Division had had a very baleful effect. The 5th New Zealand Brigade was a highly capable and experienced formation and Kippenberger, its brigadier, later noted that the attack was launched from 'the Alam Nayil Ridge, the same area as that on Ruweisat six weeks previously, but in exactly the opposite direction'.[110] However, 132nd Brigade was going into its first battle. The brigadier and his men were highly inexperienced and far from ready to mount an effective night assault in the desert. Freyberg noted that 'Corps Comd very glad 132 Bde is being used' but he felt it was because of the needs of 'propaganda' that 132nd Brigade had to take part in the assault.[111] Horrocks had commanded 44th (Home Counties) Division in England and it is clear that he felt a certain sense of ownership towards the men of 132nd Brigade. He knew the brigadier and had trained the brigade. Not surprisingly, Horrocks wanted some of his 'own' troops to take part in 'his' attack. If the attack had been conducted 24 hours earlier, it is likely that it would have hit little but desert sand but it might have complicated the withdrawal of 90th Light Division. The operation had the main objective of gaining observation over the supply routes of the Panzerarmee. However, by the evening of 3 September, the attack was far too late to interfere seriously with the withdrawal of the main striking elements of the Panzerarmee as the 90th Light had concentrated its units during the day west of Deir el Munassib. The blow now fell on the positions of the Italian Brescia Division, which had been reinforced by elements of the Ramcke Parachute Brigade and the 155th Panzergrenadier Regiment of 90th Light Division.[112]

All the units involved in the attack had to make gaps in the 600-yard wide minefield that covered the southern front of the New Zealand Division box. The attack was to be 'silent' in the hopes of passing the assaulting infantry and their supporting arms through the minefield gaps before the German and Italian infantry known to be in the Munassib depression were alerted of the impending attack. Consequently, there would be no supporting artillery fire but each brigade was supported by a squadron of Valentines from 50th Royal Tank Regiment. Given the level of artillery support which the New Zealand divisional artillery could muster, mounting a silent attack was a mistake. The attacking formations would advance south in the corridors between the three British minefields that stretched south from the New Zealand box. 26 Battalion was to cover the right flank of 132nd Brigade and did not expect to meet much opposition. The 132nd Brigade was to make the furthest advance with its final objective to reach the northern edge of the Deir el Munassib. However, the 4th and 5th Battalions, Royal West Kent Regiment, owing to the central British minefield, were separated from the 2nd Battalion the Buffs by nearly a mile. On the left, the Maori Battalion of 5th New Zealand Brigade was also ordered to reach the northern lip of the depression and to use their carrier platoon to exploit into the depression itself. Meanwhile, 21 Battalion had a shorter advance to the Deir el Muhafid where they were to act as the flank guard.

Kippenberger's experience was evident by his issue of verbal orders to his battalions before midday; these were confirmed later without change. Unfortunately, the verbal orders were not issued in 132nd Brigade until late that afternoon which gave very little time for the battalion commanders to prepare their own orders. Some company and platoon commanders had to issue their orders while the troops were on the march to the assembly areas.[113] Brigadier Robertson of 132nd Brigade called on Kippenberger that afternoon for advice. While Kippenberger made light of his experience of night attacks he did make 'two points very strongly'. He explained that during Ruweisat and El Mreir Burrows, Clifton and himself had all followed up the assault by moving brigade headquarters forward. He emphasised that 'each had got into serious trouble and had been unable to command effectively'. Kippenberger suggested that it was far better to establish brigade head-quarters as far forward as possible before the attack with the brigadier then able to go forward personally if needed without disrupting the function of the headquarters. Kippenberger's second point was that the supporting arms and brigade transport should be 'sent forwards with guides on lighted routes as required and as necessary' but not follow behind the assault or move on a timed programme.[114] This was very sound advice from a desert veteran who acknowledged his own mistakes and learned from them. Robertson did not take the advice.

Kippenberger had indeed learned from Ruweisat. The contrast between the techniques for night movement in Beresford with those used during Bacon and Splendour was striking. In 5th New Zealand Brigade the supporting transport was to assemble in groups close to brigade headquar-ters which had been established close to the gap in the New Zealand mine-fields. A provost section of military police was tasked with planting a line of lamps along the inter-battalion boundary of the brigade which the trans-port could then follow once called forward. Even if communications broke down, runners would be able to navigate back to brigade headquarters by following the lampposts.[115]

However, 132nd Brigade's plan for the advance betrayed their inexperi-ence. The direction of advance was to be maintained by the brigade intelli-gence officer sitting in a jeep with a red lamp attached to a pole. Experience had shown that navigation in the desert at night was difficult enough on foot but any mistake in direction or pacing calculated from a moving jeep would be magnified. Each battalion of the brigade had two troops of anti-tank guns under command, a platoon of machine guns and a section of Royal Engineers. All these supporting arms were carried in vehicles along with all the compressors, picks and shovels for digging in. When the men of 132nd Brigade passed 26 Battalion in their assembly areas, they 'commented on the size of the New Zealanders' picks and shovels and seemed amused when told each soldier carried one or other into action'.[116] The carrier and mortar platoons were also to follow their battalions which meant that each battalion would have 40 vehicles moving immediately behind the assault troops grinding along in bottom gear. This plan no doubt made perfect sense when training on a bleak moor 'somewhere in England' but it was to lead to disaster in the coming action.

Matters began to go wrong even before the troops had reached their assembly points. As the soldiers of the two West Kent battalions were moving up, two enemy fighters flew over and their pilots 'saw the numerous little parties of men and vehicles all moving south'.[117] 90th Light Division now had advance warning of the impending attack. The brigade also experienced constant delays in moving up to the start line because the sappers had difficulty in clearing the New Zealand minefield. The experience of the 4th and 5th West Kent battalions was very different from that of the 2nd Battalion the Buffs. As the West Kent battalions waited on the start line tightly grouped in platoon columns just 50 yards apart, the transport and tanks drove up and were directed to their allotted positions. The noise made by more than 80 vehicles alerted the nearest units of the Ramcke Brigade and Brescia Division to the danger. All prospects of a successful 'silent' attack were now gone.

Major T. H. Bevan was the New Zealand artillery liaison officer attached to the 132nd Brigade Headquarters. He remembered that the headquarters vehicles had just gone over a ridge when:

> Without any warning, a lone shell or most likely mortar bomb, burst square on a truck & set it on fire immediately, with flames that lit up the whole column & surrounding ground. Of course the area was promptly plastered with everything the enemy had – mortars, 75s & 88s – & before the column could break up there were several more trucks blazing, including a couple loaded with mines which went up like atom bombs.[118]

The light from the burning trucks silhouetted the advancing infantry who then came under intense machine-gun and small-arms fire. Bevan could not understand why the brigade headquarters had moved so far forwards as 'another few hundred yards would have seen us in the enemy lines'. Even though the headquarters was close to the attacking battalions, all communications broke down amidst the chaos. Brigadier Robertson was soon wounded and evacuated, leaving the brigade major in command: 'It was bad luck for him that his first action should be such a mess.'[119] Unfortunately, the brigade major refused to pull the few remaining headquarters vehicles back onto the reverse slope and they had to endure heavy fire throughout the night.

The infantry companies pressed on for some distance but could make little progress in the face of fierce enemy resistance. It was now imperative to dig in: casualties were mounting rapidly but all the tools were in the burning trucks. The seemingly amusing practice of the New Zealanders in carrying their picks and shovels was understood too late. Almost all the vehicles of the two battalions were now burning and parachute flares dropped by Axis aircraft simply added to the light, enabling the Italian defenders to pour murderous fire into the West Kents. With most of the senior officers of both battalions killed or wounded, it fell to junior officers and sergeants to organise some semblance of withdrawal. This quickly dissolved into rout.

(*Above*) Command. Auchinleck stands beside the desert road at El Daba and watches retreating elements of the Eighth Army on 28 June 1942.

(*Left*) El Alamein. The insignificant railway halt which gave its name to the fighting in the surrounding desert.

(*Above*) Anti-tank. The crew of a six-pounder anti-tank gun portee in early July. The men of this battalion, 2nd Rifle Brigade, later won lasting fame in the 'Snipe' action on 27 October 1942.

(*Below*) Gunners. The crew of a 25-pounder field gun in action. These men, as part of 'Robcol', fought the critical action on 2 July 1942.

(*Right*) Supply. Valentine tanks of 23rd Armoured Brigade being unloaded at Port Tewfik after a journey of over 12,000 miles.

(*Below*) Disaster. Two of the 99 Valentine tanks lost by 23rd Armoured Brigade on 22 July 1942. These wrecked tanks, from 40th Royal Tank Regiment, bear mute testimony to the ferocity of the German defence.

(*Above*) 'A little like being caged with a gorilla.' Churchill's displeasure is evident as he confronts Auchinleck, Gott and Dorman-Smith at Eighth Army tactical headquarters on 5 August 1942. (*Below*) Alam el Halfa Ridge. The new army commander, Bernard Montgomery, wearing an Australian bush hat, confers with his recently arrived 13 Corps commander, Brian Horrocks, and, on his right, 'Pip' Roberts, the newly appointed brigadier of 22nd Armoured Brigade.

(*Above*) Mine warfare. Sappers with detectors practice the new drill at the Eighth Army Mine Clearance School in September 1942.

(*Below*) Infantry. A platoon from 5th Seaforth Highlanders march in the desert during training. Pipers went into action with their units.

(*Above*) Deception. A Crusader tank with its 'sunshield' disguising it as a normal three-ton lorry. Although crude in close-up, such camouflage was remarkably effective from a distance.

(*Below*) Lightfoot. The opening bombardment of Eighth Army's offensive on 23 October 1942. The first 882 shells fired landed virtually simultaneously on their targets across the 40-mile front.

(*Above*) Defence. Well dug-in Axis positions, such as this Italian 47mm anti-tank gun pit, were all but invisible at a distance. The difficulty of locating defences from the ground reinforced the importance of aerial reconnaissance.

(*Below*) Combat support. Rearming a Sherman during a lull in the fighting. The Sherman saw its baptism of fire at El Alamein and proved a battle winner.

(*Above*) Thompson's Post. An Australian convoy passes wrecked Valentines of 40th Royal Tank Regiment. These tanks were knocked out by fire from Thompson's Post on 31 October 1942 as they moved up to support the Australian infantry. Barrel Hill can be seen in the distance.
(*Below*) Defeat and victory. General von Thoma, still covered in dust and bruised from battle, meets Montgomery at his tactical headquarters on 4 November 1942.

As the transport of 26 Battalion was about to move up in support, Lieutenant Barnett, the battalion adjutant, found the two West Kent battalions 'streaming back into the area. They seemed hopelessly disorganised. Some of them were unarmed.'[120] Barnett 'made strenuous efforts to reorganise the British troops, not so much to get them to return to the attack but so that they could cover the gap'.[121] Eventually, the remnants of both battalions were reorganised on a ridge 2,000 yards north of the Munassib Depression. Bevan remembered that as the stragglers came back into the New Zealand box the next morning, 'they all had the same story – that it was bloody murder out there'.[122]

Meanwhile, the experience of the 2nd Buffs was rather different. The leading companies advanced the 4,000 yards to the low feature named the 'Stony Ground' without any opposition except ill-aimed machine-gun fire. However, the men could see 'a big blaze' and heavy hostile fire to the west; that marked the advance of the rest of the brigade. An attempt by D Company to push forward to the depression across 'perfectly flat ground' was met by constant flares and heavy mortar shelling. Lieutenant-Colonel Nicholson decided to halt the advance and dig in on the Stony Ground. Increasingly heavy fire pinned down the battalion for the rest of the night but the forward positions were held throughout the rest of the day in the face of mounting casualties.

On the right, 26 Battalion moved off in two columns towards the minefield gap. But once they reached the gap they came under heavy mortar and artillery fire. German planes also dropped 'butterfly' bombs over the area. Nonetheless, the three companies of the battalion were able to reach their objectives without encountering opposition. Unfortunately, C Company advanced too far to the south west and became cut off. Since the battalion headquarters was fully absorbed trying to help reorganise 132nd Brigade, no one realised for some time that one company was out of touch. Attempts to extricate the company failed and after fighting an isolated battle for most of the night and following day, the survivors surrendered. Brigadier Clifton, who went forward to investigate, ran into an Italian post and was captured for the second and final time.[123]

21 Battalion and the Maori Battalion of 5th New Zealand Brigade moved off from their start lines on time, although each was missing a company which had been delayed. 21 Battalion reached its objective with few casualties and dug in. Its supporting arms came forward without any mishap. The Maori Battalion, on the other hand, became badly scattered after a fierce fight to reach the objective. Two companies followed their carriers into the Munassib Depression and attacked the large groups of Axis trucks sheltering there. Kippenberger later noted that the Maoris had killed 'an exceptional number' of Germans and Italians during their attack. Kippenberger sent forward the supporting transport and tanks for the Maoris and 'as an

insurance' ordered his reserve unit, 22 Battalion, to move forward and dig in on a line extending from the flank of 21 Battalion. This line was 2,000 yards behind the Maoris but acted as a backstop. Unfortunately, the tanks and transport found that the line of lights ran out after only 2,000 yards and, even with the help of flares sent up to guide them, lost their way and ran into fierce German opposition in the Muhafid depression. Worried by the disorganisation of the Maori Battalion and the loss of its supporting arms, Kippenberger ordered the battalion to fall back behind the 22 Battalion and reorganise on the Alam Nayil ridge.[124] By early morning the Germans were indeed organising armour and infantry for a counterattack but, this time, with the two forward battalions well dug in and supplied with all their supporting arms, 5th New Zealand Brigade was in a firm posture to meet any counterattack. The brigade called in defensive fire from the divisional artillery: it responded in just 11 minutes. Kippenberger recalled that the concentration came down 'like the hammer of Thor' and broke up the supporting waves of the Italian counterattack. The leading elements were halted by the infantry and anti-tank guns of the well-positioned battalions. Kippenberger was delighted: 'For the first time in our experience, the immediate counter-attack had been crushingly defeated.'[125]

5th New Zealand Brigade fought off three counterattacks that day which were all repulsed largely by Brigadier Weir's skilfully wielded 'hammer of Thor'. Freyberg noted that his 'artillery had a good day both 25 pr and medium – one regiment fired 350 r.p.g.'.[126] The artillery's expenditure of ammunition was prodigious. 6th Field Regiment had fired 5,307 rounds of high explosive, while 4th Field had fired the comparatively small total of 1,008 shells. 107th Battery, in 7th Medium Regiment, fired 1,000 rounds which the New Zealand History called an 'astonishing total' for medium guns.[127] Kippenberger noted that this artillery support was: 'before the practice had developed of having defensive fire prepared, codenamed and issued to gunners, infantry and armour, before any operations'.[128] This much was true but in fact the artillery support received by his brigade that day represented a real advance in technique.

Weir was instrumental in reintroducing concentrated artillery fire to Eighth Army. He had disagreed with Auchinleck's policy of brigade groups and had insisted on maintaining the right of his divisional artillery headquarters to fight the guns of the division. In line with this principle, he had carried out a series of exercises, practising regimental and divisional artillery coordination, while the division was in Syria in the early months of 1942.

At El Alamein, Weir later explained, the division:

> developed our fire drill to as near perfection as possible. All the details worked out in Syria now came in for practice and adoption. We were aided by good communications, maps survey, flash spotters, air photos, air co-operation,

counter-battery and a close liaison with infantry and other arms. We improved
our wireless technique. It would not have been possible in my view to have
fledged this machine during the defensive battle at Alamein but for the ground
work laid in Syria.[129]

By Alam Halfa the divisional artillery had 'really learnt and practised its
drill for fighting as a single fire Unit'.[130] Once the fighting was over, Weir
maintained in discussions with Horrocks and Standford that, instead of
sending a collection of individual regiments to reinforce a divisional artillery,
it would be preferable to send a formation of regiments under one
commander. This would ease the command and control of large numbers
of guns. Weir continued to advocate this approach and believed that his
constant pressure eventually paid off at Enfidavelle when 'the first A.G.R.A.
[Army Group Royal Artillery] appeared (5 A.G.R.A.) and it contained mostly
the Regts. which used to come to me individually'.[131] Alam Halfa and
Beresford thus represented an important watershed for the New Zealand
divisional artillery and encouraged the evolution of standard fire drills which
were then put into practice by all Eighth Army's artillery in the October
battle of Alamein.

The New Zealand Division had fought off every counterattack but
Freyberg decided that the troops should withdraw from their exposed posi-
tions. He spoke to Horrocks that evening and explained that 5th New Zealand
Brigade had:

> stopped the second attack but if they bring in a lot of artillery, more than
> they have there now, I think our casualties would be heavy . . . Under the
> circumstances unless there were any future operations affected by holding on
> I think we ought to come back tonight.[132]

Horrocks replied that he would refer to Montgomery for agreement but
Freyberg then admitted that, 'I hope they will agree for, taking your word,
I have told them to go ahead.'[133] Both Horrocks and Montgomery agreed
to the *fait accompli* but relations between Horrocks and Freyberg were
undoubtedly strained by the episode.

The remarkable success of 5th New Zealand Brigade, even in the face of
difficulties, and the utter collapse of 132nd Brigade's attack, was striking.
Montgomery commented that the 'enemy was extremely sensitive to any
attempts to close the gap'[134] when in fact 132nd Brigade's advance had turned
into a bloody shambles even before the Axis counterattacks and was probably the worst debacle suffered by a British brigade in the course of the
entire desert war. Lieutenant-Colonel E. A. McPhail commented that 'the
unfortunate placing of a "green" Bde between two seasoned Bdes nullified
the full force of the operation'.[135] The failure of Beresford is usually cited

as evidence that Montgomery's judgement of the Eighth Army as insufficiently trained to mount mobile operations was sound. In fact, Beresford revealed two contrasting facets of Eighth Army's performance in battle. First, the improvised nature of Beresford showed that Alam Halfa was not fought entirely to Montgomery's 'masterplan'. Moreover, Horrocks' enthusiasm for using 'his' untried brigade revealed that he had not understood the importance of ensuring that troops were not committed to battle before they were ready. The brigade had paid a heavy price for its inexperience and the West Kent History remarked that 'the operation will remain as a ghastly memory for the survivors'.[136]

However, this gloomy analysis of Beresford should not obscure what had gone right with the operation. When experienced Eighth Army infantry took ground within range of their supporting artillery the inevitable German counterattack could be stopped in its tracks. Brigadier Weir's use of divisional – and larger – artillery concentrations was a harbinger of increasingly sophisticated British artillery techniques. In this sense at least, Beresford should have given the Panzerarmee pause for thought.

With the failure of Beresford, Eighth Army's active attempts to interfere with the Panzerarmee's withdrawal came to an end. Patrols from 7th Armoured Division and both 8th and 22nd Armoured Brigade followed up the Axis rearguards but did not pressure them. The Axis formations could breathe a little more easily since a ship had successfully docked that day with 800 tons of fuel. The fuel situation was still precarious but there was now enough for the next seven days. Dust storms limited the light bomber sorties to the morning and the air crews found much less satisfying targets. The Panzerarmee was no longer under any pressure to concentrate so its formations adopted very wide dispersal as protection against the air attacks. By the evening, the vast majority of the Panzerarmee had retired behind the protection of the British minefields and the battle was, to all intents and purposes, over.

By 5 September, Rommel was able to report that the day had passed quietly and that all of his formations had completed their withdrawals. Montgomery spent that day conducting Wendell Wilkie, the American politician and one-time contender for the Presidency, around the front, proudly taking him to the positions of 22nd Armoured Brigade. The fact that the Army Commander had time to engage in a public relations exercise was a clear sign that the fighting was at an end. This meant that Montgomery's official declaration, two days later, that the battle was then over was faintly ridiculous.

The 'six days' race', as the Axis troops called Alam Halfa, was over. Rommel had not broken the Eighth Army or reached the Delta and it was the Panzerarmee which had received 'a pretty thorough beating'.[137] The cost, in the context of the desert war, had been comparatively light. Eighth Army had suffered 1,750 casualties and lost 67 tanks and 15 anti-tank guns. By comparison, the Panzerarmee had lost a great deal of transport, as well as 55 guns and 49 tanks. The Germans had suffered 1,859 casualties and the Italians 1,051.[138] Montgomery was proud of his first victory in the desert. He named the action the 'Battle of Alamein' and in conversation with Freyberg said that he 'considered Alamein one of [the] historic battles of [the] war'.[139] The British later renamed it 'Alam Halfa', emphasising the importance of the successful repulse of Rommel's armour and conveniently ignoring the debacle of Beresford. Like most defeats, Beresford became an orphan. Although subsequently seen by both sides as an important turning point in the fortunes of the war, the battle received relatively little coverage at the time. This was deliberate. Rommel's attempt to reach the Delta had been repulsed, but it was imperative that the Panzerarmee remain in its defences around Alamein. If Rommel had taken the decision to pull out to the Egyptian frontier and thus shorten his lines of communications, Montgomery would have been severely embarrassed by the fact that his opponent had slipped from his grasp.

The Axis also had no wish to point out the fact that their last all-out attempt to reach the Delta had failed disastrously and Goebbels' Propaganda Ministry referred to the events merely as a 'reconnaissance in force'. Yet Rommel's 'flaccid reconnaissance'[140] will always remain one of the more hotly contested subjects for 'what might have been'. It is impossible to know whether a properly planned and prepared counterstroke could have finished off the Panzerarmee once and for all. Nehring believed that:

> If the British High Command had conducted the operations on mobile prin-
> ciples, for which purpose armoured formations had after all been created, the
> result would probably have been disastrous for the German-Italian formations.[141]

Volumes of fierce criticism have been levelled at Dorman-Smith's plan for a 'modern defensive battle' stressing mobility and manoeuvre, but it is rarely noted that in early August Eighth Army had to plan on the assumption that Rommel *would* receive sufficient fuel for his offensive.

Montgomery's decision to mount a static defensive battle has generally been lauded but Eighth Army might have been in terrible danger 'if Rommel had had freedom of action'.[142] L. C. F. Turner, another South African official historian, believed that 'if the Afrika Korps had been capable of serious manoeuvre 22 Armd Bde and 8 Armd Bde might have got into serious trouble on 1 September'.[143] With sufficient fuel, the Afrika Korps would have presented a much more fleeting and mobile target to the bombers of the Desert Air Force and could have masked the positions of 22nd Armoured Brigade with an anti-tank-gun screen while leaving it in its 'rigid defence position severely alone'.[144] As the Afrika Korps advanced it would then have encountered 8th Armoured Brigade moving up in support. Exactly as at Gazala, the British armoured brigades could have been dealt with individually by the concentrated power of the Afrika Korps.

Similarly, Beresford resembled Operation Aberdeen in its improvised manner and disastrous outcome. L. C. F. Turner believed it to have been 'merely a continuation of the series of un-coordinated corps, divisional, brigade and "battle group" actions in which Eighth Army had indulged so unsuccessfully during the last three months'.[145] This highlights a point not often made concerning Alam Halfa: Montgomery fought the battle with only a fraction of the strength available to him, just as Ritchie had done at Gazala. The difference in outcome between the two battles lay in the power of the Desert Air Force and the Panzerarmee's lack of fuel.

Nehring realised that both commanders had made mistakes and missed opportunities in almost equal measure:

> The Goddess of Victory offered both the opponents a unique chance to revert the situation in that war theatre. The one has the chance firmly in his hands, but – over cautious and stubbornly sticking to the dogma of strategic defence – he refuses to make use of it; the other frantically tries everything in his power to get hold of it but for technical reasons is unable to grasp it.[146]

In adopting a rigidly static defensive scheme, Montgomery was fortunate that the Panzerarmee lacked the fuel to make its offensive truly powerful. At the same time, Rommel was fortunate that when he found his main striking force was virtually immobilised in front of the Alam el Halfa ridge, the Eighth Army was not launched in an all-out bid to destroy him.

Montgomery's insistence that the armour must not be loosed even in the face of an obvious Axis withdrawal has generally been praised. It is usually assumed that, had the British armoured brigades advanced to the attack, the British tanks would have sacrificed themselves on the teeth of the carefully deployed German and Italian anti-tank-gun screen. However, this interpretation is hardly fair to British armoured tactics as they had evolved by August 1942 and indeed sits uneasily with the accusations of excessive caution that were levelled against the British armour during the most recent fighting in July. The fact is that British armour had learned by its experience since Operation Crusader. The reckless charging of German gun screens was a thing of the past even before Montgomery took command.

Rommel made a fundamental mistake: he committed his main striking force to an advance deep behind Eighth Army's lines with insufficient fuel to complete the movement. On 2 and 3 September, Eighth Army did have an opportunity to punish Rommel for that mistake. A cautious advance by the armoured brigades of Eighth Army, constantly searching for the flanks of the German and Italian formations, would have forced the Panzerarmee to deploy its anti-tank guns and kept the panzers in motion – if only in redeploying to meet a possible threat. With the full support of the Desert Air Force and artillery of Eighth Army, this pressure would have fixed the Panzerarmee and probably made Montgomery's plan of cutting off its supplies successful.

Perhaps the greatest 'might have been' relates to Gott's death. Gott is generally judged not to have been the right commander to plan and conduct an intense breakthrough battle in the manner of the October battle of Alamein. This may be true but, although Montgomery rejected Gott's plan for Alam Halfa, there has to be at least a vague suspicion that, with Eighth Army under the command of 'Strafer' Gott, there may have been no need for another battle after Alam Halfa. However, battles and campaigns are filled with unforeseen events, chances and missed opportunities. The friction and fog of war are easy to disperse in hindsight but impossible to penetrate in the heat of the moment.

Rommel never seems to have fully understood the true importance of the 'technical reasons' why his offensive failed. He certainly recognised the significance of the power of the Desert Air Force but to the end he always maintained that the supply problems were ultimately and primarily due to Italian failures of organisation and inefficiency. He seems never to have understood the full complexity of the interdependencies that ensnared the Panzerarmee's logistics.

The Italian Navy and merchant marine made a supreme effort to get supplies across the Mediterranean during August 1942 and suffered heavy losses doing so.[147] The restricted capacity of the North African ports available for use only made matters worse but the main problem remained the same: Rommel had outrun his lines of supply. The advance to El Alamein placed excessive strain upon the Axis lines of communication. At the same time as Rommel was demanding increased supplies for the battlefront, the Axis had to transport large amounts of materiel to improve the inadequate facilities of the ports while also consuming vast quantities of fuel simply transporting supplies to the now far distant front.[148] This became a desperate situation thanks to a revitalised Malta and the growing power of the RAF to hit convoys at sea, bomb the ports where Axis ships docked, strafe the coastal shipping used to bring supplies forward and interdict the long land lines of communication. Rommel never understood that when supplies failed to reach Africa because the vessel carrying them was sunk more was lost than the cargo. It meant the loss of a valuable ship, and possibly its crew, out of a limited and finite number of Italian and German merchant vessels which then had serious knock-on effects throughout the complex logistics chain. Given this appalling logistics situation, Rommel revealed the final bankruptcy of his method of war. Rather than assess the situation as a whole, he still gambled on success in the midst of logistics breakdown and began his attack without the fuel to finish it. Rommel's offensive failed for more than mere 'technical reasons'.

Eighth Army may not have ruthlessly exploited its advantages during the 'six days' race' but the obvious and conclusive proof was that Rommel had been defeated. While much of the combat power of Eighth Army had remained passive during the battle, the Desert Air Force had put everything into the struggle. For the first time, the army and air force had fought a joint battle. The Desert Air Force could not provide the same kind of 'flying artillery' as the now obsolete Stuka, but it had found a way for its medium bombers to influence the land battle directly. The army had held the ring and the air force had punished the Panzerarmee repeatedly. Indeed, the laurels of the fight largely belonged to the Desert Air Force. Its campaign of strategic interdiction combined with round-the-clock battlefield support had produced victory. Montgomery's greatest achievement at Alam Halfa was that he did not allow himself or Eighth Army to make any serious mistakes. By combining the efforts of Eighth Army and Desert Air Force into a joint team, Montgomery and Coningham ensured that, this time, it was Rommel who made the forced errors that cost dearly.

Montgomery had perhaps not fought the battle with as much 'grip' or prescience as he later claimed. Morever, his 'historic' 'Battle of Alamein' was perhaps less impressive than it seemed at the time. But the real significance of Alam Halfa was its influence upon the officers and men of Eighth Army. Montgomery had repeatedly told them that they would win the next fight with Rommel and he had been proved right. The morale of the army and their confidence in their white-kneed general soared. Just as importantly, once the Panzerarmee had withdrawn, it still remained pinned to the stretch of desert near El Alamein. Having conclusively beaten off the Axis offensive, the Eighth Army could prepare to mount its own.

THIRTEEN

The Crest of a Wave

Sweat saves blood
Prussian military maxim

Rommel's attempt to reach the Delta had failed. There could be no doubt now that Eighth Army would make the next major offensive move. Although the 'sound and fury' of the interregnum, Alam Halfa and Montgomery's own version of events have tended to obscure the process, even by 7 September 1942, when Montgomery officially 'closed' his first battle in the desert, Eighth Army planning for its own offensive was already well advanced.

Auchinleck's appreciation of 2 August had provided a clear template for the future direction of Eighth Army policy. An offensive would be mounted in the northern sector while making full use of deception measures to mislead Axis observers as to its scale and scope. However, within that broad policy, a vast range of decisions had to be taken before such a 'tight' battle could be executed.

Montgomery began planning what became known as Operation Lightfoot within days of his arrival at Eighth Army Headquarters. Right from the start, he made much more effective use of his team of staff officers than Auchinleck had. Charles Richardson, who had been deeply unhappy, found the new regime gave him 'clear and definite' tasks.[1] This was in large part due to the efficient functioning of Montgomery's 'chief of staff' system. Montgomery delegated the entire running of Eighth Army's Main Headquarters to Freddie de Guingand.

Every morning at 07.00 hours, de Guingand met with the headquarters staff in the operations caravan to discuss the matters for attention that day. The meetings 'though very informal, were highly expeditious'.[2] Briefs of the present operational 'sitrep' and intelligence summaries were given, followed by de Guingand's list of points for action. Any further points would be raised and dealt with and the meeting would then break up – generally after only twenty minutes. Thanks to these meetings, the entire staff knew exactly what they were responsible for and could work to achieve it imme-diately. Freddie de Guingand's days were busy. He liaised closely with the Army Rear Headquarters on all issues of supply, stayed in touch with the staff of each corps and contacted General Headquarters Middle East in Cairo on a daily basis amongst a multitude of other tasks. Every evening, he reported to Montgomery on developments, the actions executed that day and future issues. Soon after his arrival, Montgomery had hinted that he might replace de Guingand but clearly thought better of it. Although Montgomery and de Guingand had very different personalities and tastes – perhaps because of this – they made a highly efficient team.

Richardson's first job as planner under de Guingand was to write an appreciation and plan for Lightfoot. 'Chink' Dorman-Smith had appropriated this task to himself while at Eighth Army HQ so it was not surprising that Richardson's morale improved considerably under de Guingand's direction. He was 'amazed to learn from Freddie that Monty already had very firm ideas where, when and how he would fight the battle; these ideas were passed on to me'.[3] There can be little doubt that Monty's 'very firm ideas' concerning the future offensive were informed at least in part from the work that had already been done by Auchinleck, de Guingand and Ramsden.

Richardson's appreciation was ready by 19 August, only six days after Montgomery had taken command. The object remained exactly the same as it had done since Auchinleck's 'My Draft for Counter-Offensive' scribbled on 1 July; Eighth Army was to 'destroy the enemy's forces in the area they now occupy'.[4] In assessing the various possibilities in the various sectors, Richardson identified the northern sector as 'the most suitable for a breakthrough', just as Auchinleck had done and for very similar reasons:

i)   The right flank rests securely on the sea.
ii) The MITEIRIYA Ridge is a strong tactical feature giving security to the left flank.
iii) A threat here forces the enemy away from his L. of C. and threatens him with encirclement.
iv) A 'breakthrough' in this area produces an immediate threat to the enemy's landing grounds.
v)   A landing from the sea may be possible to support the operation.
vi) Maintenance is easier.[5]

The projected axis of the attack was to be on either side of the coast road. This, too, accorded with Auchinleck's thinking. The attack, envisaged as taking place on 1 October, was timed to take advantage of the September full moon to help the sappers in their mine-lifting tasks. Four brigades, two each from the 9th Australian and 51st (Highland) Divisions, would mount the assault with a further two brigades tasked with 'holding the gap'. The plan was to breach the Axis defences rapidly and 'with the greatest measure of surprise'. This would enable 10 Corps, formed from 1st and 10th Armoured Divisions with the 2nd New Zealand Division, to penetrate the gap and drive deep into the Panzerarmee's rear. The penetration had to be deep to ensure that 'the enemy must attack us to restore the situation and cannot merely adjust his forward dispositions to conform'.[6] 10 Corps would take up positions around Ghazal station and attack any Axis armoured formations moving north in the flank. Meanwhile, 4th Light Armoured Brigade would be sent on to raid El Daba and possibly Fuka. Two hours later, a small regimental group of tanks and supporting arms would land at Ras Abu el Guruf to attack the Panzerarmee in its rear. Although it is possible to detect at least a glimpse of Auchinleck's planning in Richardson's appreciation, this document marked the beginning of an intensive period of planning, debate and discussion that transformed Lightfoot into a much larger operation.

Eighth Army and Montgomery were fortunate that Rommel did attack at the end of August. Richardson's appreciation was a very bold and daring plan which was predicated on the relatively limited, and possibly inadequate, resources which would be available to Eighth Army by the end of September. While the plan integrated all three services, an initial breakthrough attack mounted by just two divisions was too small to succeed against the increasingly elaborate defences of the Panzerarmee. The timing for the offensive was also too tight and Freyberg noted in his diary on 9 September that the 'Target date for next show is impossible. Training will go on into October.'[7] The Joint Planning Staff in Cairo prepared a detailed breakdown of the readiness states for all the units in Eighth Army. This showed that 10th Armoured Division would not be ready until 8 October while 1st Armoured, along with many other units, could not be ready until 15 October.[8] It was not possible to undertake all the detailed planning, preparations and training necessary for the attack by 1 October. Recognising this, Montgomery was determined not to attack until the period of the next full moon – sometime around 24 October. Rommel's offensive at the end of August derailed Eighth Army's timetable but it gave Montgomery something very precious. He now had a good reason to delay the attack, and a strong argument for doing so. It would have been very difficult to resist Churchill's insistent demands for an 'immediate offensive' without the reassuring defensive victory at Alam Halfa.

On 11 September, Churchill wrote to Alexander concerning plans for the coming offensive:

> I assume that LIGHTFOOT is what you and Montgomery explained to me in the caravan by the sea. It would be a help to me to know about when you think it will come off. I know you will be thinking about general problems as well as your own. I had hoped to have heard from you before.[9]

Since Churchill had appointed Alexander on the basis that he would mount an 'immediate offensive', the Prime Minister had been remarkably patient in waiting until Alam Halfa was well and truly over before raising this issue with Alexander. Nonetheless, he wanted results from his new team as soon as possible. Alexander had been astute in simply not raising the issue.

It was not until 19 September that Alexander replied and finally broke the unwelcome news to the Prime Minister: the projected date for Lightfoot was now 24 October. He explained that 10 Corps would not receive all its equipment until 1 October and, given the fact that 'the battle must be so stage managed that a hole is blown in the enemy front and 10 Corps passed through this hole in daylight', the full moon at the end of October would be needed for the operation.[10] Alexander insisted that the minimum period of training for 10 Corps once it received all its equipment was one month but 'in view of the moon period I am forced to make it only 3 weeks. It is therefore clear that 24th October is the earliest date possible.'[11] Alexander stood in a long line of British generals who had tried to explain to the Prime Minister why they had to delay their plans for attack but, unlike his predecessors, he won the political fight.

Churchill replied that he was 'greatly distressed to receive such bad news for which I was not prepared having regard to your strength compared with the enemy'.[12] Churchill desperately needed a British victory before the Torch landings took place in North Africa not only to show the value of Britain to the alliance but also to influence the French and Spanish attitude towards those landings. Churchill insisted that 'the time you mention does not give sufficient time for impression to soak in'.[13] Alexander's reply rebuffed Churchill on every point. He was adamant that 'to attack before we are ready will be to court failure' and explained in greater detail the training needs and timings which made the delay essential.[14] Montgomery had assisted Alexander in writing out the main four points on which to base a reply[15] but Alexander's reputation and standing with the Prime Minister were vital in achieving the result that both men wanted. The fact was that, for once, Churchill's new Commander-in-Chief Middle East had all the political capital he needed to stave off the Prime Minister's demands. The command changes of August, combined with the defensive victory of Alam Halfa, made it impossible for Churchill to threaten further changes to 'encourage' his generals. He was forced to accept the delay and replied, 'We are in your hands and of course a victorious battle makes amends for much delay.' Brooke insisted that Churchill finished the telegram with, 'Whatever happens we shall back you up and see you through.'[16] Alexander had won the political battle with consummate skill and Eighth Army was able to reap the benefits in full.

At the same time as he prepared his initial outline plan for Lightfoot, Montgomery began to purge the commanders of the Eighth Army and replace them with members of his own team – men he knew he could trust to fulfil his intentions. Ramsden, who had done so much to prepare the groundwork for Lightfoot, was summoned to Eighth Army Headquarters while on leave in Alexandria. Montgomery curtly informed him that he was to be replaced by Sir Oliver Leese, who had been one of Montgomery's students at Staff College. Ramsden was understandably aggrieved, but Montgomery's only explanation was, 'You're not exactly on the crest of a wave, Ramsden.'[17]

Just as Freyberg had resented Horrocks' appointment to 13 Corps, so Morshead was aggrieved at being passed over yet again for the command of 30 Corps. Leese's appointment started a fresh flurry of telegrams over the issue.[18] In fact, Churchill accepted that Morshead had justifiable claims and only agreed to Leese's appointment because Alexander had asked for him specifically.[19] Had Churchill realised that Leese was Montgomery's nomination it may well have been refused. Callum Renton, the commander of 7th Armoured Division who had quarrelled with Horrocks during Alam Halfa, was sacked. Michael Carver later noted sadly that Renton was not a good divisional commander but had the misfortune to be sacked over an argument with his superior when 'he was in the right'.[20] Nonetheless, Carver believed that John Harding, Renton's replacement, was a superb choice as 'he infused the whole division with his own energy, enthusiasm and commonsense'.[21]

Noel Martin, the Brigadier Royal Artillery of Eighth Army, who had done sterling work during the July battles in concentrating the fire of the guns and attempting to reverse the previous policies of dispersion, was blamed by Montgomery for these very practices and was replaced by Brigadier Sidney Kirkman. He had already served as Montgomery's artillery commander in England and thus was a natural choice to take charge of Eighth Army's artillery.

Montgomery's purges also swept through the brigadiers and colonels of Eighth Army. Of course, Monty could only sack British officers; officers of the three Dominion divisions and the 4th Indian Division were all immune from his broom. Montgomery undertook this stream of command changes as a means of bending what he saw as a recalcitrant army to his will. These purges undoubtedly created ill feeling within the officer corps of Eighth Army. Still, there is no question that Montgomery chose his new commanders wisely.

On 13 September, Montgomery set down his ideas for a radically expanded offensive. His memorandum covered not only the overall plan but the importance of training and morale in the coming fight. Montgomery broke from the mould of the Staff College appreciation and produced a document that was a model of clarity. During July, Eighth Army had been bombarded with multiple plans and cancellations. Montgomery's 'Memorandum No. 1' clearly laid out the overall plan and purpose yet it was only the starting point, designed as it was to 'form the basis of all our plans and preparations for operation "LIGHTFOOT"'.[22]

The plan, although incorporating some of Richardson's ideas, was very different from the 'appreciation and plan' of 19 August. Instead of a two-division assault, 30 Corps would now launch four divisions, supported by 23rd Armoured Brigade, in an attack designed to capture all the 'enemy main defended positions' between the coast and the Miteiriya ridge. The frontage of the attack was far wider but also much deeper as it was to seize the Panzerarmee's 'main gun areas'. Meanwhile, in the south 13 Corps was to seize Himeimat and thus 'draw enemy armour away from the main battle in the North'. 4th Light Armoured Brigade was to be squeezed around the southern flank to raid El Daba and destroy the enemy landing grounds there. A direct survival from Richardson's appreciation was the idea of a small combined force being landed on the coast at Ras Abu el Guruf. In common with Auchinleck and Richardson's appreciations was the emphasis on deception operations to 'deceive the enemy as to our intentions to attack at all and, if this fails, as to the direction of our main attack'. The assault was to be mounted during the hours of darkness and the bridgehead secured and 'thoroughly cleared of all enemy troops and guns' before the armoured brigades of 10 Corps moved up to pass through the gap. The armour was to be in position 'ready to fight at first light' so that they could 'complete the victory'.[23]

This seemingly simple plan was very ambitious. The infantry divisions of 30 Corps, supported by a 'great weight of artillery fire', would have to make a night advance of at least four and in some cases nearly six miles to reach the rear of the Axis defences and gun lines. The final objective for the four divisions was known as the 'Oxalic' line. 9th Australian Division would attack nearest the coast, with 51st (Highland) Division next in the line. Further south, 2nd New Zealand Division would capture and hold the Miteiriya ridge west of the Qattara track while 1st South African Division brought up its right flank to meet up with them on the ridge. One gap in the Axis defences and minefields would be made for 10 Corps within 51st (Highland) Division's front with the other in the 2nd New Zealand Division's area. Following Kisch's advice, 10 Corps would be responsible for marking, policing and clearing its own gaps in the complex series of minefields and all this would have to be achieved in just one night. Meanwhile, the infantry would have to ensure that deployment areas and routes to be used by 10 Corps were 'thoroughly cleared of all enemy troops and guns' before the armoured brigades began to move through them.[24]

The armour of 10 Corps was then meant to pass 'unopposed through gaps in the enemy minefields and be launched into territory West of these main minefields'. Having reached the objective line known as 'Pierson', the corps would then pivot on the Miteiriya ridge and take up 'ground of its own choosing astride the enemy's supply routes'. At this point, Montgomery's plan gave out as 'further operations will depend on how the enemy re-acts to this initial thrust'. The main idea was to force the panzer divisions to counterattack the British armour. This would enable Eighth Army to wear down the panzers to the point of destruction. Once this had been achieved, the rest of the Panzerarmee could then 'be rounded up without any difficulty'.[25] This concept was the reverse of Auchinleck's policy of wearing down Italian formations so that the Panzerarmee had no infantry left to hold the front.

The lack of any clear plan for the exploitation phase was striking. German operational art was founded upon a common understanding of the exploitation of a breakthrough. Panzer divisions were designed to break through enemy defences on a narrow front and then encircle the enemy.[26] Soviet operational art was even more sophisticated. Soviet 'deep battle' envisaged a series of offensives along the full length of a front. Once a breakthrough had been made, second echelon forces were tasked with driving deep into the enemy's 'operational depth' and destroying headquarters and rear area installations to bring about 'operational shock'.[27] In 1941, Soviet forces were quite unable to implement their sophisticated offensive doctrine but the doctrine of 'deep battle', as refined through the traumatic experiences of 1941 and 1942, provided the intellectual underpinnings for Soviet offensives from late 1942 onwards.[28] Montgomery had created a *corps de chasse* but he gave 10 Corps no clear role other than passing through the breach and then awaiting the Axis reaction. The lack of any clear, well-thought-out British doctrine on the exploitation of a breakthrough was a serious intellectual handicap. Montgomery's unwillingness or inability to plan for the exploitation phase demonstrated the limits of his military thinking.

Yet the initial assault to be mounted in Lightfoot was far more ambitious than Bacon and Splendour had been. Four infantry divisions, aligned along a corps frontage of 12,000 yards, had to assault the Axis defences and seize a 'bridgehead' at least 6,000 yards deep. The frontage at the final corps objective actually widened to 16,000 yards. As the 2nd New Zealand Division had shown on the night of 14 July it was just possible to mount a night advance of six miles through defended territory. However, an advance of that distance made it very difficult to ensure that all enemy posts had been mopped up. Axis defences were also far stronger by mid-September than they had been in mid-July. There was no precedent for attempting a break-in assault of this size, clearing gaps in a series of minefields and passing four armoured brigades through all in one night.

On 15 September, Montgomery held a conference with his three corps commanders and all the divisional commanders to explain his plan for the coming offensive. However, when the commanders returned to their units and began tackling the challenge of implementing the plan, most realised that it was far too ambitious. Leese, the newly appointed commander of 30 Corps, spent three days in observing the ground for the attack. He took his old friend Douglas Wimberley[29] along with him on his reconnaissances who thought that 'all the ground looked horribly open and bare'.[30] The two dominating features were the coastal ridge and the Miteiriya ridge with open desert between. However, Leese believed that even with a total of 432 field guns and 48 medium guns at his disposal:[31]

> Four Divisions were insufficient with the number of guns available to attack on the whole frontage. I was, therefore, faced with the problem of whether to attack in the north or in the south, or whether to attack in two different places.[32]

He later admitted that 'this frontage was very large and I have often looked back on it and felt that if I did the attack again I would somehow have shortened it more'.[33]

On 21 September, Freyberg sent a detailed memo to Leese outlining his concerns. He noted that the:

> capture of the position may be achieved with greater ease than the holding of the final ridge. It is certain that the enemy will launch a counter attack as soon as possible after first light. Our F[orward] D[efended] L[ocalitie]s are upon a forward slope that may be solid stone and it will therefore be most difficult to get cover for the anti-tank guns, machine guns, infantry posts, OPs etc. Further the enemy is known to have a group of guns in position to shoot at the final objective and these gun positions are out of range of the majority of our bombardment guns.[34]

Freyberg need not have speculated about the geology of the Miteiriya ridge. The Australian infantry had had all too much experience of Ruin ridge in July and it is surprising that there does not appear to have been any liaison between the two divisions on this matter. Lieutenant-Colonel Whitehead, of the 2/32nd Australian Infantry Battalion which attacked the ridge on 16 July, had noted in his report that:

> The ability of tps to dig in quickly and obtain adequate cover may decide whether the posn can be held or not. Consideration should be given to objectives where suitable cover can be obtained. . . . Posns must not be occupied where adequate Atk defence cannot be given. Fwd slopes of escarpments are difficult in this regard.[35]

However, Whitehead's excellent report was filed with 9th Australian Division Headquarters and not disseminated throughout the army. It was unfortunate that the same kind of information failure experienced by the New Zealanders on 14 July was still possible. Freyberg also noted, 'The area to be attacked and the depth to which the attack is planned to penetrate makes the operation one of great difficulty. It will require two full infantry brigades.' Given the distance to be covered, and the amount of mopping up that would be required, Freyberg recognised that battalions would not be able to go 'straight through to the final objective'. He argued that battalions would have to 'leapfrog' through to the final objective and that there would have to be a pause in the artillery programme to enable the mopping up of the first objective area and the move up to a fresh start line for the second objective. Freyberg suggested:

> The operation will accordingly divide naturally into two separate attacks. There will be the attack on the first objective when the barrage lifts, then a pause followed by concentrations of fire to cover the advance of the second wave to the final objective. I see no difficulty in either of these attacks provided we allow sufficient time and co-ordinate our start lines, bombardments and pauses with the SA Division and 51 Division.[36]

Freyberg had already recognised that 'this operation approximates to the battles fought in 1918' and the familiarity of the three key divisional commanders, Morshead, Wimberley and Freyberg, with those attacks of twenty years before was critical to the success of Lightfoot.

Thus there was a great distance between Montgomery's bold and clear overall plan and its execution. The ongoing discussions concerning the plan also highlight the sharp difference in the planning process between July and September 1942. In July, divisional commanders had been confronted with difficult tasks yet the hurried conferences before each attack had given them no time to think through the consequences or find solutions to the problems.

Although Montgomery had stated that orders were no longer to be considered a basis for discussion, this was exactly what occurred during the planning process for Lightfoot. Freyberg wrote a concerned memo to Leese on 21 September while his division prepared to carry out a full-scale rehearsal of the attack. Freyberg explained:

> We are carrying out an Exercise framed to embody as many of the conditions we are likely to meet as possible . . . The 9 Armd Brigade will co-operate in the attack which will be carried out under live artillery trench mortar and machine gun fire. We shall lift minefields and mark them under conditions as nearly approaching battle as possible.[37]

The full-scale rehearsals that each infantry division underwent during September and October were crucial in the development of the plan. These ensured that each of the infantry divisions was properly trained and prepared to achieve the ambitious objectives set for them.

Ever since the Great War, the British Army had understood the value of troops rehearsing the role they would undertake during an offensive. The importance of such training was not in doubt but during the desert campaigns there had rarely been sufficient time to undertake proper preparation, as the Australian report on Lightfoot sadly acknowledged:

> So often when the Army in the Western Desert was living from hand to mouth, troops have been thrown into battle without preparation. The value of preparing, or presenting troops to the battle was shown particularly by the achievements of 51 (H) Div in this battle.[38]

The performance of 132nd Brigade in Beresford was just one example out of many of what could happen to poorly prepared troops. The experience of 51st (Highland) Division formed a complete contrast to almost every other British unit in its comprehensive preparation for battle.[39] 51st (Highland) Division was a fresh formation which had landed in Egypt in mid-August, but the division was allowed almost two months to acclimatise and train before being sent into action. This was a luxury which no other British unit had enjoyed in nearly two years of fighting.

In many respects 51st (Highland) Division was a unique formation within the British Army. The original division, composed of the regular battalions of the Highland regiments, had been captured en masse at St Valéry in 1940. Thus the division which sailed to Egypt, formed mainly from the Territorial battalions of the same regiments, possessed a fierce desire to avenge the previous disaster. Major-General Douglas Wimberley, known as 'Lang Tam' because of his height, was very protective of his division and its distinctive Scottish character. He insisted on maintaining this and although the 7th Middlesex Regiment was the division's machine-gun battalion Wimberley rationalised this as '"mascots" to the Jocks'.[40] He refused to accept an English anti-aircraft regiment and saw to it that the battalions that went into action at Alamein were 80 per cent Scottish. Beyond that, the division had a high *esprit de corps* based on the shared traditions of the Highland regiments and the example of the previous 51st (Highland) Division in the Great War. Leese noted that 'there was a terrific spirit in the Division and great enthusiasm to learn'.[41]

The division began its acclimatisation at Qassassin and Mena camps. It was later noted that the:

> Highlander who had trained hard for nearly three years in England and Scotland was fast adapting himself to desert conditions. He dug one-man weapon pits in the sand and camouflaged them, judged distance in the unfamiliar light, conserved as a matter of routine his precious ration of water, learnt more about laying our mines and lifting those of the enemy, and began to move with certainty in an empty landscape by day and night.[42]

The necessity of dispersing the troops in the desert as a precaution led to one distinctive problem for the division. The divisional headquarters piper had to mount the tailboard of a lorry and be driven round the dispersed bivouacs to pipe the morning reveille.[43] Once the troops had become acclimatised, the division was moved up to El Hammam where the work and training became more intense. During September, each battalion of the division served in the front line with the 9th Australian Division. This enabled each unit to receive some front line experience and learn from the Australian veterans.

Wimberley was impressed with the Australians' ability as soldiers but when he first visited them he found that the soldiers were 'all half naked and burnt brown as berries. They took a bit of getting used to. I was dressed as a General and they treated me in the most "matey" way.'[44] Wimberley sent a stiff memo around his division emphasising the fact that although his division should 'copy the Australians and do our level best to absorb all they can teach us' for the officers and men he would not tolerate similar standards of discipline in his division.[45] There is no doubt that the Scottish soldiers were initially:

> startled by their apparent lack of discipline. The Aussie soldiers – uniform [of] boots and shorts – referred to their officers by their first or even nicknames, an unheard of liberty to Seaforth ears. But there was little doubt about their military efficiency.[46]

At the same time, the Australians were astonished to learn that Scottish soldiers had to salute their officers even when in action! However, when the Scottish battalions went into the line with the Australians they learned the craft of desert warfare and patrolling from masters. 51st (Highland) Division certainly never adopted the habits of the Australians but a strong bond of mutual respect grew up between the two divisions and the inexperienced Scottish units were given the best possible training.

While one Scottish battalion was serving with the Australians in its turn, the rest of the division was undergoing intensive training behind the lines. On 13 September, a training instruction outlined the programme for one month of intensive preparation. The main purpose was to study and practise the 'procedure for breaking through prepared defences, including minefields to a depth sufficient to form a bridgehead for the passage of an Armoured Division'. All arms were to practise carrying out their tasks at night and learn to cooperate with the infantry tanks of 23rd Armoured Brigade and the RAF.[47] Wimberley explained:

> We were in a fortunate position, only a small proportion of our fighting troops were in the line at one time with the 9th Australians, and we were able to

take our troops for some hours out of the 'boxes' to give them preparatory training for the forthcoming battle . . . I laid out an exact replica of the part of the enemies defences which it was our job to attack. Then I took my troops, a Brigade at a time, and practised every Battalion in the exact job I had decided it was to do in the initial attack.[48]

The first divisional level exercise was held on the night of 26–27 September with the object of studying 'the break-in to an organised prepared enemy position defended by minefields by night and reorganisation of a posn taken ready to meet c/attack'.[49] This was a full-scale rehearsal which involved two infantry brigades with all the supporting arms of the division. The divisional artillery fired a barrage in support to accustom the soldiers to the noise and dust they would encounter in battle. These exercises were not without incident. During one divisional exercise, one gun failed to lift with the barrage and six members of 1st Black Watch were killed, including the second in command, Major Arthur Wilmot. In all, the division held a total of four divisional scale exercises to ensure that every soldier understood his part in the as yet undisclosed operation.[50] When 51st (Highland) Division went into battle on 23 October 1942, it was immeasurably better prepared for its task than the men of 23rd Armoured Brigade had been three months before.

Every one of the assaulting divisions underwent a similar process of training and rehearsal designed to simulate as closely as possible the conditions the soldiers would encounter in battle. Battalion and brigade training exercises culminated in full divisional rehearsals involving the advance of the infantry, movement of transport, artillery support, minefield gapping and tank cooperation. 23rd Armoured Brigade also underwent intensive training alongside the soldiers of 51st Highland and 9th Australian Divisions. Each regiment in the brigade was rotated through the infantry exercises so that all the tank crews and infantry got to know one another. The essential trust between tanks and infantry that had been so lacking during July developed through hard training on these exercises.

The discussions over the plan in 30 Corps, combined with the vital information gained from the exercises, meant that, unlike the plans of July, the divisional and unit commanders all played a part in shaping their tasks. Leese noted:

From the start there was a most extraordinary spirit of co-operation in the Corps. This was very remarkable, taking into consideration the very strong personalities of the Commanders concerned and the divergent types of Divisions represented. From a Corps point of view one could not have wanted a more capable or helpful team.[51]

Even though Leese's appointment had been controversial, his personality and affable approach were very important in smoothing out many difficulties. He may not have had great experience of desert warfare but was willing to listen and learn from his divisional commanders and incorporate their ideas. There is no doubt that Leese handled Pienaar's prickly personality, Morshead's proud independence and Freyberg's gruff caution far more expertly than either Norrie or Ramsden had.

However, while the commanders of 30 Corps dealt with the problems in a spirit of cooperation, the same could not be said of Lumsden's 10 Corps. Although Lumsden was held in high regard by Briggs, his relations with Gatehouse had not improved since Alam Halfa. All three men began to have doubts about the feasibility of passing their armoured divisions through the minefield gaps in just one night. Freyberg's recommendation for a two-phase infantry assault with a one-hour pause was eminently sensible, indeed essential, if the infantry were to carry out their part of the plan. However, this meant that the time available for passing the armour through would be short. While Montgomery had confidently asserted that the infantry would reach the enemy gun line and completely clear the sectors earmarked for 10 Corps gaps, Lumsden and his divisional commanders knew that this was virtually impossible. The experience of Bacon no doubt loomed large in their thinking. The reservations of the armour commanders also grew after they had held their series of full-scale rehearsals.

Each armoured division held a series of exercises to practise:

(a) An approach march by night by restricted routes to a minefield area
(b) The passage of a minefield or minefields by night
(c) The deployment of fighting tps beyond the minefield.[52]

1st Armoured Division held its first exercise on 25 September, even though, before Splendour, Fisher had insisted to Brigadier Clifton that his tanks could not move at night. Now the armour of Eighth Army was practising to ensure that it could move in darkness. Yet it was also significant that, while the entire division including the tank regiments, motor battalions, lorried infantry brigade and artillery took part in the exercise, little thought was given to the need to fight alongside the infantry divisions of 30 Corps. It was stated in the division's report that, 'In all training, the presence of an Infantry Division clearing the bridgehead with all its attendant transport, guns, etc. must be remembered',[53] but at no point did the rehearsals actually include training with those divisions.

However, there was an exception to this situation within 10 Corps. After the bitter experiences of July, Freyberg refused to take part in any future attack without armour under his command. Freyberg had hoped that a New

Zealand armoured brigade might be sent out in time but eventually it was agreed that the 9th Armoured Brigade should be allotted to 2nd New Zealand Division. This meant that the division would be composed of one armoured brigade and two infantry brigades along with a full complement of supporting arms. This new organisation for a 'mobile' division was precisely the composition that Auchinleck had envisaged in his controversial plans for reorganisation in July. It made perfect sense to begin the experiment with the 2nd New Zealand Division. There were no further replacements available for the foreseeable future and thus the division could not be expected to engage in a sustained infantry battle. By providing the division with an armoured brigade, its offensive value would be increased and, given the New Zealanders' expertise in desert warfare, the division would be well placed to provide the infantry component of 10 Corps.

It was also significant that 9th Armoured Brigade had few ingrained prejudices about tank–infantry cooperation. Its three regiments had been brought to Palestine as Yeomanry cavalry regiments in 1939, and had been involved in the Syrian campaign in 1941 as horsed cavalry. The regiments were re-equipped with the latest Sherman tanks and had to learn the art of armoured warfare from scratch. Freyberg first met Brigadier John Currie of 9th Armoured Brigade on 12 September and noted that he 'seems keen to come on with New Zealand Division'.[54] Freyberg went with Currie to see a fire-power demonstration which tested the new Sherman and Crusader III tanks.

By 11 September, 318 Sherman tanks and 100 'Priest' 105mm self-propelled guns had arrived at Suez.[55] These were the tanks which Roosevelt and Marshall had promised Churchill on 21 June. The Sherman M4 Medium Tank was better than any German tank in the Afrika Korps with the possible exception of the Panzer Mk IV 'Special'. The Sherman was essentially an improved version of the Grant with its main gun in a fully rotating turret. This meant that the crews could take full advantage of the dual-purpose 75mm gun. The Sherman 75 mm could fire a high-explosive shell and, importantly, a capped armour-piercing round which could penetrate any existing German tank. The tank shared the mechanical reliability and toughness of the Grant and these characteristics made the Sherman a battle-winner.[56]

The same could not quite be said of the Crusader Mk III, which, although it mounted the six-pounder gun, was not provided with capped ammunition and could not fire an effective high-explosive shell. The small turret was cramped by the large gun breech and the reliability of the tank, just like its predecessors, was still suspect. Freyberg declared that he was 'very impressed with the performance of both tanks'.[57] However, the full allocation of 'Swallows' (as the British codenamed the Sherman) for 9th Armoured Brigade did not arrive until early October. This gave the brigade only a short time to prepare for their role in battle. The regiments of the brigade had been serving in Iraq and were collected together for training in mid-September, only six weeks before the battle. It was later related by the historian of the Royal Wiltshire Yeomanry:

Those six weeks were very hectic. They were principally devoted to rehearsing the Brigade's role in the coming offensive but besides this, there 'was so much to do and so little time in which to do it'. A deal of training had to be rounded off as recent events had sadly hampered training. Then the new Sherman tanks were beginning to arrive and these held a thousand mysteries. New machinery, new types of gun, new gadgets galore. All had to be studied and mastered.[58]

John Currie had a reputation for fearlessness in action but he also knew what could happen to untried troops in their first battle and he drove his men without mercy during this period. Six weeks was a very short time to prepare a fresh armoured brigade for battle but it was a great deal longer than had been allowed for the 23rd Armoured Brigade in July. By the time 9th Armoured Brigade went into action, John Currie had ensured that it was ready for the challenge.[59]

1st Armoured Division's exercise, in common with all the rehearsals conducted by the units of 10 Corps, threw up a mass of detailed points concerning lighting, organisation, width of gap necessary, march speed and communications. Since Kisch had insisted that each armoured division should be responsible for making its own gaps in the enemy minefields, the exercise underlined the need for a well-organised minefield task force to clear, hold and police the gaps.[60] This was a welcome, if belated recognition of the fact that 'Sappers can either work or fight, they cannot do both at once'.[61] However, the timings of each unit in passing through the minefield gaps were far from encouraging. The Bays regimental group had taken 43 minutes longer than expected while the 2nd Rifle Brigade motor battalion had taken an extra 90 minutes. Such delays were reflected throughout the division. The exercise showed the complexity and difficulty of moving an entire armoured division through narrow minefield gaps.

Lumsden, Briggs and Gatehouse all began to doubt the feasibility of the plan. Leese remembered that he:

had not been at all happy during the planning stage of the armour to break out. On arrival in this country I had been horrified at the controversy between infantry and armour. Neither had confidence in the other . . . At several Conferences the armour had expressed doubt as to whether they would in point of fact break through on the first morning.[62]

He ascribed this to the fact that the armoured divisions were too 'mine and 88mm conscious' but then he did not have personal experience of how those two weapons could easily wreck an armoured brigade in a matter of minutes. The enormous delays experienced in moving the armoured brigades through the minefield gaps during rehearsals offered concrete proof that passing them through in one night would be very difficult indeed.

Meanwhile, the Panzerarmee Afrika was far from idle in preparing for the coming blow. There is no question that the morale of the German and Italian soldiers at Alamein had sagged under the realisation that their attempt to break through to the Delta had failed. Joseph Goebbels' Propaganda Ministry could explain away the offensive as a 'reconnaissance in force' but this did not fool any desert veterans. Rommel was bitterly disappointed and increasingly ill. Eventually, his doctor insisted that he return to Germany for a rest cure. On 22 September, Rommel handed over command of the Panzerarmee to General der Kavallerie Georg Stumme who had served with distinction in Russia. However, before Rommel left for Germany he had already outlined the defensive plan to be adopted and started the preparations to meet the British attack.

Rommel's subsequent account of the fighting at Alamein, entitled 'Battle without Hope – Alamein',[63] overlaid a heavy dose of hindsight onto the Axis preparations for the coming battle in September and October 1942. In fact, it is clear that even in the face of their obvious supply difficulties Axis senior commanders were far from despondent about the coming British offensive.

Confidence within the Panzerarmee can only have increased after the series of failed operations mounted by General Headquarters Middle East and Eighth Army during September. Auchinleck's plans for combined operations on the coastal flank of the Panzerarmee, which he had outlined in his appreciation of 1 August, bore bitter fruit in September 1942. More detailed plans for large-scale raids on Tobruk and Benghazi were subsequently developed by the Joint Planning Staff in Cairo.[64] These involved Special Air Service and Long Range Desert Group forces which were tasked with penetrating the Tobruk perimeter from the desert. Meanwhile, a force of destroyers and motor torpedo boats would land a party of Marines on the seaward side of the town. These forces would approach Tobruk under cover of a heavy bombing raid by the Desert Air Force. This was a boldly conceived combined operation but when Operation Agreement was executed on the night of 13 September, it quickly developed into a costly fiasco. The anti-aircraft cruiser *Coventry* and the destroyer *Zulu* were both sunk by German bombing attacks. Three hundred Royal Marines, 280 sailors and 160 soldiers became casualties.[65] Operation Bigamy, which was conceived as a smaller special forces raid on Benghazi, had to be abandoned in the face of alert enemy defences.[66] These raids proved that Axis defensive measures along the vulnerable coastal flank were difficult to overcome and this undoubtedly led to the shelving of any thought of actual seaborne landings in the rear of the Panzerarmee during the coming offensive.

The last and perhaps most significant failure was the Eighth Army's dismal attempt to capture the Munassib depression on 29 September. This depression had remained in Axis hands after Alam Halfa but both sides recognised its importance as a key piece of defensive terrain. It was decided that the 131st Brigade[67] of 44th (Home Counties) Division should make an attempt to seize the depression before the main offensive and thus threaten the Axis hold on their forward minefields in the area. Unlike the ill-fated previous attempts to seize the depression, the brigade trained intensively for the operation, codenamed Braganza, for five days and carried out a full rehearsal on the day before the attack. At 05.25 hours the barrage fired by nine regiments of field artillery crashed down in support of the advancing infantry. The 1/6th Queen's advanced along the northern lip of the depression and met with little opposition. Similarly, the 1/7th Queen's encountered no difficulty in taking the eastern edge of Munassib. However, its sister battalion, the 1/5th Queen's, had the more difficult task of seizing the southern lip of the depression. When its C Company approached the minefield in front of the enemy positions, the defenders, drawn from the Folgore Parachute Division, put down heavy mortar and machine-gun fire which pinned the troops to the ground. Meanwhile, A Company penetrated the Italian positions only to find itself surrounded and overwhelmed. The reserve companies were then held up by fierce defensive fire and made little progress. After a day of heavy shelling, the 1/5th Queen's were withdrawn from their exposed posts. The operation cost the brigade 328 casualties for little gain.[68] Although the 21st Panzer Division was alerted by the Afrika Korps when it was clear that a 'major operation' was underway against the Munassib Depression its assistance was not required by the Folgore Division. The Afrika Korps paid the troops of the Folgore a rare compliment when it noted that the Italian division 'bore the brunt of the attack. It fought well and inflicted heavy losses on the enemy.'[69] Operation Braganza must have suggested to the commanders of the Panzerarmee that Eighth Army had learned little from its previous disastrous attempts to seize the Munassib depression.

On 3 October, Stumme wrote to Marshal Cavallero outlining the position of the Panzerarmee. He mentioned that he was carrying on with Rommel's policy 'in all respects'. There seemed little doubt that the British were preparing for a major offensive, Stumme said:

The Pz Army is taking all possible steps to be able to defeat such a British offensive. We are in a position, as far as numerical strength goes, to defend ourselves against a frontal attack on the Alamein positions.[70]

This bullish statement confirms that Rommel's pessimistic views were developed with the benefit of hindsight. In fact, Stumme had every reason to be confident that his army could deal with another British attack. Every attack that the British had mounted in July had ended in clumsy failures, the raids on Benghazi and Tobruk had been fiascos and now the Folgore Division had been able to repulse an assault at Munassib. Stumme was only too aware of the Eighth Army's growing materiel superiority but there was little to suggest to him that it would be able to capitalise upon its advantage.

The most important change to the defensive posture of the Panzerarmee began on 24 September but took until 20 October to complete. It was explained that 'the daily casualties in this static warfare compel us to loosen up our front and site it in depth'. The forward outpost line was thinned out but also extended in depth and the existing company strongpoints were augmented by additional platoon and section posts. These battle outposts were sited to a maximum depth of 1,000 yards. A commanders' conference of 164th Division on 9 October explained that German and Italian companies alternated in front of the mine 'boxes' along the whole divisional sector. The company strongpoints were laid out like a chequer board to ensure that each strongpoint could support the flank of another. The purpose of this continuous line of forward occupied posts was to protect the division and to simulate the presence of a 'strong force in occupation'.[71] Behind the outpost line, there was then a gap of one to two kilometres before the main line defences. The battalion sectors occupied a frontage of 1,500 metres and were five kilometres deep. Only one company per battalion was deployed in the outpost zone. The number of troops deployed in the forward posts of the main line was reduced and more mines laid between the strongpoints.[72]

The German engineers had recent experience of how difficult it could be to gap minefields under fire. To this end, Colonel Hecker, the Panzerarmee's Chief Engineer, had overseen the laying of 445,358 mines. German and Italian engineers laid 249,849 anti-tank mines and 14,509 anti-personnel mines from 5 July to 20 October while 181,000 mines in captured British minefields around Deir el Shein and Bab el Qattara were incorporated into the defences. A further 180,000 British mines from captured dumps had been relaid along the front.[73] No other army had incorporated so many mines into its defences up to this point in the war. All this hard labour was to ensure that Eighth Army would be confronted by a series of mine boxes designed to hem in any attacking force and contain it so that it could be counterattacked by the Panzerarmee's mobile reserves. Such deep defences combined with the minefields confronted Eighth Army with a severe challenge. Rommel placed great faith in his 'Devil's Gardens' and he believed that any future British offensive would come to grief amongst the dense tangle of wire, outposts and mines. When he took command, Stumme was converted to this belief and later even suggested that a successful defensive action could be followed by a counteroffensive designed 'to destroy the Eighth Army and later take Alexandria'.[74]

On 1 October, Captain Kircher, 15th Panzer Division's intelligence officer, wrote a prescient appreciation of the most likely methods Eighth Army would adopt in its offensive.[75] Kircher surmised that the offensive would take place in mid-October and would be carried out in close cooperation with both the Desert Air Force and the Royal Navy. He expected continual night and day bombing combined with naval gunfire support in the Sidi Abd el Rahman area and even a landing around El Daba to seize the Panzerarmee's supply dumps. Kircher expected that the main weight of the offensive would develop between the coast and the Ruweisat ridge. He had divined the actual axis of the coming attack, and while his estimation of the forces involved was less accurate, he was also surprisingly accurate on the likely methods:

> The initial penetration and breakthrough, and the clearing of gaps in the mine-fields for the armour, will be done by the infantry divisions with armoured formations under command. The sectors of our line which are not immediately attacked will be tied down by shellfire and kept busy by feint attacks. To ensure success and smash our defences the enemy will site all his artillery, including that of the armoured divisions, to support the infantry divisions' attack.[76]

Kircher also recognised that Eighth Army would use deceptive measures including camouflage for the artillery so that 'we will not realize when the positions are occupied'.[77] His estimation that the three armoured divisions would not come forward until the day of the attack was quite correct.

At the same time as Kircher was producing his accurate assessment of British intentions, the intelligence staff of Eighth Army were also building up a clear picture of the Panzerarmee's defences. Lieutenant-Colonel 'Spud' Murphy, Eighth Army's chief intelligence officer, produced a very detailed report concerning the likely 'Enemy reaction to Operation "Lightfoot"'.[78] Murphy noted that the Axis defensive system 'has already achieved a state of elaboration hitherto unparalleled in NORTH AFRICA'. Two main defensive belts of mutually supporting posts and gun positions roughly three kilometres apart stretched from the coast to Deir el Shein. This defensive system was at least three to four kilometres in depth and as much as six to seven kilometres deep in some places. Murphy observed that there was frequently 'little in the way of defences between them' but noted:

> Connecting 'walls' are formed by lines of defensive positions running generally EAST to WEST and connecting the two NORTH to SOUTH belts at intervals of 4–5km and thus forming a series of 'hollow' areas.[79]

Murphy had identified the existence of Rommel's 'mine boxes'. He correctly assessed that these 'hollows' were designed to act as traps for attacking troops. He also noted that at least 150 Axis guns could be brought to bear on each one of the hollows. Murphy commented:

Not only does the attack lose its direction but, after making a limited advance, it runs a gauntlet of fire into an angle of minefields and gun positions formed by one of the connecting 'walls' and the second belt.[80]

He had divined exactly the design and intent of Rommel's defensive system. The complex series of defensive positions in the northern sector were designed to dissipate the force of any attack while, in the more loosely defended south, the minefields were designed to channel any attack into more defensible terrain.

Murphy also noted that the distance between the 21st Panzer Division in the south and 15th Panzer Division in the north was not 'great enough to prevent Africa Corps fighting as an entity once the direction of the main thrust is ascertained'. The forward battlegroups of the panzer divisions would be available for immediate counterattacks while the British point of main effort was being identified. The panzers would have the time and freedom to concentrate 'uninterrupted save from the air'. The Afrika Korps would then be launched in a 'full-scale counter-attack against the main British effort'. Murphy's conclusions must have been sobering for Montgomery:

(1)   The enemy will fight the battle according to the principles of the system he is developing at ALAMEIN. The factor of surprise will not affect these principles, which do not demand immediate knowledge of the direction of our main attack.

(2)   90 Light Division will abandon its coastal role so soon after the enemy appreciates a major attack is coming, probably after our first air blitz, i.e. D minus 1.

(3)   Meanwhile the armoured divisions will concentrate on their chosen ground.

(4)   Immediate counter-attacks by forward armoured battle-groups must be expected on D night wherever our penetration makes them necessary. These will, however, leave the main weight of the enemy armour uncommitted.

(5)   Enemy air activity will concentrate on reconnaissance on D plus 1, possibly supporting his land forces in the Southern sector with fighter-bombers.

(6)   So soon as the main direction of our attack is appreciated, German Africa Corps will be concentrated for counter-attack. Responsibility for the SOUTH will pass to ARIETE, stiffened by a battle-group of 90 Light Division.

(7)   Stukas will be conserved for use against our main effort.[81]

Murphy had provided Montgomery and his commanders with an excellent intelligence briefing of the Axis defences and probable reaction to any offensive. While Montgomery had placed considerable emphasis upon surprise and deception as a means of wrong-footing his opponent, Murphy's analysis suggested that Rommel's defence plan would be effective even if the British did achieve tactical surprise. The defences which confronted Eighth Army in the northern sector were also far more formidable than Montgomery had realised when he first wrote his battle plan. In these circumstances it was indeed highly unlikely that 10 Corps would be able to pass through six miles of defences in one night. Even if the British armour was able to navigate its way through the Axis 'cockpit' in one night, they would then have to face a counterattack from the full weight of the Afrika Korps within hours. The plan would have to be changed.

FOURTEEN

'Born For This Battle'

On 6 October 1942, Montgomery issued his second memorandum on Lightfoot. It re-emphasised the need for secrecy and surprise but he now admitted that the enemy would know that a British offensive was coming. Instead, tactical surprise had to be gained by hoodwinking 'the enemy as to exactly where the blows will fall. We must not slip up in these arrangements.'[1]

Montgomery also acknowledged that the Axis defences were being strengthened and that both 13 and 30 Corps must patrol vigorously to locate the 'exact positions of defences, wire, booby traps etc'. In discussing the plan of battle, he stated:

> It is a regrettable fact that our troops are not, in all cases, highly trained. We must therefore ensure that we fight the battle in our own way, that we stage manage the battle to suit the state of training of our troops, and that we keep well balanced at all times so that we can ignore enemy thrusts and can proceed relentlessly with our own plans to destroy the enemy.[2]

Montgomery used the state of training within Eighth Army to justify his caution just as he had at Alam Halfa. Certainly, some units like 44th (Home Counties) and 51st (Highland) Divisions did require more training and experience in desert fighting. He stated, 'we should keep well within ourselves, and should not attempt ambitious operations beyond the capabilities of our somewhat untrained troops'. However, Montgomery could not admit, either at the time or subsequently, that his plan asked too much of Eighth Army regardless of its training.

The changes to the plan were relatively minor. 30 Corps was still to seize a bridgehead. 10 Corps was still tasked with passing through the minefields in one night. 13 Corps' objective remained the conduct of a diversionary attack but now it was explicitly stated that 7th Armoured Division was to be kept 'in being' and that 4th Light Armoured Brigade would 'not be launched to DABA until order by Army H.Q.'.

The real difference in the altered plan lay in its intent. While the original plan had envisaged 10 Corps fighting a rapid and decisive battle with the Afrika Korps, the new plan emphasised the 'methodical destruction' of the Axis troops holding the defences. 30 Corps, having seized the bridge-head, would engage in a series of 'crumbling' attacks to destroy the Axis infantry. 9th Australian Division would attack to the north, while 2nd New Zealand and 1st South African were to work southwards from the Miteiriya ridge. Meanwhile, 51st (Highland) Division would have to hold an increasing area of the original bridgehead.

Nigel Hamilton has argued that Montgomery altered his plan because of a 'mutiny' amongst his armoured commanders at the 10 Corps Conference on 7 October,[3] but in fact Montgomery had already altered his plan the day before. It is clear that the alterations were forced by Murphy's intelligence appreciation.[4] The new plan did not change the fact that the armour had to break through the minefields in one night but altered their task once they had fought their way through. Montgomery insisted that the armoured brigades had to move into the mine corridors before it was known whether they were completely clear. He also demanded that if the corridors had not been fully cleared during the night, the armoured brigades were to fight 'their own way out into the open'.[5] He left Lumsden in no doubt that the armour 'must and shall go through'.[6] 10 Corps' func-tion remained the destruction of the Axis armour but now also included preventing the panzers from interfering with the infantry's 'crumbling' operations.

The new plan was avowedly attritional. Eighth Army would now slowly 'eat the guts' out of its enemy while fending off Axis counterattacks until the destruction of the Panzerarmee was assured. These 'crumbling' attacks were a modification of Auchinleck's previous strategy which targeted the Italian infantry divisions. Eighth Army could not now direct attacks solely at Italian formations because of the 'corseting' of the Axis army but would, over time, destroy the Axis infantry so that eventually the Panzerarmee could no longer hold its defences. Montgomery fully acknowledged that fierce fighting would have to take place and emphasised the importance of 'determined leading' in what was now going to be a 'killing match' over a 'prolonged period'.[7] However, Montgomery still did not discuss what would happen when the killing match was over and the Panzerarmee obviously defeated. The lack of any developed plan for exploitation and pursuit was highly significant. Montgomery's failure to plan beyond the killing match was to have important consequences at the conclusion of the forthcoming battle.

Montgomery's eventual decision to fight an attritional battle has to be seen within its proper context. When Lightfoot began, Eighth Army had what appeared to be a significant advantage in numbers over its opponent:

Strength of Opposing Armies on 23 October 1942

	Eighth Army	Panzerarmee Afrika
Troops	220,476	108,000 (53,736 Germans)
Serviceable tanks	1,029 (170 Grants, 252 Shermans, 216 Crusader IIs, 78 Crusader IIIs, 119 Stuarts, 194 Valentines)	548 (249 German – 31 Mk IIs, 85 Mk IIIs, 88 Mk III 'Special's, 8 Mk IVs, 30 Mk IV 'Special's)
Artillery	892	552
Anti-tank guns	1,451 (554 two-pounders, 849 six-pounders)	1,063
Mines	–	445,358
Serviceable aircraft	530	350

However, Eighth Army's numerical superiority was never as great as the bald statistics would suggest. Overall, Eighth Army possessed a rough two to one advantage over the Panzerarmee. It has to be said that Montgomery encouraged his men to think in these broad terms when he wrote:

If every tank crew, and every 6-pdr A.Tk. gun team, will hit and disable one enemy tank, then we must win.

If every disabled enemy tank is destroyed at once by the RE before it can be towed away, our win becomes all the easier.

These, and other facts, must be got across to the troops in no uncertain voice.

They must be worked up to that state which will make them want to go into battle and kill Germans.[8]

This simplistic statement was highly reminiscent of Hilaire Belloc's much ridiculed view of trench fighting[9] in the Great War and about as realistic.

The force ratios that would determine the outcome of the battle were those within the 30 Corps bridgehead. Eighth Army's four assaulting infantry divisions were confronted by two dug-in infantry divisions. The German 164th Light Division had roughly 9,000 men, 180 5cm anti-tank guns, 24 field guns and 18 75mm infantry guns. The Trento Division was composed of just 4,600 men with 48 field guns and 70 anti-tank guns. There were also 16 88mm guns deployed within the various strongpoints. Deployed behind these two divisions were three mixed battlegroups of the 15th Panzer and Littorio Divisions. The two infantry divisions were also supported by 13 heavy, 70 medium and 160 field guns – a total of 243 artillery pieces.[10] Thus, at the point of attack, 30 Corps did not quite have a two to one superiority ratio in artillery and actually had fewer medium guns. This was well below the three to one ratio of forces which was generally considered necessary before a straightforward frontal assault could succeed.

An additional problem lay in the fact that only a few of Eighth Army's assaulting infantry divisions could actually sustain heavy fighting for long periods. The 9th Australian Division and 51st (Highland) Division were up to strength and had sufficient replacements in Egypt to make up significant losses. Leese considered that these divisions were capable of 'sustained offensive action'.[11] Although he described the 2nd New Zealand Division as a 'grand division', there were no reinforcements available and this meant that the division was 'incapable of sustained action'.[12] The same was true of the 1st South African Division which was under strength, had no replacements and was due to be reorganised into an armoured division immediately after the battle. This meant that of the four infantry divisions in 30 Corps, only two were capable of mounting more than one major assault. 4th Indian Division, commanded by Major-General Francis Tuker, had two brigades which were 'only capable of holding the line and could only be relied on provided they were very well mined and wired in'.[13] Only the 5th Indian Brigade, under Brigadier Russell, was considered capable of attacking. The original plan had tasked 4th Indian Division with mounting a series of raids from its position on the Ruweisat ridge but de Guingand advised strongly against this. He felt that 'until the enemy really crumples up it is better to keep a solid defence on RUWEISAT Ridge'.[14]

There were two root causes of the limits of 'sustained action' that each infantry division could undertake. The first was that, although an infantry division might muster as many as 17,000 men, the strength of rifle companies that could actually go forward into an assault was much lower. Many soldiers in each division were absorbed into the supply and administrative echelons as well as the multitude of specialised and supporting arms. This meant that each of the nine infantry battalions in a division held only 400 to 500 riflemen. Heavy casualties in the rifle companies would not shatter the division but they would render it incapable of mounting attacks.

Although the total number of men available within Eighth Army looked impressive there were distinct limits as to how that manpower could be used. Eighth Army contained many weak infantry battalions which could not be amalgamated to provide reinforcements for others. It was politically quite impossible, for example, to break up an Indian battalion to provide replacements for the New Zealand Division or vice versa. The lack of flexibility inherent in the make-up of this Imperial army meant that much of its manpower advantage simply could not be brought to bear effectively.

At the same time, Eighth Army did have a significant superiority in tanks but, crucially, not in artillery or anti-tank guns. The Sherman and Grant tanks certainly outmatched the vast majority of the German tanks and were available in quantity but Eighth Army's superiority in tanks was less profound when the large numbers of 'obsolete' Crusaders, Valentines and Honeys still equipping British units were taken into consideration. Eighth Army's numerical superiority in tanks would also count for very little unless the armoured brigades could reach the open desert and deploy properly.

Although the Panzerarmee was heavily outnumbered in tanks, this was less important in defence than the number of Axis anti-tank guns. Indeed, the Panzerarmee's anti-tank and mine defences were specifically designed to negate Eighth Army's advantage in armour and the large number of Axis anti-tank guns available meant that the British armoured brigades faced a real challenge. Most were dug in with only their barrels showing above the surface of the desert. This meant that British tank regiments were likely to suffer heavy losses before they could even see the guns that inflicted the damage. Unless the infantry of 30 Corps could break through these defences, the armour of 10 Corps would not be able to press home its numerical advantage and might well sustain crippling losses from the Panzerarmee's anti-tank-gun defence.

Thus, even in its altered form, the plan for Operation Lightfoot remained highly ambitious. It was only after the plan had been changed that Montgomery and de Guingand became fully aware of the misgivings held by the armour commanders. On 7 October, Lumsden held a 10 Corps Conference to discuss the details of the plan. Montgomery was absent, delivering a lecture to the Staff College at Haifa, and de Guingand attended in his stead.[15] The armour commanders of 10 Corps went on to have a much fuller and franker discussion than would have occurred had Montgomery been present. Monty's use of de Guingand as his eyes and ears at such conferences was actually a very clever management technique.

There was a lengthy discussion on the movement of the corps from its assembly areas in the rear to the forward defended localities of the British line. 30 Corps' rear areas would already be crammed with all the supporting transport required by the attacking divisions and the gun positions of the artillery. At the same time, 10 Corps had to drive forward, refuel and then be ready for the signal to pass through the minefield gaps. Lumsden emphasised the need for the leading regiments to be close to the British front line otherwise 'his armoured brigades could not get through to the West of the "bridgeheads" by first light'.[16] Brigadier Walsh, the Brigadier General Staff of 30 Corps, believed that, because of the congestion, 10 Corps should not be moved west of the 'Springbok' track before 03.00 hours. This gave very little time for 10 Corps to make the move through the minefields before dawn and the consensus within 10 Corps was:

In order to get the armoured brigades through in time, they must start from the general line of SPRINGBOK Road not later than 0100 hours. The

Divisional commanders were very insistent that they must not be caught with their Brigades in the 'funnels' by daylight.[17]

Lumsden informed his commanders that the order to advance would be decided by the Army Commander and might well be given 'even before 30 Corps had entirely completed their gaps'.[18]

There was simply not enough time to make the plan work. If the infantry divisions began their attack as planned at 22.00 hours, 30 Corps calculated that it would be at least 03.00 hours before the bridgehead had been seized, mopped up and all the supporting transport brought up. However, this left very little time for the armour to move forward, negotiate a three to four-kilometre stretch of cleared minefield in single file and then emerge in open country at the far side. The armour commanders had an understandable horror of being caught with their brigades still in the minefields during daylight. An armoured regiment which was still in single file in a minefield gap could not develop sufficient combat power to fight its way out of such a 'funnel'. To do so in the face of an Axis anti-tank-gun screen would simply result in the destruction of Eighth Army's armoured formations for no result. Yet 30 Corps could not possibly do its job by 01.00 hours, enabling the armour to move up early and have sufficient time to clear the gaps by dawn. The armour commanders felt that 'in order to get the armoured brigades right through into position by first light, everything would have to go very well. With a few delays 10 Corps might not have sufficient time to do so.'[19]

The conference then explored the possibility of moving the armoured brigades up during the following day. This would mean that 30 Corps would have to 'withstand an attack by a Panzer Division against their bridgehead at first light' alone. Not unsurprisingly, Brigadier Walsh refused to give a definite answer. Gatehouse even suggested that it might be preferable to delay 10 Corps' move forward until the second night. Not surprisingly, de Guingand reported to Montgomery that the 'armoured Divisional commanders of 10 Corps are obviously not quite happy as to their being able to get through the gaps by daylight'.[20] The next day, Montgomery had a stormy interview with Lumsden in which he insisted that his intentions must be carried out as planned. It remained to be seen whether the plan would actually work in practice.

The final 10 Corps orders for Lightfoot emphasised the importance of moving through the bridgehead seized by 30 Corps and deploying on the first bound, codenamed Pierson, to receive an attack by the Axis armour. Lumsden stressed the need to make a coordinated plan if the armoured brigades were faced with armour and anti-tank guns before they reached open country and that all screens of anti-tank guns should be 'immediately engaged by fire' to prevent them becoming 'firmly established'.[21] Lumsden had, by this time, decided to send only the armoured brigades through that night and to keep the motor brigades of the armoured divisions back behind the Springbok track to minimise the congestion. De Guingand believed that this was the 'right answer' even though the armoured brigades would then lack the infantry support necessary to fight their way out of the minefields. These were sensible orders but could not deal with the reality of the dilemma that would face the armoured regiments if they were not clear of the minefields by dawn.

The 30 Corps Conference, held on 9 October, was a much happier occasion. De Guingand commented that it was 'an excellent Conference, and well-run'.[22] Leese asked the assembled divisional commanders and their staff whether zero hour could be brought forward. There was a desperate need to find extra time to help 10 Corps with its timings but:

> all considered it wiser not to in view of the fact that their men had to lay up all day in slit trenches, and they would have to be fed and mustered before the advance started, and the 2200 hours zero only just gave them reasonable time for this.[23]

Nonetheless, the aim was to enable 10 Corps to start from the Springbok track at 01.30 hours. Each of the divisional commanders also had different views on the timings for the operation. Wimberley remembered that he had:

> A difficult time over deciding the rate of advance for the attack. On my right Morshead decided, very firmly, that he wanted to order his Australians to advance behind the barrage at a certain speed, which experience had taught him was the best, and to have certain lengths or pauses on the objectives before the barrage moved on. Freyberg, with his New Zealanders, had equally firm views on the rate of advance, and pauses that suited his troops; but unfortunately for me, as the Division sandwiched between them, the views of these two very experienced Commanders did not agree.[24]

While Freyberg wanted the total timing to amount to 215 minutes to keep the 'enemy on the hop' and give a greater density of artillery support during the advance, Morshead wanted 255 minutes and Wimberley had timed the operation at 292 minutes. 51st (Highland) Division could not move its two brigades at different speeds so a further conference on timings had to be held before the matter was settled to 'everyone's satisfaction'.[25]

Each divisional commander then outlined his tasks. Morshead would protect and reorganise on the northern flank and await orders before attacking north. 51st (Highland) Division would prepare to take over the Miteiriya ridge from the New Zealanders while they pushed south in exploitation. However, Freyberg emphasised that 'any major exploitation S.W. from Miteiriya Ridge must depend on whether 8 Armd Bde got through or not'.[26]

Leese followed up the conference with a letter to his divisional commanders the next day. He informed them that 'we must have zero hour a bit earlier' and hoped to bring it forward to 21.30 hours unless it was considered 'definitely not feasible'.[27] While Wimberley and Pienaar do not seem to have had any objection, Morshead was adamant that 'there must be some relaxation before the fight'. He explained that after a day of 'solitary confinement in a tight-fitting grave-like pit awaiting the hard and bloody battle' the men had to eat their dinner, listen to final instructions, make final preparations and then march up to the start line.[28] Leese deferred to Morshead's experience of handling men in battle.

On 12 October, Leese wrote to Wimberley concerning the attack frontage of the Highland Division. Morshead had mentioned to Leese that he did not think it was possible for 'a Bn. to maintain its momentum and have sufficient weight to attack available if it has to go to the extreme depth allotted by you to two of your battalions'.[29] The problem was that the frontage of 51st (Highland) Division increased from 2,500 yards at the start line to 5,000 yards at the final objective. Wimberley had solved this difficult problem by tasking the 7th Argyll and Sutherland Highlanders and the 7th Black Watch with going through from the start line all the way to the final objective. Leese, after taking advice from both Morshead and Freyberg, suggested that Wimberley should increase his battalion frontage from 600 to 800 yards to enable his division to cover the wide frontage allotted to him. Leese also passed on useful hints from the New Zealanders and Australians drawn from their wide battle experience. He concluded by reminding Wimberley that Montgomery was willing 'to accept casualties in tanks in order to ensure during the night we gained the bridge-head'. In fact, given the extensive front that his division had to cover, Wimberley felt forced to stick with his original plan and push his central battalions all the way to the final objective.

On 14 October, with the time for planning and preparation running out, Leese addressed a final letter to his divisional commanders. He emphasised the need to 'seize the bridge-head in time to pass the armour of 10 Corps through by first light'[30] and reminded his commanders that they could use the Valentine tanks of 23rd Armoured Brigade, the Scorpion mine-clearing tanks and 'any other means at your disposal in any way during the battle which you consider best to achieve this object'.[31] Leese noted that all the tanks allotted to each division should practise close cooperation with infantry through small exercises of a company of infantry and a squadron of tanks.

The striking feature of all the debates and discussions within 30 Corps is how well Oliver Leese coordinated the planning of three very different divisions with three contrasting commanding officers. Leese used the experience and expertise of the Australians and New Zealanders to help the Highlanders while at the same time ironing out as many problems as possible.

It is remarkable that neither of Montgomery's plans sketched out the contribution of the artillery or engineers in any detail. Instead, he delegated complete responsibility for the planning and preparation of these two vital areas to Brigadier Sidney Kirkman, the Brigadier Royal Artillery of Eighth Army, and Frederick Kisch, the Chief Engineer of Eighth Army. Montgomery trusted both men and their technical expertise to deliver what was needed.

Kisch had an awesome responsibility in ensuring that his sappers would gap the formidable Axis minefields in one night. Eighth Army's previous experience of mine-clearing operations, particularly in July, was not encouraging and the fact that the engineers of Eighth Army largely overcame the problem of the minefields was a major achievement.

In each division, all the engineers were under the control of the Commander Royal Engineers who then allotted resources to brigades for the operation. The engineers of 10 Corps had to make two main 'corridors' through the Axis minefields. The 1st Armoured Division corridor lay on the boundary between the 51st (Highland) and the 9th Australian Divisions, while the gaps for 10th Armoured Division would be made within 2nd New Zealand Division's area. Each armoured division needed three lanes at least 40 yards wide cut through the minefields. The engineers of each division's minefield task force expected that they would have to clear gaps in as many as four minefields, each 400 yards deep, to a total depth of 6,000 yards.[32] At the same time, the sappers attached to the assaulting infantry divisions needed to cut at least three 16-yard wide lanes through the minefields so that their supporting arms and equipment could be brought up to the front line. At least 18 lanes would have to be cut during that first night by the sappers of 30 Corps.

A task of such unprecedented difficulty and complexity required thorough preparation because, as the Royal Australian Engineers' report emphasised, 'The Preliminary Work was, and always will be as far as Engineers are concerned, the most important part of the operation.'[33] The engineers' preparations, which began in early August, were crucial to the success of the coming battle.

Kisch held a conference in early August with all the corps and divisional Commander Royal Engineers on the problem of mine clearance. The whole issue was discussed and he asked every commander to submit a written report on their views of current methods and possible improvements. Lieutenant-Colonel F. M. H. Hanson, of the 2nd New Zealand Division, took a jaundiced view of this request. He replied, 'Reports on mine-clearing along the lines requested have at various times been prepared by 2 NZ Div for EIGHTH ARMY, NINTH ARMY, 13 Corps, 30 Corps, 10 Corps and others'.[34]

To the experienced engineers of the New Zealand Division much of this effort must have seemed like the reinvention of the wheel. So many attempts to regularise mine-lifting had been made but no central authority had collated the reports and made concrete progress. Nonetheless, Hanson provided useful information concerning the minefield clearance drill which operated in his division. He suggested that each party should consist of one non-commissioned officer, eight men and one mine detector. During daylight it was estimated that this party could clear a four-yard gap through a 400-yard minefield in 30 minutes. Therefore to clear a 50-yard gap through a 400-yard minefield at night in the same time would require 12 mine parties.[35]

This time, the valuable experience contained in such replies from all the units of Eighth Army did not go to waste. Kisch sent for Major Peter Moore, a highly experienced sapper officer who had just left hospital,[36] handed him all the reports and said, 'I am sure that there should be a drill for this . . . When you have worked out a drill and I have approved it, you will form the Eighth Army School of Mine Clearance.'[37] Moore later explained:

> The lack of uniform method had led to Divisional Engineers being asked to perform impossible tasks or being asked to make gaps which were quite inadequate for the tactical operations in view. CsRE also had no reliable data on which to give advice to their divisional commanders.[38]

The school was duly established at Burg el Arab[39] and Moore, assisted by the chief instructor, Major A. R. Currie, worked hard on experiments to discover the best way to gap minefields. The engineers of each division brought experience from different operations but all had encountered similar problems. The New Zealand sappers had the bitter experiences of Bacon and Splendour to reflect upon, the South African sappers had considered the problems highlighted by Manhood, while the Australians' first experience of the difficulties in mine-gapping came as late as Bulimba.[40] The main lessons from all the experiments and exercises conducted by the engineers were that:

> The Detector, except on very rocky ground or in newly laid fields, was the quickest means of clearing mines, and the only reliable one.
> The choice of ground for any proposed gap was extremely important.
> Tapes were required to keep clearance parties going straight.
> Operation of the detector itself was an important skill which must be taught as a drill.[41]

Through the medium of the school, all these points and the lessons from accumulated experience were collated and used by Moore to produce the final standard drill for mine-lifting and the marking of minefield gaps. The engineers of each division were able to modify the standard drill but the uniform method provided a benchmark for all future operations.[42]

The Eighth Army drill was designed to clear a 40-yard gap in a mine-field 400 yards deep with the sappers using mine detectors to assist them. The Australian sappers noted drily that it was only after Bulimba that the mine detector 'emerged from the status of a rare museum piece and appeared in quantities approaching reasonable proportions'.[43] In fact, the relative shortage of detectors remained a problem throughout the preparatory period and even during the battle.

The British Mark IV, the 'Polish' and the 'Goldak' were the three main types of detectors available to the sappers, although all three used the same basic technology. These devices were all based on an early form of a metal detector with a metal search loop which was mounted on the end of a pole. This was connected to a man-pack battery and a set of earphones. The oper-ator would 'sweep' the ground with the detector while listening to a constant hum in the earphones and, when the search loop entered the magnetic field of a metal object, the hum would change in tone or stop, depending on the model of the detector.[44] Of course, the detector could not differentiate between a metal mine and other debris such as shell fragments or food tins. Nonetheless, the detector provided a far superior and faster method of searching for mines than the crude method of prodding with the bayonet. However, it was noted:

> Should detectors not be available, or the fire be too heavy for the operators to work effectively standing upright, approximately the same drill . . . is used, substituting prodding with bayonets for searching with detectors, but the results are far less sure.[45]

The drill was found to be efficient and successful by all the divisions of Eighth Army, although most adapted the drill so that it worked efficiently with fewer sappers. The standardisation of mine-lifting and gapping meant that the timings for this complex operation were relatively consistent throughout the army.

The drill was designed to begin once a minefield was located. The activ-ities of the engineers enacting their drill under fire was likened to a 'Dante-esque edition of the Lord Mayor's show'.[46] A 'confirming recce party', composed of one officer, a non-commissioned officer and three sappers, went ahead of the tape-laying and detector parties to seek the edge of any suspected minefield. As soon as a minefield had been encountered and scouted, the tape-laying party comprising one non-commissioned officer and four pairs of men went forward to lay white tape marking the boundaries of an initial eight-yard gap which could then be widened into a 40-yard gap. The tapes were checked and pegged at 30-yard intervals through the field. Finally, two men returned to the forward edge of the field to mark the boundary. The tape-laying party was followed by six detector parties each composed of three detector operators, a mine marker who relieved the detector every 15 minutes, a non-commissioned officer in charge of the party, two sappers to disarm and lift the mines and four sappers to mark the cleared lanes. Three detector operators worked in echelon, with each sweeping across an area of nine feet so that the overlap of their work ensured that the eight-yard gap would be completely searched. The detectors were followed by the mine marker who placed a metal cone on each mine that was found.[47]

Sweeping for mines placed enormous strain on the sappers. The sapper using the mine detector had to walk upright while continually sweeping the ground in front of him and constantly looking for the telltale signs of mines. With a high-pitched tone whining in his ears from the earphones the sapper was deaf to the sounds of battle around him and had to rely on the other members of the team to warn him of any immediate danger. It was as well that the drill had been designed to be simple and that the sappers practised its evolutions until they became instinctive. Every sapper was trained in all the tasks so that casualties would not halt the work.[48]

The first detector party began its work as soon as the tape-laying party was 30 yards through the minefield. Meanwhile, once the first group had covered 270 yards, the second party went forward and began to clear in the same lane. With the initial eight-yard gap clear, the other four detector parties would then start searching, each clearing a further eight-yard lane to widen the gap to 40 yards.

The disarming and lifting party followed 50 yards behind the detector parties and had the task of lifting the mines and placing them just outside the white tapes.[49] This job was made extremely dangerous by the German use of anti-lifting devices. Mines were often encountered with a length of wire fastened to the bottom running to a pull switch and a block of explosives. Sometimes two mines were linked together by wire and switches. Tripwires might set off concealed aerial bombs. The Germans also reacted to the advent of detectors by using a small number of wooden mines. These were simple wooden boxes filled with slabs of captured British gun cotton and a detonator.[50] All these German innovations were designed to make the job of clearing the gap as difficult and costly as possible.

Once the gap had been cleared, the gap-marking party placed signs on each edge of the cleared lane. These were wooden signposts painted half white and half red to indicate the gap. During night operations, a green electric light was clipped to the safe side and an amber light to the danger side of the sign.[51] At the entrance to the gap, a control post, manned by sappers and military police, was established to control the movement of traffic. An important feature of the control posts was that, for the first time, engineers were allotted their own wireless sets and frequencies to ensure rapid communications. It was estimated that it took two hours using the drill to clear a 16-yard gap through a 400-yard minefield, but of course the timing varied according to the amount of fire which the sappers had to endure while carrying out their dangerous job.[52]

The School of Minefield Clearance also experimented with a number of devices to assist the sappers in their difficult task. The most famous of these devices was the Scorpion Mk I Flail Tank which was designed to clear a path through a minefield. The Scorpion was a Matilda Infantry Tank with two steel arms fitted to its front. The arms held a circular steel drum three feet above the ground. Wire ropes with short lengths of heavy steel chain at the end were fixed to the drum which was spun by a Ford V8 engine mounted in a small armour-plated compartment on the side of the tank. When a minefield was detected, the Scorpion would turn on its rotor and move forwards at little more than one mile an hour. The spinning chains thrashed the ground in front of the tank to explode any mines in its path. Each Scorpion could clear a nine-foot gap and three moving in echelon could clear an eight-yard gap. Throughout all of the tests, the Scorpions never missed a mine but the V8 engine was poorly ventilated and tended to overheat. Another problem was that a Scorpion 'made an almost incredible amount of dust when operating, and the driver had to be sealed into his compartment while the sapper driving the flail engine had to wear a respirator'.[53] Not surprisingly, it was fully recognised that the Scorpion was still an experimental vehicle and could not be relied upon for the main mine-clearing effort.[54] There were only a few Scorpions available so each assaulting division held them in reserve for emergencies.

One of the great difficulties encountered with minefields was actually finding the edge of them. German engineers often scattered unmarked mines in front of the main field to complicate the task. Wheelbarrow or pram detectors, consisting of a tubular frame mounted on bicycle wheels, were designed to deal with this problem. These held an eight-foot wide search loop which could be pushed along by an operator looking for the edge of a minefield.[55] A series of pilot vehicles were also developed to find the edge of a minefield or 'prove' a gap by driving along it. Lorries, their floors protected with sandbags, were used for this purpose. Punctured drums of diesel dripped onto the sand thus marking the width of the gap. These pilot vehicles became known as 'snails'.[56] Another type of pilot vehicle was a lorry with concrete-filled spiked rollers attached. The three-inch-long spikes on the rollers would set off any mines in the path of the vehicle giving a noisy indication of the front of the minefield. While none of these experimental vehicles were found to be completely satisfactory they demonstrated the ingenuity which Eighth Army's engineers brought to the enormous task that confronted them.

In its short existence, the Eighth Army School of Minefield Clearance enabled Eighth Army's engineers to collate and combine their experience into practical developments. The school had eight training teams which taught seven courses, each lasting eight days, from 26 August until 20 October.[57]

In the course of just two months, the engineers of Eighth Army, using their previous experience and taking advantage of the new equipment that was becoming available, developed a rapid and flexible drill that would enable any minefield to be gapped efficiently and in a standardised way. This drill formed the bedrock for all future mine-clearance operations. At the same time, the experimental Scorpions began a path of development that led to the highly effective Sherman 'crab' mine clearance tank. All these developments were crucial to the later success of the Allied armies in Europe.

Similarly profound developments were affecting Eighth Army's use of artillery. Its concentrated power had been one of the few encouraging developments during the July fighting and the static nature of the fighting at Alamein, combined with the breathing space from early August onwards, gave the Royal Artillery the time and space it needed to develop very sophisticated and effective tactics.

Even before Sidney Kirkman arrived in September 1942, important changes had been instituted. However, he was a firm believer in the centralisation of artillery. Kirkman had been instrumental in restoring the artillery chain of command and introducing proper training for fireplans back in England. With Montgomery's full backing, Kirkman restored the command authority of each divisional Commander Royal Artillery.[58] However, these changes only applied to the British division in Eighth Army as none of the Dominion divisions had ever demoted their artillery commanders.

Not surprisingly, the fireplan for 30 Corps received by far the greatest attention. The artillery available to 30 Corps for Lightfoot consisted of the guns from each of the four assaulting divisions, the 48 guns of 4th Indian Division, three medium regiments and three field regiments on loan from 10 Corps which made an impressive total of 408 field guns and 48 medium guns.[59] This meant that the artillery was 'very thick on the ground'[60] particularly in the salient between Tel el Makh Khad and the sea.

Although Montgomery's orders placed Brigadier Mead Dennis, the commander of 30 Corps artillery, in overall control of these guns, it was decided to establish a separate headquarters to coordinate the activities of the three medium regiments. The field regiments loaned by 10 Corps were broken up and their regimental and battery headquarters were not used, in an effort to avoid further congestion.

As much of the artillery as possible had to be sited within 1,000 yards of the front line to ensure that it could reach out beyond the final objective which, at its deepest point, would be 8,000 yards from Eighth Army's front. Reconnaissance of the likely sites had to be completed rapidly so that the ammunition dumping programme could be complete by 14 October. Dennis chose the gun areas and then conferred with each divisional artillery commander to make sure 'he could fit his guns into the area'.[61]

All the ammunition for the opening bombardment had to be pre-positioned and this became a Herculean task for the gunners. Six hundred rounds per field gun and 500 rounds per medium gun were dumped at each battery position.[62] Every night for six nights groups of gunners in every divisional area had to work ferociously on this job in silence and with no smoking permitted. Every morning:

> when the lorries departed in the half-light with loads of muffled and dishev-
> elled gunners, a new batch of pits had been levelled off and disguised with
> stones and planted bushes, to simulate the surrounding desert.[63]

The gunners who dug the pits and dumped the ammunition were told that it was an 'ammunition dumping exercise' but, not surprisingly, the men knew that something 'big' must be happening. Yet more ammunition was dumped in the wagon lines five miles behind the front which meant that every gun in 30 Corps had 1,000 rounds of ammunition before any more needed to be brought forward.

The fireplan of 30 Corps has been described as a 'classic'[64] but it also represented a considerable advance from the methods used during the Great War. Much of the plan had to be designed around the infantry's rate of advance which was eventually fixed at 100 yards every three minutes. This, at the very least, did hark back to the Great War. It was decided that 'no useful purpose could be achieved by a barrage which would be thin every-where and thick nowhere' while also wasting ammunition.[65] Ultimately, Freyberg and Wimberley did use some of their field regiments to fire a very thin barrage to guide the infantry forward but this was not a main feature of the fireplan. Far greater emphasis was placed upon counter-battery fire to neutralise the Axis guns and heavy concentrations on the Axis defended localities.

The plan was divided into six distinct phases. Twenty minutes before zero hour the whole artillery of 30 Corps was tasked with firing a complex counter-battery programme. Each shoot against a hostile battery was to last just three minutes to ensure that every battery was shelled. Five minutes before zero the guns were to stop firing their counter-battery tasks and prepare for the next phase. Meanwhile, the RAF were to take over responsibility for hammering the Axis guns. At zero hour, the entire artillery was tasked with firing concentrations on the Axis Forward Defended Localities. These had all been carefully plotted and mapped. From Z + 7 until Z + 115, all the field artillery and one medium regiment were tasked with firing at targets just in front of the advancing infantry while the two other medium regi-ments continued on counter-battery tasks. At Z + 115, while the infantry reorganised after capturing their first objectives, three field regiments and all three medium regiments would fire counter-battery while the rest of the artillery provided a covering barrage in front of the first objective. From Z + 175 to Z + 185 all the artillery would fire concentrations on the main enemy positions. After Z + 185 all the artillery would return to providing covering fire in front of the forward infantry positions.[66]

Given the Axis superiority in heavy and medium guns which lay beyond the reach of most of the 25-pounder batteries, the counter-battery programme loomed large in the artillery preparations. In fact, work on the counter-battery organisation had been ongoing since early July. The 30 Corps counter-battery party office began in a very small way with just one officer and two clerks who were attached to the 7th Medium Regiment in the Alamein box. As the work increased and the sources of information grew more sophisticated, the party eventually grew and the small team had a great impact on the effectiveness of Eighth Army's artillery.[67]

The counter-battery office used a range of techniques to fix the locations of the Axis batteries. Observers from each battery in Eighth Army helped in counter-battery work by giving information on every shelling that occurred near them. However, the work of artillery intelligence officers was greatly complicated by the mixture of British, French, German, Italian and Russian guns used by the Axis artillery. It was often very difficult to identify the various Axis artillery formations.[68]

The techniques of flash spotting and sound ranging, which had both been developed during the Great War, were also used to pinpoint the location of enemy batteries. Flash spotting depended on good observation of the enemy gun lines. Observers positioned across the length of the front would watch for any gun flash and, when spotted, estimate the range and bearing to the gun. These estimates could then be collated and, particularly if the enemy battery did not move, reasonably accurate locations could be built up over time.[69]

Eighth Army had lost its survey battery in Tobruk and it was not until the middle of July that No. 1 Composite Survey Battery was deployed on the 30 Corps front. Ground visibility during the day was poor because of the effects of haze and mirage so a series of survey towers, between 30 and 80 feet high, were constructed behind the lines from the Ruweisat ridge to the coast. Bizarrely enough, the Axis batteries did not seem to understand the purpose of the platforms and only a few towers were ever shelled, probably because of the need to conserve limited ammunition stocks. From these platforms, observation parties from the survey battery surveyed the entire front and produced highly accurate maps of the enemy defences. From late July onwards, the observation posts were able to give very accurate and rapid locations at night and during the day when visibility permitted. The Axis batteries soon stopped firing at night altogether, as the heavy counterbombardment which any night firing provoked made such fire too dangerous.[70]

The sound-ranging troop of the survey battery did not reach the front until early September. Sound ranging worked by picking up the noise of an enemy gun or battery firing through a series of microphones positioned across the front. Measuring the split-second differences at which each microphone picked up the sound of each firing enabled very accurate ranging of individual enemy batteries.[71]

Just as in the Great War, aerial reconnaissance photographs provided the best form of intelligence for counter-battery work:

> It is doubtful if the enemy fully realises the extent and frequency with which he is photographed, or the uses to which the photos are put. Many of his methods of 'foxing' CB were rendered abortive by our air photos.[72]

During July, aerial reconnaissance photographs were only available intermittently and after long delays. This caused real problems for the counter-battery office and for operational planning. Given the importance of the aerial photographs provided by the Desert Air Force's tactical reconnaissance aircraft, the facilities were rapidly improved. By the end of July it had been arranged that the whole Army front would be covered every four days. This engaged the tactical reconnaissance squadrons in a never-ending stream of work but the results were impressive. The photographs, taken at a height of 25,000 feet (which gave a scale of 1/15,000), provided good detail and could often give useful information on the damage caused by counter-battery fire. These detailed pictures meant that a large-scale map was slowly plotted of the entire length and depth of the Axis defences which included coordinates of strongpoints, minefields, wire, infantry posts and sometimes even individual guns.[73]

By the beginning of October, most of the battle and alternate positions of Axis batteries had been located to within 100 yards. It was realised that heavy counterbombardments would now be counterproductive as they might force the Axis batteries to move to new locations. A silent policy was introduced and Eighth Army's guns turned to minor harassing tasks instead. The success of the counter-battery policy of Eighth Army meant that 'all the enemy artillery, as far as is known, was teed up in its battle positions ready to be hit' when the offensive began.[74]

The sophistication of Eighth Army's counter-battery techniques were never matched by the Panzerarmee. It was noted that, 'The enemy proved himself very adept in adopting evasive measures against our CB fire but, as usual, singularly inept at carrying out CB work himself.'[75] This was due partly to the fact that the Afrika Korps had relied largely on the Luftwaffe to deal with hostile batteries in the past. Stuka dive-bombing of British batteries and aerial reconnaissance for Axis artillery had been very successful. However, by July 1942, the Luftwaffe in the desert was no longer the force that it had once been. The combination of fighters and effective anti-aircraft fire had made Stuka attacks very dangerous and the low-level reconnaissance necessary for artillery spotting impossible. Yet when Luftwaffe support disappeared, the German and Italian gunners did not invest in the other counter-battery methods which, more than ever, were essential in dealing with Eighth Army's artillery. Over the four months of fighting in the Alamein line, Eighth Army only recorded ten counter-battery shoots on its guns and the German flash-spotting and sound-ranging teams were entirely inadequate. Maps captured in October showed that the German artillery had only a vague idea of the location of Eighth Army batteries and often identified old or dummy positions. Counter-battery work was never given the priority within the Panzerarmee Afrika that it required. Once the Axis forces lost their habitual advantages, they seemed unable to adopt alternative methods to restore its previous dominance.

In contrast, Eighth Army's artillery had painful experience of the former German air superiority and hitherto had been unable to rely on airpower to deal with enemy batteries. This was why they went to such lengths to ensure their own counter-battery capability at the very time that the Desert Air Force was finally able to assist them. The work of the counter-battery office progressed steadily over the months at Alamein and its contribution to the October offensive was immense. It played a major part in developing an inter-locking system of artillery capabilities that the Panzerarmee Afrika was unable to match.

The detailed picture of the Axis positions developed for the counter-battery office also provided important intelligence for the entire army's preparations. This detailed mapping enabled an elaborate system of defensive fire to be developed. Every Axis-defended locality was given a code name based on the counties of Ireland:

> These names were passed on to each Division. Thus if one Division was being heavily attacked, it merely had to ask for help on 'Wexford' on the wireless and all guns that could bear engaged 'Wexford' provided they were not busy on a timed programme of their own.[76]

This system enabled the artillery to give an unprecedented level of support to the forward troops.

Such support depended on reliable communications. A complete system of telephone cables linked each battery to its parent formation to provide reliable communications. A system of static land lines would have been a hopeless anachronism in the earlier desert campaigns but at El Alamein this 'catered for all artillery communications and worked smoothly'.[77] More generous allocations of wireless sets were also made to ensure reliable radio links and each battery received an extra three No. 19 sets for communication with armoured formations. Wireless communications were organised from each corps commander to all of the divisional artillery under his command, along with a lateral link to the two other corps. Each corps artillery commander also had a forward link to the field regiments which were tasked with counter-battery fire. This comprehensive system ensured that if wireless communication broke down for whatever reason, there was the alternative system of telephones and cable. Such a complicated system required a great deal of practice to bring about the required level of expertise and large-scale artillery exercises were held in August 1942 in each corps to practise the use of the wireless net.[78]

With such a comprehensive communications system, the artillery of Eighth Army could then experiment with larger concentrations of fire. These had been practised in Britain but had been literally impossible to employ in previous desert operations. Brigadier Weir, as we have seen, was instrumental in developing proper fire drills within 2nd New Zealand Division and these techniques were disseminated throughout Eighth Army.

Weir had recognised the need to develop standard techniques for delivering large volumes of fire on impromptu targets in a matter of minutes. While in Syria, the New Zealand training exercises had demonstrated the practicality of firing all 72 guns of the division on a single area target. He devised a rectangle 1,200 yards long and 600 yards deep whereby the coordinates of the centre point and the grid bearing of the perpendicular axis could be used to lay in every gun. The entire divisional artillery, firing seven rounds per gun, could put 504 evenly spaced rounds into the rectangle in three minutes. Weir discussed the technique with Brigadier Standford, 13 Corps artillery commander, and suggested that he might use it as a standard technique within the corps. It was important to find a convenient code name and Weir suggested 'STANK' as closest to Standford's name. Eventually, after 'STINK' had been rejected, 'STONK', 'which appeared to offend nobody',[79] was accepted as the code name. The 'STONK' was adopted as a fire drill by 2nd New Zealand Division in early 1942 and used to great effect during the July fighting and at Alam Halfa. During September 1942, once the New Zealand Division had moved to 10 Corps, Oliver Leese showed interest in the technique and ordered that it be adopted as a compulsory method for defensive fire throughout 30 Corps.

The method was also modified by Brigadier Dennis, the 30 Corps artillery commander, to produce a standard technique for the concentrated fire of the medium artillery regiments. Major John Gibbon, one of the chief staff officers who planned the 30 Corps artillery programme, recalled:

A standard concentration of Medium artillery was laid down and known as a 'STONK'. Details were circulated to formations but authority to call for this concentration was not delegated below Brigades . . . The standard concentration used was rectangular and covered 1,200^x x 400^x. It was primarily designed to stop an attack by enemy armour.[80]

The 'STONK' enabled the medium regiments to provide extremely heavy concentrations of fire very rapidly and Weir commented that 'the effect of this in Desert country against troops in the open was fairly devastating'. The 'STONK' soon became a standard technique throughout the Royal Artillery.

Weir was also instrumental in reintroducing the creeping barrage as a form of infantry support. 2nd New Zealand Division carried out its major training exercise near the Wadi Natrun on 26–27 September in which the New Zealand infantry and artillery trained together with the newly joined 9th Armoured Brigade. Before the exercise, Freyberg remarked to Weir that the main difficulties for the infantry were the depth of the minefields and the problems of controlling the infantry battalions in the dark. Weir suggested the use of a creeping barrage to guide the infantry as they advanced. The curtain of shells, although thin by Great War standards, also helped to set the pace of advance with 100 yard 'lifts' every two minutes. Major John White, Freyberg's personal assistant, suggested firing tracer shells from 40mm Bofors anti-aircraft guns to mark the brigade boundaries. Oliver Leese saw the rehearsal and subsequently endorsed the ideas to the other assault divisions. It is no surprise that he considered Weir to be the best gunner in Eighth Army.[81] His dissemination of Weir's ideas throughout 30 Corps was crucial to the evolution of Eighth Army's artillery techniques. Two of the four assault divisions eventually adopted a thin creeping barrage to support and guide the infantry while also firing heavy concentrations on known enemy localities.

One difficulty which had afflicted the Royal Artillery throughout the desert campaigns was the problem of synchronising time throughout an artillery regiment. Since the Great War, gunner officers had been responsible for fixing the time before an operation and the synchronisation of time was vital if artillery fire was to be effective. However, poor wireless communications and the need for wireless silence, combined with the lack of telephone lines, had made the synchronisation of time between batteries and regiments very difficult. However, during August 1942, it was realised that batteries could tune in to the BBC time signals and thus achieve synchronisation easily without compromising security.[82] This simple solution ensured that every battery of guns in the army worked to the same time.

Important changes also took place in the organisation of the anti-tank guns. The first six-pounder anti-tank guns had reached Eighth Army just before the battle of Gazala but there had been little time for training in the use of this new weapon. The value of the gun had been proved during the July fighting but it had been noted as early as June 1942 that:

it is an awkward gun to fire owing to the difficult posture which has to be adopted by the No. 1 . . . These difficulties make it necessary to carry out considerable training and to allot a generous number of rounds for practice before a crew can be considered proficient.[83]

Until August 1942, Eighth Army could not implement the training that was necessary. In the breathing space before the British offensive, every British anti-tank gunner was able finally to receive the training necessary to ensure proficiency in the new gun.

At the same time, the intense fighting and subsequent retreat into Egypt had completely disrupted the proposed changes in organisation whereby the anti-tank regiments were to be equipped with the six-pounder gun and the infantry battalions would receive the now surplus two-pounder guns. By late August, Eighth Army had a full complement of six-pounder guns and these changes could finally be implemented. For the first time, each infantry battalion now had eight two-pounder guns to provide its own organic protection against the panzers.

The development of artillery tactics during the Alamein campaign can be seen as a microcosm of the learning process which went on throughout Eighth Army. There was an awareness of repeated mistakes. Numerous training pamphlets had advocated the use of sound tactics, but the nature of desert fighting and the development of bad habits amongst many commanders and their troops had hampered their adoption. The static positions at El Alamein provided the time and conditions the artillery needed to reorganise itself and actually adopt tactics that were known to work. Before the October battle, it had become a sophisticated, responsive and flexible weapon of enormous power.

A vast amount of work also took place behind the lines. The first convoys of new supplies, ammunition and equipment reached Suez only in mid-August but soon turned into a veritable flood. By the end of July, most of the administrative chaos caused by the retreat into Egypt had been cleared away and proper planning to support an offensive could begin. The geographical balance now favoured Eighth Army, which was just 60 miles from its main base area at El Amiriya, with depots there fed by excellent road and rail connections to the main port at Suez. Panzerarmee Afrika, on the other hand, had pushed far beyond its safe supply limit.

The importance of local resources and manufacturing capacity to the British forces in the Middle East has often been overlooked. In 1939, General Wavell had grasped the importance of developing Egypt into an enormous supply depot and manufacturing base for British operations. Success in achieving this by 1942 was truly astonishing. By that time, much of the food consumed by Eighth Army was produced in the Middle East, potatoes were grown in Egypt and Syria, cattle imported from the Sudan, jams and marmalades bottled in

Palestine, to name only a few of the items. Such local production schemes saved over a million tons of shipping over the course of 1942.[84]

While the Royal Army Service Corps developed large local produce schemes for food, the Royal Army Ordnance Corps found means of manufacturing equipment and tools in Egypt. By June 1942, there were 25,380 military personnel employed on ordnance duties in the Middle East Command and there were more than 30,000 Egyptians in workshops and factories.[85] In July 1942, a Royal Army Ordnance Corps officer wrote:

> During the last 34 months, the Corps . . . has been coping, day after day, with the imminent and enormous task of supplying a force which has grown in less than two years from 15,000 to over 800,000 men, scattered now from Malta to the borders of Baluchistan. It has had to improvise, by local purchase, and manufacture in its own workshops, many millions of things which otherwise would have had to come 3000 miles by sea from India, or 15,000 miles from the United Kingdom round the Cape. It has had not only to supply the needs of, but to maintain at every turn, the fighting soldier in the field. What that simple statement implies is something which no previous Corps of Ordnance in the world has ever had to do.[86]

Base depots and workshops constructed in Egypt coped with these demands and churned out an enormous quantity and variety of equipment, tools and supplies. The amount of work accomplished was enormous. The workshops at Abbasia were the largest production centre in Egypt, employing 12,000 men by July 1942 and producing:

> an immense variety of work . . . in June 1942 the workshops had over 900 separate jobs on hand, from notice boards to A. A. mountings, from meat-safes to carriers for sterilised blood-bottles, from 12,000 crates for Molotov cocktails to 25,000 trestle tops for tables. Shell and ammunition gauges and extractors of all kinds, fire ladders, open sights for 25 pounders, chairs, covers for machine guns, magnetic detectors of A/T mines, hospital trolleys, jigs, pistons, saddlery, yakdans [the sheepskin jacket beloved by Eighth Army officers], swivelchairs for tanks, tool chests, steel tent pins, special armourers instruments etc. were only a few of these varied and special requirements.
>
> Perhaps the greatest compliment paid to this shop was by an Ordnance Mechanical Engineer newly out from England who visited it and remarked that 'if the War Office were to see this, they simply wouldn't believe their own eyes'.[87]

The true achievement of the Royal Army Service Corps and Royal Army Ordnance Corps in planning, constructing and managing such a vast enterprise has rarely been acknowledged, but without such endeavours the Eighth

Army could not have operated in the desert. Beyond that, the factories, workshops and supply dumps that had been slowly developed in Egypt made it possible for Middle East Command to prepare, process and deliver the vast quantities of men, materiel and equipment that now began to arrive at Suez.

In addition to the complete formations that joined Eighth Army, more than 41,000 reinforcements flowed through two personnel reinforcement camps from August until 23 October. All these men had to receive training and equipment before being sent on to their units.

One of the critical shortages consistently hampering operations was that of motor transport.[88] Service in the desert wore out trucks and lorries faster than they could be repaired or replaced and after the losses of the retreat into Egypt, Eighth Army was 25 per cent under strength in transport.[89] However, the efforts to establish assembly plants in Egypt were almost complete by July 1942. Vehicles had initially been transported to Egypt fully assembled, which wasted a great deal of shipping space. In June 1941 the first assembly plant was erected at Ataka, west of Suez. Parts could be shipped to Egypt far more efficiently and by August 1942 there were four such assembly plants in operation able to turn out a total of 180 vehicles a day.[90] By October, vehicles for the equivalent of 36 three-ton general transport companies, nine water tank companies, six tank transporter companies and one bulk petrol transport company had all been assembled and delivered to Eighth Army. General Headquarters also held a reserve of seven general transport companies. This comparative abundance of transport meant that the Royal Army Service Corps was able to meet the voracious demands of Eighth Army and prepare for an eventual advance.[91]

Perhaps more important than the mass of ordinary vehicles and lorries which filled the roads behind Eighth Army were the recovery vehicles, tractors and tank transporters, which were vital for recovering damaged tanks. Eighth Army had suffered from a crippling lack of such vehicles throughout its existence, and even by scouring the entire Middle East Command only 29 tank transporters, 51 six-wheeled breakdown tractors and 79 three-ton breakdown vehicles reached Eighth Army for the offensive. Nonetheless, such numbers, even though they did not meet the full demands of the recovery units, were an undreamt of luxury for troops who had become used to chronic shortage.[92]

This effort was coordinated with a major administrative change in the way that Eighth Army handled vehicle maintenance, recovery and repair. The crisis in tank repair in early July that had threatened to starve the army of tanks finally forced recognition that this important task had not been given the status or resources it needed. There was a widespread belief, often unfounded, that German recovery, repair and maintenance methods were superior. An aggrieved ordnance officer wrote in July 1942:

The British Army, true to its studied habit of under statement and self-depreciation has somehow tacitly assumed that the Germans miraculously whisked crippled tanks out of battle and put them back whole a few days later.[93]

The Royal Army Ordnance Corps engineering workshops and recovery sections had in fact achieved impressive results in very difficult circumstances. It was also found later that the high standards achieved by the Afrika Korps in Libya were not matched by the rest of the Wehrmacht's maintenance services.[94] However, the multiplication of different corps responsible for vehicle maintenance and repair within Eighth Army was complicated and unhelpful. The Royal Engineers, Royal Army Service Corps and Royal Army Ordnance Corps maintained their own vehicles and equipment while the vehicles of all the other arms and corps in the Army were maintained by the Royal Army Ordnance Corps engineering branch.[95] This led to considerable overlap and blurred responsibilities in an area of vital importance. In August 1942 it was decided to detach tank maintenance, repair and recovery from the overworked and overburdened Royal Army Ordnance Corps, and vehicle maintenance and repair from the Royal Army Service Corps, establishing instead an entirely new corps: the Royal Electrical and Mechanical Engineers. This was formed officially on 1 October 1942 through the amalgamation of the various engineering and maintenance units. While some members of the previous organisations were understandably upset at the changes, the formation of the Royal Electrical and Mechanical Engineers recognised the importance of vehicle maintenance in a mechanised war. By placing all such work in one organisation it also gained economies of scale. Since its formation generally required only a change in title and cap badge[96] for most of the formations and personnel involved, Eighth Army and Middle East Command soon had a complete set of Army and base workshops with a single chain of command.

The Royal Army Ordnance Corps had had to struggle throughout 1940–42 with a dearth of personnel and equipment and the exponential demands of intense mechanised warfare. The formation of the Royal Electrical and Mechanical Engineers, and the resulting priority and status given to vehicle maintenance and repair, meant that Eighth Army's maintenance finally 'surpassed Rommel with enormous benefit to the hitting power of our Armies everywhere'.[97] As in so many spheres of effort, the sore trial of the desert campaigns had finally brought results by October 1942.

Middle East Command built up considerable reserves of fuel, ammunition, spares and supplies to feed the coming offensive:

Supplies: 7 days for 10 Corps, 5 days for 13 and 30 Corps
P.O.L.:   500,000 gallons for 10 Corps

Ammunition: 268,000 rds for 25-pdr; 12,800 rds for 4.5in; 6,400 rds for
5.5in[98]

Yet the Eighth Army operational dumps were slim compared to the gargan-
tuan quantities moved up before the battle of Gazala. The lesson had been
learned: holding large stocks too close to the front risked their loss if the
operational situation worsened. Nonetheless, these stocks, compared with
the meagre supplies of the Panzerarmee whose supply lines had been
comprehensively choked by the Desert Air Force and Royal Navy, were more
than sufficient. When Eighth Army went into action on 23 October, it was
better supplied and equipped than ever before.

Critical intelligence work was also taking place behind the lines. In Cairo,
intelligence officers were assimilating the lessons from the capture of
Seebohm's Kompanie 621. Not surprisingly, the vital importance of the
British 'Y' Service was finally recognised. The personnel engaged in Army
'Y' work almost doubled from 1,300 in May to 2,400 in October 1942.
Learning the secrets of Seebohm's success enabled the 'Y' Service to enhance
their techniques and become more proficient in intercepting, translating and
disseminating German tactical messages to the units which needed it. The
signals intelligence work done in Cairo was finally coordinated with that
undertaken at corps level and these developments made Eighth Army's 'Y'
Service much more effective.[99] The destruction of Kompanie 621, moreover,
reversed the balance of advantage in signals interception. From July 1942
onwards, British Army 'Y' gained far more from the airwaves than their
German counterparts.

Similar developments were also taking place within the Army's 'J' Service.
The concept of a 'J' Service was first broached during Operation Crusader
in November 1941, when Major Hugh Mainwaring had the idea of listening
in to the forward wireless traffic of the advancing British armoured regiments. This served to give Eighth Army Headquarters a more rapid and
impressionistic picture of the progress of the fighting than could be gained
by waiting hours for divisional and corps reports to get back and enabled
commanders to react more swiftly and appropriately to events on the battlefield. 'J' also became an important means of providing the RAF with rapid
up-to-date information which could be used for planning air-support
missions. 'J' was first extensively employed by Auchinleck during July and
much valuable experience in its use was gained during the July battles. By
August 1942, the 'J' Service was firmly established.[100]

Eighth Army intelligence, signals interception and security thus made
great strides during July and August 1942 and could be capitalised upon for
the next phase of operations. That they developed so rapidly was perhaps
due to the fact that their implementation did not depend on the heavily
engaged front line units, but their effects were nonetheless profound. The

flow of Enigma decrypts and 'Y' intercepts revealed a much clearer picture of the enemy at the same time as the 'J' Service was making much more rapid command decisions possible. The flaws present in Eighth Army's conduct of operations in one key area had thus already been overcome by the end of July 1942. The British advantage in signals intelligence, security and command and control only became greater as the months passed.

The possibility that Panzerarmee Afrika might discover when and where Eighth Army was about to attack entailed considerable risk. Advance warning would enable the Axis forces to prepare to meet the attack and, through a counter-bombardment, break up the offensive before it had even begun. This vital point had been recognised early. Auchinleck's final appreciation had underlined the importance of a deception plan. After the failure of Rommel's last attempt to reach the Delta, it was obvious to both sides that Eighth Army would mount an attack at some point in the next few months. Any deception operation would be unable to disguise this fact, but it could mislead Axis intelligence officers as to its scale, scope, timing and direction.

There was almost no natural concealment possible in the desert. Both sides could use aerial reconnaissance and photography to investigate the 'other side of the hill'. However, methods of concealment and camouflage had been developed by Eighth Army to a high standard by Lieutenant-Colonel Geoffrey Barkas, the Director of Camouflage at General Headquarters Middle East. Prior to both Operation Compass and Crusader, deception measures had been undertaken with great success. At the start of Crusader strict wireless silence and the use of camouflage and dummy vehicles had enabled Eighth Army to drive far behind Axis lines before Rommel realised what was happening. Thus, while the static front at Alamein made such deception measures vital, their application by Eighth Army was not new.

Operation Bertram relied on the accumulated knowledge, developed over the previous three years, of deception measures effective in desert conditions. After writing the 'appreciation and plan' for Lightfoot, Richardson was given the task of planning the deception operation. Richardson had had experience with Special Operations Executive's 'Black' propaganda branch in 1941, and turned this to good use in planning Bertram. He considered the principal axis of attack in the north 'horribly obvious'[101] but hoped to conceal the advent of offensive preparations and, even once this was no longer possible, to deceive the Axis intelligence officers as to the timing and sector where the offensive would be mounted.[102] The orders for Bertram were issued on 14 September as part of Montgomery's operation order for the offensive and work started very soon afterwards.

Within the overall operation a number of different schemes were undertaken. The dumps of stores, ammunition and petrol required by 10 and 30 Corps in the northern sector were comprehensively camouflaged. Food and supplies were built up into stacks to look like lorries and 'the more coveted items (i.e. milk and sugar) were kept in the centre of the dump' to guard against pilfering. Each dump had a resident unit to simulate normal camp life. The ammunition dump at Imayid covered an area of three square miles and contained every type of ammunition in use. An additional 500 stacks of ammunition were added to the existing stacks but were buried and covered by hessian and sand. Ordnance stores were also hidden under dummy vehicles while petrol tins were stacked in trenches that had been dug in 1941 and so were already familiar to Axis air reconnaissance.[103] In Operation Brian open preparations and dumping were simulated in the south. Stacks of dummy stores including all kinds of engineer, ordnance, ammunition and supply dumps were mocked up from green steel wool, hessian, camouflage nets, old petrol tins and wire. The 'Diamond' dummy water pipeline was laid for 20 miles stretching into the southern sector.[104] This elaborate affair included fake pumphouses, reservoirs and vehicles filling up with imaginary water.

Just as important was the concealment of the concentration and movements of forces for the attack. Under 'Martello' the future assembly areas of 2nd New Zealand and 51st (Highland) Divisions and the armoured divisions of 10 Corps were concealed. The assembly areas were filled up with 4,000 real and 450 dummy vehicles by 6 October so that Axis observers would become familiar with them. Perhaps the most important element of 'Martello' was the concealment of 360 guns in their assembly and battle positions. The 25-pounder guns, limbers and distinctively shaped Quad artillery tractors were all made to appear to be ordinary lorries using what was called the 'cannibal' method: the gun was pushed next to its limber and a hessian 'lorry' placed over them. Then the Quad tractor was given a false square rear. The result was that each 25-pounder gun, with its limber and Quad tractor, appeared to be two ordinary lorries. This simple yet effective method meant that the Axis could not detect the build-up of artillery positions prior to the attack. Unfortunately, rain and windstorms on 16 and 17 October blew about and damaged a large number of 'sunshields' and dummy vehicles. The camouflage sections had to work hard to repair the damage and maintain the ruse.[105]

In 'Murrayfield North' and 'Murrayfield South' the moves of 1st Armoured Division and 24th Armoured Brigade were completed in two stages. The first stage was conducted openly and each division was deployed seemingly for use in the southern sector. 10th Armoured Division's moves, codenamed 'Melting Pot', used a staging area in the far south to reinforce this picture. The second move to the real assembly areas by the armoured divisions was completed on the nights of 21 and 22 October and full replicas of all the tanks and transport of the divisions were left behind when the real ones had departed. One officer remembered:

A fleet of lorries drove up to the leaguer and commenced unloading mountains of steel tubes and canvas. These were sorted out and in a few minutes an army of engineers was putting up structures in the tracks of the tanks. After a short while it could be seen that these were replicas of the tanks, and as the Regiment pulled out in the fading light it seemed rather as if they were departing spirits leaving their bodily structures in their last resting place.[106]

'Ghost' radio traffic was provided by signal sections to complete the illusion. Once in the northern sector, all the tanks were concealed under 'sunshields'. More than 700 of these camouflaged frames, which made the tanks look like lorries, were built. One type was suitable for Grants and Shermans and the other for Crusaders.

The Royal Army Ordnance Corps and Royal Engineer camouflage sections constructed a total of 8,400 different dummy vehicles, dumps and devices of all kinds.[107] Bertram represented an effort in deception and camouflage 'unequalled in military history'.[108]

In fact, this statement might well be extended to include all of Eighth Army's preparations for battle. In the space of less than three months, it had engaged in the task of evolving its techniques and capabilities in a vast range of areas. The opportunity arose from the unique operational pause and the static nature of the front, but the incentive was the bitter experience garnered from two years of intense fighting. The Eighth Army as it was about to embark upon the largest offensive of the desert war was not a new force standing upon the grave of its predecessor, but a renewed and reinvigorated military machine resting upon the shoulders of the 'old' desert army.

Leese later wrote, 'The battle was fought by one man – the Army Commander. It was conceived and carried out by him and was a great personal triumph for him.'[109] This is certainly what Montgomery himself also believed. However, the complicated negotiations within the 30 Corps planning process reveal a more interesting picture. The offensive plans used in July had indeed sprung from the mind of one man and had been littered with flaws and contradictions. There was never any time for proper debate and discussion. This encouraged 'bellyaching', and it also meant that the attacks had failed.

The strength of the Lightfoot plan lay in the fact that there were multiple authors and contributors. Montgomery provided the clear overall framework but the details were developed and settled further down the command chain. Eighth Army Headquarters worked rapidly and efficiently under Freddie de Guingand. In 30 Corps, Oliver Leese and his staff had translated Montgomery's intentions into a practical corps plan. The divisional commanders had then sorted out all the fine details. This process had worked well throughout the army with the exception of 10 Corps where the personal animosity between Lumsden and Gatehouse created friction. Sidney

Kirkman and Frederick Kisch had been given almost complete freedom to accomplish their part of the plan and succeeded brilliantly. So it may be said that Montgomery's real strength lay not in the production of cast-iron omniscient plans but in his ability and skill to energise Eighth Army by using the talents and experience of the commanders serving under him.

Montgomery also insisted that every soldier within Eighth Army should understand his part in the plan. The demands of security meant that relatively few officers knew about it at first. But all brigadiers and Royal Engineer commanders knew the plan by 29 September. On 10 October, Montgomery spoke to every unit commander. The company and battery commanders were let into the secret on 17 October and on that day all leave was quietly stopped and all travel to Cairo and Alexandria forbidden. Montgomery insisted that 21 and 22 October had to be spent in 'the most intensive propaganda as regards educating the attacking troops about the battle, and to getting them enthusiastic'.[110] Every divisional commander held a series of conferences to ensure that his subordinates understood their tasks. At the last conference for all commanders held by 9th Australian Division, Morshead echoed Montgomery's strictures for the coming fight. He told his commanders, 'This battle will be real rough house' that would require 'determined leading'. Soldiers must not surrender even if surrounded: 'They must be staunch Australians and not emulate the Italians.' Morshead exhorted his commanders to 'work, think, train, prepare, enthuse. We must regard ourselves as having been born for this battle.'[111] By the time the offensive opened, every soldier in Eighth Army knew his part in it.

The Desert Air Force was also gearing up for the coming fight. 'Mary' Coningham also had many concerns in preparing his force. The growing number of American fighter and bomber squadrons available had to be integrated into the experienced ranks of the Desert Air Force while the existing squadrons were rested and trained.[112] Coningham also had to struggle against the withdrawal of the Albacore squadrons and the sharp decline in his force of Wellington bombers. The Albacores were retained but while 130 serviceable Wellingtons had been available during July, by October there were only 80 left. This limited the capabilities of the night bomber force at exactly the moment their contribution was most needed.[113] Nonetheless, in the months before the British offensive, the medium and heavy bombers of the Desert Air Force and the USAAF continued to pound Tobruk and Benghazi in night raids, as well as the other smaller harbours along the coast. The anti-shipping campaign continued and scored a number of successes against Axis merchant shipping.

On 9 October, Coningham mounted a 'weather Blitz' against the Axis forward airfields around El Daba, which had become waterlogged by heavy rains. The results for more than 400 fighter sorties and 88 tons of bombs were somewhat disappointing: only ten German aircraft were destroyed and another 13 damaged.[114] Although this 'blitz' was an exceptional effort, the

Desert Air Force maintained a constant pressure against the Axis landing grounds to ensure that the Luftwaffe and Regia Aeronautica were always kept on the back foot.

The Axis air effort in Egypt was limited during September and October but not over Malta. Stocks of aviation fuel on the island were falling rapidly during September and British air operations had to be drastically curtailed. On 11 October, the Axis launched a final air offensive against the island in an attempt to neutralise it before the expected land battle in Egypt. The raids continued for eight days but even though 319 aircraft, fully a third of the Axis aircraft available in the theatre, had been committed to the attacks, the onslaught simply confirmed the superiority of the defending Spitfires. The strike force based on Malta was able to continue harrying Axis shipping even during the raids. In fact, the last Axis air offensive against Malta proved to be a major strategic blunder, drawing off air strength from Egypt at precisely the time when the beleaguered squadrons at El Daba and Fuka most needed reinforcements.[115]

Montgomery had made clear on taking command of the Eighth Army that there must be close cooperation with the Desert Air Force. He emphasised that 'whatever the military plan, it is vital that the air should be brought in from the start; it is not sufficient to decide on the plan and then to ask the R.A.F. how it can help'.[116] In fact, Eighth Army planning during July had already begun this process but Montgomery's move of Eighth Army's Main Headquarters to Burg el Arab to join the Desert Air Force Headquarters certainly encouraged close cooperation.

Although Montgomery had acknowledged the need for coordination, his plans for Lightfoot barely mentioned the RAF. He quite clearly expected Coningham to undertake the detailed planning necessary to support the ground offensive. Yet the army's need for deception and surprise before the attack and its insistence that the Panzerarmee itself should not be disturbed by heavy preparatory bombing frustrated Tedder and Coningham. Tedder even wrote to Portal, the Chief of the Air Staff, explaining:

> I am not very happy about Montgomery's plans. . . . one of the main lessons of the past few months has been that the enemy strength has really been broken by the twenty-four hour day of almost incessant air attack . . . This factor should, I feel, have been exploited to the utmost in the next battle. . . . He will only concentrate if he is threatened on the land . . . I feel we should have made such a threat, giving us the opportunity from the air to hammer him and weaken him for three or four days before delivering the vital blow on land.[117]

Quite clearly, Tedder was guilty of overestimating the ability of airpower to force a decision. It seems remarkable that Tedder, after two years' experience in the Middle East, could so misunderstand the realities of the challenge facing the Eighth Army or the importance of its carefully orchestrated deception plan. The Eighth Army and the Desert Air Force were now working together systematically and to great effect but they still did not necessarily understand one another.

However, although Operation Bertram denied the Desert Air Force the opportunity for round-the-clock bombing before the ground offensive, fighter squadrons provided almost continuous local air superiority, which severely limited the amount of Axis air reconnaissance over the Eighth Army. Coningham's air plan for the offensive was designed to dovetail with the army's requirements. The most important element was the retention of air superiority and the main guiding policy, once the ground battle began, was to give the maximum possible round-the-clock support to the army with fighter bombers, light bombers and medium bombers.

The Desert Air Force had built up an impressive total strength of 730 aircraft before the beginning of the offensive.[118] However, out of the front-line strength of 420 fighters only 50 were Spitfires and nearly half were the now obsolete Hurricanes. The growing obsolescence of the majority of the fighters was a serious problem since the Luftwaffe in Egypt had been re-equipped with the Me109G. This matched the performance of the Spitfire and outclassed the Hurricane. The Axis air forces in North Africa possessed a similar strength with 770 aircraft but, crucially, a much lower serviceability rate.[119] Coningham realised that the Desert Air Force had to overwhelm the Luftwaffe in Egypt before the offensive began to give his obsolete, but more numerous, fighters a fighting chance.

The air offensive actually began on 19 October, four days before the ground battle. A series of intensive attacks were concentrated on all the main Axis landing grounds at El Daba and Fuka. Over the next few nights Tobruk was heavily bombed while the forward landing grounds were attacked around the clock. These raids did not necessarily destroy many Axis aircraft but they certainly made it difficult for the Axis ground crews to keep their aircraft serviceable. By 23 October, the Stuka force had a serviceability rate of just 50 per cent and the fighter force was even more badly affected. On 23 October, not a single enemy aircraft was seen over Eighth Army's positions and throughout the day a continuous fighter patrol was maintained over the Axis forward fighter landing grounds without challenge.[120] This meant that the vast and complicated moves of Eighth Army into its battle positions went unobserved by any Axis air reconnaissance. The pre-battle air offensive was a considerable success and ensured that there was no serious challenge to the Desert Air Force's dominance throughout the coming battle.

While British preparations reached their final pitch of intensity, Axis units across the front watched anxiously for signs of the imminent offensive. 33 Reconnaissance Battalion, which had been watching the sector south of the

Munassib depression since early September, reported on 9 October that it discounted any major attack from the Qattara Depression but thought such an attack was very likely between Point 153 (two miles north of Himeimat) and Deir el Munassib.[121] Operation Bertram had been designed precisely to mislead the Panzerarmee into believing that this would be the main axis of attack. However, on 10 October, the Panzerarmee reported to Kesselring:

> The British may launch an offensive soon. The enemy will need at least 3–4 days to bring up his artillery and assault troops. Pz Army thinks that the main weight of the enemy attack will be south of Ruweisat, and perhaps also on either side of the coast road.

Axis intelligence had correctly identified the most likely sectors for attack but made the erroneous assumption that the British would not be able to conceal the massing of forces beforehand.

Under Stumme's direction, the units of the Panzerarmee had continued to develop their defences. He was fully aware of the supply crisis and ordered the utmost economy in the use of petrol. Furthermore, 'the ammunition situation compels us to be most sparing in its use, especially while the present quiet period lasts'.[122] The enforced economy made October the quietest month at Alamein, although infantry patrols and artillery bombardments continued. Even with these difficulties, Stumme estimated that 'with reasonable care in the expenditure of ammunition and in the movement of motorised formations it will be possible to conduct a defensive campaign'.[123]

Indeed, Stumme was planning to mount an ambitious counterattack against any Eighth Army breakthrough. On 15 October, he explained that if Eighth Army broke through south of Deir el Munassib, on either side of Ruweisat or on the coast road, the plan would be:

> to hold him frontally and use the motorised formations to launch pincers counter attacks against him, surround him and destroy him. It may become necessary . . . for battle groups of Afrika Korps and 20 Corps to move east through our minefields to launch a concentric attack, in order to make the pincer movement as effective as possible.[124]

The Panzerarmee was certainly not a passive force awaiting its doom. On 20 October, just as the commanders of Eighth Army were boosting their own troops' morale, Stumme reminded his commanders:

> The enemy is by no means certain of victory. We must increase that uncertainty every day. . . . The feeling of complete moral superiority over the enemy must be awakened and fostered in every soldier, from the highest commander to the youngest man. . . . From this moral superiority comes

coolness, confidence, self-reliance and an unshakeable will to fight. This is the secret of every victory.[125]

Eighth Army was about to face a stern test of determination, not just a trial of strength.

Yet as the vast collection of men, tanks, vehicles and guns moved forward to their assembly points, Bertram, in a triumph of organisation, concealed their movements. While the operation did not deceive the Axis intelligence officers as to the scale or scope of the coming offensive, or even fully convince them that the attack would fall in the south, the British deception measures ensured that the Panzerarmee's intelligence officers did not gain the clear evidence of the British build-up they needed to make full preparations.

As late as 23 October, the Panzerarmee's daily report stated: 'Enemy situation unchanged. Quiet day all along the front, with normal enemy artillery H[ostile] F[ire].'[126]

The German and Italian troops of the Panzerarmee Afrika were tense and expectant. They knew that the British would launch their attack soon but they had no notion of the storm that was about to break upon their heads.

FIFTEEN

Operation Lightfoot

Stane Jock in the mantrap field
Walking saftly[1]

As the sun set over the desert at El Alamein on 23 October 1942, the military machine that was Eighth Army began to stir into life. Throughout that long hot day, the infantrymen of the assaulting divisions, having moved up the night before, were confined to their narrow slit trenches. Even visits to the latrines were strictly controlled.[2] A member of the Highland Division recalled the scene:

> It was difficult to imagine that all along the 2,500 yards of the Divisional front, there were some ten thousand men similarly concealed, and behind them tanks and guns, vehicles and stores and more men, and that was the situation all along the whole Eighth Army Front.[3]

Meanwhile, unit commanders and staff officers had gone around carefully checking that all their preparations were complete. Most units held a final battalion 'O' Group to check the final details and read out Montgomery's 'Personal Message From the Army Commander'. Unlike Auchinleck's 'Special Order of the Day' written on 30 June just before the crisis at El Alamein, Montgomery's message did reach the troops. Pienaar went round all his formations and 'found everywhere an air of quiet confidence in the outcome of the battle'.[4]

Freyberg held a final divisional conference in the morning. All the moves up and deception measures seemed to have gone well. The New Zealand staff gnawed over every detail of the plan and worried about the timings, the weather and the strength of the enemy defences on the other side of the Miteiriya ridge. Brigadier W. G. Gentry commented: 'Even if the thing goes like an exercise the thing is virtually impossible!'[5] But it was far too late for changes.

In the dusk, thousands of men emerged from their cramped slit trenches to stretch their stiff limbs. B Echelon trucks brought up the welcome hot evening meal which was meant to sustain the men for the next 24 hours. Water bottles were topped up, grenades and ammunition issued. The battalions

formed up and then marched as silently as possible along dusty tracks past
the existing front line and through the gaps in the protective minefields to
their start lines in 'no-man's-land'. Sappers had already marked these with
miles of white tape. Wimberley watched:

> Jocks filing past in the moonlight. Platoon by platoon they filed past, heavily
> laden with pick and shovel, sandbags and grenades – the officer at the head,
> his piper by his side. There was nothing more that I could do now to prepare
> for the battle, it was only possible to pray for their success.[6]

Once the battalions reached their positions the men then lay down to wait.
After the infantry had moved off, a gunner officer noted that, after the
crowding of the past few days, his gun position became 'uncannily quiet and
lonely'.[7] The gunners wiped the sand off the first rounds of ammunition
and checked and rechecked their guns.

Further back, the tanks of Eighth Army emerged from their protective
camouflage as the crews threw off the hessian 'sandshields'. Engines were
warmed up and then squadron after squadron of tanks drove off on to their
designated tracks. There were six of these, named 'Sun', 'Moon', 'Star',
'Boat', 'Bottle' and 'Hat'; they led from 10 Corps Assembly areas and passed
through Eighth's Army's minefields. All had been completed only in the last
few days to ensure that Axis observers would not understand their significance. Along each track were hurricane lamps set inside petrol tins which
had the appropriate symbol punched in them. As the tanks moved slowly
along the tracks, nose to tail, they quickly ground the surface into a fine
powder 'which felt almost liquid if you let it run through your hands. This
powder drifted and settled everywhere and gave us all clowns' faces.'[8] Then
the tanks began to pass the gun lines, 'heavies, mediums and field. Beside
each gun, deep in its sandy pit with its snout pointing westwards, lay stacks
of shells and boxes of charges, and the gunners rested on the ground alongside.'[9] Meanwhile, the infantry, now with little to do, anxiously waited for
'Z - 20'. The desert pendulum that had been held for so long was about to
swing back with a vengeance.

The guns of Eighth Army did not all open fire at the same time. The fireplan had been calculated precisely to include the time of flight for each shell
to its target. The exact timing for each gun was calculated so that every one
of the first 882 shells would land on its target across the entire 40-mile front
simultaneously:

> Gradually the heavy guns at the rear opened up, only flashes on the horizon,
> then others joined in, flashes and bangs crept closer – suddenly the Regiment's
> 25-pounders roared! Seconds seemed longer than minutes – the spectators
> counted – 5, 4, 3, 2, 1, NOW!'[10]

The sophistication of the barrage, with its incorporation of BBC time signals to ensure accurate timing and 'time-on-target' calculations, was lost on most of the watching soldiers but all were impressed by the curtain of gun flashes that lit the sky from horizon to horizon and the wall of sound that assaulted their ears.

Montgomery claimed in his *Memoirs* that he went to sleep in his caravan just before the bombardment began but, like so many other statements in his autobiography, this was a strange embroidery of the truth.[11] De Guingand wrote in his notes on the battle that he had a quiet dinner that night and moved to a view point on the coast road at 'about 9.30'.[12] It is quite clear that Montgomery was with him. Montgomery wrote in his own diary of 'The Battle of Egypt' that the bombardment was:

> a wonderful sight, similar to a Great War 1914/18 attack. It was a still moonlit night, and very quiet. Suddenly the whole front burst into fire, it was beautifully timed and the effect was terrific; many large fires broke out in enemy gun areas.[13]

This was not a 'thousand-gun' bombardment and the Army Commander did not sleep through the noise.

An Australian soldier of the 2/17th Battalion, waiting near a gun battery, remembered how:

> From far back to the Hill of Jesus a tongue of flame leapt out. The first gun had fired.
>
> For a split second all was dark again. We heard the Sergeant shout, his voice no longer subdued, but wild, loud, excited: 'Fire!'
>
> The whole horizon to the east spewed heavenwards in a fount of orange and blood-red flame, stabbing at the sky. The thunder of the barrage drowned the bang of the lone gun; it struck us, a tidal wave of sound; it hammered on our ear drums and whipped our shirts against our chests. . . . I could hear nothing but the crashing thunder of the barrage, thunder born of the flame that was the horizon and the sky and the whole earth. All was flame and thunder, and there was no world left to us.[14]

The patient work of the counter-battery office that had developed the detailed picture of the Axis batteries over the previous months was now put to the test. The Axis batteries which had been located in front of 30 Corps were battered by the concentration of fire from 10 troops onto each enemy troop position.[15] The medium guns shelled the furthest gun positions with a series of 'murders' where, over a period of two minutes, each enemy troop of four guns was hit by 100 4.5 or 5.5-inch shells. Axis battery positions in range of 25-pounder batteries were deluged by a similar weight of shells.[16] Some

Axis batteries were subjected to concentrations of twenty to one while one battery received a thirty-six to one concentration – which destroyed it.[17] Although this initial counter-battery fire wrecked some Axis gun positions, its main effect was severely to disrupt Axis communications and shock the German and Italian defenders. Some of Eighth Army's infantry commanders had worried that a counter-battery shoot before zero hour might alert the Axis defence but the ferocity of the bombardment stunned the Axis gunners – and the Axis army – into silence.

At 22.00 hours, the first Albacores arrived over their target area at Tel el Aqqaqir. For the next six hours, 60 Wellington bombers, guided by flares dropped by 20 Albacores, attacked targets in the northern sector with the aim of destroying gun positions and causing the 'maximum amount of irritation and loss of sleep'.[18] Other Wellingtons jammed Axis wireless traffic while four Bostons were used to lay a smoke screen to assist the 24th Australian Infantry Brigade at Tel el Eisa. Finally, the Desert Air Force could put its whole force into the fight.

Immediately the bombardment began, the Headquarters of 15th Panzer Division attempted to identify where the main British effort was being made. However:

> Clarification of the situation was made very difficult by the heavy artillery fire, smoke shoots, bombing attacks, the early destruction of communications by artillery fire and the failure of Italian front-line troops to make situation reports.[19]

The heavy artillery fire had destroyed most of the telephone connections to forward units and the aerial wireless jamming was also effective. This meant that the Panzerarmee Headquarters received very little information from forward units during the assault.[20] Stumme, for the first few vital hours, was unable to react properly to the British offensive.

However, the Dundonian sapper who, on hearing the barrage, quipped, 'By Goad, that will break up a few o' the Gerry pontoon schools'[21] was perhaps more accurate than he realised. After another quiet day, the opening of Eighth Army's offensive had been completely unexpected by the Panzerarmee and this meant that the German and Italian gunners had not been standing by their guns when the bombardment began. Although the counter-battery fire caused a good deal of material destruction and disruption, it does not seem to have killed or wounded many Axis gunners who had been in their slit trenches when the bombardment began. The Axis batteries were largely neutralised for the first few hours of the offensive but many were able to recover from their shock and bring their guns into action in the days ahead.

At 21.55 hours, the gunfire stopped. There were five minutes of 'uneasy quiet'[22] while the gunners checked their tables and relaid their guns onto the first of their targets within the Axis forward defended localities. When the guns opened up again on their timed concentrations, it was zero hour and eight brigades of infantry from 30 Corps moved into the attack.

In the coastal sector, the 24th Australian Infantry Brigade kept a firm hold on the vital area around Tel el Eisa and carried out a simulated or 'Chinese' attack as a diversion.[23] This was to mislead the Axis defenders into believing that the northern flank of the attack extended to the sea so that defensive fire would be dispersed over a wider area.[24] The diversions were timed to coincide with the main phases of the real attack. Two platoon-sized raids attacked at zero hour and managed to penetrate the enemy defences under heavy fire. Meanwhile, a company of 4.2-inch mortars, along with all the mortars, anti-tank guns and machine guns of the brigade, simulated 'artillery' fire along the front. A smoke screen was laid by a Boston guided by flares while, just before midnight, searchlights 'accidentally' illuminated 75 dummy figures which had 'stood up' by remote control.[25] These were sited in two groups in front of the brigade's forward positions and drew considerable fire. Axis defensive fire continued for four hours in the northern sector and prisoners, who were taken later, confirmed that they believed they had defeated part of the main attack.[26] The brigade had achieved its objective with its 'Chinese' war and, for the rest of the month, was held in reserve. It 'watched, waited and helped when asked'.[27]

Under the cover of the timed concentrations falling on the listening post area in front of the Axis wire, the 26th Australian Infantry Brigade advanced with just the 2/24th Battalion in its first wave. On its left, the 2/17th and 2/15th Battalions of the 20th Australian Infantry Brigade moved forwards onto the first enemy posts. There was very little return fire as the three Australian battalions began their attack. The detailed picture that had been built up of the Axis defences meant 'there were no surprises in the move through the enemy minefield and wire'.[28] The wire caused little delay and the moon was so bright that many of the anti-personnel mines were avoided as the infantry advanced.[29] The standard methods for forming up and navigating at night, which had been practised time after time in exercises, worked flawlessly.[30] Although the left-hand company of the 2/24th Battalion encountered one post which put up a stiff fight, most of the assaulting companies encountered only light opposition and were able to reach the first objective line with few casualties. It was felt that 'the Germans were up to their old trick of putting Italians out in front to take the edge off the attack while they had time to prepare in the second and stronger line'.[31] Ten minutes after midnight, all three battalions were in position on the objective, just 15 minutes later than planned.[32]

After a pause of 45 minutes, fresh battalions 'leapfrogged' forward. The 2/48th Battalion continued the advance of 26th Australian Infantry Brigade and met with no opposition for 1,500 yards in the gap between the forward posts and the main Axis line of defence. Here the two leading companies were confronted with deep minefields sprinkled liberally with anti-personnel mines and strongly wired posts that put up strong resistance. However, 'due to the state of training the battalion had reached, and to the excellent work done by the engineers attached to each company, these presented few difficulties'.[33] When D Company ran into serious opposition, Sergeant Bill Kibby took command of 17 Platoon after Lieutenant Lewin was wounded. The platoon had been forced to the ground by heavy machine-gun and mortar fire and casualties were mounting. Kibby got up, shouted for the men to follow him and charged the enemy post, firing his Tommy gun.[34] After a number of the occupants were killed, the four survivors surrendered. Kibby's bravery opened the way for the advance.

Eventually, the two reserve companies leapfrogged through and reached the final objective line. Although there had been heavy artillery, mortar and machine-gun fire during the advance, casualties had been light – two dead and 27 wounded – and the companies were able to dig in amongst Italian mortar pits. Lieutenant-Colonel Hammer noted that the 'opposition had been strong but not as difficult as anticipated'. At 03.45 hours, the battalion was able to fire its success rocket which was 'almost dead on time'. Hammer also noted that the battalion's communications had worked 'almost perfectly'. He had maintained wireless contact with all of his companies through their No. 18 sets during the entire attack.[35]

Hammer's notes on the reorganisation which followed the successful attack give a real insight into how this well-drilled battalion prepared its newly won ground. Hammer pointed out:

> To picture reorganisation after a night attack you must think of the situation:-
> (a) Moonlight or dark – advanced 7–10,000 yards.
> (b) Shelling from sides – you may be amongst your own as well.
> (c) Heavy fighting may have taken place – ranks thinned – Comds hit.
> (d) Fog of war – dust, smoke, wire, mines, booby traps.
> (e) Men are tired – battle weary.
> (f) Ground – what you can see of it – is unknown.
> (g) Time before daylight limited – Rapidity is required.[36]

The first task was to select good positions for each rifle company. Each company commander had to carefully pace out the layout which each platoon commander then repeated in his own sector. The reserve companies had to pace out the distance back to their positions as 'moonlight exaggerates distance – usual disadvantage is cramping – huddling – must have depth'.[37] Once the layout had been determined, the tired men then had to dig their slit trenches for all-round defence which could then be linked up if needed.

After the success rocket went up, the battalion transport could then move through the mine gaps to bring the 'A/Tk Guns, MMG, Mortars, A Ech[elon] Vehs with more Hawkins mines, wire, sandbags, overhead cover (half sheet iron), amn, food, water'.[38] The Hawkins mines were small anti-tank mines which were laid out one per yard of front. Each man was issued with a half-sheet of corrugated iron to lay over his slit trench. The addition of some sandbags gave each man in the battalion protection from airburst shells. By the time all this work had been accomplished 'Men are contented, Amn to fight, A/Tk defence, food to eat and water to drink and a nice little bit of overhead cover stops splinters.'[39]

Hammer's attention to detail and the long hours of practice during the rehearsals all paid off for the 2/48th Battalion. By dawn, all the companies were dug in with overhead cover and the positions protected by a double row of 2,400 Hawkins mines.[40] Hammer noted:

> The whole thing takes shape now and by daylight after a long advance, a hectic fight, and a busy reorgn the whole Bn is ready for the always to be expected dawn counter attack and the inevitable day light counter attacks which always come, but the unit is sitting pretty, ready and willing to fight.[41]

The contrast between the 2/48th Battalion's experience during Lightfoot and the situation which so many of Eighth Army's infantry battalions had faced at dawn during the July attacks could hardly be greater. The application of standard procedures and battle drills combined with repeated practice meant that infantry battalions could be ready for any counterattack by dawn. However, the methods of the 2/48th Battalion represented best practice within Eighth Army and, unfortunately, they were still not universal.

For example, while almost everything went according to plan for Hammer's 2/48th Battalion, the 2/13th Battalion of 20th Australian Infantry Brigade did not make the same progress. This battalion had to attack on a front of 2,200 yards and was given the support of the Valentine tanks of 40th Royal Tank Regiment to assist in the advance. However, although the sappers were working hard to clear the minefields, the tanks were held up by mines and the battalion had to move off without tank support. The leading companies managed to advance for 1,700 yards without serious opposition but then came up against strongly held German positions. The fighting became heavy. The troops then came upon a minefield which was found to be 1,500 yards deep. This was far too big a task to be undertaken by mine detectors and two Scorpions were brought up. Unfortunately, the auxiliary engines on the Scorpions quickly overheated in the 'terrific dust' and broke down. When the reserve companies passed through to assault the main German defences they were met by a 'storm of tracer fire from the front and both flanks'.[42] Both companies were pinned down on the edge of the

German positions and suffered heavy casualties. Eventually, the two leading companies withdrew to reorganise, leaving the battalion still 1,000 yards short of the objective at dawn. Nonetheless, the battalion's supporting arms came up in support and cut a path through the minefields for the Valentines. They 'came up in line ahead like a squadron of battleships. They squatted on the F.D.L.s and the infantry pointed out the enemy posts still resisting in the vicinity.'[43] But in sum, the battalion had had a difficult night and had been unable to reach its final objective.

To the south of the Australian sector, the 51st (Highland) Division went into its first battle. The division had an even more difficult task to accomplish than the Australians as the 2,500-yard divisional front widened to two and three-quarter miles by the time the final objective was reached. Wimberley had divided the front into six lanes but there were only enough troops to leapfrog reserve battalions through on either flank. In the four central lanes, each battalion had to make the full advance of nearly five miles to the final objective. Wimberley had also inserted four objective lines, the green, red (this was the Eighth Army's first objective line), black and blue lines, to assist in coordination and pacing. This was exactly the same method used when Wimberley had learned his trade under 'Uncle' Harper, the commander of the division during the Great War. All of the Axis defended posts had been given local names familiar to each of the battalions to help them navigate through hostile territory.

Thus, in 153rd Brigade's sector, 5th Black Watch would take the advance to the red line where 1st Gordons would leapfrog through to the blue line. Further south, the 5/7th Gordons would have to advance to the final objective. In 154th Brigade's sector, the 1st Black Watch and the 7th Argyll and Sutherland Highlanders would have to make the same advance. Even then, the division did not have sufficient infantry and the fifth lane was earmarked for the recce battalion mounted in carriers with the support of the Valentines of 50th Royal Tank Regiment. On the brigade's southern flank, the 5th Camerons would make the intial advance and the 7th Black Watch would go through to the blue line.

Each battalion, in common with all the assaulting infantry that night, was formed up for night movement. The two leading companies were followed by the battalion headquarters and, in the rear, two companies in reserve. The whole battalion was led by a navigating party of an officer and two NCOs pacing out the distance on the centre line. Each company advanced with two platoons 'up' and one in reserve with the company headquarters on the inner flank. There was a five-yard gap between each soldier and each battalion covered a frontage of 600 yards and the same depth. The soldiers were heavily laden. Each man wore a small pack with a white cross of St Andrew made of scrim (a fine open-weave fabric) to aid recognition in the darkness. Every man carried a pick or entrenching tool, an extra 50 rounds of ammunition, two grenades and four sandbags. Every battalion was to be capable of fighting for 24 hours without relief or resupply although obviously the hope was that the battalion transport would reach the forward positions before dawn.

Right from the start of the advance, the thin creeping barrage fired to aid direction kicked up tremendous clouds of dust and the whole battle was fought amongst swirling clouds of dust and cordite smoke. Up to the red line, the Highlanders found the going reasonably easy. Resistance in the forward outposts was relatively light and the Axis troops seemed stunned by the bombardment. Once the advance pushed on past the red line, however, some Axis artillery batteries began to fire a defensive barrage and mortar fire increased.

In the northern lane, 5th Black Watch reached the red line at midnight after taking 'Montrose' under intense machine-gun fire. The unit suffered heavy casualties and piper Duncan McIntyre died while playing the regimental march 'Hieland Laddie'. He was found the next morning with his pipes still under his arm and his fingers 'rigid on the chanter'.[44] The 1st Gordons leapfrogged through the 5th Black Watch but met a heavy concentration of shell and mortar fire 300 yards ahead. There was doubt as to whether this was the supporting barrage or enemy defensive fire; it may actually have been both. The two leading companies pressed forwards through the smoke and dust into the barrage and were soon lost to sight. There was no more contact with the forward companies for the rest of the night. Eventually the two remaining companies were sent to go through to the final objective with a squadron of 50th Royal Tank Regiment in support but five tanks hit an unknown minefield and the advance was held up. It was decided to withdraw back to the locality of 'Kintore' to ensure that the battalion was dug in by dawn. In fact, the two leading companies had managed to reach the black line but only after very heavy fighting and severe casualties. By dawn these isolated companies were down to a total of 60 men.[45] The critical fact was that although neither the 2/17th Battalion nor the 1st Gordons had been able to reach their final objectives, this was the sector for 1st Armoured Division's corridor. The failure meant that the armour's northern corridor could not be cleared by dawn.

To the south, the 5/7th Gordons also ran into difficulty. The two leading companies met only limited resistance in reaching the red line but the reserve companies, which took up the advance at 01.00 hours, had to move nearly 1,000 yards under very heavy shell and mortar fire. Both companies were held up in front of 'Strichen' by a number of machine-gun posts and D Company tried to move round the left flank of the defences. The whole company disappeared into the smoke and dust and lost contact. Two days later, Captain J. Sharp and many of his men were found dead in the middle of a minefield. Virtually the entire company had been wiped out by machine-gun fire. Further progress was impossible and C Company dug in close to

'Strichen'. The supporting arms were able to reach the battalion head-quarters around 'Insch' so that the new defences were firmly held by dawn.[46] 153rd Brigade had had a difficult baptism of fire and had been unable to reach the black line let alone its final objectives.

1st Black Watch advanced down the northern lane of 154th Brigade's sector. The men marched very close to the creeping barrage and had to be held back. The battalion first met major resistance at the strongpoint known as 'Killin' just in front of the red line. It overran the position but suffered heavy casualties passing through the barrage. In the subsequent advance from the red line, the two reserve companies experienced real trouble. A Company ran into a minefield filled with German 'S' mines and booby-trapped 500-pound bombs. The German 'S' mine was an anti-personnel device which left only three prongs of wire above the sand. If touched, the mine was fired into the air and then exploded at chest height, showering the nearby area with shrapnel. Similarly, the 500-pound bombs were triggered by a fine tripwire. Neither the fine tripwires on the bombs nor the prongs on the 'S' mines could be easily seen, even in the bright moonlight. Nonetheless the company was able to overrun 'Perth', taking 30 prisoners, but was isolated until the morning. D Company overran 'Stanley' but had to fall back because of heavy flanking fire from the north – probably from the unsubdued post 'Keith' in the 5/7th Gordon's sector.[47]

The 7th Argyll and Sutherland Highlanders met little opposition on their march to the red line but suffered a steady drain of casualties from mines, booby traps and mortar fire. While reorganising on the red line, one platoon was wiped out by heavy shellfire. Eventually, after a further advance and more heavy casualties, the large defended locality of 'Greenock' was secured and the remnants of the forward companies, now reduced to little more than 60 men, dug in more or less on the black line.[48]

To the south, the special support force composed of the carriers of the divisional reconnaissance regiment and two squadrons of Valentines from the 50th Royal Tank Regiment worked its way slowly forwards with sappers out in front prodding with bayonets through several belts of mines. An assault platoon of the reconnaissance regiment and B Squadron of the Valentines managed to reach the final objective around 'Nairn' but heavy flanking fire forced them back to the black line.[49]

In the southernmost lane of the Highland Division, two companies of the 5th Camerons made a rapid advance to the red line under fire. They reached their objective on time and with 40 prisoners in hand. 7th Black Watch took over the advance from the red line with the task of capturing the north-western edge of the Miteiriya ridge at Point 30, known to the battalion as 'The Ben'. It became clear as the leading companies advanced that there were few Axis defenders in front of the Miteiriya ridge. Instead, this area was protected by dense fields of 'S' mines and booby traps. As the battalion advanced to the black line it was subjected to heavy and accurate shelling and suffered heavy casualties from the invisible anti-personnel mines. Six officers, each in turn acting as the battalion navigating officer, became casualties. Nonetheless, Captain C. F. Cathcart took his D Company and the one surviving platoon from B Company forwards towards the final objective. These men met very heavy resistance on the ridge, which was covered with wired-in enemy posts and minefields. After very heavy fighting, there were only one and a half platoons of soldiers left to dig in on the final objective. These men, the only ones from the Highland Division to reach the final objective, remained cut off from their battalion until the next morning but they did manage to contact the forward companies of 21 New Zealand Battalion, which had also met stiff opposition on its advance to the final objective.[50]

Wimberley had dug in his divisional headquarters on what was the existing Eighth Army front line and had to wait anxiously for news of his battalions:

Hour by hour, the code words came in, and by dawn it was clear to me that we had eaten deeply into the enemy's position, and casualties might well have been worse. The Green Line, the Red Line, and the Black Line seemed to have been taken out [on] the whole Divisional Front. Only the final objective of the Blue Line was in doubt.[51]

The Highlanders had encountered more German anti-personnel mines than any other division and casualties had been correspondingly heavy. Many of the forward positions were held by isolated companies reduced to the strength of platoons and there was considerable confusion amongst the leading troops caught in the chaos of swirling dust, smoke and shelling. Although the Highland Division had not secured its final objective, its first performance in battle had been impressive. The frontage allotted to the division had simply been too wide and the three central battalions had insufficient strength to push on to the final defences. A narrower frontage allowing fresh battalions to take over on the red line might well have achieved greater results.

To the south of the 51st (Highland) Division's sector, the infantry of the 5th and 6th New Zealand Infantry Brigades reached their objectives and exorcised the ghosts of Bacon and Splendour. When Freyberg knew that his infantry brigades had moved forwards he said: 'If there was ever justice in a cause this is it. I don't think the Itys will stick it and I don't think the Boche will either – they didn't in the last war.'[52] With rather premature optimism, he drank to the success of Eighth Army with some Burgundy.

5th New Zealand Brigade began the advance on the northern half of the New Zealand front with 23 Battalion. The left company had to deal with a series of enemy posts that caused heavy casualties from machine-gun fire but the rest of the battalion made good time to what was believed to be the first objective line. Wireless communication had failed and Lieutenant-Colonel Reg Romans was unsure of the distance travelled because of the heavy losses which had been suffered by the navigation party. He ordered his remaining three companies forward and they actually reached the Miteiriya ridge after heavy fighting. The battalion then withdrew to its own objective and dug in.[53]

Thus, 21 and 22 Battalions did not exactly leapfrog through the 23 Battalion on their advance to the final objective. In common with the 7th Black Watch, 21 Battalion suffered heavy casualties from mines in its advance up onto the Miteiriya ridge but met determined resistance only on the ridge itself. Lieutenant P. Robertson led a patrol onto the reverse slope of the ridge which overran some field guns and captured almost 100 Italian prisoners. The battalion secured its objectives only 20 minutes after the supporting artillery concentrations ceased.[54]

On the left, one of 22 Battalion's companies was held up by fire from a powerful strongpoint. C Company managed to mount a flank attack and overran the position but suffered many casualties in the process. Another large enemy post had to be cleared on the ridge itself but by 03.15 hours the objective had been taken. However, the battalion suffered heavily from airburst shelling and mortaring for the rest of the night, just as the Australian battalions which had taken the ridge in July had done.

In the 6th New Zealand Brigade's sector, 24 Battalion met with considerable opposition in its advance up to the intermediate objective but still reached the line only a few minutes later than expected. The bitter experience of the New Zealand Division during July led to the 28 (Maori) Battalion being tasked with mopping up behind the leading battalions to ensure that the supporting arms could reach the forward troops. Because of the generally weak opposition and the thoroughness with which the leading battalions had dealt with the enemy posts, the Maoris encountered few enemy troops apart from some on the southern sector where numerous enemy posts had held up the South Africans' advance.[55]

The 1st South African Division had a smaller sector to handle because of its weaker brigades; it advanced with the 1st Natal Mounted Rifles on the right, in the 2nd South African Brigade sector, and 1st Rand Light Infantry on the left, in the 3rd South African Brigade sector. As the infantry advanced, the 66 medium machine guns of the Regiment President Steyn and Die Middellandse Regiment opened fire from their enfilade positions further south and the mortar platoons sent 'a hail of bombs' into the enemy positions.[56]

By 23.50 hours, the 1st Natal Mounted Rifles had secured the first objective and taken 67 prisoners from the 61st Regiment, Trento Division, but its leading companies had suffered heavy casualties. At the same time, 1st Rand Light Infantry reported the capture of its objective but could not make contact with the 2nd South African Brigade.[57]

However, the 1/2 Field Force Battalion and the Cape Town Highlanders, which had been tasked with advancing to the final objective in the 2nd South African Brigade sector, were both held up by heavy resistance from an unsubdued strongpoint. The routine of artillery and machine-gun fire was continued for a further 30 minutes in order to support the brigade. Eventually, once a company of the Natal Mounted Rifles had been placed under the command of the 1/2 Field Force Battalion, the final objective on the ridge was taken at 06.00 hours. The Cape Town Highlanders also encountered considerable delay because their transport took time to find their minefield gap but, by first light, the battalion was digging in on the ridge. Meanwhile, 3rd South African Brigade had continued its advance with the Royal Durban Light Infantry and the 1st Imperial Light Horse but, because of the delays imposed on 2nd South African Brigade, they encountered real difficulty from the 'banana' strongpoint on their right. It was not until 05.06 hours that both battalions had secured their final objectives on the ridge.[58]

The four infantry divisions of 30 Corps had launched the largest infantry assault of the desert war and achieved considerable success. Every division had used its own methods in the attack but all of them were modified from the commonly understood doctrine. The hard training and rehearsals had clearly paid off since every battalion was able to bring up its supporting arms through the minefields and dig in before first light. This vital task had often been impossible for Eighth Army infantry in the July battles and there can be little doubt that without proper preparation the same failure might have occurred during Lightfoot. Regardless of the subsequent progress of the armour, there would be no repeat of Bacon or Splendour.

30 Corps' infantry assault was the largest but by no means the only effort made by Eighth Army that night. 4th Indian Division made two raids from the Ruweisat ridge including another 'Chinese' attack.[59] In the far south, 13 Corps made its attempt to breach the series of minefields and exploit beyond them. However, these operations turned into little more than a 'costly diversion'[60] and achieved much less than had been hoped. There were at least two reasons for this failure. 13 Corps was definitely the 'Cinderella' of the three corps during Lightfoot. The corps lacked the infantry and sappers to make a deliberate assault like that of 30 Corps. The second problem was that the artillery's counter-battery work on the southern sector had been much more difficult than in the north. When the offensive opened there was insufficient data and not enough firepower to subdue the Axis batteries opposite.[61] Horrocks was faced with making a breach in at least three minefields. Moreover, he lacked the infantry to make a deliberate assault; the corps had to hold an extended front from the Qattara Depression up to the Ruweisat ridge. 44th (Home) Counties and 50th Division were mainly engaged in holding the line. This meant that Horrocks had to use 22nd Armoured Brigade to make its own gaps in the enemy's minefields and then

use 4th Light Armoured Brigade to penetrate beyond. The minefield task force consisted of 44th Division's reconnaissance regiment mounted in carriers, six Scorpions, a squadron of the Royal Scots Greys, two companies of 1st King's Royal Rifle Corps, and sappers from the 4th Field Squadron Royal Engineers.[62] Meanwhile, 1st Free French Brigade was to capture the commanding heights at Himeimat. In his subsequent report, Brigadier de la Gause, 13 Corps Chief Engineer, stated:

> I never liked the plan for clearing the minefields, but because of the lack of infantry in 13 Corps, it was not possible to cover the mine-clearing by forming a bridgehead, and the use of Scorpions in the forefront appeared to offer the best chances of success.[63]

Roberts recalled later how Horrocks had enthusiastically described the operation to him:

> the Scorpions would lead the way through the minefields concealed in a cloud of sand, closely followed by a mass of carriers which on debouching from the minefield, would scatter like a swarm of angry bees striking terror among the enemy.[64]

Roberts certainly had misgivings; he knew how unreliable the Scorpions were and how vulnerable carriers could be under fire.

In the event, 22nd Armoured Brigade began its 10-mile approach march soon after dark. The minefield task force advanced in four columns, each headed by a Scorpion and a party of engineers. Unfortunately, the Axis artillery was not subdued by the counter-battery fire and, soon after zero hour, the task force was brought under heavy shelling, mortar and machine-gun fire. After a carrier hit a mine, the Scorpions started thrashing but it was discovered later that some very scattered mines had been laid to a depth of 900 yards before the sappers reached the main minefield.[65] Progress was so slow that, although the auxiliary engines on the Scorpions did not overheat, some broke down and others were knocked out by anti-tank gun fire. By the time the first minefield had been breached, casualties were already mounting and Roberts realised that the minefield task force could not breach the second 'February' minefield in daylight. He went forward after dawn and later reported:

> The initial impression was of complete chaos; vehicles, tanks and carriers facing in different directions, some still burning, some at curious angles, and enemy shells arriving fairly steadily but not in great quantity.[66]

It was clear that the attempt had failed. The brigade had to spend the day immobilised between the two minefields under constant fire. The positions of 22nd Armoured Brigade were still overlooked by the enemy posts at Himeimat because the Free French had been unable to take the mountain. Further north, an attempt by 1/7th The Queen's to capture a strongpoint in the Axis defences also failed. 13 Corps operations, in short, had not been attended by success.

Although the mine-gapping operations within 13 Corps had dissolved into confusion and delay, the sappers of 10 and 30 Corps accomplished a remarkable feat in the northern bridgehead. Brigadier P. A. Clauson, the 10 Corps Chief Engineer, noted that 'nothing particularly unexpected was encountered in this operation, which went more or less according to plan'.[67] The vast amount of training and preparation undertaken by the engineers proved their worth. As soon as the bombardment on the Axis forward line began, 'the RE recce parties led off, followed by the tape men, detector parties and the rest of us'.[68] The sappers had to ignore the battle going on around them and concentrate on their immediate task. The bright moonlight helped them to see the mines and many had been uncovered by the wind. Yet it took cold-blooded courage to keep upright, sweeping with a mine detector, listening for the tone in the earpieces, while the battle continued. The mine-lifting parties faced up to the awful task of lifting identified mines and placing them on the side of the track, never knowing whether the next one might be booby-trapped or fitted with a new and unknown anti-lifting device. Brigadier G. R. McMeekan praised them:

> In the face of enemy fire, which was to increase greatly on the second belt, the sappers worked steadily on, keeping to their drill. The long nights' training were amply rewarded. It takes guts to stand up, and stay standing up, under heavy fire, when everyone else is either running forward or lying down.[69]

But the sappers knew their jobs instinctively and kept at their slow, dangerous work throughout the night. Thanks to them, every infantry division was able to get its supporting weapons up well before dawn.

The sappers of 10 Corps faced an even more difficult task. They needed to cut lanes in the enemy minefields beyond the final limit of the infantry's advance. While infantry divisions were satisfied with narrow eight-yard gaps, the armour commanders needed 40-yard gaps because the leading tanks 'churned up the sand so badly that those following needed space to avoid the worst patches'. Eventually it was agreed to start with 16-yard gaps and widen them to 40 yards later.[70] 1st Armoured Division's minefield task force made good progress on the 'Sun' route which had reached the positions of the 2/17th Australian Battalion by dawn. Enemy resistance had slowed work on the 'Star' route but 'fair progress' had been made on the 'Moon' track.[71] The need to make six gaps in the minefields instead of three had slowed progress. But though the sappers had been unable to reach the final objective, the minefields had been sufficiently cleared to allow 2nd Armoured Brigade to get forward. Similarly, the minefield task force for 10th Armoured Division managed to make four gaps up to the crest of the Miteiriya ridge. On two of the routes, 'Boat' and 'Ink', the sappers eventually worked ahead of the assaulting infantry. By 04.30 hours, McMeekan felt:

> with another ninety minutes before sunrise, and with three gaps swept and marked and a fourth enemy gap clear for at least half-way over the final minefield, that I would be justified in calling the armour on. At that moment I felt all Africa was within our grasp, if only the tanks could be shepherded through within the hour.[72]

The sappers had certainly done their job. It remained to be seen whether the armour could actually break out from the narrow minefield lanes.

As the infantry went into the assault, the armoured brigades drove forward to their start points. The gun covers were taken off and the machine guns loaded while the fuel tanks were all topped up in preparation for the drive ahead:

> It was 2 a.m. and bitterly cold. Most of us were frozen to the marrow and not feeling particularly brave. The first flush of excitement had given place to the knowledge that in a very few hours we would once more be at grips with the enemy armour and that the slaughter would begin all over again.[73]

The drivers revved their engines and the long columns began to snake their way through Eighth Army's minefields. The shaded green and white lights that marked the edges of the minefields helped the columns navigate through the narrow lanes. But:

> Even before reaching the enemy minefields, the dust begins to make itself felt. Gradually at first, then with increasing intensity, a heavy choking fog builds up as the tracks churn the desert into powder. When all the tanks are on the move this fog is blinding as well as physically unpleasant. Visibility is only a few yards and it is all the drivers can do to keep in touch with the tank ahead of them.[74]

It was little wonder, then, that some of the tank columns became delayed in the middle of this 'pea-souper' dust cloud. 9th Armoured Brigade,[75] now an organic part of the New Zealand Division, was the first to reach the New Zealand infantry along the Miteiriya ridge. Its leading regiment, the Royal Wiltshire Yeomanry, attempted to get over the ridge but its squadrons hit a scattered minefield on the ridge itself:

The extent of the calamity becomes increasingly apparent as the daylight grows. The two heavy squadrons are dotted about on the near approach to the ridge in grotesque attitudes which show clearly how they have tried, but failed, to avoid the menace which is hidden in the sand.[76]

Only 12 tanks managed to get through onto the reverse slope of the ridge (the loss of six Shermans and 13 Grants would have spelt disaster for Eighth Army in July but in October these were only the first losses of many).[77] To the left, the Warwickshire Yeomanry followed the Crusaders of the New Zealand Divisional Cavalry Regiment and so avoided the mines. The tanks took up hull-down positions along the ridge as the sun rose. For the first time, the New Zealand infantry had tank support at dawn and 'those 75 millimetre guns poking out of the turrets give the infantry great encouragement'.[78]

However, the whole Eighth Army plan had been predicated on the armour breaking through *before* dawn. 24th Armoured Brigade was held up and had only reached the former enemy front line by dawn. 133rd Lorried Infantry Brigade was even further back and had not moved past the Springbok track by first light.[79] 8th Armoured Brigade[80] had experienced some delays but the two leading regiments, the Nottinghamshire Yeomanry and the Sherwood Rangers, managed to drive up to the ridge by dawn. When they attempted to press on, however, they encountered 'heavy opposition from A.Tk guns and S.A. fire'.[81] Major Peter Moore, whose 3rd (Cheshire) Field Squadron Royal Engineers had worked hard clearing the minefields throughout the night, found 'the 'leading squadron of the Sherwood Rangers all ready to go, and guided the leading tank up to and through the gap as the first light was coming'.[82] Unfortunately, when the leading tanks crossed onto the far side of the ridge:

> suddenly all hell broke loose. Every kind of tracer fire came flying towards us from all directions. The tank crews waiting behind in the packed gaps through the minefield saw armour-piercing tracer shells screaming from all over the place towards A Squadron's tanks – then the explosions of tanks blowing up, sheets of flame as they caught fire, and the dull cherry red of red-hot tank turrets.[83]

The regiment lost ten tanks from the deluge of anti-tank gun fire that greeted them. The remaining squadrons then had to accomplish the difficult task of turning round in the minefield gaps and deploying behind the ridge. With the advance held up because of a few scattered mines:

> The ridge was becoming a congested mass of tanks as the whole of 8 Armd Bde. who had been intended to pass through on this sector were all piling up

behind the mines and there must have been over 200 tanks on a frontage of less than 2 miles.[84]

An enormous armoured traffic jam had not been part of the plan.

Gatehouse moved forward to sort out the problem, contacting the main headquarters of the New Zealand Division and informing them that he was 'about to form his Tac HQ'.[85] Brigadier McMeekan remembered that as he sat down for some tea:

> General Gatehouse roared by with his Tac. H.Q. in three Crusaders. The General, looking larger than ever in his white sheepskin coat and black beret, was sitting calmly on top of his tank. He went right up to the ridge, and toured round to see the situation. It was an encouraging sight, and a well-timed visit.[86]

At the same time, Freyberg was also in his tactical headquarters, which consisted of three Honey tanks. One of the difficulties encountered during the morning was that Freyberg and Gatehouse were not able to speak to one another directly. Each had radio links back to their main headquarters and forward to their own subordinates but not to one another. Nor did they happen to meet during their tours of the front line. This situation led to misunderstandings and confusion between the two most important commanders on the ground during the most complex and difficult phase of the battle.

Gatehouse quickly realised that there could be no question of sending his armoured brigades over the ridge in the face of intense anti-tank gun fire. His regimental commanders worked hard to sort out the confusion and deploy the armoured regiments along the ridge:

> By about 0900 hrs the situation had stabilised with all three Armd Regts occupying good positions on the reverse side of the MITEIRIYA Ridge, supported by their Btys RHA and two Btys 84 A.Tk Regt.[87]

Gatehouse explained to the New Zealand Headquarters later that morning that if his armoured brigades went 'forward of M. Ridge now they will have heavy casualties'.[88] His plan was to:

> sit on the M. Ridge and if there is any question of counter-attack he will intervene but he does not want to go out in front unless there is something to go out in front for. . . . Don't want to go out and get A/Tked and shelled to hell.[89]

However, this mass of armour had never been expected to remain on the ridge. The New Zealand Division front was now completely congested with its infantry brigades having to share elbow room with three complete armoured brigades.

Meanwhile, although Gatehouse had already decided to hold firm on the Miteiriya ridge, Freyberg was convinced that the armour should still attempt to break out and kept calling up his main headquarters 'asking us to please put some energy into 10 Armd Div'.[90] Part of this confusion was because of the communication difficulties and partly because of the very different perspectives of the infantry and armour commanders.

The failure to break through on the Miteiriya ridge was in fact predictable. 9th Australian Division had made three unsuccessful attempts during July to seize and hold this key piece of terrain. On each occasion, the Australian battalions had been able to reach the ridge but then found themselves exposed to intense fire from every Axis gun position to the south of the ridge. These facts should have given some warning to Eighth Army that exploitation beyond the ridge might be difficult. In fact, by making the capture of the Miteiriya ridge the limit of the infantry objective, Eighth Army had fallen into an Axis defensive trap. After July, the Germans and Italians were well aware of the ridge's importance but also of the defensive measures they should adopt to prevent any exploitation from it. Combined with the higher level orders to thin out the outpost zone, the Axis main defence was deployed in depth on the reverse slope of the ridge. Eighth Army was able to take the ridge but any troops which attempted to advance beyond it were exposed to a torrent of fire from the web of positions beyond the ridge.

While Freyberg believed that the armour was simply not trying hard enough, Gatehouse knew that bravery and willpower were no longer enough in an armoured battle. Even at the time, the New Zealand Headquarters noted that 'thin-skinned stuff cannot cross M. Ridge'.[91] While an infantry brigade could advance, seize ground, mop up any remaining enemy posts and then bring up its soft transport with the supporting weapons to consolidate the ground, the same was not necessarily true for an armoured formation. Tank formations relied as much, if not more, on their B Echelon soft vehicles than did the infantry. The armoured brigades could conceivably have pressed forward that morning at the cost of very heavy casualties. The problem was that their petrol and ammunition trucks could not possibly have followed them through the storm of artillery and anti-tank gun fire that was falling on the forward slopes of the Miteiriya ridge. This meant that the tanks, after fighting an intense and costly battle, would have been unable to refill their petrol tanks or restock with ammunition. The result would have been disastrous. Gatehouse may have been acting with caution but doing so ensured that his armoured regiments would not be devastated. It also made certain that any Axis counterattack could be easily repulsed.

The Crusader squadron of the Stafford Yeomanry and the 12 remaining tanks of the Wiltshire Yeomanry maintained their positions on the forward slope of the ridge. These tanks fought 'a most gallant action throughout the early morning until every tank was either knocked out or blown up on mines coming back to replenish'.[92] Major Peter Farquar, M.C., the Crusader squadron leader, had to bale out of three tanks that morning.[93] While the decision of the armoured commanders to pull back behind the Miteiriya ridge was criticised at the time and has been many times since, there seems little doubt that both 8th and 24th Armoured Brigades would have shared the same fate as these leading squadrons had they attempted to move beyond the ridge. However, the congested mass of infantry, armour and vehicles made a perfect target and the ridge was heavily shelled throughout the morning.

The activity of the Axis gunners soon brought a reaction from Eighth Army's artillery. The counter-battery office prepared plans for shoots and soon the Axis fire was diminished although never completely silenced. The gunners had little respite after their exertions the night before. 7th Medium Regiment also noted that the '"STONK" – the Corps Arty concentration used for the first time with great success. Lengthy periods of fire at intense rate have proved a great strain on both 4.5 and 5.5 guns.'[94] The improved tactics and techniques which the gunners had spent so long in perfecting were now being used in anger and, from the start, Eighth Army's artillery was able to assert its superiority.

Meanwhile, 1st Armoured Division also failed to break out of the mine-fields. As the armour advanced up to them, the situation ahead was very confused. The 10th Hussars received word from their liaison officer, attached to the 1st Gordons, that the infantry was held up by a strongpoint and their leading two companies were out of touch. The liaison officer also claimed 'that they could go no farther that night'.[95] The reconnaissance troop confirmed the lack of movement. The armoured regiments were faced with a difficult decision. First light was fast approaching and the regimental groups were 'still in column nose to tail and hemmed in by minefields'.[96] To push on without knowing whether gaps had been made in the next minefields 'was likely to end in disaster'. If the regiments simply halted, they would be 'strung out along a single track in daylight', yet to deploy where they stood also risked heavy losses from mines.[97] Lieutenant-Colonel Archer-Shee of the 10th Hussars had decided to press the attack when he received orders from Briggs to deploy on the ground his regiment occupied. It was the right thing to do. As the sun came up, anti-tank gun fire became 'hot' but with the sun at their backs the 10th Hussars managed to avoid casualties by skilful manoeuvring.[98]

It did not take long before the Axis reaction to Eighth Army's offensive became apparent. By 23.00 hours on 23 October, the Afrika Korps had managed to alert all units even in the face of communication difficulties. It soon became clear that the front held by the three battalions of 62nd Infantry Regiment, Trento Division, and I Battalion of the 382nd Panzergrenadier Regiment of 164th Light Division had been overrun. Early the next morning,

Stumme assessed the situation and decided upon a counterattack. During the morning, the central and southern battlegroups of the 15th Panzer Division and the Littorio Division were committed to 'counter-attack and regain the main defence line'.[99]

The armoured brigades on the Miteiriya ridge were deployed in sound hull-down positions when the southern battlegroup of 15th Panzer Division came into the attack. The survivors of the Royal Wilts saw a mass of German and Italian tanks in one large column which moved up and down in front of the British armour's positions: 'For several hours these massed tanks "swan" up and down as a moving target for gunners', which they did without pressing home their attack.[100]

In the northern sector, 2nd Armoured Brigade noted that, by 08.20 hours, the Bays were 'engaging 20 enemy tanks at 3,000 yards range'.[101] 10th Hussars also engaged these tanks, noting that at least one was a Mk IV 'Special'. However, when the panzers advanced they were 'obviously surprised by our new tank guns with greater effective range [and] they turned away north-wards across our front'.[102] These first engagements fought on 24 October between the battlegroups of 15th Panzer Division and the British armoured brigades were of profound tactical significance. The 24th Armoured Brigade report later commented:

> His tanks seemed usually to open fire at about 2000x, halting to shoot. His fire at that range did not penetrate. Our own gunners were repeatedly drawn into opening fire at that range too. The German tanks started to get knocked out at 1500x or so and when several had been knocked out, the rest withdrew, even when numerous.[103]

It was an established part of the Afrika Korps battle drill to open fire at maximum range. For almost two years, German tank crews had been accustomed to engaging British tanks at an advantage. In the past, long-range fire had often goaded British tanks into a hasty and costly advance. On the morning after Lightfoot, the German tank crews had expected their well-tried tactics to work but the balance of advantage had now shifted against them. 1st Armoured Division reported that the '75mm on the Sherman is as good or better than any German tank gun and with good gunners there is nothing to be feared from the German tanks'.[104] Now the British tank crews could expect to win every long-range duel. Moreover, the German battle drill, which had worked successfully for so long, could not be changed in the middle of a fierce battle.

While the 88mm gun remained deadly, it began to lose at least some of its tactical advantage. A Sherman crew was able, due to its improved sights, to lob high-explosive shells accurately to beyond 2,000 yards. Under favourable circumstances, therefore, armoured regiments could deal with 88mm guns once they were spotted. The Desert Air Force's bombing runs also had an important tactical effect on the ground battle. The force broke its own records with 1,000 fighter and bomber sorties recorded during 24 October. The light bomber force flew 274 sorties over the northern sector of the battlefield but met intensive anti-aircraft fire; three aircraft were shot down and 27 badly damaged.[105] As the flights of 18 Boston bombers went overhead, 'up went the barrels of the 88's to engage our bombers, and this gave our tank commanders their opportunity to engage a number of guns previously unlocated'.[106] The 75mm fire from the Shermans was thickened by the accompanying Royal Horse Artillery troops of self-propelled 105mm guns. For the first time, the air and ground effort were directly linked even though the effect was unplanned.

Indeed, there was in many respects more tactical cooperation, however fortuitous, between the bombers of the Desert Air Force and the armour than there was between the tanks and the infantry. Once the infantry had dug in and secured their positions with their supporting weapons, there was little they could do apart from wait. To move about in the open simply brought down heavy fire on the position. The infantrymen could do little to assist the tanks with their combat and so 'this battle was fought, as it were, over the heads of the infantry . . . Though shelled and mortared, and sometimes under machine gun fire, they were spectators of what, to them, was a new kind of warfare.'[107] Many of the infantry battalions had to endure heavy shelling and suffered casualties from 'overs' – armour piercing rounds meant for tanks that hit slit trenches instead. The infantry commanders raced about in scout cars, dodging fire, as they attempted to plan further operations for the next night to 'improve' their positions. The infantry and armour continued to fight two separate battles on the same ground.

It is not surprising that the situation led to confusion. Fierce arguments began over map reading between the staffs of 51st (Highland) Division and 1st Armoured Division. 51st (Highland) Division recorded, 'It has been significant, ever since the morning of the 24th, how difficult it has been for troops to know exactly where they are in this featureless country.'[108] The main argument concerned the location of the 'Kidney feature'.[109] This was a kidney-shaped ring contour which was marked on Eighth Army's maps as a rise but which in fact was, and is, a very shallow – and almost imperceptible – depression in the desert. Arguments arose because the 1st Gordon's final objective for Lightfoot, the strongpoint known as 'Aberdeen' lay across the Kidney feature.

Wimberley had a very heated argument with Fisher that morning concerning the location of his troops. The artillery grids used by the two divisions varied by 1,000 yards. This meant that the armour insisted that the forward troops of 1st Gordons were 'not in Aberdeen at all but in Stirling. They further insisted that the two enemy localities [named by 1st Armoured Division] Snipe and Woodcock were far further east than they in fact were.'[110]

Wimberley did not take kindly to these assertions and what he saw as an accusation that the Gordons had not 'done their stuff'.[111] Although the Highland Division had paced out its advance on compass bearings from its start lines and were confident that they were correct, Wimberley noted 'in that waste of sand with few features, and a battle raging, it was not easy to be dogmatic'.[112] In fact, the Highland Division was correct. The arguments had profound tactical repercussions; for most of the battle 1st Armoured Division was 1,000 yards off in its map reading.

Given these disagreements it is not surprising that it took time for the divisional and corps commanders to sort out why the armour had failed to break out. By 10.27 hours, Freyberg learned that Lumsden had 'decided against going forward'[113] and Montgomery later stated:

> I began to form the impression at about 1100 hours that there was a lack of 'drive' and pep in the action of 10 Corps. I saw Herbert Lumsden and impressed on him the urgent need to get his armoured divisions out into the open where they could manoeuvre, and that they must get clear of the minefield area.[114]

Montgomery did not seem to recognise that the armoured divisions were still hemmed in by the minefields and that the application of more 'drive' and 'pep' might simply result in large numbers of disabled tanks. Just after midday, Leese spoke to Montgomery from the New Zealand Division Headquarters. Montgomery's version of events was that he issued verbal orders to both corps commanders with the following plan:

1. To get 1 Armd Div and 10 Armd Div out into the open as soon as possible. This to take priority of everything else. The whole artillery resources of 30 Corps to be used to assist.
2. The N.Z. Div to begin its move to the South-West, and its 'crumbling' operations as soon as possible. This to be the next priority.
3. 30 Corps to put in a strong battalion raid Westwards from the RUWEISAT Ridge on night 24/25 October.
4. 13 Corps to break through the second enemy minefield and into open country on night 24/25 October.[115]

However, the verbatim account provided by Freyberg's diary suggests a less one-way briefing. Leese had ordered Freyberg to meet with Gatehouse and Briggs and had already formulated a corps plan of attack even before he spoke to Montgomery. He then spoke to Montgomery on the telephone and informed him that 'B. [Bernard Freyberg] is confident he could get on. . . . He thinks he could go well through provided one of Gatehouse's bdes goes with him.' Leese felt that Gatehouse's 'main preoccupation is to get 10 Armd Div into position to receive attack from someone else'.[116] He explained to

Montgomery that he had placed the whole of 30 Corps artillery at Freyberg's disposal and suggested:

> that under smoke they try and do something later in day . . . Shall I send word that it is your wish providing it is feasible that they break out with support of whole Corps arty . . . You want them to get into position so that they can manoeuvre on the far side of M. Ridge.[117]

Thus, Leese developed the core ideas for the next attempt by the armour and simply referred to Montgomery for confirmation. While the plan appears in Montgomery's diary as entirely his idea, it is obvious that Leese was acting exactly as a good corps commander should. Lumsden then arrived and discussed the plan with Leese. He felt:

> question is whether you are going to sit down and accept static phase or whether we go for it baldheaded. We may get through to where his guns are now. It is a tremendous decision. If we don't do it the battle just fizzes out.[118]

This exchange suggests that, although Lumsden understood the need for caution, he was not perhaps as 'sticky' as often portrayed. Through these discussions, the eventual details of the plan were thrashed out. 10th Armoured Division was to advance over the Miteiriya ridge with its two armoured brigades and reach the 'Pierson' line, which had been the original objective for the previous night. Meanwhile, the 133rd Lorried Infantry Brigade would take over the positions of the 5th New Zealand Infantry Brigade on the ridge to act as a 'pivot of manoeuvre'. 9th Armoured Brigade would assist in the operation by advancing on the left of 8th Armoured Brigade. The advance would be supported by 300 guns drawn from the 10th Armoured, 2nd New Zealand and 51st (Highland) Divisions along with 30 Corps medium artillery.[119]

Montgomery's application of 'ginger' to Lumsden certainly worked its way down the command chain in 1st Armoured Division. That afternoon, at 15.25 hours, Briggs ordered Brigadier Frank Fisher 'to push on as fast as [you] can'.[120] No doubt mindful of Montgomery's explicit order that the armour had to fight its own way forward Fisher ordered his regiments to 'drive straight through whatever the casualties'.[121] After checking that the orders were correct, C Squadron of the 9th Lancers drove forward into an uncleared minefield:

> On the skyline could now be seen the grey shapes of approaching German tanks, and a considerable amount of small-arms and anti-tank gun fire began to come down, followed by the ugly sizzle of 88-mm shells.[122]

Lieutenant Thwaites, one of the leading troop commanders, got out of his tank and led his troop forward on foot while kicking mines out of the way until he was ordered to stop. Lieutenant Agate's troop was preceded by sappers from 1st Field Squadron Royal Engineers, who managed to clear a path through the minefield. Once the two troops had weaved their way through the minefield, they drove towards the high ground. Even when Agate's tank was hit and burning, the crew continued to fire at the distant German tanks until specifically ordered to leave the burning turret. C Squadron eventually reached the crest where it was joined by the rest of the regiment. Twelve enemy tanks were knocked out at a cost of four Shermans.[123] Although Montgomery believed that more 'drive' would have seen 1st Armoured through the minefields it is clear that the armoured regiments were fighting as hard as they could under extremely difficult conditions. They knew, even if Montgomery could not admit it, that to drive through uncleared minefields under intense anti-tank gun fire would lead to large numbers of burning tanks – and immolated crewmen – for little gain.

Wimberley was the only infantry commander to order a daylight attack that day. The 2nd Seaforths made a 'gallant daylight attack'[124] to take 'Stirling', going forward almost a mile in the bright afternoon sunshine with no artillery or tank support. The soldiers advanced at a 'slow methodical pace' with their rifles at the high port. Captain Allan Gilmour remembered:

> After a few yards, the trouble started. The first thing we knew was a long-range machine-gun opening up . . . jocks started dropping but the company still just carried on. At the foot of the final slope nearing the top, the fire became very heavy and there were a lot of casualties. The jocks went to ground.[125]

The battalion held onto its gains just short of 'Stirling' and repulsed a German counterattack that night. The men then had to hang on throughout the rest of the next day under heavy fire.[126] This costly daylight assault did help the 9th Lancers to push forward but during the day it was clearly best to leave the fighting to the armour, anti-tank guns and artillery. It was only at night that the infantry battalions came into their own again.

As the sun set on the first day of battle, it was plain that Operation Lightfoot had not gone entirely according to plan. 30 Corps had achieved considerable success in seizing its bridgehead and even though 10 Corps had not broken out, the armoured brigades had held and deterred every Axis counterattack. The fact remained that unless further progress could be made, the battle would indeed just 'fizz' out. Eighth Army had reached the limits of the original programme and its commanders were being forced to improvise. During Lightfoot, Eighth Army had proved that it could produce a well-conducted orchestral movement but it remained to be seen whether it could now invent the next crucial step.

SIXTEEN

Battle Without Hope

Still no sleep since the show commenced,
this pace cannot last something will crack[1]

Late in the evening of 24 October 1942, a small piece of buff-coloured paper landed on Churchill's desk. The blue typescript was headed 'VERY SECRET' in red at the top of the form; this document came from Bletchley Park. That particular piece of paper carried much more significant information than many of the decrypts which Churchill received: 'Report by Fliegerfuehrer at 1400 hours. General Stumme has been wounded and probably taken prisoner.'[2] The decoders at Bletchley Park had become so proficient in their decryption of high-priority messages that the German High Command in Berlin received the news that Stumme was missing less than twelve hours before Churchill did.

That morning, Stumme had left Panzerarmee Headquarters with Colonel Buechting, the Chief Signal Officer, to 'form a personal impression of the enemy penetration at Minefield L' in the Australian sector.[3] Stumme was just about to get out of his staff car when it was fired upon. Buechting was shot through the head and Corporal Wolf, the driver, panicked. He turned the car around and drove off at full speed with Stumme clinging on to the side. Stumme suffered a heart attack and fell off. When the driver returned to headquarters, Stumme was missing and his body was not found until the following day.[4] The Panzerarmee Afrika was without a commander. General der Panzertruppe Ritter von Thoma, commander of the Afrika Korps, took over temporary command. Although he knew that the British had begun a major offensive, von Thoma decided that large-scale counterattacks were not yet necessary and believed that the local counterattacks by 15th Panzer Division might well be enough to seal off the penetration.[5] He also expected that the British would launch another major attack that night and wanted to wait before committing any reserves.

However, the confusion and delay that beset the Panzerarmee with Stumme's death helps to explain why the northern panzer battlegroups failed to press home their attacks. The customary daily report sent to Berlin gave a misleading impression as it suggested that, although the British had 'succeeded in penetrating the main battle line in several places' over a 10 kilometre front, by that evening 'the line was almost all in our hands again'. While the rations of the army were not a cause for worry, and ammunition stocks were 'sufficient for 8 to 10 days fighting' the German forces had only three consumption units of fuel in Africa and one of those was in Benghazi. The report noted that, 'if the tanker due to arrive on the 26th fails to arrive there will be a serious crisis. The Italian fuel situation is already very precarious.'[6] The joint air and naval effort in the Mediterranean had achieved its purpose even before the guns at El Alamein opened fire.

When the German High Command received the report, which also suggested that the British attack would 'be strongly renewed along the whole front' the next day, Hitler ordered Rommel to return to Egypt immediately. Eighth Army had suffered a 'fortnight of confusion' when Auchinleck was replaced but this had occurred during an exceptionally quiet period. The Panzerarmee suffered its interregnum in the middle of intense fighting. Stumme's death gave Eighth Army the most precious commodity in the middle of a battle: time.

Dusk on 24 October saw both armies prepare for another night of fighting. In the south, 13 Corps prepared to make another effort to breach the 'February' minefield, while 4th Indian Division organised itself for another raid along the Ruweisat ridge. Further north, the battalions of 51st (Highland) Division mounted a series of small company and even platoon-sized attacks to take the final objective line. They were of limited effectiveness. These small, piecemeal attacks, messy and confused affairs, were fought by men who were already exhausted from the battle the night before and the long day of constant shelling and sniping. The extended frontage of 51st (Highland) Division offered more problems, placing great strain on the forward battalions. It was not until the night of 26 October that the division finally reached its original objective line along its full length.

At the same time as the Highlanders were making these small-scale attacks, 20th Australian Brigade made a further advance to reach its final Lightfoot objective. The attack was to have been made under the cover of a repeat of the original artillery programme for this attack but patrols which went out after dark on 24 October found little opposition and the advance was made silently. Both the 2/17th and 2/13th Battalions reached their objectives against only sporadic resistance and were able to dig in to their new positions without difficulty. This did not mean that the attack was without some bitter incidents. At one point, the tanks of 40th Royal Tank Regiment mistook the Australian infantry, digging into their new positions, for Germans and opened fire on the soldiers they were meant to support.[7] However, the advance meant that the sappers could also complete their task and they proceeded to finish four tracks up to the final objective as well as a lateral track to link them together.[8] Just before dawn the next day, the 7th

Rifle Brigade of 1st Armoured Division, which was new to the desert,
arrived amongst their new positions in 'columns of lumps'.[9] The riflemen
could not disperse their large numbers of soft vehicles amongst the minefields and soon drew hostile fire. The mass of vehicles proved to be an
'obvious and vulnerable target. Shelling was heavy and accurate.'[10] The
Australians found:

> the carnage terrible to watch. The Diggers were sorry for the Tommies but
> cursed them for drawing the crabs. Soon there were dozens of shattered
> burning vehicles, and dead and wounded soldiers littering the desert.[11]

Even after intensive training, inexperience could lead to expensive mistakes.
The costly deployment of 7th Rifle Brigade also showed the difficulties in
coordination arising when two separate corps attempted to deploy and
advance through the same patch of desert.

Meanwhile, on the evening of 24 October, 10th Armoured Division
made preparations to get beyond the Miteiriya ridge once more. At last
light, 9th Armoured Brigade withdrew to replenish and reorganise before
moving up in support behind 10th Armoured Division; the seven remaining
tanks of the Wiltshire Yeomanry were handed over and the regiment withdrawn.[12] The minefields confronting the 24th Armoured Brigade were
found to be deeper than expected and considerable confusion developed
over the routes. It was not until 03.45 hours that one gap had been cut
and it took yet more time to report this back to headquarters. Meanwhile,
the advance of 8th Armoured Brigade had got underway at 22.00 hours
but, soon after, disaster struck the Sherwood Rangers on the centre gap.
Just as its tanks and soft transport were passing through the narrow minefield gaps which had been cleared by the sappers, a stick of bombs, dropped
by a circling Ju88 bomber, fell on the column moving up the 'Boat' track:
'The fires and explosions which followed set alight to about 25 vehicles
which formed a huge conflagration thereby giving the enemy a good aiming
mark for further raids.'[13] A number of Ju88 bombers had flown over from
Crete that evening and, although they were flying singly looking for targets,
the large fire from the burning lorries soon attracted more of them, along
with hostile artillery fire. As the Sherwood Rangers' historian pointed out,
the ridge:

> was a highly uncomfortable place that night. In the din of battle you couldn't
> hear the bombers coming, and the first you knew was an almighty roar as one
> dropped near you. Streams of tracer fire of all kinds sped through the night.[14]

The Sherwood Rangers and 3rd Royal Tank Regiment, which were following
them through, had no alternative but to disperse their vehicles as quickly

as possible. Custance, 'in view of the possibility of an enemy attack following the bombing', ordered these two regiments to reform on their original positions back behind the ridge. This bombing raid was the only real success of the Luftwaffe during the early stage of the battle. The Stuka dive bombers had been hardly present over the battlefield due to the fact that there were barely 20 serviceable fighters to escort them.[15] Yet the disproportionate effect of these few Ju88 bombers demonstrated just how difficult, if not impossible, Eighth Army's offensive would have been without the air superiority that had been won by the Desert Air Force.

Meanwhile, the Staffordshire Yeomanry managed to pass through the second minefield gap without incident and pushed on towards 'Pierson'. 9th Armoured Brigade, after reorganising, had pushed up to the ridge again by midnight, where it came upon:

> a scene of considerable confusion, 8th Armd Bde formed up in close formation to pass through the gap had been bombed and there was a mass of burning vehicles. It was difficult to find the gap and no one seemed to know what was happening.[16]

Currie took matters into his own hands and, after a personal reconnaissance, found the gap and passed his regiments through. As the regiments moved forward they took 150 German prisoners including a battalion commander and his staff. The tanks linked up with the Staffordshire Yeomanry and waited for daylight.

It is not surprising that, with 24th Armoured Brigade completely held up, and two of his own regiments now in disorganised chaos, Custance believed that his brigade's advance should be abandoned. Gatehouse agreed and asked Lumsden for approval who, in turn, spoke to de Guingand. Montgomery's Chief of Staff had also been receiving worrying reports from liaison officers and he decided that 'this was an occasion when the Army Commander must intervene'.[17] De Guingand called Leese and Lumsden to a conference at Eighth Army Tactical Headquarters at 03.30 hours. Meanwhile, in the absence of any confirmation to withdraw, Custance had sent 3rd Royal Tank Regiment and the Sherwood Rangers forward again to link up with the Staffordshire Yeomanry.

De Guingand commented, '3.30 a.m. is not a good time to hold a conference'.[18] As reported at the time, Montgomery and de Guingand believed the situation to be that 24th Armoured Brigade was clearing its gaps and was 'hopeful of getting through by daylight'; 8th Armoured Brigade was 'somewhat disorganised by heavy shelling and bombing but would follow later'; and 9th Armoured Brigade was through the gap and moving towards the south west.[19] Montgomery believed:

the situation was developing as well as could be expected, and that there was a great need for determination and resolution, and that he was quite decided that the original Army plan of battle should be proceeded with.[20]

De Guingand felt that Montgomery's decision not to alter his plan was 'a brave one' and that, without this conference, the 'attack might well have fizzled out'.[21]

During these discussions, it would appear that Montgomery spoke to Gatehouse over a field telephone. There are two versions of the following conversation and they are diametrically opposed. Montgomery claimed that he was horrified to learn that Gatehouse's main headquarters was 16,000 yards behind the front and that he spoke to Gatehouse 'in no uncertain voice, and ordered him to go forward at once and take charge of his battle; he was to fight his way out, and lead his division from in front and not from behind'.[22]

Gatehouse had kept his main divisional headquarters far back to avoid yet more congestion at the front but this did not mean that he had not been leading from the front with his tactical headquarters. He claimed he had pointed out to Lumsden when given the orders in the evening that he considered them 'so suicidal and stupid that I must refuse to obey such an order'. He claimed that he then telephoned Montgomery himself and that Montgomery 'ordered me to carry out this operation with ONE Armd. Regt'.[23] Montgomery may well have emphasised his determination to keep to his original plan in discussions with Lumsden and Leese but this was not the result on the ground. In fact, both Montgomery and Gatehouse appear to provide garbled versions of the actual decisions. Lumsden returned from Montgomery's 'crisis' conference and engaged in an hour-long discussion with Gatehouse. Throughout this period the forward brigades had no orders. At 03.50 hours, 10th Armoured Division Headquarters noted:

> Corps Comd's decision had already been sought as to whether it was not adviseable to withdraw to original posn but although this had been asked for some three hours previously no decision was yet forthcoming.[24]

Far from Lumsden insisting that Montgomery's original orders had to be carried out, the result of the telephone conversation was that:

> orders were given to 8 Armd Bde to maintain one regt forward (Staffs Yeo) with role protection and contact west flank of 9 Armd Bde. Meanwhile to improve the gap in minefields behind them so as to allow movement backwards and forwards.[25]

This was exactly the kind of compromise solution that had bedevilled Eighth Army in the past. However, improving the minefield gap was of critical importance because, without a secure route to the new position, the forward tanks would not be able to resupply.

Meanwhile, unaware of the higher level discussions, the armoured regiments of 8th Armoured Brigade had continued their advance. By 05.00 hours, 3rd Royal Tank Regiment had managed to drive forward along the 'Bottle' route and could see the Staffordshire Yeomanry 1,000 yards ahead.[26] However, the forward tanks of the Staffordshire Yeomanry:

> came under heavy fire at some 300–400yds range from enemy A. Tk guns which the tanks crews were quite unable to see. Heavy casualties ensued and the C.O. ordered a slight withdrawal. The tanks hit however burst into flames immediately they were hit and again provided a beacon for enemy aircraft which caused further casualties.[27]

This situation was 'an unforgettable nightmare never to be erased from the memory of all those present'.[28] The Sherman tank had one major flaw: the majority of its ammunition was stored in lightly armoured bins in the turret. If the turret received a direct hit the ammunition inside invariably exploded with fatal consequences.[29] The Germans nicknamed the tank the 'Tommy cooker' while its own crews soon began to call it the 'Ronson' because, like the cigarette lighter, it lit first time. 3rd Royal Tank Regiment noted that the position was not a good one, with no hull-down positions available, and no further reconnaissance was possible. Custance ordered his units to incur 'no unnecessary casualties' and at 06.00 hours, orders were received from division to reoccupy the original positions on the Miteiriya ridge.[30]

This sudden movement to the rear confused 9th Armoured Brigade. It rapidly found itself alone when it saw 3rd Royal Tank Regiment 'suddenly and for no apparent reason' turn round and retire 'rapidly through the rear elements' of the brigade.[31] 24th Armoured Brigade did not encounter this confusion and had finally managed to push its way through the gaps. Although the regiments believed that they had reached 'Pierson' they were in fact little more than 1,000 yards in front of the ridge.[32]

Thus, Montgomery's 'crisis' conference had hardly had the effect that he desired. The whole of 10 Corps was not 'out in the open' by 08.00 hours as he later claimed.[33] Perhaps the greatest irony of the situation was that even the armoured regiments which did remain in the open beyond the Miteiriya ridge did not have the shattering effect that Montgomery had envisaged. 24th Armoured Brigade found that the two regiments 'forward of the ridge engaged enemy tanks at long range, silenced some A.Tk guns near, [and] killed numbers of enemy inf in the area'. However, with no hull-down positions available and no resupply possible, the tanks were unable to achieve any more decisive effect. The brigade had open flanks and was:

under long range arty and tank fire all day, they maintained their posn, using smoke, such movement as was possible in the minefields forward and by mutual support, did useful work and suffered very few casualties.[34]

24th Armoured Brigade's actions were certainly skilful but did not represent the hoped-for break-out. Further north, 9th Armoured Brigade was also isolated and fought:

an abortive action . . . throughout the day . . . It was not possible to find any reasonable battle position in the area and the Brigade was in a very exposed position from the WEST. No reasonable targets were presented, gun flashes, enemy posts and Tks. were engaged at long range. The continual shelling took a heavy toll.[35]

Late in the afternoon, Currie finally persuaded Freyberg that 'no useful purpose was being served' and was allowed to withdraw his brigade to its previous positions behind the ridge. Currie still believed that a real opportunity had been missed to make a 'vigorous thrust SOUTH and S.W.' that morning but the withdrawal of 8th Armoured Brigade had made that impossible.[36] In fact, it seems likely that even if all the armour had remained out in the open, little more could have been achieved. Any major push towards the south west would have taken the brigades away from their umbilical cord of soft transport. As dusk fell the armoured brigades would have been forced to withdraw towards the Miteiriya ridge. The armour might have taken more ground during the day but they could not have held it.

Meanwhile, at first light, in the northern corridor 2nd Armoured Brigade had attempted to push further west. The Queen's Bays and the 9th Lancers soon came under fire from an anti-tank gun screen 'which seemed to include a large proportion of 88-mm guns'.[37] Since the guns could not be spotted, both regiments halted but not before six Shermans of the Bays were left burning. The brigade could take no further action during the morning, although one gunner of the 9th Lancers knocked out a lone Mk IV at over 4,000 yards range; this was considered by the regiment to have been 'the best shot of the whole war'.[38] One squadron of 10th Hussars also indulged in indirect shooting with armour-piercing shot against tanks. The regiment had experimented with this technique during training and found that the relatively high trajectory of the American 75mm gun mounted in the Sherman made indirect fire possible:[39]

The tank comd had his tank some way back from a low ridge and he himself stood on the top of the tank from which he could see the target. He then engaged the target giving fire orders in the same way as for H.E. shooting. The result of this was that he knocked out and burnt five German tanks in the course of one afternoon for an average of about six rounds per tank. During this proceeding his own tank was not liable to enemy fire.[40]

Thus, while the higher commanders engaged in fierce argument about the armour not being in the 'open', the tank regiments were being highly inventive and engaging their opponents with a 'considerable measure of success'.[41] At the same time, these long-range gunnery duels were detested by the infantry because the presence of tanks within their defences brought down heavy retaliatory shelling.

2nd Armoured Brigade continued to suffer from considerable confusion about its location. In the morning, the brigade reported that, although it had previously thought it had reached the 'Pierson' line, it now found that it was much further east. 7th Rifle Brigade had linked up with its parent formation during the morning. In the early afternoon, an Axis battlegroup of 40 tanks, formed from a mix of Italian M.13s and German Mk IIIs, drove 'suddenly from behind a ridge with the dust blowing in front of them', crossed the front of the brigade and attacked the positions of 7th Rifle Brigade.[42] After their bitter experience that morning, the riflemen put up determined resistance in the face of an actual attack. As the riflemen 'kept up a continuous and accurate stream of small-arms fire' to keep the attacking tanks buttoned up, the crews of the six-pounder anti-tank guns began to take their toll.[43] The battalion knocked out at least 14 tanks and forced the rest to withdraw into the dust.

Meanwhile, Fisher had held a conference to discuss ways of helping '10 H to get forward'.[44] It was decided to push forwards C Squadron of the 10th Hussars, with the support of five batteries of the divisional artillery, to reach the ridge in front of the brigade. When reports were received that the situation in front of 24th Armoured Brigade was 'critical', C Squadron went forward through the minefield towards the Kidney feature to divert attention. The squadron believed that it had reached the objective but, when the artillery support ceased, five tanks were knocked out in a matter of minutes by 88mm guns. The survivors were forced to withdraw under the cover of a renewed artillery bombardment.[45]

Soon afterwards, 55 panzers came into the attack with the setting sun behind them, but met with no success. 2nd Armoured Brigade had spent the day fighting a series of confusing tank battles but still faced severe difficulties, being hemmed in by minefields. Losses, particularly amongst the valuable Shermans, were mounting.[46] However, the rate of attrition remained in Eighth Army's favour. The brigade claimed to have knocked out 39 enemy tanks that day.[47]

Eighth Army had already achieved far more than during any of the July attacks but Montgomery's plans were being frustrated by the realities of the situation on the ground. During the morning, Lumsden went to see Freyberg and their discussion on the possibilities of launching the projected 'crumbling' attack by the New Zealand Division was revealing. There were real difficulties in relieving the 5th New Zealand Brigade with the 133rd Lorried Infantry Brigade and Freyberg was adamant that a firm hold had to be maintained on the Miteiriya ridge because 'if he gets observation he will make things very nasty'.[48] Freyberg believed the answer was to 'get the armour together and fight a battle' but the results of the previous night had made that impossible. Lumsden remarked:

> Playing with armour is like playing with fire. You have got to take your time with it. It is like a duel. If you don't take your time you will get run through the guts. It is not for tanks to take on guns.[49]

Certainly, the caution displayed by 15th Panzer Division the day before suggested that the armour of both armies were still sparring rather than engaging in a close fight. Lumsden's arguments, and the experience of the armoured brigades that day, revealed the fundamental disagreement between Montgomery and his armour commanders. Montgomery believed that, once through the minefields, the armour would be able to use its combat power to full effect. However, the experience of the armour commanders had taught them of the danger of German anti-tank gun screens even in open country and they believed that only infantry, supported by artillery, could clear away the screen thus enabling the armour to manoeuvre.

At the same time, Lumsden knew that his armoured divisions 'must produce something constructive' but he also stated that 'I don't think the attack south is on. I never wanted it.' Freyberg responded with 'I very much agree.'[50] He knew that his division could only make one more set-piece attack and that this would ruin it for a mobile role in exploitation. Yet the 'crumbling' attacks by 2nd New Zealand Division, which were to have been launched south once the Miteiriya ridge had been taken, were an integral part of Montgomery's original plan. It was significant that, just as Lumsden had not fully explained his objections about the armour's role in the plan to Montgomery, so Freyberg had not entirely aired his misgivings about the projected 'crumbling' attacks to be launched by his division.

By this time, the 13 Corps effort in the south had been called off. It was not surprising that the ill-resourced attempts of 7th Armoured Division to penetrate beyond the 'February' minefield failed. The defence, comprising the Folgore Division and elements of the Ramcke Brigade, was fully alert and observation from Himeimat precluded any attempt at surprise. At 22.30 hours, the 1/5th and 1/6th Queen's from 131st Brigade attacked under a barrage in an attempt to form two small infantry bridgeheads beyond the 700-yard deep 'February' minefield. The two battalions managed to follow the barrage over the 2,400-yard advance but suffered heavy casualties from anti-personnel mines and found the whole area 'swept by intense fire'.[51] The attack was simply too limited to unlock the Axis defences and the two battalions were soon pinned down under heavy fire just 400 yards beyond the minefield. The two leading armoured regiments, 1st Royal Tank Regiment and 4th County of London Yeomanry, then attempted to pass through the narrow gaps cleared by the sappers. Unfortunately, they made perfect targets for the Axis gunners whose anti-tank guns enfiladed the gaps. Most of the leading tanks were knocked out at close range. Harding decided to postpone the venture until daylight when it was hoped that artillery support could silence the Italian anti-tank guns. By daylight, it was clear that Axis fire was so intense that any renewed attempt would be very costly.

Just as Custance had done, Harding asked for confirmation of his decision to abandon the attempt but he met with an entirely different response. Horrocks reported Harding's request to Montgomery and asked whether further casualties could be accepted. Montgomery said, 'No, and that 7 Armd Div must remain in being on the Southern flank.'[52] The forward tanks of the 22nd Armoured Brigade remained between the 'February' and 'January' minefields supporting the remnants of the two Queen's battalions who had to remain in position throughout that day. The survivors remembered this as 'a terrible experience as they were on a forward slope and in full view of the enemy positions, sometimes less than a hundred yards away'.[53] The following night, the remnants withdrew as best they could until heavy fire halted them. Some small groups, which found it impossible to retire, were captured. Any attempt to break through on the 13 Corps front was now abandoned, although units still had to make large-scale raids to maintain the illusion of a threat.

A few days later Horrocks told Roberts, 'You know you could have got through there if you had really tried.'[54] Just like Montgomery, Horrocks was a firm believer in the importance of 'drive' and 'pep'. Unlike his corps commander however, Roberts understood what happened when tanks were confronted with well-positioned anti-tank guns. This was the fundamental misunderstanding between the armour and infantry in Eighth Army; infantry commanders believed that, with willpower, any objective could be assaulted successfully. Eighth Army's infantry battalions had demonstrated this ability in night attack after night attack. However, the armoured commanders also knew that no amount of willpower could silence a web of anti-tank guns or protect tanks against hidden mines. The armoured battle was a far more technological contest where willpower and bravery remained important but technical superiority mattered far more than it did in the infantry. Horrocks was, of course, bitter about the fact that his corps would now fulfil a largely passive role. Although the 44th and 50th Divisions continued to mount large-scale raids in the southern sector, units were now stripped from 13 Corps to supply troops for the fighting in the north. Horrocks' 13 Corps was eventually reduced to just six brigades of infantry holding a front of 28 miles.

With his battle plan unravelling before his eyes, Montgomery held a conference with Leese, Lumsden and Freyberg at the New Zealand Division's Headquarters at noon. Montgomery clearly realised that his original plan would no longer work and decided that 'exploitation is off'.[55] Freyberg urged Montgomery:

> to put in another timed bombardment with infantry attacking as before to a depth of about 4000 yards to push him off his guns. They could have had the tanks following behind. We could have been clear of his minefields . . . The armour would then have to fight. Thought it was better to face another 500 casualties to each Division and use our guns which is our great asset to whack him.

This idea eventually grew into Operation Supercharge. A Soviet commander would have recognised this argument as the need for a 'second echelon' which could deepen and then penetrate an existing breach. Once again, the limitations placed on British operations by the absence of any higher level doctrine for the conduct of breakthrough battles were only too apparent. Montgomery had no 'second echelon' because his entire *corps de chasse* had been committed on the first night and there were no reserve formations which could put in a fresh set-piece attack on 25 October.

The lack of reserves to exploit success, which had been one of Auchinleck's main complaints in July, was now afflicting Montgomery. While there were strong arguments in favour for a renewed infantry assault this could now only be mounted by the divisions that were already engaged. This meant that such an attack would take time to organise and might well allow the Panzerarmee to recover from its initial shock. It was now clear that 13 Corps operations in the south had failed and that any 'crumbling' operations launched from the Miteiriya ridge 'would be a most costly undertaking';[56] the entire offensive might stall. Montgomery needed to keep up the pressure on the Panzerarmee and could not wait before launching a further set-piece attack.

Montgomery's decisions were clearly influenced by his subordinates but they were nonetheless of great importance in shaping the battle. The New Zealand Division was now 'NOT to operate S.W.' from the Miteiriya ridge.[57] The 'crumbling' attacks would instead be directed northwards to the coast by 9th Australian Division. 10th Armoured Division, with the exception of 24th Armoured Brigade, which would join 1st Armoured Division, was to be withdrawn but 1st Armoured Division's task remained the same: to break out of the minefields. The thinking behind these decisions was obvious. While 2nd New Zealand Division was a one-shot weapon and 51st (Highland) Division was committed to an extensive frontage that precluded it from mounting any serious attack, 9th Australian Division had suffered relatively few casualties and was physically concentrated. Under the original plan, 9th Australian Division had been tasked with preparing to launch 'crumbling' attacks to the north under the shield of 1st Armoured Division. In the absence of any viable alternative, Montgomery was forced to order the Australians to work 'Northwards towards the coast' without the protection of the armour. The skill and experience of the Australian units, which had made their attack and consolidation during Lightfoot so successful, meant that they would now face the toughest task of any division at Alamein: to fight northwards through the teeth of Axis resistance. Montgomery hoped that this change in the axis of attack would 'catch the enemy unawares'.[58]

Montgomery was, quite unwittingly, outthinking the staff of the Panzerarmee. Kesselring, von Thoma and Westphal, the acting Chief of Staff, held a conference at the Panzerarmee Battle Headquarters soon after Montgomery's meeting. They decided that the penetration had to be 'sealed off'. The Italian 21 Corps was to attack from the south while 15th Panzer Division would attack from the north.[59] The Australian attack towards the coast was to derail such plans. Kesselring was reminded of the desperate supply situation; von Thoma begged for more air support. The fighters of the Desert Air Force now ruled the skies and on 25 October many of the fighter patrols flew directly over the Axis landing grounds at El Daba. The lack of enemy fighter activity meant that a growing number of fighters were able to act as fighter bombers. No. 208 (Army Cooperation) Squadron was able to make all five of its vital tactical reconnaissance flights over the battlefield without escort on 25 October.[60] The light bomber force maintained a relentless 'milk run' of bombing attacks against the Panzerarmee during the day while the Wellingtons and Albacores continued the pounding during the night. The Luftwaffe did rush units forward from Sicily and Crete into North Africa but the hard truth was that the air battle had already been lost.

What was worse, from von Thoma's perspective, was that every attempt to seal off the penetration that day had failed. Montgomery wrote in his diary that three enemy counterattacks had been beaten off that afternoon and noted: 'So long as the enemy will attack us, that is excellent; and especially if his attacks are isolated and piecemeal.'[61] Even though Montgomery's original plan to get his armour out into the open was in tatters, the British armour was achieving the desired effect of engaging the German and Italian armour and slowly wearing down its strength in long-range gunnery duels. In fact, the habitual Axis counterattacks were playing into Eighth Army's hands. Since at least 2 July, Eighth Army had proved that a properly deployed defence could beat off a German armoured counterattack. Thus, although the British could make little headway against the Axis anti-tank gun screen, the panzers' counterattacks had simply resulted in mounting German and Italian tank losses.

On 25 October, the German High Command and the Italian Commando Supremo decided that the Panzerarmee should be renamed and known as the Deutsch-Italienische Panzerarmee. While the Axis High Command were busying themselves with nomenclature, the army they had just renamed was facing a real crisis. The daily report noted that 15th Panzer and Littorio Divisions had been forced to make costly counterattacks during the day and by that evening 15th Panzer Division's tank strength had been reduced from 119 to 32 tanks. The supply situation remained precarious and the lack of fuel limited the 'mobility of the motorised formations to an almost unbearable extent'.[62]

Rommel arrived at the Panzerarmee Battle Headquarters that evening and took command. He had stopped briefly in Rome where he met von Rintelen. The military attaché had bad news: several battalions of the 164th and Trento Divisions had already been wiped out and there were only three issues of petrol left in Africa. Rommel was 'bitterly angry'[63] at the lack of fuel but the truth was that he had ignored the clear warning provided by the events of late August. Alam Halfa had served notice that the British air and naval forces were now in a position to severely restrict the flow of Axis supplies to the front. If Rommel feared that he would now 'fight this battle with but small hope of success',[64] the fault lay largely with his refusal to withdraw from the Alamein line after Alam Halfa. Rommel immediately ordered that the panzer forces must be held back for mobile operations. Enemy tanks were to be dealt with by guns in position, not armoured counterattacks.[65] It remained to be seen whether Rommel's presence could stem the crisis.

On the night of 25 October, 51st (Highland) Division mounted two battalion attacks to reach its final objective line all along the divisional front. 5th Black Watch was ordered to take the strongpoint codenamed 'Stirling' and Lieutenant-Colonel Rennie decided on an unconventional approach. The full weight of the divisional artillery pounded the position for three hours in the early evening but the battalion attacked 'silently' at 23.00 hours in the hope that the artillery preparation had fooled the enemy survivors into 'thinking that no attack was coming after all'. The dodge worked perfectly and the only fire they received was some 'stray shells from Eighth Army guns'. 'Stirling' was found to be filled with 'dead and dying Germans'. By dawn on 26 October, the battalion was well dug in with 20 anti-tank guns in position and a squadron of 50th Royal Tank Regiment deployed close behind its positions.[66]

The 7th Argylls were not so fortunate in their attack on the 'troublesome place "Nairn"'.[67] As they advanced, 'Enemy machine guns kept chattering viciously during the attack, and very soon casualties began to mount up.' Eventually, the position was taken, and the battalion consolidated on the reverse slope of a shallow depression on the objective. Such were the casualties that the two companies which had made the attack had to be amalgamated into one composite force.[68] 5th Black Watch considered the next day, 26 October, to be a 'black day for the Battalion'[69] because of the heavy mortar fire and accurate sniper fire the soldiers had to endure throughout the day. However, Wimberley was pleased: 'Now at last we were in possession of the whole Blue

Line.'[70] Just as importantly, the tanks of 2nd Armoured Brigade could now take up hull-down positions along the entire line of the 'northern ridge'.

Ultimately, these two small-scale attacks revealed the dilemma facing Eighth Army in the days after Lightfoot. The pressure had to be maintained against the Panzerarmee but Eighth Army could only mount attacks on a limited scale. These were nonetheless very costly. However, 9th Australian Division mounted a larger-scale operation that night which seized a dominating piece of ground and later set the stage for a series of attacks towards the coast.

9th Australian Division had been warned in its orders for Lightfoot that the next stage of operations would see it mounting 'crumbling' attacks towards the coast. However, it had also been assumed that it would make these assaults with the assistance of at least some armour from 10 Corps which had 'broken out'. At noon on 24 October, 26th Australian Infantry Brigade was told to prepare plans for an attack against Point 29 the next day but now it 'would have to be done without the assistance of or threat of our own armd forces'.[71]

The main objective was to capture and hold the area to the north of its current right flank, including Point 29.[72] This feature, although only perhaps 20 feet higher than the surrounding desert, provided excellent observation. The Australians had already suffered from shelling directed by observers on Point 29. Its capture would give the Australians command of the dominant ground in the area and protect their current positions. In the first phase, the 2/48th Battalion would capture the area around Point 29, while in the second phase the 2/24th Battalion was to capture an enemy locality, known as the 'Fig Garden', from the south east.[73]

The forward companies of the 2/48th received warning orders to prepare for an attack that night which included the phrase 'Admin normal'. The battalion historian later explained what the simple phrase meant:

> Preparation in detail for battle was to be made – arrangements for mines, wire, ammunition, food, water, overhead cover, sandbags, tools, anti-tank guns, and all the rest, and holding the present position while preparing to launch another attack. And while all this was being done the battalion was subjected to murderous fire from artillery and mortars.[74]

The fact that all the preparations were completed on time proved the importance of the now well-practised battle drills of the battalion and brigade. 26th Australian Brigade was now one of the most experienced and effective formations within Eighth Army.

They experienced a lucky break. At dusk on 25 October, just hours before the attack was due, a German reconnaissance party was captured. The prisoners included the acting regimental commander of the 125th Panzergrenadier Regiment and the acting commander of its II Battalion. Both officers were carrying detailed sketch maps of the defences that showed the tracks through the minefields used by the Germans.[75]

At midnight on 25 October, the two leading companies of 2/48th Infantry Battalion pushed forward 1,100 yards to an intermediate objective with artillery support from six field and two medium regiments in the form of timed concentrations crashing down in front of the infantry.[76] This level of artillery support was impressive: 14,508 rounds of 25-pounder shell and 1,066 rounds of 5.5-inch shell were fired in the planned concentrations.[77] This enabled the forming-up area for the battalion to be cleared but this time, with fresh tactical intelligence to hand, Lieutenant-Colonel Hammer had decided on an unconventional plan of attack in a repeat of the carrier raid his battalion had mounted in July.

The two leading companies, which had advanced on foot, suffered very heavy casualties and had 'to fight every inch of the way' to reach their objectives 900 yards from the start line.[78] Then, ten carriers carrying the two leading platoons of C Company, and towing anti-tank guns, raced up four abreast from the start line following the tracks that the German officers' maps had shown were clear of mines. They crossed the 1,200 yards of desert from the start line to Point 29 in just nine minutes. The infantry jumped out of the carriers onto the spur of high ground just one minute after the artillery lifted onto the next target. The German defenders were caught completely by surprise. The noise and dust of the artillery bombardment had kept the German defenders' heads down so that they had not even seen the carriers as they sped along the track. After a quick but bloody fight, Point 29 was in Australian hands.[79]

The later moves by the battalion to exploit this early success by pushing a company towards the north east ran into very determined resistance. During this fighting, when the company was held up, Private Percy Gratwick charged an enemy machine-gun post and killed its crew. He then ran forward again and killed a mortar crew before himself being killed by machine-gun fire. Gratwick's action enabled the company to consolidate its position and won him a posthumous Victoria Cross.[80] The battalion was badly depleted and exhausted after this night of fighting but maintained a firm foothold on the ground it had captured.[81] 2/17th Infantry Battalion took over the positions vacated by the 2/48th Battalion around Point 29[82] and engineers laid more Hawkins mines to extend the protective minefield around the new positions.

Forty minutes after the start of the initial attack the 2/24th Battalion mounted its attack but, after an advance of 800 yards, it ran into a web of incredibly strong defences, including some deep concrete shelters. This delayed the attack and the infantry fell behind the artillery programme. The companies still pressed on with mounting casualties and at last seized the final objective at the Fig Garden. Both companies came under intense close-range fire and were ordered to withdraw. The remaining two companies had to fight their way forward to make contact and also suffered heavy casualties.

Once again, the reorganisation, resupply and arrival of the supporting arms which had proved so difficult in July functioned efficiently in line with the practised drills. This was remarkable given the fact that, early in the attack, a truck stacked with Hawkins mines had been hit by a shell while waiting to go forward. Soon another seven trucks loaded with mines had caught fire.[83] The ordered convoy of battalion transport descended into 'a ghastly raging inferno. As trucks burned and exploded a great wall of fire shot into the sky. The gun flashes seemed dimmed; night was turned into day. The concussion was terrific.'[84] The blaze brought down immediate Axis artillery fire. In July, a disaster such as this would have prevented proper reorganisation and probably resulted in the eventual capture of the battalion. On this occasion, the quartermasters worked frantically to replace the lost equipment and relays of carriers were used to race through the heavy shell-fire to bring the supplies forward.[85] Both battalions were dug in and re-organised on their new ground before dawn on 26 October.

26th Australian Infantry Brigade's attack was a highly successful limited assault by two experienced battalions. It was very similar in many respects to the brigade's first attack at Alamein on 10 July; the brigade had seized important high ground with heavy artillery support. There the similarities ended; this attack was only one of many in the middle of an intense and large-scale battle. However, the loss of key ground like Point 29 was bound to provoke a reaction from the Panzerarmee. Rommel's attention was drawn to the northern sector just as it had been on 10 July.

On the same night, 25 October, 8th Armoured Brigade was withdrawn to an assembly area six miles behind the front line to reorganise and re-equip.[86] 9th Armoured Brigade withdrew behind the Miteiriya ridge but was held ready to counter any attack on the New Zealand front line. Over the next two days, although no major attack developed against them, 9th Armoured Brigade suffered from intermittent shelling that caused numerous casualties. The brigade argued:

> This proved once again the error of using tanks for this purpose. Tank crews cannot sit all day in their Tanks or slit trenches, they must be out doing essential maintenance and when this has to be done under shell-fire casualties will occur.[87]

Here was another example of how difficult it could be to combine tanks and infantry in the desert. While the presence of the tanks boosted the morale of the New Zealand and South African infantry who held the ridge, the tank crews found the conditions very difficult. At last light on 27 October, the New Zealand Division was relieved by 1st South African Brigade and 9th Armoured Brigade was finally able to move into reserve positions at Alam el Onsol, well away from the shellfire of the Miteiriya ridge.

While 8th and 9th Armoured Brigades withdrew from their exposed positions, 24th Armoured Brigade, which had so far suffered fewer casualties than its counterparts, was ordered to move north to contact the flank of 1st Armoured Division. Reconnaissance revealed that this would not be possible without 'serious mine trouble' so the brigade drove back down its existing lanes and then through the cleared lanes of 1st Armoured Division. The tour also 'proved the need for caution in mine-clearing in many unreconnoitred minefields up to our new posn on the ridge N of EL WISHKA'.[88] By midday on 26 October, the two remaining armoured brigades of 10 Corps had linked up in the vital sector between El Wishka and Kidney ridge. 24th Armoured Brigade came under the command of 1st Armoured Division and both were told by Lumsden, 'the armour was to stop worrying about going to the rescue of inf divs, and to concentrate on getting out of the minefields and into the open spaces to destroy the enemy armour.'[89] The frustration at the lack of progress was now almost palpable. However, a heavy sandstorm blew up in the afternoon which prevented the regular Axis afternoon counter-attack and the cautious movement of the armour up to the newly won positions in the Highland Division's sector did draw some attention away from the Australians at Point 29.

This was just as well, since 'Intense arty fire' had rained down for three hours in the early morning of 26 October on the men of 2/48th and 2/24th Battalions with the main concentrations landing around Point 29. Rommel had placed 164th Light Division under the command of the Afrika Korps and gave the main objective for the day to 'restore the situation at Hill 28'.[90] Von Thoma went to the division's headquarters to direct the preparations for the counterattack personally.[91] As light came that morning, the Australian artillery observers now posted at Point 29 understood its importance: they could see clearly for at least 4,000 yards in every direction.[92] The historian of the 2/13th Battalion, which was posted further south, remembered:

> The battlefield within vision was seething. To the south thirty Shermans were having a set-to with enemy tanks . . . and in the west forward of 20th Brigade, a large force of enemy tanks and troop carriers moved parallel to the F.D.L.s probing for weak spots in our defences. Overhead the Bostons went by every 30 minutes trailing clouds of flak in their wake.[93]

Rommel's account gives the impression that numerous attacks were launched against Point 29 but the 26th Brigade's report later noted that, 'The day passed without any tank or infantry counter-attack.'[94] This was only because the Australian artillery observers managed to maintain communications throughout the day and directed crushing artillery concentrations from at least four artillery regiments onto every suspected group of German and Italian soldiers as they attempted to assemble for an attack. Rommel bemoaned the fact: 'Rivers of blood were poured out over miserable strips of land which, in normal times, not even the poorest Arab would have bothered his head about.'[95] This much was true but such losses over patches of sand had never concerned Rommel when he had believed in victory.

The sector held by the III Battalion 382nd Panzergrenadier Battalion, opposite the Highland Division, was threatened in the afternoon by what the 15th Panzer Division believed was a major tank attack. All the artillery support for 164th Division was diverted to defend against this. But a retaliatory attack was out of the question. Eighth Army's artillery had made any such gesture pointless and 15th Panzer Division was forced to recognise that 'with the available forces and relatively weak artillery support the hill could no longer be captured.'[96] In the afternoon, Rommel ordered the main body of the 90th Light Division to assemble in the area around Sidi Abd el Rahman while the Trieste Division was to form up at El Daba.[97] Slowly but surely, the reserves of the Panzerarmee were being sucked into the intense fighting in the northern sector.

The Luftwaffe showed some signs of recovery during 26 October. Reinforcements had been rushed from Sicily and Crete to bolster the front line squadrons. Strong fighter sweeps flew over the battle area and six small-scale bombing raids ventured over the lines of Eighth Army, yet this level of effort was far exceeded by the Desert Air Force. However, the most significant air action of the day took place far from the battlefield itself. The sailing of the Italian tanker *Proserpina*, of 4,870 tons, and the *Tergestea*, of 5,809 tons, with an escort of four destroyers, had been tracked carefully by the code-breakers at Bletchley Park. A Baltimore based on Malta spotted the convoy on the afternoon of 25 October, having been directed to the search area by Enigma intelligence. An unsuccessful torpedo attack by four Wellingtons that night was soon followed up by the preparation of another three strike forces. The first strike force on 26 October sighted the convoy 18 miles from Tobruk and its attacks managed to hit the *Proserpina* and set it alight. The ship sank the next morning. The second force missed the convoy but the third torpedoed and sank the *Tergestea* when the ship was just one mile from the relative safety of Tobruk harbour.[98] Rommel had been depending upon the fuel carried in the *Proserpina* to restore his army's ability to manoeuvre. Now that hope had been dashed.

The lack of progress – by either side – on 26 October proved that the battle had indeed 'fizzed out'. Freyberg commented to his staff, 'We have to be clear that the advance to this present position will not win the war.'[99] Montgomery held a conference with his corps commanders at Morshead's headquarters that morning. He declared a change of policy:

> 30 Corps needed a short period with no major operations. Divisions had been fighting hard since 2200 hours 23 October, and were somewhat disorganised:

a period was wanted in which Div areas could be tidied up, and things sorted out.[100]

This was a convenient way of making the best use of the time granted him by the fact that the battle had stalled.

Montgomery worked de Guingand hard that day. The Army Commander needed information on the state of the army and its ability to sustain the 'dogfight' before he worked out a solution to his problems. De Guingand provided Montgomery with a detailed statement of the tank position which revealed that casualties had been heavy. In just two days of fighting, 10 Corps had suffered the loss of 191 tanks, of which 122 were valuable Shermans and Grants. This meant that nearly 29 per cent of the crucial 'heavies' had been damaged. 23rd Armoured Brigade had suffered 63 tank casualties and 7th Armoured Division had lost 62 tanks but this included only eight Grants.[101] These statistics showed that, whatever Montgomery's opinions about the lack of 'ginger' in the armoured formations, 10 Corps had engaged in intense fighting and really had been held up on the Axis minefields. Eighth Army could now muster 754 tanks but it had gone into the battle with 1,060. This was still an overwhelming superiority in numbers, but the losses to the heavy armour were worrying. Nonetheless, de Guingand's conclusions were upbeat:

> Probably the great proportion of tank casualties have been caused on mine-fields, i.e. they are short-term repairs, and provided shops go all out we should get a reasonable flow back into units within the next day or two.
>
> We might expect a daily flow of 40/50 tanks of all types from all shops and base into units during the next week or so.[102]

The reorganisation of tank recovery and repair certainly proved its worth during this battle. The workshops were able to recover, repair and return tanks to units very quickly. From Montgomery's perspective, de Guingand's paper confirmed that, even with this rapid attrition of the tank force, Eighth Army could still maintain its pressure on the Panzerarmee.

De Guingand also presented Montgomery with a staff paper on 'Future Plans' which dealt with the eventual movement of 21st Panzer Division to the northern sector. He argued that, once 21st Panzer Division left the southern sector, 7th Armoured Division could be safely moved north as it was 'a thousand to one against the Italians attempting any major offensive operation' and 13 Corps could then hold the southern sector defensively.[103]

> We can either go on 'crumbling' the enemy's defences in the extreme North, or we can aim at placing a force (Infantry) to the West, and thereby isolating the remainder of 164 Division, and then concentrate guns and bombs upon their positions until they have had enough.[104]

In common with Freyberg's views on the necessity for a renewed infantry offensive, de Guingand's arguments helped to shape the future course of the battle.

Montgomery also spoke with Kirkman to ensure that Eighth Army's artillery would be able to sustain its effort for longer than originally expected. Montgomery noted:

> The artillery ammunition situation is good but has to be watched. If we fire 150 rounds a gun per day, we can continue the battle for three weeks. I have now limited 13 Corps to 40 rounds a gun per day for 25 pdrs.[105]

In fact, Kirkman had been understandably worried about the ammunition consumption. One hundred and fifty rounds per gun a day was nowhere near enough ammunition to continue the battle at its present intensity and Kirkman had warned Montgomery that stocks of ammunition would be exhausted after another ten days of firing at the current rate. Kirkman believed that Montgomery was relaxed and still full of confidence as they discussed the ammunition situation.[106] It would appear that much of Montgomery's confidence was feigned. Liddell Hart later discussed the battle with Briggs who, according to Liddell Hart:

> revealed an interesting and significant point – that Montgomery himself confessed in conversation afterwards that the confident and assured way in which he had talked during the first week of the battle had been assumed, and that towards the end of the first week he had actually felt that the battle might have to be broken off, in face of the stiff resistance that he was meeting.[107]

Rommel was not alone in confronting sinking hopes about the course of the fighting. Yet Montgomery's 'projection of personality', which had been a key part of his method of command since the twenties, continued to serve him well. Whatever his doubts concerning the battle, Montgomery continued to infuse his subordinates with a sense of purpose and, crucially, belief in victory.

Kirkman also commented that Lumsden was not using his corps artillery commander properly. Montgomery wrote in his diary:

> I have just discovered that LUMSDEN has been fighting his battle without having his CCRA with him. I ordered him up at once.
>
> There is no doubt that these RAC Generals do not understand the co-operation of all arms in battle. I have had many examples of this since the battle started.
>
> LUMSDEN is not really a high-class soldier.[108]

Kirkman's report was clearly the last straw for Montgomery. Montgomery's fury against his 'R.A.C. Generals' overlooked the fact that much of 10 Corps' artillery had been loaned to 30 Corps for the first night and considerable disorganisation had resulted. It took time before 10 Corps' artillery had reformed sufficiently to be used properly. However, Lumsden had seen no need to change his 'freelance desert technique' when he became a corps commander. He continued to move about the battlefield in a small tactical headquarters and this meant that, although his 'feel' for the fighting was good, he was not in constant contact with his Main Headquarters and therefore his artillery commander. Lumsden's style of command had worked well when he was a brigadier and had still functioned, if with some difficulties, when he was a divisional commander. It was no longer appropriate when he was in charge of a corps.

Montgomery held a further conference at his Tactical Headquarters that evening,[109] in which he developed his ideas for 'further offensive action'.[110] The most important idea was to form a new reserve. Montgomery had been forced to accept that the original plan had failed; all attempts to convert 30 Corps' break-in to a break-out had stalled. This meant that it was essential to draw some forces back into reserve to make another attempt, an action which involved the reshuffling of the existing pack of cards. 1st South African Division would take over the New Zealand posts on the Miteiriya ridge and 4th Indian Division would then fill the South Africans' original positions. Since the ridge was no longer a launching pad for the armour, it could now be held with fewer troops as a defensive shoulder. 13 Corps would take over more of the front from 30 Corps and 7th Armoured Division was to 'be prepared to move to Northern sector' dependent on the movement of 21st Panzer Division. These moves would be complete by dawn on 28 October and that night 9th Australian Division would mount another attack towards the coast.[111]

It is clear that, by this stage of the fighting, Montgomery had lost faith in Lumsden and that his *corps de chasse* concept was dying if not dead. The New Zealand Division was now handed to 30 Corps with the intention that it would make another infantry assault to break through the last of the Axis minefields. In the meantime, 9th Australian Division would bear the brunt of the fighting by drawing Axis attention towards the coast. These moves were tacit recognition that the original 30 Corps frontage had been too wide. The movement of forces essentially shortened the active northern front to the sectors held by 51st (Highland) and 9th Australian Division and thus, ironically, was more in keeping with Auchinleck's original intentions for his projected offensive in mid-September. The Australian attacks were designed to keep the Panzerarmee occupied and off balance while Eighth Army prepared its next blow. These decisions proved Montgomery's firm grasp of the dynamics of operational command and also the close attention he had paid to the views of his Chief of Staff and his senior subordinates.

That evening, Rommel also made an important decision. 21st Panzer Division was ordered to move to the northern sector.[112] The Ariete Division was left in the southern sector as a form of insurance but it was obvious now that the main British effort was in the north. Nonetheless, Rommel agonised over the decision because, once the division moved north, there would be insufficient fuel to send it south again.[113] Rommel was responding in exactly the way 'Spud' Murphy, Montgomery's chief intelligence officer, had predicted. Having determined the area of the British main effort, the German commander was gathering his armour for a major counterattack the next day.

The Panzerarmee's daily report painted an increasingly gloomy picture. Although it was claimed that the enemy had been 'held almost everywhere', the fighting had been 'heavy and costly'. With the loss of the tanker *Proserpina*, there was now only sufficient fuel to bring up supplies for the next two or three days. It was re-emphasised that, 'Unless every possible assistance is given in bringing over fuel the defensive battle cannot be brought to a successful conclusion.'[114]

Meanwhile, 1st Armoured Division now sent the two battalions of its 7th Motor Brigade into a night attack to seize the objectives 'Snipe' and 'Woodcock' which lay 3,000 yards in front of Eighth Army's present line. The two objectives were enemy strongpoints; 'Woodcock' lay to the north west of Kidney ridge while 'Snipe' lay to the south. The idea was simple: the two battalions would seize and hold these exposed positions until first light the next morning when they would be joined by advancing armour. Then, using 'Woodcock' and 'Snipe' as 'pivots of manoeuvre', the armour would attempt to push on and invite counterattack by the enemy armour. In many respects, Briggs's plan was a scaled-down version of Lightfoot but its execution had radically different results.

While the plan was simple, the map-reading errors of 1st Armoured Division led to considerable confusion. At zero hour, 23.00 hours on 26 October, the two battalions of the brigade, 2nd Rifle Brigade and 2nd King's Royal Rifle Corps began their advance over hastily reconnoitred ground and with real doubt as to their whereabouts. The experiences of the two battalions in the subsequent attack were very different. The battalions also adopted very different methods to reach their objectives. Lieutenant-Colonel Victor Turner, commander of the 2nd Rifle Brigade, conducted a dismounted attack with two rifle companies, a third in reserve and a screen of carriers in front of the infantrymen.[115] When the artillery support came crashing down the shells fell further to the south than Turner had expected. 51st (Highland) Division had been right all the time: 'The barrage proved that the existing locations of units of 1 Armd Div had been plotted 1000x too far to the NORTH throughout 25 and 26 Oct.'[116] After hastily altering the compass bearing on which the battalion was to advance, the troops advanced and reached what was thought to be 'Snipe' just after midnight, having met only limited opposition. The supporting weapons and transport were called up and 'consolidation with all-round defence proceeded rapidly'.[117] The 2nd Rifle Brigade had conducted a model night attack.

However, the 2nd King's Royal Rifle Corps, under the command of Lieutenant-Colonel W. Heathcote-Amery, decided to 'motor' 2,000 yards, debus under cover of the artillery concentrations and only then put in the final attack on foot.[118] With a large, yellow moon shining overhead, the assembled group of vehicles was:

> an impressive sight: carriers in front, motor platoons next and mechanized machine-gun trucks and anti-tank gun portees bringing up the rear, all moving on a compass bearing and marching by the centre.[119]

Unfortunately, 'motoring' forward in the middle of a web of German strong-points proved to be a mistake. During the advance one company picked up 'a dozen very surprised Germans' but just as Heathcote-Amery gave the order to 'debus', the leading vehicles were hit by machine-gun and anti-tank gun fire from a range of only 75 yards. Confusion ensued but one company did manage to bypass the enemy fire and reach what it believed was the battalion objective. Nearly 100 prisoners were taken along with six anti-tank guns but it was well after dawn before the other companies were able to link up on the objective. The battalion held the position, which was actually further east than 'Woodcock', throughout the day but encountered little opposition. It was noted:

> A large number of enemy tanks kept hovering about the position and several times it looked as though they were going to attack. They obviously did not know who or what we were, and after we had knocked out a couple at extreme range they drew off and the threat came to nothing.[120]

The battalion had thus mounted a successful, if confused, attack but their presence beyond the forward edge of Eighth Army's existing positions elicited little response.

The same was not true of 2nd Rifle Brigade which, unwittingly, had placed itself directly in the path of Rommel's intended counterattack. Thirteen six-pounder guns from the support company and six from 239th Anti-Tank Battery had managed to reach the position and these were dug in for all-round defence.[121] Even before dawn, the supporting carriers stirred up a leaguer of German and Italian tanks. One Mk IV and a Panzerjäger self-propelled gun drove blindly into the battalion position and both were knocked out at close range.[122] At first light, two leaguers of enemy tanks, one to the south west and one to the north, broke up and drove west almost certainly without spotting the battalion's six-pounder guns which were concealed in the soft, hummocky sand. The gunners claimed to have knocked out sixteen tanks and self-propelled guns before these two groups of tanks had moved out of range. From this point onwards, the battalion was to be under fire for most of the rest of the day, although little of this shelling was actually aimed at 'Snipe'.

Unfortunately, the gunner officer who was meant to act as the forward observation officer for the battalion had become lost during the night and, even with repeated calls from the battalion, no gunner officer was able to make it through to the exposed and indistinct position during the day. Nonetheless, the undulating ground which enabled the guns to be well dug in and camouflaged certainly helped to ensure that 'Snipe' was never overrun. It would appear that, for most of the day, the Axis armour simply did not realise there was a reinforced British motor battalion in their path.

Indeed, at 07.30 hours on 27 October, the tanks of 24th Armoured Brigade began to shell the collection of anti-tank guns that they could see ahead of them, believing them to be German. The battalion's intelligence officer had to drive back and ask them 'to desist'.[123] When the leading Shermans of the brigade moved forward to the battalion position it was apparent that it could not be used as a 'firm base' by the armour. Seven Shermans were soon burning after being hit by 88mm armour-piercing rounds from guns firing from near Kidney ridge. The tanks withdrew, leaving the battalion isolated. However, when a group of 25–30 German tanks followed up the withdrawal of the British tanks, they were caught between the guns of the riflemen and the retreating British tanks; at least eight panzers were destroyed. Later, a group of 13 Italian M.13s which drove towards the position was soon halted when four were hit. By 11.00 hours, after these intense actions, only 13 of the original 19 six-pounders were in action and ammunition was running short.

Yet another group of Italian tanks attacked at 13.00 hours and could be engaged by only one gun. This was manned by Sergeant Calliston, Lieutenant-Colonel Turner and Lieutenant Toms. The gun had only two or three rounds of ammunition left and Calliston later recalled that Toms ran to 'his Jeep, which had four boxes of ammo on board. God knows how he got to it – they were machine gunning the whole way.'[124] The jeep was set on fire but Toms and Turner managed to bring more ammunition to the gun: 'The gun was re-loaded and all 3 remaining M.13s were hit and set on fire at about 200 yards range.'[125] Turner was badly wounded in the head but, fortunately, there was a lull in the action until later in the afternoon.

The men of 2nd Rifle Brigade did not know it but 21st Panzer Division had moved up from the southern sector. Rommel had decided early that morning to launch a concerted counterattack with 90th Light Division directed on Hill 28 (Point 29) and 21st Panzer Division advancing from the south west to reach the old battle line around Kidney ridge. The attack was timed for 16.00 hours and all available artillery, along with as many panzergrenadier battalions as could be mustered, were ordered to support the attack.[126]

The first dawn reconnaissance flight by a Hurricane of No. 208 Squadron spotted a concentration of at least 1,000 vehicles in the area of Tel el Aqqaqir. The entire light-bombing effort of the Desert Air Force was directed against this target which happened to be the assembly point for the 21st Panzer and 90th Light Divisions. Nearly 200 light bombers attacked the area during the day, using the Rahman track as a convenient aiming mark. These raids caused considerable disruption to the assembling divisions. The strong air cover of the Desert Air Force also foiled the dive-bombing raid that should have preceded the counterattack. The Stukas and their escorting Me109s were driven off before they could reach the battle area. The cooperation between the Luftwaffe and Afrika Korps, which had been central to the success of the Panzerarmee in the past, was being pulled apart.[127]

However, by mid-afternoon, the panzers were ready. After a brief bombardment, the tanks of 5th Panzer Regiment attacked in waves towards the 'Snipe' position. As the panzers drove forward to take on the tanks of 24th Armoured Brigade, a southern group of 30 tanks passed within 500 yards of 2nd Rifle Brigade. Guns of 239th Battery, which had not been able to fire since the early morning, hit at least nine tanks. 21st Panzer Division noted that 'the attack was halted as a result of strong fire on the flanks from anti-tank guns and dug-in Pilot [Sherman and Grant] tanks'.[128] The combined efforts from 2nd Rifle Brigade and 24th Armoured Brigade stopped 21st Panzer Division's attack cold and the panzers withdrew to hull-down positions further north.

The most desperate fight developed at 17.30 hours when 15 Mk IIIs obviously spotted the battalion's position and drove straight towards it with machine guns blazing. Only three guns were able to fire at their approach but the leading three tanks were hit and burst into flames; the remainder drew off to hull-down positions. These tanks kept the position under machine-gun fire until darkness fell. It was stated that 'the A.Tk guns in this sector now had an average of 3 r.p.g. but providentially no further attack developed although there were 20 enemy tanks within about 100 yards'.[129] The Germans noted: 'the defensive effort of the extremely well dug-in enemy . . . remained undiminished' and that 'the 5th Panzer Regiment task . . . could not be achieved'.[130]

Eventually, after spending the evening fearing that the position would finally be overrun by German infantry, the battalion pulled out, taking one six-pounder and the breechblocks of all the other guns back with them. 2nd Rifle Brigade and 239th Anti-tank Battery had just fought one of the most celebrated anti-tank actions of the war. During one day of constant danger and exertion, they had destroyed at least 32 enemy tanks and knocked out 15 to 20 more, which were later recovered, at a cost of 14 killed, 44 wounded and one missing. Briggs, Lumsden and Montgomery were naturally delighted. The action at 'Snipe' is generally viewed as an heroic action by a single battalion but, although 2nd Rifle Brigade was isolated, it did not fight alone. The panzers had already been attacked from the air by the time they reached them. In fact, though it might have been impolitic to note it at the time, 2nd Rifle Brigade had just fought a very successful 'battlegroup' action along the lines that the 'old' Eighth Army had developed during July. 'Snipe' was simply the brightest and best example of Eighth Army's now fully developed method of anti-tank defence, the same as had been used by Robcol on 2 July, 433rd Battery on 16 July and 1st Rifle Brigade at Alam Halfa. None of this should detract from the remarkable performance of the battalion, of course; the entire combat on 27 October demonstrated that Eighth Army was now able to outfight its opponent.

Meanwhile, the soldiers of 9th Australian Division had to endure repeated counterattacks during the day. Before dawn, a mixed battlegroup composed of at least 15 tanks and 9 half-tracks followed by infantry from 15th Panzer and the Trento Division pushed forward against the 2/13th Battalion. It was said that the Axis troops 'came within an ace' of the forward Australian positions as they drove straight through the protective barrage.[131] The Australian infantry, supported by the Valentines of 40th Royal Tank Regiment, eventually drove off the attack. The attempt cost the Axis battlegroup at least two M.13 tanks and heavy casualties amongst their infantry.[132] A more determined attack in the afternoon managed to get within 400 yards of the positions of 2/17th Battalion but was eventually driven off by artillery and small-arms fire.[133] In the evening, a group of tanks and lorried infantry forming up behind a smoke screen was dispersed by artillery concentrations.[134]

26th Australian Brigade spent a 'comparatively quiet morning' but this was only because Rommel's 90th Light Division was organising a major attack to retake Point 29.[135] The division's war diary commented acidly: 'Two attacks by other formations (on Height 28) having misfired, the Division is now entrusted with the task of winning back this position.'[136] During the morning, 20 German tanks had driven up and down in front of the positions and tried to draw anti-tank fire but had not pressed home an attack. Late in the afternoon, the Axis forces opened a 'furious bombardment' of Point 29 and put down large amounts of smoke to blind the Australian artillery observers. The Australians responded by putting down all the artillery available onto the last known position of what 'appeared to be a bn of inf' that was assembling for an attack. This was Battlegroup 155 of 90th Light Division, supported by the Italian Falconi group, which now came into the attack. At one point, Lieutenant-Colonel Hammer had to stop the artillery support because the dust and smoke was so intense that he could not see the movements of the German infantry. The Panzergrenadiers pushed forward even in the face of the artillery concentrations and heavy fire from 2/48th battalion. Some of the German infantry got to within 400 yards of the Australian positions but had to withdraw to positions further back.[137]

Even after this unsuccessful attack, 90th Light kept up the pressure. A further assault was launched that night which pressed right up to the wire around the Australian positions before being driven back. A prisoner later stated that his battalion had suffered 80 dead and at least 200 wounded during one of these attacks[138] and that night the air was 'filled with cries of the wounded'.[139] 90th Light Division had displayed considerable resolution in mounting these assaults but the Australian defences had held firm.

So the determined resistance at 'Snipe' had completely broken up 21st Panzer Division's counterattack and 9th Australian Division had held firm against the repeated attempts of 90th Light Division to retake lost ground. Rommel later claimed that the lack of petrol prevented the Afrika Korps from mounting a 'concentrated and planned counter-attack' and that this compelled him to 'allow the armoured formations in the northern part of our line to assault the British salient piecemeal'.[140]

Yet, although Rommel described the counterattacks by 90th Light and 21st Panzer Divisions on 27 October as 'local',[141] it is clear that they were meant to be well-prepared and concentrated attacks. The Panzerarmee daily report stated:

> The mass of the Army was engaged throughout the day in the northern sector in heavy fighting, which fluctuated the whole time. In spite of employing the whole of the Luftwaffe and the artillery we did not succeed in our counter-attack, in winning back the lost sector of the main battle line.[142]

The failed counterattack and constant pressure had cost the Panzerarmee dearly. By that evening, the III Battalion of the 382nd Infantry Regiment, 164th Light Division, could only muster one officer and 10 soldiers. Similarly, the 62nd Infantry Regiment of the Trento Division now consisted of just 150 men. The petrol situation remained 'catastrophic' and Kesselring had been pressed that morning to agree to transport at least 300 tons of fuel each day by air until the supply situation improved.[143] Indeed, the increased level of air transport, in the face of the virtual strangulation of the sea lines of communication to Africa, became the primary means of supply for the Panzerarmee. This method could not possibly provide the full needs of the Axis army but it did stave off complete disaster.

Rommel could not admit that the techniques that had served the Afrika Korps so well for so long were simply no longer effective against Eighth Army. It was becoming clear that the habitual method of counterattack could no longer restore the situation and simply resulted in mounting German and Italian casualty figures. Thus, while the opposing Army Commanders both had to fight their own personal daemons of doubt in the midst of the battle, Montgomery was preparing his forces for another blow. Rommel had little option but to continue a policy of immediate counterattack that was no longer effective.

SEVENTEEN

'Round and Round the Mulberry Bush'

We've at last got those bloody Germans by the knackers[1]

There was a tragic sequel to the 'Snipe' action the next morning. On the evening of 27 October, 133rd Lorried Infantry Brigade[2] had been ordered to relieve 7th Motor Brigade around 'Snipe' and 'Woodcock' that night.[3] However, the brigade's advance was 'ill conceived'.[4] Still under the misconception that 1st Armoured Division's map reading was correct, the 4th and 5th Royal Sussex advanced along the wrong axis. The 5th Royal Sussex, sent to relieve the 2nd Rifle Brigade, reached what was believed to be 'Snipe' and dug in without ever contacting Turner's men. Meanwhile, the 4th Royal Sussex, 'thinking they were advancing in the gap between ABERDEEN and STIRLING in fact advanced in the dark straight through the 1 Gordons and shot at them'.[5] Wimberley commented, 'Luckily for us, little damage was done, but this incident did not enhance our opinion, at the time, of the Armoured Divisions.'[6]

Worse was to follow. After the incident with the Gordons, 4th Royal Sussex advanced towards 'Woodcock'. One company was destroyed in heavy fighting with the 115th Panzergrenadier Regiment but eventually the battalion deployed with one company on the eastern edge of 'Woodcock' and one company on the western edge of Kidney ridge.[7] These positions were directly in front of the guns of III Battalion, 33rd Artillery Regiment, 15th Panzer Division.[8] They were far more exposed than Turner's position had been, and the men of the 4th Royal Sussex were not desert veterans. The brigade had come to Egypt as part of the 44th (Home Counties) Division and had been hurriedly converted to lorried infantry in September 1942.[9] Their inexperience proved costly. At about 08.00 hours, Lieutenant C. E. Hutchinson, who was acting as an observation officer with the 2nd King's Royal Rifle Corps, saw:

> 40 or 50 inf whom, I was told, were a coy of 4 Bn Royal Sussex Regt; they were being rounded up by two Mk.IIIs and two M.13s . . . there did not appear to be any anti-tank guns in that area, nor did I hear any A.Tk guns firing prior to the inf being rounded up.[10]

The arrival of a British battalion right in the midst of the positions of
15th Panzer Division was bound to cause a reaction. A hastily gathered
battlegroup of German and Italian tanks attacked the 4th Royal Sussex
before any help could reach them. The battalion was able to put up only
slight resistance before being forced to surrender; 342 men marched into
captivity leaving behind 47 dead.[11] 10th Hussars saw the battalion being
marched away under escort before they could intervene.[12] Yet the startling
fact about the loss of the 4th Royal Sussex that morning was that it was
a unique, although still bitter, experience during the battle. In the July
fighting, the Panzerarmee had capitalised upon the disorganisation of
Eighth Army infantry units and the lack of tank/infantry cooperation after
an attack to inflict heavy losses in immediate counterattacks. Apart from
this isolated occasion, Eighth Army had learned the lesson. The
Panzerarmee continued to counterattack but found it impossible to repeat
the successes of July.

During the night of 27 October, most of Montgomery's planned reliefs
took place. 2nd New Zealand Division handed over its positions on the
Miteiriya ridge to the South Africans 'without incident'[13] and the tired New
Zealand infantry were moved back to the rear areas to rest. The New Zealand
artillery regiments moved north into the Australian sector and Freyberg
noted that they had a 'heavy job still ahead'.[14] Meanwhile, a complicated
series of reliefs were enacted to enable the 26th Australian Brigade to move
into reserve for a short rest before its next attack the following night. The
Highland Division's 152nd Brigade took over the positions of 20th Australian
Brigade which, in its turn, then relieved 26th Australian Brigade. The men
of 2/48th and 2/24th Battalions dug shallow trenches in an area south of
Tel el Eisa and slept properly for the first time in five days.[15] Although some
of the reliefs were delayed, by 06.05 hours on 28 October all the battalions
were in their planned positions. The process of preparing to deliver another
blow was now underway.

Meanwhile, the Panzerarmee was still trying to wrest the initiative away
from its opponent. On the morning of 28 October, tanks, lorried infantry
and some of the groups of men who had dug in after previous unsuccessful
attempts gathered for another attempt to retake Point 29. The 2/17th
Battalion, which had taken over the positions around Point 29, had suffered
heavy casualties and eventually it was decided to pull the infantry back from
the exposed height to better positions in the open desert.[16] However,
Lieutenant G. A. Turner, the artillery observation officer, remained in position at Point 29 even though the position was pounded by Axis artillery. He
called down fire on the numerous counterattacks throughout the day:

> There were many targets offering . . . we called for fire on pre-planned targets,
> as no doubt, did other OPs. I will never forget seeing the devastating fall of

shot and its effectiveness in halting the attack. For me, the term 'firepower' took on a new meaning.[17]

The determined soldiers of the 90th Light Division managed to get within 150 yards of the observation post on Point 29 before being hurled back by a storm of artillery and supporting machine-gun fire. Although the attack was repulsed by 12.30 hours, both sides brought down heavy shelling around Point 29 for the rest of the day. The firepower available to Eighth Army was indeed awesome but it depended upon secure communications and the bravery of the men in the forward observation posts to function. The sophisticated system of communications, combined with the skill of the gunners and the observers, enabled the artillery to give an unprecedented level of support to the forward troops. When a call came in asking for defensive fire it took the gunners an average of four minutes to provide the necessary firepower. The record during the battle was just two minutes from the call for fire to the fall of the shells.[18] Eighth Army's artillery had become one of the dominant forces on the battlefield.

The panzer divisions prepared that morning for another series of counter-attacks. 21st Panzer Division were directed against the 'Snipe' and 'Wood-cock' area while 15th Panzer Division was to make ground towards the Miteiriya ridge. Rommel rallied his troops: 'The present battle is a life and death struggle. I therefore require that: . . . every officer and man will give of his utmost and thereby contribute to its success.'[19] However, the efforts came to naught. Not only did the divisions complain of heavy artillery fire but when tanks of 15th Panzer Division approached the Miteiriya ridge, they reported that they could not advance because there were hull-down 'pilots' (Grants and Shermans) 1,600 metres ahead.[20] Gatehouse's cautious tactics may have infuriated Montgomery but they also frustrated the Germans. As the Axis armoured formations concentrated prior to their attack, the Desert Air Force weighed into the fight. During the morning, Axis formations had been well dispersed and most of the light bombers were directed to attack forward landing grounds. However, when reconnaissance aircraft observed the panzers assembling, all the light bombing effort was concentrated on the area in front of 10th Armoured Division. For the first time in the battle, the light bombers now had decent targets and over the course of two hours, seven light-bomber formations dropped a total of 80 tons of bombs into the area south and south east of 15th Panzer Division's Battle Headquarters.[21] 21st Panzer Division gave up its half-hearted attempt to attack without making any ground.

During the morning, Freyberg, now freed from any immediate operational concerns, visited Morshead and talked over the coming Australian attack with his fellow Dominion commander. Morshead described the attack as 'round and round the mulberry bush' and explained that his brigades would attack towards the coast road and then come in behind the German defenders. On hearing the plan, Freyberg commented acerbically that it was 'obviously not thought out by a gunner and is complicated but it may succeed'.[22] Leese also believed that Morshead's plan was overcomplicated but once again deferred to his more experienced subordinate. Leese later felt that he should:

> have insisted on a simple straight-forward plan; with the enormous weight of artillery support available I think this would have succeeded. As it was, the Australians remembered very vividly the failures of earlier frontal attacks in this area and thus they did everything they could to avoid undertaking once again an attack of this nature.[23]

The fighting at Tel el Eisa in July cast a long shadow upon the 9th Australian Division. This time, Montgomery was not sending 'a boy on a man's errand' as had happened in the past but the complexity of the Australian plan made its execution as doubtful as some of the more ambitious attacks of July. It was a pity that Leese did not persuade Morshead to adopt a simpler and less sophisticated plan.

Morshead's plan to go 'round and round the mulberry bush' was indeed complex. Montgomery had given 9th Australian Division the very simple directive to 'attack north' and left the detailed planning up to Morshead and his staff. The division was given lavish support: 23rd Armoured Brigade (although two regiments of the brigade were serving with the South Africans and Highlanders respectively); three extra anti-tank batteries; the guns of 2nd New Zealand, 51st (Highland) and 10th Armoured Divisions; and all three of the medium artillery regiments. This gave an impressive total of 360 guns in support of the division, which amounted to the heaviest concentration of guns yet seen in the desert war. In Lightfoot, 472 guns had supported the advance of four divisions across a 12-kilometre front but now 360 guns would support an attack by two brigades on a front of less than a mile.

The staff of 9th Australian Division had realised that there were few enemy defences south of the railway apart from what was known as the 'switch line' and the powerful redoubt at 'Thompson's Post'. They also knew from the interrogation of the captured commander of 125th Panzergrenadier Regiment, however, that plans were afoot to strengthen these positions.[24] Essentially, the attack would be mounted by five Australian battalions in a wide 'right hook' to encircle and trap the German defenders near the coast. The attack would also clear the Axis defences south of the main road and enable the division to use the road for traffic.

To execute this plan, 20th Australian Brigade would attack from Point 29 towards the north.[25] 2/17th Battalion was tasked with holding firm around Point 29 since this area was the jumping off point for all the subsequent attacks. 2/15th Battalion would advance 2,800 yards northwards to occupy and hold the current German defences. The 2/13th Battalion was to advance north east and clear up the enemy defences which ran along the ridges that radiated from Point 29. The final objective was given as the Fig Garden lying to the south west of Thompson's Post.[26] These attacks would strengthen the hold of the division around Point 29 and 'clear the ring' for the next, ambitious phase of the attack in which the 26th Brigade would drive to the main road.[27]

In the second phase, the 2/23rd Battalion, supported by Valentines from 46th Royal Tank Regiment, would push north to the railway line and then on to the main road where they would dig in to provide a base for the further movement of the 2/48th Battalion. This unit would advance south east and move astride the road to attack the current Axis forward defended localities from the rear. Meanwhile, the 2/24th Battalion would push east from Point 29 to capture Thompson's Post and clear up the defences to the south of the main road.[28]

Freyberg had been right to comment that the attack had not been 'thought out by a gunner'. Due to the fact that many of the battalions were advancing north, the supporting artillery, which was deployed behind the existing Eighth Army front, had to fire its timed concentrations in enfilade from the direction of advance. In the case of the 2/48th Battalion which was to advance east, the guns would actually be firing into the faces of the advancing infantrymen. This spoke volumes for the technical expertise of the artillery but also for the level of trust which existed between the Australians and the gunners of Eighth Army. However, the fact that each battalion was given a separate and divergent axis of advance meant that each infantry unit was facing a difficult and essentially isolated task. Morshead had had numerous arguments with Auchinleck about the ambitious tasks allotted to his brigades and battalions during the July fighting but now he was asking the same of his own men.

9th Australian Division had to bear the brunt of the fighting for the immediate future because Montgomery was still preparing for his next blow. He held a conference at 08.00 hours on 28 October to decide on the next phase of operations.[29] In essence, Montgomery closed down the offensive across the entire front – with the exception of 9th Australian Division's sector. He finally accepted that '1 Armd Div has had a fairly hard time up in the Kidney Hill area' and had recognised that 'we now have the whole of the Panzer Army opposite the northern funnel and that we shall never get the armoured divisions out that way'.[30] The 'Snipe–Woodcock area' which had been the scene of so much fighting was now to become a defensive front and 1st Armoured Division was to be withdrawn and 'held in readiness for further use in the near future'. 10th Armoured Division would take over responsibility for the area until it, too, was withdrawn on the evening of 29 October.[31]

This considerable process of regrouping was designed to bring the armour back in reserve for the next attack. Montgomery explained to his corps commanders that after the Australian attack that night, 'the next operation would be a "drive" N.W. by 30 Corps to get SIDI RAHMAN'. De Guingand noted that Montgomery's 'first reaction' was to mount the attack along the coast[32] although Freyberg wanted to make the attack 'due west from [the] Australian front'.[33] Montgomery had already decided that 'easily my best divisional commander is FREYBERG'[34] and thus he was chosen to command and organise this thrust. The choice was particularly apt since Freyberg had originally suggested the idea of a further infantry attack. However, the New Zealand Division was far too weak to mount such an operation with its existing infantry.

Freyberg was so worried about the fact that his division might be committed to another major attack that he wrote to Leese expressing his concerns. He explained that his division had suffered heavy casualties since June and more than 800 evacuations for jaundice. During the current battle, the division had suffered nearly 900 casualties and 'they have been mostly infantry and all have come from the infantry who carry rifle and the Bren gun'.[35] The seven battalions of New Zealand Infantry averaged a strength of 27 officers and 470 other ranks, each of which:

does not appear unsatisfactory . . . it must be realised that in each infantry battalion there is an irreducible minimum of 16 officers and 328 Ors composed of men of Bn HQ and HQ Coys who cannot take part in the assault with the bayonet. They comprise the following:-

Bn HQ		4 officers	50 ORs
HQ Coy –	Coy HQ	2	12
	1 Pl Sigs	2	35
	2 Pl AA		20
	3 Pl Mortars	1	44
	4 Pl Carriers	2	41
	5 Pl A Tk	3	69
	6 Pl Admin	2	57[36]

Whatever the official strength of an infantry battalion might be, the growth of the essential 'specialist' platoons often meant that there were very few infantry soldiers left actually to mount an attack. The fighting state of the New Zealand infantry battalions meant that each battalion had roughly 200 men, in four companies of 50 men each, who could actually 'go forward with an attack as fighting men'.[37] This meant that there were only 1,400 infantrymen left in the division whose total strength was 11,774 men.[38] Freyberg argued that if his division:

took a heavy knock . . . we should cease to be of any practical value as a mobile force and the whole of our artillery and other arms would be rendered value-less, and the training of this Division to a great extent would be wasted.[39]

Freyberg only committed such sensitive material to paper because he knew that if he did not his division might well cease to exist. His figures and argu-ments give a rare glimpse into the dilemma of dwindling infantry manpower which every British infantry commander faced at El Alamein.

Morshead would appear to have been less fastidious than his New Zealand colleague. Certainly, there were more Australian replacements available, but the commander of 9th Australian Division still committed badly under strength battalions to the attack that night. His 2/13th Battalion attacked on 28 October with four rifle companies, which averaged 35 men all ranks each.[40] After days of intense fighting, every infantry division at El Alamein suffered from this problem and these difficulties explain Montgomery's caution in husbanding his infantry formations and his relative profligacy with the armoured formations.

These problems, combined with the lack of flexibility inherent in the rigid make-up of the infantry divisions present in Eighth Army, might well have led to the end of the offensive. Auchinleck had faced these same diffi-culties in July. But Montgomery hit upon an elegant and effective solution. While neither Freyberg nor Morshead would ever have agreed to detach one of their infantry brigades so that it could be placed within a British infantry division, Montgomery could place a British infantry brigade within the New Zealand Division, to keep it up to strength and 'enable it to operate offensively'.[41] This solution meant that the best use could be made of Freyberg's inspirational command style and the experience of the New Zealand divisional staff while providing enough infantry for the assault. 9th Armoured Brigade was given the highest priority for tank replacements so that it could act as the spearhead for the breakthrough. Freyberg noted, 'To destroy the Germans in Egypt is the object of this operation. The attack is to be as soon as possible but there are great difficulties about mounting it the day after tomorrow.'[42] Freyberg and his staff began to work intensively on all the detailed planning and preparations that were needed to ensure that the attack worked. The artillery, signals, armour, sappers and all the other supporting weapons all had to have their part in the plan sketched out. So many previous Eighth Army attacks had failed because they were mounted before such planning was done. The cost of a mistake this time would be defeat.

Montgomery's regrouping actually caused confusion and dismay in Whitehall. Churchill had been anxiously reading the daily situation reports. After getting the report for 28 October, he became truly alarmed. It stated, innocuously enough, 'reorganisation of Corps proceeding according to plan.

30 Corps assumes command of whole Northern Section. At 2000 hrs. 10 Corps (less 10 Armd. Div.) then coming into Army reserve.'[43] To Churchill – who was also reading Rommel's now desperate daily reports pleading for more petrol, ammunition and reinforcements – news that the *corps de chasse* was being pulled into reserve suggested something had gone very wrong indeed. He discussed the matter with Anthony Eden, the Foreign Secretary, late in the evening on 28 October and drafted a stiff telegram[44] to Alexander. He then sent a message to Brooke calling him to a meeting the next day:

> The Foreign Secretary and I are agreed that this or something like it should be sent in view of the evident slowing down of the battle. The last Cositrep is particularly disquieting . . . It is most necessary that the attack should be resumed before 'Torch'. A standstill now will be proclaimed as a defeat. We consider the matter most grave.[45]

Brooke received the Prime Minister's message before he got up on 29 October and was furious. He believed that Eden had undermined Churchill's 'confidence in Montgomery and Alexander'.[46] Brooke had to leave the Chiefs of Staff meeting that morning to speak to Churchill. He later related that he was met with:

> a flow of abuse of Monty. What was my Monty doing now, allowing the battle to peter out (Monty was always my Monty when he was out of favour!). He had done nothing now for the last three days, and now he was withdrawing troops from the front. Why had he told us he would be through in seven days if all he intended to do was to fight a half-hearted battle? Had we not got a single general who could even win one single battle?[47]

Brooke had his own doubts but he kept them to himself. At another meeting that day with Churchill and Anthony Eden, he projected confidence and explained that Eighth Army had just beaten off a series of Axis counter-attacks which had failed with heavy losses. He insisted that Montgomery was simply forming new reserves for the next blow. Yet Brooke admitted that he did suffer a desperate feeling of loneliness because 'there was still just the possibility that I was wrong and that Monty was beat'.[48]

As Churchill was agonising over the slowdown in 'my Monty's' battle, the guns began firing the artillery programme for the Australian attack towards the coast. The 90th Light Division war diary noted that soon 'the northern sector was under a barrage reminiscent of Great War days. The horizon was ablaze with the flashes of enemy guns.'[49] Rommel and von Thoma considered that 'The situation is very serious, because very strong forces may be expected to break through to Sidi Abd el Rahman.'[50]

On time, at 22.00 hours on 28 October, the two battalions of 20th

Australian Brigade attacked. The forming-up area for the troops was badly congested; every battalion had to pass through the constricted area near Point 29 and this became 'the bottleneck of the operation'.[51] There had been heavy fighting around Point 29 all day and the battalions drew hostile artillery fire even before they had crossed their start lines. A direct hit on a mortar carrier killed the entire crew.[52] Lieutenant-Colonel C. K. M. Magno, the commander of the 2/15th Battalion was mortally wounded and his adjutant, Captain Harland, badly wounded.[53] Even so, the battalion pressed on in the face of mortar and machine-gun fire, meeting only scattered Italian opposition and no minefields.[54] It was able to dig in on its objective after suffering relatively light casualties.[55] Soon after midnight, the supporting arms and stores had reached the battalion and sappers were already laying a Hawkins minefield around the new positions.

The 2/13th Battalion was so under strength that its companies could cover barely 100 yards of front during its attack.[56] Nonetheless, the unit made good progress until it reached the Fig Garden, 1,500 yards from the start line. This area, sometimes referred to as the 'Fig Orchard' and ironically named, was thickly sown with 'S' mines and booby traps. More soldiers were killed and wounded by these mines than by enemy fire. The final objective was reached just after midnight but mopping up the surrounding area caused more difficulty. Gradually, the isolated German machine-gun posts in the area were overcome and the battalion was able to establish itself in the positions it had captured.[57] By the next day, when the unit had finished its reorganisation, it was discovered that the four rifle companies were left with a total of just 100 men.[58]

The second phase of the attack commenced at 23.40 hours when the 2/23rd Battalion began its advance in conjunction with 46th Royal Tank Regiment. These units had trained together for almost a week so the infantry and tank crews knew one another.[59] Unfortunately, although the first phase of the attack had 'proceeded entirely according to plan',[60] the second phase dissolved into chaos. The battalion had a long way to go before reaching the road and so it was decided to use carriers and the Valentine tanks to carry the troops forward. The idea was to speed up the advance and enhance the element of surprise.[61] Unfortunately, the final briefing was held hurriedly and with insufficient time for Lieutenant-Colonel Clarke of 46th Royal Tank Regiment to explain the operation to his squadron leaders properly. None of the tank commanders had been able to reconnoitre the start line.[62] The result was almost inevitable: the leading tanks missed the marked gaps and ran straight onto the Hawkins minefield that the Australians had laid to protect their positions. The following tanks then began to search for the gaps but many also ran onto the Australian minefield. This led to considerable chaos; the infantry sections that had been riding on the tanks were carried far away from their platoons and it proved impossible to gather the battalion to prosecute the attack.[63] The communications between the tank commanders and the infantry broke down and even though the headquarters of 26th Australian Brigade and 23rd Armoured Brigade were located close to one another, they were also out of contact. It took an hour to sort out the mess. Then, as the tanks drove forward through the minefield lanes, they were fired on by at least six 50mm anti-tank guns enfilading the gaps. This quickly led to 'complete confusion . . . with the tks moving off in all directions'.[64] The infantry companies were now hopelessly dispersed and, in desperation, Lieutenant-Colonel Bernard Evans gathered some 60 of his men together, put them in some semblance of order and attacked the German post which had caused much of the difficulty. This determined group captured 160 prisoners and the six anti-tank guns but it was not until 04.00 hours that Evans was able to report his success. His battalion had suffered 29 killed, 172 wounded and six missing during the attack.[65]

The men of the 2/24th and 2/48th Battalions had waited with growing anxiety throughout the night. They saw the inferno of fighting ahead of them and their thoughts turned to the 'possibility of attacking over open ground in daylight' which brought 'memories of just such another attack on 22nd July at Tel el Eisa'.[66] But earlier mistakes were not repeated. The brigade did develop a new plan in which 2/24th and 2/48th Battalions would continue the attack but it was soon realised that the time was too short before first light. The whole attack was postponed. Much to the relief of the waiting infantry, they trudged back to their slit trenches for some sleep.[67]

Later that morning, Brigadier Richards was able to visit the remnants of 46th Royal Tank Regiment. He found that the commanding officer and all the squadron leaders had become casualties during the night and only eight tanks remained battleworthy. The rest lay disabled on minefields. It would take time to recover them; the regiment had almost ceased to exist.[68]

As with so many attacks in the past, this effort had broken down after its initial stages. This was probably more due to the increasing tiredness of the soldiers and tank crews than to any inability to execute the plan. Yet a simpler plan enabling each battalion to advance with mutual support on its flanks might well have been more successful. Still, and most important of all, the errors and confusion of the night had not been compounded by an ill-thought-out daylight attack. The bitter events of July, when Australian battalions had been stranded in the open after hasty attacks, would not be repeated.

The Australian attack had disrupted and confused the Axis defence, and gained more elbow room for the division. Battlegroup 155 of the 90th Light Division had suffered heavy casualties although some of its elements had managed to hold out.[69] On the morning of 29 October, two German half-tracks towing 50mm anti-tank guns drove straight towards the Australian lines because their drivers were unaware of what had happened the previous night. The first vehicle was set ablaze and the 22 surprised crewmen and their guns were captured.[70] The Australian soldiers had to endure frequent airburst shelling by 88mm and 105mm guns during the day and at least three counterattacks by the tanks and infantry of Battlegroup 200 struck at the junction between the 2/15th and 2/17th Battalions.[71] However, the crushing artillery defensive fire ensured that these attacks made no ground and cost the assaulting units dearly. The Australian intelligence officers who interrogated German prisoners noted 'a definite weakening of enemy morale and that our arty concentrations were having a devastating effect both on inf and tk personnel'.[72]

This information was very welcome but one issue still troubled the intelligence officers of 9th Australian Division. The German strongpoint known as Thompson's Post, which dominated much of the surrounding desert, remained a thorn in their sides. It was formed from a number of trenches and gun pits and covered nearly 1,000 square yards. Capturing these positions was obviously very important but there were conflicting reports about whether it was still occupied. The panzergrenadiers holding it often moved to alternative positions when under bombardment, moving back if an attack threatened. The 2/13th Battalion was ordered to send out a series of patrols on 29 October to settle the matter, but failed to do so conclusively.[73] The position was to pose a threat to the 9th Australian Division for the remainder of the battle.

Montgomery noted in his diary on 29 October: 'It is becoming essential to break through somewhere.'[74] This comment was almost certainly precipitated by the visit of Alexander, McCreery and Casey, the Minister of State, to his Tactical Headquarters on the morning of 29 October. Eden had evidently taken matters into his own hands and sent Casey to observe the real situation in the desert. As usual, Montgomery 'radiated confidence' and the visitors seemed reassured.[75] However, after the meeting, Casey drew de Guingand aside and discussed the need to send a signal preparing Churchill for the possibility of a stalemate. De Guingand replied: 'If you send that signal I will see that you are hounded out of political life!'[76] It is just as well that neither de Guingand nor Montgomery ever understood the machinations in London that had brought Casey to their headquarters. By the time Casey reported to Churchill that Alexander and Montgomery 'fully realise importance of achieving breakthrough at earliest possible moment and are directing themselves strenuously to this end', the crisis of confidence had already passed.[77]

Indeed, the planning for the next breakthrough attempt finally took shape on 29 October during a series of discussions at Eighth Army Tactical Headquarters between Montgomery and de Guingand. 9th Australian Division was to repeat its attack towards the sea on the night of 30–31 October.[78] This was to draw Axis attention to the northern salient and ensure that Rommel had to commit his reserves – including the 90th Light – to that sector. Meanwhile, Montgomery hoped that on the next night Eighth Army would 'blow a deep hole in the enemy front just north of the original Northern funnel'[79] to the north of Kidney ridge. De Guingand commented that there were few defences or minefields in this sector and that the attack should be 'child's play compared with the attack on D Day'.[80] Freyberg's continued arguments, combined with fresh intelligence that the 90th Light Division was now concentrated in the coastal sector,[81] had eventually convinced Montgomery to shift the axis of the attack further south and away from the coast road. While the Army Commander and his Chief of Staff firmed up the broad vision of what had to be achieved, Freyberg and his staff engaged themselves with the all-important details of the attack.

The plan itself was simple. Two infantry brigades – the 151st Infantry Brigade drawn from 50th Division and 152nd Infantry Brigade from the 51st (Highland) Division – would attack on a front of 4,000 yards and reach a depth of 4,000 yards with the support of at least 12 field and all three medium regiments of artillery. Wimberley, who was expected to bridle at the detachment of his Highlanders, would be informed that the loan of his brigade was 'for the common good'.[82] Meanwhile, 133rd Lorried Infantry Brigade would capture 'Woodcock' to secure the southern flank of the operation, while 28 Maori Battalion was to hold the northern shoulder. Freyberg ensured that there could be no confusion over the boundaries of the attack by selecting the objectives:

> entirely from the map. Each Brigade was to advance due west on a frontage of two grid squares to a depth of four grid squares. Consequently its execution depended on accurate navigation by maintaining true bearing and correct distance.[83]

He also encouraged the infantry brigades to issue simple diagrams down to platoon and even section levels so that every man understood his part. The infantry brigades, supported by one regiment of tanks drawn from 23rd Armoured Brigade and anti-tank guns, would then hold this new penetration firmly. A tight grasp was essential; it was clear that the newly created salient would be 'shelled and bombed and counter-attacked by 15 and 21 Panzer Divisions'.[84] 9th Armoured Brigade, made up of 132 tanks, would then drive 2,000 yards beyond the infantry objective to reach the high ground marked by the Rahman track.[85] This was designed to punch a hole in the Axis defences which would enable 1st Armoured Division, following up behind 9th Armoured Brigade, to break out to the west. Freyberg remarked that 'he would take his Tac HQ forward and lead the armour through himself if necessary'.[86] In essence, the plan was a repetition of Lightfoot but on a much smaller frontage. As with any seemingly simple plan, the devil lay in the myriad details; working out the timings, frontages, moves forward and all the other finer points was an enormous task for the staff of Freyberg's divisional headquarters.

Just as Montgomery was setting in train the planning for a renewed break-out attempt, Rommel had begun to contemplate the necessity for withdrawal. He had learned that yet another tanker, the *Luisiano*, had been sunk the previous night and was now convinced that his army would not be able to withstand the punishing attacks mounted by Eighth Army for much longer. The withdrawal would have to be made before the British made a final, decisive breakthrough but any retreat would condemn much of the non-motorised Italian infantry to capture. Yet the lack of petrol made mobile warfare impossible as well. Rommel decided that when the moment came, the only answer would be to 'whip out the infantry unexpectedly' overnight in the southern sector, load as many as possible onto transport columns and use the motorised forces to mount a fighting retreat back to the Fuka position. Even so, he was not prepared to give up just yet. He decided to make one last defensive effort against the next British breakthrough attempt before accepting that the battle was truly lost.[87]

In the early hours of 30 October, four successive attacks were launched by the 90th Light Division along the front held by the 2/15th Battalion. Each was shattered by mortar and small-arms fire. At one point German tanks drove up almost to the muzzles of the Australian anti-tank guns but then withdrew. The German attacks simply could not make headway against the determined Australian defence.[88] The rest of the day 'passed quietly'[89] because a sandstorm blew up which 'spread like a great shroud over Egypt, half-burying the dead and hid for a brief moment the hate and passion of war'.[90] Even in the midst of such an intense battle, the desert itself could still dictate the tempo of the fighting. Rommel might have been well advised to start his retreat under the cover of the sandstorm.

Instead, the lull in the fighting played into Montgomery's hands. With little fighting taking place at the front, de Guingand noted that the day 'was spent in teeing up SUPERCHARGE'.[91] The next break-in attempt now had a name. Montgomery wrote out the new directive for the operation in the morning at a conference with Lumsden and Leese. At noon de Guingand met with the senior staff officers of each corps and 'other reps' to sort out the details including 'accommodation, tracks, moves forward, traffic control, allocation of resources, timings etc'.[92] That afternoon, Montgomery and de Guingand held 'a full scale conference with all Corps Comdrs and BGS's . . . at which the plan was discussed in considerable detail and various modifications made'.[93] These meetings were evidence of the efficient operation of Montgomery's command system and the effectiveness of Freddie de Guingand as his Chief of Staff, especially compared to the planning for Bacon, Splendour and Manhood. Then, no one – with the possible exception of Auchinleck and Dorman-Smith – had actually understood the full intent of the operations.

Montgomery was under intense pressure to achieve a breakthrough but the plans for Supercharge were not rushed. Freyberg, who would command the operation, had provided much of the inspiration and his views had been incorporated into the plan; but Montgomery and de Guingand also made certain that the coordination and planning involved each corps commander and their staffs. This time the entire army understood the importance of Supercharge.

The lull in the fighting also helped Morshead and his men. The Australian soldiers gained a brief respite. The preparations for the attack that night could take place undisturbed. In essence, the plan was to carry out the part of the previous attack that had been postponed. Staff officers from divisional headquarters were allocated to the 26th Australian Brigade Headquarters to help work out the details. There were to be four phases. In the first, 2/32nd Battalion, which had been held in reserve, would 'drive the enemy from and hold the area between the MAIN rd and r[ailwa]y'.[94] Its main objective was a small hill just to the south of the road called 'B11', but soon named 'Barrel Hill' by the Australian soldiers. The battalion was to hold positions between Barrel Hill near the road and the 'Blockhouse' near the railway line. In the second phase, the 2/24th and 2/48th Battalions would follow behind this first attack and then assemble, laying out their own start lines to advance east and capture the main enemy defences astride the coast road from the rear. The 2/48th Battalion would advance to the north of the main road while the 2/24th Battalion would move in parallel south of the road. The third phase would take place once the 2/48th had reached Ring Contour 25 (the Baillieu's Bluff of July fame). Its companies would face north and attack the positions known as the 'Cloverleaf' near the coast. Meanwhile, 2/24th would then face south and secure Thompson's Post. In the last phase, the 2/3rd Australian Pioneer Battalion, which was to be used as infantry, was to attack from Barrel Hill towards the coast and reorganise facing east and west so that the survivors of 125th Panzergrenadier Regiment would be completely cut off.[95]

Once again, the Australian attack was too complicated and expected too much of the Australian soldiers. The 2/24th and 2/48th Battalions were tasked with making individual advances of nearly 10,000 yards and the plan hinged on the sequential actions of individual battalions rather than their combined effort. This meant that the tasks of each battalion were indeed 'tremendous'[96] and actually far beyond the capacity of battalions that had experienced intense fighting over the last six days. The rifle companies of the 2/48th Battalion now held just 213 men;[97] each company was now at half-strength with roughly 50 men each, yet the battalion was being launched into a more ambitious assault than at any time since the July fighting.

The brigade was careful to avoid another fiasco with its supporting tanks. The Valentines of 40th Royal Tank Regiment would not be used in the night assault; they were to move up during the night on well-marked tracks so that they would be ready to support the brigade at first light.[98] At least the battalions could rely on crushing artillery support with the same 360 guns being tasked to fire timed concentrations on the known enemy positions. This time a barrage would be fired to support the advance of 2/32nd Battalion during the first phase because information on the new enemy defences that had been dug remained sketchy. The artillery programme was a detailed masterpiece of planning but everything depended upon the timings of the successive operations.[99]

When the attack began at 22.00 hours on 30 October problems emerged almost immediately. Montgomery noted that 'the attack of 9 Aust Div went in under a terrific artillery fire. My caravan at my Tactical H.Q. shook all night.'[100] Unfortunately, there was considerable congestion at the forming up place for the 2/32nd Battalion and this slowed everything down. The leading companies moved off ten minutes late and this meant that, like many battalions in the Great War, they 'lost' the barrage which had continued to creep forward according to the programme. A barrage, or even a concentration, fired by 25-pounder field guns was unlikely to kill many well-dug-in defenders. Its main purpose was to ensure that defenders kept their heads down while the bursting curtain of shells moved past their dugouts and weapon pits. As long as the attacking infantry 'leant' on the barrage by advancing no more than 50 yards behind it, they would be able to reach the defenders while they were still stunned. 'Losing' the barrage meant that the battalion had to fight its own way forward against an active and alert defence. The battalion was fortunate to find that the 'opposition was not really determined' but it became much tougher between the railway and Barrel Hill. Nonetheless, the battalion reached the hill and took 175 prisoners from I Battalion 361st Panzergrenadier Regiment. Unfortunately, soon after the final objective was reached, the Australian battalion commander was badly wounded, and in the confusion, although the battalion reorganised according to its drill, the weak companies were not able to mop up all the enemy posts surrounding them. This caused real problems for the 2/24th and 2/48th Battalions in their subsequent advance.[101]

The steep railway embankment presented other difficulties. This was found to be 12 feet high and the bulldozer which had been brought forward to cut through the bank was disabled on a mine. The engineers finally blew the rails and gathered two parties of men to dig away the sand with their entrenching tools. Three hours of exhausting work cleared a route allowing transport to move through. The gap inevitably came under anti-tank fire but remained in use until daylight.[102]

The second phase of the attack also encountered difficulties due to the number of unsubdued posts in the area between Barrel Hill and the railway. The 2/48th Battalion reached the forming up point at the railway

embankment near the Blockhouse but found that there was 'enemy resistance . . . at every step'.[103] B Company was sent forward to clear the start
line and the men duly shot and bombed the German defenders out of their
posts. Meanwhile, the other companies were sent forward of the starting
line to get them out of the line of fire. While this was going on, the 2/24th
Battalion arrived on the start line, and, since they were already 15 minutes
late, thought that the 2/48th Battalion had gone on ahead. They went forward
into the attack alone.[104]

At 01.00 hours, according to the prearranged timetable, the supporting
artillery opened up with a 'receding' barrage. Since the Australian infantry
were attacking eastwards, the barrage and concentrations crept back towards
the Eighth Army gun positions. A much wider danger distance of 600 yards
had to be imposed and this, combined with the delay and confusion at the
start line, meant that the artillery fire had little supporting effect on the
advance. Lieutenant-Colonel Hammer faced the difficult choice of waiting
at least 45 minutes under fire before the artillery programme could be altered,
or simply pushing ahead and trying to catch up with the concentrations.
Not surprisingly, he decided to push on. However, as the infantry advanced,
the barrage and timed concentrations crashed down too far ahead of them
to do much good, leaving them to deal with an alert defence. The two battalions succeeded in getting back in touch with each other but neither could
rely on effective artillery support during their advance.[105]

The 2/24th Battalion met very determined resistance when it approached
its first objective. It was only after fierce fighting, and with the assistance
of a platoon from the 2/48th Battalion, that the battalion advanced to within
700 yards of its final objective. By this time, one of the companies had been
reduced to just six unwounded men, who withdrew to the cover of the
railway embankment. Soon the other leading company, also badly depleted,
withdrew south of the embankment. The battalion commander had received
reports that Thompson's Post had been found empty by a patrol that night
and went forward with a patrol to find out for himself. It turned out to be
all too occupied and the patrol had to withdraw. Eventually, with the battalion
in an impossibly exposed position, it was decided to withdraw the remnants
into the 2/32nd position south of the railway and dig in facing west.[106]

Once the 2/48th Battalion crossed the main road, its companies came
under heavy fire and encountered stubborn resistance from numerous enemy
positions. The depleted strength of the leading companies meant that many
of these remained unsubdued as the battalion advanced, and the reserve
companies were increasingly drawn into bitter hand-to-hand fighting. By
03.00 hours the leading companies, which had become separated, had fought
their way to the first objective. One of the rear companies had lost all its
officers. The two remaining companies pushed forward another 500 yards
towards the enemy front line. Although one of them penetrated the posts

it came out with only six unwounded men. With the 2/24th Battalion already withdrawn, Hammer took the hard decision also to pull back to the 2/32nd area and reorganise facing east. Although both battalions still had functioning battalion headquarters, the fierce fighting that had been experienced without the vital cover of close artillery support had almost destroyed them as functioning units. Any thought of further 'exploitation' was simply impossible.[107]

Even though the third phase of the operation had to be abandoned, the 2/3rd Pioneer Battalion went into its first attack from the forming up point in the congested 2/32nd area. The leading companies met little opposition and even though they were 10 minutes late, soon caught up with the artillery support. Indeed, the artillery concentrations began to hold up the advance, whereupon one company commander decided to reorganise 200 yards north of the first objective to ensure that there was time to secure the position before dawn.[108]

At first light on 31 October 'the situation of the 26 Aust Bde . . . was somewhat obscure'.[109] This was a masterly understatement and it was not until long after the battle had ended that the true situation became clear. Australian soldiers holding the front further south strained to watch the battle unfolding around the railway but 'the [26th] Brigade area could only be guessed at so heavy was the pall of dust and smoke that concealed it'.[110] 2/3rd Pioneer Battalion had two companies within 500 yards of the coast and a third just north of the road. 2/32nd Battalion was holding positions which stretched across the railway up to Barrel Hill but which did not link up with the 2/15th Battalion further south. The remnants of the 2/24th Battalion – now reduced to one officer and 84 men in its rifle companies – held two positions 200 yards apart south of the railway. The 2/48th Battalion, now composed of two officers and just 48 men, held a position 300 yards east of Barrel Hill with one post just north of the railway line.[111] Though they were little more than shattered remnants, the battalions of the brigade nevertheless steeled themselves for the inevitable counterattacks.

The railway Blockhouse, a useful landmark during the planning phase of the operation, now became a medical aid post crammed with the wounded of both sides. Australian stretcher-bearers worked until they dropped bringing in the multitude of wounded men over the thousands of yards that had been covered during the attacks. Three Australian doctors, along with three German counterparts, tended the stream of wounded men brought to the Blockhouse while ambulances braved the shelling to bring casualties out of the fighting.[112]

At first light, the 2/3rd Pioneers took stock of their exposed position while the Germans brought up mortars during the morning to bombard their shallow slit trenches. Hostile fire grew steadily throughout the morning. A misunderstanding in one company led to its withdrawal back to the railway line where it was found that part of the other forward company had pulled back as well. This precipitated the withdrawal of the rest of the battalion towards the positions of the 2/32nd and 2/48th. One Pioneer company dug in around Barrel Hill while the remaining two companies, now shorn of almost all their officers, pulled back beyond the railway line.[113] Nonetheless, the Australian attack had served to cut off 125th Panzergrenadier Regiment from its regimental and divisional headquarters.[114]

The all-important communications with the gunners held up throughout the next day. Now in defence, the observation posts were able to call down powerful artillery concentrations on the initial unsupported counterattacks by two companies of 361st Panzergrenadier Regiment. These attacks threatened the position from the west as well as north and south of the railway soon after first light on 31 October.[115]

At 07.00 hours, Rommel visited the Battle Headquarters of 90th Light Division and personally issued the orders for the principal counterattack. The 361st Battle Group of the 90th Light Division and the Pfeiffer Battlegroup of the 21st Panzer Division[116] were to advance between the railway and the coast and attack the enemy at the 'hut' (as the Germans called the Blockhouse). The attack was to drive the enemy back across the railway and re-establish contact with the 125th Panzergrenadier Regiment. Rommel placed von Thoma in overall command and ordered him to go to 90th Light Division's Headquarters immediately. Von Thoma considered this order 'incomprehensible' as it meant that he had to leave his main area of responsibility and 'direct a counter-attack on an unfamiliar front'.[117] The fact was that the Australian attack had threatened the Panzerarmee at its most vulnerable point and Rommel could not afford to lose any ground in the coastal sector.

By 11.30 hours the Australians could see this threat developing. The 15 Mk III and IV tanks of the Pfeiffer Battlegroup drove along a coastal track to the north of Barrel Hill and deployed so that they could attack from the west, just south of the coast road, at the same time as the infantry of 361st Battlegroup pushed forward north of the railway. Soon, an intense fire-fight developed between the panzers and the forward Australian positions. Meanwhile, the Valentines of 40th Royal Tank Regiment had experienced a very difficult night as they attempted to thread their way through dense minefields. The supporting detachment of engineers had to do much mine-clearing and, by mid-morning, Lieutenant-Colonel Finigan had already had two tanks blown up under him by mines. After a quick conference with Hammer, Finigan decided to cross the railway line and deploy his regiment, now reduced to 32 tanks, in hull-down positions amongst the sand hummocks to the east of 2/48th Battalion's positions. The Valentines reached these positions not long before the Pfeiffer Battlegroup began its attack. Although seriously outmatched, the Valentine crews knew that they had to hold their positions to protect the Australian infantry. The anti-tank guns of 298th Anti-Tank Battery, which were deployed along the railway embankment, added their fire to support the beleaguered Valentines. Although outranged and outgunned, the Valentine crews held their ground and employed their hull-down positions to best advantage. Although the German tanks were able to knock out many of the Valentines, several panzers were also hit and set on fire. Shocked by the unexpectedly fierce resistance, the remainder of the German battlegroup withdrew.

This was only the start of a series of counterattacks that day. The exhausted Australian infantry also had to endure heavy shelling throughout the day. Further south, the 20th Australian Brigade, which was holding the original gains around Point 29, observed a large body of enemy tanks and lorried infantry forming up to the west. The brigade put in a request for bomber support and, at noon, a 'football team'[118] of Bostons duly arrived and bombed the inviting target with pinpoint accuracy. Soon, large numbers of Axis trucks were on fire and the looming counterattack dissolved into confusion, much to the delight of the watching Diggers. It was later stated, 'the excellent and continued bombing by the RAF caused jubilation in the front line and h[eav]y casualties amongst enemy MT concentrations'.[119] Throughout the day, the fighters of the Desert Air Force gave an unprecedented level of cover over the vulnerable Australian positions. Four Stuka raids were attempted against the salient but only one got through the strong fighter cover.[120]

By 14.00 hours, 90th Light Division had organised another serious counterattack designed to retake the ground between the road and the railway. The tanks and infantry managed to break into the positions of B Company 2/32nd Battalion but after a fierce fight in which the anti-tank guns and the remaining Valentines of 40th Royal Tank Regiment destroyed one Mk III and immobilised several others, the Germans were again forced to withdraw.[121]

Just two hours later, the Pfeiffer Battlegroup spearheaded yet another attack. It carefully worked its way around the Australian positions and took up hull-down positions around the high ground to the north of the road. The German infantry made no headway against the Australian defences and suffered once again from the pounding of concentrated artillery fire.[122] The Valentines kept up the unequal contest and managed to destroy five or six of the panzers before the rest withdrew. After a day of intense fighting 40th Royal Tank Regiment was finally ordered to withdraw. Twenty-one Valentines were left behind as shattered wrecks, yet the regiment had held off every German tank attack and protected the Australian infantry. The historian of the 2/48th Battalion remarked that 'the courage of these men made their action one of the most magnificent of the war'.[123] There had been no repeat of the bitter debacles of July. The tanks, infantry, artillery and anti-tank guns of 9th Australian Division worked together as a team. As darkness fell, tank-hunting parties were sent out to deal with the tanks lurking on the high ground north of the road but none was found. They had withdrawn to safer positions away from the Australian 'cockpit'.

By the end of this fierce day of fighting, von Thoma and Bayerlein were convinced that the position of the 125th Panzergrenadier Regiment in the coastal salient was 'untenable for any length of time and is an open challenge to the enemy to make further attacks'. Since the repeated counter-attacks had failed to make significant headway, von Thoma believed that the regiment should be withdrawn that night.[124] Rommel refused to countenance this. He was still firmly convinced that Eighth Army would launch its break-through attempt in the coastal sector and that any retreat from the salient would be disastrous. He ordered the attack to be continued the next day, unaware that his fixation with the fighting along the coast was drawing his attention away from the real location for Supercharge, further south. At last, Eighth Army was outthinking as well as outfighting its opponent.

26th Australian Brigade had held onto its positions throughout the day, almost, but not quite, cut off from the rest of the division. Morshead had no clear knowledge of the dispositions or strength of his depleted battalions that hung on around Barrel Hill. Little could be seen of the brigade's positions through the palls of smoke and dust that hung in the air for most of the day. It was not until 17.30 hours that Morshead was able to go to 26th Australian Brigade Headquarters and learn from Brigadier Whitehead the desperate state of the 2/24th and 2/48th Battalions.[125] He immediately ordered the brigade's relief since the ferocity of the German counterattacks was unlikely to diminish the next day.

The relief was essential because, on the night of 30 October, Freyberg had insisted that Supercharge be postponed for 24 hours. The mass of planning and movement of troops had proved too complicated and difficult to carry out properly for an attack on the night of 31 October to succeed. This meant that Supercharge would not take place until 01.05 hours on 2 November and Morshead knew that his division would have to bear the full burden of the battle for another day. 24th Australian Brigade had been holding the coastal sector since the start of the battle. Its two battalions, the 2/28th and 2/43rd, were still effective formations. Morshead ordered this fresh brigade into the Barrel Hill salient to relieve the exhausted fragments of 26th Australian Brigade. It was now their turn to suffer the full weight of the Panzerarmee's counterattacks.

The night passed quietly and the relief was able to take place unmolested. The troops of 20th Australian Brigade holding the positions further south were even able to snatch a few hours of welcome sleep. Morshead's decision to order the relief in the middle of the battle and at short notice has been called the 'high point' of his military career[126] but it was also the moment when he ran the greatest risk. A number of tense hours elapsed

small-arms fire held off the attacks and inflicted heavy casualties upon the panzergrenadiers who had ridden into the attack on the back of the tanks. Fighter-bomber sorties were also called in and inflicted considerable damage on the Axis counterattacks, although one flight of aircraft mistakenly attacked the Australian troops on Barrel Hill.[141]

In the late afternoon, 24th Australian Brigade suffered a severe blow when its headquarters received a direct hit. Brigadier A. H. L. Godfrey was mortally wounded and several other officers killed and wounded. For the rest of the day, the battalions had to fight on without direction from brigade. It had become a 'soldier's battle'. As the sun began to set upon a day of carnage, Rommel ordered another attack using the traditional Afrika Korps tactic of driving forward with the setting sun behind them to blind the defenders. Tanks and infantry advanced from the west while fifteen trucks packed with infantry deployed and pushed on from the north east.[142] A bombing raid by a Boston 'football team' combined with heavy artillery concentrations broke up the attacks before they properly got underway.[143] Even once the sun had set the fighting continued but every attempt by the German panzergrenadiers to take ground was met with 'determined and accurate artillery and S[mall] A[rms] fire'.[144] By the end of the day, both sides were exhausted but Rommel refused to withdraw the remnants of the 125th Panzergrenadier Regiment. He still hoped to divert attention away from the coastal sector with simulated attacks along the front that night.[145]

For their part, the Australian infantry were now fearful about their future. The Blockhouse was crammed with wounded and the medics were forced to leave wounded men outside. It seemed doubtful that they would be able to hang on for another day against such fierce attacks. The soldiers of 9th Australian Division had been stretched to the limit. Too much had been demanded of them by Montgomery and their own divisional commander. Yet through sheer fighting skill and determination, the Diggers had continued to fight. Lieutenant-Colonel Hammer of the 2/48th Battalion summarised the situation:

> The fighting clearly showed we were more than a match for the enemy. We should always fight with the utmost confidence. Hun is a bogeyman. He fights well but is not impregnable and can always be beaten if you have the 'WILL TO WIN'.[146]

The Australian soldiers certainly possessed the 'will to win' but their casualties had been grievous. Through their stubborn, repeated attacks and dogged resistance they had drawn the last reserves of the Panzerarmee into the fiercest fighting ever witnessed at El Alamein.

Montgomery's initial plan for a rapid breakthrough had failed by 25 October but, by launching the 9th Australian Division towards the coast, he had managed to retain the all-important initiative. While most of the original 30 Corps breach was closed down into a defensive front, the successive Australian attacks against the vulnerable yet vital coast road forced an Axis response. Thus, the fighting might be better described as positional rather than attritional. Each time the Australian infantry seized ground and threatened future attacks, Rommel mounted counterattack after counterattack in a desperate attempt to stabilise the situation. This fighting wore down the 9th Australian Division to a virtual skeleton but it sucked in all the Axis reserves and concentrated them in the north far away from the place where Supercharge would be launched. The Australian soldiers could have been forgiven for thinking that they were fighting the battle alone but their heroism gave Eighth Army vital time to prepare its next blow. Rommel had been dragged into a frantic dance 'round and round the mulberry bush' so that Supercharge could 'topple him off his perch'.[47]

EIGHTEEN

Operation Supercharge

At 01.05 hours on 2 November 1942, 360 guns, tasked with the artillery programme for Operation Supercharge, opened fire. Freyberg was vaguely disappointed and considered the 'opening not so impressive as 23/24 October'[1] but other observers at the New Zealand divisional headquarters noted:

> The ground shuddered as mediums and 25 prs leapt into action. Flashes like lightning momentarily darted skywards showing up the landscape near the guns. Crash followed crash relentlessly merging into one tremendous rumble as the gunners behind [the] guns sent off 150,000 rounds along a 4000 yd front.[2]

The bombardment was not, of course, being fired for the benefit of the watching New Zealanders but to crush any Axis resistance along the infantry's line of advance.

The artillery fireplan for Supercharge was Brigadier 'Steve' Weir's masterpiece. For the first time he was able to put his ideas concerning the effectiveness of the creeping barrage into effect with practically every gun in 30 Corps. Intelligence concerning enemy positions was sketchy so the creeping barrage came into its own. The infantry brigade holding the start line actually withdrew 1,500 yards from its forward positions and the barrage started on the original front line to ensure that no enemy defences would be missed. After three minutes of this fire, the medium guns switched to counter-battery tasks for five minutes before the full barrage landed again on the front line and remained there for 20 minutes to give the infantry time to close up. One hundred and ninety-two guns were used to fire the creeping barrage which was divided into three lines. Five regiments of 25-pounders shelled the first line which amounted to one gun every 33 yards. Three regiments of 25-pounders opened fire on a line 200 yards further west which gave greater depth to the barrage. 64th and 69th Medium shelled a line 800 yards from the first line. There was one gun firing for every 11.3 yards of front and 150,000 shells were fired in four and a half hours into an area just 4,000 yards square. Another 168 guns fired concentrations on the flanks to shatter any resistance outside the path of advance. Just as in Lightfoot, Bofors guns fired tracer to mark the brigade boundaries and smoke was used to mark start and final objective lines. This barrage was not a single, thin line of bursting shells but a massive carpet of fire which moved inexorably forward at the rate of 100 yards every two and a half minutes.[3]

Meanwhile, the night-bombing force was used in a series of 'softening up' operations, pounding the Axis positions at Tel el Aqqaqir and Ghazal station. Wellington bombers flew over the Axis positions for seven hours dropping a total of 184 tons of bombs; this broke all telephone communications at Afrika Korps Headquarters.[4] It was a magnificent example of the coordinated application of firepower on a massive scale.

The infantry had a difficult march up to the start line through powdery sand that 'was like walking through snow'.[5] The soldiers in the Durham Brigade, dressed only in shorts, shirts and thin pullovers, were very cold as they waited for two hours on the start line.[6] Private Crawford of the 2/17th Australian Battalion gave his sweater to a young soldier in the Durhams who was shivering with the cold.[7] Right on time, the infantry of 152nd and 151st Infantry Brigades stepped out behind the barrage. The Scots advanced to the skirl of the pipes, a sound that was answered by the hunting horn of Major Teddy Worrall, a company commander in the 9th Durham Light Infantry. As far as Freyberg was concerned, the attack of 152nd Brigade on the left went 'like a drill, both objectives being taken according to schedule. It was a very fine performance.'[8]

Yet this was not the experience of the battalions that actually carried out the attack. As the infantry of the 5th Camerons and 2nd and 5th Battalions of the Seaforths walked behind the barrage:

> Clouds of dust and smoke arose, blotting out the desert which so short a time ago had seemed so vast. Each man found himself in a diminished world inhabited by himself and at most three or four others. Somewhere near him was an officer or sergeant with a compass, trying to walk a straight course through the inferno for more than two miles to an objective which was only a pencil line on the map.[9]

It was almost impossible, in such smoke and dust, to keep the advancing companies together. Sections and platoons became detached from one another and many of the inexperienced troops in the leading companies actually pressed on into the barrage. When, at 03.44 hours, the brigade reported that it was on 'Neat', the final objective line, Freyberg commented, 'On to time. Damn good.'[10] Each battalion had had to fight countless small battles against Italian and German posts, and the leading companies had suffered heavy casualties. C Company of the 5th Seaforths, which had started the night with 100 men, dug in on the objective with just twelve survivors.[11]

Unfortunately, once they reached the objective, the battalions found that the ground was iron hard – the limestone bedrock lay just two feet under the surface. As the men attempted to dig in, Axis artillery began to pound their positions. Captain George Green related:

> For the next five hours my group just lay as the shells came over, heavily and accurately. They were dead on range. All this time we were trying to dig. It was the worst ever. Stuff was landing continually within twelve yards of us, and some shells were as close as four feet.[12]

There was nothing the infantry could do now except frantically dig as much as they could and wait for the armour.

The attack by 151st Brigade did not go well. The smoke shells, designed to mark the start of the barrage, 'hindered more than they helped'[13] by obscuring vision still further. Axis machine guns, firing on fixed lines, sent their streams of tracer into the air while numerous Very lights went up into the sky calling for defensive fire. The historian of the 8th Durham Light Infantry remembered:

> The noise of battle was terrific. There was the deafening crash of the shells bursting only a hundred yards ahead and the rattle of Brens and Spandaus, interspersed with fierce bursts of fire from German and British Tommy-guns and occasionally the crash of a British hand grenade exploding in a dugout or trench.[14]

The advance fragmented into a series of fierce fights between small groups of Durhams and the German and Italian defenders. Eventually, small, isolated groups from the leading companies reached the final objective. Communications became badly disrupted and it took a long time to report success back to Freyberg's headquarters. On the flanks, the Royal Sussex and 28 Maori Battalion had stiff fighting to reach their objectives. Nonetheless, the infantry did its job. They had cut a swathe through the newly formed Axis defences and taken many prisoners. The Italian 65th Infantry Regiment and I Battalion of the 115th Panzergrenadier Regiment had been overrun and destroyed along with the regimental headquarters.[15] The funnel for the armour had been created.

The spearhead for the armoured break-out was Currie's 9th Armoured Brigade. The three regiments of the brigade, the 3rd Hussars, the Warwickshire Yeomanry and the Wiltshire Yeomanry, had an unenviable task. They were to advance under a heavy barrage and break the Axis gun line that lay along the Rahman track. Although Rommel had been convinced that the British breakthrough attempt would take place along the coast road, he had developed a formidable anti-tank gun screen further south near the high ground at Tel el Aqqaqir. The screen was deployed in a wide crescent along the Rahman track with at least 24 88mm guns dug in further back and a large number of smaller calibre guns sited in small folds in the ground.

No one in Eighth Army underestimated the difficulty of the task that faced 9th Armoured Brigade. At the briefing before the attack, Freyberg explained, 'We all realise that for armour to attack a wall of guns sounds like another Balaclava; it is properly an infantry job. But there are no more infantry available, so our armour must do it.'[16] 9th Armoured Brigade's task bore a striking resemblance to the previous 'Balaclava' charge of 23rd Armoured Brigade during Splendour. The difference was that Montgomery and Freyberg were using the costly method of charging anti-tank guns as a deliberate tactic. When informed of his brigade's part in Supercharge, Currie pointed out that the brigade would be operating on too wide a front and that no reserve would be possible. He also observed that the brigade would probably suffer 50 per cent losses.[17] Freyberg replied that Montgomery 'was aware of the risk and had accepted the possibility of losing 100% casualties in 9 ARMD Bde to make this break, but in view of the promise of immediate following through of 1 ARMD DIV, the risk was not considered as great as all that'.[18] There was little more that Currie could do except to fulfil his orders and hope for the best.

When the brigade left its assembly area near El Alamein station at 22.00 hours on 1 November, it moved off with 133 tanks but over the course of the 25-mile approach march 'many tanks fell by the wayside, and it is not certain how many tanks went into battle that morning'.[19] The brigade had been very hastily made up to numbers again with reconditioned tanks, many of which were still faulty. There was no time to check sights, wireless or compasses on many of them and this made communication and control within the brigade very difficult.

The tracks used by the brigade had been churned up constantly over a week of intense fighting and the sand ground to a fine powder which lay more than a foot deep. The dust quickly turned into a thick fog: 'It was like driving blindfolded through the rush hour . . . it was pitch dark and we were in a very thick cloud of dust. It was a real pea souper.'[20] It was not surprising that such conditions led to difficulties.

The 3rd Hussars were 'most unlucky during the advance'.[21] They suffered heavy casualties amongst their infantry and anti-tank guns from heavy shelling and thus arrived on the start line without any of their support group. Meanwhile, the Warwickshire Yeomanry drove down a blind alley in a minefield and had to turn round, retrace their steps and try to make up the time.

These delays led Currie to ask for a postponemeant of half an hour in the supporting barrage to allow his regiments to reach the start line and prepare for the advance.[22] Unfortunately, the 3rd Hussars and Royal Wilts reached the start line more or less on time and urged Currie to allow them to make the attack without waiting. Currie, all too aware that his brigade was already thinly spread, insisted on waiting for the barrage at 06.15 hours, half an hour later than planned.

Each of the regiments deployed in an irregular pattern with their B Squadrons of Crusader tanks in the lead, although the 3rd Hussars had just three tanks left in its Crusader screen because the rest had broken down. These were followed by the two heavy squadrons composed of Shermans and Grants. Currie posted himself near the lead of the attack. The barrage moved slowly forward at 100 yards every three minutes; this suited an infantryman's walking pace but not the fast Crusader tanks of the lead squadrons. Small parties of German infantry broke cover and ran but many were hit by sprays of fire from the Besa machine guns of the leading tanks. Others surrendered and were cursorily thumbed towards the rear. The Crusaders of the Royal Wilts drove through the barrage and managed to reach the Rahman track while it was still dark. Soon the tanks encountered the German anti-tank gun screen:

> Flash, flash, flash . . . in a great semi-circle the guns of the enemy wink viciously back at him as great balls of fire seem to leap out of the sand and hurtle towards the oncoming tanks. Some miss their mark and bounce on the sand, to die out gracefully like fireworks in the sky. Others land with a sick-ening metallic clang on the Crusaders and explosions add dull thuds to the pandemonium of sounds that fills the shattered air.[23]

There was literally nothing else the Crusaders could do but charge the guns. In the half-light, the tank commanders drove towards every flash that they could see and, armed only with two-pounders and Besa machine guns, they blazed away at the anti-tank guns and then actually drove over the German positions to crush the guns and their crews in their pits. It was later related that the Crusader squadron of the Royal Wilts was:

> involved in a scene of great confusion. Engaged by anti-tank guns on all sides, they were also surrounded by masses of infantry running about in all direc-tions. The Sqn fought with the greatest gallantry, charging and over-running enemy guns, until not a single tank was left[24].

At great cost, the Royal Wilts had reached the enemy gun line. As the heavy squadrons followed, the first glimmers of dawn appeared and silhouetted the tanks against the sky. Now the anti-tank guns, still shrouded in dark-ness and disposed in depth, could see the tanks and began to fire on easy targets. Some German infantry and gunners who had surrendered now ran back to their posts to fight again. As the tanks drove round crushing guns and machine gunning anything they could see, the German anti-tank guns began to knock out the tanks one by one. After a wild melee, in which the regiment destroyed 14 anti-tank guns and six tanks 'this Regt. was almost wiped out'. The Royal Wilts had begun their march with 40 tanks and were now reduced to just five. The infantry company and anti-tank guns of the 14th Sherwood Foresters that had accompanied the tanks into action dug in on the ground and held on to their advanced position throughout the day. The company was shelled by both sides before withdrawing after dark.[25]

On the right, the German guns had stayed silent as the three Crusaders of 3rd Hussars went past and only opened up when the Shermans and Grants of B Squadron were right amongst them.[26] As the light grew, 'the desert seemed a mass of guns and gun-pits, but the 3rd pressed on relentlessly . . . crushing the guns beneath them'.[27] The battlefield was soon filled with the smoke from burning tanks but the 3rd Hussars were able to hold on until 1st Armoured Division came up. They had accounted for 15 anti-tank guns but the regiment had been reduced to three Crusaders and nine Shermans or Grants.[28]

On the far left, the Warwickshire Yeomanry were especially unlucky. They emerged from the minefield lane much further south than expected and had to fight an entirely isolated action. Many of their tanks were knocked out without ever firing a shot by anti-tank guns firing from their rear. The regiment soon found that it was being engaged on three sides but managed to knock out all the guns that faced them. Eventually, the regiment was ordered to pull in towards the Royal Wilts but by that time there were only seven heavy tanks left.[29]

Meanwhile, the Panzerarmee began to react to the British break-out attempt. The tanks of 21st Panzer Division drove north and contacted 15th Panzer Division. It was decided to mount an outflanking movement to attack the British penetration by attacking towards the south east. 21st Panzer Division reached Tel el Aqqaqir[30] and was about to attack when it was ordered to halt immediately by Afrika Korps Headquarters. This was because of a misunderstanding about its location and by the time the situation was clarified, the opportune moment to drive in between the Royal Wilts and the Warwickshire Yeomanry had been lost.[31] The arrival of German tanks on the spot where the Warwickshire Yeomanry had been expected caused temporary confusion amongst the Royal Wilts before the German tanks were positively identified.[32]

In this fierce dawn battle, Currie looked anxiously over his shoulder for signs of 2nd Armoured Brigade, which was supposed to push beyond the shattered remnants of 9th Armoured Brigade. All that could be seen to his front was a mass of devastation with wrecked guns, dead crews and burning tanks littering the landscape.[33] His brigade had suffered crippling casualties; 31 officers and 198 other ranks were killed, wounded or missing.[34] Montgomery later wrote, 'If the British armour owed any debt to the infantry of the Eighth Army, the debt was paid on November 2 by 9th Armoured brigade in heroism and blood'.[35] Yet poor tactics, inexperience and inferior tanks had led to that debt being paid over and over again during the desert war. Currie's brigade, just like 23rd Armoured Brigade on 22 July 1942, or the armoured brigades at Sidi Rezegh or Gazala, had carried out its orders to the letter and the cost had been just as heavy. It was later argued:

> Although the brigade did not reach its final objectives, it is claimed that in spite of these losses, the action was a success and that only a few guns remained in the enemy position for 2 ARMD BDE to deal with, and that the break was made if exploitation had been quick and bold.[36]

In the event, 1st Armoured Division did not immediately exploit the sacrifice of 9th Armoured Brigade. At 07.35 hours, the New Zealand Division Headquarters reported to Leese that 'Currie is out where he should be' but also that 1st Armoured Division were moving very slowly and needed to be pushed out as far as possible. Just three minutes later Freyberg was asking Leese to apply 'more ginger' to 1st Armoured Division so that they got 'a bloody move on'.[37] Currie and Freyberg were convinced that 1st Armoured Division missed the opportunity to break through the Axis gun screen immediately but that was not the way that Briggs, Fisher or the leading squadrons of 2nd Armoured Brigade saw the situation confronting them that morning.

The regiments of 2nd Armoured Brigade had had an equally difficult night march with many delays caused by dust and mines but by 07.00 hours the brigade was deploying west of the minefields 600 yards behind the positions of 9th Armoured Brigade[38] and 'endeavouring to locate enemy armour and A.Tk guns'.[39] The historian of the 9th Lancers explained, 'It soon became obvious that the 9th Armoured Brigade had had a disaster: tanks were burning all over the desert in front of us.'[40] By this time the desert had changed. The sun was now up and the German 88mm guns disposed in depth beyond the Rahman track could add their fire to the guns which had not been subdued by 9th Armoured Brigade. Around this time, Currie met Lieutenant-Colonel Gerald Grosvenor, the commanding officer of the 9th Lancers, and said angrily, 'Well, we've made a gap in the enemy anti-tank screen, and your brigade has to pass through, and pass through bloody quick.' Grosvenor replied, 'I have never seen anything, sir, that looks less like a gap.'[41] 9th Armoured Brigade had sacrificed itself upon the Axis gun screen and caused great damage but had been unable to make a breakthrough. If 2nd Armoured Brigade had driven forward onto the waiting German guns it would have met the same fate as Currie's brigade.

Even though the regiments of 2nd Armoured Brigade deployed for defence and attempted to find good positions, the 9th Lancers believed that:

From then on the day was about the worst we had ever had . . . all day we were fired at continually from three sides by 88's and 105's. For hours on end the whack of armour-piercing shot on armour plate was unceasing.[42]

Rather than mounting another desperate charge, the regiments of 2nd Armoured Brigade settled down to use the tactics that were known to work. The Shermans and the supporting Priests used their high-explosive shells to good effect[43] but, 'although every endeavour was being made to push on', the 'strong A. Tk. screen, well hidden in the sand dunes, was making progress slow'.[44] This lack of forward movement also meant that the new salient was filling with tanks, troops and guns and becoming dangerously congested.

By 09.35 hours, 30 Corps had received intelligence from the 'Y' Service that the 21st Panzer Division was expected to counterattack west-south-west while the 15th Panzer Division would attack along the inter-brigade boundary.[45] The Pfeiffer Battlegroup, which had fought so hard against the Australians, was also brought south to join in the counterattack.[46]

Rommel had been expecting the British breakthrough attempt along the coast road and its unexpected direction gave the British at least some time to meet the attack. 8th Armoured Brigade had now followed up behind 2nd Armoured Brigade although it took until midday before its regiments were assembled on the southern flank of the corridor. They were not seriously engaged during the day.[47] At noon, the scattered remnants of 9th Armoured Brigade were collected into a composite regiment of 35 tanks and placed on the right of 2nd Armoured Brigade where they remained in action all day.

For the rest of the morning and afternoon, there was the greatest clash of armour seen at El Alamein. The Axis gunners redoubled their fire into the congested salient while the two German panzer divisions drove forward to stem the tide. Observers in the 90th Light Division commented:

During the morning the fighting reached its climax. Smoke and dust covered the battlefield, and visibility became so bad that the general picture was of one immense cloud of smoke and dust. Tanks engaged in single combat; in these few hours the battle of Alamein was decided.[48]

Although the German tank crews pressed home their attacks they made no headway against the British defence and suffered heavy losses. The German counterattack 'broke down in the face of the massed British armour which moved only in stages'.[49] At least 25 German tanks were destroyed by 2nd Armoured Brigade during the fighting. Eventually, after fierce fighting, the British armour was able to make some ground but 1st Armoured Division did not get any further forward than the Rahman track. The 21st Panzer Division noted:

After several more attempts during the afternoon the attack was found to be no longer practicable. Owing to the superior enemy fire power, 5th Panzer Regiment could neither be transferred nor withdrawn. However, the deep enemy penetration had been contained.[50]

Operation Supercharge had failed. The infantry of 151st and 152nd Brigades had made a deep breach in the Axis lines and 9th Armoured Brigade had attempted to punch right through the gap. It had inflicted heavy losses on the Axis gun line but had been annihilated in the attempt. Briggs had been quite right to hold back his 1st Armoured Division and wait for the inevitable Axis counterattack. 15th and 21st Panzer Divisions were virtually destroyed during the day of intense fighting. However, the fact remained that there had been no breakthrough and the Axis line had held.

The Desert Air Force operated at full pitch over the battle. The fighter cover completely protected the salient and the two Stuka raids which the Luftwaffe attempted were intercepted before they could reach the Eighth Army's lines. Targets were poor for the light-bomber force during the morning but as the Afrika Korps concentrated for its series of counter-attacks it was pounded by a shuttle service of Baltimores and Bostons.[51]

The Panzerarmee had sealed off the penetration but its line of defence was now leaking. For days Montgomery had wanted to get his armoured car regiments out into the open desert behind the Panzerarmee to attack the Axis supply lines. Supercharge provided the perfect opportunity. However, when Lieutenant-Colonel Pepys of the Royal Dragoons met with Montgomery and Lumsden at Army Headquarters there was an awkward moment:

> When the three of them stood facing the map of the battlefield which covered one whole wall of the caravan and the Army Commander talked about the 'Royals' both colonel and corps commander made the tacit stipulation that it would in fact be only two squadrons.[52]

This revealed that Montgomery was – embarrassingly – no expert when it came to armoured car operations. Lumsden had commanded an armoured car regiment in France in 1940 and realised that a regimental headquarters would only be a liability in operations behind the lines. This exchange cannot have improved relations between Montgomery and his corps commander but he did murmur assent to Pepys's plan to drive clear of the Panzerarmee's rear before coming back to attack them from the west.[53] Two squadrons of the Royal Dragoons, following in the wake of 152nd Brigade, managed to squeeze past the German anti-tank gun screen just before dawn on 2 November. Some of the cars fell into gun pits but the rest made it out into the open desert. For the next three days the armoured cars made numerous piratical attacks against Axis supply columns in the best traditions of the Jock columns and destroyed a vast amount of Axis material.[54]

But the lack of a clear breakthrough meant that Eighth Army had to begin a series of hastily improvised attacks to deal with the Axis gun screen. At 16.15 hours that afternoon, the 2nd Seaforth Highlanders mounted an attack on the 'Skinflint' objective which met little opposition. This time, unlike their previous daylight attack of 24 October, the attack went in under the support of eight field and two medium regiments of artillery, which completely shook the defence.[55] The battalion advanced 1,500 yards in just 20 minutes and collected 100 prisoners for no loss. Unfortunately, after the successful attack the Jocks suffered casualties from a German sniper concealed in a burned-out tank. A full company attack was launched to clear out the sniper and it was only with difficulty that the Jocks were restrained from shooting him.[56] Soon afterwards, the 5th Royal Sussex, part of 133rd Lorried Infantry Brigade that was temporarily under the command of 51st (Highland) Division, put in an equally successful attack on 'Snipe' and 'Woodcock'.[57] The Sussex had finally seized the ground where their 4th Battalion had come to grief. The Panzerarmee's grip on its defences was beginning to loosen.

On the evening of 2 November, after a desperate day of fighting, Rommel telephoned von Thoma to discuss the situation. Von Thoma reported that he had managed to close the gap with scant forces but the fierce fighting, and the overwhelming superiority of the enemy's tanks, artillery and aircraft, had caused very heavy casualties.[58] 15th Panzer Division's 8th Panzer Regiment now had eight tanks left and its commander, Oberst Teage, had been killed. Captain Stiffelmeyer, the commander of its I Battalion, had also been killed. The division now had a total of six Pak 38s in its anti-tank defence.[59] 21st Panzer Division could only muster 20 Mk III and Mk IVs.[60] Von Thoma estimated that no more than 35 tanks would be available for use the next day – and the British had at least four times that number at the front.[61] The infantry and artillery had fought bravely but were now reduced to one-third of their strength at the beginning of the British offensive. The flak batteries were also reduced to one-third of their 88mm guns. Von Thoma considered this particularly worrying as the 50mm Pak 38 was no longer considered effective against the heavy American tanks.[62]

Von Thoma believed that if the British attacks continued in the same strength a breakthrough would be unavoidable because there were no longer any reserves available. The moment that Rommel had feared for so long had finally arrived. He would have to withdraw to save what he could of his army. The Panzerarmee's daily report tried to put the best possible light on the desperate situation:

> After ten days of uninterrupted fighting our own losses are exceptionally high, due to the overwhelming superiority of the enemy's infantry, tanks and artillery

and the unremitting use he has made of his Air Force. . . . In the coming night and on 3 November we expect new attempts to penetrate by strong armoured forces . . . our forces are no longer sufficient to prevent new breaks through. As from 3 November the Army is therefore preparing to fight its way back step by step in face of the enemy pressure.[63]

Eighth Army had not broken through during Operation Supercharge but the skilful positional defence put up by the British units during the morning and afternoon of 2 November had doomed the Panzerarmee to defeat. By forming a new salient, Eighth Army had invited counterattacks and these had worn down the strength of the panzer divisions to the point that they could no longer resist. Rommel was finally forced to admit that his army would have to withdraw from El Alamein before it was completely destroyed.

Having taken this painful decision, Rommel worked quickly to give the retreat the best chance of success. The linchpin for the withdrawal were the remnants of the Afrika Korps and the Italian XX Motorised Corps. The Ariete Division was finally ordered north to bolster the remnants of the Littorio and Trieste Divisions in XX Motorised Corps. The motorised troops were to hold firm in the northern sector and conduct a fighting withdrawal throughout the next day towards El Daba. The Italian XXI Corps, with the Trento and Bologna Divisions, would pull out that night to a line 12 kilometres west of Tel el Aqqaqir. The Italian X Corps, still holding the line in the south, was ordered to withdraw that night to a line west of Bab el Qattara. The Ramcke Parachute Brigade would also pull out to the western edge of the Qatani minefield. It was at least hoped that if these formations could hold out during the next day, more transport could be provided from flak units during the evening of 3 November.[64]

Meanwhile, Lumsden worried that unless his armour could make some ground that night, it would be faced with an equally powerful anti-tank gun screen the next day. The historian of the Rifle Brigade noted that such a 'phase is always a dangerous one for the motor battalions'.[65] Lumsden decided to use the 7th Motor Brigade once again to punch a hole in the screen for his armour to exploit at dawn the next day. The brigade, composed of three motor battalions, 2nd and 7th Rifle Brigade and 2nd King's Royal Rifle Corps, which had already seen much action during the battle, were ordered to seize three separate objectives over the line of the Rahman track.[66] 2nd Armoured Brigade would then pass through the motor battalions and be ready to exploit the gap at first light.[67]

The three battalions went into the attack but experienced very different levels of success. The 2nd King's Royal Rifle Corps, now reduced to three companies, was given powerful artillery support, and advanced on foot towards the objective. It met fierce opposition along the line of the Rahman track and casualties were heavy. The battalion managed to dig in on what it believed was its objective but could only bring up eight anti-tank guns (two troops) because of the exposed nature of the position.[68] In fact, the battalion held a position which was still east of the Rahman track.

Meanwhile, the 2nd and 7th Rifle Brigade had mounted 'silent' attacks which came to grief against heavy opposition. After heavy fighting, the 7th Rifle Brigade reached its objective but found it impossible to bring up anti-tank guns. 2nd Rifle Brigade also cleared out a considerable number of enemy anti-tank guns, machine-gun and infantry posts around its objective but also found that the storm of fire made it impossible to bring up the six-pounder guns. Both battalions were forced to withdraw in the face of an imminent German tank attack at dawn. This experience proved just how fortunate the 2nd Rifle Brigade had been in its celebrated action at 'Snipe' just a few days before. The cost of this unsuccessful 'trifling, inconsequent, nameless battle' was almost as heavy as that suffered at 'Snipe'.[69] Eighth Army still had great difficulty in mounting improvised, hasty attacks in the face of determined, desperate German resistance. The two Rifle Brigade battalions had at least absorbed Ramsden's lesson from the July battles, that infantry battalions shorn of their supporting weapons should withdraw rather than be overrun.

However, 2nd King's Royal Rifle Corps was able to remain in its exposed forward position until the next morning. Just after first light, the riflemen could see Italian tanks driving over the ridge at Tel el Aqqaqir and coming into the attack.[70] The first shot from one of the six-pounders knocked out an M.13 tank at 800 yards range. Roughly 12 Italian tanks, formed from the remnants of the Littorio Division, moved into hull-down positions and put down heavy fire on the battalion but the anti-tank guns were able to claim another six M.13s in the fire-fight.[71]

Even though the battalion conducted a determined defence of its outpost, the Axis anti-tank gun screen had not been sufficiently shaken to allow the armoured brigades to break out. At 05.30 hours, the advance of 2nd Armoured Brigade was cancelled although 8th Armoured Brigade was ordered to move south of Tel el Aqqaqir towards the now occupied 'Skinflint' feature. Both brigades made slow progress while continuing to knock out any anti-tank guns that they encountered. The Ninth Lancers remembered that:

> the entire day was spent in shooting. The enemy tanks tried again, with no better results, and the 75's took great toll. The German infantry dug-in in front began to lose their nerve and ran from cover to cover all the time.[72]

1st Armoured Division claimed to have knocked out 22 tanks and 23 guns that day and observed that Axis transport was beginning 'to thin out to the West' but that the 'A.Tk screen, in spite of considerable losses, was still strong'.[73] The situation was, of course, intensely frustrating to the British commanders, who could sense that their opponent was about to break. The

Desert Air Force also added its weight, bombing the concentrations of Axis motor transport around Tel el Aqqaqir ceaselessly during the morning. Indeed, the 772 fighter, 272 light-bomber and 104 medium-bomber sorties flown on 3 November represented the peak effort of the Desert Air Force for the entire campaign.[74]

At 13.55 hours that afternoon, Freyberg, who was busily trying to prepare his division for its mobile role, got word of an aerial reconnaissance report stating that the road east of El Daba was solid with Axis traffic. The Desert Air Force duly switched its attention to these convoys during the afternoon. By dusk there were burning vehicles strewn along the whole length of the road from Ghazal to Fuka. Freyberg commented with satisfaction that, 'They are in a hell of a mess. We ought to attack through the south side of our bulge and get the armour out without running into their A/Tk screen.'[75] Leese made plans for a series of infantry attacks to penetrate the gun screen while Lumsden gave orders to Briggs to push his division west at first light the next morning.[76] Lieutenant-Colonel Saunders of the 5/7th Gordons was given orders to pass through the position gained by the 2nd Seaforths on the previous night and advance south west at 18.00 hours to reach the Rahman track. 8th Royal Tank Regiment of 23rd Armoured Brigade were placed in support and George Elliott, the artillery commander of 51st (Highland) Division, arranged a heavy barrage to assist the battalion.[77]

Unfortunately, during the afternoon there was considerable confusion about the location of the forward elements of 1st Armoured Division. 2nd King's Royal Rifle Corps were believed to be on Tel el Aqqaqir and 8th Armoured Brigade reported at 16.00 hours that they were 1,000 yards west of the track to the south of the salient. Briggs learned late in the afternoon of the plan to attack with the Gordons and that it was to include 'a heavy concentration of arty fire to the West of the RAHMAN track in the area of AQQAQIR'.[78] Fearing that his forward elements would be hit by the artillery barrage, Briggs took 'every possible step . . . to prevent this arty concentration being put down',[79] including a telephone call to Leese. Leese later admitted, 'I made a wrong decision and agreed to cancel the barrage and to allow the attack to go on with smoke alone in case of the odd concealed enemy light automatic gun.'[80] Wimberley was amazed:

> To be told that our Armour was already on the objective . . . and that it was only a case of moving forward. This was not my information at all, and I pleaded hard for the Tanks, if there were any there, to clear out and let my attack go in properly under a Barrage. I was told, No. It was only with difficulty that I could get leave, at least a smoke barrage to guide the Jocks.[81]

Half an hour before the attack went in, 8th Armoured Brigade reported that they were not, in fact, west of the Rahman track but it was 'too late to do anything'.[82] Briggs attempted to correct his division's error by ordering his artillery to fire in support and 8th Armoured Brigade was ordered 'to give every possible support by firing Sherman 75-mm H.E.'[83] Of course, this was no substitute for a properly organised artillery barrage. 1st Armoured Division's map-reading errors had yet again caused problems for 51st (Highland) Division – and this time there were tragic consequences.

Having been told that the enemy was withdrawing and that British tanks were already on the objective, Lieutenant-Colonel Saunders decided to send some of his men riding on the tanks of the one squadron of 8th Royal Tank Regiment that had arrived; the rest of the battalion would follow as rapidly as possible. The balance of the Valentines arrived just as the battalion was about to begin its attack and the remaining infantrymen 'climbed eagerly on to the leading tanks'.[84] But as the tanks drove forward with their passengers into the setting sun, they ran directly into positions held by the II Battalion of the 115th Panzergrenadier Regiment and the 605th Anti-Tank Battalion.[85] The German 50mm and 88mm guns opened fire from the front and both flanks: 'tank after tank was hit, many bursting into flames, and the 5/7th Gordons also suffered heavy casualties'.[86] Wimberley later saw some of the battered Valentines 'coming out of action, and they were covered with the dead bodies of my Highlanders. It was an unpleasant sight and bad for any troops morale.'[87] Six Valentines were burnt out and another 11 badly damaged. The Gordons did overrun the positions of II Battalion of the 33rd Artillery Regiment[88] and dug in on the Rahman track south of Tel el Aqqaqir, but only after suffering 68 casualties.[89]

The disastrous attack of the 5/7th Gordons proved yet again that Eighth Army found it difficult to conduct effective small-scale operations. There had been no time to organise another formal assault to break the Axis gun line and the series of improvised battalion attacks attempted instead achieved very uneven results. Indeed, this series of infantry attacks during 2–3 November 1942 had borne a striking similarity to many of the hastily organised and poorly prepared operations mounted in July. The difference lay in the ability of the Panzerarmee to respond to them. Auchinleck had genuinely believed that the Axis army was at its last gasp and that risks had to be run in order to win, yet none of the improvised offensives in July had achieved their objective. Now, in early November, after ten days of intense fighting Montgomery and his commanders likewise believed that risky attacks had to be mounted to break the Panzerarmee; this time they were right.

As if it was the exception that proved the rule, the next infantry attack mounted by Eighth Army succeeded. Immediately after he saw the tanks with their gruesome cargo, Wimberley was told that he would have to organise another two attacks that night. Like the Australians and New Zealanders, 51st (Highland) Division had run out of infantry but was given the 5th Indian Brigade for the attack (Eighth Army had virtually run out of formed infantry units that could still be used in an attack. Montgomery's stricture that 'divisions would fight as divisions' was long gone. Units were now being plugged into different formations at a moment's notice). Wimberley was informed by Leese that the Indians would attack Tel el Aqqaqir that night but he admitted:

> I was so sick at heart at being over-ruled regarding not firing my barrage for the Gordon attack, that I must have shewn it in the voice unmistakably. I remember Oliver said over the phone, 'Surely now you, Douglas, of all people are not going to lose heart'.[90]

Lieutenant-Colonel John Sym later commented that he did not know how Wimberley 'managed to last out the North African campaign. He never spared himself and wasted so much in nervous energy that he always looked desperately ill.'[91] Wimberley's jeep had been blown up on a mine on 24 October but he had taken no rest. After ten days of the tremendous strain of commanding his division in battle, Wimberley could have been forgiven for losing heart. However, he recovered his composure and insisted that the attacks by 5th Indian Brigade that night, and the 7th Argylls the next morning, should have the maximum possible artillery support.[92] On this final night of the battle both sides were stretched to the limit.

It was fortunate that Brigadier Russell and his men of the 5th Indian Brigade were relatively fresh. Russell received his orders from 30 Corps at midday on 3 November. His brigade was to attack on a very narrow front and advance for two miles to the south west of Tel el Aqqaqir. This, it was hoped, would push past the Axis gun screen and enable the armoured brigades to drive into the open. It was only at 16.00 hours that day that the start line had been selected and the brigade began to drive 12 miles to the assembly point. The men then had to march another five miles to reach the start line 'ankle deep in powdery sand which all but stifled the marchers'.[93] These obstacles delayed the brigade's arrival and Russell asked for the artillery programme to be postponed for an hour. George Elliott and the staff of 51st (Highland) Division worked rapidly to ensure that there would be no difficulties with the postponement. At 02.30 hours on 4 November a full artillery programme of counter-battery fire and concentrations on known enemy locations was loosed and at 04.00 hours, with tracer from Bofors guns marking the boundaries of the attack, the 360 guns of 30 Corps fired a creeping barrage which overwhelmed the Axis defences. It was a major achievement to organise what was essentially a repeat of the artillery programme for Supercharge at such short notice. The 1/4th Essex and 4/6th Rajputana Rifles advanced behind the barrage for three hours but encountered little opposition: 'It was more tidying-up – winkling out the dazed occupants of dug-outs and dusting off slit trenches where a few panzer grenadiers sought to sell their lives dearly.'[94]

There were numerous isolated combats but the Indian infantry were able to follow the barrage and reach their objective just as dawn broke on 4 November. At last there was a gap for the British armour to drive through into the desert beyond Tel el Aqqaqir.

While Eighth Army had spent a frustrating day on 3 November, quite unbeknown to the British the Panzerarmee had suffered catastrophe. The withdrawal in the south had started in the early hours of the morning and had gone unnoticed. It was very slow since much of the equipment and heavy weapons had to be manhandled back because of the lack of transport. 90th Light Division had also somehow managed to extricate the remnants of 125th Panzergrenadier Regiment from its coastal salient during the night and pull back to positions 4 kilometres east of Sidi Abd el Rahman. At midday, the Ariete and Trieste Divisions had linked up with the Afrika Korps.[95] With the Afrika Korps managing, if only just, to hold the British armour with its wide semi-circle of guns and tanks around Tel el Aqqaqir, Rommel decided that the time was ripe to order a further withdrawal of the non-motorised elements of the army. There was very little transport available so the withdrawal had to be made in short bounds. By the early afternoon, Eighth Army patrols were able to enter Deir el Munassib and Deir el Shein, the scene of so much fighting over so many months, unopposed.

However, at 13.30 hours on 3 November, Panzerarmee Headquarters received an order direct from Adolf Hitler. When the Panzerarmee's daily report for 2 November had reached the German High Command, now installed in the Wolfschanze (Wolf's Lair) in East Prussia, the news of Rommel's imminent withdrawal had struck like a 'thunderclap'.[96] Hitler sent a grandiloquent message forbidding any withdrawal:

> The German people join with me in following, with full confidence in your leadership and in the bravery of the German and Italian troops under your command, the heroic defence in Egypt. In your present situation nothing else can be thought of but to hold on, not to yield a step, and to throw every weapon and every warrior who can be spared into the fight. Strong air reinforcements will be given to the C-in-C South very soon. Also the Duce and the Italian Supreme Command will do their utmost to provide you with the means to carry on the struggle. Despite his numerical superiority the enemy must have exhausted his strength. It would not be the first time in history that the stronger will has triumphed over stronger enemy forces. You can show your troops no other road but that to victory or death.[97]

Hitler's order contained certain ironic echoes of the message that Churchill had sent to Auchinleck during the crisis in June. 'Every fit male should be made to fight and die for victory', Churchill had declared.[98] In truth, neither war leader fully understood the fighting in the desert but while Auchinleck and the Eighth Army had mastered the crisis in early July, defeat was now staring the Panzerarmee in the face. Rommel, so used to complete freedom of action in the theatre, was shocked to receive a direct order forbidding retreat.[99] Instead of sensibly ignoring this impossible order, Rommel obeyed it. The orders for further withdrawal were cancelled and all formations were ordered to 'defend their present positions to the last'.[100] Unsurprisingly, this sudden change in orders caused confusion within the Panzerarmee. Not all units received the new instructions; the Bologna Division was already marching to the west and it took a long time to bring it back to the front. Hitler's order completely disrupted what had been a relatively orderly withdrawal and doomed the non-motorised Italian infantry to capture. Rommel felt an 'overwhelming sense of bitterness' when he realised that 'even the greatest effort could no longer change the course of the battle'.[101]

Although Rommel had obeyed Hitler's order, when he read the message to von Thoma over the telephone that night the commander of the Afrika Korps protested that his force would be destroyed if it continued to hold its present positions. Von Thoma demanded that the Afrika Korps should be allowed to move back to the line 15 kilometres east of El Daba which had been arranged on 2 November. Rommel hesitated but eventually agreed.[102] Rommel also sent off Lieutenant Berndt, his personal assistant, to the Wolfshanze to persuade Hitler to change his mind.

Von Thoma's intervention ensured that the Afrika Korps would be able to escape. During the evening, its units were ordered to disengage and the remnants of 15th and 21st Panzer Division were able to withdraw six miles to their new positions 'without any particular difficulty'. The 33rd Panzer Engineer Battalion and a light flak battery were left behind as a rearguard.[103] These orders made it inevitable that, although the Afrika Korps might slip away, the Italian forces of the Panzerarmee would be destroyed.

Dawn on 4 November saw the 7th Argylls attack Tel el Aqqaqir. Unlike the Gordons the previous evening, the Argylls had the support of seven regiments of field artillery on a frontage of just 600 yards. The advance was unopposed but eight men were killed and 23 wounded by 'drop shorts' from some of the supporting artillery.[104] These 'drop shorts' were due not only to the extreme fatigue of the gunners but also to the fact that many of the field gun barrels were worn out. This was the last bombardment fired by Eighth Army's artillery during the battle. The 7th Medium Regiment noted, 'We have fired 22,000 rds of ammn since the battle began.'[105] In 12 days of battle, the artillery had fired more than one million rounds of 25-pounder ammunition. On the 30 Corps front each 25-pounder gun had fired an average of 1,909 rounds per gun.[106] These astonishing figures give some idea of the crushing weight of support that the artillery gave to the units in the front line. The physical demands on the gunners had been enormous but

Eighth Army's artillery fire had done much to determine the outcome of the battle.

Using the Argyll's attack as cover, the remaining squadron of the Royal Dragoons and the 4th South African Armoured Car Regiment were able to pass through the gap just before dawn. No information concerning the 5th Indian Brigade's attack had reached von Thoma during the night so for the first few hours of daylight the Panzerarmee was unaware that the Eighth Army was now free to exploit its victory.

The coast road became the main focus for the fighter bombers and light bombers of the Desert Air Force but the fleeing columns of Axis transport were not an easy target. Sixty Hurricanes and Kittyhawks made early morning sorties all along the coast road but had to fly through a wall of intense anti-aircraft fire. Eleven fighters were shot down during the morning alone. Nonetheless, more than 100 light bombers attacked targets around Fuka in the morning but, by the afternoon, the Axis transport on the coast road had thinned out so much that the light bombers were switched to army targets.[107] The Desert Air Force, in common with the Eighth Army, found it difficult to exploit the new conditions of the pursuit that day.

1st Armoured Division did not quite break free. 2nd Armoured Brigade moved off at dawn with the 10th Hussars in the van but although they were able to drive forward for about 4,000 yards they soon encountered the Axis rearguard, composed of the Afrika Korps and the 90th Light Division, deployed on a wide sand dune at Tel el Mampsra. Bayerlein met von Thoma just before dawn and was surprised to see the general wearing full uniform with insignia and medals. Von Thoma reputedly said to Bayerlein, 'Hitler's order is a piece of unparalled madness. I can't go along with this any longer.'[108] Von Thoma then went forward with the Afrika Korps *Kampfstaffel* to attempt to stem the British break-out. At 08.05 hours he reported, 'The situation will become critical if the 150 tanks continue their pressure. Have been engaged.' He remained with the *Kampfstaffel* throughout the morning helping to organise the withdrawal of the rest of the Afrika Korps behind the screen of the rearguard.[109] The regiments of 2nd Armoured Brigade kept up the pressure but were held up by German anti-tank guns which moved back in bounds. Around noon, when Bayerlein drove up to Tel el Mampsra to check on the situation of the rearguard, he realised that the *Kampfstaffel* had been destroyed. He saw 'a man standing erect beside a burning tank, apparently impervious to the intense fire which criss-crossed about him. It was General von Thoma.'[110] Bayerlein managed to escape but von Thoma surrendered to Captain Grant Singer of the 10th Hussars.[111] Rommel promptly placed Bayerlein in charge of the Afrika Korps.

Although 1st Armoured Division had to spend another hard day in contact with the German rearguard, the experience of the other armoured divisions was rather different. John Harding's 7th Armoured Division had been brought up ready to exploit the breach but spent an 'exhilarating and frustrating night' on 3 November.[112] Michael Carver remembered:

> We were all desperately eager to get going and be the first to break out into the open desert, but the congestion on the dimly marked tracks through the minefields, ploughed deep in dust, the changes of plan and the uncertainty about what was going on led to endless delays. John Harding could hardly contain his impatience.[113]

Nonetheless, by 08.30 hours on 4 November, the division led by 22nd Armoured Brigade was out into the open. It drove beyond Tel el Aqqaqir for five miles before encountering opposition. Harding ordered 'Pip' Roberts to outflank these 'small pockets' but the brigade was soon engaged by what remained of the Ariete Division. The Italian tanks were hopelessly outmatched but the Ariete, along with groups from the Littorio and Trieste Divisions, fought all afternoon in a desperate attempt to escape from threatened encirclement. Eventually, all three Italian divisions were destroyed. Roberts commented that 'it was very good battle practice for the brigade!'[114] However, after this sustained engagement, his brigade was only able to drive for about half an hour before stopping for the night. The often unjustly maligned Italian XX Corps had sacrificed itself and prevented the encirclement of the Afrika Korps.

8th Armoured Brigade, now returned to the command of 10th Armoured Division, was also able to press forward, but it, too, spent the day 'systematically destroying enemy tanks and A.Tk gun screen'.[115] By the late afternoon, the brigade was ordered to turn south, find the Axis right flank and drive to El Daba to cut off the enemy columns moving westwards.[116] A further sidestep proved necessary to avoid the fighting to the north but, although the brigade attempted to make a night march, the night was so dark that progress was difficult and the move was cancelled.[117]

By the evening of 4 November the issue was no longer in doubt. After 12 days of intense fighting, the resistance of the Panzerarmee had finally been broken. The British armoured brigades, which Montgomery had hoped would break out at dawn on 24 October, were at last in the open. But there had been no breakthrough in the strict definition of the military term.[118] Had Operation Supercharge succeeded and the British armour punched through the Axis defences on 2 November, the Eighth Army might well have been able to encircle and destroy the entire Panzerarmee while it remained fixed to its positions. Supercharge did not succeed as planned and the Panzerarmee had already begun to step back and make preparations for retreat on the night of 2 November. Even with Hitler's 'victory or death' order, it was this fact, more than any other, which ensured that when the British armour did reach the open desert they would find it impossible to encircle and destroy Rommel's army completely.

The 15th Panzer Division battle report later commented that, during 4 November, the Eighth Army had 'approached the German positions with great caution'.[119] This was only the first accusation of caution levelled against the Eighth Army during the pursuit and it is a cry that has been taken up by historians ever since. However, it was not caution but pure congestion that delayed and hampered Eighth Army's break-out and pursuit over the coming days. With every unit champing at the bit to be involved in the pursuit, enormous traffic jams developed that took hours to sort out. An artillery officer later explained:

> In thick clouds of thick, cloying dust, which was semi-solid up to one's waist, the Regiment disappeared into the gaps and every driver and every man peered forward to try and keep the next gun or truck in view. Battery commanders strove to keep up with their battalion or regimental commanders, whose formations were pouring through the gaps and fanning out in a great flood. Men and officers alike were in a great state of excitement, disbelief and wonder.[120]

The units of Eighth Army were still hemmed in by the narrow salient of Operation Supercharge and all the supporting transport had to make its slow laborious way through tight minefield gaps and choking dust. Given these conditions, Eighth Army did well to exert any pressure at all upon the Panzerarmee during 4 November.

The pursuit began in earnest on 5 November. 2nd Armoured Brigade reached El Daba in the early afternoon and drove on aiming for Bir Khalda just south of Mersa Matruh. 8th Armoured Brigade got on the move early and drove rapidly to Galal. There, the brigade found:

> enemy tanks and transport streaming Westwards along the Main road. The road was quickly blocked and several tanks knocked out. The enemy there, taken apparently by surprise, fell into the bag wholesale.[121]

During the afternoon, the brigade fought a sharp action at Galal station in which 20 Italian tanks were destroyed in less than 10 minutes. By the evening, the brigade had knocked out 54 Axis tanks, captured 12 guns and taken more than 1,000 prisoners in one day.[122]

7th Armoured Division spent a slightly frustrating day, during which the tanks had to change direction several times to avoid confusion with other formations. A dummy minefield caused considerable delay and progress was not as rapid as John Harding had hoped. Carver later related that Harding tried to persuade Lumsden to give 7th Armoured Division:

> priority in petrol supplies and let us, who knew this part of the desert like the backs of our hands, drive west, until we could be certain that we had

overtaken Rommel's withdrawal, then cut up north to block him, probably between Sollum and Bardia.[123]

Lumsden, however, wanted to give 1st Armoured Division, his previous command, a more prominent role in the pursuit. Moreover, there was considerable pressure to open up the coast road as soon as possible to ensure the flow of supplies and to reopen the vital landing grounds for the Desert Air Force.

Although Harding did not know it, a plan similar to his had been presented to Montgomery by de Guingand on 2 November. De Guingand had tasked Richardson with developing Operation Grapeshot for an independent force that would be capable of reaching Tobruk and sustaining itself for seven days.[124] The force would consist of 96 tanks, preferably diesel-engined Shermans and Grants, two regiments of armoured cars, two battalions of infantry, one Royal Horse Artillery battery and a light anti-aircraft regiment along with a field squadron of engineers. Once Eighth Army had taken Mersa Matruh, Major-General Gairdner would drive down the Siwa track to reach Bir Khamsa and on to Tobruk.[125] The plan certainly had potential and might well have placed the Panzerarmee in real difficulty but Montgomery did not agree to it.[126]

Montgomery's attitude towards his armoured commanders certainly did not help matters during the initial pursuit. With his trust in his 10 Corps commander at an all time low, he refused to give Lumsden full independence to conduct the pursuit.[127] Quite simply, Montgomery did not want the hard-won laurels of the victory to be won by Lumsden, Gatehouse or Briggs when he considered that their performance during the battle had been poor. Montgomery's failure before the battle began to plan adequately for pursuit meant that no unit was given overall priority in the chase. Each commander followed his own instincts. All three armoured divisions, along with 2nd New Zealand Division, attempted to be 'in at the kill'. The result on 5 November was a series of 'short hooks' that failed to catch the retreating Panzerarmee.

The remnants of the Afrika Korps were actually able to disengage from the pursuing elements of Eighth Army during a night march on the night of 5 November.[128] However, 21st Panzer Division was immobilised for lack of fuel the next day[129] and only really saved by the rain which fell in the early afternoon and turned the desert into a quagmire. The storm and subsequent floods on 6 and 7 November brought Eighth Army's pursuit grinding to a halt. It had missed the fleeting opportunity on 5 November and the rainstorms confirmed the failure. Ultimately, although a number of attempts were made to cut them off, the remnants of the Panzerarmee were able to escape.

However, Rommel did not escape with anything recognisable as an army.

Casualty figures for the Panzerarmee will only ever be estimates given the confusion that reigned amongst its units in the early stages of the pursuit. British estimates, based on intercepts, gave German casualties as 1,149 killed, 3,886 wounded and 8,050 captured. Italian losses amounted to 971 dead, 933 wounded and 15,552 captured. By 11 November the total number of Axis prisoners had risen to 30,000 as more were netted during the pursuit.[130] Eighth Army claimed to have destroyed or captured 259 Axis tanks and 254 guns during the fighting although these were incomplete estimates.[131]

A more revealing assessment of the damage inflicted upon the Panzerarmee came on the morning of 5 November, when the divisions of the Afrika Korps reported their current strengths. 15th Panzer Division had eight battleworthy tanks, 200 riflemen, four anti-tank guns and 12 field guns. 21st Panzer Division comprised 30 battleworthy tanks, 400 men in three weak battalions, 16 anti-tank guns and 25 field guns. 90th Light Division had three weak regiments and one depleted artillery regiment. 164th Light Division had 700 men and six anti-tank guns.[132] The Italian armoured and motorised formations were comprehensively destroyed on 4 November – one after the other the Littorio, Trieste and Ariete Divisions had sent in their final messages to Panzerarmee Headquarters. The Italian infantry formations stranded in the desert with no transport, water or food had no choice but actually to seek out units of the Eighth Army and surrender. There was only one exception to this bleak picture. On 5 November, para-troops from Ramcke's Parachute Brigade managed to capture a column of British transport, enabling nearly 600 men to rejoin the Panzerarmee two days later.[133] The vital support structure of the army, along with the head-quarters of the formations, did survive but the fighting element was reduced to little more than a weak regimental group. In these circumstances, the wreck of the Panzerarmee survived only by making a headlong flight out of Egypt.

Eighth Army paid a heavy price for its victory: 2,350 of its men had been killed during the battle. Another 8,950 servicemen had been wounded in the fighting while 2,260 were missing in action.[134] At least 332 British tanks had been knocked out during the battle and 111 guns destroyed.[135] Before the battle, Richardson had been asked by de Guingand for an estimate of the total casualties to assist the medical services in planning hospital provision. He admitted that he had no experience to help him come up with a figure so de Guingand went to Montgomery. The Army Commander 'forecast with great accuracy' a figure of 13,000.[136] The actual total was 13,560.[137]

Back at El Alamein, the rest of Eighth Army settled down to 'tidying up' the battlefield by salvaging as much equipment and materiel as possible. The soldiers of 9th Australian Division, who had been hemmed in on their dangerous salient for so long, were now free to roam the battlefield. Corporal C. W. Mears noted in his diary on 5 November:

today we inspected the battlefield. Touring around fairly intoxicated. The war is not so bad after all. There are some lonely graves in the desert, both our own boys and the enemy, just a tin hat + cross to denote the fallen.[138]

Private J. A. Crawford also walked over ground that had recently been the scene of intense fighting:

At last the armour has gone through. But for the little boy-faced Tommy there is no thrill of victory, no pride in a job splendidly done. He lies on his back as if asleep, still in my sweater, a hundred yards ahead of where I gave it to him. His chest is riddled but not very bloody; the holes are neat. Spandau Joe did not miss this time.[139]

Eighth Army had finally crushed the Panzerarmee but the human cost to both sides had been grievous.

NINETEEN

Ring Out the Bells!

One of the most enduring myths concerning the final battle at El Alamein is that when Churchill heard the news he ordered the church bells, silent since 1939, to be rung out all over Britain in celebration of the victory. The ringing of the bells has entered British legend along with the supposed thousand-gun barrage that opened the battle.

The reality is, unfortunately, more prosaic. The celebration of the victory was not as spontaneous a gesture as might be supposed. Alexander composed a statement announcing the Eighth Army's victory over the Panzerarmee on 4 November 1942:

> The Axis Forces in the Western Desert after 12 days and nights of ceaseless attacks by our land and air forces are now in full retreat. Their disordered columns are being relentlessly attacked by our land forces and by the Royal Air Forces by day and night.[1]

He reported that Stumme had been killed, that von Thoma had been captured, and that 'the enemy's losses in killed and wounded have been exceptionally high'. Casey immediately sent this to Churchill in the hope that he would be able to make the 'most of defeat of enemy in interests of TORCH'.[2] It was now vital, with the invasion of French North Africa imminent, to influence French and Spanish opinion in favour of the Allies. Britain had finally proved to the world that her armed forces could win a battle. Alexander issued the statement to the press in Cairo that night and the British public heard the news on a special BBC news bulletin.[3]

Churchill was, of course, delighted to learn of Rommel's defeat. Alexander and his 'brilliant lieutenant Montgomery' (there was no mention of the 'my Monty' of just a few days before) had delivered the victory that Churchill had desired for so long. The Prime Minister was already thinking about the possible impact upon Torch and he informed Alexander:

> If the reasonable hopes of your telegram are maintained and wholesale captures of the enemy and a general retreat are apparent I propose to ring the bells all over Britain for the first time this war. Try to give me the

moment to do this in the next few days. At least 20,000 prisoners would be necessary.[4]

Churchill's reply sheds interesting light on the scale of victory he considered necessary to order a general celebration. The number of captives Churchill required paled into insignificance next to the 150,000 Italian prisoners that the Western Desert Force had taken during Operation Compass in 1941 but the victory at Alamein represented something much greater: it was clearly the end for the Axis in Africa.

The very next day, Alexander was able to signal the Prime Minister: 'Ring out the Bells!'[5] Eighth Army had already captured more prisoners than Churchill's minimum requirements. Churchill hesitated; he had not expected the battle to be so long or hard-won. When the Prime Minister mentioned to the CIGS his desire to ring the bells, Brooke 'implored him to wait a little longer till we were quite certain that we should have no cause for regretting ringing them'.[6] 'Brooke's mind was already turning to the prospects facing the invasion fleet nearing the coast of North Africa for Operation Torch. Churchill and the British people had already experienced so many shocks and disappointments. Churchill replied to Alexander that he would delay ringing the bells until it was known that Torch was a success, to avoid the eventuality of any 'accident which would cause distress'.[7]

On 8 November 1942, British and American troops landed on the shores of North Africa at Oran, Casablanca and Algiers. Operation Torch had begun, and, with it, the birth of full-scale operations by the Anglo-American alliance. The commitment of thousands of American troops to the Mediterranean theatre served final notice that Axis ambitions in North Africa were doomed, and, indeed, that Fascist Italy and Nazi Germany could not long endure. Yet Torch also represented the final eclipse of British independence in the Second World War. Churchill was well aware that Britain was now part of an Anglo-American coalition and the bells were rung in joint celebration for Alamein and Torch on November 15.[8]

Although Eighth Army's victory at El Alamein was crushing, it represented the end of Axis ambitions in Africa only because of the impact of the Torch landings. The Axis forces in Africa were now faced by threats from two directions. Units which might have rebuilt the Deutsch–Italienische Panzerarmee had to be sent to Tunisia. In these circumstances the Axis defence of Libya could not be prolonged.

Nonetheless, Montgomery was absolutely determined to ensure that there could be no revival in Rommel's fortunes. In complete contrast to Rommel's hasty logistic improvisations for his invasion of Egypt, the supply of Eighth Army during its rapid pursuit of the remnants of the Panzerarmee was a masterpiece of forward planning. Even before the British offensive opened in October important planning meetings were held at General Headquarters

Middle East to decide on the logistic support needed to sustain Eighth
Army's advance beyond El Alamein.[9] Indeed, Eighth Army's pursuit was
even quicker than its retreat into Egypt had been. The forward elements of
Eighth Army entered Tobruk on 13 November having covered 376 miles in
ten days of pursuit. Agedabia was reached on 23 November after a total
advance of 778 miles in 20 days.[10] This was astonishingly rapid by any
standards and it was sustained by one of the most efficient logistic systems
hitherto devised. The Eighth Army halted in front of El Agheila until 12
December but this temporary pause was vital to ensure that the subsequent
advance to Tripoli could be sustained. Rommel made a brief stand at El
Agheila but on 23 January, three months after the start of the offensive at
El Alamein, Eighth Army entered Tripoli.[11] The desert pendulum would not
swing again.

Alamein represented another kind of watershed. Great Britain, since its
formation in 1707, had rarely gone to war except as part of a coalition.
However, by 1942 Britain could no longer pretend to be the dominant partner
in any coalition. The country was essentially bankrupt and dependent upon
American largesse, through the Lend-Lease programme, to feed and clothe
her population as well as to continue the war. In this sense, Alamein represented the final 'British' victory of the war and this fact explains much of
the nostalgia which has surrounded the last 'Battle of Egypt' ever since.

Alamein also signalled the final collapse of the system of Imperial Defence.
The 9th Australian Division paraded as an entire formation at Gaza on 22
December 1942 and was reviewed by an appreciative Alexander.[12] Yet this
marked the last time that an Australian formation would serve under British
command in the Middle East. There was to be no repeat of the Australian
experience in the Great War when, after service in the Mediterranean theatre
at Gallipoli, Australian forces were transferred to France. Similar thinking
had been behind the despatch of the Australian corps to Egypt in 1939 but,
by 1942, John Curtin's Australian government needed its troops to fight
against the Japanese in the Pacific theatre. Curtin had in fact demanded the
return of his division on 24 October and, after a flurry of telegrams, Churchill
had had no choice but to agree to the request.[13] On 19 November 1942, the
New Zealand government also requested the return of its division but was
persuaded to allow it to remain in the Mediterranean theatre.[14] The 2nd
New Zealand Division continued to serve in the Eighth Army until the end
of the war in Europe. However, the negotiations between the British,
Australian and New Zealand governments in late 1942 proved that the
assumptions that had underpinned the concept of Imperial defence were
now obsolete.

As quiet returned to what had been the battlefield at El Alamein, the
Eighth Army had an opportunity to take stock of what had been learned
during the fighting. While there had been a dearth of official pamphlets and

publications detailing the Eighth Army's experience between May and October 1942, a veritable flood of reports, lessons learned and other documents was produced after the final victory.[15] There was a difference between assessing defeat and explaining victory. Eighth Army was justifiably proud of its success in breaching the Axis minefield defences and finally defeating Rommel's panzer divisions. Thus, the concentration upon the October battle of Alamein at the expense of the more awkward experiences of the July fighting began as soon as the battle ended.

Eighth Army had, eventually, taken stock of its previous experience and used this knowledge to educate its units in a more coherent system of war. There is no doubt that the operational pause and static nature of the front at Alamein were vital for Eighth Army's development. The extended lull had seen the re-education of Britain's desert army on an enormous scale. It is also clear that the three battles of El Alamein cannot be seen as separate and distinct events but, crucially, as an important continuous experience in the development of the Eighth Army.

Eighth Army learned more from its defeats than the Panzerarmee had ever learned from its victories. The Panzerarmee trained and fought with well-proven tactics but its early string of victories meant that it had stopped learning. After the battle, the main British report on the lessons from Lightfoot criticised the tactics of the Axis forces, arguing that the enemy:

> maintained and fought in mixed battle groups long after their usefulness had ended. His counter attacks were piecemeal and bore no resemblance to his massed effort of the past, and he was in fact forced to repeat many of our faults of certain earlier operations.[16]

Ultimately, the Panzerarmee was unable to adapt its tactics to less favourable circumstances.

The profusion of reports demonstrated just how much Eighth Army had learned during its sojourn at El Alamein. They covered every conceivable military subject but the main developments influenced British fighting methods for the rest of the war. The reconcentration of artillery, which had begun under Auchinleck, meant that 'artillery correctly handled is a battle winning factor of first importance. It dominated the Alamein battle.'[17] After experiencing the doldrums in the previous desert campaigns, the Royal Artillery had regained its central place in the British Army's method of fighting. The 'dominating influence' of the minefield had been overcome by the mine-gapping techniques developed by the Royal Engineers. The importance of complete coordination between the army and air force 'bred of knowledge and mutual understanding of each other's problems and methods'[18] meant that the Desert Air Force had been able to provide an unprecedented level of battlefield support to the army. The infantry, through the development of robust battle drills and proven techniques for consolidation, had become 'capable of attacking by night with the bayonet against any form of defence'.[19] The lessons for the armour were less clear. The 24th Armoured Brigade report complained that 'many principles of armoured tactics had to be violated' during the battle.[20] Arguments concerning the proper use of armour at Alamein continued for many years. The exception to these problems was the 23rd Armoured Brigade. Its intensive training with the infantry divisions of 30 Corps meant that, with certain exceptions, the brigade had supplied flexible and close tank support 'with excellent results'.[21] The path of the 23rd Armoured Brigade from disaster in July to the 'excellent results' of October and November illustrates the process of development that all units of Eighth Army underwent during the summer and autumn of 1942.[22]

It was the combination of all these developments into a complex and interlocking system of war that enabled Eighth Army finally to master its opponent. Subsequent battles at Wadi Akarit and Mareth[23] demonstrated that Eighth Army had become a confident and effective fighting formation. It did so not by copying German tactics but, as David French has commented, by finding its own solutions to its problems and fighting in a distinctively British manner. Eighth Army came to rely upon firepower as well as fighting skill and careful movement rather than risky manoeuvre.[24] This sort of success may not have looked as dramatic as Rommel's offensive dashes to Tobruk and Alamein, but it was nonetheless profound.

British fighting methods for the rest of the war generally followed the pattern set by El Alamein. Under Montgomery's now considerable influence, 'set-piece' attacks in which infantry attacked with the support of concentrated artillery fire became the favoured approach. British forces also came to rely on close cooperation with the air arm which could generally guarantee air superiority. The British use of armour, however, was never as spectacular as the early German successes or as effective as the later Soviet offensives. The lack of a clear doctrine for the breakthrough battle remained an unsolved problem for the rest of the war. However, the development and application of this system owed as much to Eighth Army's previous combat experience as to Montgomery's style of command.

Eighth Army, after a period of intense combat lasting nearly two years, had finally learned how to master its opponent in desert warfare. Yet this did not mean that the British Army as a whole could rest on these laurels and assume that it now knew how to defeat the vaunted German Wehrmacht. Indeed, the reverse could be true, as this conversation between two soldiers during the war reveals:

One soldier remarked at a later date on hearing a man from the Desert expound his theory and practice, 'Very right and proper. What you don't realise is that the story of El Alamein and beyond is just as much a part of history as the Waterloo Campaign. We shall never fight again in the Desert – in this war.'[25]

The difficulty for the Eighth Army and indeed the entire British Army after Alamein was that the lessons learned in the bare deserts of Egypt were not necessarily of value elsewhere.

After the fighting in Sicily, the now highly experienced 152nd Brigade of the 51st (Highland) Division held a discussion on the lessons it had learned since its baptism of fire at El Alamein. At one point, the discussion turned to an examination of the relative merits of day and night attacks:

Ever since El Alamein we have been very night attack minded – in fact we have very seldom even thought of attacks except in terms of night attack. The reasons for this are obvious – El Alamein was probably the biggest night attack ever carried out: it was a great success: therefore night attack stock went very high. It is equally obvious however that there were very special conditions and considerations at El Alamein which do not exist now and are never likely to exist again. Over such flat and open country as the desert was there, a day attack to the same depth (fully 7000 yards) could never have been successful: Rehearsals over ground almost exactly similar to the ground over which the actual attack was to be made were carried out to an extent and on a scale very unlikely ever again to be possible.[26]

British soldiers were justifiably proud of the achievements of the Eighth Army at El Alamein but the fighting there came to be seen as part of a unique set of circumstances that could not necessarily be replicated.

It is significant that the two British arms that maintained their reputations throughout the rest of the Second World War were the Royal Artillery and the Royal Engineers – and this can be explained by the fact that the lessons they learned at Alamein were of direct relevance in *any* theatre of operations. Once the Royal Artillery had learned the effectiveness of concentrated fire – and gained the wireless communications to manage it properly – these tactics could be applied with effect on every battlefield. Yet even in the use of artillery there were caveats. 152nd Brigade recognised that:

in the flat desert each shell had a more or less guaranteed performance i.e. a guaranteed beaten zone, but in broken hilly country this is not so and many shells will have little or no destructive performance.[27]

The Royal Artillery had to learn how to adapt its proven techniques to the very different terrain encountered in Tunisia, Italy and Europe.

The mine-clearance techniques that the Royal Engineers developed during the Alamein campaign became the standard procedure for tackling any mine obstacle for the rest of the war. The concept of an armoured engineer vehicle first pioneered in the unreliable Matilda 'Scorpion' was later developed into a whole family of armoured engineer vehicles that proved invaluable in the European theatre.

Similarly, although the principles of tank/infantry cooperation remained the same as in the desert, they required radically different tactical execution in the mountainous terrain of Italy or the dense hedgerows of Normandy. With much shorter ranges and obscured vision, along with the greater lethality of infantry anti-tank weapons, the infantry and armour had to learn new tactical lessons all over again.

Perhaps most important of all, the 'winning team' that Eighth Army had become by October 1942 did not remain together for long. Both the 9th Australian and 1st South African Divisions returned home soon after the end of the battle. The rapidly changing demands for troops that had afflicted Eighth Army so severely during 1941 and 1942 quickly cropped up again in 1943 and 1944. 44th (Home Counties) Division was broken up soon after the battle. The same fate befell the 24th Armoured Brigade, which considered it 'a sad waste that circumstances compel breaking up the trained team. It is more vital to success than the equipment – and not so easily produced.'[28] Unfortunately, the British Army found it difficult to follow this principle when it was stretched by demands for troops in Italy and Burma and for the coming campaign in North West Europe.

Unfortunately, the British Army never seemed able to ensure that inexperienced units would not be flung into battle without proper preparation. This critical problem that had affected the performance of Eighth Army so severely before October 1942 continued to dog the British Army for the rest of the war. The comprehensive preparation for battle which had made such a difference to the combat effectiveness of the 51st (Highland) Division at El Alamein was never repeated. The majority of the British units that fought in Normandy had not seen action before and although they trained hard in Britain this could not provide the same level of preparation that the 51st (Highland) Division had undergone in Egypt. In many cases, the home army was forced to learn the lessons of Alamein from pamphlets alone.[29]

During the Alamein campaign, the Eighth Army was granted the breathing space it needed to assimilate lessons which transformed it from a clumsy and inept fighting formation into an effective and battle-winning army. But the British Army did not have an effective means of transferring that experience and knowledge onto other untested and untried units. This was a serious limitation on the effectiveness of the British Army in the Second World War and a tragedy for inexperienced troops who had to learn the same lessons the hard way in battle after battle.

APPENDICES

Appendix A

MOST SECRET

APPRECIATION BY COMD 13 CORPS.

1 August 1942

OBJECT

1. To consider plans for offensive action at an early date:

FACTORS

2. My own strength:-

> One infantry Division – not up to strength
> One Armoured Division consisting of 22 Armd Bde
> > 4 Lt Armd Bde
> > 7 Motor Bde

Comment These forces are barely sufficient to hold present Corps front. No opportunity to train or prepare these forces specially for offensive operations.

3. Enemy's Strength:-
See Appendix 'A' [not reproduced]

Comment. The enemy has suffered very severe losses in his African trained infantry and these are not easily replaced. Quality will drop but numbers likely to be made up. In spite of losses in tank crews and his Armd Divs generally it would be dangerous to assume that they will not be picked troops. The Italian morale is low and likely to remain so.

4. Relative Strength. Recent unsuccessful offensive action by us will have reassured enemy that his present position is strong enough as a screen behind which to build up a striking force. For reasons of general policy as well as reasons of expediency in this theatre of war, enemy may be expected to continue the offensive at earliest possible date.

This date depends on when he can build up a large enough striking force for his purpose. Therefore what sized force does he aim at?

It is considered that he must have a minimum of:-

One German Armd Div at almost full strength (i.e. 12,000 men 150–180 tanks)

90 Lt Div – 50% of strength (6,000 men)

One Italian Armd Div – 75% strength (i.e. 6,000 men 100 medium tanks)

One Italian Motor Div – 75% strength (5,000 men)

Totals Approx 30,000 men, 250 tanks,

plus supplies, transport, and services for above to maintain to Alexandria and continue battle for seven days. In addition sufficient Air Force to give local air superiority over area for attack and sufficient holding troops (who would be mainly Italian) to contain the forces opposite to them.

A striking force of this size could be ready by 15 Aug.

5.   Ground.

(a) Looking East. Barrel track and to South bad going but not impossible for light specially equipped vehicles or tracked vehicles. Maintenance of large forces not likely. Strong raids are possible to Delta. Danger exists as long as our left flank is not secured on QATTARA depression.

North of barrel track there is an expanse of good going as far North as 88 grid and as far East as 46 grid. East of 46 'going' deteriorates. None of this bad 'going' is an obstacle to tanks but it restricts the maintenance of wheeled vehicles of such forces. ALAM EL HALFA and GEBEL BEIN GABIR point like fingers to SW and provide all the observation and the good going to the coast road. These features and particularly ALAM EL HALFA are vital for any advance down the Coast to Alexandria – they are also vital to us for holding our present positions.

(b) Looking West, Coast road main artery of communication and supply – Also area of enemy Landing Grounds. Road passes through one defile at FUKA. The escarpment curves round SE to QATTARA but is not serious obstacle except near FUKA. QARET EL ABD important locality as it commands best route to high ground and FUKA escarpment. ABU DWEISS important only as a hold on the QATTARA depression.

Comment. Coast road vital and particularly vulnerable at FUKA which is best approached South of QARET EL ABD.

6.   <u>Courses open to us.</u>

(a)   To attack between QATTARA and ABU DWEIS with a view to gaining
      a footing on the FUKA escarpment for further exploitation.
      An attack on this part of the front would be less impeded by our own
      minefields than elsewhere. On present dispositions the opposition
      would be largely Italian. There is scope and opportunity for tactical
      surprise. The attainment of the objective would open a way to the vital
      ground at FUKA. Counter attack would be possible only from the
      North. Even if we were frustrated in making a full break through it
      would greatly strengthen the left flank of the Corps if we captured
      and consolidated ABU DWEIS – QATTARA. The disadvantage to
      the plan is that if the enemy is contemplating an offensive himself it
      is most probable that he would collect his striking forces South of the
      QATTARA position and therefore opposite to our point of attack.

(b)   An attack North of QATTARA would meet very strong opposition
      and minefields, it offers no suitable objective. It is known to contain
      well organised defensive fire and is adjacent to enemy tanks. Limited
      success here would have no advantages. An attack North of QATTARA
      has nothing to recommend it.

(c)   Lure the Enemy out in front of his minefields to fight on ground
      disadvantageous to him. Such a plan would surrender the initiative to
      the enemy which might be difficult to regain. Such a plan might fit
      naturally into the scheme of defence and might be the only practical
      plan if by reason of superiority in armour the initiative clearly rests
      with the enemy. It would not be sufficient to await attack, the enemy
      would have to be lured out by some bait before he is ready and incur
      some unexpected risk which he is taking only because he has been
      misled. Details of such a plan will be more apparent after considering
      courses open to the enemy.

7.   <u>Courses open to the enemy.</u>

(a)   An attack with ALAM EL HALFA as his first objective, going round
      anywhere South of the ALAM NYAL ridge – subsequently cutting
      the road in the HAMMAN area and thrusting straight for Alexandria.
      A raid down the Barrel track towards the Delta might be combined
      with this. This is much the most likely course and the most difficult
      to meet. An attack anywhere North of ALAM NYAL would meet
      strong minefields, bad going and prepared positions. There are many
      possible variations in the details of such a plan but it is the only one
      which he could carry out with his present shortage of infantry if he
      is making ALEXANDRIA his objective.

(b)   A strong raid down the Barrel track aimed at the DELTA. As already
       explained a strong force could not be maintained but it cannot be ignored
       that the Barrel track and South of it is a route to Cairo which is not
       strongly covered. He might expect results from panic and general alarm
       out of all proportion to the military objective gained. If the raiding party
       was strong enough in tanks it would be difficult to attack effectively from
       Air or ground and it is possible, that the anti-tank defences of the Delta
       would be insufficiently mobile to meet such a thrust.

(c)   An attack North of the ALAM NYAL ridge is unlikely owing to present
       enemy weakness in infantry.

8.   Conclusion.

(a)   It is considered that our best course is 6 (a) but that arrangements to
       put into effect course 6 (c) should be undertaken until we are ready
       for course 6 (a).

(b)   The enemy's most likely course is 7 (a) but he is likely to have suffi-
       cient strength to carry out this course before 15 Aug.

(c)   Enemy could carry out course 7 (b) now but is more likely to make
       this part of course 7 (a) at a later date.

(d)   Additional forces necessary to plan course 6 (a) would be:-
              One Armoured Div (one Armd Bde)
              One Infantry Div.

                                                              Lt. Gen.
                                                      Comd. 13 Corps.

Appendix B

[Reproduced from WO201/556, TNA]

MOST SECRET

Appreciation by C in C, M.E. at Eighth Army at 0800 hrs 1st August 1942.

GENERAL POSITION

1. As a result of my last full appreciation on 27th July, 42 I was reluctantly forced to the conclusion that I would gain less than I stood to
lose if I continued to attack the enemy's strengthened positions with
insufficient and insufficiently trained troops, and it was therefore
necessary to reorganise, refit, and train until the Eighth Army could
be substantially reinforced in infantry and tanks. This cannot be till
the middle of September at the earliest. Orders have been issued to
meet this situation and Eighth Army is now on the tactical defensive,
though the enemy is to be harried by every means in our power and
is not to be allowed to regain strength undisturbed.

OBJECT.

2. While Eighth Army is on the defensive, to cause the greatest possible
loss to the enemy and to disturb his plans.

FACTORS.

3. Strengths.
    The relative strength of the enemy and ourselves has not changed
greatly in the last week. He has received reinforcements for his depleted
formations and two thirds of the newly arrived 164 Div are up as are
some Italian parachutists. It is probable that there are now about 120
German tank runners against our 50 Grant tanks. The enemy is also
hastening the arrival of a regiment of parachute troops.

Deductions.
    We still have a numerical superiority in infantry though this is diffi-
cult to assess. We are beginning to be inferior in 'Capital A.F.Vs' and
must therefore be careful of those we have. They should be kept for

a main action. We have a considerable qualitative superiority in infantry owing to the fact that the Germans will have either to rely on his German infantry for all fighting or to bring his Italians again into close contact with our troops. We must force the Germans to bring forward Italians by keeping up pressure all along the enemy front, so as to force him to use Italians to hold it if he is to be able to concentrate his Germans for an offensive.

4. So much for the forces in contact on the main front between the sea and the QATTARA DEPRESSION. We also dispose of certain mobile and partisan forces not possessed by the enemy. These are:-

  a) 7th Armoured Division, comprising, 7th Motor Brigade Group and 4th Light Armoured Brigade Group.

  b) The Long Range Desert Group.

  c) Certain forces working under the general control of the Directorate of Combined Operations which could be used against the sea-ward flank.

ADMINISTRATION.

5. The enemy has serious transportation difficulties. His L of C extends from BENGHASI to EL ALAMEIN supplemented by intake through TOBRUK and MATRUH. To mount an offensive at EL ALAMEIN he requires considerable reserves of ammunition and P.O.L. He probably has not sufficient transport to bring forward stores for an offensive and also defence stores. The more, therefore, he has to consider defence measures such as mining, wiring, etc., the longer will it take him to stage an offensive. Every mine we compel him to lay helps us in the short term, though it may not do so in long term.

VULNERABLE POINTS.

6. The enemy is vulnerable on his main front in the whole area from BAB EL QATTARA northwards to the sea. He cannot risk a break through by us in this area; it must therefore be held strongly by Germans until he can fix our attention elsewhere by taking the offensive.
DEDUCTION We should do everything possible to keep his Germans in the NORTHERN and Central sectors. The greater our success in this the more will he be forced to use Italians in the sector SOUTH of BAB EL QATTARA. Alternatively the enemy may consider his northern sector sufficiently strengthened to permit of a higher proportion of Italians being used there. We should be ready to take advantage

of this. But we should also interfere as much as possible with any strengthening of the enemy's forward positions.

7. The southern sector of the enemy front (south of BAB EL QATTARA) although vulnerable to infantry in darkness or smoke, is largely TANK proof except in the six mile gap between GEBEL KALAK and BAB EL QATTARA. The enemy holds this area with infantry posts possibly supported by Italian armour. This area might be vulnerable to large scale infantry infiltration. The front SOUTH of GEBEL KALAK might offer an opportunity to infantry action particularly if it were held by Italians. Any action of this sort would have to be carefully planned and rehearsed.

The northern edge of the QATTARA depression runs from about MINQAR ABU DWEIS to QARA, about 130 miles. So far as is known the depression and the northern cliffs can only be crossed at one place, RAS EL QATTARA where a track leads north to MATRUH from BAHARIYA. There is water here and this place is used as a L.R.D.G. base. It is presumably a place which the enemy should hold, for if he did we would be restricted to the SIWA approach. Alternatively if we established a bridgehead here from which to operate raiders in strength we could be a thorn in the enemy side. The possibility of getting a strong mobile force into the country NORTH of RAS EL QATTARA seems a good one.

SIWA is accessible to us from BAHARIYA or QARA. The OASIS area is well known to us. The enemy have some 500 Italians there. These should be vulnerable to attack from SOUTH or NORTH. We may have administrative difficulties in maintaining a strong enough force to attack this area.

DEDUCTION. The enemy has a vulnerable flank here and could be forced to make a considerable detachment to protect it. Moreover, provided we could maintain reasonable forces at BAHARIYA this is a flank which has offensive possibilities.

The Sea Flank. The exploitation of the sea flank is a very large subject and there are at present projects varying from the landing of tanks, etc. near DABA to the blocking of MATRUH and a large scale attack on TOBRUK. Attacks on the sea flank might also be combined with frontal attacks and operations from QATTARA.

The REAR. The experiences of our escaped prisoners of war show how lightly the enemy back areas east of the Egyptian frontier are occupied, and the area west of the Egyptian frontier must also be very lightly held. There is scope for the L.R.D.G. and air-borne troops in this area. We might also in certain circumstances exploit the use of our prisoners of war in TOBRUK.

COURSES OPEN TO THE ENEMY

8.   To the extent to which we have been forced temporarily to act on the defensive, we have surrendered initiative to the enemy. It seems we should therefore think first what he can do. His first course will clearly be to strengthen his front from the sea to the QATTARA Depression and to develop this in depth. In doing this he must be certain that his northern sector is strong, for it is from behind this that he will develop an offensive.

Deductions. Although it may not suit our future plans that the enemy should make the northern sector very strong, it will pay to keep him apprehensive and busy here even at the risk of his strengthening it further. The enemy will regard his front SOUTH of BAB EL QATTARA as a starting line for any turning movement against the southern flank of our present front. A well-timed capture of GEBEL KALAK and the TAQA plateau might dislocate this project even though we could not consolidate our gains. It would almost certainly force the enemy to detach German troops to hold this area.

The enemy is likely also to clear up his QATTARA flank and to hold RAS EL QATTARA and SIWA. We will also reconnoitre and defend any areas suitable and vulnerable to attack by us from the sea.

COURSES OPEN TO US.

9.   Our policy should be to harass the enemy by all possible means (moral as well as physical), so as to keep him stretched and impede his preparations for attack. All this while keeping ourselves concentrated. The targets for action are:-

LAND AND AIR:-   a) KALAK – TAQA sector.
                        b) Raids across QATTARA Depression.
                        c) Feint attacks on central or northern sectors.

LAND, SEA AND AIR:-

                        a) Raids on TOBRUK and BENGHASI
                        b) Raids or feint at DABA.
                        c) Folbot landings as minor enterprises.

PLAN.

> This interim plan does not deal with our resumption of the general offensive but for action in the interim period which will last until either the enemy takes the general offensive or we do.

10. 30 Corps.

> To prepare for large scale raids in the MITEIRIYA and DEIR EL SHEIN areas. To be launched if by any chance either of these areas are taken over by Italians. Meanwhile to miss no chance of taking prisoners and harassing the enemy by patrol action, fire, etc. Preparation for the large scale raid should be complete by 10th August.

11. 13 Corps.

> To prepare,
>
> a) for a large scale raid on the area KALAT – TAQA to be launched if this sector is taken over by Italians. Meanwhile to miss no chance of taking prisoners and harassing the enemy by patrol action, fire, etc. Preparation for the large scale raid should be complete by 10th August.
>
> b) an advance into the enemy's rear areas via RAS EL QATTARA with a battle group of armoured cars, motor troops and artillery. This to take place possibly when L.R.D.G. begin to operate further west. Possible date, 14th August.

12. The strengthening of our front by wire and mines should enable both Corps to withdraw troops into reserve in preparation for offensive action.

13. L.R.D.G. etc. To operate as required.

14. R.N. To prepare attacks on MATRUH and TOBRUK and in conjunction with D.C.O. to raid TOBRUK or BENGHASI.

15. R.A.F. To support these operations as they occur and also by air action on the EL ALAMEIN front to convey the impression that we are interested in northern sector.

Signed C. Auchinleck

General.
Commander-in-Chief
Middle East Forces

Appendix C

[Reproduced from WO201/556, TNA]

<u>MOST SECRET.</u>

<u>WESTERN FRONT</u>

Appreciation of Situation,
2 Aug 42.

1. <u>OBJECT.</u>

To destroy the enemy where he is.

2. <u>ENEMY.</u>

(i) Enemy has two secure flanks, NORTH on sea, SOUTH on QATTARA depression.

(ii) Enemy northern and central sectors as far SOUTH as DEIR EL QUATTARA are strongly mined and entrenched. Defences of his SOUTHERN sector though strong probably less continuous and not so deep.

(iii) To hold all his front reasonably strongly and at same time be able to keep strong mobile reserve for counter attack or defensive, enemy probably will have to use ITALIANS again in his forward zones on one part of his front or another.

(iv) Enemy centre opposite RUWEISAT ridge obviously vital to security whole position and has been made correspondingly strong. Depressions in this area give admirable cover for his mobile armoured reserve, which increases permanent strength this sector.

(v) Enemy NORTHERN flank already forced back by our occupation TEL EL EISA covers main road, railway and coast, and therefore his main communications. Hence this is his most vulnerable flank, security of which is vital to him. Therefore sure to be strongly held in depth.

(vi) Enemy SOUTHERN flank well posted in difficult ground and can be refused for considerable distance before his rear areas and communications are endangered. On other hand a breach here would give opening for deep raid against his communications by armoured and motorised forces.

(vii) Enemy army is practically all concentrated in forward area. Garrisons of important points in rear, such as TOBRUK BENGHASI, appear very weak.

(viii) Enemy ITALIAN troops are now unreliable even in defence unless stiffened by Germans.

(ix) Enemy has parachute troops with which he can operate behind our lines.

(x) Enemy's maintenance system is most precarious and provided we can continue to weaken it by our attacks, seems unlikely to get stronger in the near future.

(xi) Enemy for political reasons can not recede from his present positions, however much he may wish to do so for military reasons. He is likely to resume the offensive at the earliest opportunity also for political reasons and because he knows we are likely to be reinforced.

(xii) If we make an offensive enemy is likely to expect it to develop round his SOUTHERN flank as this would be in accordance with previous practice, rather than in the NORTH.

3. OURSELVES.

(i) We must secure at all costs the NORTHERN half of our position from the sea to the high ground running parallel to and four miles SOUTH of RUWEISAT ridge. Loss of this ridge, the RUWEISAT ridge or the coastal ridge, would make our general defensive zone untenable.

(ii) Our positions in the NORTH are now fortified in depth and can be defended by the forces available using if necessary our existing forward zone from TEL EL EISA SOUTHWARD to DEIR EL HIMA as an outpost position covering the main defensive zone should the enemy threaten to breach it or isolate parts of it from the remainder.

(iii) In the SOUTH we have no fixed defences beyond some minefields designed to delay and break up a rapid enemy advance with armoured and motorised troops. Our intention is to use our light troops to delay and harass an enemy advance in this section until our main reserves can strike it in flank from the NORTH.

(iv) We have the resources to land forces behind the enemy's positions or to raid and destroy his ports and other vital points on his lines of communication.

(v)   We have fortified zones in rear of the EL ALAMEIN – HAMMAM defensive zone and garrisons with which to hold them against a sudden enemy raid around the SOUTHERN flank of Eighth Army.

(vi)   We now have a light armoured brigade and also a special R.A.F. wing designed for low flying attack on enemy troops.

4.   <u>DEDUCTIONS.</u>

(i)   We can not turn the enemy flanks, therefore we must break his centre or force our way through one or other of his flanks with the object of enveloping the rest of his line and striking at his rear areas.

(ii)   An attempt to break the enemy's centre is unlikely to succeed unless we can build a greater superiority over the enemy than seems probable at the moment, even though it does facilitate the concentration of a mass of artillery and tanks at the decisive point. Therefore we must strike at one flank or the other.

(iii)   The enemy's SOUTHERN flank may be easier to break through than his NORTHERN flank and offers far reaching possibilities for deep movements by motorised and light armoured forces against the enemy's rear and communications. On the other hand it is not easy to concentrate troops, particularly artillery, in the extreme SOUTH without unduly depleting the centre and NORTH and thus inviting an enemy counter stroke in this vital sector. Moreover the distances to be covered by any force breaking through are great and much of the country is difficult for movement. Decisive results, therefore, may be slow to mature.

(iv)   An attack against the enemy's NORTHERN flank is bound to meet strong opposition organised in depth and strongly supported by artillery and aircraft. The results, however, of a break through here would have immediate and perhaps decisive effect. Moreover it should be possible to ensure the maximum concentration of artillery on this front without unduly weakening the centre, though the area for the deployment of artillery WEST of EL ALAMEIN is limited, and would need enlarging. An attack here could well be combined with a landing from the sea in rear of the enemy, thus increasing the concentration of force at the decisive point. It would also give early access to the landing grounds round DABA urgently needed by the R.AF for further operations.

(v)   Whether the attack be made in the NORTH or the SOUTH, the enemy must be kept stretched and prevented from forming a strong mobile reserve. Every effort should be made to induce the enemy to concentrate his GERMAN infantry on the sector it is proposed not to attack.

(vi) No chance of striking at the ITALIANS by means of raids, limited attacks and air attacks, must be missed, so as to keep their morale at low ebb.

(vii) Utmost and unremitting pressure must be maintained on the enemy lines of supply whenever and wherever these can be reached.

(viii) We must organise our rear areas and all really vital points against attack by parachute troops.

(ix) We must be ready for a sudden enemy thrust round the SOUTHERN flank of our main defensive zone, which must therefore be occupied to some degree at all times, especially in its SOUTHERN sector.

(x) The enemy must be led to believe that we are incapable of taking the offensive for many months to come.

5. PLAN.

(i) To make all preparations for a deliberate attack on the extreme NORTH of the enemy's position.

(ii) To disguise this intention by inducing the enemy to believe that when able to resume the offensive we intend to attack in the SOUTH. Overt preparations should be made to this end.

(iii) To attack and harass the enemy communications to the greatest possible extent.

(iv) To perfect the organisation of our main defensive zone in rear of the EL ALAMEIN position and be ready to meet an enemy attempt to turn or by-pass our SOUTHERN flank.

(v) To train and rehearse intensively for the main operation against the enemy NORTHERN flank.

(vi) To prepare our motorised and armoured forces to take immediate advantage of the break through when made.

Signed C. Auchinleck

General.
Commander-in-Chief.
Middle East Forces.

Appendix D

[Reproduced from WO201/556, TNA]

APPRECIATION AND PLAN: OPERATION 'LIGHTFOOT'.

1.   OBJECT.

To destroy the enemy's forces in the area they now occupy. The enemy must not be allowed to withdraw any elements back to CYRENAICA.

2.   SCOPE OF OPERATION.

This plan deals with the 'break-through' and the destruction of the enemy, but not with the pursuit of any elements that may escape, nor with the re-occupation of LIBYA.

3.   CODEWORD.

The codeword for the operation is 'LIGHTFOOT'.

CONSIDERATIONS.

4.   GROUND.

(a) Northern Sector.

In the Northern sector we hold ground giving good observation, the strongly fortified ALAMEIN area, and a flank on the sea which we can turn to our advantage.

The 'going' map is not complete between ALAMEIN and DABA, but from such information as is available it appears that there is a belt of fair going running six miles South of, and parallel to, the main road. North of this, the going is similar to that near IMAYID Station, but is not impassable.

The area East of EL ALAMEIN for deploying a large force, and also the area West and North of the MITEIRIYA Ridge, is restricted. Great difficulty must be expected in deploying a large force quickly in this area, and detailed organisation will be required. This problem is being investigated urgently.

A thrust in the Northern sector brings an immediate threat to bear on the

enemy's L. of C. and landing grounds. Success here would tend to cut off
the enemy forces in the South. Should a landing from the sea also be possible
to support this thrust, it will derive some air protection from that already
provided for our forces in the area.

An attack in this sector is the easiest for us to maintain.

(b) Central Sector.

The enemy shares the RUWEISAT Ridge with us, and we have not got the
best observation. The ground to the West is difficult and contains depressions such as DEIR EL SHEIN, EL MIREIR, and DEIR EL ABYAD which
afford protection to the enemy and can be strongly held.

(c) Southern Sector.

In the sector South of QARET EL ABD, there is only a narrow gap between
DEIR EL QATTARA and the EL TAQA plateau which would be suitable
for the passage of a large force. A series of impassable escarpments runs N.W.
and S.E. from QARET EL ABD to EL QUSEIR. This barrier would make
exploitation against a force North of the barrier difficult if not impossible.

(d) Conclusion.

Provided the difficulty of congestion can be overcome, the Northern sector
is the most suitable for a 'break-through' for the following reasons:

(i)   The right flank rests securely on the sea.
(ii)   The MITEIRIYA Ridge is a strong tactical feature giving security to
        the left flank.
(iii)   A threat here forces the enemy away from his L. of C. and threatens
        him with encirclement.
(iv)   A 'break-through' in this area produces an immediate threat to the
        enemy's landing grounds.
(v)   Landing from the sea may be possible to support the operation.
(vi)   Maintenance is easier.

5.   ENEMY'S PRESENT DEFENSIVE LAY-OUT.

The enemy defensive lay-out North of DEIR EL SHEIN rests on a series
of thickening and planned minefields covered by fire. Irregular and smaller
minefields are laid in front of the main fields. He has developed DEIR EL
SHEIN itself and appears to be building a second position there behind his
present one. South of RUWEISAT Ridge he has mined less thickly and less
systematically, and makes use of those defended localities, such as BAB EL
QATTARA, which he captured from us.

6.   AIR SITUATION.

As we advance, the increased distance of our forward troops from our fighter aerodromes will reduce the effectiveness of our fighter cover. An increased weight of enemy air attack must therefore be expected and the need for dispersion and A.A. protection will be greater until a threat to the enemy forward landing grounds forces him to withdraw his air forces.

7.   ENEMY SUPPLY SYSTEM.

The enemy's main dumps are in the areas around DABA, and South of SIDI ABD EL RAHMAN. Tracks used for supplying his forward troops are shown on the 1:100,000 map. If he is forced to maintain his forward troops from DABA by the desert route, he will be faced with difficulties owing to shortage of serviceable transport. We should, therefore, aim at occupying ground South of SIDI ABD EL RAHMAN in order to make a detour by the enemy necessary.

DABA is of great importance to the enemy for the following reasons:

(a)   His advanced air bases are located there.
(b)   His forward supply dumps and workshops are located there.
(c)   Tracks across the desert to maintain the Southern sector of the enemy front converge at DABA.

A force sent to DABA will, therefore, interfere considerably with the enemy's air and supply organisations.

8.   THE 'BREAK-IN'.

(a) Speed and Surprise.
It is essential that the 'break-in' should be carried out rapidly and with the greatest measure of surprise.

(b) Our object is to position ourselves on ground vital to the enemy's security and force him to fight at our advantage and against guns in position. Our penetration must therefore be sufficiently deep to ensure that the enemy must attack us to restore the situation and cannot merely adjust his forward dispositions to conform.

(c) We must also select ground which will give us protection on our Southern flank against the enemy's counter-attack. The MITEIRIYA Ridge is such a feature.

(d) Force required.
It is considered that four Infantry Brigades are required; two on the right and two on the left, to break-in. For re-organisation and holding the gap

two further Brigades will be required. It is recommended that the Aust Div and 51 Div complete be used for this purpose. The Infantry Brigade required for 1 Armd Div could be provided by 50 Div.

9.   DIRECTION OF ATTACK.

Two courses are open:

(a)   To attack from the S.E. in a N.W. direction from the present South African positions.

(b)   To attack S.W. from the area of 20 Aust Bde, combined with a thrust N.W. along the main road.

The advantages and disadvantages of these courses will be considered during the detailed planning stage, but on a first examination it appears that an initial attack from the North is preferable.

10.   POSITIONING OF OUR ARMOURED FORCES.

Once the gap is created, our armoured force must be so positioned that it threatens the enemy with encirclement and can deal with an enemy counter-attack. It is recommended that the force should be sited N.W. of the MITEIRIYA Ridge and include the feature TEL El AQQAQIR (861297) which gives good observation to the South and S.E.

11.   SIZE OF ARMOURED FORCE REQUIRED.

It is estimated that by 1 October German tank strength may be 350 and Italian 200. To ensure adequate superiority, it is recommended that the whole of 10 Corps be employed to meet the enemy's armour, and 1 Armd Div be held in reserve to reinforce 10 Corps if required.

12.   LANDINGS FROM THE SEA.

Naval forces are available for the following:

(a)   To raid TOBRUK and BENGHAZI.

These operations are already planned to take place on 9 September. They will therefore precede the main offensive and cannot take place soon enough to interfere seriously with the enemy's reinforcement programme. It is for consideration whether they should be delayed for another month (to suit the moon) and be synchronised with the main offensive.

On the other hand these operations should weaken the enemy's position generally and thereby make our task easier.

(b)   <u>Landing a force of approximately one Regt tanks with supporting arms and infantry on the coast between DABA and ALAMEIN to support our main thrust.</u>

Suitable beaches for this operation are shown in Appendix 'A' [not reproduced] from which it will be seen that the most favourable beach is RAS ABU EL GURUF. The object of this landing would be to disrupt the enemy's rear areas and cause the maximum alarm and despondency. By this means we should compel the enemy to divert forces which might be used to oppose our main 'break-in' thrust.

The time of landing is governed by the following considerations:-

To avoid the force being sighted by air recce after leaving ALEXANDRIA the earliest time of the main landing would be approximately two to three hours before first light.

Landing at this time also has the advantages that it:-

(i)   Reduces risk to T.L.C. by allowing them to be well clear of the beaches by first light.
(ii)   Assists in obtaining an undetected approach in the moon conditions prevailing on the target date.
(iii)   Allows time for any ships supporting the landing by bombardment time to get well clear before daylight.

The landing should precede, or at latest be simultaneous with, the main attack.

13.   <u>NAVAL BOMBARDMENT.</u>

Naval forces are available to bombard targets near the coast during darkness. Suggested targets are gun positions and reserves in the rear area beyond the reach of our own artillery. Careful timing will again be required to ensure that surprise is not jeopardised. A heavy bombardment should be timed to take place with the opening of the main attack; on subsequent nights bombardments will be of value to harass the enemy's rear areas.

14.   <u>ATTACKS AGAINST THE ENEMY'S REAR.</u>

(a)   Landings from the sea in the enemy's rear are not considered worthwhile as they would not contribute to the main object of defeating the enemy in his present position, and would result in a diversion of our air effort to produce fighter cover.
(b)   From the landward side small parties of STIRLING'S men could operate from KUFRA provided that they have returned in time from

the BENGHAZI operation. It is recommended that the most profitable targets would be enemy aircraft, M.T. and locomotives, and that every effort should be made to carry out these attacks just before the main offensive starts.

(c)   The operation of a larger force to interfere with the enemy's L of C, and rear organisation can only be done by first securing SIWA. This is likely to require a force of at least the equivalent of an infantry Brigade and a Lt armoured Brigade, and it is considered that such a force could produce better results if employed in the North. The factor of surprise also causes difficulties, as it would not be possible to disguise the advance of any but very small forces towards SIWA from the East.

There is also the question of air support that will tend to reduce the air effort on the main front.

If the enemy has accumulated considerable reserves in the forward area by the time of our offensive starting, the attacks on his L. of C. from SIWA would not produce any immediate effect on the main battle.

To maintain such a force would take at least 13 G.T. Coys. This project is therefore not recommended.

15.   <u>COURSES OPEN TO THE ENEMY.</u>

Assuming that the enemy does not attack first, the following are his possible reactions to a 'break-through' in the North:

(a)   To attack the base of the salient created by our 'break-in'.
(b)   To attack our main armoured and mobile forces.
(c)   To send a force to deal with our raiding forces operating in rear.

In each case our counter measure will be:

(a)   To attack the enemy force from the flank and rear.
(b)   To defeat his armour on ground of our own choosing.
(c)   To allow him to weaken his main forces whilst keeping our own concentrated and then destroy the D.A.K.

16.   <u>FORCES REQUIRED TO HOLD SOUTHERN SECTOR.</u>

The force required to hold the sector South of the RUWEISAT Ridge is estimated at two Brigade Groups forward in the present N.Z. positions. One armoured division will be required initially in the Southern sector to deal with any enemy counter-attack.

17. DIVERSIONS AND DECEPTION.

In order to contain enemy forces opposite them, formations holding the RUWEISAT Ridge and the area South of it will be required to act as vigorously as possible within the limits of the artillery available to support them. A cover plan will be necessary and deceptive measures will be required to show the main thrust taking place in the South, e.g. construction of additional dummy landing grounds, movement of artillery, wireless deceptive measures etc.

18. ZERO HOUR.

The choice of zero is governed by the lifting of the minefield, co-ordination with the landing from the sea, and, to a lesser extent, by co-ordination with Naval bombardment. Training exercises are being carried out to determine whether the operation of 'breaking-through' can be more easily carried out at first light than during darkness. If, as seems probable, it is decided that the minefield must be lifted by night, then the landing from the sea will not take place until one or two hours after the main attack has already started. Although enemy vigilance would be increased there would be a shorter time between the landing of the party and the arrival of the main exploiting force. This combination of timings is therefore preferable, and it will also be possible to synchronise the Naval bombardment and achieve surprise.

19. MOON.

Full moon – 25 September.

1 October: sunrise 0653 hours; sunset 1847 hours; moonrise 0045 hours; moonset 1300 hours.

20. ORGANISATION OF RELIEFS AND DATE OF READINESS.

See appendix 'B' [not reproduced]

21. FORCES AVAILABLE AND PROPOSED ALLOTMENT.

See Appendix 'C' [not reproduced]

22. OUTLINE PLAN.

(a)   9 Aust Div and 51 Div will 'break-through' the enemy's front between 874287 and the coast and will secure the following objectives: SIDI ABD EL RAHMAN Station, Pt. 30 (869292).

(b)   Zero hour – approximately 0100 hours.

(c)　10 Corps (10 Armd Div, 8 Armd Div, N.Z. Div) with 4 Lt. Armd Bde under command, advance through gap created, and take up position in the general area Pt. 36 (855312), Pt. 47 (852300), Pt. 43 (860297), with the tasks of:

(i)　Attacking in flank enemy armoured forces moving North or N.W.;
(ii)　Sending a column of 4 Lt. Armd Bde to DABA to raid landing grounds and destroy enemy supply dumps, and, if the situation warrants, sending a column to FUKA to raid landing grounds.

(d)　A force of the approximate size of one Regt tanks and supporting arms will be landed at about 0300 hours at RAS ABU EL GURUF (852925) to attack the enemy in rear with the object of drawing off his forces from the sector of our main attack.

(e)　Naval bombardment will be carried out at zero hour of the main attack on located targets West of RAS ABU EL GURUF.

23.　R.A.F.

Before D1 the main air effort will be concentrated on attacking enemy supplies on L. of C., enemy aerodromes and on sustained bombing at night of D.A.K. with the object of lowering morale.

On D1 and after maximum air effort will be concentrated in support of the battle in the Northern sector.

De Guingand
B.G.S.
19/8/42.

Glossary

AFV	Armoured fighting vehicle
AP	Armour-piercing
A.Tk	Anti-tank gun
Arty	Artillery
BEF	British Expeditionary Force
BGS	Brigadier General Staff
BRA	Brigadier Royal Artillery
Bde	Brigade
Bn	Battalion
CB	Counter-battery
CCS	Casualty clearing station
CE	Chief Engineer
CGS	Chief of the General Staff
CIGS	Chief of the Imperial General Staff
CLY	County of London Yeomanry
CRA	Commander Royal Artillery
CRE	Commander Royal Engineers
C-in-C	Commander-in-Chief
Coy	Company
DAK	Deutsches Afrika Korps
DCGS	Deputy Chief of the General Staff
DF	Defensive fire
Div	Division
FDL	Forward defended localities
FOO	Forward observation officer
GHQ	General Headquarters
GOC	General Officer Commanding
GSO 1	General Staff Officer 1
HE	High explosive
Ia	German staff officer responsible for operations (The roman numeral indicates members of the staff of army, corps and division)
Ib	German staff officer responsible for materiel; his duties corresponded roughly to those of British 'Q' and ordnance officers

Ic	German staff officer responsible for intelligence
Id	German staff officer responsible for training
Inf	Infantry
'J' Service	Wireless intercept of forward friendly units
KRRC	King's Royal Rifle Corps
Main HQ	Main Headquarters
OKH	Oberkommando der Heeres (High Command of the Army)
OKW	Oberkommando der Wehrmacht (High Command of the Armed Forces)
OP	Observation post
PAK	Anti-tank
Panzerjager	Literally means 'tank hunter'. German term for self-propelled (and often armoured) anti-tank guns
Pl	Platoon
Pz	Panzer
QF	Quick-fire
QM	Quartermaster
RAF	Royal Air Force
RAOC	Royal Army Ordnance Corps
RAP	Regimental Aid Post
RASC	Royal Army Service Corps
RE	Royal Engineers
REME	Royal Electrical and Mechanical Engineers
RHA	Royal Horse Artillery
RTR	Royal Tank Regiment
R/T	Radio Telephone
Rear HQ	Rear Headquarters
Regt	Regiment
SAA	Small-arms ammunition
SIM	Italian Military Intelligence Service
SP	Self-propelled
Tac HQ	Tactical Headquarters
'Y' Service	British wireless intercept service

NOTES

Introduction

1. Angus Calder, *The People's War*, p. 304.
2. Martin Gilbert, *Churchill: A Life*, p. 734.
3. Winston S. Churchill, *The Second World War*, Volume IV: *The Hinge of Fate*, p. 354.
4. Bernard L. Montgomery, *The Memoirs of Viscount Montgomery of Alamein*.
5. Churchill, *The Hinge of Fate*.
6. Desmond Young, *Rommel*, p. 162.
7. See in particular Nigel Hamilton, *Monty: The Making of a General 1887–1942*, and Nigel Hamilton, *The Full Monty: Montgomery of Alamein 1887–1942*.
8. Denis Falvey, *A Well-Known Excellence: British Artillery and an Artilleryman in World War Two*, p. 83.
9. Charles Richardson, *Flashback: A Soldier's Story*, p. 105.
10. See Battle of Alamein: Notes by Commander Eighth Army, WO106/2254, TNA.
11. See The Battle of Egypt 23 Oct. 1942–7 Nov. 1942: Some Notes by Lt-Gen. B. L. Montgomery, BLM28/1 Montgomery MSS, IWM.
12. Peter Bates, *Dance of War: The Story of the Battle of Egypt*, p. 230.
13. C. E. Lucas Phillips, *Alamein*.
14. Michael Carver, *El Alamein*; *Tobruk*; *Dilemmas of the Desert War: A New Look at the Libyan Campaign 1940–1942*. These are only the most important books from Carver's prolific body of work.
15. Corelli Barnett, *The Desert Generals*.
16. Barton Maughan, *Tobruk and El Alamein*.
17. See J. L. Scoullar, *Battle for Egypt: The Summer of 1942*, and Ronald Walker, *Alam Halfa and Alamein*. These are only the main New Zealand official histories of the period and there are a whole range which cover the war service of each arm and battalion in the New Zealand Expeditionary Force.
18. Mark Johnson and Peter Stanley, *Alamein: The Australian Story*.
19. John Latimer, *Alamein*; Stephen Bungay, *Alamein*; Richard Doherty, *The Sound of History: El Alamein, 1942*.
20. See Shelford Bidwell and Dominic Graham, *Firepower: British Army Weapons and Theories of War 1904–1945*; Dominic Graham, *Against Odds: Reflections on the Experiences of the British Army, 1914–45*; Stephen Hart, *Montgomery and 'Colossal Cracks': The 21st Army Group in Northwest Europe, 1944–45*.
21. David French, *Raising Churchill's Army: The British Army and the War Against Germany, 1919–1945*.

22. Jeremy Crang, *The British Army and the People's War 1939–1945*.

23. Timothy Harrison Place, *Military Training in the British Army, 1940–1944: From Dunkirk to D-Day*.

Chapter One: War in the Desert

1. Winston S. Churchill, *The Hinge of Fate*, p. 344.

2. Macgregor Knox, *Mussolini Unleashed: Politics and Strategy in Fascist Italy's Last War*, p. 125.

3. J. R. M. Butler, *Grand Strategy*, Volume II: *September 1939–June 1941*, p. 295.

4. Mussolini had considered the British Empire a strategic competitor for control of the Mediteranean since the 1920s. See Knox, *Mussolini*, p. 39–40.

5. ibid., p. 89.

6. Butler, *Grand Strategy*, Volume II, p. 298.

7. ibid., p. 295.

8. Michael Howard, *The Mediterranean Strategy in the Second World War: The Lees-Knowles Lectures at Trinity College, Cambridge 1966*, p. 9.

9. I. S. O. Playfair, *The Mediterranean and Middle East*, Volume I, *The Early Success Against Italy (to May 1941)*, pp. 31–5.

10. John Connell, *Wavell: Scholar and Soldier*, p. 209.

11. Playfair, *The Mediterranean and Middle East*, Volume I, p. 92–3.

12. James J. Sadkovich, *The Italian Navy in World War II*, p. 45.

13. Playfair, *The Mediterranean and Middle East*, Volume I, pp. 150–54.

14. John Baynes, *The Forgotten Victor: General Sir Richard O'Connor*, p. 122.

15. Carl von Clausewitz, *On War*, pp. 568–9.

16. ibid., p. 569.

17. JKS, 'The Royal Army Ordnance Corps in the Middle East (September 1939 to June 1942)', GHQ ME, 18 July 1942, unpublished history found in RAOC Campaigns (History of the RAOC in the Middle East and 8th Army 1939–42) WW2 Box 1, RLCM.

18. Gerhard Schreiber, Bernd Stegemann and Detlef Vogel, *Germany and the Second World War*, Volume III: *The Mediterranean, South-east Europe, and North Africa 1939–1941*, p. 181.

19. Knox, *Mussolini*, p. 272.

20. Schreiber et al., *Germany*, Volume III, pp. 183–97.

21. ibid., pp. 654–5.

22. ibid., p. 655.

23. The literature on Erwin Rommel is vast. Some of the more important works are: Basil H. Liddell Hart, *The Rommel Papers*; Desmond Young, *Rommel*; David Irving, *The Trail of the Fox: The Life of Field-Marshal Erwin Rommel*; Ronald Lewin, *Rommel as Military Commander*; David Fraser, *Knight's Cross: A life of Field Marshal Erwin Rommel*.

24. Erwin Rommel, *Infantry Attacks*.

25. This was Napoleon's name for Marshal André Massena.

26. German Army High Command.

27. F. H. Hinsley et al., *British Intelligence in the Second World War: Its Influence on Strategy and Operations*, Volume One, pp. 191–223; Ralph Bennett, *Ultra and Mediterranean Strategy 1941–1945*, pp. 15–30.

28. A. G. Dudgeon, *Hidden Victory: The Battle of Habbaniya, May 1941*.

29. Playfair, *The Mediterranean and Middle East*, Volume III: *British Fortunes Reach their Lowest Ebb (September 1941 to September 1942)*, pp. 216–21.

30. ibid., p. 224.

31. ibid., pp. 224–5.

32. ibid., pp. 225–6.

33. ibid., pp. 228–9.

34. J. A. I. Agar-Hamilton and L. C. F. Turner, *Crisis in the Desert May–July 1942*, pp. 39–42.

35. Playfair, *The Mediterranean and Middle East*, Volume III, pp. 235–7.

36. ibid., pp. 232–4.

37. ibid., pp. 239–44.

38. Air Officer Commanding Middle East, and Commander-in-Chief Middle East respectively.

39. Andrew B. Cunningham, *A Sailor's Odyssey: The Autobiography of Admiral of the Fleet Viscount Cunningham of Hyndhope*, pp. 464–5.

40. The best estimated figures give the totals as 19,000 British, 13,400 South African and 2,500 Indian troops. See Agar-Hamilton and Turner, *Crisis in the Desert*, p. 221.

41. Playfair, *The Mediterranean and Middle East*, Volume III, pp. 261–75.

42. The Contribution of the Information Service to the May–June 1942 Offensive in North Africa, RG457/1035, USNA.

43. Auchinleck to Winston Churchill, PREM3/290/6, TNA.

44. *The Times*, 22 June 1942.

45. Agar-Hamilton and Turner, *Crisis in the Desert*, pp. 236–40.

46. ibid.

47. 'German tank tactics as viewed by the British', HW1/676, TNA.

48. ibid.

49. The Contribution of the Information Service to the May–June 1942 Offensive in North Africa, RG457/1035, USNA.

50. Fellers to Washington, 16 June 1942, in The Contribution of the Information Service to the May–June 1942 Offensive in North Africa, RG457/1035, USNA.

51. Fellers to Washington, 20 June 1942, in The Contribution of the Information Service to the May–June 1942 Offensive in North Africa, RG457/1035, USNA.

52. The Contribution of the Information Service to the May–June 1942 Offensive in North Africa, RG457/1035, USNA.

53. ibid.

54. Auchinleck's Despatch, Supplement to the *London Gazette*, 15 January 1948, with unpublished appendices, WO32/10160, TNA.

Chapter Two: The Swing of the Pendulum

1. Hereafter CIGS.
2. Auchinleck to CIGS, 25 June 1942, MUL957, Auchinleck MSS, JRL.
3. Auchinleck to CIGS, 23 June 1942, MUL950, Auchinleck MSS, JRL.
4. CIGS to Auchinleck, n.d., MUL960, Auchinleck MSS, JRL.
5. Churchill to Auchinleck, 28 June 1942, PREM3/290/6, TNA.
6. Eric Dorman O'Gowan, A1: The Worst Possible Case, p. 12, unpublished memoir, 1/2/16 Dorman O'Gowan MSS, JRL. Eric Dorman-Smith changed his surname to the Irish Dorman O'Gowan in 1949. See Lavinia Greacen, *Chink: A Biography*, p. 295.
7. Auchinleck's Despatch, WO32/10160, TNA.
8. Galloway to Auchinleck, 31 August 1942, MUL1000, Auchinleck MSS, JRL.
9. Ritchie was able to rebuild his career in the army. He later served as a corps commander under Montgomery in 1944–5. John Keegan, *Churchill's Generals*, p. 214.
10. Dorman O'Gowan, A1: The Worst Possible Case, p. 12, 1/2/16 Dorman O'Gowan MSS, JRL.
11. J. L. Scoullar, *Battle for Egypt: The Summer of 1942*, pp. 55–8.
12. I. S. O. Playfair, *The Mediterranean and Middle East*, Volume III pp. 288–9.
13. ibid., pp. 14–15.
14. Auchinleck's Despatch, p. 328, WO32/10160, TNA.
15. ibid.
16. 13 Corps Intelligence Summary, up to 27 June 23.59 hrs, WO169/4006, TNA.
17. Playfair, *The Mediterranean and Middle East*, Volume III, pp. 289–90.
18. ibid., p. 290.
19. ibid., pp. 291–2.
20. Scoullar, *Battle for Egypt*, pp. 91–135.
21. Playfair, *The Mediterranean and Middle East*, Volume III, p. 294.
22. ibid., p. 295.
23. Von Clausewitz, *On War*, pp. 595–6.
24. Appreciation of the situation regarding the defence of Egypt, 28 June 1942, reproduced in unpublished appendices to Auchinleck's Despatch, WO32/10160, TNA.
25. ibid.
26. ibid.
27. ibid.
28. Gott, who was out of contact with Eighth Army Headquarters, was dismayed by Corbett's order. See Howard Kippenberger, *Infantry Brigadier*, p. 139.
29. Churchill to Auchinleck, 24 June 1942, PREM3/290/6, TNA.

30. ibid.
31. Auchinleck's Despatch, p. 328, WO32/10160, TNA.
32. J. A. H. Carter and D. N. Kann, *The Second World War 1939–1945 Army: Maintenance in the Field*, Volume 1, p. 223.
33. JKS, 'The Royal Army Ordnance Corps in the Middle East', RLCM.
34. ibid.
35. Air Historical Branch, RAF Narrative (First Draft), The Middle East Campaign, Operations in Libya and the Western Desert 21 January 1942 to 30 June 1942, n.d., Air Ministry, pp. 193–203, JSCSC.
36. ibid., p. 202.
37. ibid., pp. 193–203.
38. JKS, 'The Royal Army Ordnance Corps in the Middle East', RLCM.
39. ibid.
40. Enemy Documents Section, Appreciation No. 9, pp. 477–486, CAB146/13, TNA.
41. JKS, 'The Royal Army Ordnance Corps in the Middle East', RLCM.
42. ibid.
43. Nichol was awarded the Military Cross for his actions. The 12 tanks represented fully one-fifth of all the Grants available to Eighth Army. See RAOC Campaigns (History of the RAOC in the Middle East & 8th Army 1939–42), WW2 Box 1, RLCM.
44. JKS, 'The Royal Army Ordnance Corps in the Middle East', RLCM.
45. Kirk to Department of State, 30 June 1942, RG165/78, USNA.

Chapter Three: The Armies at El Alamein

1. Dorman O'Gowan, A1: The Worst Possible Case, p. 21, 1/2/16 Dorman O'Gowan MSS, JRL.
2. For Auchinleck's life and career see John Connell, *Auchinleck: A Biography of Field-Marshal Sir Claude Auchinleck*; Phillip Warner, *Auchinleck: The Lonely Soldier*; Alexander Greenwood, *Field-Marshal Auchinleck*; Roger Parkinson, *The Auk: Auchinleck, Victor at Alamein*.
3. Charles Richardson, *Flashback: A Soldier's Story*, p. 101.
4. Dorman-Smith to Liddell Hart, 29 November 1942, 1/242/49 Liddell Hart MSS, LHCMA.
5. Michael Carver, *Tobruk*, p. 253.
6. Richardson, *Flashback*, p. 99.
7. For an unrivalled biography of 'Chink' Dorman-Smith, see Lavinia Greacen, *Chink: A Biography*.
8. Richardson, *Flashback* p. 103.
9. Saul Kelly, *The Hunt for Zerzura: The Lost Oasis and the Desert War*.
10. Military Report on the North-Western Desert of Egypt, 1937, The General Staff, The War Office, WAII/1/DA 491.23/4, NANZ.
11. A. N. Hadfield, 'British success or Italian Failure: To what extent was Operation

Compass a successful use of superior doctrine?', Defence Research Paper, Watchfield, Joint Services Command and Staff College, 2002.

12. Lessons of the Operations in the Western Desert, December 1940, RG167, Box 627, USNA.

13. ibid.

14. Brian Bond, *British Military Policy Between the Two World Wars.*

15. JKS, 'The Royal Army Ordnance Corps in the Middle East', RLCM.

16. A.H. Fernyhough, *History of the Royal Army Ordnance Corps 1920–1945*, pp. 108–16.

17. Timothy Harrison Place, *Military Training in the British Army, 1940–1944*, pp. 128–52.

18. David French, *Raising Churchill's Army*, pp. 185–9, 217; Jeremy Crang, *The British Army and the People's War 1939–1945*, pp. 2–17.

19. J. N. Whiteley, 'Notes on Main Lessons of Recent Operations in the Western Desert', 7 July 1942, WO201/452, TNA.

20. ibid.

21. Harrison Place, *Military Training*, pp. 8–18.

22. Dorman O'Gowan, A1: The Worst Possible Case, p. 15, 1/2/16 Dorman O'Gowan MSS, JRL.

23. French, *Raising Churchill's Army*, pp. 37–40.

24. Eighth Army Training Instruction No. 1/1942, WO201/452, TNA.

25. A. L. Pemberton, *The Development of Artillery Tactics and Equipment*, p. 10.

26. Ian V. Hogg, *British & American Artillery of World War 2*, pp. 25–6.

27. ibid., pp. 42–3, 46–9.

28. Pemberton, *Artillery Tactics*, pp. 44–6.

29. The two-pounder gun had a 40mm diameter bore and could penetrate 42mm of armour plate at 1,000 yards. See Hogg, *British & American Artillery*, p. 75.

30. Hogg, *British and American Artillery*, p. 73.

31. Lessons from Operations, Cyrenaica No. 10, 13 January 1942, WAII/1/DA491.24/15, NANZ.

32. The six-pounder gun had a 57mm diameter bore and could penetrate 74mm of armour plate at 1,000 yards. See Hogg, *British & American Artillery*, p. 77.

33. Hogg, *British & American Artillery*, p. 73.

34. W. E. Murphy, *2nd New Zealand Divisional Artillery*, p. 328.

35. W. Heinemann, 'The Development of German Armoured Forces 1918–40', in F. H. Toase and J. P. Harris, *Armoured Warfare*, pp. 60–61.

36. L. C. F. Turner, The Problems of Desert Warfare, WAII/2/Box 1, NANZ.

37. Pemberton, *Artillery Tactics*, pp. 66–7.

38. R. F. H. Nalder, *The Royal Corps of Signals: A History of its Antecedents and Development (circa 1800–1955)*, pp. 223–64.

39. R. F. H. Nalder, *The History of British Army Signals in the Second World War*, pp. 9–26.

40. ibid., pp. 42–50.

41. Turner, The Problems of Desert Warfare, WAII/2/Box 1, NANZ.

42. Nalder, *British Army Signals*, p. 50.

43. Shelford Bidwell, *Gunners at War: A Tactical Study of the Royal Artillery in the Twentieth Century*, pp. 83–97.

44. P. G. Griffith, 'British Armoured Warfare in the Western Desert 1940–43', in Toase and Harris, *Armoured Warfare*, p. 77–80.

45. Tom Corbett to Tom Hutton, 6 September 1942, 2/32 Hutton MSS, LHCMA.

46. Dorman O'Gowan, A1: The Worst Possible Case, p. 15, 1/2/16 Dorman O'Gowan MSS, JRL.

47. CinC's Operation Memorandum No. 4, 13 July 1942, WO201/408, TNA.

48. Peter Chamberlain and Chris Ellis, *British and American Tanks of World War II: The Complete Illustrated History of British, American and Commonwealth Tanks, 1939–1945*, pp. 37–8.

49. Lessons from Operations, Cyrenaica No. 2, 10 December 1942, WAII/1/DA 491.24/15, NANZ.

50. Lessons of the Operations in the Western Desert, December 1940, RG167, Box 627, USNA.

51. Chamberlain and Ellis, *British and American Tanks*, p. 56.

52. ibid., p. 60.

53. ibid., pp. 88–9.

54. Peter Beale, *Death By Design: British Tank Development in the Second World War*, pp. 93–4.

55. ibid., pp. 100–101.

56. Lieutenant-Colonel H. E. Pyman, Lectures and Demonstrations by 8 Armoured Brigade Syndicate, n.d., 4/9 Pyman MSS, LHCMA.

57. Lieutenant-Colonel H. E. Pyman, Tactical Notes on Handling of Anti-Tank Guns, 4/7 Pyman MSS, LHCMA.

58. Lessons from Operations, Cyrenaica No. 2, 10 December 1942, WAII/1/DA491.24/15, NANZ.

59. Ian V. Hogg, *German Artillery of World War Two*, pp. 194–7. The Pak 38 could penetrate 61mm of armour at 1,000m.

60. ibid., pp. 162–70. The German Flak 18, 36 and 37 guns were all broadly similar weapons. The armour-piercing round could penetrate 105mm of armour plate at 1,000m.

61. ibid.

62. Chamberlain and Ellis, *British and American Tanks*, pp. 108–09.

63. David Fletcher, *The Great Tank Scandal: British Armour in the Second World War*, Part 1, pp. 90–92; Chris Ellis and Peter Chamberlain, *The Great Tanks*, pp. 120–31.

64. Fernyhough, *History of the Royal Army Ordnance Corps*, pp. 199–201.

65. Frederick Myatt, *The British Infantry 1660–1945: The Evolution of a Fighting Force*, pp. 199–200.

66. ibid., p. 203.

67. The official allocation was eight one-cwt trucks, 33 15-cwt trucks, two water trucks, an office truck, 12 30-cwt trucks, two RASC three-ton trucks attached to carry rations. Each rifle company also had four 15-cwt trucks to carry baggage: see ibid., p. 200.

68. Operations of the 7th Armoured Division, 1 May 1941, RG167, Box 627, USNA.

69. Francis Tuker, *Approach to Battle: A Commentary, Eighth Army, November 1941 to May 1943*, p. 151.

70. Dorman O'Gowan, A1: The Worst Possible Case, p. 14, 1/2/16 Dorman O'Gowan MSS, JRL.

71. ibid., p. 15.

72. School for Armoured Troops, Wunsdorf, 16 Oct. 41 – Experiences from the African Theatre of War, translated in Australian Intelligence Diary, Morshead Papers, 3DRL 2632/6/28, AWM.

73. See R. L. DiNardo, *Mechanized Juggernaut or Military Anachronism? Horses and the German Army of World War II*.

74. 164th Light Division and the Ramcke Parachute Brigade which arrived in theatre during July–August 1942 were foot-bound infantry formations which caused great strain upon the motor transport of the Panzerarmee.

75. Heinemann, 'The Development of German Armoured Forces', in Toase and Harris, *Armoured Warfare*, p. 58.

76. ibid., p. 59.

77. The official name was *Panzerkampfwagen* II. See F. M. von Senger and F. M. Etterlin, *German Tanks of World War II: The Complete Illustrated History of German Armoured Fighting Vehicles 1926–1945*, p. 15.

78. The Pz Kw II was armed with a 20mm cannon and had 35mm of frontal armour: ibid., pp. 24–5.

79. This was the 5cm L/42 Panzerkanone which had a muzzle velocity of 450–685 metres per second: ibid., pp. 34–8.

80. This was the 5cm (KwK 39) L/60 which had a muzzle velocity of 1,180 metres per second: ibid.

81. The 7.5cm KwK L/24 possessed a muzzle velocity of 450 metres per second: ibid., p. 44.

82. John A. English and Bruce I. Gudmundsson, *On Infantry*, p. 108.

83. John J. T. Sweet, *Iron Arm: The Mechanization of Mussolini's Army, 1920–1940*.

84. Macgregor Knox, *Hitler's Italian Allies: Royal Armed Forces, Fascist Regime, and the War of 1940–43*, p. 153.

85. ibid., p. 152.

86. ibid., pp. 51–2.

87. ibid., p. 124.

Chapter Four: The Crucial Day

1. Lieutenant-Colonel H. E. Pyman 'The Development of Armoured Warfare', 4/10 Pyman MSS, LHCMA.
2. Artemis Cooper, *Cairo in the War 1939–1945*, p. 195.
3. Paulo Monelli, *Mussolini: An Intimate Life*, pp. 9–10.
4. Corbett to Auchinleck, 1 July 1942, WO201/2007, TNA.
5. Charles Richardson, *Flashback: A Soldier's Story*, p. 101.
6. R. H. W. S. Hastings, *The Rifle Brigade in the Second World War, 1939–1945*, p. 134.
7. Paulo Caccio-Dominioni, *Alamein: An Italian Story 1933–1942*, p. 14; the name can also be translated as 'two cairns'.
8. Written statement by Lieutenant-General C. W. M. Norrie, Comd 30 Corps from 6 Oct. 41 to 8 Jul. 42, WO106/2235, TNA.
9. Fellers to Washington, 20 June 1942, in The Contribution of the Information Service to the May–June 1942 Offensive in North Africa, RG457/1035, USNA.
10. F. W. von Mellenthin, *Panzer Battles 1939–1945: A Study of the Employment of Armour in the Second World War*, p. 132.
11. ibid.
12. My Draft for Counter-Offensive, MUL 963, Auchinleck MSS, JRL.
13. Dorman O'Gowan, A2: Alamein, July 1st–July 17th: The Decisive Battle, p. 22, 1/2/17, Dorman O'Gowan MSS, JRL.
14. John Connell, *Auchinleck: A Biography of Field-Marshall Sir Claude Auchinleck*, p. 628.
15. German tank tactics as viewed by the British, HW1/676, TNA.
16. Lieutenant-Colonel K. F. May, Report on Action of 18th Ind. Inf. Bde. at Deir el Shein, 1 July 1942, 12 April 1944. May was taken prisoner on 1 July 1942 but managed to escape during the Italian armistice in 1943. WO106/2233, TNA; 18th Indian Brigade was composed of 2/5th Essex, 2/3rd Gurkhas and 4/11th Sikhs.
17. ibid.
18. ibid.
19. T. A. Martin, *The Essex Regiment 1929–1950*, p. 464.
20. Statement by Dennis, WO106/2235, TNA.
21. Statement by Norrie, WO106/2235, TNA.
22. ibid.
23. ibid.
24. Lieutenant-Colonel K. F. May, Report on Action of 18th Ind. Inf. Bde. at Deir el Shein, 1 July 1942, WO106/2233, TNA.
25. Martin, *The Essex Regiment*, p. 470.
26. Statement by Norrie, WO106/2235, TNA.
27. 4th Armoured Brigade War Diary, 1 July 1942, WO169/4216, TNA.

28. Written Statement by Brig. G. S. Hatton, BGS 30 Corps from 23 May 42 to 19 Jul. 42, WO106/2235, TNA.

29. Statement by Major-General H. Lumsden, Account of Operations 1 Armd Div – 1 July 42, WO106/2235, TNA.

30. Statement by Dennis, WO106/2235, TNA.

31. Bisheshwar Prasad, *The North African Campaign 1940–43*, pp. 549–550.

32. 30 Corps Intelligence Summary No. 119, 2 July 1942, WO169/4034, TNA.

33. ibid.

34. 90th Light Division War Diary, 1 July 1942, WAII/1/DA438.24/2, NANZ.

35. Translates as 'battle staff'. This was a company-sized unit tasked with the protection of Panzerarmee Afrika's Headquarters.

36. 90th Light Division War Diary, 1 July 1942, WAII/1/DA438.24/2, NANZ.

37. Air Historical Branch, RAF Narrative (First Draft), The Middle East Campaign, Operations in Libya, the Western Desert and Tunisia, July 1942–May 1943, n.d., Air Ministry, pp. 22–3, JSCSC.

Chapter Five: Ruweisat Ridge

1. Francis Tuker, *The Pattern of War*, p. 53.

2. Auchinleck's Despatch, p. 328, WO32/10160, TNA.

3. Afrika Korps War Diary, 2 July 1942, WAII/1/DA438.23/1, NANZ.

4. Air Historical Branch, The Middle East Campaigns, July 1942–May 1943, pp. 24–5, JSCSC.

5. 90th Light Division War Diary, 2 July 1942, WAII/1/DA438.24/2, NANZ.

6. 'Operational Report – 1 S A Div El Alamein Defensive Battle 29 Jun. 42–30 Sep.42', WO201/393, TNA.

7. 21st Panzer Division War Diary, 2 July 1942, WAII/1/DA 438.24/3, NANZ.

8. Basil H. Liddell Hart, *The Rommel Papers*, p. 248; F. W. von Mellenthin, *Panzer Battles, 1939–1945. A Study of the Employment of Armour in the Second World War*, p. 133.

9. 90th Light Division War Diary, 2 July 1942, WAII/1/DA438.24/2, NANZ.

10. J. A. I. Agar-Hamilton and L. C. F. Turner, *Crisis in the Desert May–July 1942*, p. 306.

11. L. Inglis, Comments on Ruweisat, WAII/1/DA21.1/10/9, NANZ.

12. HQ 2 NZ Div G Branch War Diary, 2 July 1942, WAII/1/DA21/1/31, NANZ.

13. HQ formed from HQ 10 Indian Div, A Battery HAC, 11th Field Regiment, RE detachment from 10 Indian Div, Signals from 10th Indian Division, 1/4 Essex Regiment, 100 men from Gurkhas of 18 Indian Brigade, RIASC and Field Ambulances from 10th Indian Division, see Anon., *The Royal Artillery Commemoration Book 1939–1945*, p. 225.

14. ibid., p. 224.

15. ibid.

16. 4th County of London Yeomanry War Diary, 2 July 1942, WO169/1399, TNA.

17. Afrika Korps War Diary, 2 July 1942, WAII/1/DA438.23/1, NANZ.

18. Auchinleck to Alanbrooke, 25 July 1942, 6/2/14 Alanbrooke MSS, LHCMA.

19. Liddell Hart, *The Rommel Papers*, p. 248.

20. 90th Light Division War Diary, 2 July 1942, WAII/1/DA438.24/2, NANZ.

21. Air Historical Branch, The Middle East Campaign, July 1942–May 1943, p. 26, JSCSC.

22. 30 Corps Intelligence Summary No. 132, 15 July 1942, WO169/4034.

23. Agar-Hamilton and Turner, *Crisis in the Desert*, p. 307.

24. Operational Report, 1 S A Div, El Alamein Defensive Battle 29 Jun. 42–30 Sep. 42, WO201/393, TNA.

25. Agar-Hamilton and Turner, *Crisis in the Desert*, p. 307.

26. Dorman O'Gowan remembers the event as having taken place on the evening of 1 July and that Pienaar asked for his entire *division* to be relieved; see Dorman O'Gowan, A2: Alamein. July 1st-July 17th, The Decisive Battle, p. 24, 1/2/17 Dorman O'Gowan MSS, JRL.

27. ibid.

28. Operational Report, 1 S A Div, El Alamein Defensive Battle 29 Jun. 42–30 Sep. 42, WO201/393, TNA.

29. Dorman O'Gowan, A2: Alamein, July 1st-July 17th, The Decisive Battle, p. 24, 1/2/17 Dorman O'Gowan MSS, JRL.

30. ibid.

31. ibid.

32. ibid.

33. Panzerarmee Daily Report, 2 July 1942, AWM54 492/4/76, AWM.

34. Panzerarmee War Diary, 3 July 1942, AWM54 423/4/103, AWM.

35. Operational Report, 1 S A Div, El Alamein Defensive Battle 29 Jun. 42–30 Sep. 42, WO201/393, TNA.

36. Air Historical Branch, The Middle East Campaigns, July 1942–May 1943, pp. 33–7, JSCSC.

37. 30 Corps Intelligence Summary, No. 120, 3 July 1942, WO169/4034, TNA.

38. Gott to Auchinleck, 10.00 hrs 3 July 1942, MUL966 Auchinleck MSS, JRL.

39. ibid.

40. Afrika Korps War Diary, 3 July 1942, WAII/1/DA438.23/1, NANZ.

41. 21st Panzer Division War Diary, 3 July 1942, Union War Histories Translation, WAII/1/DA 438.24/3, NANZ.

42. Joan Bright, *The Ninth Queen's Royal Lancers 1936–1945*, p. 88.

43. ibid., pp. 88–9.

44. 4th Armoured Brigade War Diary, 3 July 1942, WO169/4216, TNA.

45. Panzerarmee Battle Report Appendices, 3 July 1942, AWM54 492/4/76, AWM.

46. Panzerarmee Daily Report, 3 July 1942, AWM54 492/4/76, AWM.

47. Carl von Clausewitz, *On War*, pp. 568–9.

48. 21st Panzer Division War Diary, 3 July 1942, WAII/1/DA 438.24/3, NANZ.

49. Panzerarmee Daily Report, 4 July 1942, AWM54 492/4/76, AWM.
50. Auchinleck's Despatch, p. 328, WO32/10160, TNA.
51. For a full analysis of this disaster see David M. Glantz, *Kharkov 1942: Anatomy of a Military Disaster.*
52. Churchill to Auchinleck, 12 July 1942, PREM3/290/6, TNA.
53. Auchinleck to Churchill, 15 July 1942, PREM3/290/6, TNA.
54. Eighth Army Operation Order No. 90, 4 July 1942, WO201/408, TNA.
55. ibid.
56. ibid.
57. Agar-Hamilton and Turner, *Crisis in the Desert*, p. 322; Panzerarmee Afrika War Diary, 5 July 1942, AWM54 423/4/103, Part 101, AWM.
58. A brief account of the 2/48th Battalion's move from Syria to Egypt, AWM54 526/2/6, AWM.
59. This exchange is related in Barton Maughan, *Tobruk and Alamein*, p. 552.
60. ibid., pp. 345–52; see also John Connell, *Auchinleck: A Biography of Field-Marshall Sir Claude Auchinleck*, pp. 277–83.
61. Dorman O'Gowan, A2: Alamein, 1/2/17, Dorman O'Gowan MSS, JRL.
62. H. Kippenberger, *Infantry Brigadier*, p. 150.
63. Air Historical Branch, The Middle East Campaigns July 1942–May 1943, pp. 95–6, JSCSC.
64. Eighth Army Operation Order No. 91, 6 July 1942, WO201/408, TNA.
65. Dorman O'Gowan, A2: Alamein, 1/2/17 Dorman O'Gowan MSS, JRL.
66. Agar-Hamilton and Turner, *Crisis in the Desert*, p. 324.
67. Report on Operations 24 Aust Inf Bde 3–29 Jul. 42, AWM54 526/6/5, AWM.
68. Anon., *Red Platypus: A Record of the Achievements of the 24th Australian Infantry Brigade*, p. 45.
69. Eighth Army Operation Order No. 91, 6 July 1942, WO201/408, TNA.
70. See Eighth Army Intelligence Summaries Nos 251, 252, 253, 254, 5–9 July, WO201/2154, TNA.
71. Liddell Hart, *The Rommel Papers*, p. 252.
72. Dorman O'Gowan, A2: Alamein 1/2/17, Dorman O'Gowan MSS, JRL.
73. Liddell Hart, *The Rommel Papers*, p. 252.

Chapter Six: Tel el Eisa

1. 2/48th Infantry Battalion: The Attack of 10 July 1942, AWM54 526/6/15, AWM.
2. John G. Glenn, *Tobruk to Tarakan: The Story of the 2/48th Battalion A.I.F.*, p. 107.
3. 2/48th Infantry Battalion, The Attack of 10th July 1942, AWM54 526/6/15, AWM.
4. David Goodhart, *We of the Turning Tide*, p. 27.
5. Basil H. Liddell Hart, *The Rommel Papers*, p. 253.
6. Literally, 'drumfire'.

7. 26th Australian Infantry Brigade Narrative of Operations 5th to 31st July 1942, AWM54 526/6/16, AWM.

8. ibid.

9. Glenn, *Tobruk to Tarakan*, p. 108.

10. Eighth Army Intelligence Summary No. 254, 8/9 July 1942, WO201/2154, TNA.

11. Von Mellenthin, *Panzer Battles*, pp. 164–5.

12. General Walter Nehring, Der Feldzug in Afrika, Part IV: The Battles in the El Alamein positions from 4 July to 22 October 1942, p. 15, Union War Histories Translation No. 16, WAII/1/DA438.23/2, NANZ.

13. Liddell Hart, *The Rommel Papers*, p. 252.

14. 26th Australian Infantry Brigade Narrative of Operations 5th to 31st July 1942, AWM54 526/6/16, AWM.

15. ibid.

16. The other half of the division, along with 15 tanks, was deployed behind the Brescia Division on the Ruweisat ridge; see 15th Panzer Intelligence Diary, 10 July 1942, WAII/11/24, NANZ.

17. The No. 74 ST Grenade, known as a 'sticky bomb', was an infantry anti-tank grenade which was literally sticky so that it could be attached to an enemy tank. It was heavy, weighing two pounds four ounces, and had to be handled carefully once the protective cover had been taken off the adhesive. Needless to say, it required courage to use one in action.

18. Glenn, *Tobruk to Tarakan*, p. 112.

19. J. A. I. Agar-Hamilton and L. C. F. Turner, *Crisis in the Desert, May to July 1942*, p. 328.

20. Dorman O'Gowan, A2: Alamein, p. 31, 1/2/17, Dorman O'Gowan MSS, JRL.

21. See J. P. Harris with Niall Barr, *Amiens to the Armistice: The BEF in the Hundred Days Campaign, 8 August–11 November 1918*, p. 44, and Gary Sheffield, *The Forgotten Victory: The First World War, Myths and Realities*, pp. 149–54, for details of the 'Bite and Hold' method in the First World War.

22. The concept of the indirect approach first appeared in print in Liddell Hart, *The Decisive Wars of History*, 1929, which was then expanded in Liddell Hart, *The Strategy of the Indirect Approach*, 1941, and then in a number of subsequent revised editions. Dorman-Smith took the 1941 edition with him to Alamein, and later wrote the foreword to the 1946 edition.

23. See Brian Bond, *Liddell Hart: A Study of his Military Thought*; Alex Danchev, *Alchemist of War: The Life of Basil Liddell Hart*; and John Mearsheimer, *Liddell Hart and the Weight of History*.

24. Greacen, *Chink*, pp. 120–23.

25. Liddell Hart, *The Strategy of the Indirect Approach*, 1946, p. 7.

26. Dorman O'Gowan, A1: The Worst Possible Case, p. 12, 1/2/16, Dorman O'Gowan MSS, JRL.

27. ibid., p. 16.

28. Liddell Hart, *The Strategy of the Indirect Approach*, p. 16.

29. ibid., p. 178.

30. ibid., pp. 179–80.

31. Inglis to Freyberg, 11 July 1942, WAII/8/24, NANZ.

32. 26th Australian Infantry Brigade Narrative of Operations 5th to 31st July 1942, AWM54 526/6/16, AWM.

33. 2/24 Aus Inf Bn, Intelligence Summary No. 8, 24/25 July 1942, AWM54 526/5/5, AWM.

34. Translates as 'Strategic Signals Intercept Company'. Seebohm's unit was previously called the 3rd Intercept Company of Signals Battalion No. 56 but changed to the more important title on 17 April 1942. See German Wireless Intercept Organisation, WO201/2150, TNA.

35. Hans Otto Behrendt, *Rommel's Intelligence in the Desert Campaign*, p. 170.

36. German Wireless Intercept Organisation, WO201/2150, TNA.

37. Evidence of Enemy Intercept Success June 1941 to October 1943, RSM.

38. Hugh Skillen, *Spies of the Airwaves: A History of Y Sections During the Second World War*, p. 186.

39. German Wireless Intercept Organisation, WO201/2150, TNA.

40. Evidence of Enemy Intercept Success June 1941 to October 1943, RSM.

41. Problems of Desert Warfare, WAII/2/Box 1, NANZ.

42. Behrendt, *Rommel's Intelligence*, p. 173.

43. 15th Panzer Division Intelligence Diary, 10 July 1942, WAII/II/24, NANZ.

44. 26th Australian Infantry Brigade Narrative of Operations 5th to 31st July 1942, AWM54 526/6/16, AWM.

45. ibid.

46. Liddell Hart, *The Rommel Papers*, p. 254.

47. ibid.

48. 26th Australian Infantry Brigade Narrative of Operations 5th to 31st July 1942, AWM54 526/6/16, AWM.

49. Liddell Hart, *The Rommel Papers*, p. 255.

50. Operational Report, 1 S A Div, El Alamein Defensive Battle 29 Jun. 42–30 Sep. 42, WO201/393, TNA.

51. ibid.

52. 'PAK' translates as 'anti-tank'.

53. Operational Report, 1 S A Div, El Alamein Defensive Battle 29 Jun. 42–30 Sep. 42, WO201/393, TNA.

54. 26th Australian Infantry Brigade Narrative of Operations 5th to 31st July 1942, AWM54 526/6/16, AWM.

55. Max Parsons, *Gunfire!: A History of the 2/12 Australian Field Regiment 1940–46*, p. 100.

56. ibid.

57. Auchinleck to Brooke, 25 July 1942, 6/2/14 Alanbrooke MSS, LHCMA.

58. JKS, 'The Royal Army Ordnance Corps in the Middle East', RLCM.

59. Memo on Ammunition Policy, 14 July 1942, WO201/408, TNA.

Chapter Seven: Raw Bacon

1. A line often quoted by Gott, from John Bunyan, *The Pilgrim's Progress*.

2. Dick Vernon, *'Strafer' Gott*, p. 18.

3. Agar-Hamilton to Kippenberger, 19 April 1949, WAII/11/6, NANZ.

4. Inglis to Freyberg, 11 July 1942, GoC's Papers, Minqar Qaim and Ruweisat, WAII/8/24, NANZ.

5. J. L. Scoullar, *Battle for Egypt: The Summer of 1942*, pp. 204–19.

6. Inglis to Freyberg, 11 July 1942, GoC's Papers, Minqar Qaim and Ruweisat, WAII/8/24, NANZ.

7. See Martin Middlebrook, *The First Day on the Somme: 1 July 1916*, Allen Lane, 1971; Robin Prior and Trevor Wilson, *Command on the Western Front: The Military Career of Sir Henry Rawlinson 1914–1918*, Blackwell, 1991.

8. Comments by Inglis on New Zealand Draft Official History, WAII/1/DA 21.1/10/9, NANZ.

9. ibid.

10. ibid.

11. Narrative of Operations Compiled from New Zealand Intelligence Summaries, WAII/8/24.

12. Comments by Inglis, WAII/1/DA21.1/10/9, NANZ.

13. ibid.

14. ibid.

15. C-in-Cs Operation Memorandum No. 4, 13 July 1942, WO201/408, TNA.

16. Comments by Inglis, WAII/1/DA21.1/10/9, NANZ.

17. ibid.

18. Lessons from Operations, Cyrenaica No. 11, 19 January 1942, WAII/1/ DA491.24/15, NANZ.

19. Report on the night attack carried out by 4 NZ Inf Bde on the night of 14/15 July and on the subsequent overrunning of the position by enemy tanks, Act Brig. J. T. Burrows, WAII/8/24, NANZ.

20. ibid.

21. ibid.

22. HQ 2 NZ Div 'G' Branch War Diary, 15 July 1942, DA 21/1/31, NANZ.

23. Howard Kippenberger, *Infantry Brigadier*, p. 165.

24. D. J. C. Pringle and W. A. Glue, *20 Battalion and Armoured Regiment*, p. 264.

25. ibid., p. 237.

26. Kippenberger, *Infantry Brigadier*, pp. 165–6.

27. Report on the night attack carried out by 4 NZ Inf Bde, WAII/8/24, NANZ.

28. ibid.

29. Pringle and Glue, *20 Battalion*, p. 266.

30. Written Statement by Lieutenant-General C. W. M. Norrie, Comd 30 Corps from 6 Oct. 41 to 8 Jul. 42, WO106/2235, TNA.

31. E. H. Smith, *Guns Against Tanks: L Troop, 7th New Zealand Anti-Tank Regiment in Libya, 23 November 1941*, p. 3.

32. ibid., p. 30.

33. Notes on Main Lessons of Recent Operations in the Western Desert, 7 July 1942, WO201/452, TNA.

34. Pringle and Glue, *20 Battalion*, p. 272.

35. ibid., p. 271.

36. HQ 2 NZ Div 'G' Branch War Diary, 15 July 1942, DA21/1/31, NANZ.

37. ibid.

38. 15th Panzer Division Intelligence Diary, 15 July 1942, WAII/11/24, NANZ.

39. ibid.

40. ibid.

41. ibid.

42. Bisheshwar Prasad, *The North African Campaign, 1940–43*, pp. 422–3; Compton Mackenzie, *Eastern Epic*, p. 586.

43. 21st Panzer Division War Diary, 15 July 1942, WAII/1/DA438.24/3, NANZ.

44. HQ 2 NZ Div 'G' Branch War Diary, 15 July 1942, DA21/1/31, NANZ.

45. Kippenberger, *Infantry Brigadier*, pp. 169–70.

46. Major-General A. H. Gatehouse, 'Certain Aspects of the battles of Alam El Halfa and El Alamein', n.d., Liddell Hart 9/28/42, LHCMA.

47. Comments by Inglis, WAII/1/DA21.1/10/9, NANZ.

48. HQ 2 NZ Div 'G' Branch War Diary, 14 July 1942, DA21/1/31, NANZ.

49. 1st Armoured Division Operation Order No. 15, 14 July 1942, WO169/4006, TNA.

50. 2nd Armoured Brigade War Diary, 15 July 1942, WO169/4210, TNA.

51. ibid.

52. Prasad, *North African Campaign*, p. 422; Mackenzie, *Eastern Epic*, p. 586.

53. 2nd Armoured Brigade War Diary, 15 July 1942, WO169/4210, TNA.

54. ibid.

55. Pringle and Glue, *20 Battalion*, p. 268.

56. 2nd Armoured Brigade War Diary, 15 July 1942, WO169/4210, TNA.

57. Pringle and Glue, *20 Battalion*, p. 269.

58. ibid., p. 270.

59. J. F. Cody, *New Zealand Engineers, Middle East*, pp. 301–02.

60. 22nd Armoured Brigade War Diary, 15 July 1942, WO169/4251, TNA.

61. 2nd Armoured Brigade War Diary, 15 July 1942, WO169/4210, TNA.

62. Kippenberger, *Infantry Brigadier*, p. 172.

63. 4th New Zealand Brigade was rebuilt and converted to an armoured brigade but it never served in North Africa again.

64. Scoullar, *Battle for Egypt*, p. 300.

65. ibid., p. 301.
66. Brigadier C. E. Weir, 14 April 1948, WAII/11/6, NANZ.
67. ibid.
68. Comments by Inglis, WAII/1/DA 21.1/10/9, NANZ.
69. Lessons from Operations, Cyrenaica No. 11, 19 January 1942, DA 491.24/15, NANZ.
70. Brigadier C. E. Weir, 14 April 1948, WAII/11/6, NANZ.
71. Nehring, Der Feldzug in Afrika, p. 24, WAII/1/DA 438.23/2, NANZ.
72. Inglis to Freyberg, 18 July 1942, WAII/8/24, NANZ.
73. Dorman O'Gowan, A2: Alamein, p. 33, 1/2/17, Dorman O'Gowan MSS, JRL.

Chapter Eight: Ruin Ridge

1. 9th Australian Division Operation Orders, 16 July 1942, 3DRL2632/ 6/23 Morshead MSS, AWM.
2. 21st Panzer Division War Diary, 16 July 1942, WAII/1/DA438.24/3, NANZ.
3. 20 Infantry Brigade War Diary, 16 July 1942, AWM52 8/2/20, AWM.
4. Representations made to Commander-in-Chief Sir Claude Auchinleck then Commanding Eighth Army 15 July 1942, 3DRL 2632/16 Morshead MSS, AWM.
5. G. H. Fearnside, *Bayonets Abroad: A History of the 2/13 Battalion AIF in the Second World War*, pp. 216–17.
6. The British troops were probably from the 2nd Battalion, West Yorks Regiment, part of 5th Indian Division.
7. Private J. A. Crawford, Forward from El Alamein, p. 363, DRL/0368, AWM.
8. Compton Mackenzie, *Eastern Epic*, p. 586.
9. 21st Panzer Division War Diary, 16 July 1942, WAII/1/DA438.24/3, NANZ.
10. Howard Kippenberger, *Infantry Brigadier*, p. 181.
11. Fearnside, *Bayonets Abroad*, p. 217.
12. Walker provides a detailed account in Anon., *The Royal Artillery Commemoration Book 1939–45*, p. 574. He remembers the action as having taken place on 15 July but it is clear that it was actually on 16 July 1942.
13. ibid.
14. ibid., p. 574.
15. ibid.
16. See Mackenzie, *Eastern Epic*, pp. 586–7; Bisheshwar Prasad, *The North African Campaign 1940–43*, p. 423; E. W. C. Sandes, *From Pyramid to Pagoda: The Story of the West Yorkshire Regiment (The Prince of Wales's Own) in the War 1939–45 and Afterwards*, p. 138.
17. Mackenzie, *Eastern Epic*, p. 587. These figures have been challenged and may be an overestimate. It is certain that at least 18 German tanks were knocked out during the action, although the number permanently destroyed may have been lower. There is no doubt that 5th Indian Brigade achieved a notable defensive victory.

18. Dorman O'Gowan, A2: Alamein, p. 33, 1/2/17, Dorman O'Gowan MSS, JRL.

19. 9th Australian Division Operations in the El Alamein Area July 1942, 3DRL2632 6/15 Morshead MSS, AWM.

20. ibid.

21. ibid.

22. ibid.

23. Statement by Private J. M. Welsh, captured Alamein 17 July 1942, AWM54 526/1/4, AWM.

24. Report of the Attack on Ruin Ridge by 24 Aust Inf Bde, AWM54 527/6/14, AWM.

25. Anon., *Red Platypus: A Record of the Achievements of the 24th Australian Infantry Brigade*, p. 34.

26. ibid., p. 35.

27. Report of the Attack on Ruin Ridge by 24 Aust Inf Bde, AWM54 527/6/14, AWM.

28. ibid.

29. ibid.

30. Report on Carrier Raid on Tel el Eisa Ridge, at last light on 17 July 1942, AWM54 526/6/18, AWM.

Chapter Nine: Operation Splendour

1. Basil H. Liddell Hart, *The Rommel Papers*, p. 257.

2. Mark Adkin, *The Waterloo Companion*, p. 163.

3. Dorman O'Gowan, A2: Alamein, p. 33, 1/2/17 Dorman O'Gowan MSS, JRL.

4. Eighth Army Operation Order No. 100, 17 July 1942, WO201/408, TNA.

5. ibid.

6. Eighth Army Operation Order No. 101, 19 July 1942, WO201/408, TNA.

7. ibid.

8. Gott to Freyberg, 20 July 1942, WAII/8/24, NANZ.

9. Inglis Private Diary, 20 July 1942, WAII/1/DA441.23/5, NANZ.

10. ibid.

11. GoC's Diary, Part II, 20 July 1942, WAII/8/44, NANZ.

12. ibid.

13. Report on Attack by 6 (NZ) Inf Bde on 21/22 Jul. 42 against El Mreir Depression, WAII/8/24, NANZ.

14. ibid.

15. 23 Armd Bde Gp Operation Order No. 2, 21 July 1942, WO169/4260, TNA.

16. A. H. Gatehouse, Notes on Operation on Ruweisat Ridge on July 22 1942, 9/28/42 Liddell Hart MSS, LHCMA.

17. ibid.

18. Dorman O'Gowan, A3: 'Splendour' and Aftermath, p. 47, 1/2/18 Dorman O'Gowan MSS, JRL.

19. Known to the Australians as 'Baillieu's Bluff'.

20. 9th Australian Division Operations in the El Alamein Area July 1942, 3DRL2632 6/14 Morshead MSS, AWM.

21. Morshead's diary, 21 July 1942, 3DRL/2632/3/2 Morshead MSS, AWM. There is considerable confusion about the date and timing of these events. Morshead's diary gives the date as 21 July and therefore before Operation Splendour. Corelli Barnett's *The Desert Generals*, relying on testimony from Ramsden and Dorman-Smith, places the events on 22 July. However, the idea that these commanders would have time for such fierce arguments during a major operation is implausible and it is much more likely that they engaged in debate the day before the operation. Dorman-Smith argues that Morshead's intransigence delayed the subsequent Operation Manhood but it is clear that Morshead's complaint was made about his division's role in Splendour and not Manhood.

22. Dorman O'Gowan, A3: 'Splendour' and Aftermath, p. 47, 1/2/18 Dorman O'Gowan MSS, JRL.

23. Barnett, *The Desert Generals*, p. 222.

24. ibid., p. 223.

25. Morshead's diary, 21 July 1942, 3DRL/2632/3/2 Morshead MSS, AWM.

26. Greacen, *Chink*, p. 223.

27. Bryan Perrett, *The Valentine in North Africa 1942–43*, p. 11.

28. 23rd Armoured Brigade War Diary, 7 July 1942, WO169/4260.

29. Prime Minister to General Auchinleck, 3 July 1942, MUL967 Auchinleck MSS, JRL.

30. David Fletcher, *The Great Tank Scandal: British Armour in the Second World War*, p. 110.

31. The Royal Army Ordnance Corps in the Middle East, RLCM.

32. R. L. McCreery, 'Recollections of a Chief of Staff,' *The Twelfth Royal Lancers Journal*, April 1959, p. 35.

33. Perrett, *Valentine*, p. 13.

34. Narrative of Events, 23rd Armoured Brigade Group, WO169/4260, TNA.

35. C. T. Witherby, unpublished memoir, p. 12, Witherby MSS, IWM.

36. 23 Armd Bde Gp Demonstration 'Start', 14 July 1942, WO169/4260, TNA.

37. G. P. B. Roberts, *From the Desert to the Baltic*, p. 87.

38. C. T. Witherby, pp. 10–11, IWM.

39. Clifton to Kippenberger, 14 July 1949, WAII/11/6, NANZ.

40. J. F. Cody, *New Zealand Engineers, Middle East*, p. 304.

41. Appendix 'C' to 30 Corps Operation Order No. 66, 21 July 1942, 3DRL2632 6/23 Morshead MSS, AWM.

42. 15th Panzer Division Intelligence Diary, WAII/II/24, NANZ.

43. Nehring, Der Feldzug in Afrika, p. 28, WAII/1/DA438.23/2, NANZ.

44. ibid.

45. W. H. E. Gott, Loss of Point 63, 26 July 1942, WO201/536, TNA.

46. HQ 2 NZ Div 'G' Branch War Diary, 21 July 1942, WAII/1/DA21/1/31, NANZ.

47. Report on Attack by 6 (NZ) Inf Bde on 21/22 Jul. 42 against El Mreir Depression, WAII/8/24, NANZ.

48. Frazer D. Norton, *26 Battalion*, p. 160.

49. ibid.

50. ibid., pp. 163–4.

51. ibid.

52. Report on Attack by 6 (NZ) Inf Bde on 21/22 Jul. 42, WAII/8/24, NANZ.

53. ibid.

54. ibid.

55. See Clifton to Kippenberger, 14 July 1949, WAII/11/6, NANZ and 2nd Armoured Brigade War Diary, 22 July 1942, WO169/4210, TNA.

56. ibid.

57. HQ 2 NZ Div 'G' Branch War Diary, 22 July 1942, WAII/1/DA21/1/31, NANZ.

58. ibid.

59. ibid.

60. W. E. Murphy, *2nd New Zealand Divisional Artillery*, pp. 349–50.

61. 21st Panzer Division War Diary, 22 July 1942, WAII/1/DA 438.24/3, NANZ.

62. Murphy, *2nd New Zealand Divisional Artillery*, p. 350.

63. Report on Attack by 6 (NZ) Inf Bde on 21/22 Jul. 42, WAII/8/24, NANZ.

64. 2nd Armoured Brigade War Diary, 22 July 1942, WO169/4210, TNA.

65. 6th Royal Tank Regiment War Diary, 22 July 1942, WO169/4509, TNA.

66. HQ 2 NZ Div 'G' Branch War Diary, 22 July 1942, WAII/1/DA21/1/31, NANZ.

67. Clifton to Kippenberger, 14 July 1949, WAII/11/6, NANZ.

68. Howard Kippenberger, *Infantry Brigadier*, p. 189.

69. A. H. Gatehouse, Notes on Operation on Ruweisat Ridge on July 22 1942, 9/28/42 Liddell Hart MSS, LHCMA.

70. ibid.

71. 1st Armoured Division War Diary, 22 July 1942, WO169/4006, TNA.

72. ibid.

73. Four tanks in brigade headquarters and 52 tanks in each regiment (49 Valentines and three Matilda close-support tanks). The 22 July was the last occasion in which the Matilda tank saw action as a gun tank in the Middle East.

74. 21st Panzer Division War Diary, 22 July 1942, WAII/1/DA438.24/3, NANZ.

75. Nehring, Der Feldzug in Afrika, p. 30, WAII/1/DA438.23/2, NANZ.

76. Perrett, *Valentine*, pp. 18–20.

77. 21st Panzer Division War Diary, 22 July 1942, WAII/1/DA438.24/3, NANZ.

78. 23rd Armoured Brigade War Diary, 22 July 1942, WO169/4260, TNA.

79. C. T. Witherby, p. 16, Witherby MSS, IWM.

80. 'Tank state: 4/II, 12/III, 5/III Long, 1/IV, two command tanks', 21st Panzer Division War Diary, 22 July 1942, WAII/1/DA 438.24/3, NANZ.

81. 23rd Armoured Brigade War Diary, 22 July 1942, WO169/4260, TNA.

82. Narrative of the assault on Point 63, WAII/1/DA516.23/1, NANZ.

83. W. H. E. Gott, Loss of Point 63, 26 July 1942, WO201/536, TNA.

84. ibid.

85. ibid.

86. 26 Infantry Bde Narrative of Operations 5–31 July 1942, AWM54 526/6/16, AWM.

87. ibid.

88. ibid.

89. ibid.

90. Geoffrey Giddings, 'Oppa's War Years', 93/4/1, Giddings MSS, IWM.

91. Perrett, *Valentine*, p. 25.

92. Report on Operations 24 Aust Inf Bde 3–29 Jul. 42, AWM54 526/6/5, AWM.

93. ibid.; Anon., *Red Platypus: A Record of the Achievements of the 24th Australian Infantry Brigade*, p. 34.

94. Andrew Gordon, *The Rules of the Game: Jutland and British Naval Command*, John Murray, 1996.

95. Inglis, Private Diary, 25 July 1942, WAII/1/DA441.23/5, NANZ.

96. Clifton to Kippenberger, 14 July 1949, WAII/II/6, NANZ.

97. ibid.

98. Panzerarmee Daily Report, 22 July 1942, AWM54 492/4/76, AWM.

99. Nehring, Der Feldzug in Afrika, p. 33, WAII/1/DA438.23/2, NANZ.

Chapter Ten: Emasculation

1. Auchinleck, Special Order of the Day 25 July 1942, MUL987 Auchinleck MSS, JRL.

2. 30 Corps Operation Order No. 68, WO169/4034, TNA.

3. ibid.

4. Report on Operations by 24 Aust Inf Bde Gp 26/27 Jul. 42, AWM54 526/6/17, AWM.

5. ibid.

6. Statement by Private R. J. Sharp – captured Alamein 27 July 1942, AWM54 527/1/3, AWM.

7. Report on Operations by 24 Aust Inf Bde Gp 26/27 Jul. 42, AWM54 526/6/17, AWM.

8. P. J. Lewis and I. R. English, *Into Battle with the Durhams: 8 DLI in World War II*, p. 129.

9. 2nd Armoured Brigade War Diary, 27 July 1942, WO169/4210, TNA.

10. ibid.

11. Report on Operations by 24 Aust Inf Bde Gp 26/27 Jul. 42, AWM54 526/6/17, AWM.

12. Statement by Private R. J. Sharp – captured Alamein 27 July 1942, AWM54 527/1/3, AWM.

13. G. H. Fearnside, *Bayonets Abroad: A History of the 2/13 Battalion AIF in the Second World War*, p. 222.

14. Report on Operations by 24 Aust Inf Bde Gp 26/27 Jul. 42, AWM54 526/6/17, AWM.

15. 9 Australian Division attack on El Miteiriya Ridge 27 July 1942, 4 August 1942, AWM54 526/6/17, AWM.

16. Lewis and English, *Into battle with the Durhams*, pp. 129–30.

17. 2nd Armoured Brigade War Diary, 27 July 1942, WO169/4210, TNA.

18. Douglas Wimberley, A Scottish Soldier, Volume II, unpublished memoir, p. 30, PP/MCR/182 Wimberley MSS, IWM.

19. Barrie Pitt, *The Crucible of War 2: Auchinleck's Command*, p. 322.

20. Brigadier Kisch, Mine Clearance – Operation Night 26/27 Jul., WO201/679A, TNA.

21. ibid.

22. Nehring, Der Feldzug in Afrika, p. 38, WAII/1/DA438.23/2, NANZ.

23. ibid.

24. Fearnside, *Bayonets Abroad*, p. 222.

25. Brigadier Kisch, Mine Clearance – Operation Night 26/27 Jul., WO201/679A, TNA.

26. ibid.

27. Taylor to Barnett, 18 January 1965, 1/27/9 Dorman O'Gowan MSS, JRL.

28. G. Isserson, 'The Evolution of Operational Art', in Harold Orenstein, *The Evolution of Soviet Operational Art 1927–1991: The Documentary Basis*, Volume 1, pp. 75–6.

Chapter Eleven: Interregnum

1. Inscription on the memorial to Lieutenant-General William Henry Ewart Gott and Major-General John Charles Campbell in All Saints Cathedral, Cairo.

2. Appreciation of the Situation, 27 July 1942, in the unpublished appendix to Auchinleck's Despatch, WO32/10160, TNA.

3. Dorman O'Gowan to Horrocks, 11 July 1959, 1/13/1 Dorman O'Gowan MSS, JRL.

4. See, for example, Francis de Guingand, *Generals at War*, pp. 184–8, and Corelli Barnett, *The Desert Generals*, pp. 224–30. Barnett reproduced Dorman-Smith's appreciation of 27 July 1942 which has been subsequently quoted by many authors. Auchinleck and Gott's appreciations of 1 and 2 August 1942 have hitherto been ignored.

5. This is in part due to the fact that Auchinleck only made brief reference to them in his Despatch. The only copies of the originals which survive were deposited in GHQ Middle East papers (WO201/556 TNA) rather than Eighth Army papers.

6. No copies survive in his papers.

7. Charles Richardson, *Flashback: A Soldier's Story*, p. 102.

8. Michael Carver, *Harding of Petherton*, pp. 92–3.

9. McCreery, 'Recollections of a Chief of Staff', *The Twelfth Royal Lancers Journal*, April 1959, p. 36.

10. ibid.

11. Dorman O'Gowan, A3: 'Splendour' and Aftermath, p. 63, 1/2/18 Dorman O'Gowan MSS, JRL.

12. Douglas Wimberley, A Scottish Soldier, Volume II, unpublished memoir, p. 33, PP/MCR/182 Wimberley MSS, IWM.

13. Appreciation by C in C, M. E. at Eighth Army at 0800 hrs 1st August 1942, WO201/556, TNA; see Appendix B.

14. ibid.

15. Combined forces, in Second World War parlance, meant the combined use of air, sea and ground forces.

16. Appreciation by Comd 13 Corps, 1 August 1942, WO201/556, TNA; see Appendix A.

17. ibid.

18. Ramsden's appreciation has yet to be found, if it was in fact written.

19. 30 Corps Operation Instruction No. 69, 30 July 1942, WO169/4034, TNA.

20. Lieutenant-General W. H. C. Ramsden to Lieutenant-General L. Morshead, Major-General D. H. Pienaar and Major-General R. Briggs, 2 August 1942, 3DRL2362/2/6 Morshead MSS, AWM.

21. ibid.

22. ibid.

23. Auchinleck, Western Front, Appreciation of Situation, 2 Aug. 1942, WO201/556, TNA: see Appendix C.

24. ibid.

25. Training in breaking through minefields, 5 August 1942, WO201/2590, TNA.

26. ibid.

27. ibid.

28. Dorman O'Gowan, A2: Alamein, p. 34, 1/2/17 Dorman O'Gowan MSS, JRL.

29. Adrian Stewart, *The Early Battles of Eighth Army: 'Crusader' to the Alamein Line 1941–1942*, p. 142.

30. Nigel Hamilton, *Monty: The Making of a General 1887–1942*, pp. 581–2.

31. See Paddy Griffith, *Forward into Battle: Fighting Tactics from Waterloo to Vietnam*, p. 95.

32. 30 Corps Operation Instruction No. 71, 30 July 1942, WO169/4034, TNA.

33. 9 Aust Div, 13 August 1942, Morshead Papers, 3DRL2632/6/23, AWM.

34. Inglis Private Diary, WAII/I/DA441.23/5, NANZ.

35. ibid.

36. ibid.

37. Churchill to Auchinleck, 27 July 1942, PREM3/292/1, TNA.

38. ibid.

39. ibid.
40. Alex Danchev and Daniel Todman (eds), *War Diaries 1939–1945, Field Marshal Lord Alanbrooke*, p. 275.
41. ibid., p. 278.
42. ibid., p. 286.
43. Brooke to Auchinleck, 17 July 1942, 6/2/14 Alanbrooke MSS, LHCMA.
44. ibid.
45. Auchinleck to Brooke, 25 July 1942, 6/2/14 Alanbrooke MSS, LHCMA.
46. Danchev and Todman, *Alanbrooke*, p. 286.
47. Auchinleck to Brooke, 25 July 1942, 6/2/14 Alanbrooke MSS, LHCMA.
48. ibid.
49. Danchev and Todman, *Alanbrooke*, p. 291.
50. Dorman O'Gowan, A4: Liquidation in Cairo, p. 68, 1/2/19 Dorman O'Gowan MSS, JRL.
51. ibid.
52. Private J. A. Crawford, Forward from El Alamein, 3 DRL/0368, AWM.
53. Dorman O'Gowan, A4: Liquidation in Cairo, p. 68, 1/2/18 Dorman O'Gowan MSS, JRL.
54. Churchill to Mrs Gott, 29 August 1942, quoted in full in Dick Vernon, *'Strafer' Gott*, p. 55.
55. ibid., p. 54.
56. ibid.
57. Nigel Nicolson, *Alex: The Life of Field Marshal Earl Alexander of Tunis*, pp. 111, 150.
58. Inglis Private Diary, WAII/I/DA441.23/5, NANZ.
59. Vernon, *Gott*, p. 76.
60. ibid.
61. ibid., pp. 61, 107.
62. Agar-Hamilton to Kippenberger, 19 April 1949, WAII/II/6, NANZ.
63. Lieutenant-Colonel Ian Jacob's Diary, 8 August 1942, 6/7/3 Alanbrooke MSS, LHCMA.
64. Churchill to Auchinleck, 8 August 1942, MUL 990 Auchinleck MSS, JRL.
65. Lieutenant-Colonel Ian Jacob's Diary, 8 August 1942, 6/7/3 Alanbrooke MSS, LHCMA.
66. ibid.
67. Danchev and Todman, *Alanbrooke*, p. 296.
68. I. S. O. Playfair, *The Mediterranean and Middle East*, Volume III.
69. Carver, *Harding*, p. 94.
70. Charles Richardson, *Send for Freddie: The Story of Montgomery's Chief of Staff Major General Sir Francis de Guingand, KBE, CB, DSO*, p. 67.
71. Bernard L. Montgomery, *The Memoirs of Viscount Montgomery of Alamein*, p. 94.
72. Harding, quoted in Nicolson, *Alex*, p. 157.

73. Montgomery, *Memoirs*, p. 92.

74. ibid.

75. Wimberley, A Scottish Soldier, p. 32, PP/MCR/182 Wimberley MSS, IWM.

76. Montgomery, *Memoirs*, p. 97.

77. Quoted in Barnett, *The Desert Generals*, p. 258.

78. Francis de Guingand, *Operation Victory*, p. 136.

79. ibid., pp. 136–7.

80. Dorman O'Gowan, Piece IV: Cairo around 20th August 1942, 1/2/15 Dorman O'Gowan MSS, JRL. Dorman-Smith had been a student at Staff College when Montgomery was a member of the Directing Staff.

81. Barnett, *The Desert Generals*, p. 251.

82. Montgomery did command a battalion in Egypt 1931–3 but the dynamics of military time and space in 1942 were very different. Montgomery, *Memoirs*, pp. 42–3; Hamilton, *Monty*, pp. 215–21.

83. De Guingand, *Operation Victory*, p. 139.

84. Freyberg to Kippenberger, 5 November 1947, WAII/11/6, NANZ.

85. ibid.

86. GoC's Diary, 14 August 1942, WAII/8/44, NANZ.

87. Carver, *Harding*, p. 93.

88. ibid., pp. 93–4.

89. 44th (Home Counties) Division War Diary, 18 August 1942, WO169/4133, TNA.

90. Playfair, *The Mediterranean and Middle East*, Volume III, p. 314.

91. ibid., pp. 318–22.

92. GoC's Diary, 14 August 1942, WAII/8/44, NANZ.

93. Horrocks even attempted to mend some fences in his memoirs concerning the controversy between Auchinleck and Montgomery over whether it was Auchinleck's intention to retreat in August. He corresponded with Dorman O'Gowan on this point. See Sir Brian Horrocks, *A Full Life*, pp. 110–14, and Dorman O'Gowan to Horrocks, 11 July 1959, Dorman O'Gowan MSS, JRL.

94. Horrocks, *A Full Life*, p. 107.

95. Montgomery, *Memoirs*, p. 103.

96. Phillip Roberts to Lieutenant-Colonel W. B. Roberts, 4 August 1942, G. P. B. Roberts MSS, LHCMA.

97. Montgomery, *Memoirs*, p. 104.

98. Horrocks, *A Full Life*, p. 116

99. Roberts, *From the Desert to the Baltic*, p. 94.

100. Personal Memorandum from Comd 13 Corps, 23 August 1942, WO169/4006, TNA.

101. ibid.

102. Horrocks, *A Full Life*, p. 118.

103. Winston S. Churchill, *The Second World War*, Volume IV: *The Hinge of Fate*, p. 462.

104. De Guingand, *Operation Victory*, p. 151.

105. Churchill, *The Hinge of Fate*, p. 463.

106. Horrocks, *A Full Life*, p. 119.

107. ibid.

108. Lieutenant-Colonel Ian Jacob's diary, 20 August 1942, 6/2/7 Alanbrooke MSS, LHCMA.

109. Auchinleck to Brooke, 14 August 1942, 6/2/14 Alanbrooke MSS, LHCMA.

110. Tom Corbett to Tom Hutton, 2/32 Hutton MSS, LHCMA.

111. Dorman-Smith was given command of a brigade at Anzio but was removed under controversial circumstances and left the army in 1945. See Greacen, *Chink*, pp. 246, 279–91, 294.

112. Dorman O'Gowan to Horrocks, 11 July 1959, Dorman O'Gowan MSS, JRL.

113. Agar-Hamilton to Kippenberger, 2 July 1951, WAII/II/6, NANZ.

114. Playfair, *The Mediterranean and Middle East*, Volume III, p. 371.

115. 1st Armoured Division War Diary, 2–5 August 1942, WO169/4054, TNA.

116. 8th Armoured Brigade was composed of: 3rd Royal Tank Regiment, Nottinghamshire Yeomanry and the Staffordshire Yeomanry.

117. Development of Armoured Warfare, 4/10 Pyman MSS, LHCMA.

118. See, for example, J. N. Whiteley, Notes on Main Lessons of Recent Operations in the Western Desert, 7 July 1942, WO201/452, TNA; F. Messervy, Some Lessons from the Battle in Libya 27 May to 19 June 42, as seen by Comd 7 Armd Div, MUL962 Auchineck MSS, JRL.

119. A. H. Gatehouse, 'Notes on certain aspects of the battles of Alam el Halfa and El Alamein', 9/28/42 Liddell Hart MSS, LHCMA.

120. 8th Armoured Brigade War Diary, WO169/4230, TNA.

Chapter Twelve: The Six Days' Race

1. 21st Panzer Division War Diary, 29 August 1942, WAII/11/23, NANZ.

2. Basil H. Liddell Hart, *The Rommel Papers*, p. 275.

3. Enemy Documents Section, Appreciation No. 9, p. 40, CAB146/14, TNA.

4. James L. Sadkovich, *The Italian Navy*, p. 283.

5. ibid.

6. Martin van Creveld, *Supply in War: Logistics from Wallenstein to Patton*, p. 197.

7. ibid.

8. Enemy Documents Section, Appreciation No. 9, p. 44, CAB146/14, TNA.

9. ibid., p. 42.

10. ibid., pp. 43–5.

11. ibid., p. 42.

12. ibid., p. 41.

13. Air Historical Branch, The Middle East Campaigns, July 1942–May 1943, p. 140, JSCSC.

14. Enemy Documents Section, Appreciation No. 9, p. 48–53, CAB146/14, TNA.

15. ibid., pp. 45–7.

16. ibid., pp. 54–6.

17. ibid., pp. 58–62.

18. One *Versorgungsstaffel* (translated as 'consumption unit') was enough fuel to move a formation 100km over good terrain with all its vehicles. The actual distance which could be travelled on one consumption unit varied widely according to the nature of the terrain. See translator's note to Union War Histories Translation No. 2B War Diary of 21st Panzer Division 14 June–28 July 1942, AWM54 492/4/79 Part 2, AWM.

19. Enemy Documents Section, Appreciation No. 9, p. 84, CAB146/14, TNA.

20. ibid., p. 79.

21. The Italians lost the *Lerici* on 16 August, *Rosolino Pilo* on 17 August, the cargo of the auxiliary sailing vessel *Agia Maria* on 19 August and the tanker *Pozzarico* on 21 August. See Air Historical Branch, The Middle East Campaigns, July 1942–May 1943, p. 140, JSCSC.

22. Ralph Bennett, *Ultra and Mediterranean Strategy, 1941–1945*, pp. 148–51; F. H. Hinsley et al., *British Intelligence in the Second World War: Its Influence on Strategy and Operations*, Volume II, pp. 417–25.

23. Enemy Documents Section, Appreciation No. 9, p. 98, CAB146/14, TNA.

24. Liddell Hart, *The Rommel Papers*, p. 271.

25. Nehring, Der Feldzug in Afrika, p. 57, WAII/1/DA438.23/2, NANZ.

26. ibid.

27. Enemy Documents Section, Appreciation No. 9, pp. 87–95, CAB146/14, TNA.

28. Michael Carver, *Out of Step*, p. 136.

29. Air Historical Branch, The Middle East Campaigns, July 1942–May 1943, p. 165, JSCSC.

30. ibid., p. 168.

31. 21st Panzer Division War Diary, WAII/11/23, NANZ; Air Historical Branch, The Middle East Campaigns, July 1942–May 1943, p. 168, JSCSC.

32. Vincent Orange, *Coningham: A Biography of Air Marshal Sir Arthur Coningham*, p. 109.

33. Hereward Wake and W. F. Deedes, *Swift and Bold: The Story of the King's Royal Rifle Corps in the Second World War 1939–1945*, p. 96.

34. Air Historical Branch, The Middle East Campaigns, July 1942–May 1943, p. 172, JSCSC.

35. R. H. W. S. Hastings, *The Rifle Brigade in the Second World War, 1939–1945*, p. 145.

36. 21st Panzer Division War Diary, 30 August 1942, WAII/11/23, NANZ.

37. ibid.

38. Air Historical Branch, The Middle East Campaigns, July 1942–May 1943, p. 172, JSCSC.

39. Afrika Korps War Diary, 31 August 1942, WAII/11/20, NANZ.

40. 21st Panzer Division War Dairy, 31 August 1942, WAII/11/23, NANZ.

41. E. W. C. Sandes, *From Egypt to Pagoda: The Story of the West Yorkshire*

Regiment (The Prince of Wales's Own) in the War 1939–45 and Afterwards, pp. 143–6.

42. Enemy Documents Section, Appreciation No. 9, p. 106, CAB146/14, TNA.

43. German maps referred to the high point on the Alam el Halfa ridge as Height 132, while British maps showed it as Point 102.

44. Carver, *Out of Step*, p. 137.

45. G. H. Mills and R. F. Nixon, *The Annals of the King's Royal Rifle Corps*, Volume VI: *1923–1943*, p. 286.

46. Dorman-Smith to Liddell Hart, 27 November 1942, 1/242/48 Liddell Hart MSS, LHCMA.

47. Air Historical Branch, The Middle East Campaigns, July 1942–May 1943, p. 178, JSCSC.

48. Battle of Alamein: Notes by Commander Eighth Army, WO106/2254, TNA.

49. 22nd Armoured Brigade War Diary, 31 August 1942, WO169/4251, TNA.

50. G. P. B. Roberts, *From the Desert to the Baltic*, p. 99.

51. 21st Panzer Division War Diary, 31 August 1942, WAII/11/23, NANZ.

52. These tanks were Panzer IV Ausf F2, armed with the 7.5cm KwK 44 L/43 gun which had a muzzle velocity of 990 metres per second. See von Senger and Etterlin, *German Tanks of World War II*.

53. Hastings, *The Rifle Brigade*, p. 146.

54. 21st Panzer Division War Diary, 31 August 1942, WAII/11/23, NANZ.

55. ibid.

56. 22nd Arm Bde War Diary, 31 August, 1942, WO169/4251, TNA.

57. 21st Panzer Division War Diary, 31 August 1942, WAII/11/23, NANZ.

58. Nehring, Der Feldzug in Afrika, p. 65, WAII/1/DA438.23/2, NANZ.

59. 21st Panzer Division War Diary, 31 August 1942, WAII/11/23, NANZ.

60. Von Mellenthin, *Panzer Battle*, p. 145.

61. Air Historical Branch, The Middle East Campaigns, July 1942–May 1943, p. 181, JSCSC.

62. Named after a Queensland brand of beer rather than the Melbourne suburb.

63. Operation Bulimba, Report on the operation from 2/15 Aust Inf Battalion, AWM54 526/6/3, AWM.

64. ibid.

65. Morshead's Diary, 23 August 1942, 3DRL2632/3/2 Morshead MSS, AWM.

66. Operation Bulimba, AWM54 526/6/3, AWM.

67. ibid.

68. Perrett, *The Valentine in North Africa*, pp. 29–30.

69. Operation Bulimba, AWM54 526/6/3, AWM.

70. ibid.

71. ibid.

72. ibid.

73. Nehring, Der Feldzug in Afrika, p. 63, WAII/1/DA438.23/2, NANZ.

74. German military term meaning 'point of main effort'.

75. Battle of Alamein: Notes by Commander Eighth Army, WO106/2254, TNA.

76. ibid.

77. ibid.

78. 30 Corps Operation Order No. 69, 30 July 1942, WO169/4034, TNA.

79. Appreciation by Comd 13 Corps, 1 August 1942, WO201/556, TNA.

80. 21st Panzer Division War Diary, 1 September 1942, WAII/11/23, NANZ.

81. 8th Armoured Brigade War Diary, 1 September 1942, WO169/4230, TNA.

82. ibid.

83. 44th (Home Counties) Division War Diary, 1 September 1942, WO169/4133, TNA.

84. Weir to Scoullar, 9 June 1948, WAII/1/DA491.2/18, NANZ.

85. 4th and 7th Field Regiments and 3rd Royal Horse Artillery.

86. 11th Field Regiment.

87. Air Historical Branch, The Middle East Campaigns, July 1942–May 1943, p. 187, JSCSC.

88. 21st Panzer Division War Diary, 1 September 1942, WAII/11/23, NANZ.

89. Afrika Korps War Diary, 2 September 1942, WAII/11/20, NANZ.

90. Air Historical Branch, The Middle East Campaigns, July 1942–May 1943, p. 190, JSCSC.

91. Panzerarmee Daily Report, 1 September 1942, AWM54 492/4/77, AWM.

92. Air Historical Branch, The Middle East Campaigns, July 1942–May 1943, p. 189, JSCSC.

93. Afrika Korps War Diary, 2 September 1942, WAII/11/20, NANZ.

94. 21st Panzer Division War Diary, 2 September 1942, WAII/11/22, NANZ.

95. Panzerarmee Afrika Daily Report, 2 September 1942, AWM54 492/4/77, AWM.

96. ibid.

97. Battle of Alamein: Notes by Commander Eighth Army, WO106/2254, TNA.

98. Roberts, Desert to Baltic, p. 105.

99. J.A.I. Agar-Hamilton and L.C.F. Turner, Crisis in the Desert May–July 1942, pp. 56–7.

100. Major-General A. H. Gatehouse, 'Notes on certain aspects of the battles of Alam El Halfa and El Alamein', Liddell Hart Papers, 9/28/42, LHCMA.

101. Air Historical Branch, The Middle East Campaigns, July 1942–May 1943, p. 193, JSCSC.

102. ibid., p. 197.

103. The Afrika Korps estimated that 300 aircraft dropped 2,400 bombs when, in reality, 100 bombers dropped 1,000 bombs; Afrika Korps War Diary, 3 September 1942, WAII/11/20, NANZ; Air Historical Branch, The Middle East Campaigns, July 1942–May 1943, p. 197, JSCSC.

104. Afrika Korps War Diary, 3 September, WAII/11/20, NANZ.

105. Battle of Alamein: Notes by Commander Eighth Army, WO106/2254, TNA.

106. Air Historical Branch, The Middle East Campaigns, July 1942–May 1943, p. 197, JSCSC.

107. ibid., pp. 214–15.

108. GoC's Diary, 1 September 1942, WAII/8/44, NANZ.

109. Maori Battalion and 21st New Zealand Infantry Battalion.

110. Howard Kippenberger, *Infantry Brigadier*, pp. 207–8.

111. GoC's Diary, 3 September 1942, WAII/8/44, NANZ.

112. 90th Light Division WD, 2 September 1942, WAII/11/23, NANZ.

113. H. D. Chaplin, *The Queen's Own Royal West Kent Regiment, 1920–1950*, pp. 214–15.

114. Kippenberger, *Infantry Brigadier*, pp. 210–11.

115. ibid., pp. 209–11.

116. Frazer D. Norton, *26 Battalion*, p. 172.

117. Chaplin, *West Kent Regiment*, p. 215.

118. Major T. H. Bevan, The Attack on the Munassib Depression by 132 Bde 4 September 1942, WAII/1/DA359.01/10/1, NANZ. Bevan wrote his account from memory after the advent of the atomic bomb. A truck filled with mines could produce an enormous explosion.

119. ibid.

120. Norton, *26 Battalion*, p. 173.

121. ibid., p. 174.

122. Bevan, The Attack on the Munassib Depression, WAII/1/DA359.01/10/1, NANZ.

123. Norton, *26 Battalion*, p. 166.

124. Kippenberger, *Infantry Brigadier*, p. 213.

125. ibid., p. 216.

126. GoC's Diary, 4 September 1942, WAII/8/44, NANZ.

127. W. E. Murphy, *New Zealand Divisional Artillery*, p. 369.

128. Kippenberger, *Infantry Brigadier*, p. 216.

129. Weir to Kippenberger, 9 June 1948, WAII/1/DA491.2/18, NANZ.

130. Weir to Scoullar, 9 June 1948, WAII/1/DA491.2/18, NANZ.

131. ibid.

132. GoC's Diary, 4 September 1942, WAII/8/44, NANZ.

133. ibid.

134. Battle of Alamein: Notes by Commander Eighth Army, WO106/2254, TNA.

135. Lieutenant-Colonel. E. A. McPhail, Account of 132 Bde Ops, WAII/1/DA 359.01/10/2, NANZ. McPhail was the brigade intelligence officer of 5th New Zealand Brigade at the time of the attack.

136. Chaplin, *West Kent Regiment*, p. 217.

137. Liddell Hart, *The Rommel Papers*, p. 275.

138. I. S. O. Playfair, *The Mediterranean and Middle East*, Volume III, pp. 390–91.

139. GoC's Diary, 6 September 1942, WAII/8/44, NANZ.

140. Dorman-Smith to Liddell Hart, 27 November 1942, 1/242/48 Liddell Hart MSS, LHCMA.

141. Nehring, Der Feldzug in Afrika, p. 74, WAII/1/DA438.23/2, NANZ.

142. ibid.
143. Turner to Walker, 26 September, 1955, WAII/11/7, NANZ.
144. Nehring, Der Feldzug in Afrika, p. 74, WAII/1/DA438.23/2, NANZ.
145. Turner to Walker, 26 September, 1955, WAII/11/7, NANZ.
146. Nehring, Der Feldzug in Afrika, p. 75, WAII/1/DA438.23/2, NANZ.
147. Sadkovich, *The Italian Navy*, p. 277.
148. ibid., p. 280.

Chapter Thirteen: The Crest of a Wave

1. Charles Richardson, *Flashback: A Soldier's Story*, p. 111.
2. Charles Richardson, *Send for Freddie: The Story of Monty's Chief of Staff Major-General Sir Francis de Guingand*, p. 78.
3. Richardson, *Flashback*, p. 113.
4. Appreciation and Plan: Operation 'Lightfoot', 19 August 1942, WO201/432, TNA; see Appendix D.
5. ibid.
6. ibid.
7. GoC's Diary, WAII/8/44, NANZ.
8. Dates of Readiness, Eighth Army, Appendix A to JPS Paper No. 108, WO169/3793, TNA.
9. Churchill to Alexander, 11 September 1942, PREM3/299/1, TNA.
10. Alexander to Churchill, 19 September 1942, PREM3/299/1, TNA.
11. ibid.
12. Churchill to Alexander, 20 September 1942, PREM3/299/1, TNA.
13. ibid.
14. Alexander to Churchill, 23 September 1942, PREM3/299/1, TNA.
15. Francis de Guingand, *Operation Victory*, p. 158.
16. Churchill to Alexander, 23 September 1942, PREM3/299/1, TNA.
17. Corelli Barnett, *The Desert Generals*, p. 268.
18. Morshead to Blamey, 15 September 1942, 3DRL2632/15 Morshead MSS, AWM.
19. Churchill to Alexander, 11 September 1942, PREM3/299/1, TNA.
20. Michael Carver, *Out of Step*, p. 139.
21. ibid.
22. 'Lightfoot', General Plan of Eighth Army, 14 September 1942, WO201/444, TNA.
23. ibid.
24. ibid.
25. ibid.
26. W. Heinemann, 'The Development of German Armoured Forces 1918–40', in Toase and Harris, *Armoured Warfare*, pp. 58–62.
27. David M. Glantz and Jonathan House, *When Titans Clashed: How the Red Army Stopped Hitler*, pp. 8–12.

28. ibid.

29. Leese had been the adjutant of 3rd Coldstream Guards and Wimberley the adjutant of 79th Cameron Highlanders in the 1st Guards Brigade garrisoned in Aldershot in the early twenties. They had gone to Staff College at the same time and served at the War Office together. See Douglas Wimberley, A Scottish Soldier, Volume II, unpublished memoir, p. 36, PP/MCR/182 Wimberley MSS, IWM.

30. ibid.

31. These guns included the regiments from all four divisions, three medium regiments each of 16 guns and 18 troops of 25-pounders drawn from 10 Corps that were attached to 30 Corps for the operation.

32. Account by Gen. Sir Oliver Leese of 30 Corps Operations, WAII/1/DA491.2/17, NANZ.

33. ibid. The final plan and orders for 30 Corps' part in Lightfoot can be found in WO169/4035, TNA.

34. 'Lightfoot', 21 September 1942, WAII/8/25, NANZ.

35. Report on Operations of 2/32nd Aust Inf Bn 16/17 Jul. 42, AWM54 526/4/7, AWM.

36. 'Lightfoot', 21 September 1942, WAII/8/25, NANZ.

37. ibid.

38. 9th Australian Division Report on Lightfoot, CAB106/777, TNA.

39. J. B. Salmond, The History of the 51st Highland Division, 1939–1945.

40. Wimberley, A Scottish Soldier, p. 24, PP/MCR/182 Wimberley MSS, IWM.

41. Account by Oliver Leese, WAII/1/DA491.2/17, NANZ.

42. Wilfrid Miles, The Life of a Regiment: The Gordon Highlanders 1919–1945, pp. 152–3.

43. Wimberley, A Scottish Soldier, p. 35, PP/MCR/182 Wimberley MSS, IWM.

44. ibid., p. 30.

45. Douglas Wimberley, Memo, 18 September 1942, WO169/4164, TNA.

46. Andrew Todd, The Elephant at War: 2nd Battalion Seaforth Highlanders 1939–1945, p. 34.

47. 51st (Highland) Division Training Instruction No. 2, WO169/4164, TNA.

48. Wimberley, A Scottish Soldier, p. 36, PP/MCR/182 Wimberley MSS, IWM.

49. 51st (Highland) Division Training Exercise No. 1, WO169/4164, TNA.

50. 51st (Highland) Division War Diary, September–October 1942, WO169/4164, TNA.

51. Account by Oliver Leese, WAII/1/DA491.2/17, NANZ.

52. 1st Armoured Division War Diary, WO169/4054.

53. 'The Following Notes are made as a result of 1 Armd Div Exercise No. 1', 29 September 1942, WO169/4054.

54. GoC's Diary, 12 September 1942, WAII/8/44, NANZ.

55. I. S. O. Playfair, The Mediterranean and Middle East, Volume IV, p. 8.

56. Chamberlain and Ellis, British and American Tanks of World War II, pp. 114–15.

57. GoC's Diary, 12 September 1942, WAII/8/44, NANZ.

58. Pitt, *Royal Wilts*, p. 123.

59. Lucas Phillips, *Alamein*, p. 110.

60. This was composed of a motor battalion less one company (the 2nd Rifle Brigade), 7th and 9th Field Squadrons Royal Engineers, 572nd Field Company Royal Engineers and three troops of Crusader tanks. The organisation of 1st Armoured Division's Minefield Task Force became the standard model within Eighth Army as taught at Haifa. See 1st Armoured Division War Diary, September 1942, WO169/4054.

61. Brigadier P. N. Moore, 'Mine Clearance – El Alamein', *The Royal Engineers Journal*, Vol. 106, No. 3, December 1992, p. 193.

62. Account by Oliver Leese, WAII/1/DA491.2/17, NANZ.

63. Liddell Hart, *The Rommel Papers*, pp. 287–326.

64. JPS Staff Paper No. 110, 8 September 1942, WO169/3793, TNA.

65. For a detailed account of Operation Agreement, see Peter C. Smith, *Massacre at Tobruk: The Story of Operation Agreement*.

66. Playfair, *The Mediterranean and Middle East*, Volume IV, pp. 20–23.

67. The 131st Brigade consisted of the 1/5th, 1/6th and 1/7th Battalions of the Queen's Royal Regiment.

68. R. C. G. Foster, *History of the Queen's Royal Regiment*, Volume III, *1924–1948*, pp. 167–70.

69. Afrika Korps War Diary, 30 September 1942, WAII/11/20, NANZ.

70. Stumme to Cavallero, 3 October 1942, Translation of Appendices to Panzerarmee Afrika War Diary, September to October 1942, AWM54 492/4/77, AWM.

71. Appendix D to MI GHQ MEF, 30 October 1942, Morshead Papers, 3DRL2632 6/19, AWM.

72. Panzerarmee to Lower Formations, 20 September 1942; 21 Corps to Panzerarmee, 24 September 1942, German–Italian Forces in Africa, September – October 1942, Translation of Appendices to Panzerarmee Afrika War Diary, AWM54 492/4/77, AWM.

73. Pz Army Engineer HQ to Pz Army G Branch, 20 October 1942, Translation of Appendices to Panzerarmee Afrika War Diary, September to October 1942, AWM54 492/4/77, AWM.

74. Stumme to Cavallero, 3 October 1942, Translation of Appendices to Panzerarmee Afrika War Diary, September to October 1942, AWM54 492/4/77, AWM.

75. Captain Kircher, Probable tactics of the British Eighth Army in the Offensive against the Alamein Front, 1 October 1942, Afrika Korps Records, WAII/11/22, NANZ.

76. ibid.

77. ibid.

78. Enemy Reaction to Operation 'Lightfoot', GSI Eighth Army, 7 October 1942. Morshead Papers, 3DRL 2632 2/5, AWM. The report was disseminated to

the corps and divisional commanders on 7 October but obviously Montgomery knew of its contents before he issued his 'Memorandum No. 2'.

79. ibid.
80. ibid.
81. ibid.

Chapter Fourteen: 'Born For This Battle'

1. 'Lightfoot, Memorandum No. 2 by Army Commander', 6 October 1942, WO201/444, TNA.
2. ibid.
3. See Hamilton, *Monty*, pp. 706–10.
4. Montgomery issued his changed plan in 'Lightfoot, Memorandum No. 2' on 6 October 1942 but the 10 Corps Conference, which de Guingand attended, did not take place until the next day. See Hamilton, *Monty*, pp. 704–10, and Notes on 10 Corps 'Lightfoot' Conference, 7 October 1942, 1/2/10 De Guingand MSS, LHCMA.
5. Montgomery, *Memoirs*, p. 120.
6. ibid.
7. 'Lightfoot, Memorandum by Army Commander,' 28 September 1942, WO201/444, TNA.
8. ibid.
9. Belloc became famous for his newspaper articles which featured suggestions that every Allied soldier should throw a grenade over the top at the same time. If every grenade accounted for at least one German then the war would be won!
10. Information – Enemy, Appendix A to 30 Corps Operation Order No. 83, 12 October 1942, WO169/4035, TNA.
11. Account by Oliver Leese, WAII/1/DA491.2/17, NANZ.
12. ibid.
13. ibid.
14. Notes on 30 Corps 'Lightfoot' Conference, 9 October 1942, 1/2/11 De Guingand MSS, LHCMA.
15. Hamilton, *Monty*, p. 708.
16. Notes on 10 Corps 'Lightfoot' Conference, 7 October 1942, De Guingand Papers, 1/2/10, LHCMA.
17. ibid.
18. ibid.
19. ibid.
20. ibid.
21. 10 Corps Operation Instruction No. 2, 21 October 1942, WO169/3990, TNA.
22. Notes on 30 Corps 'Lightfoot' Conference, 9 October 1942, De Guingand Papers, 1/2/11, LHCMA.

23. ibid.

24. Douglas Wimberley, A Scottish Soldier, Volume II, unpublished memoir, p. 38, PP/MCR/182 Wimberley MSS, IWM.

25. ibid.

26. Notes on 30 Corps 'Lightfoot' Conference, 9 October 1942, De Guingand Papers, 1/2/11, LHCMA.

27. Leese to Morshead, Wimberley and Pienaar, 10 October 1942, WO201/645, TNA.

28. Morshead to Leese, 11 October 1942, AWM54 526/6/6, AWM.

29. Leese to Wimberley, 12 October 1942, WO169/4164, TNA.

30. Leese to Morshead 14 October 1942, AWM54 526/6/6, AWM.

31. ibid.

32. R. P. Pakenham-Walsh, History of the Corps of Royal Engineers, Volume VIII: 1938–1948, p. 385.

33. RAE 9 Aust Division, Report on 'Lightfoot' Operation, AWM54 527/6/11, AWM.

34. CRE 2 NZ Div to CE 13 Corps, 12 August 42, WAII/1/DA37/1/36, NANZ.

35. ibid.

36. Brigadier P.N. Moore, 'Mine Clearance – El Alamein', The Royal Engineers Journal, p. 193.

37. Lucas Phillips, Alamein, p. 95.

38. Moore, 'Mine Clearance – El Alamein', p. 193.

39. J. F. Cody, New Zealand Engineers, Middle East, p. 343.

40. RAE Report on 'Lightfoot', AWM54 527/6/11, AWM.

41. Moore, 'Mine Clearance – El Alamein', pp. 193–4.

42. Pakenham-Walsh, Royal Engineers, p. 369.

43. RAE Report on 'Lightfoot', AWM54 527/6/11, AWM.

44. Cody, New Zealand Engineers, p. 343.

45. Lessons from Lightfoot, WO201/449, TNA.

46. P. W. Pitt, Royal Wilts, p. 124.

47. Lessons from Lightfoot, WO201/449, TNA.

48. Pakenham-Walsh, Royal Engineers, p. 370.

49. Lessons from Lightfoot, WO201/449, TNA.

50. RAE Report on 'Lightfoot', AWM54 527/6/11, AWM.

51. Lessons from Lightfoot, WO201/449, TNA.

52. ibid.

53. RAE Report on 'Lightfoot', AWM54 527/6/11, AWM.

54. Lessons from Lightfoot, WP201/449, TNA.

55. ibid.

56. ibid.

57. CE Eighth Army, War Diary, August–October 1942, WO169/3942, TNA.

58. R. G. S. Bidwell, 'The Development of British Field Artillery Tactics 1940–42: The Desert War', p. 89.

59. John Gibbon, Arty at Battle of El Alamein, Staff School Haifa, War Course No. 8, 9 February 1943, Gibbon MSS, Royal Artillery Library, RAHT.

60. John Gibbon, Report on the Action of the Artillery of 30 Corps at El Alamein October 23 to November 4 1942, Gibbon MSS, RAHT.

61. John Gibbon, Arty at Battle of El Alamein, Gibbon MSS, RAHT.

62. ibid.

63. 'Sterno', 'A Field Regiment in the Battle of Egypt October–November, 1942', pp. 189–99.

64. Bidwell, 'British Artillery Tactics 1940–42', p. 90.

65. John Gibbon, Arty at Battle of El Alamein, Gibbon MSS, RAHT.

66. 30 Corps Artillery Operation Order No. 18, 13 October 1942, Gibbon MSS, RAI.

67. Report on Counter Battery Work at EL ALAMEIN July to November 1942, WO201/2821, TNA.

68. ibid.

69. ibid.

70. ibid.

71. ibid.

72. ibid.

73. ibid.

74. ibid.

75. ibid.

76. John Gibbon, Arty at Battle of El Alamein, Gibbon MSS, RAHT.

77. A. L. Pemberton, *The Development of Artillery Tactics and Equipment*, p. 141.

78. ibid.

79. Weir to Kippenberger, 9 June 1948, WAII/1/DA491.2/18, NANZ.

80. John Gibbon, Arty at Battle of El Alamein, Gibbon MSS, RAHT.

81. Lucas Phillips, *Alamein*, p. 106.

82. Pemberton, *Artillery*, p. 129.

83. Lieutenant-General Frank Messervy, 'Some Lessons From the Battle in Libya 27 May to 19 June '42 as seen by Comd. 7 Armd Div', 29 June 1942, MUL 962, Auchinleck MSS, JRL.

84. Anon., *The Story of the Royal Army Service Corps 1939–1945*, p. 106.

85. JKS, 'The Royal Army Ordnance Corps in the Middle East', RLCM.

86. ibid.

87. ibid.

88. Anon., *Royal Army Service Corps*, p. 112.

89. Eighth Army held 32,700 vehicles instead of its establishment of 43,500 at the beginning of August; Anon., *Notes on the Maintenance of the Eighth Army and the Supporting Royal Air Force by Land, Sea and Air from El Alamein to Tunisia*, p. 2.

90. Anon., *Royal Army Service Corps*, p. 125.

91. Anon., *Notes on the Maintenance of the Eighth Army*, p. 2.

92. ibid.

93. JKS, 'The Royal Army Ordnance Corps in the Middle East', RLCM.

94. Anon., *Royal Electrical and Mechanical Engineers*, Volume I, p. 6.

95. ibid., p. 1.

96. A supply of the new cap badges was flown to Egypt just in time for the formation of the new corps. There was universal disappointment when the badges were found to be made of brown Bakelite. See B. B. Kennett and J. A. Tatman, *Craftsmen of the Army: The Story of the Royal Electrical and Mechanical Engineers*, p. 94

97. ibid.

98. Anon., *Notes on the Maintenance of the Eighth Army*, p. 5.

99. Hugh Skillen, *Spies of the Airwaves: A History of Y Sections During the Second World War*, p. 206.

100. R. J. T. Hills, *Phantom Was There*, pp. 85–93.

101. Charles Richardson, *Flashback: A Soldier's Story*, p. 115.

102. Operation Bertram, WO201/2023, TNA.

103. ibid.

104. ibid.

105. Richardson, *Flashback*, p. 115; Operation Bertram, WO201/2023, TNA.

106. D. F. Underhill, *Queen's Own Royal Regiment The Staffordshire Yeomanry: An Account of the Operations of the Regiment during World War II 1939–1945*, p. 6.

107. Operation Bertram, WO201/2023, TNA.

108. ibid.

109. Account by Oliver Leese, WAII/1/DA491.2/17, NANZ.

110. Lightfoot, Memorandum by Army Commander, 28 September 1942, WO201/444, TNA.

111. Notes in connection with Lightfoot, AWM54 526/6/6, AWM.

112. Air Historical Branch, The Middle East Campaigns, July 1942–May 1943, pp. 223–6, JSCSC.

113. ibid., pp. 227–8.

114. ibid., p. 236–7.

115. ibid., pp. 241–3.

116. Air Historical Branch, The Middle East Campaigns, July 1942–May 1943, p. 250, JSCSC.

117. ibid., p. 253.

118. The force was divided into 420 single-engined fighters, 30 twin-engined fighters, 150 light bombers, 100 medium bombers and 30 reconnaissance aircraft: ibid., p. 264.

119. In North Africa, the Luftwaffe possessed 195 fighter and 80 dive bombers while the Regia Aeronautica had 400 fighters, 70 bombers and 25 coastal aircraft. In the Mediterranean theatre as a whole, however, the Axis air forces had the much higher total of 1,925 aircraft: ibid., pp. 261–2.

120. ibid., pp. 258–9.

121. 33 Reconnaissance Battalion to Panzerarmee, 9 October 1942, AWM54 492/4/77, AWM.

122. Panzerarmee to Lower Formations, 8 October 1942, German–Italian Forces in Africa, September to October 1942, Translation of Appendices to Panzerarmee Afrika War Diary, AWM54 492/4/77, AWM.

123. Panzer Army Headquarters to Field Marshal Rommel, 13 October 1942, German–Italian Forces in Africa, September to October 1942, Translation of Appendices to Panzerarmee Afrika War Diary, AWM54 492/4/77, AWM.

124. Stumme to Afrika Korps, 15 October 1942, German–Italian Forces in Africa, September to October 1942, Translation of Appendices to Panzerarmee Afrika War Diary, AWM54 492/4/77, AWM.

125. Stumme to Lower Formations, 20 October 1942, German–Italian Forces in Africa, September to October 1942, Translation of Appendices to Panzerarmee Afrika War Diary, AWM54 492/4/77, AWM.

126. Panzerarmee Daily Report to OKW, 23 October 1942, AWM54 492/4/77, AWM.

Chapter Fifteen: Operation Lightfoot

1. From the poem 'Stane Jock' by W. H. Burt, in Victor Selwyn, Dan Davin, Erik de Mauny and Ian Fletcher, *From Oasis into Italy: War Poems and Diaries from Africa and Italy 1940–1946*, pp. 15–16.

2. Miles, *Life of a Regiment*, p. 135.

3. John McGregor, *The Spirit of Angus: The War History of the County's Battalion of the Black Watch*, p. 37.

4. Operational Report – 1 S A Div 30 Sept. 42–10 Nov. 42, WO201/2828, TNA.

5. GoC's Diary, WAII/8/44, NANZ.

6. Douglas Wimberley, A Scottish Soldier, Volume II, unpublished memoir, p. 41, IWM.

7. 'Sterno', 'A Field Regiment in the Battle of Egypt October–November, 1942', *Royal Artillery Journal*, p. 190.

8. T. M. Lindsay, *Sherwood Rangers*, p. 37.

9. Joan Bright, *The Ninth Queen's Royal Lancers 1936–1945*, p. 110.

10. Max Parsons, *Gunfire!: A History of the 2/12 Australian Field Regiment 1940–46*, p. 123.

11. Bernard L. Montgomery, *The Memoirs of Viscount Montgomery of Alamein*, p. 128.

12. BGS's Notes on Battle, 1/2/19 De Guingand MSS, LHCMA.

13. The Battle of Egypt 23 Oct. 1942–7 Nov. 1942: Some Notes by Lt Gen B. L. Montgomery, BLM28/1 Montgomery MSS, IWM.

14. Private J. A. Crawford, Forward from El Alamein, 2/17th Battalion, 3DRL368, AWM.

15. RA Notes on the Offensive by Eighth Army from 23 Oct.–4 Nov. on the El
    Alamein Position, WO201/2877, TNA.

16. Walker, *Alam Halfa and Alamein*, p. 254.

17. John Gibbon, Arty at Battle of El Alamein, Gibbon MSS, RAHT.

18. Air Historical Branch, The Middle East Campaigns, July 1942–May 1943,
    p. 273, JSCSC.

19. 15th Panzer Division Report on the Battle of Alamein and the Retreat to Marsa
    el Brega, 23rd October–20th November 1942, AWM54 423/4/103, AWM.

20. Translation of German Official War Narrative, 23 October–5 January 1943,
    AWM54 492/4/74, AWM.

21. McGregor, *The Spirit of Angus*, p. 38.

22. G. H. Fearnside, *Bayonets Abroad: A History of the 2/13 Battalion AIF in the
    Second World War*, p. 265.

23. 24 Aust Inf Bde Operation Order No. 20 'Lightfoot', AWM54 527/4/4, AWM.

24. 9th Australian Division Report on Lightfoot, CAB106/777, TNA.

25. Operation Bertram, WO201/2023, TNA.

26. 9th Australian Division Report on Lightfoot, CAB106/777, TNA.

27. Gordon Combe, Frank Ligertwood and Tom Gilchrist, *The Second 43rd,
    Australian Infantry Battalion 1940–1946*, p. 118.

28. 26 Australian Infantry Brigade – report on operation 'Lightfoot', AWM54
    527/6/9, AWM.

29. An account of 20 Brigade Operations El Alamein October–November 1942,
    AWM54 527/6/13, AWM.

30. Lessons from Operations, 24 Aust Inf Bde, 17 November 1942, Morshead
    Papers, 3DRL2632 6/14–15, AWM.

31. Fearnside, *Bayonets Abroad*, pp. 265–6.

32. 9th Australian Division Report on Lightfoot, CAB106/777, TNA.

33. John G. Glenn, *Tobruk to Tarakan: The Story of the 2/48th Battalion A.I.F.*,
    p. 145.

34. ibid.

35. Night Attack, Summary of El Alamein Battle, AWM54 527/6/5, AWM.

36. Reorganisation Alamein, Summary of El Alamein Battle, AWM54 527/6/5,
    AWM.

37. ibid.

38. ibid.

39. ibid.

40. Glenn, *Tobruk to Tarakan*, p. 146.

41. Reorganisation Alamein, AWM54 527/6/5, AWM.

42. Fearnside, *Bayonets Abroad*, p. 267.

43. ibid., p. 269.

44. McGregor, *Spirit of Angus*, p. 39.

45. Miles, *Life of a Regiment*, pp. 137–9.

46. ibid., pp. 136–7.

47. 51st (Highland) Division War Diary, 23 October 1942, WO169/4165, TNA.

48. Ian C. Cameron, *History of the Argyll and Sutherland Highlanders 7th Battalion: From El Alamein to Germany*, pp. 42–4.

49. 51st (Highland) Division War Diary, 23 October 1942, WO169/4165, TNA.

50. D. F. O. Russell, *War History of the 7th Bn. The Black Watch, R.H.R., Fife Territorial Battalion. August 1939–May 1945*, pp. 17–19.

51. Wimberley, A Scottish Soldier, p. 42, PP/MCR/182 Wimberley MSS, IWM.

52. GoC's Diary, WAII/8/44, NANZ.

53. R. Walker, *Alam Halfa and Alamein*, p. 266.

54. ibid., p. 269.

55. ibid., p. 267.

56. Operational Report – 1 S A Div 30 Sep. 42–10 Nov. 42 Lightfoot, WO201/2828, TNA.

57. ibid.

58. ibid.

59. Compton Mackenzie, *Eastern Epic*, p. 600.

60. Walker, *Alam Halfa and Alamein*, p. 281.

61. Report on Counter Battery Work, WO201/2821, TNA.

62. Roberts, *From the Desert to the Baltic*, p. 112.

63. Notes on mine lifting operations, 13 Corps, 23–25 Oct., WO201/448, TNA.

64. Roberts, *Desert to the Baltic*, p. 113.

65. Notes on mine lifting operations, 13 Corps, 23–25 Oct., WO201/448, TNA.

66. Roberts, *Desert to the Baltic*, p. 115.

67. Engineer Operation Report No. 56, WO201/448, TNA.

68. Brigadier G. R. McMeekan, 'The Assault at Alamein', *The Royal Engineers Journal*, p. 326.

69. ibid., p. 327.

70. ibid., pp. 319–20.

71. The first 16-yard gap was made in the sunrise field by 00.50, 1st Armoured Division War Diary 24 October 1942, WO169/4054, TNA.

72. McMeekan, 'The Assault at Alamein', pp. 329–30.

73. Bright, *Ninth Lancers*, p. 110.

74. Pitt, *Royal Wilts*, p. 137.

75. 9th Armoured Brigade was composed of Royal Wiltshire Yeomanry, Warwickshire Yeomanry and 3rd Hussars.

76. Pitt, *Royal Wilts*, p. 140.

77. 9th Armoured Brigade War Diary, 24 October 1942, WO169/4233, TNA.

78. Pitt, *Royal Wilts*, p. 140.

79. I. S. O. Playfair, *The Mediterranean and Middle East*, Volume IV, p. 41.

80. 8th Armoured Brigade was composed of 3rd Royal Tank Regiment, Nottinghamshire Yeomanry and Staffordshire Yeomanry.

81. Operation Lightfoot, 8th Armoured Brigade War Diary, WO169/4230, TNA.

82. Moore, 'Mine Clearance – El Alamein', pp. 197–8.

83. Lindsay, *Sherwood Rangers*, p. 39.

84. 9th Armoured Brigade War Diary, 24 October 1942, WO169/4233, TNA.

85. GoC's Diary, 24 October 1942, WAII/8/44, NANZ.

86. McMeekan, 'The Assault at Alamein', p. 331.

87. Operation Lightfoot, 8th Armoured Brigade War Diary, WO169/4230, TNA.

88. GoC's Diary, 24 October 1942, WAII/8/44, NANZ.

89. ibid.

90. ibid.

91. ibid.

92. 9th Armoured Brigade War Diary, 24 October 1942, WO169/4233, TNA.

93. D. F. Underhill, *Queen's Own Royal Regiment The Staffordshire Yeomanry: An Account of the Operations of the Regiment during World War II 1939–1945*, p. 7.

94. 7th Medium Regiment War Diary, 24 October 1942, RAHT.

95. D. Dawnay, *The 10th Royal Hussars in the Second World War 1939–1945*, pp. 77–8.

96. Bright, *Ninth Lancers*, p. 111.

97. Dawnay, *10th Royal Hussars*, p. 78.

98. ibid.

99. 15th Panzer War Diary, 24 October 1942, WAII/11/22, NANZ.

100. Pitt, *Royal Wilts*, p. 142.

101. 2nd Armoured Brigade War Diary, 24 October 1942, WO169/4210, TNA.

102. Dawnay, *10th Royal Hussars*, p. 79.

103. 24th Armoured Brigade, Notes for MG AFV on Operations 23–29 Oct. 42, WO201/545, TNA.

104. Reports on Operations, 1st Armoured Division, 11 November 1942, WO201/439, TNA.

105. Air Historical Branch, The Middle East Campaigns, July 1942–May 1943, p. 278, JSCSC.

106. Dawnay, *10th Royal Hussars*, p. 79.

107. Miles, *Life of a Regiment*, pp. 139–40.

108. Notes for War Diary, 51st (Highland) Division, WO169/4165, TNA.

109. The kidney-shaped feature was also variously described as Kidney ridge and Kidney Hill. Even these different descriptions have caused confusion amongst historians, a problem exacerbated by the portrayal in the film *Desert Victory* of 'Kidney Ridge' as a piece of dominating ground. Even though the modern road, which runs through the battle area, bisects the kidney feature, and it is clearly marked upon maps, it remains difficult to locate. It is little wonder that, in the middle of the battle, its location, and even its existence, became the source of heated arguments.

110. Notes for War Diary, 51st (Highland) Division, WO169/4165, TNA.

111. Wimberley, A Scottish Soldier, p. 42, PP/MCR/182 Wimberley MSS, IWM.

112. ibid., p. 43.

113. GoC's Diary, 24 October 1942, WAII/8/44, NANZ.

114. The Battle of Egypt 23 Oct. 1942–7 Nov. 1942: Some Notes by Lt Gen B. L. Montgomery, BLM28/1 Montgomery MSS, IWM.

115. ibid.

116. GoC's Diary, 24 October 1942, WAII/8/44, NANZ.

117. ibid.

118. ibid.

119. Playfair, *The Mediterranean and Middle East*, Volume IV, p. 45.

120. 2nd Armoured Brigade War Diary, 24 October 1942, WO169/4210, TNA.

121. Bright, *Ninth Lancers*, p. 111.

122. ibid.

123. ibid, p. 112.

124. Wimberley, A Scottish Soldier, p. 44, PP/MCR/182 Wimberley MSS, IWM.

125. Todd, *The Elephant at War*, p. 39.

126. ibid., pp. 40–41.

Chapter Sixteen: Battle Without Hope

1. Corporal C. W. Mears, 2/17th Battalion, personal diary entry for 26 October 1942, PR84/379, AWM.

2. HW1/1007, TNA.

3. 'German–Italian Forces in Africa, 23 Oct. 42–5 Jan. 42', Translation of German Official War Narrative, AWM54 492/4/74, AWM.

4. Basil H. Liddell Hart, *The Rommel Papers*, p. 305.

5. 'Translation of German Official War Narrative, 23 October–5 January 1943, AWM54 492/4/74, AWM.

6. ibid.

7. G. H. Fearnside, *Bayonets Abroad: History of the 2/13 Battalion AIF in the Second World War*, p. 232.

8. 9th Australian Division Report on Lightfoot, CAB106/777, TNA.

9. Fearnside, *Bayonets Abroad*, p. 274.

10. Hastings, *The Rifle Brigade*, p. 156.

11. Fearnside, *Bayonets Abroad*, p. 274.

12. 9th Armoured Brigade War Diary, 24 October 1942, WO169/4233, TNA.

13. 8th Armoured Brigade Report on Operations, WO201/439, TNA.

14. T. M. Lindsay, *Sherwood Rangers*, pp. 40–41.

15. Air Historical Branch, The Middle East Campaigns, July 1942–May 1943, p. 283, JSCSC.

16. 9th Armoured Brigade War Diary, 25 October 1942, WO169/4233, TNA.

17. Francis de Guingand, *Operation Victory*, p. 199.

18. ibid. There is some doubt as to the timing of this conference. De Guingand's *Operation Victory* states '3.30 am' while the original minutes give the time as 02.30 hours. See Minutes of Conference held at Tac HQ, Eighth Army, at 02.30 hours 25 October 1942, 1/2/12 De Guingand MSS, LHCMA. It would

appear that, given the subsequent hour-long conversation between Lumsden and Gatehouse, the original time of 02.30 hours is correct.

19. ibid.
20. ibid.
21. De Guingand, *Operation Victory*, p. 200.
22. Bernard L. Montgomery, *The Memoirs of Viscount Montgomery of Alamein*, p. 130.
23. A. H. Gatehouse, Notes on certain aspects of the battles of Alam el Halfa and El Alamein, Liddell Hart 9/28/42, LHCMA.
24. 10th Armoured Division War Diary, 25 October, 1942, WO169/417, TNA.
25. ibid.
26. 3rd Royal Tank Regiment War Diary, 25 October 1942, WO169/4506, TNA.
27. 8th Armoured Brigade Report on Operations, WO201/439, TNA.
28. Underhill, *The Staffordshire Yeomanry*, p. 7.
29. The alarming tendency of the Sherman to ignite when hit was also partly due to the fact that many versions of the tank were powered by a Wright radial aircraft engine that ran on high-octane aviation spirit. The majority of Shermans used at Alamein were first-production models designated as the M4A1 by the US Army and the Sherman II by the British. See Chris Ellis and Peter Chamberlain, *The Great Tanks*, p. 133–4. Some of the regiments at Alamein were lucky enough to be equipped with diesel-engined Shermans which were much less likely to catch fire when hit in the engine but just as likely to explode when hit on the turret (the M4A2, known to the British as the Sherman III); see Joan Bright, *The Ninth Queen's Royal Lancers 1936–1945*, p. 110.
30. 10th Armoured Division War Diary, 25 October 1942, WO169/417, TNA.
31. 9th Armoured Brigade War Diary, 25 October 1942, WO169/4233, TNA.
32. 24th Armoured Brigade, Notes for MG AFV on Operations 23–29 Oct. 42, WO201/545, TNA.
33. The Battle of Egypt 23 Oct. 1942–7 Nov. 1942: Some Notes by Lt Gen B. L. Montgomery, BLM28/1 Montgomery MSS, IWM.
34. 24th Armoured Brigade, Notes for MG AFV on Operations 23–29 Oct. 42, WO201/545, TNA.
35. 9th Armoured Brigade War Diary, 25 October 1942, WO169/4233, TNA.
36. ibid.
37. Bright, *Ninth Lancers*, p. 112.
38. ibid., p. 113.
39. D. Dawnay, *The 10th Royal Hussars in the Second World War 1939–1945*, p. 73.
40. Reports on operations, 1 Armd Div, 11 November 1942, WO201/439, TNA.
41. ibid.
42. Hastings, *Rifle Brigade*, p. 156.
43. ibid.
44. 2nd Armoured Brigade War Diary, 25 October 1942, WO169/4210, TNA.
45. ibid.

46. The tank state of 2nd Armoured Brigade on the evening of 25 October was Queen's Bays: 5 Shermans, 16 Cruisers; 9th Lancers: 18 Shermans, 19 Cruisers; 10th Hussars: 18 Shermans, 17 Cruisers; see 2nd Armoured Brigade War Diary, 25 October 1942, WO169/4210, TNA.

47. ibid.

48. GoC's Diary, 25 October 1942, WAII/8/44, NANZ.

49. ibid.

50. ibid.

51. R. G. C. Forster, *History of the Queen's Royal Regiment*, Volume VIII: *1924–1948*, p. 172.

52. The Battle of Egypt 23 Oct. 1942–7 Nov. 1942: Some Notes by Lt Gen B. L. Montgomery, BLM28/1 Montgomery MSS, IWM.

53. Forster, *Queen's Royal Regiment*, p. 172.

54. Roberts, *From the Desert to the Baltic*, p. 117.

55. GoC's Diary, 25 October 1942, WAII/8/44, NANZ.

56. The Battle of Egypt 23 Oct. 1942–7 Nov. 1942: Some Notes by Lt Gen B. L. Montgomery, BLM28/1 Montgomery MSS, IWM.

57. Decisions given by Army Commander at Conference held at HQ 2 NZ Div at 1200 hrs 25 Oct. 42, 1/2/13 De Guingand MSS, LHCMA.

58. The Battle of Egypt 23 Oct. 1942–7 Nov. 1942: Some Notes by Lt Gen B. L. Montgomery, BLM28/1 Montgomery MSS, IWM.

59. Enemy Documents Section, Appreciation No. 9, p. 17, CAB146/17, TNA.

60. Air Historical Branch, The Middle East Campaigns, July 1942–May 1943, p. 286, JSCSC.

61. The Battle of Egypt 23 Oct. 1942–7 Nov. 1942: Some Notes by Lt Gen B. L. Montgomery, BLM28/1 Montgomery MSS, IWM.

62. Enemy Documents Section, Appreciation No. 9, pp. 24–5, CAB146/17, TNA.

63. Liddell Hart, *The Rommel Papers*, p. 304.

64. ibid., p. 305.

65. Enemy Documents Section, Appreciation No. 9, p. 26, CAB146/17, TNA.

66. McGregor, *The Spirit of Angus*, p. 40.

67. Wimberley, A Scottish Soldier, Volume II, unpublished memoir, p. 44, PP/MCR/182 Wimberley MSS, IWM.

68. Cameron, *Argyll and Sutherland Highlanders 7th Battalion*, pp. 45–7.

69. McGregor, *Spirit of Angus*, p. 40.

70. Wimberley, A Scottish Soldier, p. 44, PP/MCR/182 Wimberley MSS, IWM.

71. 26 Aust Infantry Brigade Report on Operation 'Lightfoot', AWM54 527/6/9, AWM.

72. This feature was known to the Panzerarmee as 'Hill 28'.

73. 26 Aust Inf Bde Operation Order No. 22, 25 October 1942, AWM54 527/4/4, AWM.

74. John G. Glenn, *Tobruk to Tarakan: The Story of the 2/48th Battalion A. I. F.*, p. 148.

75. 26 Aust Infantry Brigade Report on Operation 'Lightfoot', AWM54 527/6/9, AWM.

76. ibid.

77. Carver, *El Alamein*, p. 140.

78. Glenn, *Tobruk to Tarakan*, p. 150.

79. 26 Aust Infantry Brigade Report on Operation 'Lightfoot', AWM54 527/6/9, AWM.

80. Glenn, *Tobruk to Tarakan*, p. 154.

81. 26 Aust Infantry Brigade Report on Operation 'Lightfoot', AWM54 527/6/9, AWM.

82. An account of 20th Brigade Operations El Alamein October–November 1942, AWM54 527/6/13, AWM.

83. 26 Aust Infantry Brigade Report on Operation 'Lightfoot', AWM54 527/6/9, AWM.

84. Glenn, *Tobruk to Tarakan*, p. 151.

85. ibid., p. 155.

86. 8th Armoured Brigade War Diary, 26 October 1942, WO169/4230, TNA.

87. 9th Armoured Brigade War Diary, 26–27 October 1942, WO169/4233, TNA.

88. 24th Armoured Brigade, Notes for MG AFV on Operations 23–29 Oct. 42, WO201/545, TNA.

89. 1st Armoured Division War Diary, 26 October 1942, WO169/4054, TNA.

90. 15th Panzer Division War Diary, 26 October 1942, WAII/11/22, NANZ.

91. Afrika Korps War Diary, 26 October 1942, WAII/11/20, NANZ.

92. Glenn, *Tobruk to Tarakan*, p. 156.

93. Fearnside, *Bayonets Abroad*, p. 276.

94. 26 Aust Infantry Brigade Report on Operation 'Lightfoot', AWM54 527/6/9, AWM.

95. Liddell Hart, *The Rommel Papers*, p. 306.

96. 15th Panzer Division Report on the Battle of Alamein and the Retreat to Marsa el Brega, 23rd October–20th November 1942, AWM54 423/4/103, AWM.

97. ibid.

98. Air Historical Branch, The Middle East Campaigns, July 1942–May 1943, pp. 292–4, JSCSC.

99. GoC's Diary, 26 October 1942, WAII/8/44, NANZ.

100. The Battle of Egypt 23 Oct. 1942–7 Nov. 1942: Some Notes by Lt Gen B. L. Montgomery, BLM28/1 Montgomery MSS, IWM.

101. Tank Position 26 Oct. 1942, 1/2/14 De Guingand MSS, LHCMA.

102. ibid.

103. Future Plans, 1/2/15 De Guingand MSS, LHCMA.

104. ibid.

105. The Battle of Egypt 23 Oct. 1942–7 Nov. 1942: Some Notes by Lt Gen B. L. Montgomery, BLM28/1 Montgomery MSS, IWM.

106. Hamilton, *Monty*, p. 762.

107. Liddell Hart notes, 11/1943/74 Liddell Hart MSS, LHMCA.

108. The Battle of Egypt 23 Oct. 1942–7 Nov. 1942: Some Notes by Lt Gen B. L. Montgomery, BLM28/1 Montgomery MSS, IWM.

109. Decisions by Army Commander given at a Conference held at Tac HQ Army at 1900 hrs 26 Oct., 1/2/16 De Guingand MSS, LHCMA.

110. The Battle of Egypt 23 Oct. 1942–7 Nov. 1942: Some Notes by Lt Gen B. L. Montgomery, BLM28/1 Montgomery MSS, IWM.

111. Decisions by Army Commander given at a Conference held at Tac HQ Army at 1900 hrs 26 Oct., 1/2/16 De Guingand MSS, LHCMA.

112. 21st Panzer Division War Diary, 26 October 1942, WAII/11/22, NANZ.

113. Liddell Hart, *The Rommel Papers*, p. 308.

114. Enemy Documents Section, Appreciation No. 9, p. 52, CAB146/17, TNA.

115. Account of the Action by 2 RB at 'Snipe' on 26/27 Oct. 42, WO169/4054, TNA.

116. ibid.

117. ibid.

118. Wake and Deedes, *Swift and Bold*, p. 110.

119. ibid., p. 111.

120. ibid., p. 112.

121. Hastings, *Rifle Brigade*, p. 168.

122. Account of the Action by 2 RB at 'Snipe' on 26/27 Oct. 42, WO169/4054, TNA.

123. ibid.

124. H. G. Parkyn, *The Rifle Brigade Chronicle for 1942*, p. 151.

125. Account of the Action by 2 RB at 'Snipe' on 26/27 Oct. 42, WO169/4054, TNA.

126. Afrika Korps War Diary, 27 October 1942, WAII/11/20, NANZ.

127. Air Historical Branch, The Middle East Campaigns, July 1942–May 1943, pp. 297–8, JSCSC.

128. 21st Panzer Division Report on the Battle of Alamein and the Retreat to Mersa el Brega, AWM423/4/103 (Part 93), AWM.

129. Account of the Action by 2 RB at 'Snipe' on 26/27 Oct. 42, WO169/4054, TNA.

130. 21st Panzer Division Report on the Battle of Alamein and the Retreat to Mersa el Brega, AWM 423/4/103 (Part 93), AWM.

131. Fearnside, *Bayonets Abroad*, p. 277.

132. 20th Brigade Operations, El Alamein, AWM54 527/6/13, AWM.

133. 9th Australian Division Report on Lightfoot, CAB106/777, TNA.

134. 20th Brigade Operations, El Alamein, AWM54 527/6/13, AWM.

135. 26 Aust Infantry Brigade Report on Operation 'Lightfoot', AWM54 527/6/9, AWM.

136. 90th Light Division War Diary, 27 October 1942, WAII/11/23, NANZ.

137. 26 Aust Infantry Brigade Report on Operation 'Lightfoot', AWM54 527/6/9, AWM.

138. ibid.

139. Glenn, *Tobruk to Tarakan*, p. 157.

140. Liddell Hart, *The Rommel Papers*, pp. 307–8.

141. ibid., p. 309.

142. Enemy Documents Section, Appreciation No. 9, p. 50, CAB146/17, TNA.

143. ibid., p. 43.

Chapter Seventeen: 'Round and Round the Mulberry Bush'

1. A Digger's comment to Morshead on a visit to the front line during the battle, Morshead to Dowdell, 12 November 1942, AWM3DRL/2562, AWM.

2. 133rd Lorried Infantry Brigade was the infantry formation of 10th Armoured Division.

3. 10th Armoured Division War Diary, 27 October 1942, WO169/4117.

4. G. D. Martineau, *A History of the Royal Sussex Regiment: A History of the Old Belfast Regiment and the Regiment of Sussex 1701–1953*, p. 258.

5. Notes for War Diary, 51st (Highland) Division War Diary, WO169/4165, TNA.

6. Wimberley, A Scottish Soldier, Volume II, unpublished memoir, p. 45, PP/MCR/182 Wimberley MSS, IWM.

7. Report on Investigation 'C', 99/1/2, RB 2/7, Briggs MSS, IWM.

8. 15th Panzer Division Report on the Battle of Alamein and the Retreat to Marsa el Brega, 23rd October–20th November 1942, AWM54 423/4/103, AWM.

9. Martineau, *Royal Sussex Regiment*, p. 258.

10. Report on Investigation 'C', 99/1/2, RB 2/7, Briggs MSS, IWM.

11. I. S. O. Playfair, *The Mediterranean and Middle East*, Volume IV, p. 56.

12. 2nd Armoured Brigade War Diary, 28 October 1942, WO169/4210, TNA.

13. GoC's Diary, 28 October 1942, WAII/8/44, NANZ.

14. ibid.

15. Glenn, *Tobruk to Tarakan*, p. 158.

16. 9th Australian Division Report on Lightfoot, CAB106/777, TNA.

17. Parsons, *Gunfire!* pp. 124–5.

18. Pemberton, *Artillery Tactics and Equipment*, pp. 143–5.

19. Afrika Korps War Diary, 28 October 1942, WAII/11/20, NANZ.

20. 15th Panzer Division War Diary, 28 October 1942, WAII/11/22, NANZ.

21. Air Historical Branch, The Middle East Campaigns, July 1942–May 1943, p. 301, JSCSC.

22. GoC's Diary, 28 October 1942, WAII/8/44, NANZ.

23. Account by Oliver Leese, WAII/1/DA491.2/17, NANZ.

24. 26th Aust Infantry Brigade Report on Operation 'Lightfoot', AWM54 527/6/9, AWM.

25. 20th Aust Infantry Brigade Operation Order No. 26, 28 October 1942, AWM54 527/4/4.

26. ibid.

27. 26th Aust Infantry Brigade Report on Operation 'Lightfoot', AWM54 527/6/9, AWM.

28. 26th Aust Infantry Brigade Operation Order No. 26, 28 October 1942, AWM54 527/4/4.

29. Decisions of Army Commander at Conference held at Tac HQ Army 0800 hrs 28 Oct. 1942, 1/2/17 De Guingand MSS, LHCMA.

30. The Battle of Egypt 23 Oct. 1942–7 Nov. 1942: Some Notes by Lt Gen B. L. Montgomery, BLM28/1 Montgomery MSS, IWM.

31. Decisions of Army Commander at Conference held at Tac HQ Army 0800 hrs 28 Oct. 1942, 1/2/17 De Guingand MSS, LHCMA.

32. BGS's Notes on Battle, 1/2/19 De Guingand MSS, LHCMA.

33. GoC's Diary, 28 October 1942, WAII/8/44, NANZ.

34. The Battle of Egypt 23 Oct. 1942–7 Nov. 1942: Some Notes by Lt Gen B. L. Montgomery, BLM28/1 Montgomery MSS, IWM.

35. Freyberg to Leese, 27 October 1942, WAII/8/25, NANZ.

36. ibid.

37. ibid.

38. ibid.

39. ibid.

40. Fearnside, *Bayonets Abroad*, p. 281.

41. The Battle of Egypt 23 Oct. 1942–7 Nov. 1942: Some Notes by Lt Gen B. L. Montgomery, BLM28/1 Montgomery MSS, IWM.

42. GoC's Diary, 28 October, WAII/8/44, NANZ.

43. C.-in-C. Middle East to the War Office, COSITREP [Chief of Staff's Situation Report] No. 566, 28 October 1942, PREM3/299/1, TNA.

44. Unfortunately, the draft telegram does not appear to have survived.

45. Churchill to CIGS, 28 October 1942, PREM3/299/1, TNA.

46. Danchev and Todman, *War Diaries 1939–1945, Field Marshal Lord Alanbrooke*, p. 335.

47. ibid.

48. ibid., p. 336.

49. 90th Light Division War Diary, 28 October 1942, WAII/11/23, NANZ.

50. Enemy Documents Section, Appreciation No. 9, p. 63, CAB146/17, TNA.

51. 20th Brigade Operations El Alamein, AWM54 527/6/13, AWM.

52. ibid.

53. Ronald J. Austin, *Let Enemies Beware! 'Caveant Hostes': The History of the 2/15th Battalion, 1940–45*, p. 165.

54. 20th Brigade Operations El Alamein, AWM54 527/6/13, AWM.

55. Six killed, 36 wounded and three missing: Austin, *Let Enemies Beware!*, p. 165.

56. Fearnside, *Bayonets Abroad*, p. 282.

57. 20th Brigade Operations El Alamein, AWM54 527/6/13, AWM.

58. Fearnside, *Bayonets Abroad*, p. 285.

59. 26th Aust Infantry Brigade Report on Operation 'Lightfoot', AWM54 527/6/9, AWM.

60. 20th Brigade Operations El Alamein, AWM54 527/6/13, AWM.

61. 26th Aust Infantry Brigade Report on Operation 'Lightfoot', AWM54 527/6/9, AWM.

62. Perrett, *The Valentine in North Africa 1942–43*, p. 45.

63. 26th Aust Infantry Brigade Report on Operation 'Lightfoot', AWM54 527/6/9, AWM.

64. ibid.

65. ibid.

66. Glenn, *Tobruk to Tarakan*, p. 160.

67. 26th Aust Infantry Brigade Report on Operation 'Lightfoot', AWM54 527/6/9, AWM.

68. 23rd Armoured Brigade Group, Report on Operations Lightfoot and Supercharge, 23rd October to 6th November 1942, WO169/4261, TNA.

69. 90th Light Division War Diary, 29 October 1942, WAII/11/23, NANZ.

70. Austin, *Let Enemies Beware!*, p. 166.

71. 2/15 Aust Inf Bn, 30 October 1942, Morshead Papers, 3DRL2632/6/14, AWM; 90th Light Division War Diary, 29 October 1942, WAII/11/23, NANZ.

72. 20th Brigade Operations El Alamein, AWM54 527/6/13, AWM.

73. ibid.

74. The Battle of Egypt 23 Oct. 1942–7 Nov. 1942: Some Notes by Lt Gen B. L. Montgomery, BLM28/1 Montgomery MSS, IWM.

75. de Guingand, *Operation Victory*, p. 206.

76. ibid.

77. Casey to Churchill, 30 October 1942, PREM3/299/1, TNA.

78. The Battle of Egypt 23 Oct. 1942–7 Nov. 1942: Some Notes by Lt Gen B. L. Montgomery, BLM28/1 Montgomery MSS, IWM.

79. ibid.

80. BGS's Notes on Battle, 1/2/19 De Guingand MSS, LHCMA.

81. De Guingand, *Operation Victory*, p. 206.

82. GoC's Diary, 29 October 1942, WAII/8/44, NANZ.

83. Col. John M. Sym, unpublished memoir, Sym MSS, LHCMA.

84. GoC's Diary, 29 October 1942, WAII/8/44, NANZ.

85. The Rahman track, which runs from Sidi Abd el Rahman down to the Qattara Depression, remains one of the few obvious landmarks in otherwise nondescript desert.

86. GoC's Diary, 29 October, WAII/8/44, NANZ.

87. Basil H. Liddell Hart, *The Rommel Papers*, p. 314.

88. Austin, *Let Enemies Beware!*, p. 166.

89. 9th Australian Division Report on Lightfoot, CAB106/777, TNA.

90. Glenn, *Tobruk to Tarakan*, p. 162.

91. BGS's Notes on Battle, 1/2/19 De Guingand MSS, LHCMA.

92. ibid.

93. ibid.

94. 26th Aust Inf Bde Operation Order No. 24, 30 October 1942, AWM54 527/4/4.

95. 26th Aust Infantry Brigade Report on Operation 'Lightfoot', AWM54 527/6/9, AWM.

96. Glenn, *Tobruk to Tarakan*, p. 162.

97. ibid.

98. 23rd Armoured Brigade Group, Report on Operations Lightfoot and Supercharge, 23rd October to 6th November 1942, WO169/4261, TNA.

99. RAA 9 Aust Div Operation Order No. 11A, 30 October 1942, AWM54 527/4/4.

100. The Battle of Egypt 23 Oct. 1942–7 Nov. 1942: Some Notes by Lt Gen B. L. Montgomery, BLM28/1 Montgomery MSS, IWM. Montgomery's own account gives the final proof that it would be very difficult indeed to go to sleep and stay asleep just as 800 guns opened fire!

101. 26th Aust Infantry Brigade Report on Operation 'Lightfoot', AWM54 527/6/9, AWM.

102. ibid.

103. Glenn, *Tobruk to Tarakan*, p. 163.

104. 26th Aust Infantry Brigade Report on Operation 'Lightfoot', AWM54 527/6/9, AWM.

105. ibid.

106. ibid.

107. ibid.

108. ibid.

109. 9th Australian Division Report on Lightfoot, CAB106/777, TNA.

110. Fearnside, *Bayonets Abroad*, p. 287.

111. 9th Australian Division Report on Lightfoot, CAB106/777, TNA.

112. Glenn, *Tobruk to Tarakan*, p. 170.

113. 26th Aust Infantry Brigade Report on Operation 'Lightfoot', AWM54 527/6/9, AWM.

114. 90th Light Division War Diary, 31 October 1942, WAII/11/23, NANZ.

115. ibid.

116. This battlegroup was commanded by Major Pfeiffer, the commanding officer of the 39th Panzerjager Battalion, and was composed of a tank battalion of 15 tanks, the self-propelled guns of 39th Panzerjager, a company of 617th AA Battalion with one heavy and two light field howitzer batteries in support. This battlegroup now represented almost half the strength of the division. See Afrika Korps War Diary, 31 October 1942, WAII/11/20, NANZ.

117. Afrika Korps War Diary, 31 October 1942, WAII/11/20, NANZ.

118. This was the Australian nickname for the tight formation of 18 bombers used by the Desert Air Force.

119. 20th Brigade Operations El Alamein, AWM54 527/6/13, AWM.

120. Air Historical Branch, The Middle East Campaigns, July 1942–May 1943, p. 312, JSCSC.

121. 26th Aust Infantry Brigade Report on Operation 'Lightfoot', AWM54 527/6/9, AWM.

122. ibid.

123. Glenn, *Tobruk to Tarakan*, p. 170.

124. Afrika Korps War Diary, 31 October 1942, WAII/11/20, NANZ.

125. Situation reports leading up to and including Alamein, 3DRL2632/6/20 Morshead MSS, AWM.

126. David Coombes, *Morshead: Hero of Tobruk and El Alamein*, p. 152.

127. It took only two troop carriers to carry the remnants of the 2/48th Battalion: Glenn, *Tobruk to Tarakan*, p. 171.

128. Air Historical Branch, The Middle East Campaigns, July 1942–May 1943, p. 314, JSCSC.

129. Gordon Combe, Frank Ligertwood and Ian Gilchrist, *The Second 43rd Australian Infantry Battalion, 1940–1945*, p. 121.

130. ibid., p. 128.

131. The 2/43rd always referred to the area as the 'Blockhouse', ibid., p. 121.

132. Enemy Documents Section, Appreciation No. 9, p. 87, CAB146/17, TNA.

133. 90th Light Division War Diary, 29 October 1942, WAII/11/23, NANZ.

134. Glenn, *Tobruk to Tarakan*, p. 171.

135. Combe, Ligertwood and Gilchrist, *The Second 43rd*, p. 122.

136. Air Historical Branch, The Middle East Campaigns, July 1942–May 1943, pp. 315–16, JSCSC.

137. 9th Australian Division Report on Lightfoot, CAB 106/777, TNA.

138. Combe, Ligertwood and Gilchrist, *The Second 43rd*, pp. 122–3.

139. 9th Australian Division Report on Lightfoot, CAB106/777, TNA.

140. 90th Light Division War Diary, 1 November 1942, WAII/11/23, NANZ.

141. 9th Australian Division Report on Lightfoot, CAB106/777, TNA.

142. ibid.

143. Combe, Ligertwood and Gilchrist, *The Second 43rd*, p. 124.

144. 9th Australian Division Report on Lightfoot, CAB106/777, TNA.

145. Afrika Korps War Diary, 1 November 1942, WAII/11/20, NANZ.

146. Summary of El Alamein Battle, AWM54 527/6/5, AWM.

147. Montgomery to Brooke, 1 November 1942, BLM49/1 Montgomery MSS, IWM.

Chapter Eighteen: Operation Supercharge

1. GoC's Diary, 1/2 November 1942, WAII/8/44, NANZ.

2. ibid.

3. Information concerning the artillery programme taken from W. E. Murphy,

2nd New Zealand Divisional Artillery, pp. 402–5, and 'Battle for Egypt October–November 1942' (New Zealand Account) WO201/425, TNA.

4. Air Historical Branch, The Middle East Campaigns, July 1942–May 1943, pp. 316–19, JSCSC.

5. Lewis and English, *Into Battle with the Durhams*, p. 147.

6. ibid.

7. Private J. A. Crawford, Forward from El Alamein, 2/17th Battalion, 3DRL368, AWM.

8. Battle for Egypt October–November 1942 (New Zealand Account) WO201/425, TNA.

9. Alistair Borthwick, *Battalion: A British Infantry Unit's Actions from El Alamein to the Elbe 1942–1945*, p. 28.

10. GoC's Diary, 2 November, WAII/8/44, NANZ.

11. Borthwick, *Battalion*, p. 30.

12. ibid., p. 33.

13. Lewis and English, *The Durhams*, p. 148.

14. ibid., p. 149.

15. 15th Panzer Division War Diary, 2 November 1942, WAII/11/22, NANZ.

16. Lucas Phillips, *Alamein*, p. 334.

17. 9 Armd Bde Group Report on Supercharge, WO201/554, TNA.

18. ibid.

19. ibid.

20. Pitt, *Royal Wilts*, p. 149.

21. 9 Armd Bde Group Report on Supercharge, WO201/554, TNA.

22. GoC's Diary, 2 November 1942, WAII/8/44, NANZ.

23. Pitt, *Royal Wilts*, p. 156.

24. 9 Armd Bde Group Report on Supercharge, WO201/554, TNA.

25. ibid.

26. ibid.

27. Hector Bolitho, *The Galloping Third: The Story of the 3rd King's Own Hussars*, p. 278.

28. 9 Armd Bde Group Report on Supercharge, WO201/554, TNA.

29. ibid.

30. The Germans called it 'The Monolith'.

31. 21st Panzer Division Report on the Battle of Alamein and the Retreat to Mersa el Brega, AWM423/4/103 (Part 93), AWM.

32. 9 Armd Bde Group Report on Supercharge, WO201/554, TNA.

33. Lucas Phillips, *Alamein*, p. 356.

34. 9 Armd Bde Group Report on Supercharge, WO201/554, TNA.

35. Derek Jewell, *Alamein and the Desert War*, p. 90.

36. 9 Armd Bde Group Report on Supercharge, WO201/554, TNA.

37. GoC's Diary, 2 November 1942, WAII/8/44, NANZ.

38. Report on Investigation 'B', 1st Armoured Division War Diary, 2 November 1942, WO169/4054, TNA.

39. 1st Armoured Division War Diary, 2 November 1942, WO169/4054, TNA.

40. Bright, *Ninth Lancers*, p. 118.

41. Lucas Phillips, *Alamein*, p. 362.

42. Bright, *Ninth Lancers*, pp. 118–19.

43. 1st Armoured Division War Diary, 2 November 1942, WO169/4054, TNA.

44. ibid.

45. GoC's Diary, 2 November 1942, WAII/8/44, NANZ.

46. 21st Panzer Division Report on the Battle of Alamein and the Retreat to Mersa el Brega, AWM423/4/103 (Part 93), AWM.

47. 8th Armoured Brigade Operation Supercharge, WO201/439, TNA.

48. 90th Light Division War Diary, 2 November 1942, WAII/11/23, NANZ.

49. 15th Panzer Division Report on the Battle of Alamein and the Retreat to Mersa el Brega, 23rd October–20th November 1942, AWM54 423/4/103, AWM.

50. 21st Panzer Division Report on the Battle of Alamein and the Retreat to Mersa el Brega, AWM423/4/103 (Part 93), AWM.

51. Air Historical Branch, The Middle East Campaigns, July 1942–May 1943, pp. 319–20, JSCSC.

52. J. A. Pitt-Rivers, *The Story of the Royal Dragoons 1938–1945*, pp. 59–60.

53. ibid., p. 60.

54. Their total 'bag' amounted to 181 vehicles, 3 tanks, 1 half-track, 1 medium gun, 3 field guns, 17 anti-tank guns, 20 Breda cannons and 1 aeroplane!: ibid., pp. 60–63.

55. I. S. O. Playfair, *The Mediterranean and Middle East*, Volume IV, p. 70.

56. Todd, *Elephant at War*, p. 42.

57. 10th Armoured Division War Diary, 2 November 1942, WO169/4117, TNA.

58. Afrika Korps War Diary, 2 November 1942, WAII/11/20, NANZ.

59. 15th Panzer Division Report on the Battle of Alamein and the Retreat to Mersa el Brega, 23rd October–20th November 1942, AWM54 423/4/103, AWM.

60. Afrika Korps War Diary, 2 November 1942, WAII/11/20, NANZ.

61. Enemy Documents Section, Appreciation No. 9, pp. 91–2, CAB146/17, TNA.

62. ibid.

63. Translation of German Official War Narrative, 23 October–5 January 1943, AWM54 492/4/74, AWM.

64. ibid.

65. Hastings, *The Rifle Brigade*, p. 157.

66. 1st Armoured Division War Diary, 2 November 1942, WO169/4054, TNA.

67. 2nd Armoured Brigade War Diary, 2 November 1942, WO169/4210, TNA.

68. Wake and Deedes, *Swift and Bold*, pp. 113–14.

69. Hastings, *The Rifle Brigade*, pp. 158–60.

70. This was proof that 2nd King's Royal Rifle Corps never reached the crest of Tel el Aqqaqir during the night.

71. Wake and Deedes, *Swift and Bold*, p. 114; 1st Armoured Division War Diary, 3 November 1942, WO169/4054, TNA.

72. Bright, *Ninth Lancers*, p. 119.

73. 1st Armoured Division War Diary, 3 November 1942, WO169/4054, TNA.

74. Air Historical Branch, The Middle East Campaigns, July 1942–May 1943, p. 324, JSCSC.

75. GoC's Diary, 3 November 1942, WAII/8/44, NANZ.

76. 1st Armoured Division War Diary, 3 November 1942, WO169/4054, TNA.

77. Miles, *Life of a Regiment*, p. 143; Wimberley, A Scottish Soldier, Volume II, unpublished memoir, p. 48, PP/MCR/182 Wimberley MSS, IWM; Account by Oliver Leese, WAII/1/DA491.2/17, NANZ.

78. 1st Armoured Division War Diary, 3 November 1942, WO169/4054, TNA.

79. ibid.

80. Account by Oliver Leese, WAII/1/DA491.2/17, NANZ.

81. Wimberley, A Scottish Soldier, p. 48, PP/MCR/182 Wimberley MSS, IWM.

82. Account by Oliver Leese, WAII/1/DA491.2/17, NANZ.

83. 1st Armoured Division War Diary, 3 November 1942, WO169/4054, TNA.

84. Miles, *Life of a Regiment*, pp. 143–44.

85. 15th Panzer Division Report on the Battle of Alamein and the Retreat to Mersa el Brega, 23rd October–20th November 1942, AWM54 423/4/103, AWM.

86. Col. John M. Sym, unpublished memoir, Sym MSS, LHCMA.

87. Wimberley, A Scottish Soldier, p. 48, PP/MCR/182 Wimberley MSS, IWM.

88. 15th Panzer Division Report on the Battle of Alamein and the Retreat to Marsa el Brega, 23rd October–20th November 1942, AWM54 423/4/103, AWM.

89. Miles, *Life of a Regiment*, p. 144.

90. Wimberley, A Scottish Soldier, p. 49, PP/MCR/182 Wimberley MSS, IWM.

91. Sym Memoir, Sym MSS, LHCMA.

92. Wimberley, A Scottish Soldier, p. 49, PP/MCR/182 Wimberley MSS, IWM.

93. G. R. Stevens, *Fourth Indian Division*, p. 195.

94. ibid., p. 196.

95. Translation of German Official War Narrative, 23 October–5 January 1943, AWM54 492/4/74, AWM.

96. Walter Warlimont, *Inside Hitler's Headquarters 1939–45*, p. 268.

97. Translation of German Official War Narrative, 23 October–5 January 1943, AWM54 492/4/74, AWM.

98. Churchill to Auchinleck, 24 June 1942, PREM3/290/6, TNA.

99. Liddell Hart, *The Rommel Papers*, p. 322.

100. German Official War Narrative, 23 October–5 January 1943, AWM54 492/4/74, AWM.

101. Liddell Hart, *The Rommel Papers*, p. 322.

102. Afrika Korps War Diary, 3 November 1942, WAII/11/20, NANZ.

103. 15th Panzer Division Report on the Battle of Alamein and the Retreat to Mersa el Brega, 23rd October–20th November 1942, AWM54 423/4/103, AWM.

104. Cameron, *Argyll and Sutherland Highlanders 7th Battalion*, p. 52.

105. 7th Medium Regiment War Diary, 5 November 1942, RAHT.

106. R.A. Notes on the Offensive by Eighth Army from 23 Oct.–4 Nov. on the El Alamein Position, WO201/2877, TNA.

107. Air Historical Branch, The Middle East Campaigns, July 1942–May 1943, pp. 333–4, JSCSC.

108. William Richardson and Seymour Freidlin, *The Fatal Decisions*, p. 106.

109. Afrika Korps War Diary, 4 November 1942, WAII/11/20, NANZ.

110. Richardson and Freidlin, *The Fatal Decisions*, p. 107.

111. Singer was tragically killed the next day: D. Dawnay, *10th Hussars*, pp. 84–5.

112. Carver, *Out of Step*, p. 142.

113. ibid., pp. 142–3.

114. Roberts, *From the Desert to the Baltic*, p. 119.

115. 10th Armoured Division War Diary, 4 November 1942, WO169/4117, TNA.

116. 8th Armoured Brigade Operation Supercharge, WO201/439, TNA.

117. ibid.

118. A true breakthrough requires a penetration of an enemy's positions in depth while the enemy is still attempting to hold those positions.

119. 15th Panzer Division Report on the Battle of Alamein and the Retreat to Mersa el Brega, 23rd October–20th November 1942, AWM54 423/4/103, AWM.

120. Anon., *The Royal Artillery Commemoration Book 1939–1945*, pp. 234–5.

121. 8th Armoured Brigade Operation Supercharge, WO201/439, TNA.

122. ibid.

123. Carver, *Out of Step*, p. 143.

124. Richardson, *Flashback*, p. 123.

125. Notes on Conference regarding 'Grapeshot' held at Tac HQ Army at 12.00 hrs 2 November, 1/2/24 De Guingand MSS, LHCMA.

126. de Guingand, *Operation Victory*, p. 216.

127. Carver, *Out of Step*, p. 143.

128. 15th Panzer Division Report on the Battle of Alamein and the Retreat to Mersa el Brega, 23rd October–20th November 1942, AWM54 423/4/103, AWM; 21st Panzer Division Report on the Battle of Alamein and the Retreat to Mersa el Brega, AWM423/4/103 (Part 93), AWM.

129. ibid.

130. Middle East Strategy, CAB106/2291, TNA.

131. 8th Army Claims up to 2359 hrs 3 November, WO201/439, TNA.

132. Afrika Korps War Diary, 5 November 1942, WAII/11/20, NANZ.

133. Volkmar Khun, *German Paratroops in World War II*, pp. 154–5.

134. 'Casualties Eighth Army' 23 October–7 November 1942, GHQ MEF, WO201/439, TNA.

135. 'Tank Losses' 10 November 1942. Another 100 tanks remained unaccounted for in the forward area. WO201/439, TNA; Playfair, *The Mediterranean and Middle East*, Volume IV, p. 78.

136. Richardson, *Flashback*, p. 121.

137. 'Casualties Eighth Army' 23 October–7 November 1942, GHQ MEF, WO201/439, TNA.

138. Corporal C. W. Mears, 2/17th Bn, PR84/379, AWM.

139. Private J. A. Crawford, Forward from El Alamein, 2/17th Battalion, 3DRL368, AWM.

Chapter Nineteen: Ring Out the Bells!

1. Mideast to Air Ministry, 4 November 1942, PREM3/299/1, TNA.

2. ibid.

3. Calder, *The People's War*, p. 304.

4. Churchill to Alexander, 4 November 1942, PREM3/299/1, TNA.

5. Alexander to Churchill, 5 November 1942, PREM3/299/1, TNA.

6. Danchev and Todman, *War Diaries 1939–1945, Field Marshal Alanbrooke*, p. 338.

7. Churchill to Alexander, 7 November 1942, PREM3/299/1, TNA.

8. Calder, *The People's War*, p. 305.

9. Record of a Meeting Held at GHQ MEF on 5 Oct. to Discuss the Future Maintenance of Eighth Army by Sea, 7 October 1942, WO69/3794, TNA.

10. Middle East Forces, *Notes on the Maintenance of the Eighth Army*, p. 19.

11. ibid., p. 48.

12. Johnson and Stanley, *Alamein: The Australian Story*, pp. 267, 268.

13. Maughan, *Tobruk and El Alamein*, pp. 748–50.

14. Anon., *Documents Relating to New Zealand's Participation in the Second World War 1939–45*, Volume II: pp. 141–55.

15. These include Lessons from Lightfoot, WO201/449; 8th Armoured Brigade Reports on Operations, WO201/439; 9th Armoured Brigade Report on Operations, WO201/554; 9th Australian Division Report, CAB106/777; 2nd New Zealand Division Report, WO201/425, TNA, amongst many others.

16. Lessons from Lightfoot, WO201/449, TNA.

17. ibid.

18. ibid.

19. ibid.

20. 24 Armoured Brigade, Notes for MG AFV on Operations 23–29 Oct. 42, WO201/545, TNA.

21. Lessons from Lightfoot, WO201/449, TNA.

22. 23rd Armoured Brigade Group, Account of Operations from 23 Oct. to 6 Nov. 1942, WO106/2263, TNA.

23. I. S. O. Playfair, *The Mediterranean and Middle East*, Volume IV, pp. 329–76.

24. French, *Churchill's Army*, pp. 274–85.

25. Hills, *Phantom Was There*, p. 85.

26. 152nd Infantry Brigade, Discussion on lessons learned during the year of fighting from El Alamein to Messina, WO231/16, TNA.

27. ibid.

28. 24 Armoured Brigade, Notes for MG AFV on Operations 23–29 Oct. 42, WO201/545, TNA.

29. Harrison Place, *Military Training*, pp. 14–17.

Bibliography

Unpublished Primary Sources

(Abbreviations in parenthesis refer to sources in Notes to individual chapters, pp. 439-495.)

The National Archives, Kew (TNA)

PREM3
CAB106, 146
HW1, 8
WO32, 69, 106, 169, 201, 214, 231

Imperial War Museum, Department of Documents (IWM)

Montgomery MSS
Wimberley MSS
Briggs MSS
Giddings MSS
Witherby MSS

Liddell Hart Centre for Military Archives, King's College London (LHCMA)

Liddell Hart MSS
Sym MSS
Alanbrooke MSS
De Guingand MSS
Pyman MSS
Hutton MSS
GPB Roberts MSS

Joint Services Command and Staff College (JSCSC)

Air Historical Branch, RAF Narrative (First Draft)

Royal Artillery Library, Royal Artillery Historical Trust (RAHT)

Gibbon MSS
Kirkman MSS

Royal Logistics Corps Museum (RLCM)

RAOC Campaigns WW2 Box 1

Royal Signals Museum (RSM)

Australian War Memorial, Canberra (AWM)

Morshead MSS
AWM52, 54
3DRL
PR84

National Archives of New Zealand, Wellington (NANZ)

WAII/1, 2, 8, 11

United States of America National Archives, Washington, DC (USNA)

RG457
RG167

John Rylands Library, Manchester University, Manchester (JRL)

Auchinleck MSS
Dorman O'Gowan MSS

Published Secondary Sources

Abraham, Sir William, *Time Off For War: The Recollections of a Wartime Staff Officer*, privately published, 1982
Adair, Robin, *British Eighth Army, North Africa, 1940–1943*, Arms & Armour Press, 1974

Adkin, Mark, *The Waterloo Companion*, Aurum Press, 2001

Agar-Hamilton, J. A. I. and L. C. F. Turner, *Crisis in the Desert May–July 1942*, Oxford University Press, 1952

—*The Sidi Rezeg Battles 1941*, Oxford University Press, 1957

Anon., *Documents Relating to New Zealand's Participation in the Second World War 1939–45*, Volume II, War History Branch, 1951

—*Notes on the Maintenance of the Eighth Army and the Supporting Royal Air Force by Land, Sea and Air from El Alamein to Tunisia*, Middle East Forces GHQ, Cairo, 1943

—*Red Platypus: A Record of the Achievements of the 24th Australian Infantry Brigade*, Imperial Printing Company, 1946

—*Royal Electrical and Mechanical Engineers*, Volume I, War Office, 1951

—*The Story of the Royal Army Service Corps 1939–1945*, G. Bell and Sons, 1955

—*The Army Field Manual*, Volume IV: *All Arms Tactics in Special Environments*, Part 3: *Desert: Historical Supplement*, HMSO, 1993

—*The Royal Artillery Commemoration Book 1939–1945*, G. Bell and Sons, 1950

Austin, Ronald J., *Let Enemies Beware! 'Caveant Hostes': The History of the 2/15th Battalion, 1940–45*, Slouch Hat Publications, 1995

Bailey, J. B. A., *Field Artillery and Firepower*, The Military Press, 1989

Baker, A. H. R. and B. A. Rust, *A Short History of the 50th Northumbrian Division*, 50th Division, 1966

Barkas, Geoffrey, *The Camouflage Story (from Aintree to Alamein)*, Cassell, 1952

Barnett, Corelli, *The Desert Generals*, William Kimber, 1960

—*Hitler's Generals*, Weidenfeld & Nicolson, 1989

Bates, Peter, *Dance of War: The Story of the Battle of Egypt*, Leo Cooper, 1992

Baynes, John, *The Forgotten Victor: General Sir Richard O'Connor*, Brassey's, 1989

Beale, Peter, *Death by Design: British Tank Development in the Second World War*, Sutton, 1998

Beaton, Cecil, *Near East*, Batsford, 1943

Behrendt, Hans Otto, *Rommel's Intelligence in the Desert Campaign*, William Kimber, 1985

Belchem, David, *All in a Day's March*, Collins, 1978

Belot, Raymond D., *The Struggle For The Mediterranean 1939–1945*, Princeton University Press, 1951

Bennett, Ralph, *Ultra and Mediterranean Strategy 1941–1945*, Hamish Hamilton, 1989

Bickers, Richard Townshend, *The Desert Air War 1939–1945*, Leo Cooper, 1991

Bidwell, R. G. S., 'The Development of British Field Artillery Tactics 1940–42: The Desert War', *Royal Artillery Journal*, September 1967.

Bidwell, Shelford, *Indirect Fire Artillery as a Battle Winner/Loser: A Historical Study*, MOD, n. d.

—*Gunners at War: A Tactical Study of the Royal Artillery in the Twentieth Century*, Arms and Armour, 1970

—and Dominic Graham, *Firepower: British Army Weapons and Theories of War 1904–1945*, George Allen & Unwin, 1982

Bingham, James, Kilburne Wordsworth and Werner Haupt, *North African Campaign 1940–1943*, Macdonald, 1969

Bolitho, Hector, *The Galloping Third: The Story of the 3rd King's Own Hussars*, John Murray, 1963

Bond, Brian, *Liddell Hart: A Study of His Military Thought*, Cassell, 1977

—*British Military Policy Between the Two World Wars*, Oxford University Press, 1980

Borthwick, Alistair, *Battalion: A British Infantry Unit's Actions from El Alamein to the Elbe 1942–1945*, Baton Wicks, 1994

Bowron, J. H., 'The Battle of Alam Halfa 30 August–6 September 1942', Defence Research Paper, JSCSC, 2000

Bradford, Ernle, *Malta 1940–43*, Hamilton, 1985

Brett-James, Anthony, *Ball of Fire: The Fifth Indian Division in the Second World War*, Gale & Polden, 1951

Bright, Joan, *The Ninth Queen's Royal Lancers 1936–1945*, Gale & Polden, 1951

Brooks, Stephen (ed.), *Montgomery and the Eighth Army: A Selection from the Diaries, Correspondence and Other Papers of Field Marshal The Viscount Montgomery of Alamein, August 1942 to December 1943*, Bodley Head for the Army Records Society, 1991

Bungay, Stephen, *Alamein*, Aurum Press, 2002

Butler, J. R. M., *Grand Strategy*, Volume II: *September 1939–June 1941*, HMSO, 1957

—*Grand Strategy*, Volume III, Parts I and II, *June 1941–August 1942*, HMSO, 1964

Caccio-Dominioni, Paulo, *Alamein: An Italian Story 1933–1942*, George Allen & Unwin, 1966

Calder, Angus, *The People's War*, Jonathan Cape, 1986

Cameron, Ian C., *History of the Argyll and Sutherland Highlanders 7th Battalion: From El Alamein to Germany*, Thomas Nelson and Sons, 1947

Carell, Paul, *The Foxes of the Desert*, New English Library, 1961

Carter, J. A. H., and D. N. Kann, *The Second World War 1939–1945 Army: Maintenance in the Field 1943–1945*, Volume I, The War Office, 1952

—*The Second World War 1939–1945 Army: Maintenance in the Field 1943–1945*, Volume II, The War Office, 1961

Carver, Michael, *The History of Fourth Armoured Brigade*, Gale & Polden, 1945

—*Tobruk*, Batsford, 1962

—*El Alamein*, Batsford, 1962

—*Harding of Petherton*, Weidenfeld & Nicolson, 1978

—*Dilemmas of the Desert War: A New Look at the Libyan Campaign 1940–1942*, Batsford, 1986

—*Out of Step*, Hutchinson, 1989

Chalfont, Alun Jones, *Montgomery of Alamein*, Weidenfeld and Nicolson 1976

Chamberlain, Peter, and Chris Ellis, *British and American Tanks of World War II: The Complete Illustrated History of British, American and Commonwealth Tanks, 1939–1945*, Arms & Armour Press, 1969

Chaplin, H. D., *The Queen's Own Royal West Kent Regiment, 1920–1950*, Michael Joseph, 1954

Chappell, F. R., *Wellington Wings: An RAF Intelligence Officer in the Western Desert*, William Kimber, 1980

Churchill, Winston S., *The Second World War*, Volume IV: *The Hinge of Fate*, Cassell, 1951; Penguin, 1985

Clay, Ewart W., *The Path of the 50th: The Story of the 50th (Northumbrian) Division in the Second World War, 1939–1945*, Gale & Polden, 1950

Clayton, Aileen, *The Enemy is Listening*, Crecy, 1993

Clayton, Anthony, *Forearmed: A History of the Intelligence Corps*, Brassey's, 1993

Clifford, Alexander, *Three Against Rommel: Wavell, Auchinleck and Alexander*, Harrap, 1943

Close, Bill, *View from the Turret: A History of the 3rd Royal Tank Regiment in the Second World War*, Dell & Bredon, 1998

Cody, J. F., *New Zealand Engineers, Middle East*, New Zealand Historical Publications Branch, Department of Internal Affairs, 1961

Combe, Gordon, Frank Ligertwood and Tom Gilchrist, *The Second 43rd, Australian Infantry Battalion 1940–1946*, Second 43rd Battalion AIF Club, Adelaide, 1972

Connell, John, *Auchinleck: A Biography of Field-Marshal Sir Claude Auchinleck*, Cassell, 1959

—*Wavell: Scholar and Soldier*, Collins, 1964

Coombes, David, *Morshead: Hero of Tobruk and El Alamein*, Oxford University Press, 2001

Cooper, Artemis, *Cairo in the War 1939–1945*, Hamish Hamilton, 1989

Crang, Jeremy, *The British Army and the People's War 1939–1945*, Manchester University Press, 2000

Cunningham, Andrew B., *A Sailor's Odyssey: The Autobiography of Admiral of the Fleet Viscount Cunningham of Hyndhope*, Hutchinson, 1951

Danchev, Alex, *Alchemist of War: The Life of Basil Liddell Hart*, Weidenfeld & Nicolson, 1998

—and Daniel Todman (eds), *War Diaries 1939–1945, Field Marshal Lord Alanbrooke*, Weidenfeld & Nicolson, 2001

Dawnay, D., *The 10th Royal Hussars in the Second World War 1939–1945*, Gale & Polden, 1948

De Guingand, Francis, *Operation Victory*, Hodder & Stoughton, 1947

—*Generals at War*, Hodder & Stoughton, 1964

Denholm-Young, C. P. S., *Men of Alamein*, Schindler, 1943

D'Este, Carlo, *World War II in the Mediterranean: 1942–1945*, Algonquin, 1990

DiNardo, R. L., *Mechanized Juggernaut or Military Anachronism? Horses and the German Army of World War II*, Greenwood, 1991

Doherty, Richard, *The Sound of History: El Alamein, 1942*, Spellmount, 2002

Domenico, Petracarro, 'The Italian Army in Africa 1940–1943: An Attempt at Historical Perspective', *War & Society*, Vol. 9, No. 2, October 1991, pp. 103–27

Douglas, Keith, *Alamein to Zem Zem*, Oxford University Press, 1979

Dudgeon, A. G., *Hidden Victory: The Battle of Habbaniya, May 1941*, Tempus, 2000

Ellis, Chris and Peter Chamberlain, *The Great Tanks*, Hamlyn, 1975

Ellis, John, *Brute Force: Allied Strategy and Tactics in the Second World War*, André Deutsch, 1990

English, John A., and Bruce I. Gudmundsson, *On Infantry*, Praeger, 1994

Everrett, H., 'The Secret War in the Desert', *British Army Review*, December 1978, pp. 66–8

Falvey, Denis, *A Well-Known Excellence: British Artillery and an Artilleryman in World War Two*, Brassey's, 2002

Fearnside, G. H., *Bayonets Abroad: A History of the 2/13 Battalion AIF in the Second World War*, 1993

Fernyhough, A. H., *History of the Royal Army Ordnance Corps 1920–1945*, Royal Army Ordnance Corps, 1967

Fletcher, David, *The Great Tank Scandal: British Armour in the Second World War*, Part 1, HMSO, 1989

Forster, R. G. C., *History of the Queen's Royal Regiment*, Volume VIII: *1924–1948*, Gale & Polden, 1953

Forty, George, *Tanks Across the Desert: The War Diary of Jake Wardrop*, Kimber, 1981

Fraser, David, *Alanbrooke*, Collins, 1982

—*Knight's Cross: A Life of Field Marshal Erwin Rommel*, HarperCollins, 1993

French, David, *Raising Churchill's Army: The British Army and the War against Germany, 1919–1945*, Oxford University Press, 2000

Freyberg, Paul, *Bernard Freyberg VC: Soldier of Two Nations*, Hodder & Stoughton, 1991

Gilbert, Martin, *Churchill: A Life*, William Heinemann, 1991

Gladman, Brad W., 'Air Power and Intelligence in the Western Desert

Campaign, 1940–43', *Intelligence And National Security*, Vol. 13, No. 4, Winter 1998, pp. 144–62

Glantz, David M., and Jonathan House, *When Titans Clashed: How the Red Army Stopped Hitler*, Kansas University Press, 1995

—*Kharkov 1942: Anatomy of a Military Disaster*, Sarpedon, 1998

Glenn, John G., *Tobruk to Tarakan: The Story of the 2/48th Battalion A.I.F.*, Rigby Limited, 1960

Gooderson, Ian, *Air Power at the Battlefront: Allied Close Air Support in Europe 1943–45*, Frank Cass, 1998

Goodhart, David, *We of the Turning Tide*, F. W. Preece, 1947

Graham, Dominic, *Against Odds: Reflections on the Experiences of the British Army, 1914–45*, Macmillan, 1999

Grant, Roderick, F. W., *The 51st Highland Division at War, 1939–1945*, Ian Allan, 1977

Greacen, Lavinia, *Chink: A Biography*, Macmillan, 1989

Greene, Jack and Alessandro Massignani, *Rommel's North Africa Campaign, September 1940–November 1942*, Combined Books, 1994

—*Naval War in the Mediterranean 1940–1943*, Chatham Publishing, 1998

Greenwood, Alexander, *Field-Marshal Auchinleck*, Pentland Press, 1990

Griffith, Paddy, *Forward into Battle: Fighting Tactics from Waterloo to Vietnam*, Anthony Bird, 1981

Hamilton, Nigel, *Monty: The Making of a General 1887–1942*, Allen Lane, 1982

—*The Full Monty: Montgomery of Alamein 1887–1942*, Allen Lane, 2001

Handel, Michael I. (ed.), *Intelligence and Military Operations*, Frank Cass, 1988

Harris, J. P., with Niall Barr, *Amiens to the Armistice: The BEF in the Hundred Days Campaign, 8 August–11 November 1918*, Brassey's, 1998

Harrison, Frank, *Tobruk: The Great Siege Reassessed*, Arms & Armour Press, 1996

Harrison Place, Timothy, *Military Training in the British Army, 1940–1944: From Dunkirk to D-Day*, Frank Cass, 2000

Hart, Stephen, *Montgomery and 'Colossal Cracks': The 21st Army Group in Northwest Europe, 1944–45*, Praeger, 2000

Hastings, R. H. W. S., *The Rifle Brigade in the Second World War, 1939–1945*, Gale & Polden, 1950

Heckstall-Smith, Anthony, *Tobruk*, Blond, 1959

Hills, R. J. T., *Phantom Was There*, Edward Arnold, 1951

Hinsley, F. H., with E. E. Thomas, C. F. G. Ransom, R. C. Knight, *British Intelligence in the Second World War: Its Influence on Strategy and Operations*, Volume I, HMSO, 1979

—*British Intelligence in the Second World War: Its Influence on Strategy and Operations*, Volume II, HMSO, 1984

Hogg, Ian V., *German Artillery of World War Two*, Arms & Armour Press, 1975

—*British & American Artillery of World War Two*, Arms & Armour Press, 1978

Horrocks, Brian, *A Full Life*, Collins, 1960

Howard, Michael, *The Mediterranean Strategy in the Second World War: The Lees-Knowles Lectures at Trinity College, Cambridge 1966*, Weidenfeld & Nicolson, 1968

—*Grand Strategy*, Volume 4: *August 1942–September 1943*, HMSO, 1972

Humble, Richard, *Crusader: Eighth Army's Forgotten Victory, November 1941 to January 1942*, Leo Cooper, 1987

Ireland, Bernard, *The War in the Mediterranean, 1940–1943*, Arms & Armour Press, 1993

Irving, David, *The Trail of the Fox: The Life of Field-Marshal Erwin Rommel*, Weidenfeld & Nicolson, 1977

Jewell, Derek (ed.), *Alamein and the Desert War*, Sphere Books, 1967

Johns, F. L. and others, *The History of the 7th Medium Regiment, Royal Artillery (now 32nd Medium Regiment R.A.) during World War II, 1939–1945*, RA Historical Committee, 1951

Johnson, Mark, and Peter Stanley, *Alamein: The Australian Story*, Oxford University Press, 2002

Jones, Matthew, *Britain, The United States and the Mediterranean War, 1942–44*, Macmillan, 1996

Keegan, John, *Churchill's Generals*, Weidenfeld & Nicolson, 1991

Kelly, Saul, *The Hunt for Zerzura: The Last Oasis and the Desert War*, John Murray, 2002

Kennett, B. B., and J. A. Tatman, *Craftsmen of the Army: The Story of the Royal Electrical and Mechanical Engineers*, Leo Cooper, 1970

Kesselring, A., *The Memoirs of Field Marshal Kesselring*, Greenhill, 1997

Khun, Volkmar, *German Paratroops in World War II*, Ian Allan, 1978

Kippenberger, Howard, *Infantry Brigadier*, Oxford University Press, 1949

Knox, Macgregor, *Mussolini Unleashed, 1939–1941*, Cambridge University Press, 1986

—*Hitler's Italian Allies: Royal Armed Forces, Fascist Regime, and the War of 1940–43*, Cambridge University Press, 2000

Koburger, Charles W., *Naval Warfare in the Eastern Mediterranean 1940–1945*, Praeger, 1993

Latimer, John, *Alamein*, John Murray, 2002

Levine, Alan J., *The War Against Rommel's Supply Lines, 1942–1943*, Praeger, 1999

Lewin, Ronald, *Rommel as Military Commander*, Batsford, 1968

—*Montgomery as Military Commander*, Batsford, 1971

—*The Life and Death of the Afrika Korps*, Batsford, 1977

Lewis, P. J., and I. R. English, *Into Battle with the Durhams: 8 DLI in World War II*, London Stamp Exchange, 1990

Liddell Hart, Basil H., *The Decisive Wars of History*, G. Bell and Sons, 1929

—*The Strategy of the Indirect Approach*, Faber & Faber, 1941; revised edition 1946

—*The Rommel Papers*, Collins, 1953

—*The Tanks: The History of the Royal Tank Regiment and its Predecessors, Heavy Branch Machine-gun Corps, Tank Corps and Royal Tank Corps, 1914–1945*, Cassell, 1959

Lindsay, T. M., *Sherwood Rangers*, Burrup & Mathieson, 1952

Lucas, James, *War in the Desert: The Eighth Army at El Alamein*, Arms & Armour Press, 1982

Lucas Phillips, C. E., *Alamein*, William Heinemann, 1962

Lucio, Ceva, 'North African Campaign 1940–43: A Reconsideration', *Journal of Strategic Studies*, March 1990, pp. 84–104

Luck, Hans von, *Panzer Commander: The Memoirs of Colonel Hans von Luck*, Praeger, 1989

MacIntyre, Donald, *The Battle For The Mediterranean*, Batsford, 1965

Mackenzie, Compton, *Eastern Epic*, Chatto & Windus, 1951

Macksey, Kenneth, *Afrika Korps*, Macdonald, 1968

—*Rommel, Battles and Campaigns*, Arms & Armour Press, 1979

Majdalany, Fred, *The Battle of El Alamein*, Weidenfeld & Nicolson, 1965

Martin, T. A., *The Essex Regiment 1929–1950*, The Essex Regiment Association, 1952

Martineau, G. D., *A History of the Royal Sussex Regiment: A History of the Old Belfast Regiment and the Regiment of Sussex 1701–1953*, Moore & Tillyer, n.d.

Maughan, Barton, *Tobruk and El Alamein*, Australian War Memorial, 1966

McCreery, R. L., 'Recollections of a Chief of Staff', *The Twelfth Royal Lancers Journal*, April 1959

McFetridge, Charles D., 'In Pursuit: Montgomery after Alamein', *Australian Defence Force Journal*, March/April 1993, pp. 29–41

McGregor, John, *The Spirit of Angus: The War History of the County's Battalion of the Black Watch*, Phillimore, 1988

McKee, Alexander, *El Alamein: Ultra and the Three Battles*, Souvenir Press, 1991

McMeekan, G. R., 'The Assault at Alamein', *The Royal Engineers Journal*, Vol. LXIII, December 1949

Mearsheimer, John, *Liddell Hart and the Weight of History*, Brassey's, 1988

Miles, Wilfrid, *The Life of a Regiment: The Gordon Highlanders 1919–1945*, Aberdeen University Press, 1961

Mills, G. H., and R. F. Nixon, *The Annals of the King's Royal Rifle Corps*, Volume VI: *1923–1943*, Leo Cooper, 1971

Monelli, Paulo, *Mussolini: An Intimate Life*, Thames & Hudson, 1953
Montgomery, Bernard L., *El Alamein to the River Sangro*, Hutchinson, 1948
—*The Memoirs of Viscount Montgomery of Alamein*, Collins, 1958
Moore, P. N., 'Mine Clearance – El Alamein', *The Royal Engineers Journal*, Vol. 106, No. 3, December 1992
Moorehead, Alan, *African Trilogy*, Hamish Hamilton, 1944
Murphy, W. E., *2nd New Zealand Divisional Artillery*, New Zealand Historical Publications Branch, Department of Internal Affairs, 1966
Myatt, Frederick, *The British Infantry 1660–1945: The Evolution of a Fighting Force*, Blandford, 1983
Nalder, R. F. H., *The History of British Army Signals in the Second World War*, Royal Signals Institution, 1953
—*The Royal Corps of Signals: A History of its Antecedents and Development (circa 1800–1955)*, Royal Signals Institution, 1958
Neillands, Robin, *The Desert Rats: 7th Armoured Division, 1940–1945*, Weidenfeld & Nicolson, 1991
Nicolson, Nigel, *Alex: The Life of Field Marshal Earl Alexander of Tunis*, Weidenfeld & Nicolson, 1973
Norton, Frazer D., *26 Battalion*, New Zealand Historical Publications Branch, Department of Internal Affairs, 1952
Orange, Vincent, *Coningham: A Biography of Air Marshal Sir Arthur Coningham*, Methuen, 1990
Orenstein, Harold, *The Evolution of Soviet Operational Art 1927–1991: The Documentary Basis*, Volume 1, Frank Cass, 1995
Pakenham-Walsh, R. P., *History of the Corps of Royal Engineers*, Volume VIII: *1938–1948*, The Institution of Royal Engineers, 1958
Parkinson, Roger, *The Auk: Auchinleck, Victor at Alamein*, Granada, 1977
Parkyn, H. G., *The Rifle Brigade Chronicle for 1942*, The Rifle Brigade Club and Association, 1943
Parsons, Max, *Gunfire!: A History of the 2/12 Australian Field Regiment 1940–46*, Globe Press, 1991
Pemberton, A. L., *The Development of Artillery Tactics and Equipment*, The War Office, 1950
Perrett, Bryan, *The Valentine in North Africa 1942–43*, Ian Allan, 1972
Piekalkiewicz, Janusz, *Rommel and the Secret War in North Africa: Secret Intelligence in the North African Campaign*, Schiffer, 1992
Pitt, Barrie, *The Crucible of War 1: Wavell's Command*, Papermac, 1986
—*The Crucible of War 2: Auchinleck's Command*, Papermac, 1986
—*The Crucible of War 3: Montgomery and Alamein*, Papermac, 1986
Pitt, P. W., *Royal Wilts*, Burrup & Mathieson, 1946
Pitt-Rivers, J. A., *The Story of the Royal Dragoons 1938–1945*, Williams Clowes, 1956

Playfair, I. S. O., *The Mediterranean and Middle East*, Volume I: *The Early Successes Against Italy (to May 1941)*, HMSO, 1954

—*The Mediterranean and Middle East*, Volume II: *The Germans Come to the Help of their Ally (1941)*, HMSO, 1956

—*The Mediterranean and Middle East*, Volume III: *British Fortunes Reach their Lowest Ebb (September 1941 to September 1942)*, HMSO, 1960

—*The Mediterranean and Middle East*, Volume IV: *The Destruction of the Axis Forces in Africa*, HMSO, 1966

Prasad, Bisheshwar, *The North African Campaign 1940–43*, Combined Inter-Services Historical Section, 1956

Pringle, D. J. C., and W. A. Glue, *20 Battalion and Armoured Regiment*, New Zealand Historical Publications Branch, Department of Internal Affairs, 1957

Richardson, Charles, *Flashback: A Soldier's Story*, William Kimber, 1985

—*Send for Freddie: The Story of Montgomery's Chief of Staff Major General Sir Francis de Guingand, KBE, CB, DSO*, William Kimber, 1987

Richardson, William, and Seymour Freidlin, *The Fatal Decisions*, Michael Joseph, 1956

Roach, Peter, *The 8.15 to War: Memoirs of a Desert Rat*, Secker & Warburg, 1982

Roberts, G. P. B., *From the Desert to the Baltic*, William Kimber, 1987

Robertson, John, and McCarthy, John, *Australian War Strategy 1939–1945: A Documentary History*, University of Queensland Press, 1985

Rommel, Erwin, *Infantry Attack*, Stackpole Books, 1990

Roskill, S. W., *The War at Sea 1939–1945*, Volume II: *The Defensive*, HMSO, 1954

—*The War at Sea 1939–1945*, Volume II: *The Period of Balance*, HMSO, 1956

Royal Air Force, *Air Support: Second World War 1939–1945*, Air Ministry, 1955

Russell, D. F. O., *War History of the 7th Bn. The Black Watch, R.H.R., Fife Territorial Battalion, August 1939–May 1945*, Markinch Printing Co., 1948

Ryder, Rowland, *Oliver Leese*, Hamish Hamilton, 1987

Sadkovich, James J., *The Italian Navy in World War II*, Greenwood Press, 1994

Salmond, J. B., *The History of the 51st Highland Division 1939–1945*, Blackwood, 1953

Samwell, H. P., *An Infantry Officer with the Eighth Army: The Personal Experiences of an Infantry Officer During the Eighth Army's Campaign through Africa and Sicily*, Blackwood, 1945

Sandes, E. W. C., *From Pyramid to Pagoda: The Story of the West Yorkshire Regiment (The Prince of Wales's Own) in the War 1939–45 and Afterwards*, F. J. Parsons, 1951

Schmider, Klaus, 'The Mediterranean in 1940–41: Crossroads Of Lost Opportunities?', *War & Society*, Vol. 15, No. 2, October 1997, pp. 19–41

Schmidt, Heinz W., *With Rommel in the Desert*, George Harrap & Co., 1951

Schreiber, Gerhard, Bernd Stegemann and Detlef Vogel, *Germany and the Second World War*, Volume III: *The Mediterranean, South-east Europe, and North Africa 1939–1941*, Clarendon Press, 1995

Scoullar, J. L., *Battle for Egypt: The Summer of 1942*, New Zealand Historical Publications Branch, Department of Internal Affairs, 1955

Selwyn, Victor, Dan Davin, Erik de Mauny and Ian Fletcher, *From Oasis into Italy: War Poems and Diaries from Africa and Italy 1940–1946*, Shepheard-Walwyn, 1983

Sheffield, Gary, *The Forgotten Victory: The First World War, Myths and Realities*, Hodder Headline, 2000

Simpson, Michael (ed.), *The Cunningham Papers: Selections from the Private And Official Correspondence of Admiral of the Fleet Viscount Cunningham of Hyndhope*, Volume 1: *The Mediterranean Fleet, 1939–1942*, Ashgate Publishing, 1999

Skillen, Hugh, *Spies of the Airwaves: A History of Y Sections During the Second World War*, Hugh Skillen, 1989

Smith, F. H., *Guns Against Tanks: I Troop, 7th New Zealand Anti-Tank Regiment in Libya, 23 November 1941*, New Zealand War History Branch, 1948

Smith, Peter C., *Massacre at Tobruk: The Story of Operation Agreement*, William Kimber, 1987

'Sterno', 'A Field Regiment in the Battle of Egypt, October–November, 1942', *Royal Artillery Journal*, Vol. LXX, No. 3, July 1943

Stevens, G. R., *Fourth Indian Division*, McLaren & Sons, 1949

Stewart, Adrian, *The Eighth Army's Greatest Victories: Alam Halfa To Tunis 1942–1943*, Leo Cooper, 1999

—*The Early Battles of Eighth Army: 'Crusader' to the Alamein Line 1941–1942*, Leo Cooper, 2002

Strawson, John, *El Alamein: Desert Victory*, Dent, 1981

Sweet, John J. T., *Iron Arm: The Mechanization of Mussolini's Army, 1920–1940*, Greenwood, 1980

Tedder, Arthur W., *With Prejudice: The War Memoirs of Marshal of the Royal Air Force, Lord Tedder*, Cassell, 1966

Terraine, John, *The Right of the Line*, Hodder & Stoughton, 1985

Toase, F. H., and J. P. Harris, *Armoured Warfare*, Batsford, 1990

Todd, Andrew, *The Elephant at War: 2nd Battalion Seaforth Highlanders 1939–1945*, Pentland Press, 1998

Trainor, Bernard E., 'Deception', *Marine Corps Gazette*, October 1986, pp. 57–61

Tuker, Francis, *The Pattern of War*, Butler and Tanner Ltd, 1958

—*Approach to Battle: A Commentary, Eighth Army, November 1941 to May 1943*, Cassell, 1963

Underhill, D. F., *Queen's Own Royal Regiment the Staffordshire Yeomanry:*

An Account of the Operations of the Regiment during World War II 1939–1945, Staffordshire Libraries, 1994

Van Creveld, Martin, *Supplying in War: Logistics from Wallenstein to Patton*, Cambridge University Press, 1977

Verney G. L., *The Desert Rats: The History of the 7th Armoured Division 1938–1945*, Hutchinson, 1954

Vernon, Dick (ed.), *'Strafer' Gott*, Culverlands Press Ltd, Winchester, n.d.

Von Clausewitz, Carl (edited and translated by Michael Howard and Peter Paret), *On War*, Princeton University Press, 1976

Von Mellenthin, Friedrich Wilhelm, *Panzer Battles, 1939–1945: A Study of the Employment of Armour in the Second World War*, Cassell, 1956

Von Senger and Etterlin, F. M., *German Tanks of World War II: The Complete Illustrated History of German Armoured Fighting Vehicles 1926–1945*, Arms & Armour Press, 1971

Wake, Hereward, and W. F. Deedes, *Swift and Bold: The Story of the King's Royal Rifle Corps in the Second World War 1939–1945*, Gale & Polden, 1949

Walker, Ronald, *Alam Halfa and Alamein*, New Zealand Historical Publications Branch, Department of Internal Affairs, 1967

Warlimont, Walter, *Inside Hitler's Headquarters 1939–45*, Weidenfeld & Nicolson, 1964

Warner, Phillip, *Alamein*, William Kimber, 1979

—*Auchinleck: The Lonely Soldier*, Buchan & Enright, 1981

—*Phantom*, William Kimber, 1982

Wilmott, H. P., *The Great Crusade*, Michael Joseph, 1989

Winterbotham, F. W., *The Ultra Secret*, Weidenfeld & Nicolson, 1974

Wood, Derek (ed.), *The End of the Beginning: A Symposium on the Land/Air Co-Operation in the Mediterranean War, 1940–1943*, Royal Air Force Historical Society/ Royal Air Force Staff College, Bracknell, 1992

Young, Desmond, *Rommel*, Collins, 1950